CHICAGO PUBLIC LIBRARY
WOODSON REGIONAL
9525 S. HALSTED ST. 60628

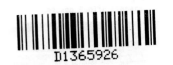

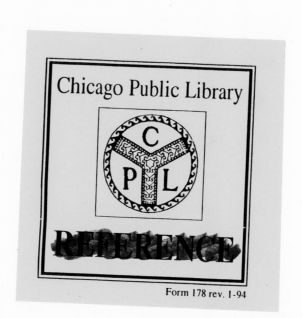

Women Playwrights in England,
Ireland, and Scotland
1660 – 1823

Women Playwrights in England, Ireland, and Scotland 1660 – 1823

David D. Mann & Susan Garland Mann,
with Camille Garnier

INDIANA UNIVERSITY PRESS
Bloomington and Indianapolis

The paper used in this publication meets the minimum requirements of American National Standard for Information Sciences—Permanence of Paper for Printed Library Materials, ANSI Z39.48-1984.

Manufactured in the United States of America

Library of Congress Cataloging-in-Publication Data

Mann, David, date
Women playwrights in England, Ireland, and Scotland: 1660–1823 / David D. Mann and Susan Garland Mann, with Camille Garnier.
p. cm.
ISBN 0-253-33087-4 (alk. paper)
1. English drama—Women authors—Bio-bibliography—Dictionaries. 2. English drama—18th century—Bio-bibliography—Dictionaries. 3. English drama—17th century—Bio-bibliography—Dictionaries. 4. English drama—19th century—Bio-bibliography—Dictionaries. 5. Women dramatists, English—Biography—Dictionaries. 6. Women and literature—Great Britain—Dictionaries. I. Mann, Susan Garland. II. Title.
PR635.W6M36 1996
822.009'9287—dc20
[B] 95-48939

1 2 3 4 5 01 00 99 98 97 96

THIS BOOK IS DEDICATED TO OUR MOTHERS —

Jeannette Kneer Mann-Lackey

Mary Margaret Tully Garland

Camille Janvier

CONTENTS

Preface

To attempt an extensive treatment of a subject that has been shrouded in anonymity and mystery for many years means that this must be a book in progress, examining the sparsely explored field of early women dramatists. Even with as much factual detail and critical commentary as we have assembled, we have not managed to resolve some vexing questions that elude us about female dramatists from 1660 to 1823. Nevertheless, readers and users of this volume are likely to discover new information about plays written by women in this period; we anticipate further progress by readers and users of this book. We intend a wide audience for this book: students of the Restoration, the Eighteenth Century, and the Romantic era; theatre historians; feminist scholars; researchers of drama; theatre directors; analyzers of popular culture; as well as general readers. Our purpose in this book is to advance investigations into female playwrights and their dramas from the late seventeenth century through the early nineteenth century.

Beginning with the reestablishment of the theatres in 1660 when women were first allowed on stage, we include all English dramatic texts by women we have been able to obtain. Although some were intended as reading texts (i.e., closet dramas or plays to be read in the privacy of one's own room), most of these dramas were performed. When theatre history is closely considered, Robert Hume has pointed out, it is "infuriatingly untidy" (1976; 9). Our terminal date goes beyond the eighteenth century to incorporate those manuscripts licensed for performance by the Lord Chamberlain from 1737 to 1823; included in the Larpent Collection are quite a few manuscripts plays by women. Although some of the plays were published, the Larpent Collection at the Huntington Library contains a number of dramas never printed. We read all those manuscripts from the collection available to us in the Readex Microprint series, but we were unable to visit the Huntington to read all the manuscript plays by female dramatists.

Several women wrote plays in two centuries, e.g., Joanna Baillie (1762–1851) and Harriet Lee (1757–1851), whose first comedy *The New Peerage* appeared in 1787 and whose last play *The Three Strangers* was produced in 1825. Like most women dramatists of the Romantic period, Baillie learned her dramaturgy in the eighteenth century, and her plays succeeded more with reading rather than with theatre audiences. We follow Baillie, Lee, and other playwrights (such as Mary Russell Mitford whose plays began to appear in 1823) through their theatrical careers, examining those dramas written or produced after 1823. In the early nineteenth-century, spectators clamored for Gothic-inspired exhibitions and sensational melodramas.

Our research shows that more than 160 women wrote almost 600 plays, or close to twenty percent of the drama produced during this period. (A chronological list of these dramas by women can be found in an appendix at the end of this volume.) Of course, because women playwrights often sought anonymity, this number represents those plays we have been able to identify as having a female author. Many English women writers during this period wrote both plays and novels (e.g., Behn, Haywood, Griffith, and

Inchbald), but prose fiction has recently received the majority of the critical attention. Perhaps the many parts that make up the history of drama—set design, staging, theatres, playwrights, and actors—complicated the research and may account for the limited exploration into the subject of eighteenth-century female playwrights.

This book is organized alphabetically, intermixing play titles with the playwrights. Entries for playwrights begin with their last name given in boldface, upper-case letters. We provide a brief biographical sketch of the dramatist, beginning with what we can discover of her parentage, social background, education and early interest in the theatre, the composition and publication history of her plays, her other prominent works (novels, poetry), principal themes and ideas that emerge from her dramas, and the theatrical genres in which she excelled. Each biographical entry is followed by a brief selective bibliography of useful primary material, significant secondary information, and critical essays focusing on her career as a dramatist and her connections with the theatres.

Entries for individual dramatic works appear in upper/lower case, boldface type. Because playwrights in this period usually gave their dramas double titles (for example, Susanna Centlivre's *The Cruel Gift; or, The Royal Resentment*), we consistently set off the first title with a semicolon. Our entries are generally organized in these paragraph divisions: 1) the production history (when and where performed and with what significant actors) and publication information; 2) a brief plot synopsis; 3) a concise evaluation of the play, and 4) when plays are translated or adapted from non-English sources, we examine the way a female translator/ adaptor transposes the drama into English or adapts a play for the English stage. Does she go beyond a fairly literal translation? How has she altered the text for performance? Finally, we endeavor to note useful biographical and critical materials where they exist. Repeatedly mentioned reference works are given in acronyms or abbreviated names, such as *BD* to refer to *Biographia Dramatica; or, A Companion to the Playhouse*, compiled by D. E. Brown, I. Reed, and S. Jones (3 vols., published 1812); or Tobin, which cites Terance Tobin's *Plays by Scots, 1660–1800* (1974). These short-titles are given in the list of "Frequently Cited Works," placed at the end of the Introduction.

We customarily list the playwright by the name she used when she wrote her dramas. Because Catharine Trotter wrote all of her plays before she married the Rev. Patrick Cockburn, we consistently refer to her as Catharine Trotter. This method gets trickier in the case of Lady Elizabeth Berkeley Craven, who later became the Margravine of Anspach. For her early dramas (1778–1784), we cite her first married name, "Lady Elizabeth Berkeley Craven, later the Margravine of Anspach." After the death of Lord Craven in 1791, she married the Margrave of Anspach, and we refer to her later dramas as written by the "Margravine of Anspach, formerly Lady Elizabeth Berkeley Craven." Cross references in the text should help the reader out of any quandaries.

We have retained some pieces, wrongly assigned to women playwrights or to a particular female dramatist, in order to make the reader aware of longstanding misattributions. *The East Indian*, for instance, has been ascribed by a few early commentators to Fanny Burney, "a lady," or "a woman author." Since Burney is in fact *not* the author, we have marked the work as "misattrib" to her.

Various editions and printings are distinguished at the end of drama entries with capital letters. MODERN EDITIONS are those that supply a reading text of the play without detailed bibliographical notes about the early editions. One example would be Maureen Duffy's *Five Plays* by Behn (1990): it provides a play text (from Montague Summers) without notes. Paddy Lyons and Fidelis Morgan, in *Female Playwrights of the Restoration* (1991), also furnish a modern text of several plays with some explanatory notes but without detailed attention to texts and bibliography. A FACSIMILE EDITION copies the early printing exactly. Often these facsimile editions appear in a series, such as E-CED (i.e., *Eighteenth-Century English Drama*, general editor, Paula Backscheider). Specific editors follow the entry for the play, such as Richard C. Frushell for Centlivre and Frederick Link for Cowley. CRITICAL EDITIONS may also show up in a series, like "Satire and Sense" (general editor, Stephen Orgel), but any critical edition should have a detailed apparatus with attention to bibliographical problems, explanatory notes, and textual alterations. Good examples of critical editions from that series are Behn's *The Luckey Chance*, edited by Jean Coakley, and Behn's *The City Heiress*, edited by William Hersey. Although Janet Todd has prepared a critical edition of Behn's works, the volumes containing the plays are in press. This multi-edition should be in print soon from Ohio State University Press.

Many of the texts we read came from the Readex Microprint series on microcards; these are now in microfiche. With the wide acceptance and availability of computers now used in scholarly pursuits, many readers with access to The Eighteenth-Century Short-Title Catalogue (ESTC) on disk can readily find printings that occurred from 1700 to 1800. Copies of many of the texts in ESTC are available in microfilms in THE EIGHTEENTH CENTURY (TEC) series. Although we record those we have been able to find in the ESTC, we only include first editions and later ones that have significant textual changes.

Much of our research could not have been done without those three wonderfully full compendiums of information: *The London Stage, 1660–1800*, complied by W. Van Lennep, E. L. Avery, A. H. Scouten, G. W. Stone, and C. B. Hogan; *A Biographical Dictionary of Actors, Actresses, Musicians, Dancers, Managers, and Other Stage Personnel in London, 1660–1800* by P. H. Highfill, Jr., K. A. Burnim, and E. A. Langhans; and *The Prologues and Epilogues of the Eighteenth Century, 1660–1737* by Pierre Danchin. Among the solid and practical secondary sources on English women dramatists we have found most useful are noteworthy books by Jacqueline Pearson, *The Prostituted Muse: Images of Women and Women Dramatists, 1642–1737* (1988), Nancy Cotton's earlier study *Women Playwrights in England, c. 1363–1750* (1980), and Constance Clark's *Three Augustan Woman Playwrights* [Mary Pix, Delarivere Manley, and Catharine Trotter] (1986). Robert D. Hume's *The Development of English Drama in the late Seventeenth Century* (1976) and William J. Burling's *A Checklist of New Plays and Entertainments of the London Stage, 1700–1737* (1993) have helped us place the early dramas in their theatrical contexts. Janet Todd has organized and compiled *A Dictionary of British and American Women Writers, 1660–1880* (1984), with signed entries written by different scholars. Both *An Encyclopedia of British Women Writers* (1988), edited by Paul and June Schlueter, and *The Feminist Companion to Literature in English* (1990), compiled by Virginia Blain, Isobel Grundy, and Patricia Clements, have been especially helpful. Gwenn Davis and Beverly A. Joyce gathered a serviceable listing of titles in their *Drama by Women to 1900: A Bibliography of American and British Writers* (1992).

A few specific bibliographies on individual playwrights, such as Mary Ann O'Donnell's distinguished catalogue of Aphra Behn's works (1986), have made our task easier. We have found several biographies on individual dramatists and authors most helpful; among the most notable were works on Behn (George Woodcock, Angeline Goureau, Frederick Link), Centlivre (John W. Bowyer, F. P. Lock), Haywood (George Whicher, Mary Ann Schofield, Christine Blouch), Burney (Kristina Straub, Margaret Anne Doody, Judy Simons), and Edgeworth (Marilyn Butler). A valuable collection of essays on various aspects of women and the theatre may be found in *Curtain Calls: British and American Women and the Theatre, 1660–1820*, edited by Schofield and Cecilia Macheski (1991). As beneficial as we have found these secondary works, none encompasses women's writing for the theatre over such an extended period in England. Thus, we feel that the following material should enhance modern scholarship on drama by women from 1660 to 1823.

ACKNOWLEDGEMENTS

Camille Garnier has been actively involved with this project since its inception. An eighteenth-century French specialist who has worked with women translators, Camille has read all of the English plays included here that are based on French sources, and she has compared these translations or adaptations to the French originals. This was in itself a remarkable accomplishment: although British women during this period translated from German and other continental sources, the majority of the translation work was from French to English. Beyond this role, she joined us as we each proofread the entire manuscript. Camille's contributions are always substantial and precise: her partnership invaluable.

We also wish to thank scholars who have made recommendations about the content, organization, or final arrangement of the book: Professors Rob Hume (Penn State), Douglas White (Loyola of Chicago), Helene Koon (California State University at San Bernardino), William Burling (Southwest Missouri State University) and Paula Backscheider (Auburn University). Archibald Irwin (Indiana University Southeast) assisted the research by discussing our work with us.

We spent much time in rare book libraries, and this volume could not have been written without the resources provided by the Lilly Library at Indiana University-Bloomington, the Newberry Library in Chicago, and the Beinecke Library at Yale University. Specific thanks go to librarians at Indiana University Southeast (Stacey Russell), at Miami University (Bill Wortman, Elizabeth Brice, Liz Ping, Becky Morganson, and John Diller), and at the Lilly Library (William R. Cagle, Sue Presnell). For providing us with information from various libraries we were unable to visit, we thank Robert Bator, William W. Hardesty, and Richard W. Momeyer. Henry H. H. Remak and Ivona Hedin, Director and Assistant Director of the Institute for Advanced Study, Bloomington, not only provided office space and secretarial support while we were working at the Lilly but offered considerable hospitality.

Both Miami University and Indiana University provided much needed research support: we gratefully acknowledge a funded research leave from Miami; summer faculty fellowships from Indiana University Southeast; a release-time fellowship from Indiana University Southeast; an Inter-Campus Scholar appointment from the Research and the University Graduate School and the Institute for Advanced Studies, Bloomington; and a Ball Brothers Fellowship to work at the Lilly Library.

We would like to acknowledge the support and encouragement provided by Drs. James Nordlund, Debra Breneman, and John Breneman of the University of Cincinnati Medical Center, and by Dr. Kristie J. Paris of the James Graham Brown Cancer Center, Louisville, KY.

We also wish to acknowledge graduate students at Miami University who in several seminars on women playwrights have helped us sharpen our judgments. Some of these students have gone on to do further work on female playwrights and their plays from this period: Emily Detmer, Kim Tyo-Dickerson, Susan Grambsch, Jerry Hakes, Shawn Hutchinson, Kim Jacobs, Rich Lane, Teresa Lyle, Carol Morison, Eleni Siatra, Thayer Talbot, Alan Taylor, and Shannon Wilson.

We very much appreciate the continuing support of Joan Catapono at the Indiana University Press. Her confidence in the work assisted us immeasurably. John Zeigler, production editor at the Press, provided detailed commentary, enabling William Rumsey to prepare camera-ready copy. A philosopher turned typesetter, Bill never lost his sense of humor as he selflessly devoted himself to balancing pages and checking headers. The production of the book would have been delayed considerably, and would have been far more painful, had he not come to our aid. Finally, we were blessed that someone as perceptive and as good-natured as Frances Purifoy agreed to copyedit the final draft.

D. D. M., S. G. M.

INTRODUCTION

After the Puritans closed the English theatres in 1642, they thought they had put an end to what they considered "those licentious representations." But when the short-lived Puritan-Commonwealth experiment failed and the English invited Charles II to assume the monarchy in 1660, one of his first orders reinstated the theatres—with women acting for the first time on the English stage. And women did take to the stage: while some acted, others wrote for theatrical presentation. Within a decade, Aphra Behn began to establish herself as a professional dramatist, but it was twenty-five years before other women would attempt a livelihood by writing for the stage.

The profession of playwrighting has always been hazardous, but in Behn's case it was made more difficult because she had to compete in a world controlled entirely by men; nevertheless, she wrote nearly twenty plays, as well as poetry and novels. Few playwrights composed more, except perhaps her friend John Dryden, the poet laureate, who wrote for the King's players under Thomas Killigrew. It was the Duke's company, however, that produced most of Behn's most enduring works—comedies of intrigue.

From 1660 onward, only these two companies held patents and were allowed to stage plays. Many previous dramas were apportioned to each house—including Shakespeare and Ben Jonson—but both Killigrew and William Davenant, the director of the Duke's company, began to look for new playwrights to provide dramas for their post-Commonwealth audiences. While men supplied much of the early Restoration drama, Katherine Philips translated two plays by the popular French dramatist Pierre Corneille before her early death, and both were staged. An original tragicomedy by Frances Boothby and a tragedy by Elizabeth Polwhele were also staged before Behn entered the arena of playwrighting.

Holding her own against such dramatists as Sir George Etherege and William Wycherley, Behn continued writing about a drama a year —sometimes more—from the 1670s through the end of the 1680s. When the two theatre organizations consolidated to form the United company in 1682, playwrights were less in demand as the single company mounted fewer new plays. With the death of Charles II and the advent and sudden departure of James II, the drama underwent a number of changes, but Behn didn't live to see these, for she died just as the new Protestant rulers, William and Mary, came to the throne. Under the moral aegis of the new rulers, plays gradually became less bawdy and a reformed exemplary drama became established.

About the time of Queen Mary's death in 1694, a group of the leading actors had become so dissatisfied with the tyranny of Skipworth and Rich, who had bought the theatre patents, that they broke with these manipulative entrepreneurs. Thomas Betterton led the new company, organized with women as shareholders (Elizabeth Barry and Anne Bracegirdle) for the first time; the players' company opened at a refurbished Lincoln's-Inn-Fields Theatre on 30 April 1695 with Congreve's *Love for Love*. Having two companies in operation demanded more plays, and a second wave of female dramatists arrived to supply this need for the 1695–96 season. "Over one-third of all the new plays that season were by women or adapted from women's work," Paula Backscheider points out in *Spectacular Politics* (71). The new playwrights included "Ariadne," Delarivere Manley, Catharine Trotter, and Mary Pix, most of whom would continue writing for the theatre into the eighteenth century, despite Jeremy Collier's attack on the salaciousness of the stage.

After two plays in that first season, Manley drifted into novels and journalism. She did not finish another play for ten years (*Almyna*, 1706), and it was more than ten years until her last one was produced (*Lucius*, 1717). Trotter accomplished more in her authorship of drama, but she became sidetracked as a defender of John Locke's philosophical views; later she was preoccupied as a wife and mother. Pix doggedly turned out a dozen dramas while befriending Susanna Carroll, who is best remembered by her married name—Susanna Centlivre—and who was destined to become one of the great playwrights of the eighteenth century.

Centlivre turned her career from acting on the provincial stage to playwrighting for London audiences in 1700 with her first play, *The Perjur'd Husband*, though she continued intermittently both to act and write until her marriage in 1707. Concentrating on playwrighting after marriage, Centlivre produced rollicking but chaste comedies that proved extraordinarily successful; performances of her plays continued long into the nineteenth century. A staunch supporter of Queen Anne, Centlivre became as closely identified with the politics of the Whigs as Behn was with the Tories. After Centlivre died in 1723, however, women seemed to write plays only sporadically. Eliza Haywood spent her early career as a novelist who occasionally wrote plays and sometimes acted in them; she spent several seasons with Henry Fielding's company until the Licensing Act of 1737. In the following decade Haywood created a periodical for women and reactivated her career as a novelist, but she never returned to the stage as performer or as playwright.

The biting political satire Fielding put on stage during the 1730s at the Haymarket Theatre (and Haywood acted in) caused the Parliament to pass the Licensing Act, mandating only two playhouses, Covent Garden and Drury Lane. The law also specified that each new play to be performed had first to be approved by the Lord Chamberlain. Many dramatists besides Fielding were displaced by this political maneuver, and for almost twenty years there was very little dramatic writing on the part of women; some, like Haywood, turned to prose fiction.

It may have been the benefit nights of the mid-eighteenth century that motivated several female performers to write plays. In a once-a-year benefit performance, the actor entreated the public to attend the theatre on a designated night; after the performance the total amount of money for tickets was reckoned, and house charges were then deducted, the remaining funds going to the actor. For instance, when Kitty Clive wrote *The Re-*

hearsal; or, Bayes in Petticoats as an afterpiece to be played on her benefit night at Drury Lane (15 March 1750), the receipts were £240 and the house charges £60, so Clive took home £180. Clive prepared several plays for her benefit nights in the later part of her long-running stage career (which continued to 1768). Susannah Cibber, another female actor turned playwright, presented a play she had adapted for her benefit night; her afterpiece *The Oracle* debuted on 17 March 1752 at Covent Garden.

If benefit nights encouraged authorship, it was the managers who accepted the plays that they felt would draw audiences. Dr. Samuel Johnson's prologue for David Garrick written for the opening of Drury Lane in the 1747 season makes this point:

> The Stage but echoes back the publick Voice.
> The Drama's Laws, the Drama's Patrons give,
> For we that live to please, must please to live.

In Garrick's thirty-year reign at Drury Lane (1747–1776), he may have condescended to women dramatists, but he was also their advocate. Garrick produced dramas by nine women playwrights in 128 performances at Drury Lane, while Covent Garden produced three women dramatists for a total of twenty performances (Ellen Donkin in *Curtain Calls* 144). Thus, Garrick took greater risks in presenting women playwrights, whereas the management at Covent Garden seemed only interested in women who were proven dramatists. The willingness to take risks gave Garrick greater selectivity of women's manuscripts, and as Donkin notes he was "an excellent judge of what would succeed with his audiences" (147).

Despite Garrick's willingness to take risks with inexperienced female dramatists, it was still difficult for playwrights to get their works performed because of limited venues. During the summer after the main theatres ended their season, the Haymarket Theatre filled the gap, allowing some new plays to be performed, and providing employment for the younger actors who were just breaking into the profession. While Garrick presided at Drury Lane, Samuel Foote ran the summer theatre at the Haymarket. When R. B. Sheridan followed Garrick at Drury Lane, Thomas Harris had just taken over at Covent Garden where he began a long run as manager (1774–1809). At the Haymarket, George Colman the Elder assumed the managership from Foote at the end of the season in 1776. With new management at the end of the 1770s, theatres changed direction and women playwrights—now more accepted—became part of this change.

Regardless of the manner in which women were treated, it was their experience in the theatre that enabled many to succeed as playwrights. Because Garrick coached Hannah More, Hannah Cowley, and Elizabeth Griffith, each of these women had learned enough about writing for the stage that they continued to produce plays after his retirement. Frances Brooke learned her craft managing operas and music programs at the King's Theatre in the 1770s. Elizabeth Inchbald's years on the provincial stage taught her what would succeed in the theatre. Although More and Griffith gave up being dramatists, Brooke and Cowley were joined by Inchbald as the best-known female playwrights in that decade.

While some critics complain that women playwrights brought excessive sensibility to the stage, men began this trend as early as Richard Steele's *The Conscious Lovers* in 1722, and later male dramatists (for example, Cumberland and Holcroft) continued it at the end of the century and into the 1800s. Audiences seemed to enjoy watching disreputable male characters being reformed—sometimes by long-suffering women, at other times by spirited females who insisted on their change. Tender feelings for the suffering of others brought out true emotions: in a play like Inchbald's *Such Things Are*, prison reform is central to the action, and audiences see anguished political prisoners forced behind bars because of their views against a reigning government. A character's responsiveness to natural beauty (e.g., Sir George Evelyn in Inchbald's *Wives as They Were*) gives an index to how the audience should evaluate that character. And these sensitive feelings in the drama parallel those emotions developing concurrently in romantic poetry.

As the last decade of the century began, more women turned to playwrighting as a literary outlet, and even Hannah More took up her pen to write a dramatic dialogue, *Village Politics*, a conservative pamphlet opposing the revolutionary politics of Tom Paine's *Common Sense*. An interest in medievalism with heavy gothic overtones opened the way for other women. So while Ann Radcliffe's gothic thrillers excited readers of novels, Mary Darby Robinson's *The Sicilian Lover*, an unacted gothic drama, drew a good deal of attention—if judged by the relatively large number of reviews it received. Women also began to write dramas of moral instruction for adolescents and young children. When Maria Edgeworth, Elizabeth Pinchard, and Charlotte Turner Smith prepared didactic plays for their own families, publishers (Elizabeth Newbery among them) thought the juvenile dramas would interest the general public. These works helped to develop the genre of a novel written for children in dramatic form: speech prefixes indicated the youthful or adult speakers, stage directions helped reveal the action, and occasional prose segments explained settings and situations. While poorer children were being taught bible stories through pamphlets prepared for the Sunday School Movement by reformers such as Hannah More and Sarah Trimmer, dramatic novels helped middle-class children learn morals and values.

Much of this "theatre of education" came from Madame de Genlis, and it is worth noting that plays based on French sources—dramas, tales, fables, and histories—are far more plentiful than translations from German or Spanish origins. Until the French Revolution, adaptations and translations from French literature occur regularly on the English stage. One comedy in particular, Sophia Lee's *The Chapter of Accidents* (1780)—based on Diderot's *Le Pére de famille* and Marmontel's moral tale "Laurette"—stands out as the most popular adaptations of French materials. Acted one hundred times through the end of the century, *The Chapter of Accidents* was repeated almost every season until Lee's death in 1824.

Other continental sources enjoyed a vogue on the English stage, and women adaptors and translators had a large part in this trend. In the fall of 1798, performances of *Lover's Vows* by Kotzebue—adapted for the English stage by Inchbald—ran forty-two nights its first season at Covent Garden, and this gave rise to a greater interest in German dramas by Goethe, Schiller, and Kotzebue. English women interested in drama and with a knowledge of the German language became major translators for the many plays that were in demand: Anne Plumptre translated seven plays by Kotzebue, and her sister Belle translated a play by Iffland; Maria Geisweiler translated three by Kotzebue and one by Iffland; Rose D'Aguilar Lawrence rendered a play by Goethe into English; and the Margravine of Anspach (formerly Lady Elizabeth Craven) not only translated but produced her version of Schiller's *Die Räuber* at Brandenburgh House in Hammersmith; her translation was published in 1799. R. B. Sheridan's adaptation of Kotzebue's *Pizarro*, based on Anne Plumptre's word-for-word translation, ran for thirty-one nights at the end of the Drury Lane season in 1799.

While the popularity for German drama quickly subsided, Joanna Baillie put her dramatic theory of the passions into practice on stage, and the nineteenth century saw a theatrical change in Baillie's prominently exhibiting the single, powerful emotion of a protagonist. Focusing on such passions as love, hate, or jealousy, Baillie wrote plays where emotion dominated, but action in her plays was necessarily restricted; her dramas, thus, lack a stageable dramatic intensity. Tragedy, she believed, would demonstrate the danger of uncontrolled passions, whereas comedy would display the effect of a passion held in check. Although the foremost actors of the day, Sarah Siddons and her brother John Philip Kemble, appeared in a production of Baillie's *De Monfort* at Drury Lane on 29 April 1800, the play ran just eight times. Of the twenty-seven dramas Baillie wrote, only a few were actually staged; nevertheless, her plays gained an extensive readership.

In contrast to plays based on Baillie's dramatic theory were the energetic stage performances of Jane M. Scott at the Sans Pareil (later the Adelphi) Theatre, which her father built to showcase her talents. In the family's thirteen years at the theatre, Scott wrote, produced, directed, and acted in some fifty of her creations, including pantomimes, burlettas, melodramas, farces, spectacles, and comic operas. Seldom considered highbrow fare, Scott's dramas, as well as her acting and directing, point to her versatility and popularity. The varied entertainment offered by Scott at the Sans Pareil may have prompted a movement toward music-hall fare and vaudeville performances which developed in the later part of the century.

In an age where melodramas were growing more popular, serious drama seldom received a hearing. Still, Mary Russell Mitford wished to produce critically significant tragedies of high quality. Yet another female dramatist neglected in theatre histories of the period, Mitford packed the playhouse with her dramas, especially *Rienzi*, which ran for thirty-four nights its first season at Drury Lane.

Class, Education, and Marital Status

Making any sort of generalization about the various women who wrote plays is difficult, for on the social scale they ranged from titled women (Lady Sophia Burrell) to farmhands (Mary Leapor), and they came from virtually every class. Hannah Brand was a daughter of a tanner; Marianne Chambers the daughter of the first mate on an East the King's company in London probably staged a performance in the spring. That August, William Davenant burlesqued Philips's tragedy in his farce *The Playhouse to be Let*.

As Aphra Behn developed into a professional dramatist through the 1670s, she too was attacked by name-calling because she "invaded" the male domain of playwrighting. Behn fought back in the Prefaces to her plays, refuting charges of plagiarism, immorality, and prejudice. Behn's artful intrigue plots and her well-developed characters created a popularity matched by few male dramatists. Another instance of public mockery of female playwrights occurred when three different women wrote producible plays in the 1695–96 theatrical season, and several men joined forces to parody these playwrights in *The Female Wits* (1696). Yet each of these women—Mary Pix, Catharine Trotter, and Delarivere Manley—went on to produce a number of notable stage plays. Other seventeenth-century women dramatists, such as Margaret Cavendish, the Duchess of Newcastle, were scorned with denigrating titles—"Mad Madge"—and repudiated in public. Yet Cavendish would not give up her writing, and she composed a number of prose works and more than two dozen plays.

Another example of denigration of female playwrights came from the players themselves. When reading through one of Susanna Centlivre's comedies in the greenroom, one actor became so upset at his part that he threw down his book and refused to act in the play. Centlivre asserted it "was much easier to write a play than to get it represented" (quoted in *The Female Tatler* no. 69, for 12–14 December 1709): she claimed the cast seemed always to wrangle over minutiae and to consider their judgment better than the author's. However, continual nagging adversity didn't keep Centlivre from turning out a score of successful plays.

To avoid harsh criticism, several women dramatists masked their names: for instance, the author of the witty comedy *She Ventures and He Wins* (1695) wrote under the pseudonym of "Ariadne," and only the initials "M. N." identify the female author of *The Loyal General* (1706). Anonymous printings may be merely inscribed "by a lady," or by initials, and dedications remain unsigned. Knowing they could anticipate male prejudice, a few female playwrights disguised themselves under a male persona. Because many women dramatists used pseudonyms to disguise their real identities, while other women writers may have wished to preserve their "good" names and chose to remain anonymous, a significant number of female playwrights have passed into oblivion. The many anonymous plays in this period should remind us that numerous works by women went unacknowledged. After three hundred or more years, it is almost impossible to determine authorship.

Over the course of the eighteenth century, many obstacles remained for women who wrote dramas. Women playwrights seemed almost decimated by the Licensing Act of 1737, and very few of them wrote plays for the next twenty years. In his managerial capacity at Drury Lane from 1747 to 1776, David Garrick did assist some female playwrights during his patriarchal reign. Still many female playwrights found getting their plays produced a difficult proposition. Consider the case of Sarah Gardner, who submitted her play to Colman in April 1777 in hopes of seeing it performed that summer season at the Haymarket. It took more than two months for him to read her play, *The Advertisement; or, A Bold Stroke for a Husband*, and to speak with her about it. He then asked her to turn the comedy into a farce, but he insisted on putting it off until the following summer since the present summer season was nearly half over. Through the intercession of a subordinate, Colman finally agreed to put on the play for Gardner's benefit night, and if it succeeded the play would be revived the following summer. Instead of keeping the author's name secret as he had promised, Colman announced it at the players' first reading. Knowing Gardner was the author, the actors were not predisposed to take the play seriously. Nevertheless, author and work received an enthusiastic response from the audience. Back in the greenroom, however, the actors abused her, and Colman swore he would never perform the play again (for a detailed discussion, see Isobel Grundy, *TSWL* 7 [1988]: 7–25, where she notes "in addition, Mary Latter, Jean Marishall [also Marshall] and Sophia Lee all published complaints about the procrastination and broken promises of managers").

In addition to irresponsibility by managers and mistreatment by actors, intolerance toward female dramatists was a problem that women often had to contend with at home. Prejudicial attitudes about the theatre caused fathers to discourage their daughters from writing dramas. Such was the case with Fanny Burney when her father demanded she suppress *The Witlings* in 1779.

Despite various forms of resistance, however, theatre managers put on more women's plays in the last two decades of the eighteenth century than ever before. Hannah Cowley and Elizabeth Inchbald became two of the best known in their ability to draw audiences. With the retirement from the stage of Cowley in 1795 and Inchbald in 1805, there seemed to be different opportunities for female playwrights. Early in the nineteenth century gothic plays, melodramas, and *comédie sérieuse* rose in popularity. New female dramatists appeared on the theatrical scene, such as Marianne Chambers, who left two witty comedies and then vanished from the stage milieu. Even those who never succeeded in getting their plays staged—such as Ann M'Taggart—often persisted in writing and publishing plays. The range of these early nineteenth-century women playwrights is established in the main section of this volume. Despite whatever public bias that lingered against women dramatists, works by these playwrights overcame gender antipathy, showing a remarkable change of attitudes toward female dramatists from the Restoration period through the Romantic era.

Generic Choices and Restrictions

Most women who wrote dramas were women who read or saw dramas; consequently, they had in mind how a play should appear on the page or the stage. Because audiences tend to be unpredictable in their dramatic preferences, theatrical trends follow no tidy pattern. A play that may be popular today could be considered old-fashioned next month. Several twentieth-century critics, beginning with Allardyce Nicoll, have tried to refine generic classifications of Restoration and eighteenth-century drama beyond comedy and to write about themes radically different from what men chose, women concentrate upon affairs of the heart, love, honor, and truth" (322).

While women were attracted to certain specific genres, they also seemed to avoid others. Female playwrights, for instance, seldom choose to write satirical plays or sardonic burlesques, perhaps because satires are usually written by insiders, and women were generally excluded from the political or social world often satirized by men. Exceptions do exist, but in many of these cases the playwright/actor parodies herself. For example, when she wrote an afterpiece for her benefit night, Clive creates the role of Mrs. Hazard for herself as the target of her farce *The Rehearsal; or, Bayes in Petticoats* (1750). In another self-parody, Sarah Gardner casts herself as a distracted poet in *Mrs. Doggrell in Her Altitudes* (1795). Other than plays by women who performed on stage (Centlivre included), women dramatists seem to show little interest in parody and satire. From the evidence of the dramas in this period, it appears accurate that women view the world differently from men.

While they might naturally have gravitated toward or avoided certain topics or themes, as well as certain genres and subgenres, women dramatists also had to respond to the potential economics of the theatre market. If a particular kind of play is popular enough to run six nights, this will provide the author with two benefit performances. In crass terms, the dramatists are forced to ask themselves—what will bring audiences into the theatre? Blood-and-gore tragedies were popular and less difficult to write than a thoughtful tragedy. The several sources that the early playwrights used—early English plays, French drama, and historical pieces—could recreate a well-known story in a new guise, and often stock plots were brushed up with some alterations and original touches. Dramas may also have developed from political motives. Several of Behn's plays abuse the narrow-minded Puritans (*The Roundheads*), while Centlivre's comedies frequently support the Whigs (*The Gotham Election*). In the revolutionary spirit of the 1790s, the arch-conservative Hannah More chose a contrasting dramatic dialogue in *Village Politics* to censure Thomas Paine's *Common Sense*, which she considered ultraradical.

Topics, Themes, Motifs, Settings

In looking at some of these contrasting visions, users of this volume will discover that dramas by women illustrate wide interests in many subjects. Certain confrontational issues probably led writers to produce work in dramatic form because of the inherent nature of conflict in theatrical works. Most topics that stirred women dramatists in this 163-year period, linking these three centuries, still have universal qualities that make the subjects of many dramas germane to modern readers.

Moral education.

Women characters are often portrayed by female playwrights as the primary advocates of ethical principles, providing a moral force in an immoral world. In the latter part of the eighteenth century, the moral education of the young in acquiring appropriate behavior and virtuous precepts comes in part through drama, mostly written by women.

Beginning with the English translation of Madame de Genlis's *Theatre of Education* in 1781, dramas for young people illustrate negative and unacceptable characteristics, such as stealing, cruelty to animals, arrogant behavior, anger, tardiness, and false sentiments. Positive traits include hard work, kindness to animals, helping the less fortunate, and keeping up with one's lessons. These overtly didactic plays, written by Elizabeth Pinchard, Charlotte Sanders, and Charlotte Turner Smith, found a wide audience in the last decade.

In another mode of instruction that ran parallel to the "theatre of education," More wrote her *Sacred Dramas* (1782). Wholly taken from the Old Testament, these plays dramatize Daniel in the lion's den, David fighting Goliath, and the discovery of the baby Moses hidden in the bulrushes. Beyond the education of adolescents, female dramatists illustrate behavioral excesses for adult edification: for instance, Baillie's exhibition of ruling passions demonstrates mature predicaments. In *De Monfort*, hatred drives the title character to murder, whereas in her contrasting comedy, *The Election*, Baltimore is motivated by a class hatred toward Freeman, who would be his benefactor. These plays are not simply moral lessons for adults; they develop a strong dramatic tension.

Marriage.

Many dramas by women deal with marriage—approaching, present, and past. Arranged and forced marriages come in for a great deal of censure, and several of the later plays even examine divorce. Behn's first play, *The Forced Marriage* (1670), demonstrates Erminia's predicament: she is secretly pledged to Philander, the King's son, but without her approval the King agrees to give her to Alcippus because of his military victories. Despite this forced marriage, Erminia remains faithful to Philander until the predicament can be resolved. Readers can follow several treatments of forced marriages in almost every play Behn wrote.

Nearly one hundred years later, Lord Medway in Frances Sheridan's *The Discovery* (1763) forces his children (a son and a daughter) to marry for money in order to reconcile their father's exorbitant expenditures. The fathers who demand that marriages take place in both these dramas are atypical in one way, however; they recognize their mistakes and in the end publicly acknowledge they have been wrong. More commonly, fathers or other patriarchal figures acknowledge no guilt or wrongdoing, so far as arranged or forced marriages are concerned. In numerous dramas, it is the woman herself who seeks forgiveness even though the patriarchal figure has been discredited by the end of the play. While demanding fathers usually attempt to control marriages, some sympathetic male figures help young lovers bypass these blocking figures. In *Cross Partners* (1792), for example, Sir Charles Callender generously provides the money for Cleveland and Louisa to marry, relieving them both from forced marriages.

Second marriages often show that hope has failed to triumph over experience, and such marriages in the drama usually depict an older man and a younger wife. Mary Pix in her *Deceiver Deceived* (1697) shows a young wife, Olivia, learning to defend herself against her husband's deceit and to defend her honor against the slander of others; but at the conclusion of the play she finds there is no easy exit from the misalliance she has been forced into. Lady Byfield has married an older man in Kitty Clive's *Every Woman in Her Humour* (1760), and while she cannot love him, she explains to her stepdaughter that she will never injure (cuckold?) him. Over the course of the play, Lady Byfield becomes a stronger figure and in the concluding scene orders the caustic-tongued Miss Croston (played by Clive herself) from the house. Baillie titles an early drama *The Second Marriage* (1802), in which Seabright marries Lady Sarah for her family connections, and his ambitions cause a breakup in their relationship. One play that treats divorce is Inchbald's *Every One Has His Fault* (1793). Sir Robert and Lady Ramble end up in a Scottish divorce, as a result of his shabby treatment of her, but the divorce doesn't improve her situation, for she comes under the control of her guardian, Lord Norland. The play also deals with other problematic marriages involving disinheritance and poverty; women in this drama seem to get the worst of domestic situations, but they manage to survive through sheer pluck and tenacity.

Class structure.

Class has a decided impact on marital circumstances in many of the plays written during this period. For women dramatists, especially, class played an important role in marriage. Margaret Cavendish, who could never forget that she was the "Duchess of Newcastle," emphasizes the importance of noble breeding in several plays. A number of later dramas by women turn on the well-worn plot device that the abandoned child brought up by humble parents is found to have descended from aristocratic stock. An example of this plotting can be seen in the cradle exchange that occurs in Hannah Brand's *Adelinda* (1798), whose title character—brought up in the castle—is actually the daughter of a farm couple, whereas Zella (raised by Dorcas, the rural wife) is proved to be the real daughter of the Marquis and Marchioness d'Olstain. Frances Brooke's popular *Rosina* (1782) operates on the same principle that "blood will tell," because of the eighteenth-century notion that one's heredity is more significant than the environment in which one is reared. The virtuous orphan who gives her name to the play is beloved by Belville, the local landowner, but he cannot marry her until he discovers Rosina to be the daughter of a now deceased gentleman. These sorts of fairy tale elements might lead to wish-fulfillment in audiences: they may dream of themselves as foundlings who discover that they have come into their rightful inheritance of wealth, power, and position.

In the early nineteenth century, greater resistance to class structure is evident in some of the plays, no doubt a reaction in part to the French Revolution and other social and political upheavals. In Caroline Boaden's *Fatality* (1829), for instance, the comments about class seem contradictory. General Loverule has engineered a marriage between Susanna and Bernard, a soldier wounded defending his son, because the General disapproved of his son Edward's desire to marry Susanna. Repeatedly, the play criticizes the General's interference and his class snobbery. Yet, Susanna's dissatisfaction with her husband seems to be rooted in his social status, and Bernard begs like a servant for clemency from the General at the end of the play—"Oh, my benefactor! do not curse me!" (28)—even though Edward was disloyal to him by making advances to Susanna.

Boaden's *Don Pedro the Cruel and Don Manuel the Cobbler!* (1838) contains less ambiguity and a much stronger criticism of oppressive class structure. In this melodrama, a lowly cobbler is given the title of Corregidor for twenty-four hours and told that he will be executed if he cannot feed the starving poor. With the help of his old friend and lover, Paquita the beggar, the cobbler succeeds by breaking up a grain monopoly. Given a second task, Don Manuel discovers that Don Pedro, the King, is a murderer. By setting the play in Seville during the 14th century, Boaden emphasizes that classes barriers have long existed in European societies.

Disguises, masks, and cross-dressing.

Because some female dramatists distrust happy endings and fairy-tale solutions, they create women protagonists who know what they want to achieve and who take risks to accomplish their goals. In *She Ventures and He Wins* (1695), for example, the anonymous playwright (who calls herself Ariadne) has Charlot, the main character, test Lovewell, the man she wishes to marry. Part of the testing involves Charlot's wearing men's clothes: in her male guise, Charlot sets up three tests of Lovewell with consummate cleverness, establishing that he loves her and not her money. In Centlivre's *The Gamester* (1705), Angelica puts on a male costume to test the resolve of her lover Valere not to gamble. He unquestionably fails the test, however; not only does he lose all his money to her, but he also forfeits Angelica's picture, wagered on the last cast of the dice. She ultimately forgives Valere, who vows to gamble no more, though his reform is not altogether convincing.

Women sometimes take on disguises in order to assist others. In *The Fate of Sparta* (1789), Chelonice disguises herself as a priestess to go the camp of the enemy's army in an attempt to deter the destruction of her father and her city, and she succeeds in getting the attack postponed. Other female protagonists dress as men to serve in some way the men they love. In Cavendish's *Love's Adventures*, Lady Orphant dresses as a page and assumes the name of Affectionata to assist Lord Singularity, who has become a general to the Venetians. Pearson points out the homoerotic component in this plot, for Singularity begins to eschew women in favor of "his Affectionata," who finally declares her real identity.

Behn's *Feign'd Curtizans* (1679) features Marcella and Cornelia, who flee parental control (a forced marriage and the convent) and go to Rome where they disguise themselves as courtesans. During the night's intrigue, the women find that with this disguise they have a freedom and independence from class distinctions and parental requirements. Their demands for personal autonomy succeed because they are willing to take risks. The many disguises women assume provide them with a freedom they would not have if they were recognized as themselves. Cross-dressing also frees women from the numerous gender restrictions commonly conferred on them by a male hierarchy. In many dramas by women, then, the playwrights urge the breaking of the existing hegemony so that society becomes less inhibited. By disregarding restrictive codes and male-dominated governance, many women in dramas by female playwrights achieve an autonomy they have established as their prerogative. (Kristina Straub's *Sexual Suspects* [1992] provides an excellent treatment of cross-dressing, especially concerning gender roles and sexual identities.)

Women helping other women.

Central to many of the plays covered in this volume, women's friendship emerges as something quite different from those relationships depicted by most male writers. The female characters in many of these plays know how to sympathize with each other's problems, offer assistance to one another, and protect a female friend in a desperate predicament. Female friendships even occur between women who might oppose each other or who are competitors for the same end. Two romantic rivals in Sarah Richardson's *Ethelred* (c. 1810), for instance, transcend sexual jealousy: Emma agrees to care for Ethelgive's children after her death. A different example of female friendship can be found in Pix's *Deceiver Deceived* (1697), where a mother and daughter combine energies to overcome male plots. One of the best examples of women befriending and helping one another comes from Centlivre's *The Wonder: A Woman Keeps a Secret* (1714). At no small emotional expense to herself, Violante conceals Isabella to save her from a forced marriage. The importance of women's friendships in so many of these dramas cannot be overstated. Since women are often compelled to develop cooperative strategies, there is less competition among women in these plays than in those plays written by men.

Attention to the theme of female friendship may have resulted in part from the fact that women playwrights generally assisted one another. When Centlivre wrote her first play in 1700, Mary Pix had already established herself as a playwright, but Pix befriended the novice. The two became lasting friends so that after Pix's death, Centlivre's *Busie Body* was performed for the benefit of Mrs. Pix's executor (at Drury Lane on 28 May 1709), causing newspapers to speculate that Pix had written "the greatest part" of the play (*LS* 2: 193). Despite such easy slander, Pix and the few women playwrights at the beginning of the eighteenth century cooperated in support of one another, still acknowledging Behn's renown for her pioneering work as a professional dramatist.

Exotic settings and historical subjects.

To talk about the problems in their own land and in their own time, English women playwrights sometimes set their plays in foreign lands, where powerful—and often barbaric—men seem to have absolute control over women. The exotic settings extend from the Far East (Siam in *The Unnatural Mother*, 1698, and India in *The Widow of Malabar*, 1790) to the Near East (*The Royal Mischief*, 1696, and *A Day in Turkey*, 1791) and many lands bordering the Mediterranean (Spain in *The Midnight Hour*, 1787; Greece in *The Fatal Legacy*, 1723; Italy in *The Rover*, 1677). The staging of battles between the Moors and the Christians takes place on the shores of North Africa and Spain in Lady Dacre's *Xarifa* (1821). Several of Centlivre's plays are set in Lisbon: *Marplot* (1710), *The Wonder* (1714), and *The Wife Well Managed* (1715). A few playwrights even set their dramas in North America—*The Siege of Quebec* (Forsyth, 1789), *Virginia* (Plowden, 1800), and *The Widow Ranter; or, The History of Bacon in Virginia* (Behn, 1689). The last two feature Indians to generate a sense of danger and to provide local color.

Historical settings nearer home take up Scottish, Irish, or British events in antiquity, usually the middle ages. Historical plays, too, have a similar set of unwritten regulations where men govern and women produce children, preferably male heirs to continue the lineage. Ann Yearsley attempts to rehabilitate the character of Earl Godwin, in the play of that title, during the time of Edward the Confessor. Similarly, Burney's *Edwy and Elgiva* (1795) dramatizes a tenth-century conflict between the King of the West Saxons and the Catholic clergy. In her play called *Malcolm* (1779), Roberts probes the events that follow the death of the usurper in Shakespeare's *Macbeth. Mary Queen of Scots* (1792) focuses on Queen Elizabeth's rival in Mary Deverell's closet drama. Even recent English history becomes a reality in Mitford's *Charles the First*—but not easily. The play was first prohibited by the Lord Chamberlain in 1826, and it didn't make its way to the stage until 1834 when—with changes—it was finally approved by a new Lord Chamberlain, to whom Mitford shrewdly dedicated the play. Although oppressive male figures in British history are less barbaric than foreign rulers (perhaps for patriot reasons), their exercise of authority reinforces the status of women, who have no place in the governing hierarchy nor any other position in the power structure. Cavendish creates a new world order because of the actions of her protagonist, Victoria, in *Bell in Campo* (1662), which is not set in any definite historical period. Victoria successfully leads a women's army through a triumphant battle, and because of their success abroad the women win new rights at home.

Racial and religious prejudice.

Especially when set in exotic lands, many of these plays must have appealed to British racial and religious prejudice. If not treated merely as exotic local color, non-Europeans—especially Middle-Eastern Indians, Turks, Africans, and South Americans—are typically described as primitive, cruel, and devoted to religions that are obviously inferior to Christianity. In Brand's *Huniades* (1791), for instance, when Mahomet offers to make peace with Belgrade if the Princess will marry him, Agmunda is horrified: "a Turk! a murderer! An Infidel!" (47). It is no wonder that the most enlightened of these non-Europeans generally convert by the end of the play. When he goes to strike the Spaniard Alphonso while he is sleeping, the Indian Houaco in Dacre's *Pedrarias* succumbs to his friend's Christian goodness: "The virtues *I* have prized are savage Nature's—*Thine* are from Heaven" (185). Nonetheless, there are exceptions or at least slightly more complex treatments of race and religion. Although the African princess in *Incle and Yarico* (attributed to Mrs. Wendell, 1742) puts off a man from her own tribe in order to leave with a white man, the behavior of the white man is strongly condemned when he sells the pregnant Yarico into slavery because he believes he cannot marry her. Several themes arise from the events: a condemnation of slavery, a denunciation of racial injustice, and a castigation of disloyalty. In *La-Peyrouse*, Anne Plumptre's translation of Kotzebue's *La*

are the plays that deserve to be revived on stage. While a few of Aphra Behn's comedies have enjoyed twentieth-century performances, other of her plays merit consideration for the stage, especially such fast-moving intrigue comedies as *Sir Patient Fancy* and *The City Heiress*. Aside from *The Wonder*, two of Centlivre's comedies that would have theatrical attractiveness are *The Busie Body* and *A Bold Stroke for a Wife*: both plays would be likely to captivate audiences with their high-spirited characters and their clever plotting. Cowley created lively drama in over a dozen plays, and several of her comedies were quite successful in her own day. Her best comedies are generally conceded to be *The Belle's Stratagem* (1780), which was performed into the early twentieth century, and *A Bold Stroke for a Husband* (1783) which held the stage for nearly a hundred years. Both comedies are worthy of revival for their brilliant female characters who take charge of their own destinies. As the bibliography of secondary sources that follows the Introduction demonstrates, many female dramatists from this period still warrant critical attention, including not only Behn, Centlivre, Inchbald, and Cowley, but also less well-known playwrights such as Mary Pix, Eliza Haywood, Elizabeth Griffith, Frances Sheridan, and Fanny Burney.

At least two dramatists also were well recognized as drama critics and theorists in their day. After writing plays for twenty years, Inchbald was asked by the publisher Longman to prepare brief commentaries and critical prefaces to some 125 plays currently being acted—to illustrate their dramatic and intrinsic values. The twenty-five volumes of *The British Theatre* (1808) conferred upon Inchbald the appellation of "Britain's First Woman Drama Critic" (the title of a convincing essay by Katharine M. Rogers included in *Curtain Calls*). Rogers discusses some of the difficulties Inchbald encountered because of her "gentle criticism": despite male detractors however, Inchbald maintained her position and earned the name of a genuine drama critic. If Inchbald gained a reputation as a critic, Baillie could be said to be one of the earliest female theorists of drama. She illustrated her theory of the passions in many plays, written over a forty-year period. Her first plays in 1798 were prefaced with a lengthy essay explaining the importance of a single passion to unify a drama.

Even with the resistance to women playwrights and the prejudice that they experienced from managers, actors, and their own families, female dramatists made remarkable advances in the number of plays written as well as those performed. While women's plays were not always popularly successful, female dramatists deserve recognition for their achievements. We hope this volume will promote a reevaluation of what these woman did achieve in plays that they wrote for the reading public and for stage performance. In the last quarter of the eighteenth century, as documented by the chronological list of female playwrights at the end of this volume, more women wrote, translated, published, and produced more plays than at any earlier time. This quantity, as well as the quality of these plays, favorably compares with the number of dramas by women in the Victorian age and rivals women playwrights in twentieth-century Britain.

ABBREVIATIONS

We have used standard MLA abbreviations for journal titles within the text of this work.

Biblical references are to the King James Version (KJV).

Frequently Cited Works

Adelphi = *The Adelphi Theatre Calendar*. Ed. Alfred L. Nelson and Gilbert B. Cross. Westport, CT: Greenwood, 1988.

Annals = *Annals of English Drama, 975-1700*, by Alfred Harbage, revised by Samuel Schoenbaum. Third edition, revised by Sylvia Stoler Wagonheim. London: Routledge, 1989.

Backscheider = Backscheider, Paula. *Spectacular Politics*. Baltimore: Johns Hopkins UP, 1993.

BD = Baker, David Erskine, Issac Reed, and Stephen Jones. *Biographia Dramatica; or, A Companion to the Playhouse*. 3 vols. 1812; NY: AMS, 1966. (NOTE: Baker to 1764, Reed to 1782, and Jones to 1811.)

BDAA = Highfill, Philip H., Jr., Kalman Burnim, and Edward Langhans, *A Dictionary of Actors, Actresses, Musicians, Dancers, Managers, and Other Stage Personnel in London, 1660-1800*. 16 vols. Carbondale: Southern Illinois UP, 1973-94.

BL = *British Museum Catalogue of Printed Books*. 263 vols. London: Trustees of the British Museum, 1965-66.

BNA = Backscheider, Paula R., Felicity Nussbaum, and Philip B. Anderson, eds. *An Annotated Bibliography of Twentieth-Century Studies of Women and Literature, 1660-1800*. NY: Garland, 1977.

Bevis 1980 = Bevis, Richard W. *The Laughing Tradition: Stage Comedy in Garrick's Day*. Athens, GA: U of Georgia P, 1980.

Bevis 1988 = Bevis, Richard W. *English Drama: Restoration and Eighteenth-Century*. London: Longmans, 1988.

Bowyer = Bowyer, John Wilson. *The Celebrated Mrs. Centlivre*. 1952; Westport, CT: Greenwood, 1968.

Burling = Burling, William J. *A Checklist of New Plays and Entertainments on the London Stage, 1700-1737*. Madison, N. J.: Fairleigh Dickinson UP, 1991.

Butler = Butler, Marilyn. *Maria Edgeworth: A Literary Biography*. Oxford: Oxford UP, 1972.

CAM = *Catalogue of Additions to the Manuscripts: Plays Submitted to the Lord Chamberlain, 1824-1851*. London: British Museum, 1964.

Clark 1955 = Clark, W. S. *The Early Irish Stage, the Beginnings to 1720*. Oxford: Clarendon, 1955.

Clark 1965 = Clark, W. S. *The Irish Stage in the County Towns, 1720-1800*. Oxford: Clarendon, 1965.

Conolly = Conolly, L. W. *The Censorship of English Drama 1737-1824*. San Marino, CA: Huntington Library, 1976.

Cotton = Cotton, Nancy. *Women Playwrights in England, c. 1363 to 1750*. Lewisburg, PA: Bucknell UP, 1980.

Curtain Calls = *Curtain Calls: British and American Women and the Theatre, 1660-1800*. Ed. M. A. Schofield and Cecilia Macheski. Athens, OH: Ohio UP, 1991.

Davis & Joyce = *Drama by Women to 1900: A Bibliography of American and British Writers.* Comp. Gwenn Davis and Beverly A. Joyce. Toronto: U of Toronto P, 1992.

DBAWW = Todd, Janet, ed. *A Dictionary of British and American Women Writers, 1660-1800.* 1984; London: Methuen, 1987.

DLB = *Dictionary of Literary Biography. Restoration and Eighteenth-Century Dramatists.* Vols. 80, 84, 89. Ed. Paula R. Backscheider. Detroit: Gale, 1989. [DLB vols. 39, on Aubin, and 93, on Baillie.]

DNB = *Dictionary of National Biography.* 22 vols. Ed. L. Stephen and S. Lee. London: Smith and Elder, 1908-09.

Donohue 1970 = Donohue, Joseph W. *Dramatic Character in the English Romantic Age.* Princeton: Princeton UP, 1970.

Donohue 1975 = Donohue, Joseph W. *Theatre in the Age of Kean.* Totowa, NJ: Rowman and Littlefield, 1975.

Doody = Doody, Margaret Anne. *Frances Burney: The Life in the Works.* New Brunswick, NJ: Rutgers UP, 1988.

Downes = Downes, John. *Roscius Anglicanus.* Ed. Judith Milhous and Robert D. Hume. London: Society for Theatre Research, 1987.

E-CED = *Eighteenth-Century English Drama.* 58 vols. Gen. ed. Paula Backscheider. NY: Garland, 1980-84. Facsimile reprints with critical introductions by various scholars.

EEB = Early English Books, Wing 1641-1700. Microfilms. Ann Arbor: Xerox, in progress.

ESTC = *Eighteenth-Century Short Title Catalogue.* London: British Library, 1992.

EBWW = *An Encyclopedia of British Women Writers.* Ed. Paul and June Schlueter. NY: Garland, 1988. (2nd ed. forthcoming in 1996).

Eshleman = Eshleman, Dorothy Hughes. *Elizabeth Griffith.* Philadelphia: U of Pennsylvania, 1949.

FCLE = Blain, Virginia, Isobel Grundy, and Patricia Clements, *The Feminist Companion to Literature in English: Women Writers from the Middle Ages to the Present.* New Haven: Yale UP, 1990.

Forster = Forster, Antonia. *Index to Book Reviews in England, 1749-1774.* Carbondale: Southern Illinois UP, 1990.

Genest = Genest, John. *Some Account of the English Stage, from the Restoration in 1660 to 1830.* 10 vols. 1832; NY: Franklin, 1965.

Halliwell = Halliwell, James O. *Dictionary of Old English Plays.* London: J. R. Smith, 1860.

Hazlitt = Hazlitt, W. C. *A Manual for the Collector...of Old English Plays [to 1700].* 1892; NY: Franklin, 1966.

Hobby = Hobby, Elaine, *Virtue of Necessity: English Women's Writing, 1649-88.* London: Virago, 1988. Chapter 5 (102-27) on Newcastle, Boothby, Polwhele, and Behn.

Hume 1976 = Hume, Robert D. *The Development of English Drama in the Late Seventeenth Century.* Oxford: Clarendon, 1976.

Hume 1983 = Hume, Robert D. *The Rakish Stage: Studies in the English Drama, 1660-1800.* Carbondale: Southern Illinois UP, 1983.

Inglis = Inglis, Ralston. *The Dramatic Writers of Scotland.* Glasgow: G. D. Mackellar, 1868.

Jackson = Jackson, Mary V. *Engines of Instruction, Mischief, and Magic: Children's Literature in England from Its Beginnings to 1839.* Lincoln: U of Nebraska P, 1989.

Keener & Lorsch = *Eighteenth-Century Women and the Arts.* Ed. Frederick M. Keener and Susan E. Lorsch. Westport, CT: Greenwood, 1988.

Kendall = *Love and Thunder: Plays by Women in the Age of Queen Anne.* London: Methuen, 1988.

Kinne = Kinne, Willard Austin. *Revivals and Importations of French Comedies in England, 1749-1800.* NY: Columbia UP, 1939.

Larpent = MacMillan, Dougald. *Catalogue of the Larpent Plays in the Huntington Library.* San Marino, CA: Huntington, 1939.

Levy = Levy, Jonathan. *The Gymnasium of the Imagination: A Collection of Children's Plays in English, 1780-1860.* Westport, CT: Greenwood, 1992.

Link = Link, Frederick M. *Aphra Behn.* NY: Twayne, 1968.

Lock = Lock, F. P. *Susanna Centlivre.* NY: Twayne, 1979.

Lonsdale = *Eighteenth-Century Women Poets: An Oxford Anthology.* Ed. Roger Lonsdale. Oxford: Oxford UP, 1989.

LS = *The London Stage, 1660-1800.* 11 vols. Carbondale, IL: Southern Illinois UP, 1960-68. Part 1, 1660-1700, ed. William Van Lennep, with Introduction by Emmett L. Avery and Arthur H. Scouten (1965); Part 2, 1700-1729, ed. Emmett L. Avery (2 vols., 1960); Part 3, 1729-1747, ed. Arthur H. Scouten (2 vols., 1961); Part 4, 1747-1776, ed. George W. Stone (3 vols., 1962); Part 5, 1776-1800, ed. Charles B. Hogan (3 vols., 1968).

Mendelson = Mendelson, Sara Heller. *The Mental World of Stuart Women.* Amherst: U of Massachusetts P, 1987.

Milhous = Milhous, Judith. *Thomas Betterton and the Management of Lincoln's Inn Fields, 1695-1708.* Carbondale: Southern Illinois UP, 1979.

Milhous & Hume = Milhous, Judith, and Robert D. Hume. "Attribution Problems in English Drama, 1660-1700." *Harvard Library Bulletin* 31 (1983): 5-39.

Morgan = Morgan, Fidelis. *The Female Wits: Women Playwrights on The London Stage, 1660-1720.* London: Virago, 1981.

NCBEL = *New Cambridge Bibliography of English Literature.* 5 Vols. Ed. George Watson. Cambridge: Cambridge UP, 1969.

NUC = *National Union Catalog. Pre-1956 Imprints.* London: Mansell, 1968–81.

Nicoll = Nicoll, Allardyce. *A History of English Drama, 1660-1900.* Rev. ed., 6 vols. Cambridge: Cambridge UP, 1952-59.

O'Donnell = O'Donnell, Mary Ann. *Aphra Behn: An Annotated Bibliography of Primary and Secondary Sources.* NY: Garland, 1986.

OCEL = *The Oxford Companion to English Literature.* 5th ed., revised and altered by Margaret Drabble. Oxford: Oxford UP, 1985.

Pearson = Pearson, Jacqueline. *The Prostituted Muse: Images of Women and Women Dramatists, 1642-1737.* NY: St. Martin's, 1988.

Readex Microprint = Listed in *Three Centuries of English and American Plays: A Checklist: England: 1500-1800, United States, 1714-1830.* Ed. G. William Bergquist. NY: Hafner, 1963. From 1801-1900: James Ellis, Joseph Donohue, and Louise Allen Zak, eds., *English Drama of the Nineteenth Century: An Index and Finding Guide.* New Canaan, CT: Readex, 1985.

Revels = *The Revels History of Drama in England.* Gen. eds. T. W. Craik and C. Leech. Vol. 5: 1660-1750 [includes specific discussions of Behn, Centlivre, S. Cibber, Clive, Manley, Pix, and Trotter] Vol. 6: 1750-1880 [arranged by decade rather than playwright]. London: Methuen, 1975-83.

Straub 1987 = Straub, Kristina. *Divided Fictions: Fanny Burney and Feminine Strategy.* Lexington: U of Kentucky P, 1987.

Straub 1992 = Straub, Kristina. *Sexual Suspects: Eighteenth-Century Players and Sexual Ideology.* Princeton: Princeton UP, 1992.

Scouten = *Restoration and 18th Century Drama.* Ed. A. H. Scouten. NY: St. Martin's, 1980. See also his volumes in *LS*.

Small = Small, Miriam R. *Charlotte Ramsay Lennox, An Eighteenth Century Lady of Letters.* New Haven: Yale UP, 1935.

Smith, D. F. = Smith, Dane Farnsworth. *Plays about the Theatre in England from "The Rehearsal" to the Licensing Act in 1737 or, The Self-Conscious Stage and its Burlesque and Satirical Reflections in the Age of Criticism.* London: Oxford UP, 1936.

Smith & Lawhon = Smith, Dane Farnsworth, and M. L. Lawhon. *Plays about the Theatre in England, 1737-1800 or, The Self-conscious Stage from Foote to Sheridan.* Lewisburg: Bucknell UP, 1979.

Smith & Cardinale = *Women and the Literature of the Seventeenth Century: An Annotated Bibliography Based on Wing's Short-Title Catalogue.* Complied by Hilda L. Smith and Susan Cardinale. Westport, CT: Greenwood, 1990.

Smith, J. H. = Smith, John Harrington. *The Gay Couple in Restoration Comedy.* 1948; NY: Octagon, 1971.

Souers = Souers, P. W. *The Matchless Orinda.* Cambridge, MA: Harvard UP, 1931.

Stanton = Stanton, Judith Philips, "'This New-Found Path Attempting': Women Dramatists in England, 1660-1800." *Curtain Calls: British and American Women and Theatre, 1660-1820.* Ed. M. A. Schofield and C. Macheski. Athens: Ohio UP, 1991.

Staves = Staves, Susan. *Players' Scepters: Fictions of Authority in the Restoration.* Lincoln: U of Nebraska P, 1979.

Stratman = Stratman, Carl J. *Bibliography of English Printed Tragedy, 1565-1900.* Carbondale: Southern Illinois UP, 1966.

Tobin = Tobin, Terance. *Plays by Scots, 1660-1800.* Iowa City: U of Iowa P, 1974.

TEC = The Eighteenth Century (microfilm collection). Woodbridge, CT: Research Publications, in progress .

Waldo = Waldo, Lewis P. *The French Drama in America in the Eighteenth Century and its Influence on the American Drama of that Period, 1701-1800.* Baltimore: Johns Hopkins UP, 1942.

Ward = Ward, William S. *Literary Reviews in British Periodicals, 1789-1797.* NY: Garland, 1979; *Literary Reviews in British Periodicals, 1798-1820,* 2 vols. NY: Garland, 1972; *Literary Reviews in British Periodicals, 1821-1826.* NY: Garland, 1977 [NB: for each reference in the text to Ward, consult the volume that includes the year of the play in question.]

Whincop = Whincop, Thomas [i.e., John Mottley]. *Scanderbeg . . . to which is added a List of all the Dramatick Authors . . . and of all the Dramatick Pieces . . . to the Year 1747.* London: W. Reeve, 1747.

Wing = Wing, Donald. *Short-Title Catalogue. . .1641-1700.* 2nd ed. 3 vols. NY: MLA, 1972-88.

London Theatres

The Introduction to each part of *The London Stage* contains a detailed history of active theatres in the period. After 1800, we have used *The Oxford Companion to the Theatre*.

Bridges = Theatre Royal in Bridges St. (1662–72)

CG = Theatre Royal Covent Garden (1732–1808, 1809–1843)

DG = Duke's Theatre in Dorset Garden (1671–1706)

DL = Drury Lane (1674–1791, 1794–1809, 1812–1878)

EOH = Royal Lyceum and English Opera House, rebuilt after the Lyceum burnt down (1834–1902)

GF = Goodman's Fields: [1] Odell's Theatre in Ayliffe St. (1729–1732); [2] The New Theatre in Ayliffe St. (1732–42)
HAY = Haymarket (1720–1820, 1821–1879), often referred to as the Little Theatre in the Haymarket.
James St. = The Tennis Court in James Street (1713–1756)
King's = King's Theatre in Haymarket. Opened in 1705 as the Queen's Theatre; name changed to the King's Theatre after the death of Queen Anne in 1714 (1705–1789, 1791–1867)
LIF = Lincoln's Inn Fields, converted from a tennis court to a theatre (1661–1674, 1695–1705, 1714–33, for hire until 1744)
LYC = Lyceum (licensed for plays 1809–1830; burnt down)
Queen's = Opened 1705; name changed to King's Theatre after the death of Queen Anne in 1714; renamed Queen's on the accession of Victoria in 1837 (1705–1789, 1791–1867)
SP = Sans Pareil, forerunner of the Adelphi Theatre in the Strand, originally built by John Scott to display the talents of his daughter, Jane M. Scott, in 1806. Sold in 1819, the theatre reopened under new ownership as the Adelphi (1819–1858)
YB = The Great Room or Theatre in York Buildings, Villiers St. (1703–1737)

Dublin Theatres

Plays by women were performed at the following Dublin venues. A detailed history of these theatres may be found in La Tourette Stockwell's *Dublin Theatres and Theatre Customs, 1637–1820*. 1938; NY: Blom, 1968.

Smock-Alley = Smock-Alley Theatre (1662–1787)
Capel-St. = Capel-Street Theatre [1] (1745–1750); [2] (1770–1784)
Crow-St. = Crow-Street Theatre (1758–1820)
Hawkins-St. = Hawkins-Street Theatre (1821–1880)

the Moor overreaches himself once too often and is killed by the very people he planned to kill.

TEXTS: Wing B1715; EEB Reel 167: 5 (1677). Wing B1716; EEB Reel 1324: 3 (1693). Readex Microprint of 1677 edition.

MODERN EDITIONS: *Works*, ed. Montague Summers (1915; NY: Phaeton, 1967) 2: 1–98; Behn, *Five Plays*, with introduction by Maureen Duffy (London: Methuen, 1990), reprints Summers's text: 370–474.

ABINGTON, Frances Barton (1737–1815). Fanny Barton grew up in poverty near Covent Garden. Her first acting break came with Theophilus Cibber's company in the summer of 1755 at the Haymarket. She performed at Bath and Richmond the following season, and in the fall of 1756, she began three seasons at DL. In the summer of 1759, she married James Abington, a trumpeter of the King. Since she had little encouragement from Garrick, she accepted an invitation to Dublin, where she performed at both Smock Alley and Crow Street from 1759 to 1765, when she returned to the London stage. Her success in Dublin caused her to become estranged from her husband. At the retirement of Kitty Clive in 1769, Abington took over her roles, and for the next twenty years, she was the leading comic actress in the London theatre. After quarrelling with Garrick again, she finished her acting career at CG, from which she retired in 1790. She was lured out of retirement for a couple of years at the end of the century. To Abington has also been attributed *Matrimony; or, The Sleep Walker*, an unpublished comic afterpiece, prepared for her benefit at CG on 27 April 1798, and based on *Le Somnambule* by Antoine de Ferriol, Comte de Pont-de-Veyle. Abington continued to live in London until her death in 1815. [BDAA]

Adela; or, The Barons of Old, Jane West. This five-act verse tragedy was printed in the first volume of her *Poems and Plays* (1799), published by Longman and Rees. West comments in the preface that it was rejected by both theatres; there is no known performance.

Set in medieval times, the play opens with Gertrude and her father, Osbert, watching a tournament, which is won by "Albert," who is in disguise; he is actually Herbert, the son of the Earl of Pembroke. Theodore, the son of Lord Conway, plots with Mordaunt to rid the kingdom of Herbert. Adela, Theodore's sister, has no wish to marry Mordaunt, to whom she is betrothed. Herbert's cousin Bertrand warns him to flee because Theodore and Mordaunt are planning to kill him. Guiscard is hired by Theodore and Mordaunt to spy on Herbert. When Adela rejects Mordaunt, he and Theodore plan to abduct her. Herbert hears of the plan, and in Bertrand's attire kills Theodore and saves Adela, leaving his own scarf and helmet behind. Mordaunt and Guiscard blame Herbert and take their case to Lord Conway, who puts off the trial until the next morning. During the night, Mordaunt gives Guiscard a dagger to kill Herbert. Meanwhile Herbert asks Lord Conway to question Guiscard, who cannot be found, but Herbert goes after him. Guiscard is brought before Lord Conway, and he says he is "caught in his own bloody toils." Herbert returns, wounded in a fight with Mordaunt, whom he has killed. Herbert dies from his wounds amid a general lament for his tragic loss.

Often, in the play, important events must be reported since they take place off stage, and several scenes do not always contribute to forwarding the plot. The villainy of Theodore and Mordaunt forces the admirable characters to be on the defensive throughout the play. These moral characters, then, must react to what is thrust upon them; they seem to have no definite plans. On the other hand, Adela knows that she wants no part of a forced marriage to Mordaunt, and she would rather enter a convent than be pushed into wedlock. Otherwise the eighteenth-century idea of medieval paternalism (as suggested by the subtitle "The Barons of Old") prevails.

TEXT: Readex Microprint of *Poems and Plays*, vol. 1 (London: T. N. Longman and O. Rees, 1799) 1–122.

Adelaide, Amelia Alderson Opie. This tragedy, written in Opie's early twenties, was twice performed at Plumptre's Private Theatre in her hometown of Norwich on 4 and 6 January

1791 (*BD* 2: 4). The play was apparently not printed, and there is no known copy. Cecilia Brightwell's biography (1854) provides no information about the plot of this lost tragedy.

Adelinda, Hannah Brand. This five-act comedy, an adaptation of Destouches's *La Force du Naturel* (1750), was never produced. Brand collected the play in her *Poems and Plays*, published at Norwich by Beatniffe and Payne, 1798.

Set in Paris, *Adelinda* examines the issue of heredity vs. environment, which was often debated in the eighteenth-century. Marquis d'Olstain insists that Adelinda marry Count d'Olstain, a relation of his and heir to his title. Adelinda has always felt closer to Dorcas, her country nurse, than to her noble parents; she has no inclination for the Count and has secretly wedded Strasbourg, her father's steward. Strasbourg, however, is thought to be in love with Zella, the daughter of Dorcas, who is as charming and refined as Adelinda is boisterous and unsophisticated; he encourages this supposition to conceal his real attachment. The Count, though engaged to Adelinda, cannot help admiring Zella. In the fourth act, Adelinda gets a posthumous letter from Dorcas's dead husband, confirming what his wife has just confessed to her: Adelinda is indeed the farmer's daughter, whereas Zella is the child of the Marchioness and Marquis. The final act reveals all: Dorcas has exchanged the children in order to ensure a brilliant life for her own daughter. The Marquis is pleased to have Zella as a daughter, and he gladly accepts her marriage to the Count. The Marquis also approves of Adelinda's marriage to Strasbourg. The heredity vs. environment question is settled, Adelinda says, by "internal evidence": she is more like Dorcas in temperament, whereas Zella is more like the Marchioness, and no upbringing could alter these facts.

Brand's *Adelinda* is a close adaptation in prose of Destouches's comedy in verse; his title *La Force du Naturel* unambiguously announces the theme of the play. Little change has been made in the characters, except for their names. Brand has switched some scenes around in the first three acts, while retaining some word-for-word translations. Phrasing is altered to give a few characters (Adelinda, Dorcas, and Zella) more forceful personalities than their French counterparts.

While cradle exchanges are the stuff of eighteenth-century literature, they seem improbable when reported on stage, which may explain why *Adelinda* was not accepted for production, though its length may also have been a prohibiting reason. Moreover, Brand has a tendency to lace the text with didactic passages. The use of a regional dialect, however, makes Dorcas an effective "low" character as it did in the French original. "Blood will tell" emerges as a theme in both cultures because each had a hierarchical structure with the nobility clearly separated from other classes.

TEXT: Readex Microprint of *Poems and Plays*, 1798.

The Adventures in Madrid, Mary Pix. This three-act comedy was produced at the Queen's Theatre in June 1706 and printed for William Turner, James Knapton, Bernard Lintot, and B. Bragg. No publication date appears on the title page, but some critics give 1706 as the year of production. Because "1709" is written in an eighteenth-century hand at the bottom of the (Yale) Readex Microprint copy, and because the ESTC (British Library) affirms that year, Burling accepts 1709 as the play's publication date. We believe that the advertisements for William Turner at the end of the quarto imply a publication date of 1706.

Shortly after two Englishmen (Gaylove played by Barton Booth and Bellmour by Benjamin Husbands) arrive in Madrid at the English Ambassador's, they meet and fall in love with two Spanish women (Clarinda played by Elizabeth Barry and Laura by Anne Bracegirdle). In the intrigues that follow, the men try to win the women away from Don Gomez, who is husband to one and guardian to the other. They are assisted by Don Phillip, a nephew who has been bilked of his estate by Don Gomez, and by Gusman, whose love (Lisset) has been imprisoned by Don Gomez. In the final act, the men bring Gomez into the Inquisitor's court, where his dastardly deeds are revealed, allowing five couples to unite by joining hands in a dance: Gaylove and Laura (Don Phillip's sister), Bellmour and Clarinda (Don Gomez's niece who has been forced to act as his wife), Don Phillip and Emilia (Gayman's sister), Gusman and Lisset, and Jo (Bellmour's cowardly servant) and Beatrice (Clarinda's woman).

While the play may have been a "failure" on stage (Milhous), Paula Barbour compares it favorably with Pix's *The Innocent Mistress* (1697) and labels *The Adventures in Madrid* "one of Pix's best." Cotton, on the other hand, finds it "sentimentalized." Hume says the play "provides breezy treatment of semi-serious intrigues," whereas Clark stresses the contrasts of the Spanish and English cultures. Janet McLaren, in her essay in *Gender at Work*, feels that *The Adventures in Madrid* is less successful than Pix's earlier comedies (Detroit: Wayne State UP, 1990: 110). Edna Steeves has written the fullest discussion of the play in *Curtain Calls*, where she elaborates on Lisset's breeches role that brings about the plot resolution, and on the importance of the secret passage connecting Gomez's house with the Ambassador's. Even though the play was not revived, it could be considered influential on Susanna Centlivre's later—and quite successful—use of Spanish settings, particularly in *The Busie Body* (1709), which one contemporary newspaper, *The Post-Boy*, claims Pix had a hand in writing (Burling). The dialogue of the play seems flat when contrasted to its high action. More important, however, Don Gomez goes far beyond a mere blocking figure. He could have been borrowed from a blood-and-thunder tragedy. Not only has he tried to have his nephew Don Phillip killed, but he has forced his niece to act as his wife to solidify his own financial holdings, and he plans to cheat his ward out of her estate. Don Gomez is not the fumbling Cit of Behn's comedies, but he is a serious threat and a downright villain. His presence also underscores dishonest acquisition of wealth, and the monetary and economic themes of Pix's last play.

TEXT: Readex Microprint.

FACSIMILE EDITION: E-CED, with introduction by Edna L. Steeves (NY: Garland, 1982).

The Advertisement; or, A Bold Stroke for a Husband, Sarah Cheney Gardner. This three-act comedy was produced at the Haymarket Theatre on 9 August 1777 for her benefit night; it was not printed. Originally titled *The Matrimonial Advertisement*, the play featured Gardner in the role of Mrs. Holdfast. The numerous difficulties that she encountered in getting her play accepted, rehearsed, and finally produced are well described by Isobel Grundy in *TSWL* 7 (1988): 7–25. Her article goes into much more detail than earlier pieces in *TN* by F. Grice and A. Clarke, 7 (1952–53): 76–81, and by Godfrey Greene, 8 (1953–54): 6–10. Bevis points out that the play "contains as perfect a statement of Shaftesburian moral optimism as will be found in Georgian drama" (1980; 104).

Mrs. Epigram has the job of writing an advertisement for a wealthy widow, Mrs. Holdfast, who is looking for a "deserving mate." The candidates include O'Cannon, a disinherited Irishman; George Wydham, an Englishman who has a lost love; and McLocust, a Scotsman. But they begin to eliminate themselves: O'Cannon becomes suddenly rich, Wydham's lost love reappears, and McLocust leaves when Mrs. Holdfast pretends poverty. Testing all these suitors, Mrs. Holdfast chooses O'Cannon, who expresses a mixture of "sentiment and whimsical humor." Wydham's reunion with Lydia, his lost love, causes the Widow, her physician, and O'Cannon to set them up with financial contributions, but it is only the Widow who sends money to support Mrs. Epigram.

In her extended discussion of Gardner's play, Grundy answers charges of plagiarism by eighteenth-century critics, and she points out the feminine aspects of the comedy. The Widow chooses the outsider O'Cannon rather than the conventional Englishman, George Wydham. Moreover, a friendship develops between the Widow and Mrs. Epigram, and the Widow's respect for her "gives Epigram her happy ending." Finally, Grundy finds that Gardner's play presents "unfamiliar female angles on familiar situations."

MANUSCRIPTS: Larpent 435; the Colyton Ms., discussed by Grundy, was revised sometime after the production.

Agmunda, Hannah Brand. This altered version of *Huniades* was performed by the DL company at the King's Theatre on 2 February 1792, with Brand in the title role. The character of Huniades was omitted in this revision (*BD* 2: 9). It was not repeated.

MANUSCRIPT: Larpent 932.

TEXT: Readex Microprint from *Poems and Plays*, 1798, retitled *Huniades; or, The Siege of Belgrade*.

Agnes de Castro, Catharine Trotter. This five-act tragedy in blank verse, based on the novel with the same title by Aphra Behn (1688), was produced at DL in December 1695 and printed the following year by H. Rhodes, R. Parker, and S. Briscoe. Written when Trotter was in her sixteenth year, the tragedy is a promising first play, adding dramatic action and a heroic element to Behn's novel. Later dramatizations of this tale were done by Barbarina Wilmot (*Ina* in 1815 with an English setting) and Mary Russell Mitford (*Inez de Castro*, 1841).

Agnes, a Spanish aristocrat, has come from Spain to Portugal and is the favorite of the Princess Constantia, who tells Agnes her husband doesn't love her: he loves Agnes. Nevertheless, the Princess will continue to love the Prince because he loves her best friend Agnes. In opposition to this unhappy triangle are Elvira (a former mistress of the Prince), her brother Alvaro, and her favorite Bianca. They are angry that the Princess has chosen a Spaniard as a confidant rather than a Portuguese woman; also Alvaro lusts after Agnes. When the King offers Agnes a chance to marry Alvaro, she says that she values freedom more than the "golden chains" of matrimony. The King encourages Alvaro to capture Agnes by force. Later, Elvira stabs the Princess as she is waiting for Agnes. When Agnes arrives, she is charged by the Princess's dying words to love and marry the Prince. Agnes starts to kill herself and swoons. When the King and his party arrive, Elvira blames Agnes for the murder of the Princess, and her story is supported by Bianca. But when the Princess's ghost appears to Elvira, she goes mad and stabs Bianca. In a dying speech, Bianca bears witness to Elvira's treachery. Once again, the Prince sues for Agnes's hand, but she cannot entertain his passion. Alvaro, who has overheard all, comes forward to attack the Prince, causing Agnes to shriek. The Prince sidesteps the blow, and Alvaro inadvertently stabs Agnes. The Prince kills Alvaro, and Agnes dies from her fatal wounds. After the Prince is prevented from falling on his sword, the King tells his son that he must forebear in life.

Though Cotton believes the tragedy, in the Senecan mode, is "a hundred years out of date," the play is strong in its handling of female friendship. Clarke points out that the two heroines of unassailable virtue meet tragic ends through no fault of their own. "Bred together from Infancy," Agnes and the Princess continue to trust and support one another in spite of the Prince's desire for Agnes. The relationship between the two women—not the Prince's attraction to Agnes—is the central focus of the play. Male power and parental authority, in the person of the King, appear to be culpable for the blood bath: he has acted foolishly and has been morally compromised without any self-realization. Yet in the final speech of the play, the King's moral stature is somewhat reestablished; he pronounces that his son must live and confront his pain of life.

TEXTS: Wing C4801. EEB Reel 87: 12. Readex Microprint.

FACSIMILE EDITION: *The Plays of Mary Pix and Catharine Trotter*, vol. 2, with introduction by Edna L. Steeves (NY: Garland, 1982).

Albina, Countess Raimond, Hannah Cowley. After being rejected both by Sheridan at DL and Harris at CG, Cowley took the play to George Colman the Elder, who produced it in the summer season at the Haymarket. First performed on 31 July 1779, Cowley's five-act tragedy ran for seven nights, three of which were benefits for the author. *Albina* did not enjoy a revival, though T. Spilsbury printed the play for J. Dodsley and others in 1779. In her preface, Cowley remarks on the resemblance between her tragedy and those of Hannah More. This acrimonious debate spilled over into press. When a second edition appeared later in 1779, Cowley had dropped her preface (*BD*). Ellen Donkin provides a good discussion in her essay "The Paper War of Hannah Cowley and Hannah More" (*Curtain Calls*, 143–62).

Cowley's tragedy takes place during the time of the English crusades. When Edward returns from the holy wars, he wishes to marry Albina whose husband died during the fighting. Edward asks the help of Westmoreland, Albina's father, in his suit. Although Albina loves Edward, she thinks she should continue her widowhood longer. Her father prevails, however; she accepts Edward. High-born Editha, who is dependent on Albina, wants to stop the marriage because if she can marry Edward she will regain her noble status. Editha exploits Gondibert, brother of Raimond, to help her subvert the marriage. They tell Edward that Albina has a low-born lover, and Editha shows him Gondibert in disguise going into Albina's chambers the night before the wedding. When Edward tells Westmoreland that Albina is unchaste, Westmoreland challenges him to a fight in the lists. Just before they are to draw lances, Gondibert's old tutor Egbert, who has overheard the plotting, tells the King the truth, and Gondibert is banished. The hot-headed Gondibert intends to kill Albina, but by mistake he kills Editha and then turns the dagger on himself. Edward, thinking Albina is dead, is going to kill himself, but she herself stops him.

Unfortunately, Albina is a passive heroine, and she arouses less interest than Editha, who prompts so much revenge. Gagen praises Cowley's drawing of Gondibert's character as well as his mad scene, gaining the audience's pity (DLB 89: 88). Pity, too, may be extended to Albina when she is unjustly accused of licentiousness. In his introduction to Cowley's dramas in the E-CED volumes, Frederick Link provides an extended discussion of the play and its context within eighteenth-century verse drama. Readers should be aware that the 1813 version of Cowley's *Works* contains a number of verbal alterations from the first edition of 1779. The second part of the title, *Countess Raimond*, is dropped, and the time of the play is moved from the reign of King Henry II to King Richard I. In the cast of characters, the most important change is that Editha (1779) becomes Elfrida (1813). Also functionary characters are given names: an "Officer" becomes "Hengist"; Oswald's function is now explained as "Steward to Westmoreland," and "A Servant" becomes "Gwillim Albina's Servant." Although the verbal changes may result from the performance, it is more likely that Cowley's preparation of a reading edition for posterity is the reason for most of the changes. Cowley's earlier diatribe about More's plagiarism and Garrick's complicity is reduced from eight pages in 1779 to a brief paragraph. In another prefatory paragraph in 1813, Cowley nods in the direction of Joanna Baillie's theory of passions in the drama by remarking that *Albina* "has its natural foundation in the Passion of Envy."

MANUSCRIPT: Larpent 486. Readex Microprint of manuscript.

TEXT: Readex Microprint of 1779 edition.

FACSIMILE EDITION: E-CED, with introduction by Frederick Link (NY: Garland, 1982).

Alfred the Great, Anne Gaudry Faucit or Fawcett (1780?–1849), although Davis and Joyce credit Harriet Elizabeth Diddear Faucit (1789–1857). This historical drama in three acts was produced at the Theatre Royal, Norwich on 16 May 1811 for her benefit night. Apparently the play was not published.

The second Mrs. John Savile Fawcett seems less likely to have written this piece, since she and her husband were mostly in London, and the writer of this drama must have had a strong connection with the Norwich theatre.

MANUSCRIPT: Larpent 1665.

The Alienated Manor, Joanna Baillie. This five-act comedy was printed in her *Dramas*, published by Longman and others, 1836. There is no known performance.

The title refers to a country estate that has passed from the family of Mr. Crafton to Mr. Charville because it was gambled away by one of Crafton's relatives. Charville is recently married; he, his new wife Harriet, and his sister Mary live in the manor. They have hired Sir Level Clumb, "an improver," to make changes in the grounds, which Crafton thinks unnecessary. Sir Robert Freemantle is visiting Crafton, his uncle, and Charville suspects that he plans an intrigue with Harriet. Sir Robert, in fact, spends time with Mrs. Charville to mask his attachment to Mary, but Charville goes to some lengths to spy on them (disguising himself as a servant in his own house), and he even opens their mail (merely a letter from Mrs. Charville to Sir Robert's sister, an old school friend). His bumbling attempts make Charville ridiculous. In the last act, when Sir Robert's plans to wed Mary are explained, Charville admits that he acted selfishly, and he agrees to return the money he won gambling with Crafton's relative, Henry.

While some of Baillie's plays reached the stage, *The Alienated Manor* may not have attracted theatre managers because it lacks focus. Besides the silly husband who thinks he is being cuckolded on the flimsiest evidence, Baillie satirizes the mania for improving land surrounding country houses. Among her characters are a fortune-hunting German philosopher, Smitchenstault, who wants to marry Charville's sister for her money; and Sancho, "a black," bent on assisting the losing gamester Henry Crafton (his master). Baillie's setting includes a haunted room, which none of the present tenants seem to know about, but which the servants have discovered. Without much judicious cutting, it is difficult to imagine this piece on stage.

TEXT: Readex Microprint of *Dramas* (1836) 1: 121–249.

All on a Summer's Day, Elizabeth Inchbald. This five-act comedy was produced only once (at CG on 15 December 1787), and it was not printed during the author's lifetime. Damned, perhaps because of Louisa's secret affair with Wildlove, the play may also have been too hastily staged by Harris, the manager at CG. In a letter to *The London Review and Literary Journal* (December 1787), Inchbald says that, contrary to her own inclination, she trusted Harris's judgment since he was right in urging the successful production of her previous play, *The Midnight Hour* (CG, 22 May 1787).

Before the action of the play, Wildlove and Louisa have had an affair that should have led to marriage, but her poverty prevented this. She then went out to join her father, Governor Moreton, in India. When the play opens in a village, Mrs. Goodly, who raised Louisa, is chiding Lady Carrol, her sister-in-law, for her argumentative nature toward Sir William, the older husband of Lady Carrol. Wildlove is their house guest for the summer: he seems to be making advances to most of the ladies, except Lady Carrol, who seems to flirt with almost all the men. Sir William receives a note that the Governor has returned with Louisa and her fiancé, Lord Henley. Learning that Wildlove is in the village, Louisa decides she must act coolly toward him. When Lady Carrol arrives, she confesses her indiscretion to Louisa: she corresponded with the son of Sir Ralph Mooneye, as if she were unmarried and Sir William were her father. Now Sir Ralph is coming to see Sir William about this matter. Lady Carrol does everything she can to get the letters before Sir William sees them. In the meantime, Wildlove and Louisa are cool toward each other, but he arranges a meeting with Governor Moreton and confesses to him. Louisa enters as the Governor is about to stab Wildlove and says she has told the whole story to Lord Henley; the Governor finally approves of Louisa's union with Wildlove. After Sir William has gotten Lady Carrol's packet of letters, he vows to leave her, but they are reconciled.

This plot lacks the usual verve of Inchbald's plays: it is loosely pieced together, and the sudden turns are neither prepared for, nor are they always justified. The characters are mostly types, but inconsistent. For example, Wildlove acts differently in almost every scene. If Inchbald intended to examine the effect of premarital sex on the participants, the topic seems to have been too explicit for the audience, and they condemned the play. Nevertheless, Inchbald exposed the double standard (one set of principles for men and another for women), and this too may have upset audiences. Had Inchbald been given more time by Harris to smooth out the details, the play could have been stronger thematically.

MANUSCRIPT: Larpent 789. Manuscript transcribed in E-CED, with introduction by Paula R. Backscheider (NY: Garland, 1980).

Almeda; or, The Neapolitan Revenge, "by a Lady." This "tragic drama" was published by H. D. Symonds in 1801, but it didn't reach the stage.

BD notes that the tragedy is based on the romance of *The Life of Rozelli*, and the play "borders on the ludicrous. A dying, but unrepentant, adulteress, procures her lover, to whose inconstancy she owes her last illness, to be locked up in a chest, intending him to be buried alive with her. When the revenge is frustrated, the lover, Count Casalia, is restored to liberty and the arms of Zelector, the object of his honourable passion" (2: 20).

TEXT: Not in Readex Microprint. NUC lists copies at LC (Longe Collection, 304: 6) and Yale.

Almeyda, Queen of Granada, Sophia Lee. This five-act tragedy in blank verse is based partly on Shirley's *The Cardinal*; it was first produced at DL on 20 April 1796, after being deferred several times because of the indisposition of John Palmer, who played Abdallah. It was performed five times that season and published the same year by Cadell and Davies. The cast was led by Sarah Siddons (to whom the play is dedicated) in the title role, with her brother, John Philip Kemble, performing Alonzo. Sophia's sister, Harriet, contributed the prologue and epilogue.

The play opens in a Moorish castle overhanging the Guadalquiver River. Although the Moors rule in Granada, the King of Castile, Ramirez, possesses the castle. He has raised Almeyda from infancy with his own children (Victoria and Alonzo), even though she is the daughter of the former King of Granada. In the first act, she is restored to the Moors, and Orasmyn, the son of the regent of Granada, falls in love with Almeyda. The ambitious regent, Abdallah (Almeyda's uncle), wants his son to marry Almeyda, but she is still in love with Alonzo, who visits Almeyda in disguise. Abdallah discovers his identity and sends him to prison. Knowing Alonzo is his rival, Orasmyn generously sets Alonzo free. Almeyda asks Hamet, the captain of the Moorish guard, to take her to Alonzo, but they arrive at the prison just after Orasmyn and Alonzo have left. Not finding Alonzo, Almeyda assumes he has been murdered by Abdallah and loses her senses. Because of her frenzy, Almeyda is brought before the Council of State and is told to resign her crown to Abdallah. She recovers her reason and refuses to submit. Abdallah, then, lies to his son, telling him that Almeyda is poisoned. Orasmyn implores his father to give Almeyda an antidote. Abdallah agrees to the request and a goblet is brought in: Abdallah first drinks himself, and then he gives it to Almeyda who drinks. Abdallah exalts because the pretended antidote was actually poison, but he is carried off in the throes of death. Alonzo enters, and as Almeyda dies, she unites the Castilians (Alonzo) with the Moors (Orasmyn).

Lee's poetry provided an effective vehicle for Sarah Siddons's talents. Occasional hints of Shakespearean lines augment the text (as when Abdallah says "There is too much of *method* in this frenzy"). Still, the play did not go beyond its opening season, perhaps because of a cumbersome plot and insufficiently developed characters. The strong friendship between Victoria and Almeyda, established in the first act, lapses in the remainder of the play because Victoria stays with her father. As a blocking figure, the Regent of Granada is little more than an ambitious misogynist, and Alonzo cannot stand against the political wiles of Abdallah. Still, it is Almeyda who, despite her apparent madness, rallies to display a mental toughness against the Council of State, convincing them she's every inch a queen.

MANUSCRIPT: Larpent 1113. Readex Microprint of the manuscript.

TEXT: Readex Microprint.

Almida, Dorothea Mallet Celisia. Her one five-act tragedy in blank verse was taken from Voltaire's *Tancrède* (1760). The first production occurred on 12 January 1771 at DL where it was acted nine nights and once the following season. Anne Barry, who acted Almida, got much critical praise for her performance. The play was printed three times the same year by T. Beckett.

Two houses in Syracuse (one ruled by Arnolph, the other by Orbassan) have been fighting a civil war, and the weakened country is no match for the Saracen emperor, Solyman, who is planning to invade. As an act of reconciliation, Arnolph offers his daughter, Almida, in marriage to Orbassan. Earlier, Tancred was banished from Syracuse, and at the court of Byzantium he met and was privately engaged to Almida. She explains her dilemma in a letter to Tancred, but the letter is intercepted. The senate concludes that the letter was meant for Solyman, and Almida is sentenced to death for treason. Tancred comes to Syracuse as an unknown knight. Even though he thinks Almida has been false to him, he wishes to preserve her life. Off stage, Tancred fights Orbassan and kills him. Almida recognizes Tancred, but he will not speak to her. Tancred replaces Orbassan as the head of the army, and under him the Syracusans defeat the Saracens. Tancred, however, is mortally wounded. Brought to court, he becomes convinced of Almida's innocence. When he dies, she throws herself on his dead body and dies in despair. Arnolph is left alone with the disastrous results of his choices: he has failed as a father and as a statesman.

Almida is not just "based partly on Voltaire": it is a faithful translation of his tragedy *Tancrède*, with a mere change of names for some of the characters—Amenaides becoming Almida, and Argire becoming Arnolph. Celisia at times translated literally, at others rendered the original in her own words with a few liberties. Although she kept all the scenes in each of the five acts, she did reduce their lines, thus toning down Voltaire's pathos. Unhappy with the curt French ending, a mere two lines pronounced by the dying Arnolph, she successfully brought the work to a firmer end by expanding on the father's grief and by adding a warning about "our too violent tho' virtuous passions." Celisia displayed an effective dramatic sense that Nicoll does not credit her with (3: 82).

Almida realizes that she is a pawn to both her father and to the state. Nevertheless, she will not accept the marriage to Orbassan that is being forced upon her, and she is willing to die on the scaffold rather than accept the state's charge of treason. Almida shows that she can take a stand, for when Tancred is on the battlefield, she vows to outdo him, saying her "bosom bar'd shall meet the vengeful steel" (54). From all contemporary reports, Ann Barry must have been splendid in the role of Almida.

MANUSCRIPT: Larpent 314.

TEXT: Readex Microprint.

Almyna; or, The Arabian Vow, Delariviere Manley. This five-act verse tragedy was first produced at the Queen's Theatre on 16 December 1706 and published the following year without Manley's name by William Turner and Egbert Sanger. In the preface, Manley praises the "unwearied care" that Betterton took with the performance, and she dedicates the tragedy to Elizabeth Barry, who played the title role. Manley also mentions problems (i.e., Bracegirdle leaving the stage and Mills's prolonged illness) that prevented a revival of the tragedy. *Almyna* is the first English drama to use the *Arabian Nights* as its source.

Because Caliph Almanzor, Sultan of the East, has found his first wife unfaithful, he decides all women are potential adulteresses and without souls. The morning after each of his many marriages, he has his brides executed. His heir and brother, Abdalla, has deflowered Zoradia while Almyna studied in Memphis. Upon Almyna's return, Abdalla is smitten with her and gives up Zoradia. Almyna, however, will not marry her sister's betrayer and, instead, agrees to marry Almanzor even with the awful consequences. When Almanzor meets the beautiful Almyna, he is struck by her beauty and her persuading tongue, and he instantly falls in love with her. Knowing what Almyna's fate will be the morning following her marriage, Zoradia and Abdalla independently plan to save her. Expecting to die, Almyna demonstrates extreme fortitude awaiting her death, but it is the Sultan who halts the execution, and she becomes his Queen for good. Unaware of the reprieve, Zoradia and

Abdalla lead forces to save Almyna and are killed.

Almyna parlays her education into more advantages for women by making the Sultan see that women have souls and that they can be virtuous. Moreover, she argues her case very convincingly. Nevertheless, she is put to a fearful test and nearly executed. The jilting of Zoradia by Abdalla brings about the test of female (in this case, sisterly) friendships. This strong friendship contrasts sharply with brotherly relations between Almanzor and Abdalla. The two principals, Almanzor and Almyna, are fully drawn characters, whereas neither Zoradia nor Abdalla are strong enough to cope with difficulties that face them. While Zoradia has reasons to complain, Abdalla whines his way through the play, and it is hard to understand what Zoradia sees in him. Although she writes strong speeches, Manley provides little action. Several important events (e.g., Almyna's halting the marriage to Abdalla, and Almanzor's being informed of Almyna's intention to marry him) take place off stage. What the play, and especially the character of Almyna, argues for is the value of education for women.

TEXT: Readex Microprint.

Amana, Elizabeth Griffith. A five-act dramatic tragedy based on Hawkesworth's prose tale in *The Adventurer*, nos. 72 and 73, Griffith's dramatic poem was published in 1764 for W. Johnston, but it was not performed. Although the title page has "By a Lady," the dedication is signed "Eliza Griffith." Some of the subscribers to this tragedy include Edmund Burke, David Garrick, Dr. Johnson, and Frances Sheridan.

An oriental tale, popular in this period, *Amana* illustrates, according to the preface, "the folly of human wishes." The only daughter of an Englishman and a now deceased Egyptian woman, Amana has just married Nouradin, a young merchant, in Cairo. In revenge for a slight, Caled recommends Amana for the Sultan's pleasure, and before the newly wedded pair can consummate their marriage, she is taken to the Sultan, who believes women are "formed solely for [male] use." Meanwhile, Nouradin and his father-in-law plan to rescue Amana by Nouradin's dressing as the Sultan. At the same time, the prime minister suggests the Sultan would be more acceptable to Amana if he dressed as Nouradin. In the harem, Amana meets Fatima, the Sultan's first wife, and Fatima gives her a vial of poison since Amana says she would rather die than become mistress to the Sultan. When the disguised Sultan comes to her room, Caled challenges him, thinking the Sultan is really Nouradin; they fight and kill each other. Nouradin disguised as the Sultan calls for Amana. She drinks the poison before she finds out it is actually Nouradin. When she dies, he stabs himself.

This tale of unrelenting tragedy shows the disastrous effects of tyranny and despotism. Male characters in *Amana* and other plays of the period generally employ disguises for sexual purposes; while this is the Sultan's intent, Nouradin alters his costume to save Amana. Susan Staves, writing in DLB, points out that Elizabeth Griffith turned to writing comedies after this unsuccessful dramatic tragedy; it was panned in both the *Monthly Review* and *The Critical Review* (89: 175–76). Nevertheless, Griffith alters her source by having Amana strongly resist the Sultan's advances, and Amana becomes a tragic heroine worthy of being the title character.

TEXTS: Readex Microprint. TEC Reel 1465: 1.

The Ambiguous Lover, Elizabeth [Betsy] Sheridan. This farce, written by the daughter of Frances Sheridan, was produced at the Crow-Street Theatre, Dublin, 5 March 1781. Kinne notes that the farce was drawn from Patrat's *L'Heureuse Erreur* (191n). Since the piece was never printed, the text is presumed lost.

The Amorous Prince; or, The Curious Husband, Aphra Behn. This five-act play has been called a "romantic comedy" (Cotton), "tragicomedy" (Link), and "serious intrigue play" (Hume). Behn's second staged drama, it was produced at LIF on 24 February 1671, and printed for Thomas Dring the same year.

The play, set in Florence, opens on the amorous Prince Frederick, leaving after a nocturnal sexual encounter with Cloris to whom he is engaged. When Frederick returns to Florence, Lorenzo suggests he meet his sister Laura, even though she is engaged to Curtius, Cloris's brother. In a second plot, Clarina, recently married to Antonio, and her sister, Ismena, are dressed identically; knowing that Antonio has asked Alberto to test his wife's faithfulness, Ismena chooses to act as Clarina in order to meet Alberto. Ismena says she will make all come right: "This unlucky restraint upon our Sex, Makes us all cunning." And through her clever machinations, she does just that. Antonio learns to repent his jealousy over Clarina, who forgives him; Ismena herself wins Alberto; Curtius is able to marry Laura; and the Prince goes back to Cloris. The silly Lorenzo has compromised himself and must marry Isabella, Clarina's servant.

Disguises and cross-dressing play an important part in this drama. To deal with the Prince's inconstancy, Cloris dresses as a young man and aids him in his distress. Even as a fallen maid, she has enough pluck to act in a difficult situation. Another creative woman, Ismena, shows great ability in bringing the true lovers together. While love is pitted against friendship in both plots, as Link points out, it is the clever women who force events in this comedy.

TEXTS: 1st Wing B1718; 2nd Wing B1717; EEB Reel 483: 3. Readex Microprint.

MODERN EDITION: *Works*, ed. Montague Summers (1915; NY: Phaeton, 1967) 4: 117–213.

Angelica; or, Quixote in Petticoats, although attributed to Charlotte Ramsey Lennox, this comedy in two-acts, based on Lennox's novel *The Female Quixote*, is not in fact by her, as noted by both *BD* and Small. In the "Advertisement," the unknown male author "thinks *himself* under an indispensible [sic] obligation to inform the public that the character of Angelica and the heroic part of Careless, is not only borrow'd, but entirely taken, from the female Quixote, of the ingenious Mrs. Lennox" (emphasis added). Printed in 1758 "for the Author," the comedy was not acted because David Garrick, the dedicatee, noted its strong resemblance to Steele's *The Tender Husband*. Indeed, the second title comes from Act II, scene 3, line 1 of that comedy (Steele, *Plays*, edited by Shirley S. Kenny [Oxford: Clarendon, 1971]: 241).

TEXT: Readex Microprint.

Angelina, Mary Goldsmith. This comic opera in two acts was probably produced at Margate in late August or early September 1804. *BD* says it was for Mrs. Henry's benefit (2: 29). Originally titled *Walcot Castle*, the play was never printed.

MANUSCRIPT: Larpent 1431.

Animal Magnetism, Elizabeth Inchbald. This popular three-act farce, adapted from Dumaniant's *Le Médecin malgré tout le monde*, was first performed at CG on 29 April 1788 as an afterpiece to Frances Brooke's *Rosina*. Eleven performances were given the first season. The publication history is murky: it may have been pirated by P. Bryon in Dublin during 1788 or 1789, but no date appears on the title page. An edition was published in Dublin by C. Lewis in 1789; a London edition appeared that same year.

Set in Paris, the play opens with Constance telling her maid, Lisette, that she has seen the Marquis de Lancy from her window. Lisette knows that his valet, LaFleur, is dressed as a doctor. Constance's guardian, a quack doctor (never named), keeps her locked up and plans to marry her himself. He then returns home, having been refused a diploma from the medical faculty; to circumvent the faculty, he decides to become an animal magnetist. With this cue, LaFleur acts as a representative of the sect and gives the guardian a magnetic wand which, he says, will make his ward fall in love with him. When the guardian waves it around, however, both Constance and Lisette act as if they love him madly. He then gives the wand to his servant Jeffery, and the women act as if they are in love with him. LaFleur returns with the Marquis, disguised as a patient, and in the course of the quack's treatment, the Marquis pretends to die. The Marquis and LaFleur then change places, and the Marquis and two friends dressed as doctors enter and blame the quack for killing the patient. To get out of his dilemma, the quack agrees to do anything and signs an agreement allowing the Marquis to wed Constance.

Inchbald follows closely Dumaniant's three-act comedy, at times translating entire passages literally, at others slashing long scenes or eliminating shorter ones, often at the expense of Lisette, Dumaniant's insolent but generous maid, who appears somewhat blander in the English version. Nevertheless, the role as played by Isabella Mattocks, who specialized in fast-talking, resourceful maids, must have come across well. Some comical elements, such as the quack's lamentations about old age's stupidity or his fierce invectives, have been downplayed while the preparations for the wedding of the Marquis and Constance have been entirely overlooked. Finally, Inchbald discarded the French title, *Le Médecin malgré tout le monde [The Doctor in spite of every one]*, reminiscent of Molière's famous play, *Le Médecin malgré lui*. By preferring *Animal Magnetism*, Inchbald clearly indicated her intention to make the most of the farcical elements inherent to the handling, or mishandling, of the magnetic wand. Although Genest (6: 498) considered the plot "grossly improbable," audiences apparently had no objections (the piece is after all a farce). Since *Animal Magnetism* played for several consecutive seasons, the fast action on stage seems to have met with a good deal of audience approval.

MANUSCRIPTS: Larpent 802 and Harvard Library.

TEXTS: Readex Microprint of the 1792 Dublin edition. TEC Reel 548: 8 (1788 or 1789 Dublin piracy by P. Bryon).

FACSIMILE EDITION: E-CED, with introduction by Paula R. Backscheider, reprints the 1789 Dublin edition, published by C. Lewis (NY: Garland, 1980).

The Animated Effigy, Jane M. Scott. A farce in two acts, the play was first performed at the Sans Pareil Theatre on 12 February 1811. James Sanderson provided the music, and Scott herself acted the role of Lady Augusta. It ran thirty-two nights its first season and fifteen times the following season.

MANUSCRIPT: Larpent 1660.

Anna, Miss Catherine? Cuthbertson. This comedy was first produced at the King's Theatre by the DL company on 25 February 1793, but it was never printed. The *Public Advertiser* of 26 February 1793 said the play was without a plot, and it charged Palmer (who played Henry, the romantic lover of Anna) with contributing to the demise after one night. Even though it was advertised on the playbill of 26 February 1793 to be performed on 28 February, the play was deferred at the request of the author; it was never again repeated on stage.

The theatrical embroglio surrounding the production of *Anna* apparently involved both J. P. Kemble (as actor and manager of DL) and Dorothy Jordan, who made her season's debut in the play. The *Star* reported (1 March 1793) that Kemble tried to vex Jordan publicly in the third act by "pulling out his snuff-box, [and beginning] to take the *pinch of contempt*" (emphasis in the original). Rumors circulated that Jordan wrote the play, but Cuthbertson put the widespread gossip to rest by acknowledging in the *Oracle* (9 March 1793) "I am the Author of that Comedy" (Lucyle Werkmeister, *A Newspaper History of England, 1792–1793*. Lincoln: U of Nebraska P, 1967: 315–16). If the event took place on stage as described, it is difficult to credit the *Star*'s report, for J. P. Kemble does not appear in the cast list (*LS* 5: 1524) and was unlikely to be a stand-in.

Although the manuscript is difficult to read in the Readex version, the plot and characters can be deciphered. Lady Touchwood, who lives in Touchwood Castle, is the second wife of Lord Touchwood, recently deceased. The now-grown Touchwood children from the first marriage have claims on money that Lady Touchwood tries to keep for herself. Anna, the title character, is incarcerated in an ancient castle on the grounds by Lady Touchwood (called by FCLE the "wicked stepmother" of the piece—257). Lady Touchwood plans to send Anna to a convent in Antwerp, but will hold her hostage in the meantime. Although Anna's brother (Sir Frederick Touchwood) and his friends Henry and Gaythorne try to help her, Anna is naive enough to believe that her stepmother would not be cruel to her. When a letter of Lady Touchwood's is intercepted, Anna finally accepts the treachery of her stepmother, and the vicious plans are overthrown. Anna is united with Henry in the final act.

One underlying idea in the drama is that people are not what they seem, and it is difficult to tell the good characters from the bad ones. The use of some gothic trappings would have appealed to the audiences in the mid-1790s, and the fairy tale elements of being locked in a castle by a wicked stepmother create a motif that will become even more popular in the next century.

MANUSCRIPT: Larpent 969. Readex Microprint of manuscript.

ANSPACH, Elizabeth Berkeley Craven, Margravine of (1750–1828). Born in London, she was the youngest of four daughters. In her *Memoirs* (1826), she says little about her early education, but she later wrote dramas in French and German and translated works from these languages. In 1767 she married Lord Craven by whom she had seven children. Lady Craven moved in prominent social and literary circles which included Dr. Johnson, Sir Joshua Reynolds, and Horace Walpole. Boswell mentions Johnson's visit to "the beautiful, gay, and fascinating Lady Craven" in his *Life of Johnson*. Reynolds started a portrait of her which he never finished (there is a completed portrait by Angelica Kaufmann), and Walpole printed her translation of *Le Somnambule* (or *The Sleep-Walker*) at his Strawberry Hill Press in 1778. In 1780, after her play *The Miniature Portrait* was performed in Newbury for the benefit of the poor, R. B. Sheridan brought her play out at DL. Both Lord and Lady Craven were involved in extramarital affairs that caused them to separate in 1783. Lady Craven left England with her youngest son, Keppel, and traveled extensively in Europe. Part of her travels in 1786 are chronicled in *Journey Through the Crimea to Constantinople*, published in 1789. During the course of her travels, she met and became involved with the nephew of Frederic the Great, Christian Frederic the Margrave of Anspach. After the death of Lord Craven in 1791, she married the Margrave. The next year they moved to England and purchased Brandenburgh House, Hammersmith, which had a theatre where the Margravine produced her own plays for more than a decade. Performance seemed to be most important to the Margravine, for almost none of these plays were published: from this period the only extant printed pieces are the songs from *The Princess of Georgia* (1798) and her translation of Schiller's *Die Räuber* (1799). During this period, however, the Margravine did write a novel, *The Soldier of Dierenstein; or, Love and Mercy*, that came out in 1802, After the death of the Margrave in 1806, Anspach wrote no more plays or other imaginative works. Two years before her own death, she published her *Memoirs*, which proved to be her most popular book.

All of Anspach's plays reflect fashionable stage drama of the day—sentimental pieces, comic operas, and comedy farces. Her travel writings, correspondence, and autobiography show an unusually self-absorbed writer who never forgets her rank or her learning. Everything of interest seems to originate with herself: the subjects gain credit or suffer defamation according to her response. On the other hand, John Timpane, writing in EBWW, describes her literary persona as "so open and unself-conscious that her frequent discussions of herself do not seem like mordant conceit" (130). [*BD*, DBAWW, DNB, EBWW, FCLE, NCBEL 831–32]

Antiochus the Great; or, The Fatal Relapse, Jane Wiseman, later Holt. This five-act tragedy was first produced at LIF in November 1701 with Elizabeth Barry as Leodice. The play was printed on 25 November 1701 for William Turner and Richard Basset, though 1702 appears on the title page. In the front matter, Wiseman comments on the play: "The reception it met in the World was not kind enough to make me Vain, nor yet so ill, to discourage my Proceeding." Wiseman's play was not revived, though an opera, *Antiochus* (music by Francisco Gasperini), was performed in the 1711–12 season, and a play of that same title by John Mottley staged in 1721.

In the first act of Wiseman's tragedy, the King of Syria, Antiochus, returns from an Egyptian war, bringing with him Berenice, the daughter of the King of Egypt. Antiochus's former mistress, Leodice is revengeful because she was left with a child by Antiochus and her paramour is marrying a woman from another country. On her father's urging, Berenice (who has left a lover, Ormades, in Egypt) marries Antiochus, who later discovers that Ormades has followed Berenice to Syria. In a meeting with her former lover, Berenice declares that Ormades should return to Egypt because she is now Antiochus's wife. After Ormades is discovered with Berenice, he is threatened with punishment by Antiochus. But Ormades will not let Antiochus shame him, and he stabs himself. With her lover's death, Berenice rejects Antiochus, who then decides to return to Leodice, only to find she has taken poison. In a final irony, Leodice has her dying revenge by giving poison to Antiochus. At the conclusion of the play, Berenice only wishes to return to Egypt, and she asks her woman Irene to "prove the kind Companion of my Life."

Although we never see the King of Egypt on stage, it is his "forced marriage" of Berenice to Antiochus which sows the seeds of tragedy even before the play opens. She tries to do her duty, and even urges her former lover Ormades to return to Egypt. After he dies, she shuns Antiochus, and he fatally relapses to his mistress Leodice, who shows an extravagant passion in most of her actions. After the masque in Act Three, for instance, a disguised Leodice tells her story to the King, who wants the man who wronged her to repair the situation. She then throws off her disguise and confronts the King, who has wronged her. One can see why Elizabeth Barry may have coveted such a role. In her introduction to the play, Kendall points out that never in the play do Leodice and Berenice confront each other. Having reversed the usual convention of female rivalry, Wiseman explores the characters of two different women under external stress brought about by dominating male power figures.

TEXT: Readex Microprint.

MODERN EDITION: Edited with introduction by Kendall in *Love and Thunder* (London: Methuen, 1988): 113–53.

The Apocriphal [sic] Ladies, Margaret Lucas Cavendish, Duchess of Newcastle. Called a comedy by the author, this closet drama was printed in her *Playes*, published by John Martyn, James Allestry, and Tho. Dicas in 1662. It was not intended for production.

The "Unfortunate Dutchess" has married a husband who has accepted the title of Duke of Inconstancy and taken her money and power. The Duke's chief interest is in his mistress, Lady Beauty, even though she is married. When Lady Beauty's husband dies, the Duke drives the "Unfortunate Dutchess" from the country. This, he believes, allows him the right to marry Lady Beauty, who becomes the "Comical Dutchess." When the "Unfortunate Dutchess's" sister, the Princess, marries the brother of the Duke of Inconstancy, she creates the title of "Prince" for him, though he is called the "Shadow Prince" by others. The "Apocriphal Ladies" are thus the "Creating Princess" and the "Comical Dutchess." People from various social levels in the kingdom discuss the inheriting of honors and titles. Burgers' wives, waiting women, gentlemen, and two scriveners' wives have their own scenes. Toward the end of the play, Lady True Honor instructs Madame Inquirer on the degrees of princes, explaining that "True honor is derived from heaven." Moreover, she will not visit the "apocriphal ladies." The play ends with the wives of the scriveners taking a different position, asserting "mon[e]y doth all things." Perhaps this cynical, concluding remark satirizes all the nobility, and the play earns the generic title of "comedy."

The text questions the social airs put on by people who merely assume nobility (probably the Cromwell government). If so, the play was likely to have been written before 1660. While the drama exhibits little concern for characterization or plot development in the usual sense, Cavendish sets forth several points of view about what it means to be noble: is it appearance, or is it divinely ordained? By placing the discussion in a dramatic context, Cavendish lets the reader decide the merits of nobility. Several references to the playhouse and actors underscore the real vs. the make-believe. Also, Cavendish's prefiguring of fairy-tale motifs adds another dimension to the play. Aside from names that explain character (such as Lady Beauty), Cavendish presents instant acquisitions of titles, sudden marriages, discarding of rivals in a fantastic fairy-tale world.

TEXT: Wing N868. EEB Reel 502: 11. Readex Microprint.

Appearance Is Against Them, Elizabeth Inchbald. This two-act farce was first produced at CG on 22 October 1785 and acted thirteen times its first season as an afterpiece. Publication by G. G. J. and J. Robinson took place later in 1785. Originally titled *The Shawl*, the farce was revived (CG, 1 May 1804) under the title of *Mistake on Mistake; or, Appearance Is Against Them.*

The Indian shawl, the central visual symbol in the play, goes from hand to hand before it is returned to its rightful owner, Lady Mary Magpie. She first receives the shawl from her intended, Mr. Walmsley, to wear on their wedding day. She shows it to Miss Angle and her servant Fish; then she spreads it on her bed. On Fish's suggestion, Miss Angle "borrows" the shawl to send to Lord Lighthead in order to rekindle his interest in her. When he receives the shawl, instead of returning it to Miss Angle as a mistake, he sends it to his current love interest, Lady Loveall, who is then seen by Mr. Walmsley wearing it in Covent Garden. He brings her to Lady Mary Magpie's where the details are unraveled, and Lady Loveall returns the shawl to Lady Mary. At the end of the play, Lord Lighthead asks which of us has not "appeared culpable," and Mr. Walmsley says "these adventures shall be a warning to us, never to judge with severity, while the parties have only appearances against them."

Hughes and Scouten, commenting in *Ten English Farces*, note that "farces are at a disadvantage when judged by a reader rather than a spectator." They also stress the strength of the dialogue even though the characters are types. While the farce gained a strong reception, it did not stay in the repertory. Inchbald herself acted Miss Angle in the season's last performance of this piece (8 December 1785).

MANUSCRIPT: Larpent 708.

TEXT: Readex Microprint.

CRITICAL EDITION: *Ten English Farces*, edited with introduction by Leo Hughes and A. H. Scouten (Austin: U of Texas P): 239–262.

FACSIMILE EDITION: E-CED, with introduction by Paula R. Backscheider (NY: Garland, 1980).

The Arcadian Pastoral, Baroness Elizabeth Berkeley Craven, afterward the Margravine of Anspach. This musical interlude was privately produced at Burlington House in 1781 or 1782 with the children of Lords Craven, Spencer, Paget, and Southampton acting the roles (*BD*). There is no record that it was published, and the text is apparently lost.

Arden of Feversham, adaptation ascribed to Eliza Haywood. The altered version of the domestic tragedy, adapted from the anonymous Renaissance English play of 1591, was produced at the Haymarket on 21 January 1736 with Haywood in the role of Mrs. Arden. The *London Daily Post and General Advertiser*, 21 January, reported an attempt to disrupt the rehearsal and prevent the performance (*LS* 3: 545). This version has not been published.

In the original plot, Mrs. Arden and her paramour Mosby plan to murder Arden. Eventually they hire two killers—Shakebag and Black Will—who carry out the murder. But Mrs. Arden and Mosby are discovered as the ones who set the murderers on, and they are executed. George Lillo's manuscript version of this play was completed by John Hoadley and produced at DL on 12 July 1759.

"ARIADNE" (fl. 1695). This pseudonym was used by an unknown playwright who flourished in the 1690s. Her *She Ventures and He Wins* was produced at LIF in September 1695, and published in 1696. She is also thought by some critics to be the author of *The Unnatural Mother*, produced at LIF in September 1697, published 1698, since the preface mentions that the author has written a previous play. But no other evidence exists that Ariadne penned *The Unnatural Mother*. [Cotton, DBAWW, EBWW, FCLE, Hume, Pearson.]

Aristodemus; or, The Spectre, translated by Frances Burney, niece of Fanny Burney d'Arblay. Published in her *Tragic Dramas; chiefly intended for representation in Private Families: to which is added Aristodemus, a tragedy from the Italian of Vincenzo Monti*, there were no public performances of Burney's translation of this five-act tragedy.

Messina is the setting for this modern tragedy, written on an ancient Greek model. The Spartan Ambassador, Lysander, comes to work out peace proposals between the warring factions. He talks first to Palamedes, a Spartan captive, who tells about the generosity and sadness of King Aristodemus. Another Spartan captive, Cesira, reiterates stories about the King's kindness, treating her as his lost daughter. Lysander then explains the source of the King's sadness: when the Delphic Oracle required a sacrifice, the King chose his older daughter Dircea; and because he did, the King's wife killed herself. To keep his youngest daughter Argis safe, the King charged Eumeus to take her away to safety; however, she was slain, and Lysander himself led the attack. Gonippus, a counselor to the King, asks the monarch to divulge what is troubling him. The tragic story is much the same as we have heard, but Aristodemus claims his own ambition to be King caused him to murder his daughter Dircea. Now he frequently sees a "tremendous spectre." Before the peace talks, Lysander explains to Palamedes how he actually saved Aristodemus's daughter, Argis, and had her raised in Sparta, where she was called Cesira. The King knows nothing of this, and he dotes on Cesira as if she were his daughter. After the peace is settled between the Messinaians and Spartans, the King wanders among the tombs fearing the spectre of his "murdered daughter's shade." Before Cesira starts back to Sparta, she encounters Eumeus, who gives her a scroll which tells her she is not who she thinks she is, and she must seek Lysander for news of her real father. Lysander admits Cesira is Argis, the daughter of Aristodemus, and she returns to search for him among the tombs. Aristodemus can no longer live with his dreadful guilt and has plunged a dagger into his breast when Argis (Cesira) finds him. After she has revealed that she is Argis, Aristodemus blames the gods and dies.

The relationships between Aristodemus and his daughters, one he killed and one he thinks he sent to her death, become the central focus in this tragedy. His tremendous responsibility for the death of his older daughter creates a spectre of guilt that haunts him throughout the play. Before Argis can identify herself and offer him possible redemption, he has taken his own life. As he dies, he can only blame the gods, when in fact his own deeds caused his downfall. One of the strong features of the play is that it is arranged so that the audience hears the changing story of the earlier events. The details of the first story are stripped away by each succeeding story. If, as Burney recommends, the play is "chiefly intended for representation in Private Families," it could result in a very gloomy evening of pity and terror for the family viewing the performance. This is not to denigrate the tragedy, but the successive repetition of Aristodemus's murder and guilt are quite austere.

TEXT: Readex Microprint.

Aristomenes; or, The Royal Shepherd, Anne Finch, Countess of Winchilsea. The composition of the play, according to Myra Reynolds, may have begun in July 1689, when the Countess was on a visit to Eastwell, but it was at Godmersham where she completed *Aristomenes* (xxviii). Although the tragedy was never performed publicly, it is printed in Finch's *Miscellany Poems, on Several Occasions*, published in 1713 "for J. B." The source of the play is Pausanias's *Messenica*, where the 4th book relates the history of Aristomenes at length (Genest 10: 153–54).

Both love and war are central to the tragedy. In the first act, Climander (disguised as a shepherd though he is Demagetus, the son of the Prince of Rhodes and the Royal Shepherd) tells Arcasius, an old counsellor, to give him a horse and arms so that he can go fight with Aristomenes against foreign invaders. Arcasius tries to calm his passion by telling him that he must wed "the Beauteous Daughter of the Best of Men." They hear cries of the retreating Messenian shepherds who say that Sparta is victorious and Aristomenes taken. Herminia, Aristomenes's daughter, and her confidant Barina will hide from the Spartans. Meanwhile, the Spartans bring in the captured Aristomenes and take him off to a dungeon, where he hears voices—one telling him to end it all, and the other telling him to rouse himself. When a fox runs by he catches it, and the fox leads him out of the dungeon. Later, Climander (still in disguise) assists Herminia, and they fall in love. On the Spartan side, Amalintha, the daughter of Anaxander, has fallen in love with Aristor, Aristomenes's son. Aristomenes, now out of the dungeon, asks her for help; Amalintha agrees, and as a pledge gives him her dagger. Aristomenes returns to his people; Climander becomes Demagetus and is united with Herminia, and Aristor with Amalintha, who is excused for being a Spartan because she helped Aristomenes in his plight. In the final act the war is renewed again, and although the Messenians win, the Spartan Clarinthus sneaks into their camp and gets revenge on Amalintha by stabbing her. He in turn is killed by Aristor, who then dies with Amalintha. As they return victorious, the Messenians discover Aristor and Amalintha dead. Seeing the dead pair, Aristomenes is ready to kill himself, but he decides he must live until "Rhodes is rescu'd, and my Task completed."

The strength of the drama lies in its poetry, not in its dramatic intensity. Finch echoes Otway in her tender handling of several scenes: these prove quite effective. Finch also emphasizes an antiwar sentiment. For instance, love is always canceled by war: Amalintha laments "when will this Discord end! Is there no happy Land, Where only Love, and its kind Laws prevail? . . . why shou'd Men with Hearts unmov'd Seek the bold War, and leave ours trembling for them?" Throughout the play, men pursue honor in battle, but the option that they could live humbly for peace, as the recurring shepherd motif suggests, they never consider.

MANUSCRIPT: Folger Shakespeare Lib. MS N.b.3.

TEXT: Readex Microprint.

CRITICAL EDITION: *The Poems of Anne Countess of Winchilsea*, edited with introduction by Myra Reynolds (Chicago: U of Chicago P, 1903): 337–411.

The Art of Management; or, Tragedy Expelled, Charlotte Cibber Charke. This farce was performed at least three times at York Buildings beginning 24 September 1735. The farce was printed the same year by W. Rayner, with an ironic dedication to Charles Fleetwood, the manager of DL who had fired her on the grounds of immoral conduct. The piece was intended as a satire on Fleetwood, who tried to buy up all the copies.

The scene is DL Theatre where Fleetwood is the manager, Squire Brainless; Charke's brother Theophilus Cibber is Headpiece, and she is Mrs. Tragic. In addition, there are various theatrical types—leading actor, prompter, dancer, porter, boxkeeper, and dressmaker. The theatre has fallen on hard times because the manager only offers a repertory of rope dancing and pantomime instead of legitimate theatre. Moreover, good actors have been let go, and incompetent actors have had their salaries raised. After Mrs. Tragic receives her notice, she is consoled by Headpiece. When Brainless turns up, Headpiece defends his sister and advises Brainless to sell. But Brainless's decision is firm: Mrs. Tragic must go. The offended Headpiece, then, resolves on rebellion, which splits the theatre into factions: Brainless and his lieutenant, Bloodbath, on one side and the actors on the other. At this point Brainless is arrested for debt and dragged to debtors' prison. The theatre, now under the direction of Headpiece, will be able to offer legitimate dramas. The troupe then plans to stage *All for Love* or *The Earl of Essex* for the benefit of their former manager. Mrs. Tragic forgives Brainless and praises her brother Headpiece.

Dane F. Smith finds the play full of more talk than action, and he also points out that Charke is too serious to animate her play with the physical action of farce. In addition, most of the characters are undeveloped except Mrs. Tragic and Headpiece, who become sentimental heroine and hero.

TEXT: Readex Microprint.

The Artifice, Susanna Centlivre. This five-act comedy was first produced at DL on 2 October 1722 and printed the same year for T. Payne, though 1723 is on the title page. Despite a strong cast headed by Anne Oldfield as Mrs. Watchit, the play lasted only three nights and was not revived.

Four plots make Centlivre's play difficult to follow for audience or reader. Two of the plots are set up in the first act, while the other two plots are mentioned: (1) When Sir John Freeman meets Fainwell in the Park, Fainwell is in livery. Actually an Ensign in a regiment, Fainwell has taken two months leave to try to win the rich Widow Headless under the name of Mr. Worthy of Gloucestershire. To achieve this he has become a servant in her household. (2) Sir John says that he has been disinherited in favor of his younger brother Ned. Because of this reversal in fortune, Olivia's father Sir Philip Moneylove now insists that she marry Ned and break off her betrothal to Sir John. The opening conversation also foreshadows two other plots: (3) Ned has had a liaison with Louisa, a Dutch woman, by whom he fathered a son (in Dutch law they are considered married); and (4) Fainwell's uncle Watchit has come to town with a young wife. Ned believes the Watchits happen to lodge next to him, and he has a connecting door which will allow him access to Mrs. Watchit. With so many disconnected plots afoot, Centlivre does manage to keep the play going. Ned's Dutch wife arrives and lodges in back rooms at the Widow Headless's, where she asks him for one visit. When Ned comes, they drink a glass of wine; her artifice is to tell him it is poisoned. He then marries her, leaving his brother Sir John free to marry Olivia. After some jiggery-pokery with the will, Sir John inherits, while Louisa announces that she has a £40,000 bequest from her father, and Ned acquiesces. Fainwell (as Worthy) unmasks Tally, a rival adventurer posing as Lord Pharoah-Bank, and the artifice succeeds with the Widow. Finally, the Watchits reconcile after her near adultery with Ned.

After a long and successful career as a playwright, Susanna Centlivre must have been disappointed that her last play failed to please the public, and it has not pleased many of her critics since. Her biographer, John W. Bowyer, finds most of the plot lines borrowed from her own earlier work. F. P. Lock remarks that "its sheer length (106 pages) may have resulted in tedium" (117). After Centlivre's illness in 1719, she may have felt driven to pack as much as she could into what would be her last play, which "seems unusually troubled and pessimistic about the institution of marriage itself," according to Pearson (225). Moreover, the mixed values push the comedy in the direction of the sentimental mode: the archetypical sentimental drama, Steele's *The Conscious Lovers*, premiered at DL in November 1722, a month after *The Artifice*. One unusual feature of the play is that seven servants are used, not all of them in the cast list: with Fainwell acting as Jeffery, a servant in the Widow Headless's house, we learn a good deal of the activities "below stairs." To have servants requires money, and this emphasizes that most of the plot lines turn on economics—wills, legacies, fortune hunting, bribes, and bequests.

TEXTS: Readex Microprint. TEC Reel 476: 27.

FACSIMILE EDITION: E-CED: *The Plays of Susanna Centlivre*, edited with an introduction by R. C. Frushell (NY: Garland, 1982).

Asgard the Demon Hunter; or, Le Démon à la Chasse, Jane M. Scott. Called a burletta spectacle in one act, this piece was produced at the Sans Pareil Theatre on 17 November 1812 and acted forty-two times its first season. Michael Parnell composed the music.

In *The Adelphi Stage Calendar*, Frank McHugh describes this spectacle, which opened the Sans Pareil season, as a "Gothic fantasy which gave the audience plenty of lurid situations and stage effects" (15). The climax of the piece has Wildgrave being chased into a cavern beneath his castle, where at midnight Asgard appears as the Demon of Darkness, and they descend together into a pit of flames.

MANUSCRIPT: Larpent 1741.

Aspacia, Anne Hughes. This three-act, blank verse tragedy was printed in her *Moral Dramas Intended for Private Representation*, published by William Lane, 1790. There is no known public performance.

Hughes's drama raises questions about female friendships from the outset. Ismena chooses her duty to Aspacia rather than accept the crown offered by Selim. But Aspacia is misled and thinks Ismena false. Aspacia's quest for revenge leads to her own death. Despite the small cast, the relationship of the characters is not always clear. In her first speech, Ismena says she was "born obscure, an humble village maid," but why and how she became Aspacia's companion is never explained. Ambition to regain a queenly stature seems to drive Aspacia, whereas faithfulness to Aspacia motivates Ismena. The denouement of this "happy-ending" tragedy finds the revenge-seeking characters dying, while the noble and virtuous characters (Selim and Ismena) live on.

TEXT: Readex Microprint.

The Assignation, Sophia Lee. This five-act comedy was acted only once at DL on 28 January 1807. It was never printed, perhaps because, as *BD* remarks, "it was universally condemned" (2: 41).

MANUSCRIPT: Larpent 1508.

AUBERT, Isabella (fl. 1715–20). While often credited with the three-act mock opera *Harlequin Hydespes; or, The Greshamite* (27 May 1719 at LIF), Aubert is not the author. She sang in Mancini's *Hydaspes* (27 August 1715 at LIF), which was parodied in the later piece. Based on notices in the *Daily Courant*, Burling argues convincingly that the play should be credited to her husband, Mr. Aubert. Her last known performance in England was as a singer in a concert given at York Buildings on 1 June 1720. [BDAA, Cotton, Pearson]

UBIN, Penelope (1685?–1731). Born in London of Huguenot refugee parents, Aubin shared the two cultures all her life, and this is reflected in her writings. Frans De Bruyn notes that what little we know about Aubin's life comes from a satirical portrait of her "by the Abbé Prévost, who was living in London at the time of Aubin's short-lived career as an orator in 1729" (DLB 39: 11). Early in her literary pursuits, Aubin published several poems on the political and military leaders of the day—the Stuarts, Queen Anne, and the Duke of Marlborough. After a long hiatus, Aubin began publishing novels, and translations of French novels, through the decade of the 1720s.

Her activity as a public orator in 1729 rivaled that of the well-known Orator Henley. The author of one comedy, *The Merry Masqueraders; or, The Humorous Cuckold* (first performed at the Haymarket Theatre on 9 December 1730), Aubin influenced both Prévost and Richardson with her prose work (novels and histories). In her own dramatic benefit performance on 11 December 1730, Aubin wrote and delivered a new epilogue. The details of her death the following year are obscure. [BDAA, BNA, Cotton, DBAWW, FCLE, Pearson]

The Author and Bookseller, Charlotte MacCarthy. This dramatic dialogue in twelve pages, published "for the author" in 1765, was not meant for stage performance. *BD* describes it as ". . . merely designated as an introduction to proposals for printing a book, entitled 'Justice and Reason faithful guides to Truth. A Treatise under thirty-seven heads.'" Davis and Joyce describe it as a "satiric play."

TEXT: Not in Readex Microprint.

-B-

BAILLIE, Joanna (1762–1851). Born in Lanarkshire, Scotland, Joanna Baillie grew up in her father's manse. At the age of ten, she went to a boarding school in Glasgow, where she distinguished herself as an actor and improvisor. In 1776, her father was appointed

Professor of Divinity at the University of Glasgow. When he died two years later, Joanna with her mother and sister returned to Lanarkshire, while her brother Matthew went to Oxford University. Upon the death of an uncle, Dr. William Hunter, Matthew inherited his London house, and the family moved there in 1784. At age twenty-eight, Joanna published a volume of poetry, *Fugitive Verses*.

Her first play, *Arnold*, has not survived, but in 1798 she published anonymously her *Plays on the Passions*—each play unified by the dominance of a single passion. For instance, *Basil* and *The Tryal* focus on love in a tragedy and a comedy, while *De Monfort* treats hatred in a tragedy. Baillie's introduction to the *Plays* takes up the importance of sympathetic instincts as a powerful teacher. Her theories of the passions were often at variance with stage practicality and contemporary critics charged that her plays lacked incident. Nevertheless, John Philip Kemble prepared *De Monfort* for the stage: he acted the title character, while his sister Sarah Siddons acted De Monfort's sister Jane (DL, 29 April 1800). Two years later, Baillie brought out her second volume of *Plays on the Passions*, which included *The Election* (a comedy on hatred), *Ethwald* (a tragedy in two parts), and *The Second Marriage* (a comedy on ambition). In 1804, Baillie published *Miscellaneous Plays*, containing two tragedies, *Raynor* and *Constantine Paleologus*, separated by *The Country Inn*, a comedy. These plays did not focus on a single passion. Although *Constantine Paleologus* was written with the actors in mind, Kemble and Siddons did not choose to adapt the tragedy for the stage. Instead, it was performed in Surrey (as a melodrama), and later in Liverpool, Edinburgh, and Dublin. In 1806, Baillie's mother died, and she and her sister took a house together in Hampstead where they both lived for the rest of their lives. With the help of Sir Walter Scott, Baillie's play *The Family Legend* appeared on the Edinburgh stage in 1810. The drama enjoyed considerable success in Scotland, based as it was on a feud among Highland clans, and it ran fourteen nights. Several years later, *The Family Legend* was staged at DL (29 April 1815). Baillie's third volume of *Plays on the Passions* came out in 1812, with fear as the dominant passion in *Orra*, *The Dream*, and *The Siege*; a musical drama *The Beacon* illustrated hope.

After her plays were collected in 1821, Baillie turned her efforts to nondramatic poetry: *Metrical Legends of Exalted Characters* came out in 1821, and she edited *A Collection of Poems* in 1823. *The Martyr*, a poetical drama written earlier and printed in 1826, treats the martyrdom of Maro, an officer in Nero's guard, who dies for his Christian beliefs. She also published *The Bride* in 1828. At the age of seventy-four, Baillie published in three volumes her last plays, which she had intended to issue posthumously. Two of these dramas were staged in London during 1836; Charles Kemble appeared in *The Separation* at CG, and Vandenhoff acted *Henriquez* at DL. Baillie continued to write poetry into her eighties, and she saw her *Works* through the press before she died in 1851.

A number of critics praise Baillie's dramatic originality in her twenty-seven printed plays. Perhaps if she had been more familiar with stagecraft and frequented the playhouse oftener, more of her plays would have been produced. But if she did not achieve the display on stage that she wished, Baillie succeeded with the reading public. Baillie's emphasis on the passions set up moral choices that characters must grapple with. Her contemporary readers, then, found a moral content quite strong in almost every drama. Most of her plays show a natural language which reflects the romantic ideal of people speaking to one another in everyday speech rather than in an elevated or poetical language. [*BD*, BNA, DBAWW, DNB, EBWW, FCLE, Genest (9: 333–47), Lonsdale, NCBEL (3: 363–64), OCEL. Biography by Margaret S. Carhart, 1923, with bibliography. The *Series of Plays* (1798, 1802, and 1812) in 3 vols. are in facsimile, ed. D. H. Reiman (NY: Garland, 1977); the first volume (1798) also appears in a facsimile edition as part of the "Revolution and Romanticism, 1798–1834" series, ed. Jonathan Wordsworth (NY: Woodstock, 1990). Baillie's *Dramatic and Poetical Works* (1851) has been printed in a facsimile edition

(Hildesheim and NY: Georg Olms Verlag, 1976).]

BALFOUR, Mary Devens (1755?–c. 1820). Author of poetry and one three-act "grand national melodrama," *Kathleen O'Neil*, produced in Belfast on 9 February 1814, and printed the same year in Belfast by Archbold and Dugan. Kathleen is a well-known deer-slayer whose character combines intrepidity and shyness. Abducted, she is later rescued by her chief suitor. A comic subplot, a good deal of Celtic spirit, and several songs help enliven the play. [FCLE, Nicoll]

Ballynavogue; or The Lilly of Lismore, Jane M. Scott. See **The Row of Ballynavogue**.

The Barber of Seville; or, The Useless Precaution, translated by Elizabeth Griffith. Taken from Beaumarchais's comedy, *Le Barbier de Séville; ou, La Précaution inutile*, Griffith's four-act version was never produced, though it was published "for the author" in 1776 with a dedication to R. B. Sheridan. George Colman the elder may have used Griffith's translation for his three-act comic opera, *The Spanish Barber*, first acted at the Haymarket 30 August 1777. His version held the stage for a number of years.

Count Almaviva, in love with Rosina, a beautiful young orphan of noble origin, leaves Madrid for Seville where Rosina lives. There, he meets Figaro, his former servant, now barber to Dr. Bartholo, Rosina's old guardian who plans to marry her. With Figaro's help and ingenuity, Almaviva tries to enter Bartholo's house, first as a soldier in need of lodging, then as a substitute for Bazile, Rosina's music teacher, supposedly taken ill. But the ever-watchful Bartholo overhears a conversation which reveals a complicity between Rosina and Almaviva, and, still determined to get Rosina for himself, he uses a letter to prove to her that her lover is unfaithful. Out of spite, she uncovers her projected elopement with the Count. Fortunately, the Count and Figaro manage to enter through a window while Bartholo is away, and after a short quarrel, the two lovers not only reconcile but are married by the very lawyer who was to unite Rosina to the old doctor. Bartholo returns just in time to witness youth and love triumph over a selfish old man and his useless precautions.

Although Griffith intended "to alter or retrench one or two Acts" (*Advertisement*) of Beaumarchais's masterpiece, her version can be called a literal translation. Except for minor cuts noted by Kinne (143), to which should be added a highly comical episode in Act III, scene 4, described by Beaumarchais in scenic directions omitted in the English version, Griffith translated the play rather than adapting it. Her rendition is often awkward, careless, and even inaccurate as Kinne shows in his telling but incomplete list of alterations. An example of mistranslation (not included in Kinne) is in one of Figaro's most famous and biting remarks in the first act; "un grand," i.e., a noble man, is rendered "a great Man," which misses Beaumarchais's indictment of the French nobility. Devoid of the witty, mordant style of the original, Griffith's translation was not well received by the critics (Kinne 143 n.104), but Betty Rizzo notes that a second edition was called for in 1776, and published by J. Chouquet (*Curtain Calls* 140).

TEXT: Readex Microprint.

The Baron, translated by Fanny Holcroft. This two-act comedy was translated from the Spanish of Inarco Celenio. There is no known English performance. It was published in *The Theatrical Recorder*, vol. 2, no. 11, edited by Thomas Holcroft (London: C. Mercier, 1806): 287–322.

Set in Yllescas, Spain, the comedy turns on the appearance of the Baron in this rural village. His story is that he was forced to flee Madrid, short of funds, after fighting a duel. His tale completely takes in Isabella's mother Donna Monica, and he moves into their house. When Leonardo, Isabella's fiancé, returns from Toledo, he finds the Baron has taken his place, and Leonardo is no longer admitted. Don Pedro, Donna Monica's brother, is the voice of reason: he suggests the Baron is an imposter, but Donna Monica will not listen because she wishes Isabella to marry the Baron. Even though her mother wants to be called

"Lady," Isabella holds out for Leonardo. After being challenged to a duel by Leonardo, the Baron makes his escape, climbing out of a window. With Don Pedro's help, Leonardo and Isabella are reconciled to Donna Monica, who finally approves of their marriage.

In her "Remarks" at the end of the translation, Fanny Holcroft says that the play "has not sufficient incident for the English stage," but it provides an example of the current drama in Spain, where it was publicly performed at Cadiz. Isabella appears to be passive, but despite the attempts to manipulate her by the Baron and Donna Monica, she remains steadfast to Leonard.

TEXT: Readex Microprint.

BARRELL, Maria Weylar (fl. 1770–90). First known for her poetry, *Rêveries du Coeur, or Feelings of the Heart* (1770), Maria Weylar lived in London contributing to periodicals. In 1785, as Maria Barrell, she was thrown in debtors' prison. Because of this experience, she published a prose tract (1788) and a drama, *The Captive* (1790). Barrell's play was not acted. No birth or death dates established. [FCLE, Nicoll]

BARRYMORE, Mrs. William [Adams] (fl. 1823). Author of a "diversion," *Evening Revels*, produced at DL on 10 November 1823. Apparently, it was not printed. [Nicoll; not noted in Genest]

The Bashaw; or, Adventures of Three Spaniards, Jane M. Scott. This "musical Melo Dramatic Burletta" opened on 23 January 1809 at the Sans Pareil Theatre with Miss Scott in the role of the Bashaw. James Sanderson composed the music. It ran fifty-nine nights its first season and was revived twelve times the following season. There is no known text of the melodrama.

The Basset-Table, Susanna Carroll [Centlivre]. This five-act comedy, based on Regnard's *Le Divorce* of 1688, was first produced at DL on 20 November 1705 and published the same year by William Turner (dated 1706) without the name of the author. Even though the play ran only four nights and was not revived, Jonas Browne and S. Chapman published a second edition in 1706.

Lady Reveller runs a fashionable gambling (basset) table in the house of her uncle, Sir Richard Plainman. He and her cousin, Lady Lucy, try to dissuade her from these gaming activities, as does a sincere lover, Lord Worthy. Although Valeria, Sir Richard's daughter, displays a scientific and philosophical turn of mind, she is taken with Ensign Lovely. Her father thinks her scientific apparatuses are so much rubbish, and he plans to marry her off to a valiant sailor. With the assistance of Captain Firebrand, Lovely acts the sailor and weds Valeria. Sir James Courtly stages an attempted rape of Lady Reveller, until Lord Worthy rushes in to save her. When Courtly explains this plot to Lady Lucy, she finally agrees to marry him.

The popularity of Centlivre's *The Gamester* (produced LIF, February 1705) may have prompted her to create another play on the vice of gambling. Here, as Hume notes, the previous play is inverted to stop a woman (Lady Reveller), rather than a man (Young Valere), from excessive gaming (469). The use of language in the play is particularly interesting: gambling terms used in basset become metaphoric when spoken by the gamesters. Captain Firebrand speaks in nautical terms and is, then, parodied by Lady Reveller. The Sagos from the trading classes have private names for each other that they use in public: she is Keecky, and he is Puddy. Valeria speaks in scientific terms, and Lord Worthy's servant Buckle uses an exaggerated language as he makes up stories about his master. Perhaps the most important word in *The Basset Table* is "heart": the lovers desire to win hearts, not merely the person they love. Lord Worthy, for instance, says that Lady Reveller's "heart's the gem that I prefer." Alpiew thinks Lady Reveller must have "a heart of adamant" to withstand Worthy's love. Sir James Courtly can be rescued if Lady Lucy will give her heart: he says "were your heart the stake, I'd renounce all engagements to win that, or retrieve my own." When she thinks his "heart poisoned with vicious thoughts," he claims "my heart, till now unused to passion, swells at the affront." When Sir James proves his innocence, Lady Lucy's "heart yields."

TEXT: Readex Microprint.

FACSIMILE EDITION: E-CED, with introduction by Richard C. Frushell (NY: Garland, 1982).

MODERN EDITION: Everyman's Library, *Female Playwrights of the Restoration*, edited with introduction by Paddy Lyons and Fidelis Morgan (London: Dent, 1991): 235–292.

Battle in the Shadow, Jane M. Scott. This spectacle by Scott was performed forty-three times, opening on 12 January 1807 at the Sans Pareil Theatre. No copy of the play exists.

The Battle of Poictiers; or, The English Prince, Mrs. Hoper. Although this tragedy was produced at Goodman Fields on 5 March 1747, it was not printed and must be presumed lost. The historical Prince must have been a popular topic at this period since William Shirley's *Edward the Black Prince* was produced at DL on 6 January 1750.

The Battle of Waterloo, Mary Hornby. This five-act tragedy was published at Stratford-upon-Avon for the author by B. W. Barnacle, 1819. Stratman (#2408) says that there is no indication that the play was staged. A play by the same title was done by J. H. Amherst and printed for Duncombe without a date.

TEXT: Not in Readex Microprint.

The Beacon, Joanna Baillie. This "Serious Musical Drama in Two Acts" was first published in *A Series of Plays: [on] the Stronger Passions* (third series), 1812. On 9 February 1815, Larpent approved the play for performance in Edinburgh, but neither Genest, nor Margaret Carhart, Baillie's biographer, mention a production.

Set on a Mediterranean island in the fourteenth century, the play opens with a morning song designed to awaken Aurora, who is sleeping after having been up all night at her beacon. She keeps a fire burning each night on the cliffs of the island in the hope that her lover Ermingard, who has gone on a pilgrimage to the holy land, will see it and be able to guide his ship to land. The ruler of the island, Ulrick, was Ermingard's rival for Aurora's hand, and he believes that she should stop the nightly beacon fires and declares the coming night will be her last. Bastiani reports to Ulrick that the papal legate from Palestine has docked, and Ulrick leaves the women together. They include Aurora, Terentia (Ulrick's relation), Edda (a singer), and Viola (who often watches at night with Aurora). They plan to have the biggest fire ever this night. Garcio, a nephew of the papal legate, brings Aurora tokens from Ermingard, but he does not know whether he is dead or alive. That night two fishermen attend the fire, and one sings a lengthy narrative ballad. When Bastiani comes to tell them that a boat below the cliff is in danger, they go to help, leaving him to watch the fire. He is joined by Viola, Terentia, and Aurora. They hear singing, and soon some knights from St. John of Jerusalem arrive. They praise the beacon for saving them. Aurora asks about Ermingard, and the knight she asks turns out to be Ermingard, who has however taken holy vows of the order of St. John of Jerusalem. Terentia suggests they retire to her chamber where they can talk privately. When Ulrick becomes angry, Garcio goes to get the papal legate. Ulrick breaks in on Terentia, Aurora, and Ermingard; the two men fight until they are stopped by Garcio and the papal legate, who says that Ulrick must give an account of himself and his ward Aurora to the Pope, and that Ermingard may honorably leave the order and marry Aurora.

The drama only hints at the reasons for Ulrick's conflict with Ermingard—they were rivals—but no details are given. As the blocking figure, Ulrick is drawn without his motives being fully defined. Aurora's optimism that Ermingard will return appears to be based only on her feeling that if she thinks it, it must be so. Again, character is underdeveloped with a paucity of motivation. Although there are only four songs, the music functions to underscore the events in the drama: for instance, when Edda sings a cheerful song to Aurora, it concludes with the words "happy thoughts return." Later, she has a song with the refrain "long, long lost is found."

MANUSCRIPT: Larpent 1846.

TEXT: Readex Microprint of 1821 edition. 3: 267–314.

FACSIMILE EDITION: *Romantic Context: Poetry* reprints the 1812 edition (London: Longman, Hurst, Rees, Orme and Brown). Compiled by D. H. Reiman (NY: Garland, 1977).

The Beau Defeated; or, The Lucky Younger Brother, attributed to Mary Pix. This five-act comedy is partly based on F. C. Dancourt's *Le Chevalier à la Mode* of 1687. It was produced at LIF in March 1700 and probably published the same year (though without date) by W. Turner and R. Basset. Pix's name does not appear on the title page. The play has also been ascribed to Henry Barker, and sometimes called *The Beau Demolished.*

Lady Landsworth, described as a "rich widow from Yorkshire," is staying in London with Mrs. Rich, a city widow, who wishes to climb the social ladder. The contrast of the widows and their involvement with suitors highlights their different characters. Another contrast shows that the Clerimont brothers have decidedly different values: the cloddish elder brother who has inherited the family fortune cares only for dogs and hunting, whereas the decent younger brother remains troubled by the death of his father. Lady Landsworth tests the younger Clerimont until he meets with her approval, whereas the elder Clerimont ends up with Mrs. Rich, whose previous beau, Sir John Roverhead, is shown to lack the title he has given himself.

Although some critics believe Pix used Molière as a source (for instance, Clark thinks that Mrs. Rich's predicament owes a good deal to Molière's *Les Précieuses Ridicules* of 1659), the influence could easily have come from earlier English plays. The affected language lesson of Cathos and Magdelon in *Les Précieuses Ridicules* is missing, as is the smarting lesson their suitors inflict on them through their disguise as servants. While Pix's Sir John is an usurper, he has assumed a title for the purpose of finding a rich wife, not to inflict a lesson. Thus, we do not believe Molière is a direct source for Pix.

Pix's main inspiration, Dancourt's *Le Chevalier à la Mode*, features a ruthless fortune hunter who pursues several potential wives at once. At the opening of the play, Mrs. Rich/Mme. Patin and her sensible maid Betty/Lisette engage in an exchange that comically exposes the widow's silly pretensions to nobility and her resolve to acquire it at any price. Pix also borrowed the madrigal scene where three women discover not only that they were given the same lines of poetry, but also have shared the same lover. Aside from her source, however, Pix added several significant characters, such as Lady Landsworth and the Clerimont brothers. She makes Sir John a false knight instead of the real chevalier of the original. The result is that Pix's plot appears somewhat cluttered with several labored dialogues that are unlike the opening scene, lifted almost word-for-word from Dancourt, which is rightly praised by Fidelis Morgan and Allardyce Nicoll. John Harrington Smith believes Dancourt's comedy superior to Pix's because of Dancourt's tight plotting, alert dialogues, and successful comic scenes with well-rounded characters (*JEGP* 47 [1948]: 390–94). Indeed, *Le Chevalier à la Mode* stands out as Dancourt's masterpiece.

Critical opinion on Pix's comedy varies widely: Paula Barbour believes it is one of her least interesting comedies, whereas Nancy Cotton thinks it one of her best. Hume points out that the testing of young Clerimont has become standard by 1700, and Clark remarks on the play's movement toward sensibility. Certainly, the upstart city people act as ridiculously as the country bumpkins. The principal exemplary character, Lady Landsworth (played by Anne Bracegirdle), demonstrates a strong determination to choose her own husband, showing us a clear-headed woman who knows what she wants.

TEXTS: Wing P2326. EEB Reel 1192: 3. Readex Microprint.

FACSIMILE EDITION: E-CED, with introduction by Edna L. Steeves (NY: Garland, 1982).

MODERN EDITION: Everyman's Library, *Female Playwrights of the Restoration*, edited with introduction by Paddy Lyons and Fidelis Morgan (London: Dent, 1991): 161–234.

The Beau's Duel; or, A Soldier for the Ladies, Susanna Carroll [Centlivre]. This five-act comedy was acted at LIF during June 1702, but the exact date of the premiere is not known. The author adapted parts of the play from Mayne's *The City Match* (1637). Bowyer notes a revival the following season (21 October 1702), which was advertised "with a new scene," though "there is no way to trace the additions" (43), since D. Brown and N. Cox published the play in July 1702. Susanna Carroll signed the dedication. A reprinting of the play by Jonas Brown occurred in 1715 (advertised in the *Daily Courant*, 26 February 1715—Burling); ESTC notes contributing publishers W. Mears and T. Woodward. We have been unable to compare the two printings.

Set in London, the first act opens with Colonel Manly and Captain Bellmein ready to fight a duel because they think they love the same woman. However, they soon learn differently: Emilia (Bellmein's inamorata) has recently arrived at her uncle's house on a visit to her cousin Clarinda, whom Manly adores. The two soldiers watch while Clarinda is given a musical serenade provided by Sir William Mode, who has the approval of Clarinda's father, Careful. The soldiers are, thus, challenged to win their ladies despite the blocking father and several beaus; however, it is the women who bring the action to a head. Dressed in male attire, they catch the beaus faking a duel with "files," read "foils," and literally kick them around. When Clarinda's father insists on her marrying Sir William, she sends for Colonel Manly; they duck into a church and are married. Careful is so angry that he marries a meek Quaker woman (Mrs. Plotwell in disguise), only to find her the reverse of what he thought. Since the marriage had been staged (Bellmein acted a Scot's parson), he agrees to accept Clarinda and Manly, if he can be freed from the marriage. Achieving this, Careful blesses the couple, Mrs. Plotwell returns his papers, and Emilia accepts Bellmein.

The females (Clarinda, Emilia, and Mrs. Plotwell) control the play's action: they easily dispose of the fops—Ogle and Sir William—in the beau's duel; they subdue Careful with a marriage trick; and they bring their soldier lovers—Colonel Manly and Captain Bellmein—to the altar. Pearson discusses Mrs. Plotwell in some detail: as a character with a sordid and unconventional past, "Mrs. Plotwell is the most attractive of Centlivre's benevolent female intriguers, since she intrigues not for personal gain but altruistically to help the young lovers" (215). The quarto of 1702 is, unfortunately, laced with errors: several times, for instance, Toper is given the speech prefix of Roarwell. Lock suggests that the character of Toper was altered, for political reasons, from a bully to a drinker to avoid blurring him with the officers (88). As in many of Centlivre's dramas, commerce plays an important part in this comedy. While Sir William's money influences Careful in his favor, Ogle is described as a "Fortune-hunter." By duping Careful, the women force him to give Clarinda and Manly a dowry. Also, an inheritance allows Mrs. Plotwell to change her ways.

TEXTS: Readex Microprint. TEC Reels 578: 11 (1702); 589: 21 (1715).

FACSIMILE EDITION: E-CED, with introduction by R. C. Frushell (NY: Garland, 1982).

BEHN, Aphra (1640?–1689). England's first professional female dramatist, Aphra Behn said little about her early life, which has proved a vexing problem for her biographers. Add to the paucity of biographical facts her nineteenth-century reputation as a writer of "smutty" plays, and much is now obscured in the dust of history. We are unsure of where or when she was born: probably in Kent and probably 1640. While she complained later of her lack of education, Aphra clearly gained more than conventional learning. In 1663, she traveled with her family to Surinam, and on her return she married a tradesman of Dutch descent, who probably died in the plague. Shortly thereafter, she went to Antwerp to spy for Charles II, ran up debts, and returned home to go to debtors' prison.

Freed, perhaps by the help of Thomas Killigrew, she soon saw her first play, *The Forced Marriage* (produced at LIF) at the age of thirty. After this reasonable success (it ran six nights), she had produced in the same season *The Amorous Prince* (at LIF). Her comedy, *The Dutch Lover* (produced at DG, 6 March 1673), failed, as she tells us in the preface, mainly for two reasons: male critics damned it because a woman wrote it, and the actors botched her text. It was three years later that she returned to the stage with her only tragedy, *Abdalazer* (produced at DG, July 1676). With *The Town-Fopp*, *The Rover*, and possibly *The Debauchee* (all produced at DG in the 1676–1677 season), Behn found her true metier—fast-paced, rollicking intrigue comedies. Over the next five years, Behn probably wrote at least ten comedies, all of them produced at DG: *The Counterfeit Bridegroom* (attrib.), *Sir Patient Fancy*, *The Feign'd Curtezans*, *The Young King*, *The Revenge* (attrib.), *The Second Part of the Rover*, *The False Count*, *The Roundheads*, *The City Heiress,* and *Like Father, Like Son*. These comedies have an abundance of witty dialogue, frequent disguises (with much cross-dressing), mistaken identities, and near-catastrophic duels. In August 1682, her excessive Tory sympathies caused her to be arrested for an epilogue she contributed to the anonymous play, *Romulus and Hersilia*. While this passed with little incident, Behn declined to put more political feelings on stage. She turned to poetry, novels, and translations in the next four years before returning to the stage with a boisterous—non-political—comedy, *The Luckey Chance* (produced at DG, April 1686) and a clever farce, *The Emperor of the Moon* (produced at DG, March 1687). She turned mostly to fiction and poetry in the two years before her death on 16 April 1689; she was buried in Westminster Abbey. Two of her plays were produced posthumously—*The Widow Ranter* (at DL in November 1689) and *The Younger Brother* (at DL in February 1696).

Given the extreme difficulties of working in the male-dominated field of drama, Behn's achievement is considerable. The only near rivals to the sheer size of her dramatic production—nineteen known plays—are Shadwell and Dryden in a forty-year period which included Etherege, Wycherley, and Congreve. Central to many of her plays is the recurring problem of forced marriages: Behn rebelled against any enslavement. While she entertained her audience, she also instructed them in the equality and mutual respect of men and women. [*BD*, BNA, Cotton, DBAWW, DLB 80 (by K. M. Rogers), DNB, EBWW, FCLE, Hobby, Hume, Morgan, NCBEL (2: 755–57), Scouten (by F. Link), Smith & Cardinale, Revels. Biographies by Woodcock, 1948 (rpt. 1989); F. Link, 1968; M. Duffy, 1977; and A. Goreau, 1980. Bibliographies by J. Armisted, 1984, and M. A. O'Donnell, 1986]

Belisarius, Charlotte Brooke. A lost play, though *BD* suggests that one act of the drama may have been published in *The Oracle*, a daily paper, on 17 October 1795 (2: 56). We have been unable to verify this.

Bell in Campo, Margaret Lucas Cavendish, Duchess of Newcastle. A drama in two parts, printed in her *Playes*, published by John Martyn, James Allestry, and Tho. Dicas in 1662. The play was not produced.

Cavendish divides her play in two parts, but the several plot lines continue through both parts. When the play opens, the Reformation kingdom is going to war with the kingdom of Faction, but a gentleman speaks confidently about the Reformation general. The scene shifts to the general and his wife Victoria, who wants to go to war with him. She argues her case successfully, and he agrees she should accompany him. Then we hear from various women who will or will not go with their husbands to war. When the first battle appears eminent, the women are sent to a garrison town away from the fighting. Angry over this affront, the women vote Victoria as their commander. Meanwhile at home, Madame Jantil has bad dreams and worries about her husband. Shortly thereafter he and the husband of Madame Passionate are reported dead. Three men—Gravity, Compagnion, and Comerade—plan to woo the two widows. At the front, the women learn that the male army has been defeated, so they prepare themselves for battle. Victoria rallies her troops: after recovering the male prisoners captured by the enemy, they lay siege to a strong fort that is the key to the enemy's kingdom. The male contingent requests that they be allowed to join the female army, "*leaving all these affairs of War to your* [the women's] *discretion*." Lady Victoria says that by their actions the female army has proved itself equal to the male; she then recommends that the male forces be allowed the honor of capturing the fort, since "we have got honour enough in the Battel we fought, and victory we did win." On the home front, Madame Jantil erects a tomb to her husband and lives a cloistered life, while Madame Passionate enjoys spirits of distilled wine and looks around her for another husband. She decides to marry to please herself and selects Compagnion, whose eyes recall those of her late husband. Madame Jantil makes a will and dies, whereas Madame Passionate's marriage to young Compagnion is a catastrophe: her new husband spends her money on riotous living, depletes her estate, and replaces her in the marriage bed with a maid. At the front, since the female army has been so successful, the men are encouraged to advance beyond the fort, causing the kingdom of Faction to submit. When the victorious women return home, a parade is given in their honor. The King declares that women will now be mistresses in their own houses, keep the family purses, own all the jewels and plate, and go abroad freely. Lady Victoria is honored not only by the King but by her husband.

Cavendish's latest biographer, Kathleen Jones, argues that this is her most successful play (*The Glorious Fame* [London: Bloomsbury, 1988]: 131–32). Pearson says that the "main plot stresses the strengths of women, the subplot their weaknesses" (*TSWL* 4 [1985]: 36). Hobby remarks that "Lady Victoria's congratulatory speech to her soldiers emphasizes that women can do anything, if they can only escape their conditioning long enough to have faith in themselves" (109). As the play's central figure, Lady Victoria organizes her troops well and leads them effectively. She sets out the rules, gets a consensus, and pushes ahead when the men falter. Her effectiveness in war wins women's rights in peace.

TEXTS: Wing N868. EEB Reel 502: 11. Readex Microprint.

The Belle's Stratagem, Hannah Cowley. This successful five-act comedy was first produced at CG on 22 February 1780 and was acted twenty-eight times its first season. *The Belle's Stratagem* became a staple of the British stage well into the nineteenth century, as Genest documents. Because of the play's popularity, CG paid Cowley £100 to withhold publication, but a spurious copy was printed in Dublin by T. Bathe during 1781. London publication by T. Cadell was in April 1782. Inchbald included the play in her *British Theatre* collection, 1808.

When Doricourt returns from France, he signs marriage articles, by prearrangement, with Letitia Hardy, who has recently come from the country to London. He remarks to his friend Saville that she is "*only* a fine girl," lacking the spirit and fire he has encountered in European women during his travels. For her part, Letitia plans to turn Doricourt's indifference into an active dislike, for "'tis easier to convert a sentiment into its opposite, than to transform indifference into tender passion." When Doricourt visits, Letitia acts an awkward country maid. In a crucial scene at a masquerade, the masked Letitia charms Doricourt off his feet. Although he confesses that he is strongly attracted to her, she will not give in to him, at least not yet. The next part of her stratagem (feigned illness by her father) leads Doricourt to marry Letitia in her rustic guise. After the ceremony, she enters in her masquerade costume and mask, much to his mortification. She teases him until her father comes in, and she unmasks, revealing that she is the spirited Letitia, now Doricourt's wife. Her husband goes into raptures, and in his final speech regrets that he had been taken in by foreign manners and says that he is delighted with his British wife. In a secondary plot, Sir George and Lady Frances Touchwood have recently married, and after several trials they reaffirm their love for each other.

Letitia Hardy is nothing if not a strong woman. She diagnoses Doricourt's original indifferent feelings for her; by careful planning

reared by Horatio. The exchanging of the children was mutually agreed upon by the parents "in hopes of a great advantage" (224). Thus Florio's education, which may have been "insipid," has become a "lasting pleasure" (225).

The premise of the play, the conscious exchange of the children without their knowledge, appears implausible, and the lack of a strong conflict must have made the play unsuitable for the stage. Both parents' control of their children's destiny suggests to Penny's readers that "parents know best." At least these parents do not decide on a forced marriage.

TEXT: Readex Microprint of the *Poems*, 1780: 186–228.

The Blazing World, Margaret Lucas Cavendish, Duchess of Newcastle. This prose piece (called "a unique blend of fiction, philosophy, and wish fulfillment" by Kathleen Jones, in her recent biography of Newcastle, *The Glorious Fame* [London: Bloomsbury, 1988]: 167–69) was published in *The Description of a New World, called the Blazing-World* by A. Maxwell in 1668, but Cavendish apparently intended to add a dramatic portion. The fragment not included, *A Piece of a Play*, is a dramatized beast fable, which appears to be complete despite the title. Printed in her *Playes, never before printed*, published by A. Maxwell in 1668, it was not performed. A detailed discussion appears under *A Piece of a Play*.

TEXTS: Wing N867. EEB Reel 674: 2. Readex Microprint.

The Blind Child; or, Anecdotes of the Wyndham Family, Elizabeth Sibthorpe Pinchard. While this appears to be more of a novel than a play, it does include stage directions and dialogue among the children of the Wyndham family and their parents. Published in three parts by Elizabeth Newbery, the book first appeared in 1791; it was not intended for stage performance.

The children of the Wyndham family—Emily, age 14; Arthur, age 12; Helen, the title character, age 9; and Maria, age 7—live with their parents, who spend winters in London and summers in the country. After the family goes to the country, Helen's blindness requires explanations by her siblings; though she can feel the warmth, she must ask what sunshine is; though she can hear the birds, she wants to know what they are like. The first afternoon, the family drives to see Charlotte Neville and her mother, Mrs. Wyndham's oldest friend, who has been ill. While Charlotte plays outside with Maria and Helen, Mrs. Wyndham and Emily learn that Mrs. Neville does not expect to live long, and she hopes that the Wyndhams will care for Charlotte after she's gone. Emily says that she will be like a mother to the child. The next morning Mrs. Wyndham praises Emily's sensibility with Mrs. Neville. They plan a visit to the Sidney family, where the example of their ungovernable children—Edward and Harriet—provides a learning experience for the Wyndham children. Later, Mrs. Wyndham stresses the Sidney family should be pitied, not ridiculed. When she is called to Mrs. Neville, Mrs. Wyndham stays the night. The next day Mr. Wyndham joins her, but they return late in the day with Charlotte because Mrs. Neville has died. For the next few weeks, the children, especially Emily, learn about fortitude in the face of grief. To help Emily, Mrs. Wyndham gives her a story to read, "Elfrida; or, The Mirror." This tale-within-a-tale illustrates that wishes don't assist real happiness and often cause discontent. After assimilating this lesson, Emily is invited with Helen to a concert in the neighborhood, but on the day of the event a message arrives that the concert has been canceled because of a death in the family. Emily feels sorry for the family, but Helen cries at her disappointment, prompting Mrs. Wyndham to comment about bearing disappointments with patience. After the summer passes, the family and Charlotte return to London where Helen is to have an operation on her eyes. The operation appears to be a success, but Helen must remain in a darkened room for a while. In the progress of Helen's recovery, she learns to read and write, and finally to paint.

Pinchard's intent, stated in her preface, is to "awaken goodness in the rising generation," urging the young to adopt a true sensibility. At the conclusion of her preface, Pinchard quotes from "Sensibility," a poem by Hannah More. Understanding a blind child is an unusual issue for a late eighteenth-century writer, yet after some early references, little more is made of Helen's blindness until she has an operation at the end of the dramatic tale. Some attention to the problem of cruelty to animals arises when the Wyndhams visit the Sidneys. It is quite clear that Mrs. Wyndham is the teacher of the children in formal lessons, but more important she helps them learn manners and morals. While Mr. Wyndham supports her views, his chief role in the education of the children is to give Arthur Latin lessons. Emily is the foremost recipient of Mrs. Wyndham's educational schemes, for she and later Helen will help the orphaned Charlotte develop in deportment and decorum.

TEXT: Not in Readex Microprint. We read the fifth edition, printed for Elizabeth Newbery, 1798, in the King Collection at the Miami (Ohio) Univ. Library.

BOADEN, Caroline (fl. 1821–1839). Boaden wrote several plays, all produced at the Haymarket Theatre during summer seasons. She most likely grew up with the theatre: her father wrote plays and later prepared biographies of Siddons and Inchbald. Her first drama, produced under her name, was a three-act comedy, *Quite Correct* (1825); it was acted forty-eight times but not printed. *Fatality*, a one-act drama (1829), was acted eleven times. Her farce, *William Thompson; or, Which is He?* (1829) was acted twenty-two times. Another two-act farce, *First of April* (1830) was acted sixteen times. Her drama *A Duel in Richelieu's Time* was acted in 1832, and *Don Pedro the Cruel and Manuel the Cobbler* performed at the Surrey Theatre in 1838. [Genest 9: 315, 489, 531–32, Nicoll]

A Bold Stroke for a Husband, Hannah Cowley. This five-act comedy was first produced at CG on 25 February 1783 and had eighteen performances in its first season. As early as 1832, Genest noted the play's indebtedness to both Otway's *The Atheist* (1683) and Durfey's *The Virtuous Wife* (1683), but these borrowings in no way diminish Cowley's achievement. Printed first by the booksellers of Dublin in 1783, the comedy was published in London by T. Evans in 1784. Inchbald collected this comedy in her *British Theatre* (1808), and in her introduction Inchbald praises Cowley's ability to combine instruction with entertainment.

Actually, two women strike bold strokes in this comedy: one, Victoria, reclaims her wandering husband Don Carlos, and the other, her cousin Olivia, wins the man she wants after her father has urged many suitors upon her. In the serious plot, Carlos has left Victoria and foolishly signed over his wife's estate to the fortune-hunting Laura. Dressing as Florio, an attractive young man, Victoria gains Laura's affections. The unscrupulous Laura drops Carlos, who plans to kill Florio, only to discover he is actually Victoria. Without revealing her plans to him, Victoria, aided by her old friend Gasper, regains her estate and her husband. In the humorous plot, Olivia plays various roles in order to reject the many suitors provided by her father, Don Caesar, who is so driven to get heirs that he threatens to marry and to send Olivia to a convent. In the meantime, a veiled Olivia arranges to see Julio, who has recently returned from France. Convinced that Julio is the man she wants to marry, Olivia switches places with her maid, Minette, to test Julio's love. In the last scene, Julio declares his intention of marrying Olivia before the dumbfounded, but delighted, Don Caesar.

Although the title recalls Centlivre's *A Bold Stroke for a Wife* (1718) where Fainwell uses many disguises to win the hand of Ann Lovely, Cowley makes the women agents of the action. Set in Madrid, little else about the play is Spanish except the names. Jean Gagen calls the play "an English comedy of romantic intrigue except for the fact that women rather than men are the principal intriguers" (DLB 89: 94). Gagen also remarks that both women are daring, resourceful, and responsible for saving themselves from miserable situations in which the men (Victoria's husband and Olivia's father) have placed them. Cowley's dual plot is well integrated even with the contrasting women: Victoria is serious and sentimental, whereas Olivia is high spirited and witty.

Within the context of the play, Cowley demonstrates a broad knowledge of the currently fashionable European music scene, creating the character of Vincentio, one of Olivia's rejected suitors, who refers to "the gusto of [Antonio] Sacchini [1730–1786], and the sweetness of [Christoph] Gluck [1714–1787]," both important eighteenth-century opera composers. When Vincentio first sees Olivia, he says, without irony, that her presence thrills him "like a cadenza of Pachierotti" [Gasparo Pacchiarotti, 1740–1821], a castrato who sang in England from 1778 to 1784. Later, he mentions [Felice de] Giardini [1716–1796], an Italian violinist and composer who directed the orchestra at the King's Theatre, London from 1750 to 1777. In contrast with Vincento's pompous musical references, Olivia states her favorite musical instrument is the Jew's harp.

MANUSCRIPT: Larpent 617.

TEXTS: Readex Microprint of 1784 London ed. TEC Reel 3958: 5 (1784, fifth London edition by Evans).

FACSIMILE EDITION: E-CED, with introduction by Frederick Link (NY: Garland, 1982), prints the third edition (London: T. Evans, 1784).

A Bold Stroke for a Wife, Susanna Centlivre. Viewed as one of Centlivre's major contributions to the drama, this five-act comedy debuted at LIF on 3 February 1718 and ran for six nights its first season. Publication was the same year by W. Mears, J. Browne, and F. Clay. The play became a perennial favorite with actors and audiences, especially after the middle of the eighteenth century.

Before the play opens, Colonel Fainwell and Ann Lovely wish to marry, but her fortune has been entailed by her deceased father to four guardians. Unless Fainwell can get them all to consent, the couple can't afford to marry. The situation is made more difficult because each of the four is as different as possible: Sir Philip Morelove is an old beau; Periwinkle, an antiquarian; Tradelove, a broker on the stock exchange; and Obadiah Prim, a Quaker. By dressing in a borrowed suit of French clothes, Fainwell easily convinces Sir Philip. When the old beau introduces the foppish-appearing Fainwell to the other three guardians, they reject him out of hand. Fainwell, in the disguise of an Egyptian traveller, fails in his first attempt to convince Periwinkle because the antiquarian discovers who he is. Not to be put off, Fainwell tries Tradelove by dressing as a Dutch merchant and speaking in an accent. His friend Freeman reports to Tradelove news that will cause stocks to rise, and Tradelove wagers £2,000 that the information is false. Losing the bet, Tradelove gives permission for Fainwell to marry Ann in lieu of paying the debt. In a second attempt on Periwinkle, Fainwell acts Mr. Pillage, the old steward to Periwinkle's recently deceased uncle, reporting the death and Periwinkle's inheritance. In giving Periwinkle a lease to sign, Fainwell substitutes a paper allowing him to marry Ann. Finally, there is Prim to be hoodwinked: Fainwell's friend Sackbut has discovered that Prim is to be visited by Simon Pure, a Quaker from Pennsylvania, and Fainwell will go disguised as Simon Pure. In the course of his visit, he undertakes Ann's conversion. All goes well until the real Simon Pure arrives, but his identity is challenged, and when he goes off to find the coachman who drove him from Bristol, Prim consents to Ann's marriage. When the guardians assemble, they find they have been tricked. Fainwell reminds the audience and tells the guardians that he is a soldier: "I have had the honour to serve his Majesty." He concludes by saying "'Tis liberty of choice that sweetens life, Makes glad the husband, and the happy wife."

While Fainwell acts a number of characters and goes through several disguises, there are almost no actions Ann Lovely can take. Because of Ann's passivity, Pearson describes the comedy as a "a male-centered play" (209). Another way to judge the events of the play is to see the four guardians as single-minded characters whose passion for their one interest renders them eccentric enough to ignore the social world. Contrary to them, both Fainwell and Ann wish to be involved in their own and in a larger world. Fainwell succeeds because he can enter into the narrower interests of the guardians. When mewed up, Ann rightly fumes about her untenable position, but given the opportunity to participate in the "conversion" scene at Prim's, she shows her social mobility. While Fainwell must practice deceit with the guardians, he acts honestly with Ann and she with him. Centlivre demonstrates that through mutual understanding love does conquer all. To which Stathas adds, "but as intelligent people of fashion, [Fainwell and Ann] know that the god of love helps those who help themselves" (xxvi). The central focus on Fainwell's winning Ann not only provides a tightly organized plot, but also points to the social world triumphing over narrow-mindedness and intolerance. Lock points out that "alone of Centlivre's full-length plays, *Bold Stroke* has no subplot" (108).

TEXT: Readex Microprint of 1727 Dublin edition.

CRITICAL EDITIONS: Edited with introduction by Thalia Stathas (Lincoln: U of Nebraska P, 1968); edited with introduction by Nancy Copeland (Peterborough, Ontario: Broadview, 1995).

MODERN EDITION: *The Meridian Anthology of Restoration and Eighteenth-Century Plays by Women*, ed. Katharine M. Rogers (NY: Penguin-Meridian, 1994): 185–259.

FACSIMILE EDITION: E-CED, with introduction by R. C. Frushell (NY: Garland, 1982).

BOOTH, Ursula Agnes (1740–1803). An actress at Drury Lane, Booth played minor roles with the company for about twenty years. Married to the DL tailor, she adapted one play, an updated version of the Fletcher and Massinger farce, *The Little French Lawyer*, produced at CG, 27 April 1778 and printed the same year by J. Bell. Booth acted summers at HAY during the 1790s; her last performance was at that theatre on 14 September 1797. [BDAA]

BOOTHBY, Frances (fl. 1669–70). Her dedication to her one five-act tragedy, *Marcelia; or, The Treacherous Friend* (printed by Will Cademan and Giles Widdowes, 1670) gives little information about the playwright herself. Langbaine, writing in 1691, provides no further information. Boothby signed her dedication to "Lady Yate, of Harvington in Worcester-shire," from her "most humble Servant and Kinswoman." S. H. Mendelson mentions a poem complaining of the "Unjust Censure" of her play and its failure, addressed to a Mrs. Somerset, a cousin of Lady Yate (129). Could the Harvington identified in the dedication be the village halfway between Worcester and Stratford-upon-Avon, north of Evesham on the fringe of the Cotswolds, or is it, as the editors of *Kissing the Rod* suggest, Harvington Hall near Chaddesly Corbett, outside of Kidderminister? [*BD*, Cotton, DBAWW, FCLE, Hobby, Hume, Smith & Cardinale]

BOWES, Mary Eleanor, Countess of Strathmore (1749–1800). The author of one unproduced, blank-verse, five-act tragedy, *The Siege of Jerusalem* (privately printed in 1774), Bowes became involved in a cause célèbre later in her life and did not return to drama.

Bowes, an only child, was well educated and well off. In 1767, she married the Earl of Strathmore by whom she had five children. After his death in 1776, Bowes, pregnant by another man, married Andrew Robinson Stoney, who fought a duel with the Rev. Henry Bate Dudley because of what Stoney considered to be libelous remarks about her in *The Morning Post*. A marriage speculator, Stoney had previously married a wealthy woman who had died. Stoney, now taking the name of Bowes, forced the Countess to sign over her property and to write her *Confessions* (dated 3 February 1778). After they separated, she sued for divorce; he later abducted her, for which he was sent to prison. After the divorce in 1789, the depositions were published: they charge him (1) with excessive cruelty to her in private and with humiliating her in public, and (2) with seduction and rape. Once out of prison Stoney published the Countess's *Confessions* (1793). Stoney's further suits against the Countess failed to overturn the divorce settlement that returned her property to her. [*BD* notes *The Gentleman's Magazine* (56: 1079) carried a report of the kidnapping; FCLE; biography by Ralph Arnold, 1957 (rpt. 1987).]

BOYD, Elizabeth (fl. 1726–1745). The author of one unproduced play—*Don Sancho; or, The Student's Whim*, which includes in the second act the masque, "Minerva's Triumph." It was published for the author in 1739. Her first foray into the literary world, however, began in November 1726, when she published "The Variety: A Poem in Two Cantos," by "Louisa," where she praises earlier women authors—Behn, Manley, Centlivre, and Haywood. Boyd also wrote a number of poems for public occasions, a novel *The Happy Unfortunate; or The Female Page* (1732, reissued in 1737 by subscription under its subtitle), and published a periodical *The Snail*, though only one number appeared in 1745. Dates of her birth and death are not known. [*BD*, Cotton, DBAWW, FCLE, Lonsdale]

BRAND, Hannah (d. 1821). Born and raised in Norwich, she assisted her sisters in keeping a school until she took to the stage. She is the author of two comedies, *Adelinda* and *The Conflict; or, Love, Honour and Pride*, never produced, and one tragedy, *Huniades*. These plays were included in her *Poems and Plays* published by Beatniffe and Payne, Norwich, 1798. *Huniades* was first performed in Norwich on 7 April 1791 and in London on 18 January 1792 by the DL company at the King's Theatre (with Brand as Agmunda), but after one performance it was withdrawn for alterations. Revised and retitled, *Agmunda* was performed at the King's Theatre on 2 February 1792, Brand acting the title role. She was with Tate Wilkinson's company in York from February to May 1794, and she appeared in *The Provoked Husband* as Lady Townley (20 March 1794). She also took the title role in *Agmunda* on the company's last performance in York, 21 May 1794, her benefit night. Genest reports that "the play itself was as unsuccessful in York as it had been in London. ...it certainly did not deserve the treatment it met with; ...and *Huniades* would perhaps have succeeded, if Mrs. Siddons had played the principal character instead of the author, who did not aid the play by her own acting" (7: 47–50). Wilkinson describes her as being "starched in manner, virtuous in conduct and resolute in her objections to a low-cut dress." Not withstanding her self-proclaimed abilities in Italian, French, Latin, and Greek, Brand had a regional accent, which may have contributed to her lack of success on stage. When she retired from the theatre, she became a governess, caused a conflict between her employers, and had to leave England. [*BD* reproduces Wilkinson's remarks about Brand from *Wandering Patentee,* BDAA, DBAWW, DNB, FCLE, Genest]

Brian the Probationer; or, The Red Hand, Isabel Hill. Published posthumously, this verse tragedy in five acts was not staged. Hill's brother, Benson Earle Hill, added a memoir of his sister to the play; both were published together by W. R. Sams in 1842. [Stratman #2283]. This is an early psychological drama in which Isabel Hill tries to fathom the mind of a murderer. Hill's brother notes in his memoir that she read about the murders on a trip to Edinburgh and wrote a "character" for a friend to show to Charles Kemble, the manager of CG. Although Kemble said the play wasn't stageable, Isabel Hill remained interested in the title character.

Brian is a "probationer" in the Scottish church, and before he earns his ministry he tutors two sons of Kaird, the Lord Provost of Scotland. In the household is Magdalene, an orphan, whom Kaird has taken in at the suggestion of his nephew St. Clair. Brian has fallen in love with her, but while she thinks well of the probationer she is destined to marry St. Clair. Her rejection of Brian drives him away, and he plans to kill himself. But when the two sons of Kaird attempt to bring him back, he stabs them. He is caught in the act (i.e., literally red-handed), and Kaird—invoking the old law of the "Red Hand"—sentences him to death within the hour. Despite pleas for clemency from Magdalene, Brian is executed.

What Hill probes in Brian's character is the effect of his stern Calvinism, his passion for Magdalene, and his educational methods with the two boys, whom he finally murders. Brian does not appear to be angry at them but at himself. Once taken by the law, he argues his case by blaming his own orphan state, his low social status, and his desperate situation. He turns on his judges by asking who among them have not sinned, but Brian is still executed.

While Hill's portrait of a mind overwhelmed by religious fanaticism is unusual for the early Victorian age, the frequently shifting ways that Brian interacts with the other characters are not always easy to follow psychologically. For instance, Kaird vows he will never forgive him, but at the end he does; Magdalene will protect his secrets, but she cannot love him; after Brian is captured, Magdalene offers him the jewels St. Clair has given her at their marriage so Brian can buy his way out of prison and escape.

TEXT: Readex Microprint.

The Bridals, Margaret Lucas Cavendish, Duchess of Newcastle. This drama appeared in her *Plays, Never before Printed*, published by A. Maxwell in 1668. It was not produced.

In this play, the reader follows the progress of two about-to-be-married couples (Sir John Amorous and Lady Coy; Sir William Sage and Lady Vertue) through their weddings to their lives following marriage. In contrasting the married couples, Cavendish introduces Facil, who attempts to seduce the former Lady Coy (now Lady Amorous) through the efforts of Mimick, a jester. Lady Vertue, however, becomes the moral model of a wife. A second plot involves Mr. Aged and Mr. Longlife, who try to prevent their children (Sir Mercury Poet and Lady Fancy) from marrying because they are both wits, but the young people marry despite their parents' objections; and they finally win the parents' blessings.

It may be no surprise that the most successful marriage is that of Sir William Sage and Lady Vertue (Cavendish's husband was William, Duke of Newcastle, and perhaps she casts herself as Lady Vertue). Kathleen Jones, Cavendish's biographer, suggests, however, that at the beginning of Cavendish's own marriage with the Duke (he was a widower) she may have been more like Lady Coy on the wedding night (*The Glorious Fame* [London: Bloomsbury, 1988]: 53–54). The contrasting characters then might serve to remind readers of the dual aspects of single personalities. This drama from the later set of plays has more dramatic action and brisker dialogue than most of her *Playes* of 1662. Since the characters are more developed than those in her earlier dramas, it suggests that Cavendish's involvement with *The Humourous Lieutenant* (1667), also attributed to her husband, may have helped her see stage possibilities for her plays.

TEXTS: Wing N867. EEB Reel 674: 2. Readex Microprint.

The Bride, Joanna Baillie. This three-act drama in verse was first published in 1828 by H. Diggens and H. Colburn. It was later included in her collected *Dramas*, published by Longmans, et al., 1836. A comparison of the two texts shows no substantive changes; the 1828 text has end notes, the 1836 text uses footnotes. The drama was not staged.

Set in Ceylon, the play opens with the ruler, Rasinga, preparing to go into the mountains to bring back a second bride (a custom permitted in the culture), who is never named. Rasinga has been married for ten years to Artina, and they have a son, Samar, and a younger daughter (not named). Artina's brother Samarkoon becomes angry over this second marriage and plans with some freebooters to abduct the bride. Although he achieves his goal, Rasinga and his forces mount a successful counterattack and return with the bride and Samarkoon in chains. Meanwhile, an old physician, Juan de Creda, has come back to Ceylon. When he was there two years before, he had saved Rasinga's life. Now he undertakes to mediate between the two brothers-in-law. With the help of Artina, Samar, and Rasinga's mother, de Creda brings Rasinga to acknowledge that a second marriage would not be right. The ruler pardons everyone and gives his would-be bride to his brother-in-law, Samarkoon.

Part of de Creda's strategy to win over Rasinga relies on his talking to the ruler about the importance of "turning the other cheek." The physician (and apparently missionary) explains the anguish of Christ who, on the cross, forgave his enemies and betrayers. The idea that people in the subcontinent need Christianization underscores Baillie's text. Dramaturgically, the play would be difficult to mount, though most of the battles take place offstage. Women are treated as mere chattels and polygamy permitted in this culture, as

Baillie portrays it. Nevertheless, it takes the women, children, and church to bring Rasinga around in the end.

TEXTS: Readex Microprint of (1) the 1828 edition and (2) the 1836 edition. 3: 279–368.

The British Orphan, Mariana Starke. A tragedy produced only at Mrs. Crespigny's private theatre in Camberwell, 7 April 1790, by amateur performers. "The scene was laid in Spain" (*BD* 2: 69). The play was never printed, and no text of this tragedy has survived.

The Broken Vow, Mary Hornby. This five-act comedy was published in Stratford-upon-Avon, no publisher given, in 1820. Dion Boucicault published a play by the same title in 1851.

TEXT: Not in Readex Microprint.

BROOKE, Charlotte (1740–1793). Born in 1740 in Ireland, she grew up in a house where literature was important and valued. The daughter of poet, playwright, and novelist Henry Brooke, Charlotte (who never married) spent much time looking after her father in his old age. After his death in 1783, she became a full-time writer and collector of old Irish and Gallic poetry. Following Bishop Percy's collection of ancient English poetry, Charlotte published translations of her collection in *Reliques of Irish Poetry* in 1789. She edited her father's works in 1792, a year before her death in Ireland. She is also credited by the *BD* as having written one tragedy, titled *Belisarius*: although the *BD* believes the manuscript to be lost, an act of this play may have been posthumously published in *The Oracle*, 17 October 1795 (2: 56). We have been unable to verify this. [*BD*, BNA, DBAWW, DNB, EBWW, FCLE]

BROOKE, Frances Moore (1724–1789). Orphaned in early childhood, Frances and her sister Sarah were educated by clerical relatives in Lincolnshire. Brooke was over thirty when she started *The Old Maid*, a weekly periodical (1755–1756). Although she wrote several successful plays, Brooke's first effort in drama, a five-act verse tragedy *Virginia*, was rejected by both Garrick and Rich, and the play was not produced. "Printed for the author" in 1756, it was sold by A. Millar, with "odes, pastorals and translations." In her novel, *The Excursion* (1779), Brooke attacked Garrick for his practices in theatrical management.

After marrying Rev. John Brooke and writing a sentimental novel, Brooke spent several years in Quebec, where her husband was stationed as a chaplain. Her novel *The History of Emily Montague* (1769) emerged from her North American experiences. When she returned to England, Brooke assisted Mary Ann Yates in managing the King's Opera House, 1773–1778. Her first staged tragedy, *The Siege of Sinope*, debuted at CG on 31 January 1781 and featured Mary Ann Yates in a prominent role. Her most popular play was the comic opera, *Rosina*, produced at CG exactly a year later, with music by W. Shield. An operatic farce, *Marian* was produced at CG on 22 May 1788, again with music by Shield. She died in Lincolnshire in January 1789.

Brooke's work in the theatre with Mary Ann Yates gave her ideas of what would attract audiences, and her achievement as a playwright is her ability to entertain these audiences with light musical comedy. As intriguing as Brooke's tragedies are, they don't succeed in finding the right pathos to move her readers or her audiences to pity or terror. Her representation of North America in her novels stands as one of her significant literary contributions.

[*BD*, BDAA, BNA, DBAWW, DNB, FCLE, OCEL. Biography by Lorraine McMullen, 1983. Gwendolyn B. Needham, "Frances Brooke: Drama Critic," *TN* 15 (Fall, 1960): 47–52.]

BRUNTON, Anna Ross. See Anna **ROSS**.

BURGESS, Mrs. (fl. 1779–80). The author of a single play, a comedy entitled *The Oaks; or, The Beauties of Canterbury*, "which was several times acted in that city," probably in 1779 or 1780. A topical piece, it was not performed in London, but it was printed in Canterbury by Simmons and Kirkby in 1780. *The Thespian Dictionary* (1802) mentions that Mrs. Burgess "keeps a shop in St. George's

Street," Canterbury, so perhaps she was still living in 1802. [*BD*]

BURKE, Miss. (fl. 1793). *BD* describes her as "a lady from Ireland (1: 78). Her one two-act comic opera, *The Ward of the Castle*, was produced at CG on 24 October 1793, with music by Tommaso Giordani. It ran for only three nights. Although the songs were printed for the performance, the play itself was never published, and the manuscript is in the Larpent Collection (992). According to FCLE, she is not related to the novelist Anne Burke, who published from 1785–1805. [*BD*, FCLE]

BURNEY, Frances "Fanny," later Mrs. d'Arblay (1752–1840). Although well-known as a novelist, Burney wrote several dramas that were considered for the stage. Two—*Love and Fashion* and *A Busy Day*—were accepted for production but never staged, while others exist only in manuscript. *Edwy and Elgiva*, her only play actually produced (1795), failed largely because most of the cast did not know their parts. (*The East Indian*, produced 1782, has been attributed to Burney, but there is little evidence that she wrote the play.)

Daughter of Esther (Sleepe), who died when Fanny was ten, and Charles Burney, a music historian and member of the Johnson circle, Fanny began in 1768 a detailed diary that she wrote sporadically until her death (published 1889). Her first novel, *Evelina, or a Young Lady's Entrance into the World*, was published anonymously in 1778, and it was a sensational success. She then wrote a comedy, *The Witlings* (1779), which she suppressed because her father thought its satire on "bluestockings" too biting. Her next novel, *Cecilia*, was published in 1782. Burney was pressured by her family to accept the position of second Keeper of the Robes to Queen Charlotte (1786–91). During this time, separated from family and friends, she wrote a series of tragedies—*Edwy and Elgiva*, *Hubert De Vere* (first titled *Cerulia*), *The Siege of Pevensey*, and the fragment, *Elberta*. None of these dramas has been published; they are in the Burg Collection of the NYPL. After resigning her post, Burney married Alexandre d'Arblay (1793), formerly a general under Lafayette, and her only child was born in 1794. *Camilla* (1796), her third novel, was financially successful but received mixed reviews. After *Camilla*, Burney wrote three comedies—*Love and Fashion* (1799), *A Busy Day; or, An Arrival from India* (1800), and *The Woman Hater* (1800–01). These comedies satirize fashion, male prejudices about women, and both the nouveau-riche "Cits" (citizens of London) and the vain aristocracy. After England and France made peace, Burney joined her husband in France to try to reclaim property that he had lost during the French Revolution. When war broke out again, she was forced to remain in France until 1812. Her final novel, *The Wanderer; or, Female Difficulties* (begun in 1800), was published in 1814. The twelve volumes of *The Journals and Letters of Fanny Burney*, edited by Joyce Hemlow and published 1972–84, offer insight into her later life.

While Burney is better known for her novels, her dramatic comedies are entertaining and skillfully written. Burney had an excellent ear for dialogue, best demonstrated when she juxtaposes representatives of different classes. Furthermore, as Judy Simons concludes, "the journals and plays of Fanny Burney complement one another in showing us an alternative side to the increasingly restrained writer of the novels. They reveal a woman acutely observant and often outspoken in her opinions" (NY: Barnes, 1987: 133). [BNA, DBAWW, DNB, EBWW, FCLE, Lonsdale, OCEL. Burney's manuscripts are in the Berg Collection, NYPL; some detail is given in Joyce Hemlow, "Fanny Burney, Playwright," *UTQ* 19 (1949–50): 170–189. T. G. Wallace has edited *The Busy Day* (1985). Biographies by Joyce Hemlow (1958), Judy Simons (1987), and Margaret Anne Doody (1988). Bibliography by J. A. Grau, 1981].

BURNEY, Frances (1776–1828), daughter of Esther Burney and niece of Fanny Burney d'Arblay. Like her aunt, Frances Burney wrote several plays. Her collection of dramas was published "for the author" by Thomas Davidson and sold by J. Murray in 1818. In addition to plays intended for private presentation, she added a translation of a play from the Italian. Titled *Tragic Dramas; chiefly intended for representation in Private Families: to which is added Aristodemus, a tragedy from the Italian of Vincenzo Monti*, Burney's volume included her own *Fitzormond; or, Cherished Resentment* (a three-act verse drama) and *Malek Adhel, the Champion of the Crescent* (a three-act verse drama, adapted from *Mathilde* by Madame Cottin) in addition to Monti's five-act tragedy.

BURRELL, Lady Sophia Raymond (1750?–1802), later Mrs. Clay. She was known as a poet before she ventured into drama. Her first three-act play, *Comala*, was published in her *Poems*, 1793, though said to have been written in 1784. A production of *Comala* may have been given in Hanover Square Rooms during 1792. After the death of her husband in 1796, she married the Reverend William Clay the following year. She adapted two tragedies from Corneille—*Theodora; or, The Spanish Daughter* and *Maximian*—and these were published in 1800 without being acted. Her death occurred on the Isle of Wight in 1802.

Two dramas, published in 1814, twelve years after her death, have been erroneously credited to Burrell. FCLE identifies Ann M'Taggart as the author of *A Search after Perfection* and *Villario*. [*BD*, DBAWW, DNB, FCLE, Lonsdale]

BURTON, Philippina (fl. 1768–1787). Known as an actress for a couple of seasons, Burton (later Mrs. Hill) wrote one comedy, *Fashion Display'd*, that was performed at the Haymarket Theatre, 27 April 1770, for her benefit. Burton acted the main character and spoke the epilogue. It was presented two other nights that season; there was no revival. Although the play was to be printed in the spring of 1771 (*LS* 4: 1511), there is no evidence that it was. The manuscript is in the Larpent Collection (308). As Miss Burton, she published *Miscellaneous Poems* (1768); and as Mrs. Hill, an *Apology* [for acting Scrub in *The Beaux Stratagem* at Brighthelmstone] (1786) and *Portraits, Characters, Pursuits, and Amusements* (1785? with another edition in 1795?). [BDAA]

The Busie Body, Susanna Centlivre. One of Centlivre's most popular plays, this five-act comedy premiered at DL on 12 May 1709. Not only was it frequently performed during the author's lifetime, but it was acted well into the nineteenth century. Printed the same month by Bernard Lintott (*Daily Courant* 31 May 1709), the comedy has not been without its detractors: the *Post-Boy* (26-28 May 1709), for instance, asserts that the greatest parts of this play as well as *The Gamester* were written by Mary Pix (*LS* 2: 193), but there is no evidence to support this. Centlivre's biographer, J. W. Bowyer, notes that the two were good friends and may well have helped one another. Critics have identified several sources of *The Busie Body* in Jonson's *The Devil is an Ass* (1616), and in either Molière's *L'Etourdi* (1658) or Dryden's *Sir Martin Mar-all* (1667), or both. But the borrowings are, as Bowyer points out, "general and no discredit to [Centlivre]" (103).

Set in London, the comedy has two main plots that turn on romance: (1) Sir George Airy wants to marry Miranda, but he is blocked by Sir Francis Gripe, Miranda's guardian, who plans to marry her himself. (2) Charles, Gripe's son, wants to marry Isabinda, but her father, Sir Jealous Traffick, plans for her to marry a Spanish Don who will shortly arrive in England. Between these two intrigues stands the title character, Marplot, who is also a ward of Sir Francis. With the best intentions, Marplot throws additional complications in the way of the lovers because of his insatiable curiosity and his literal mindedness. In the Airy-Miranda-Gripe plot, Sir Francis, assured that Miranda loves him, agrees to Sir George's spending an hour with her under his supervision—for one hundred pounds. Angered at being a subject of barter, Miranda acts dumb through the interview, though Sir George manages to understand her through sign language. Later in front of Sir Francis, she tells Marplot to let Sir George know that he should avoid the garden at eight o'clock that night because if he comes he will be greeted with firearms. Sir George knows an assignation when he hears one and meets Miranda, but they are interrupted by Sir Francis and Marplot. Sir George hides behind the "chimney-board," and to keep Sir Francis away, Miranda tells him her pet monkey is there, which inflames Marplot's curiosity. As Sir Francis is going out the door, Marplot opens the chimney-board, and Sir George runs out unseen, breaking some china on the way. Meanwhile, Charles tries to visit Isabinda. His first attempt is thwarted by the unexpected return of Sir Jealous, whose suspicions are aroused by Marplot's loitering near his door. Charles escapes by jumping from a balcony, landing on Marplot, who cannot understand what he's done wrong. On Charles's second try to visit Isabinda, he'll use a rope ladder, but this plan is foiled by the dismissal of Patch, Isabinda's maid, who then suggests that Charles impersonate Signor Diego Babinetto, who is intended for Isabinda, since no one in the house has ever seen the Spaniard. Attired in a Spanish costume, Charles arrives at Sir Jealous's house, attended by Sir George as a merchant. Isabinda protests, for she has no intention of marrying the Spaniard, but George takes her aside and tells her it is Charles in disguise. As they are being married, Marplot shows up asking for his friend in a Spanish habit, causing Sir Jealous to suspect mischief. Sir George, however, bars the door, and a moment later Charles and Isabinda emerge married. Just then Sir Francis, Miranda, and their servants arrive to find Sir Jealous bilked. Miranda tells Sir Francis that she has secured the papers of Charles's uncle, giving Charles a sizeable legacy. Sir Francis leaves angrily, but Sir Jealous philosophically accepts his new son-in-law. Marplot is forgiven by all.

An "Augustan Intrigue Comedy" is how Hume classifies *The Busie Body*, which uses "a veritable catalogue of comic devices and formulas" (116). But these "devices and formulas" add up to effective theatre. Lock devotes a chapter to the play, calling it "a triumph of construction, timing, and the disposition of comic business" (*Susanna Centlivre* 67). In her convincing discussion of the play, Pearson believes that it "is one of the most affirmative of its age in its themes of women's power and women's language" (222). Miranda avoids being dominated through her effective use of language (with Sir Francis) and through her silence (with Sir George), proving she is no passive heroine. Almost every critic has something to say about Centlivre's characterization of Marplot: "he is the most memorable part of the play" (Hume); "he is absurd, but not contemptible" (Bateson); "again and again Marplot subverts male sexuality" (Pearson); "Marplot . . . [is] designed not for reform but for laughter" (Byrd). Audiences, then and now, enjoy seeing what blunder Marplot will commit next.

TEXTS: Readex Microprint. TEC Reel 4052: 14.

FACSIMILE EDITIONS: Augustan Reprint Society, with introduction by Jess Byrd (Los Angeles: Clark Lib., 1949); E-CED, with introduction by R. C. Frushell (NY: Garland, 1982).

MODERN EDITION: Everyman's Library, *Female Playwrights of the Restoration*, edited with introduction by Paddy Lyons and Fidelis Morgan (London: Dent, 1991): 293–363.

A Busy Day; or, An Arrival from India, Fanny Burney. This comedy was accepted for production by Thomas Harris, manager of CG, for the 1800–01 season, but never produced.

Eliza and Cleveland have recently arrived from India after their betrothal was blessed by her guardian prior to his death. Before announcing their intentions, Eliza, who is now a wealthy heiress, wishes to become reacquainted with her biological family, the Watts. The plot consists of a series of obstacles to this match, resulting from the class differences between the two families: Cleveland's pretentious aristocratic family and the vulgar band of "Cits" (citizens of London) to whom Eliza is related. The match is tested by a series of events that encourage the hero and heroine to mistrust one another. For example, Eliza is pursued by Cleveland's brother Frank, who plans to marry her in order to settle his debts; he is unaware of her attachment to his brother. Similarly, Cleveland is pursued by wealthy Miss Percival, who has agreed to pay off his uncle's mortgage if Cleveland marries her. After discovering that Cleveland loves Eliza, Miss Percival is driven by a desire for revenge to bring the Watts together with Cleveland's snobbish aunt and uncle, Lady Wilhelmina and Sir Marmaduke. When this occurs in Act V, the resemblances of the two families are as striking as their differences. Burney criticizes both families for their selfishness, disloyalty, and total indifference to suffering when it involves a member of another class or race.

A Busy Day is a play that contemporary audiences could enjoy. The class distinctions are established not only by dialogue, but by an elaborate network of detail, including characters' social behavior and actions, their attempts to mimic other classes, and their attention to fashion. Even though Miss Percival, Frank, and various minor characters conform to stereotypes, Eliza and Cleveland's sister Jemima resist being sentimental heroines. As the play opens Eliza takes refuge in an inn, following an accident with her carriage. Unlike more passive heroines, she takes charge of the situation. While Cleveland is reticent to defend his desire to marry beneath his station, Eliza has no reluctance to defend her Indian servant against the unkind treatment he receives in England. Similarly, although Jemima is a friend of Miss Percival's, she also befriends Eliza after meeting her with the Watts. Even more important, Jemima resolves the final obstacle to the marriage by arranging for Eliza to pay off her uncle's mortgage.

MANUSCRIPT: New York Public Library, Berg Collection.

CRITICAL EDITION: Edited with introduction by Tara Ghoshal Wallace (New Brunswick: Rutgers UP, 1984), based on the manuscript in the Berg Collection, NYPL.

-C-

Camilla the Amazon; or, The Mountain Robber, Jane M. Scott. This two-act musical melodrama opened 6 February 1817 and ran nineteen nights its first season and was revived the following season running for eight nights. John Jolly composed the music, and Scott took the title role.

MANUSCRIPT: Larpent 1954.

The Capricious Lady, Jael-Henrietta Mendez Pye. This farce, performed only one time as an afterpiece at DL on 10 May 1771 for the joint benefit night of Joseph Inchbald and a Mrs. Morland (of Norwich). It was never printed.

Lady Waver, the title character, wants to purchase a country place from Sir William Woodley. As they are making arrangements, she suggests their grown children wed as part of the bargain. He demurs, but Louisa Waver and Charles Woodley appear to be in agreement. They, in fact, know each other from when Louisa lived with her aunt. In one of her several caprices, Lady Waver soon decides the house doesn't suit her and wants to resell it to Sir William. Through Major Sumner's intervention, the resale will be done if Louisa and Charles can wed. Lady Waver is so eager to get back to London, she agrees immediately and rushes back to town without staying for the wedding.

Lady Waver acts as the blocking figure who stands in the way of her daughter's marriage, and it is her cousin Major Sumner who facilitates the nuptials. The brief afterpiece doesn't allow for much development of character.

MANUSCRIPT: Larpent 323. Readex Microprint of manuscript.

The Captive, Maria Barrell. This two-act drama was published in 1790 with no publisher's name on the title page. Barrell, in the Advertisement, notes that the play was not intended for the stage. The text of *The Captive*, written from prison, begins with a dedication to George, the Prince of Wales, warning him to beware of "the fatal consequences of insolvency" (iv). Barrell's Preface praises British liberty, but condemns inhumane laws that punish debt by incarceration. She implores Parliament to remove this cruel punishment through legislative reform. In the verse Prologue, Barrell reaffirms her distressing situation, imprisoned with her two children, but in hopes some pity will be shown by the "senate" to those whose only "crime [is] unseen insolvency" (xiii).

The drama opens with Amelia begging admission to the prison to see her husband, Captain Heartly. She bribes the turnkey, Surly, with her wedding ring to admit herself and her two children. The debt of £600 for which Heartly has been imprisoned resulted from a loan which enabled Heartly to purchase equipment for his troops. Surly suggests that he seek redress from the government. The Keeper of the Prison, Humanicus, comes in and sends Surly away. Trueman, Heartly's servant, blames an "ungrateful government," but Heartly accepts responsibility because of misplaced confidence. Humanicus goes to the person who brought the charges against Heartly, Teasewell, and urges him to change his mind by observing the family's distress. Teasewell claims all he wants is his principal and his interest, but Humanicus asks him to forgive the entire debt. Amelia pleads with Teasewell, and he tells her privately that he'll forgive the debt if she will make him happy. When Amelia refuses, Teasewell suggests the same idea to Heartly, who says he would not gain his freedom at Amelia's degradation. After Teasewell departs, Benevolus, a creditor of Trueman, enters and forgives his debt. Benevolus even offers to help Heartly, who thanks him in a halting voice and dies. After much lamentation—and Benevolus's gift of ten guineas—Humanicus entreats the poor family to leave "this place of sorrow" (31).

Janet Todd comments that Barrell's play exposed "the sorry condition of debtors imprisoned for many years for debts which they had no chance of paying. The play works entirely through conventional sentimental tableaux, the supreme one echoing [Edward Moore's 1753 drama] *The Gamester* in presenting a husband dying in prison surrounded by a virtuous wife and faithful servant. . . . Barrell insists on making her own sorry situation part of her written play text, a less common habit among dramatists than among novelists and poets, who often presented themselves as distressed parents or sensitive recluses in rural retreats" (*Sensibility: An Introduction* [London: Methuen, 1986]: 41).

TEXT: Not in Readex Microprint. We read a copy provided by the BL.

Cardiff Castle, Mary G. Lewis. This dramatic-historical sketch was published with a long poem *Zelinda* by Simpkin and Marshall in 1823.

TEXT: Not Readex Microprint. NUC: Copies at LC, Huntington, and Harvard.

The Carnival; or, Harlequin Blunderer, Charlotte Cibber Charke. This pantomime was produced only once, at LIF on 17 September 1735 with Charke taking the role of Harlequin. Since a description of the actions was never printed, it must be presumed lost.

CARROLL, Susanna Freeman. See **CENTLIVRE**, Susanna Carroll.

CARSTAIRES, Christian (fl. 1786). The author of a volume of poems, printed in Edinburgh, 1786, Carstaires also wrote one farce, *The Hubble-Shue*, produced in Edinburgh about 1786. Inglis describes the play as "a strange eccentric drama"; he also notes that "on the suggestion of the late Charles Kirkpatrick Sharpe, Esq., a few copies of this piece were reprinted, 1835, by W. H. Logan, Esq., Manager of the Border Bank, Berwick-on-Tweed" (30). Tobin, who reprints the piece in its entirety (71–79), notes that Carstaires was a Fyfeshire governess and that she dedicated her playlet to the "Honorable Antiquarian Society." He also nominates her "for the most *outré* dramatist of the century" (70). [Inglis, Tobin]

The Carthusian Friar; or, The Age of Chivalry, a Female Refugee. A five-act tragedy published in 1793 for J. Owen and H. D. Symonds. Nothing is known of the female refugee who wrote the play, though she may be French. *BD* (2: 86) and Stratman (#906) say that the play was not staged. The author's preface reports that the play was written at the age of eighteen, "long previous to the Author's coming to this hospitable and blessed country" (iii). She also claims that the tragedy is founded on real events with which she is connected.

Set near Toulon in Provence (except for the third and fifth acts), the play begins with St. Clair, tutor to the young Duke of Rochford, learning from Raymond, an old family servant, about the moroseness of Eugenia, the Duchess of Rochford. It seems that the Duke left her before the young Duke (Theodore) was born, has not returned, and is presumed dead. No one knows why the Duke left except the Duchess, who won't tell. The Duchess enters, reading a letter from her son, who asks that he be allowed to explore the world. Reluctantly, she agrees that he should go to Court, telling him to practice with his sword. Meanwhile, in a cottage on the estate, the peasant Montigny chides his daughter, Juliet, for trying to educate herself. Juliet counters by saying he encouraged her by engaging a teacher. When Montigny was away at Toulon, she entertained Theodore but had to put off "the transports of [his] misguided passion" (23). Just then Theodore, on his way to Court, stops at the cottage and begs Juliet to marry him, but she contends it is not fit for her to receive his vows. When Theodore arrives at Court, he encounters Melville, a courtier who insults his parents. The two fight: Melville wounds Theodore in the arm and escapes. Theodore now wants revenge, but he also has to find out the truth from his mother. Returning to Castle Rochford, he gets his mother to tell him that she was pursued by Mansoli, his father's best friend. Rochford accused her of infidelity with Mansoli and left. The Duchess asserts the charge is not true and asks her son to take revenge on Mansoli, who is in Turin. Theodore hastily departs, and upon leaving the estate he encounters Juliet. He is so full of his mission that he doesn't recognize her, tosses a sack of gold, and goes hurriedly on. Juliet decides to use the gold to follow him. She changes clothes and is hired as a page to Theodore. In Turin, she delivers the answer to the challenge to Mansoli, but when she hears of the pending duel she admits to Theodore that she is Juliet. She accompanies him to the duel, where he fatally wounds Mansoli. Before dying, Mansoli says he seduced a noble lady in Italy and fled to Provence, but the noble lady died and he was given the child to raise. He turned the child over to the Montigny family, and in a last testament he divides his fortune between his nephew Melville and his daughter, who we now know to be Juliet. As she comes forward, Mansoli asks forgiveness and dies. Officers come and arrest Theodore. Before he is taken to the scaffold for murder, he is to confess to a Carthusian Friar, who is actually Theodore's father. As Theodore is being taken away, St. Clair arrives with the news that the Duchess is dead. Theodore asks his father to care for Juliet and goes to the scaffold and dies. But the Friar concludes the play by saying he will spend the rest of his life in a dark cell repenting his misdeeds.

Even though truth may be stranger than fiction, this curious play suffers from too many coincidences. But in a dramatic poem, perhaps, that should not hinder readers from appreciating the values espoused. The head-strong Theodore wants to clear his mother's name, but the abandoned child of Mansoli, Juliet, is the more engaging character. She wants to get an education; she's able to put off the impetuous Theodore, and she still follows him by dressing as a page. The extended, blank-verse speeches render the play unsuitable for the stage. Because they provide information readers need to know, the speeches are useful to the plot, but the nondramatic exposition on stage would not engage an audience.

TEXT: Readex Microprint.

A Case of Conscience, Elizabeth Inchbald. Written in 1800, this five-act drama was originally intended for DL with J. P. Kemble to play Romono and his sister Sarah Siddons to act Adriana. Friction between the proprietor and the principal actors caused delays over several years, and the play was never produced. James Boaden printed it from the manuscript in the *Memoirs of Mrs. Inchbald*, which he edited in 1833 (2: 295–352).

The play is set at the Castle Romono and its environs near Madrid during the time of the Inquisition. Before Adriana married the Marquis of Romono, she had been promised to Duke Cordunna. Now twenty years later on flimsy evidence that he recently discovered, the Marquis believes that his son, Count Oviedo, is in fact the offspring of the Duke. Since finding this information, the Marquis has become mean spirited toward his wife and hates to hear Oviedo mentioned. With Oviedo's return from war, however, Castle Romono resounds with the young man's praise, and the Marquis becomes even more morose, causing him to send his ward Eudora, who had been promised to Oviedo, to a convent. The Marquis seeks out a hermit to help him determine if the Duke is indeed Oviedo's father. Salvador, the hermit, reluctantly returns to the Castle with him to question Adriana and reveals himself to her as Duke Cordunna. Oviedo, meanwhile, decides to rescue Eudora from the convent with the help of Girone, an old family retainer. When she is free, they ask the hermit, returning from the castle, if he will harbor Eudora in his cell. He agrees and leaves with Eudora, but Oviedo and Girone are arrested and taken before the Grand Inquisitor. The Marquis, having been told by Salvador that the Duke was Oviedo's father, will not lift a finger to help the young man. Knowing nothing of her son's plight, Adriana leaves with Duke Cordunna, and the Marquis completes his revenge by following them to report that their son is dead. When the Marquis arrives, Adriana says that the Marquis is Oviedo's father, and the Duke now says he has his revenge for Adriana's earlier broken promises. Just then, the Duke is arrested by the officers of the inquisition for having impersonated a holy hermit, but once outside he is saved by Oviedo, who has not been killed after all. The two draw swords, and Oviedo slays the Duke. As the explanations go round, Girone brings in Eudora; Adriana and the Marquis unite her with Oviedo.

The unusual double revenge produces a melodramatic turn in the plot: the Duke wants vengeance on both Adriana and the Marquis by causing the death of their son, and the misinformed Marquis wants Adriana and her former lover to suffer the loss of the son he thinks they have conceived. Readers will probably be less than pleased about the Marquis's survival at the end of the play; he has, after all, been such a tyrant through the first four and a half acts that it's hard to accept the rejoicing at the end. Adriana's role called for Sarah Siddons to act the long-suffering wife who can only muster moral fortitude when facing her husband's cruelty. Some revisions in staging the play, however, might have produced improvements in the text.

TEXT: Not in Readex Microprint.

FACSIMILE EDITION: E-CED, with introduction by Paula R. Backscheider (NY: Garland, 1980).

The Castle of Avola, Olivia Wilmot Serres. This three-act operatic scenario, printed with her miscellaneous poems in *Flights of Fancy*, was published by subscription and printed for J. Ridgway, 1805. There is no known production.

The events occur at Avola Castle and its environs in Spain. Although the Duke of Avola has recently married Lady Antonetta, he lusts after Elvina, who is beloved by the Duke's unacknowledged nephew Alphonso. In a rural cottage, Alonzo tells Elvina about her mother, Alonzo's only child: Julia was seen by a passing noble who married her, and she became the Countess of Arragon. But her husband treated her cruelly, poisoned her, and left her for dead. Julia survived and gave birth to Elvina. Before she died, Julia charged Alonzo never to reveal the name of Elvina's father. In the night, robbers in the pay of the Duke capture Elvina and bring her to the Castle of Avola, where Lady Antonetta languishes because the Duke has not announced their marriage. When the Duke comes to visit Lady Antonetta, he tells her that their marriage was not legal, causing her to faint and ultimately to go mad. Meanwhile, Elvina is freed by Alphonso, only to be recaptured by the Duke. When the Duke sees the ghost of Julia, he faints, allowing Elvina to escape. Alone in the midst of a terrible storm and lost in the forest, Elvina is rescued by Alphonso who takes her to Alonzo's cave. The three are, however, captured by robbers hired by the Duke. When they are brought before him, Alonzo (actually the Duke of Madrid) confronts the Duke with his evil deeds, particularly the discovery that Elvina is his daughter by Julia whom he attempted to murder. The Duke asks forgiveness and will spend the rest of his life in repentance. The Duke also acknowledges that Alphonso is his nephew and blesses Alphonso's union with Elvina.

The reader/audience is teased by the obscured births through much of the libretto. As the villain of the piece, the Duke seems only to lust after women, to lie with them, and to cast them aside. He nearly commits incest with Elvina,

plays were staged by the DL company: *The School for Friends* (1805) and *Ourselves* (1811), performed at the Lyceum. After these critically acclaimed plays, however, Marianne Chambers disappeared from public notice, and she apparently wrote nothing else.

Chambers's two comedies exhibit strong characterizations, and a subject matter that is humorous but at the same time raises questions about morality and reform, such as the difficulties of marriage and the ability of women to control their own destinies. Her plotting is intricate but believable. [*BD*, DBAWW, FCLE]

The Chapter of Accidents, Sophia Lee. This five-act comedy, based partly on Diderot's *Le Père de famille*, debuted at the Haymarket on 5 August 1780 and was acted fourteen times its first season. T. Cadell published the play the same year. An enormously popular play, *The Chapter of Accidents* was acted 100 times through the end of the century. It was repeated almost every season up to the year before Lee's death in 1824. Both *BD* (2: 92) and Genest (6: 158) comment on Lee's complaint—in the preface—about the first rejection of her play by Harris, the manager of CG.

Lord Glenmore has a son Woodville and is the guardian of Miss Mortimer, who is secretly married to Captain Harcourt. Glenmore's cousin, Governor Harcourt, who has just returned from overseas, explains that before going abroad he arranged for his daughter to be brought up in Wales. The fathers are concerned about young Woodville's having a mistress, and Lord Glenmore sends his servant Vane to discover the situation. Woodville talks to the Governor about having fallen for a country lass (who, the sagacious reader divines, must be the Governor's daughter). The Governor, meanwhile, speaks of his plans to marry Miss Mortimer. When Woodville pays a visit to his mistress Cecilia, he is seen by Vane, who pumps Cecilia's manservant, Jacob, about the relationship between Woodville and Cecilia. Vane reports to Lord Glenmore, who asks Vane to abduct and marry Cecilia. Woodville's cousin, Capt. Harcourt, comes in disguise with a letter for Cecilia to test her attitude toward Woodville: the letter alleges that Woodville is obliged to marry another woman. Capt. Harcourt asks Miss Mortimer to shelter Cecilia, and she agrees. The plan to abduct Cecilia is about to go forward, when Grey (a clergyman from Wales who has raised Cecilia) arrives and recognizes the Governor as Cecilia's real father. Grey tells Harcourt that Cecilia has left Wales. The Governor wants to reject Cecilia, but Grey desires only her return. Vane, who has overheard, plots to get Cecilia. When Capt. Harcourt and Miss Mortimer arrive with Cecilia (who is not named), Lord Glenmore is struck with her. Woodville goes to Cecilia's but finds she has taken asylum with a friend. He runs into Grey, and Woodville promises he will reform. When Lord Glenmore and the Governor go to Cecilia's house, they find her maid, Bridget, dressed in her mistress's clothes. They take Bridget for Cecilia, but she confesses and is taken to Lord Glenmore's. He tells Cecilia, who is still in disguise, about Bridget and then offers himself to her, but she leaves. Jacob tells Woodville of Bridget's abduction, but Capt. Harcourt explains the changed situation to Woodville. In a stable room Bridget laments her situation, but Vane, still thinking she is Cecilia, takes her to be married. Lord Glenmore then brings in Bridget and Vane, who says they are married. In the confusion about Bridget being the Governor's daughter, Vane discovers he has married the maid. When Lord Glenmore brings in Cecilia, Woodville recognizes her. Grey says Cecilia is the Governor's daughter. She gives herself to Woodville, and Grey has the last speech about how efficacious is Providence.

As she acknowledges in her "Preface," Sophia Lee found her inspiration for the character of Cecilia, Woodville's fallen but virtuous mistress, in one of Marmontel's moral tales, entitled "Laurette." But she is less candid about what she owes Diderot when she describes the similitude between her first draft and *Le Père de famille* as a "chance-similitude," which, upon her finally reading a translation of the French work, "rather flattered than grieved" her (ii–iii). Despite some disingenuousness, Lee kept Diderot's main characters while changing their names and some of their family relationships, and she generally followed the original, including its happy, moralizing ending. She skillfully meshed the Marmontel "elopement and seduction" with the rest of the plot, and introduced low comedy through the characters of Bridget and Jacob. She further enlivened Diderot's "serious drama" by introducing comic elements, such as disguises or the use of dialect. The result was a resounding stage success.

Sophia Lee, the daughter of actors, shows a good sense of theatre in the play: she handles disguised identities, testing of characters, and opinionated paternal figures well. Money and legacies figure importantly in motivation and action with the term "interest" being frequently used. Men's views of women's education are shown to be inadequate: Cecilia, after all, has been seduced by Woodville. Nevertheless, he wants to marry her, and at the end of the play their beginnings in vice will turn to virtue. While Grey's moralizing conclusion to the play strikes a sentimental tone, contemporary eighteenth-century audiences must have easily accepted his homily.

MANUSCRIPT: Larpent 526.

TEXT: Readex Microprint.

Charity, Sarah Cheney Gardner. This one-act farce, written in Gardner's manuscript book, was not performed, nor has it been printed. F. Grice and A. Clarke describe it as "a boring and far from amusing tirade, occasioned by a series of personal affronts" (*TN* 7 [1952–53]: 77). In contrast, Isobel Grundy points out how the farce "uses men to dramatize Gardner's vindication" of an episode that occurred when she was acting with an amateur troupe in Jamaica during 1785–86 (*TSWL* 7 [1988]: 15).

In the plot of the farce, Ben Budget has purportedly written a play "out of sheer love of justice." Because the publisher is "devoted to truth and principle," he will print the play. In the last scene, Gardner's persecutors are abused by O'Staunch, an Irishman.

MANUSCRIPT: The Colyton Ms., described by Grundy, is privately owned.

CHARKE, Charlotte Cibber (1713–1760). The last child of the large family of Katherine Shore and Colley Cibber (actor, dramatist, manager of DL, and ultimately poet laureate), Charlotte grew up as an impetuous tomboy. Sent to school at the age of eight, she was a tolerably good student in languages, geography, and music, as she reports in her autobiography. Moreover, she learned to hunt and ride in the country; staying with a country doctor, Charlotte gained some knowledge of gardening and pharmacy. At the age of seventeen, she married Richard Charke, a musician at DL, and she began her checkered theatrical career. (Shortly thereafter they were estranged, and he went to Jamaica where he died.)

Charlotte played minor roles at first, and after some time off for child bearing she took on larger character parts. In 1734, she managed a summer theatrical company, called "the mad company of the Haymarket" by a contemporary writer. Charlotte herself took a number of male roles, such as Macheath and George Barnwell. The following year, Charlotte walked out of DL because of an altercation with Fleetwood, the manager, whom she parodied in a play she wrote to describe the circumstances of the break, *The Art of Management; or, Tragedy Dispell'd* (YB, 24 September 1735). When the play was printed with a dedication to Fleetwood, he tried to buy all the copies in order to destroy them. During the summer, she supported herself acting with a troupe at LIF, where her farce (unpublished) *The Carnival; or, Harlequin Blunderer* was performed (5 September 1735). Later in the season, she joined Fielding's company at the Haymarket, where she played in *Pasquin* the role of Lord Place, a parody of her father.

When the Licensing Act of 1737 closed the smaller venues, Charlotte found herself out of a job, but she resourcefully set up a puppet theatre, until illness forced her to abandon the project. Deserted by her family, Charlotte was hounded by creditors. Off and on she acted where she could at fairs, unlicensed venues, and "concerts" (which included plays). She wrote for performance, *Tit for Tat; or, Comedy and Tragedy at War*, given at James Street for her benefit, 16 March 1743; it is unpublished. For a while she kept a steak and soup shop and then an ale house, where plays were performed. During this time too, she may have been married to a John Sacheverell, but this marriage seems short-lived. In an attempt to make ends meet, Charlotte became a strolling player, moving from town to town, though she did spend two seasons as prompter at Bath.

When she returned to London in 1754, she sold for £10 a novel, *The History of Henry Dumont and Miss Charlotte Evelyn*, which was published the following year. She then turned her hand to her autobiography, which was published serially in eight parts. These collected parts made a volume entitled *A Narrative of the Life of Mrs. Charlotte Charke (Youngest Daughter of Colley Cibber, Esq.) Written by Herself*; two editions were printed in 1755. Between her writing for a living, Charlotte continued her work on the unlicensed stage, acting with her brother Theophilus and his Haymarket company and later at Bartholomew Fair. She wrote two short works, both allegedly true stories: *The Mercer; or, Fatal Extravagance* (1756) and *The Lover's Treat; or, Unnatural Hatred* (1758). After acting briefly at Canterbury, Charlotte returned to London, applying for a license to perform. Permission was granted, and Charlotte took the role of Marplot in Centlivre's *The Busie Body* (HAY, 28 September 1759). It was her final performance. She died in poverty early the following year: an obituary described her as "a gentlewoman remarkable for her adventures and misfortunes."

Although Charlotte Cibber Charke led a remarkable life, her major contribution to the theatre was her ability to act a wide number of roles, male and female. Always short of money and frequently in debt, she courageously continued to write and act in the face of staggering difficulties. While Charlotte has been called "unconventional," her life demonstrated how a woman deserted by husband and family made her own way against tremendous odds. [*BD*, BDAA, BNA, Cotton, DBAWW, DNB, EBWW, FCLE, OCEL. Biography by Fidelis Morgan, 1988; autobiography, rpt. 1968. Kristina Straub, in chapter seven of *Sexual Suspects*, discusses Charke's "Protean nature" (1992).]

Charles the First, Mary Russell Mitford. This five-act historical tragedy in blank verse was refused a license in 1825 by the then Lord Chamberlain, the Duke of Montrose; later the new Lord Chamberlain—the Duke of Devonshire—approved the opening performance at the Royal Victoria Theatre on 2 July 1834. The play, dedicated to the Duke of Devonshire, was published by J. Duncombe prior to the production in 1834. Mitford says, in her introduction, she has tried to be accurate in the portrayal of the historical figures, though she has made slight alterations to tighten the dramatic effect.

The play opens in London, where the potential regicides plan how they will deal with the King, who is under house arrest at Carisbrooke Castle. Even though General Fairfax dislikes the proceedings, Cromwell says they must "arraign Charles Stuart . . . for warring on his own people" (19). When the Queen attempts to visit her husband in prison, she is stopped. Cromwell, however, permits her to go, reminding his followers that they are soldiers in God's enterprise. The King still states he will not give up his divine right. As Cromwell enters, the Queen accuses him of ambition and says he is as evil as Richard III. When Cromwell asks him to resign the crown, the King comes back with "Never." The trial at Westminster Hall covers all of the third act. Even though the King won't recognize the legitimacy of his judges, the trial proceeds. Notwithstanding Cromwell's being one of the judges, he is called to testify. His views carry the day and the King is pronounced guilty. The Queen cries out from the gallery and comes to her husband's side. Before being taken to prison, the King accuses Cromwell of acting out of jealousy. Later, when some of the judges are unwilling to sign the order of execution, Cromwell bullies and threatens them until they do so. The date of execution is set for the following day (30 January 1649). Cromwell reports this to the King, who asks that his children and the Queen be taken to safety. Then the King forgives Cromwell but reminds him not to tempt God. On the following morning (V.1, cut from the production), the Queen tries to change places with the King, but he rejects her offer. As she leaves, he turns to prayer. At the Banqueting Hall, Cromwell checks last-minute details and expresses a concern that General Fairfax's troops may try to stop the execution. The General himself comes to save the King, but Cromwell tells him he needs "a higher warranty than our wild will" (73). The King enters and makes a final speech before going to the scaffold. In the last scene, Cromwell speaks a self-justifying soliloquy. The Queen enters to plead with him, and he asks Lady Fairfax to take her out. When Cromwell hears the abbey bell, he announces that the King is dead, and he takes responsibility, saying "the deed is mine."

Mitford's historical tragedy clearly favors the royalist side, and she makes Cromwell the villain who acts out of mixed motives—ambition, jealousy, and greed for power. Cromwell claims he behaves only as an agent of the Almighty while humanly forcing the issues at every turn. The King and Queen are portrayed as exemplary characters—a loving couple and good parents—whose only hope is to strike a chord of pity in Cromwell. Both General and Lady Fairfax make efforts to help their royal friends, but Cromwell's single-mindedness pushes relentlessly forward to the King's execution. Mitford's strong blank verse is worthy of her subject.

MANUSCRIPT: BL Add. Ms. 42873, ff. 402–49.

TEXT: Readex Microprint.

Charlotte; or, One Thousand Seven Hundred and Seventy Three, Mrs. Cullum. Although the drama was not produced, it was printed by Baker and Galabin in 1775. In "To the Reader," Mrs. Cullum says the subtitle indicates the year in which the play was written.

Colonel Freeman and his sister Charlotte await the arrival of Mr. Stanley from abroad, but when he arrives Freeman won't let him see Charlotte, saying that he has a plan which requires Stanley's staying away for a day or two. Freeman's plot is to tell his sister that Stanley has lost his money in order to judge her reaction. But Charlotte outplots him by dressing as a man and going in disguise to Stanley. She gives him, as if it were a legacy, £5,000 cash and a miniature portrait. Later, upon Freeman's questioning, Stanley produces the miniature and secures Charlotte. The three then go to Stanley's house where he will introduce Freeman to his sister, newly arrived in town. In a subplot, Charlotte's snooty maid Pinwell, eavesdropping on Freeman's plot, hears him tell Charlotte that Stanley has lost all his money. Pinwell, therefore, decides to get another post, only to discover that Stanley is not poor at all. The other servants are so overjoyed that they have a dance to celebrate Pinwell's departure as well as the potential marriage of Charlotte and Stanley.

Mrs. Cullum's intent may have been to write a drama that portrayed the intersecting lives of masters and servants, for almost half of the play involves the retainers and servants of Colonel Freeman and Stanley. Dramatically, the play lacks "stageability": many speeches are too long, characters lack development, and the play exhibits a deficiency of conflict. *BD* remarks "This drama [was] never intended for the stage; being destitute of plot, or any other quality necessary for theatrical representation. The authoress confesses that she has been guilty of an artifice to bespeak the favour of the reader, by giving her play a name so justly beloved and respected by the whole nation" (2:93). Despite many dramaturgical problems, the play features Charlotte's sudden action of dressing as a man and voluntarily giving cash to "poor Stanley." This strong example of a generous and capable woman deserves more attention than it has been given.

TEXT: Readex Microprint.

The Child of Nature, Elizabeth Inchbald. As the adaptor of the play, Inchbald says that Harris, the manager at CG, sent her a literal translation "by a Lady." She then "with much care and attention, prepared it for the English stage." Based on Madame de Genlis's *Zélie; ou, l'Ingénue* (1781), Inchbald adapted the play into a four-act version which was first produced at CG on 28 November 1788, but acted only four times as a mainpiece. Beginning 6 December 1788, the play was shortened to three acts and performed twenty-three times as an afterpiece its first season. In the 1799–1800 season, Inchbald shortened several speeches but kept the plot, compressing the piece into two acts for CG (23 April 1800). DL continued to perform the three-act version. G. G. J. and J. Robinson published the four-act version in 1788.

Set in Spain, the four-act version of the play opens on the Count Valantia, who purposely has his coach break down near the country house of the Marquis Almanza and his ward. The Marquis has raised Amanthis, a supposed orphan who is now seventeen. Inchbald has altered her source in several ways: five acts are cut to four, the setting takes place in Spain rather than Normandy, and the characters are given Spanish names. While Amanthis is prohibited books, she may read—but only manuscripts handwritten by the Marquis (these are historical and moral tracts in Genlis). The cousin of the Marquis, Merida, comes for a visit; she has previously been interested in the Count. The Marquis wants to marry his ward, but his own guardian (and uncle) opposes the match. Amanthis clearly wants to marry the Marquis, not the Count who is attempting to woo her. A stranger then arrives and says he is Alberto, Amanthis's real father, and he reveals that she is not a poverty-stricken waif after all. In the end, the Marquis and Amanthis are to wed, and the Count and Merida agree to marry. (In the shorter versions, the plot and characters remain much the same, though several speeches are deleted, and the action is speeded up.)

Inchbald generally follows her source in cutting the five-act *Zélie* to four acts, though Kinne believes that the reduction causes too many abrupt transitions for which the readers/audience are not prepared. He also notes that Inchbald has larded the adaptation with a good deal of unnecessary sentiment. Yet he does state "this play is fundamentally a drama with a purpose" (206).

The question of women's education is central to the action, but the play skirts the issue of *who* should be supervising the education. By her guardian's restricting her access to books and to conversation, Amanthis can only learn what the Marquis would have her learn. Other educators are Amanthis's father and the Marquis's uncle, and she learns the male-taught lessons well. Bound up with education is the question of freedom: since Amanthis has not seen the world, how will she cope with a wider society? While the play is full of various trials, Inchbald may also want her audience to consider the real and false loyalties of the characters. The subplot of the Count's former and future relationship with Merida may be clever, but it seems disingenuous.

MANUSCRIPT: Not in the Larpent Collection.

TEXT: Readex Microprint of the 1788 edition.

FACSIMILE EDITIONS: Four-act version: E-CED, with introduction by Paula R. Backscheider (NY: Garland, 1980). Two-act version: *A Collection of Farces and Other Afterpieces*, selected by Mrs. Inchbald (1809; NY: Benjamin Blom, 1970) 1: 1–38.

CIBBER, Susanna Maria Arne (1714–66). Although not born into a musical family, Susanna (as well as her brother Thomas) were well trained in the musical arts. She began as a singer at DL, but she soon moved into acting roles. Married to Theophilus Cibber (Colley's son), Susanna found that her husband was a gambler, a rake, and a ne'er-do-well. To pay for his wagering and whoring, Theophilus arranged for private meetings between Susanna and William Sloper and then charged Sloper with adultery, asking £5,000 damages. Theophilus won a token £10. Not satisfied, Theophilus then sued Sloper for £10,000 on the charge of "detaining" Susanna (i.e., preventing him from profiting on his wife's acting). This time Theophilus was awarded £500; Susanna and Sloper left England, and she remained with him throughout her life.

It was probably in 1740–41 that she saw in Paris Saint-Foix's *L'Oracle*, which she later adapted. In the spring of 1742, Susanna was in Dublin to sing in the premiére of Handel's *Messiah*, and shortly thereafter she returned to London, performing for the 1742–43 season at CG where she also sang in the first English performance of *Messiah*. She acted off and on at both DL and CG, where *The Oracle* was first produced at her benefit night on 17 March 1752. From the season of 1753–54 until her death in 1766, she acted at DL, when the theatre was managed by David Garrick, who is reported to have said that tragedy died with her death.

By all accounts, the outstanding tragic actress of her day, Susanna Cibber wrote one afterpiece for her benefit night, which she continued to play for several years. Although she will always be known for her acting, her contribution to the dramatic literature of the eighteenth-century, an adaptation of *The Oracle* prepared for her benefit night, shows a comic side of her talents. Not debilitated by her early marriage to Theophilus Cibber, Susanna made a remarkable comeback, rising to the top of her profession.

[*BD*, BDAA, DBAWW, DNB, OCEL, Revels. E-CED series, ed. D. Mann. Biography by Mary Nash, 1977.]

The City Farce, attributed to Mrs. Weddell. Apparently the play ran up against the Licensing Act of 1737 and was not staged. Later that year, G. Hawkins published the text which was sold by J. Roberts. The title page says it was "Designed for the Theatre-Royal in Drury-Lane," and a long address "to the Gentlemen of the Pit" prefaces the text. The author intends to revive the spirit of "our old English Farce." Both the prologue and epilogue refer to the author as "he," perhaps to mask a female playwright.

When Simplex meets Colonel Counterscarp, they talk of life in military metaphors, and Simplex compares soldiers to modern beaus. Captain Truck, at home, tells his daughter, Orinda, he hopes she will marry George, a haberdasher's apprentice, whereas she favors Simplex. Smatch calls on Miss Flash who lives in the house, and he entertains her with a song. The scene shifts to the haberdasher's shop, where George works; he's so engrossed in trying on various attire than he can scarcely tend to business. Back at Captain Truck's, Miss Flash talks with her maid Liddy about marriage and freedom; when they see the Captain coming, they withdraw so he can talk to the newly arrived Squire Plowlands, George's father. When George comes in elaborately overdressed, his father doesn't recognize him. While the women and their beaus leave to talk of marriage, an old member of the militia is invited in to sing a ballad about the city forces, with which the play ends.

Most readers would be disturbed by the lack of resolution, a problem easily resolved by betrothal or marriage. While the play is labeled a farce, there is little farcical action. Moreover, the long speeches would make the play difficult to present on stage. The most amusing scene is when the country father fails to recognize his citified son who is foppishly dressed, but by 1737 this is an old canard. The play may have been rejected by the DL manager because of an unsatisfactory closure or lack of unity rather than its political content.

TEXT: Readex Microprint.

The City Heiress; or, Sir Timothy Treat-All, Aphra Behn. In this five-act comedy, Behn employs scenes from both Middleton's *A Mad World, My Masters* and Massinger's *The Guardian*; Martin S. Balch has studied these borrowings in his monograph (Salzburg Studies, 1981). Probably produced at DG in late April or early May of 1682, the play was printed the same year for D. Brown, T. Benskin, and H. Rhodes.

Tom Wilding, a young Tory, is disinherited by his Whiggish uncle Sir Timothy Treat-all, despite pleas by Sir Charles Meriwell. Sir Timothy and Sir Charles's uncle, Sir Anthony Meriwell, argue about the education of their nephews. Both Wilding and Sir Charles share an interest in Lady Galliard, a rich city widow. When Wilding meets her, he is observed by Sir Charles and Sir Anthony. Sir Charles interrupts the couple, and the two men fight, but Sir Anthony steps forward and separates them. Later, Sir Anthony tells Sir Charles that he will teach him the way "to go a Widow-wooing." The city heiress, Charlot, knows of Wilding's interest in Lady Galliard, and Mrs. Clacket suggests that Charlot observe him at Sir Timothy's party, disguised as a Scottish relation. Meanwhile, Wilding plans to have Diana, his kept mistress, go to Sir Timothy's party disguised as Charlot. Sir Anthony then accompanies Sir Charles as he goes to woo Lady Galliard, but Sir Charles's bumbling attempts draw angry reactions from his uncle. Sir Timothy comes to take Lady Galliard to his party, where Wilding has brought Diana, disguised as Charlot. Sir Timothy falls for her and offers Diana marriage. Wilding slips out and returns, disguised as a Person of Quality, who offers Sir Timothy the throne of Poland. When Charlot comes in her Scottish disguise, Wilding woos her, but he also makes an assignation with Lady Galliard at her house, where he carries her to her bedroom. When Sir Anthony and Sir Charles arrive at Lady Galliard's much the worse for drink, her woman

Closet fends them off so Wilding can flee. Sir Charles then woos Lady Galliard. Wilding and his friends go in disguise to Sir Timothy's house where they take his money and secure his papers. The next morning, Sir Timothy takes Diana, thinking she is Charlot, to be married. Charlot hears that Wilding passed the night with Lady Galliard but discovers it is Sir Charles who is about to marry her. Sir Timothy comes in with Diana having just married her. After he discovers his mistake and realizes the stolen papers are treasonable, he forgives Wilding who will wed Charlot.

One of the most political of Behn's plays, *The City-Heiress* came out in the midst of a Whig-Tory clash (the Shaftesbury brouhaha), but as Link points out "the comedy also stands on its own merits" (70). Most critics comment on the contrasting pairs: the promiscuous libertine Wilding vs. the sober, one-woman Sir Charles; the stodgy, narrow-minded Sir Timothy vs. the active, pleasure-loving Sir Anthony; the witty Charlot vs. the romantic Lady Galliard. While the uncles argue over male education, female education comes with experience: each woman must understand what is in her own best interest. Lady Galliard finds she is fortunate in securing Sir Charles after giving herself to Wilding. Diana also sees it is in her interest to hang on to Sir Timothy, even with his reduced funds. Charlot holds out and claims Wilding because her interest is a man who loves her and whom she can live with amicably.

TEXTS: Wing B1719; EEB Reel 270: 7 (1682). Wing B1720; EEB Reel 835: 4 (1698). Readex Microprint of 1682 edition.

MODERN EDITION: *Works*, ed. Montague Summers (1915; NY: Phaeton, 1967) 2: 195–300.

CRITICAL EDITION: *Satire and Sense* series. An Old-Spelling Edition, edited by William R. Hersey (NY: Garland, 1987).

Clara; or, The Nuns of Charity, Charlotte Nooth. This five-act verse tragedy was included in Nooth's *Original Poems, and a Play*, published by subscription and printed for Longman, Hurst, Rees, Orme, and Brown in 1815. There is no known performance.

The scene is the Castle of Valmonsor and its environs, on the banks of the Rhone in the sixteenth century. Count Valmonsor has lost his first wife, and he plans to marry Clara the following day. His young son Julio is being raised by his sister Amelia, who has also raised Clara at the castle. Clara's father, Baron Montalban, arrives for the wedding, but she knows almost nothing of him except that he has piled up debts and is financially ruined. With the arrival of Father Anselmo, all go to greet him except Amelia, who voices her concern about her brother marrying a Montalban. The next morning Montalban mentions the noises he's heard in the night and asks about the peasants who work on the Valmonsor estate. In a soliloquy, Montalban plans to kill Julio, but later when he has the opportunity he can't drive in the knife and throws the child into the Rhone. Clara comes on the scene, picks up the bloody knife, and realizes her father is the murderer. When Amelia comes, she thinks Clara is responsible, but Clara won't name the real criminal. Montalban blames the peasants, who probably made the noises the previous night, and he renounces Clara who is taken away. Meanwhile, the Count has a war on his hands with the Count of Rohan, and he leaves with his troops. Clara is taken to a cell and then to trial where she is pardoned but not acquitted. Father Anselmo suggests Clara go to the convent of the Sisters of Charity, where the first person she meets is Isabel, the former wife of the Count of Rohan. Eighteen years ago, after she gave birth to a daughter, the Count deserted her. Some sisters arrive to say that many were wounded in the battle, and Clara joins them to go help the victims. Making their way through the woods, Clara and Isabel stop at a hut, where a peasant brings in Julio from the river. Julio tells them Montalban tried to murder him. Nearby Valmonsor and the Count of Rohan fight each other, and Valmonsor falls. While Clara goes to bind up his wounds, Isabel takes the Count of Rohan aside. Valmonsor is remorseful because he thinks Clara can never forgive him, but she does. Father Anselmo arrives with the wounded Montalban, who confesses to the attempted murder of Julio. Before he dies, Montalban tells Clara that she is not his daughter, but the offspring of Isabel and Rohan. Father Anselmo asks Rohan to repent, and when he does, he is forgiven by Isabel. Valmonsor and Rohan are reconciled, and Father Anselmo blesses the new-found joy and harmony.

Nooth says that the basis for her drama is Madame de Genlis's story of the "Siege of Rochelle," which has been adapted for dramatic purposes. As the title character, Clara is put through much anguish because she will not name Montalban as the murderer. Ultimately, however, she finds her real parents, reconciles with her fiancé, and discovers Julio alive. But it seems more the twists of the plot than her own doing that rejoin her to the community in the end.

TEXT: Not in Readex Microprint. We read the play at the Lilly Library, Indiana Univ., Bloomington.

CLARKE, Lady Olivia (c. 1785–1845). The younger sister of Sydney Owenson, Lady Morgan, novelist and playwright, Olivia Owenson was mostly raised by her sister and life-long confidante after the death of their mother when Olivia was only two. While a governess, she met and married Dr. (later Sir Arthur) Clarke, a physician to the navy. Although not a handsome man, the doctor offered Olivia a fashionable home for her and her father. Lady Clarke had at least four children by Sir Arthur and spent a comfortable, if not happy, life in Dublin. Her sister's success emboldened her to write one five-act comedy, entitled *The Irishwoman*. She saw her play produced at the Crow-Street Theatre in Dublin, 1819, and printed the same year in Dublin and London by Henry Colburn, her sister's publisher. Although overshadowed by a more famous sister, Lady Clarke continued to write verse and prose as her health permitted. [Information gathered from Mary Campbell's biography of Lady Morgan, 1988.]

CLIVE, Catherine "Kitty" Raftor (1711–85). Irish in background, if not by birth, Kitty (as she was familiarly known) seems to have had little formal education. Stage-struck at an early age, she used to follow actors through the streets of London.

At seventeen, she was engaged by DL, and for the next forty years held the stage as the reigning comedienne of theatrical London. Her marriage to George Clive was brief and ended in separation. An excellent singer as well as actress, Clive sang the role of Dalilah in Handel's *Sampson* (CG, 18 February 1743). Angered about managerial tyranny in the fall 1744, Clive—in *The Case of Mrs. Clive Submitted to the Publick*—charged that she had been fired without due cause, and that the two managers (Rich and Fleetwood) were in league against her. She eventually acted two seasons at CG before returning to DL. In 1750, Clive wrote the first and most successful of her several plays for her benefit night, *The Rehearsal; or, Bayes in Petticoats*. Performed as an afterpiece to *Hamlet*, the farce featured Clive as the author Mrs. Hazard, who comes to the theatre to see her play acted; when Mrs. Clive doesn't show up, Mrs. Hazard must take her place. The piece was not only acted for Clive's benefit but also for others in the DL company; it was printed until 1753, though the rest of her plays remain unpublished. Clive wrote an ambitious afterpiece, again for her benefit, *Every Woman in her Humour* (DL, 20 March 1760). Taking the role of Mrs. Croston, Clive pokes fun at affectation. Frushell believes that *The London 'Prentice* (1754) and *The Island of Slaves* (1761) are probably not by Clive, but written for her. Clive's final benefit plays include *The Sketch of a Fine Lady's Return from a Rout* (1763) and *The Faithful Irishwoman* (1765); the latter enlarges and reworks the former. Although both dramas spoof card-playing women, they also celebrate Irish patriotism. Clive retired from the stage in 1769 and was given a cottage by her old friend Horace Walpole near his house at Twickenham, where she lived until her death in 1785.

It is Kitty Clive's acting that makes her a fixture in theatrical history and her clever personality that makes its way into theatrical lore. Still, her farces show that while she considers the theatre important, she doesn't take herself too seriously. Most of her plays are self-reflexive in that they cause audiences to laugh at the character she has created of herself. [*BD*, BDAA, BNA, Cotton, DBAWW, DNB, EBWW, FCLE, NCBEL (2: 828), OCEL, Revels. Biography by Percy Fitzgerald, 1888 (rpt. 1969).]

COCKBURN, Catharine. See Catharine **TROTTER**.

COLLIER Jane (1709/10?–1754/55?). The daughter of a philosophical clergyman, Jane learned classical languages at an early age. A long-time friend of Sarah Fielding and her brother Henry, she grew up in Salisbury. With her younger sister Margaret (1717–94), she was invited to London by the Fieldings, after the dissolution of Rev. Collier's estate. In London, the Collier sisters became correspondents and friends of Samuel Richardson. Jane even prepared a critique of *Clarissa*, which was never published. Later, Jane published, anonymously, *An Essay on the Ingeniously Tormenting* (1753), though she had help from another Salisbury friend, James Harris. Robin Jarvis, writing in DBAWW, describes the essay as "an early exercise in black comedy, the principle of which is 'remember always to do unto every one what you would least wish to have done unto yourself'" (89). The following year, Jane joined Sarah Fielding in preparing *The Cry*: the dramatic format has Portia telling her history with remarks by Una (who represents Truth) and by The Cry (a general public chorus). Jarvis believes the "character sketches suggest Sarah Fielding, while the satiric wit probably belongs to Jane Collier" (89). The same year, prior to his departure for Lisbon, Henry Fielding presented Jane with "a vellum-bound copy of his favorite Horace, inscribed by himself affectionately" (Battestin, *Henry Fielding* 392–93). Although Margaret Collier accompanied Fielding on his voyage to Lisbon, Jane went only as far as Gravesend to bid him farewell. Shortly thereafter, Jane Collier died. [DBAWW, FCLE]

Comala, Lady Sophia Raymond Burrell. This three-act verse drama, "taken from a poem of *Ossian*," may have been the same one produced in Hanover Square Rooms, 1792 (see *BD* 2: 112–13). It was printed in her *Poems* published by J. Cooper in 1793. The title page bears the date of "December, 1784," when the drama may have been finished.

The action, according to Burrell's notes, takes place in the year 211. Before the events of the drama take place, Comala (the daughter of Sarno, King of the Inistore or Orkeny Islands) fell in love with Fingal, the King of Morven, and has followed him disguised as a youth. She is discovered by Hidallan, one of Fingal's warriors, whose love she had slighted earlier. Knowing nothing of this, Fingal prepares to fight the Roman legions and plans to marry Comala, now undisguised, when the battle is over. While Fingal engages the Romans, Comala asks Morni, a druid, what will be the outcome, and he predicts that Fingal will return victorious. This is indeed the outcome, and Fingal sends Hidallan to tell Comala of his safe return. In revenge for Comala's earlier slight, however, Hidallan reports Fingal dead. When Fingal arrives, Comala thinks him a ghost and dies of a broken heart. The play ends with Fingal planning to punish Hidallan.

Any production of this play would face the difficulty of convincing the audience of Comala's broken heart, especially since she dies offstage. Hidallan's motivation to get revenge on Comala is not clearly enough explained to be convincing. While it is plausible that Fingal should seek revenge on Hidallan, Fingal only promises to punish Hidallan. Burrell could have expanded her imitation of the Ossian verses to make this drama more convincing. Many of the poetic lines come from MacPherson's dialogue that is printed following the play.

TEXT: Readex Microprint.

Comala, Susan Fraser. This poetic drama is included in Fraser's *Camilla de Florian and Other Poems* "By an officer's wife," printed for the author and sold by J. Dick in 1809. Davis and Joyce note that the verse drama is adapted from Ossian (James MacPherson). We assume the play treats the same tragic figure and circumstances used by Burrell in her drama taken from the identical source.

TEXT: Not in Readex Microprint. NUC lists a copy at Yale.

The Comical Hash, Margaret Lucas Cavendish, Duchess of Newcastle. Printed in her *Playes*, published by John Martyn, James Allestry, and Tho. Dicas in 1662, the drama was not produced.

There are three plot lines: 1) Lady Gadder, Lady Kindeling, and Lady Bridelhead consider how they should go about getting proper husbands; 2) Lady Examination, Lady Solitary, and Lady Censure take differing positions on problems concerning women; and 3) Sir William Admirer must decide whether to marry Lady Fraction (who loves change) or Lady Peaceable (who loves tranquility). In addition, scenes involving two or more unnamed gentlemen provide commentary on previous action or introduce other points of view.

The operative word in the title is "hash," which suggests older ideas served up in a different manner. The play could be called a comedy since it ends with a marriage. One of the more instructive scenes (V.xxi) contains a monologue by Lady Censurer, who considers what she might do with ten shillings she has earned by singing at court. Should she set up an alms house, give to the poor, invest in a ship, etc.? When she says she should build a bawdy house because it's a trade that never fails, Lady Examination calls her a "wag." Although the nuptials of Sir William and Lady Peaceable happen "off stage," it becomes the subject of a commentary by two unnamed gentlemen. The only unifying theme in this "comical hash" concerns whether to marry or not to marry.

TEXTS: Wing N868. EEB Reel 502: 11. Readex Microprint.

The Conflict; or, Love, Honour and Pride, Hannah Brand. This comedy, an adaptation of Pierre Corneille's *Don Sanche d'Arragon* (1650), was never produced. It was collected in Brand's *Poems and Plays*, published at Norwich by Beatniffe and Payne, 1798.

Donna Elvira is the rightful Queen of Arragon, but the throne has been usurped by Garcia before her birth. She was born and bred in Castile, and, at the opening of the play, the people have revolted from Garcia and have sent deputies to Elvira to hail her as Queen. The Castilians request Elvira choose a husband from among Don Manrique, Don Lopez, and Don Alvarez. But she and Isabella, the present Queen of Castile, love Carlos, General of Castile, who has distinguished himself by his valor. Even though he is respected by his enemies, the Castilians look on Carlos with some degree of contempt, because his parentage is unknown. Isabella creates Carlos a Marquis, gives him a ring, and says he shall recommend her choice. Carlos declares that he will give the ring to no one, except the person who will vanquish him in single combat. At the conclusion, Carlos turns out to be Sancho, the son and heir of the former King of Arragon. Elvira, on finding that Carlos is her brother, gives her hand to Alvarez, and Isabella marries Carlos.

Brand gets her theme of love vs. honor from Pierre Corneille. Both Isabella and Elvira have fallen for Carlos, but their passions are incompatible with their rank. Noble blood, however, will always emerge in fine deeds, and Carlos's hidden birth by his royal parents who feared for his safety vindicate both women. The conflict of the title is resolved by the love, honor, and pride of the subtitle.

Brand calls her play a "Heroick Comedy," translating Pierre Corneille's new genre which portrays characters of high rank without inspiring terror or pity. Brand followed her model closely for the first three acts, but she made some alterations in the last two acts for no apparent reason. Nevertheless, both plays end in a similar manner, except that Brand added moralizing lines in conclusion extolling the unfailing rewards of true virtue. The two plays, however, read differently: where Corneille used classical rimed verse, Brand used blank verse, which fits the subject less well. Corneille's lines are restrained and dignified, Brand's are inelegant and sentimental. That Brand's blank verse doesn't really suit the subject may explain why her work was never produced.

TEXT: Readex Microprint of *Poems and Plays*, 1798.

The Conjurer, by a lady. This three-act farce was published by S. Gosnell in 1823 with another three-act farce, titled *A Lesson for Lovers*. There is no indication that either play was performed, nor is there any clue to the author's name. A manuscript (Larpent 1882) exists of *The Conjuror; or, Blaise in Amaze*, a two-act burletta, produced 30 October 1815 at Sans Pareil by Jane M. Scott. We have not been able to determine whether the single title is the same as the dual title.

TEXT: Not in Readex Microprint.

The Conjuror; or, Blaze in Amaze, Jane M. Scott. This two-act farcical burletta opened the San Pareil season on 30 October 1815. A popular piece, it played forty-nine nights and was revived the following season. John Jolly wrote the music for the play, and Scott took the role of Laurette.

MANUSCRIPT: Larpent 1882.

The Conquest of Corsica by the French, by a Lady. The author of this tragedy is unknown: the play's title page prints "By a Lady." The five-act verse tragedy was printed for the author in 1771. *BD* (3: 120) and Stratman (#1270) say that the play was not staged.

Based on a framework of real events, the play opens just as the Corsicans have discovered that the French plan to invade their island. The Senate votes to repel the invaders. Senator Abatucci then informs his daughter, Flavonia, engaged to General Paoli, who had earlier driven the Genoese from their coasts. Senator Barbaggio also tells his wife, Leonora (the niece of the General), that he must go to fight the invading French. A third farewell occurs when the General bids adieu to Flavonia. Meanwhile, Count de Marboeuf, in charge of French operations, is concerned about the fierce patriotism among the Corsicans, and he has asked that Count De Vaux be sent to oversee the attack, in order not to bear the shame of a possible defeat. In the Corsican camp, the General's brother, Clement Paoli, joins the leaders. For a while the battle is indecisive, but through treachery the French manage to defeat the Corsicans. At home, Flavonia hears that the General and his principal officers have been killed; she becomes distracted and takes poison. In fact, all the Corsican leaders have survived the conflict, and they plan to flee to England. In her death throes, Flavonia has a final farewell with General Paoli and dies. After he laments her passing, Paoli, apparently forgetting his patriotic mission, makes a speech about one island where liberty still exists—England—where he "will take up Residence to live and die."

This timely piece was published less than two years after the real General Paoli was driven out of Corsica by the French. The several farewells before the battle show a strong anti-war theme from the women. Nevertheless, the Corsican men do their military duty only to be defeated by a betrayal from within. Modern historians do not mention Flavonia or Leonora; we assume they are invented by the author to provide a feminine point of view. That Flavonia has received misinformation about the conflict causes her to take poison, precipitating a double tragedy. About the form of the drama: the verse is an odd mix of iambic pentameter and longer (14 or 16 stress) lines. The unknown playwright uses several scenes within an act to juxtapose the feelings of the various high-ranking Corsicans as well as contrasting the attitudes of the French army commanders. The importance of freedom and liberty emerges as another thematic underpinning in the play.

TEXT: Readex Microprint.

The Conquest of Spain, Mary Pix. This five-act tragedy, based on Rowley's *All Lost by Lust* (acted 1619, printed 1633), was produced at the Queen's Theatre in mid-May 1705 (from 12–22 May has been suggested by Milhous and Hume in Downes) and ran six nights. Publication, advertised in the *Daily Courant* of 25 May 1705, was by R. Wellington, though without a date on the title page (Burling).

Julianus, an old Spanish general, comes out of retirement to face the Moors who have invaded Spain. He asks the King to take care of his daughter, Jacincta, and his ward, Margaretta. The latter has secretly married Julianus's nephew, Antonio, who also goes off to the war. While the war progresses well for the Spanish, the King plots "to enjoy" Jacincta. When she won't comply, he rapes her. She goes to her victorious father in disguise and tells him the story. Although Julianus can only lament what has happened, Jacincta's fiancé, Theomantius, vows revenge against the King. He gathers an army that includes the captured Moors and their general, Mullymumen. Once they have taken the castle, the Moors call for reinforcements, who are waiting just off the coast, and subdue the Spaniards. The King and Julianus are imprisoned together, and as Jacincta comes to her father she is wounded. Old Julianus is so fiercely loyal that he helps the King escape, but he has one last tender scene with Jacincta before he dies. When Theomantius arrives, he has a final scene with Jacincta before she dies, and Theomantius falls on his sword. In the subplot, Antonio's fellow officer Alvarez schemes to have Margaretta, but he is thwarted and stabbed by Antonio. In the end, the Moors have conquered, and Mullymumen lets the young lovers go as it was the last wish of Julianus.

Although there are only two women in the play, designs on their virtue are central to the plot. The King's lust causes the conquest of Spain by the Moors, but violated as she is by her monarch, Jacincta reaches her father on the battlefield asking for revenge. Julianus, however, is too mired in his ways and cannot raise a hand against his sovereign: given the fact that the King has raped his daughter, Julianus's loyalty seems cruel and misplaced. Though they have a strong friendship, Jacincta and Margaretta are manipulated by lustful males, and the women can do little to help one another, as Pearson notes (180). In the play, too, is a strong undercurrent of blame. When the King fails to seduce Jacincta at first, he blames his henchmen. Even Jacincta blames Theomantius for bringing the Moors to help him gain revenge on the King. And finally in a powerful scene, Julianus blames the King for the downfall of Spain.

TEXT: Readex Microprint.

FACSIMILE EDITION: E-CED, with introduction by Edna L. Steeves (NY: Garland, 1982).

Constantia, Anne Hughes. This three-act verse tragedy was printed in her *Moral Dramas Intended for Private Representation*, published by William Lane in 1790. There is no known production.

Set in Cyprus, the tragedy traces the final days of Queen Constantia, who has wrongly inherited the throne from her father, Theron. Having imprisoned the former king, Lycimacus, Theron reigned as a usurper, and on his death passed the crown to Constantia. Some Cretans, including Lysander and his counselor Glaucus, have been shipwrecked on Cyprus, and Constantia has fallen in love with Lysander, overthrowing Lysidas her former suitor. She wants the Cretans to stay one more day before they depart, and she declares a festival day. Glaucus thinks Lysander showed weakness in delaying, and the counselor strongly urges him to depart. When Lysander tries to take leave, Constantia tells him Lysidas has taken Lycimacus from prison and started a rebellion. She is ready to lead the troops, and Lysander says he will assist her with his Cretan sailors. In an interview with Lysidas, Constantia offers to marry him if he'll rid her of Lycimacus, the rightful king. In fact, she plans to imprison Lysidas for the murder, thus ridding herself of two problems at once. Discovering this plot, Lysander rebukes Constantia; she relents and tries to stop Lysidas. Glaucus then tells Lysander that Lycimacus is his real father, and that Constantia has caused him to be murdered. She is taken away to prison, and Glaucus tells him that justice demands her life. The Cypriots ask Lysander to become their king and he agrees. Because Glaucus believes Constantia must be punished, he goes to her prison cell with a bowl of poison and a dagger, giving her a choice of death. Constantia drinks the poison, but Lysander arrives saying that Lysidas has not killed his father, and that Lycimacus has approved of his marrying Constantia, who dies at his feet. Glaucus tells Lysander to take revenge by killing him, but he cannot do it. In the final speech Lysander laments that "one bad deed" has blasted "the promised joy."

Constantia shows a good deal of strength as Queen of Cyprus, but her "one bad deed," ordering the murder of Lycimacus, causes her downfall. Even with this mistake, she is imposed upon by the male worlds of her father and Glaucus, her antagonist. She seems as attractive and irresistible as Cleopatra, and Lysander's love for her is not unlike Antony's for the Egyptian Queen. Glaucus acts Enobarbus's role in urging Lysander to take responsibility. Hughes's blank verse fits her subject well, but some pertinent stage directions would help clarify the action.

TEXT: Readex Microprint.

Constantia, Ann Hamilton M'Taggart. This five-act tragedy in verse was published with *Valville; or, The Prejudices of Past Times* in 1824 by M. A. Nattali. As the preface acknowledges, the story is taken from one of the tales that Countess de Genlis wrote to illustrate moral points in her three-volume treatise on education, titled *Adele and Theodore; or, Letters on Education* (1782). When M'Taggart collected her *Plays* in 2 vols., published by A. J. Valpy in 1832, she included *Constantia*.

The play begins with Duke Manfredi in a highly agitated state, demanding vengeance against his wife, Duchess Constantia, who was in love with a stranger (Count Lorenzo) when her parents forced her marriage to Manfredi, "his princely rank, his gaudy wealth" (15). Manfredi's inability to control his wife's affection results in his condemnation of all women: "They seem so pure, and yet at heart how foul are those whom we call angels" (22). Having discovered her love for another by confiscating her letters to her parents (Count and Countess Valdi), Manfredi agrees to pardon her if she will reveal the object of her love. Refusing to do so, Constantia is given a sleeping potion, her death is announced, and she is forced to live imprisoned in her own mausoleum. After five years pass, the Count has aged and is frail. His relative Count Lorenzo appears for his first visit in ten years, and it is announced that Constantia's parents will soon be arriving. Having lost use of his limbs, Manfredi asks Lorenzo to take food to a "foe" imprisoned beneath Constantia's tomb. Although given strict instructions to leave the food and return, Lorenzo disobeys and discovers the weakened Constantia. As they stand before the mausoleum, Count and Countess Valdi witness the door opening and Lorenzo helping their daughter from the tomb. Simultaneously, the Duke is brought in on a chair, and he stabs himself when he realizes that he will never fully satisfy his desire for revenge, although at the very end he asks for his wife's and daughter's pardon.

The plot comes from Madame de Genlis's work, not just in its broad outlines, but also in such details as the waxen mannequin used to simulate Constantia's "corpse," the mirror held to the heroine's face to emphasize what she is about to lose (reminding her torturer that even if no human witnesses his horrible deed, God will observe), and Constantia's finding refuge in her mother's arms. While the works bear some similarities, the tone and purpose of each are quite different. In Madame de Genlis's text, the heroine, the Duchess of C. (her first name is never revealed), writes an autobiographical account of fifty-seven pages of the horrors she endured for seven years in her subterraneous prison, of her despair that led her to contemplate suicide, of her determination to stay alive—with the help of religion—for her daughter's sake, of her deliverance by her faithful lover Belmire, of her unbounded joy at seeing the world around her again, and of her resolution to give her fifteen-year-old daughter in marriage to Belmire, in order to give him a chance for happiness and to fulfill her vow to lead a retired life. Fully happy now, she can thank God even for her misfortunes for they have purified her heart. M'Taggart stopped her tragedy with the deliverance of Constantia, for her goal, unlike that of her French counterpart, was not to show how blissfully happy one can be with the help of religion. As a playwright, she needed a more dramatic ending, hence the duke's sudden repentance and his spectacular suicide on stage. M'Taggart illustrates how an author can completely change a source: while she is faithful to the main outlines of a scenario, the resulting drama can emphasize quite different values.

While the language of the play holds little interest, the story itself has power, primarily because the leading characters have psychological depth. Lorenzo is a Byronic figure, and Constantia is long-suffering, willing to sacrifice herself before revealing Lorenzo's name. She does, however, demonstrate verbal aggressiveness when confronting her husband: "Manfredi, I am both your wife and victim" (25). A unifying theme is the play's criticism of the marriage that Constantia's parents have forced upon her. Although Countess Valdi regrets their actions after the daughter's "death," Count Valdi does not question the wisdom of the marriage ("The envied bride of titles, wealth, and power" 82) until he discovers that his son-in-law has buried Constantia alive.

TEXT: Not in Readex Microprint. We read the play at the Lilly Library, Indiana Univ., Bloomington.

Constantine Paleologus, Joanna Baillie. This five-act tragedy first appeared in *Miscellaneous Plays*, printed by Longman, Hurst, Rees, and Orme, 1804. It was produced, as altered by Mr. Terry for his benefit, at the Theatre Royal, Liverpool, with the subtitle of *A Band of Patriots*, on 7 November 1808. Margaret Carhart mentions a performance (retitled *Constantine and Valeria*) at the Surrey Theatre the same year, a performance in Edinburgh in 1820, and a performance at the Theatre Royal in Dublin, 1825.

Set in Constantinople and in the Camp of Mahomet, near the city, the events occur just hours before an anticipated attack by the Turks. Since Mahomet (the Ottoman sultan, Muhammad II) is destined to succeed in his attack against Constantine (Constantine XI, the last Byzantine emperor), the play focuses on the effect that the tragedy has on the major characters. Two Greeks, Petronius and Marthon, who are also secret agents of Mahomet, have paid men in the street to stage an insurrection the night before the attack. In response, Constantine and his heroic supporters (Othus, a learned Greek; Rodrigo, a Genoese naval commander; and Justiniani, a brave Genoese soldier) go to subdue the crowd. Subsequently, Justiniani and Rodrigo are sent to the Sultan's camp for a last peace offering before the final battle. Although they arrive just after an attack has been made on the Sultan's life, Mahomet perceives that they are brave men and refuses to take them as prisoners. When the would-be assassin appears before Mahomet, he (Othoric) explains that he was not sent by Constantine: his action was self-devised in response to his admiration for the Greek Emperor. The peace mission fails, but Mahomet is impressed that Constantine is loved by men such as these. The next morning before the battle, Constantine gathers his supporters around, expressing his love for them, before an early church service. Then, in an interview with his wife Valeria, Constantine confesses that he fears she will become the Sultan's wife if the battle is lost. Angry that her husband believes this possible ("he who thinks me helpless thinks me mean" 398), Valeria vows to commit suicide should her husband's fears be realized. When Constantine is killed in the ensuing attack, Mahomet stops the fighting so that he can be properly buried. Then he approaches Valeria, who stabs herself after receiving the Sultan's promise that when she dies she will be buried with Constantine. Before dying, Valeria also obtains Mahomet's promise that her friend Ella (Petronius's daughter) and Rodrigo can wed. The closing speech is given to Othus the sage, who is dying. Othus informs Mahomet that Heaven still favors the Greeks in spite of their military loss: "And think not when the good and valiant perish by worldly power o'erwhelm'd, that heaven's high favour shines not on them—Oh, no! then shines it most (437).

Constantine Paleologus's strength is that the major historical characters are sympathetic, relatively complex, and surprisingly human. Although the play is heavily biased in favor of Christianity, Mahomet is allowed to become an adversary worthy of Constantine. While not important until the last two acts, Valeria directs the action after Constantine has died, including her own suicide. Although depicted in the beginning of the play as fearful and superstitious, Valeria ultimately demonstrates courage and control over her life; as Mahomet eulogizes her passing, "Great God of heav'n! was this a woman's spirit that took its flight?" (434). Finally, Constantine's nobleness and bravery are tempered by self-doubts and knowledge of his personal limitations.

MANUSCRIPT: Larpent 1557.

TEXT: Readex Microprint of *Miscellaneous Plays* (2nd ed., 1805): 279–438.

FACSIMILE EDITION: *Romantic Context: Poetry* reprints *Miscellaneous Plays* (London: Longman, Hurst, Rees, and Orme, 1804). Compiled, with an introduction, by D. H. Reiman (NY: Garland, 1977).

The Convent of Pleasure, Margaret Lucas Cavendish, Duchess of Newcastle. She labels this play "A Comedy" on the title page. Printed in her *Plays, Never before Printed*, published by A. Maxwell in 1668, it was not performed publicly.

When Lady Happy's father dies, she uses her inheritance to establish a "Convent of Pleasure," for women only, but it will be a place of freedom. While several would-be wooers of the women (Take-Pleasure, Facil, Courtly, and Adviser—all of whom appear in *The Bridals*) object to the new arrangement, there is nothing they can do. They even go so far as considering setting fire to the new establishment, or dressing as cook-maids or servants to gain entrance. But because a foreign Princess has joined the women, they decide to wait. Meanwhile, Lady Happy has the rooms changed to suit each season. The foreign Princess says she will dress in men's clothes and escort Lady Happy to a play. What follows in the third act are a series of tableaux about the woes that women must put up with in marriage: these include sickness in pregnancy, the pains of childbirth, husbands who gamble away their estates, husbands who spend money on whores and bring them home, husbands who are always drunk, adult children who take advantage of their parents, and women subjected to harassment so the man can take them to bed. Clearly, Lady Happy is smitten with the foreign Princess: "Why," she asks, "may not I love a Woman with the same affection I could a Man?" Then, "They imbrace and Kiss, and hold each other in their Arms." Act IV incorporates two other masques: (1) a poetic pastoral with Lady Happy taking the role of a shepherdess and the foreign Princess acting a shepherd and (2) a nautical masque in which the foreign Princess acts Neptune while Lady Happy plays a sea-goddess. Suddenly Madame Mediator (who also appears in *The Bridals*) breaks in, crying "there is a man disguised in the Convent." That man turns out to be the foreign Princess, who is actually a Prince. In the final scene, Lady Happy and the Prince celebrate their wedding.

In Pearson's discussion of the play, she states that "Cavendish's view of marriage can be deeply contradictory" (132), contrasting the difficulties women face in marriage (Act III) with the nuptials of Lady Happy and the Prince at the end of the play. The conventional ending shifts our view from the virtues of the women's convent to the impossibility of escaping traditional gender roles. Pearson concludes that the ideal partner for a spirited women is not "the conventional macho male but an androgyne" (142). The several characters who also appear in both *The Bridals* and *The Convent of Pleasure* suggests that in her later plays Cavendish may be trying to work out what finally makes a successful marriage.

TEXT: Wing N867. EEB Reel 674: 2. Readex Microprint.

ABRIDGED VERSION: *First Feminists: British Women Writers, 1578–1799*, ed. Moira Ferguson (Bloomington, IN: Indiana UP; Old Westbury, NY: Feminist P, 1985): 86–101.

COOPER, Elizabeth (fl. 1735–40). Nothing is known about Cooper's early life, except that she was married to Thomas Cooper (possibly an auctioneer or a bookseller or both). After his death, she gave "the first publick Tryal of [her] Muse" in her five-act comedy *The Rival Widows; or, The Fair Libertine* (acted at CG 22 February 1735). During the six-night run, Cooper took the role of Lady Bellair on her two benefit nights. The following year Cooper's less successful *The Nobleman; or, The Family Quarrel* played at the Haymarket on 17 May 1736 and ran three nights, but it was not printed and is presumed lost. In 1737, she turned to collecting poetry and, with the help of William Oldys, published it as *The Muses Library . . . From the Saxons, to the Reign of King Charles II* (1737, reissued 1741). This retrospective anthology contains brief biographies as well as a scholarly preface with original commentary. Almost no women writers are included, however. A proposed second volume never appeared. No facts have come to light about Cooper's later life. [*BD*, Cotton, DBAWW, DNB, FCLE]

The Coquet's Surrender; or, The Humourous Punster, by a lady. The first publication of this five-act comedy by an anonymous author did not indicate that the playwright was female; it was only in a later (1733) issue that "a lady" is given credit. The play had one performance on 15 May 1732 at the Haymarket Theatre under the title *The Coquet's Surrender; or, The Humorous Punster* (for the benefit of the author); it was published by E. Raynor. The following year T. Grey reissued the comedy, and the title page reads: *The Court Lady; or, The Coquet's Surrender. A Comedy. Written by a Lady.* See *The Court Lady; or, The Coquet's Surrender*.

TEXT: Not in Readex Microprint. NUC: Copies of 1732 text at Iowa and Yale; copy of 1733 at LC (Longe 152: 1), Huntington, and Yale.

The Coquettes; or, The Gallant in the Closet, Lady Eleonora Cathcart Houston. This comedy, a translation from Thomas Corneille (*BD* 2: 128), was produced at the Canongate Theatre, Edinburgh, 10 February 1759. Although *BD* reports that the play was not printed, James Boswell is said to have provided a prologue, spoken by Mr. Parsons.

Cordelia, Anne Hughes This five-act tragedy was first printed in her *Moral Dramas*, published by William Lane, 1790. There is no known production. Other than a few names from *King Lear*, such as Oswald, Edgar, and Cordelia, the plot of this "happy-ending" tragedy bears little resemblance to Shakespeare's play. The poetry, however, has some affinities with Shakespeare's blank verse.

Upon the death of Ethelbert, the King of Mercia, Segbert assumes the throne. Edgar, the son of Ethelbert, is brought up with Segbert's daughter, Cordelia. In an uprising, Segbert must ask for the help of Osric, who then demands the hand of Cordelia. Unknown to her father, however, Cordelia has wed Edgar, on the recommendation of her now-deceased mother. When the play opens, Kenred tells Oswald that the Kentish forces want to overthrow the tyrannical king, and they are waiting near the castle for Edgar to lead them. When they explain the situation to Edgar, he says that his marriage had the proviso that he wouldn't harm the King. Edgar is, thus, torn between his duty to his deceased father's followers and his love for Cordelia, but he will lead the Kentish forces, if the King is spared. Meanwhile, the King has arranged for Osric to marry Cordelia, who tries to put the wedding off, but the King won't listen. Cordelia sees death as the only way out and asks the Steward to prepare a potion, and he does so. Upon taking his leave, Edgar asks for the vial of poison; she gives it to him, but explains that she had rather suffer death before dishonor. While Cordelia hopes she will not need poison, she must be prepared. Edgar relents and returns the poison. When Cordelia appears in the chapel, she says she has no hand to give, saying "I am the wife of Edgar." The King sends her to the tower and has a search mounted for the "traitorous" Edgar. Osric boils over with anger and cannot wait to go into battle. The battle is described by Matilda, Cordelia's woman, and it appears that Edgar's forces are lost. Cordelia takes poison, but Edgar soon rushes in victorious (having killed Osric) only to find a dying Cordelia. The Steward arrives and tells them that the potion he provided isn't fatal. Their joyous reunion is dampened somewhat because when the King was returning to the castle someone in the mob shot him with an arrow. Nevertheless, Cordelia and Edgar look forward to a happy reign.

Hughes's real strength in this play is a mentally agile title character: Cordelia plans her remarks carefully and argues well. Although she is unable to convince her father to wait a few days before she will be forced to wed Osric, she puts up a spirited argument. Cordelia doesn't merely accept Edgar's wanting to take away the poison vial, but she gives it to him and explains why she should have it; he accepts her argument and returns it. Before having to go to the chapel to face her father and Osric, she asks for mental strength to handle the ordeal. Hughes's poetical lines sometimes echo Shakespeare's, but her blank verse is quite readable and occasionally memorable.

TEXT: Readex Microprint.

Corinth, Charlotte de Humboldt. This five-act poetical drama first appeared in 1821, published with her poetry by Ellerton and Henderson. The volume was expanded and published in 1838 by Longman and others. The tragedy was not staged.

Before the play opens, Cypaelas has usurped the government of Corinth, but at his death he asks his son Periander to restore to Corinth its ancient liberty. Periander, however, has ambitions beyond his father's wishes. In the first scene, two representative citizens, Lysander and Perdiceas, speak of the "perjured prince" who has continued to expropriate the rights of the Corinthians. At the palace Melissa, Periander's wife, laments Periander's failure to follow his father's wishes, but the ruler's pride will not allow him to listen to her. He plans to lead his troops to Corfu and will leave Procles in charge. As the ruler of Epidauros, Procles intends to extend his own power during Periander's absence. His first design is to gain the affections of Melissa. When she will not yield to his advances, he has her imprisoned in a tower. Procles then tries to win the approval of the disgruntled citizens, led by Lysander. A letter is sent to Periander containing false information about Melissa and Procles. Although his general tells him he is abused, Periander must return and see for himself. The denouement occurs at Cypaelas's tomb, where Periander plans to take revenge on his wife. Disguised, Melissa tries to explain the false content of the letter. Procles arrives and draws his sword against Periander and the two fight; as Procles is about to deliver a coup de grâce, Melissa rushes in front of Periander and is stabbed. Periander learns Melissa has been chaste, and as she dies Melissa tells Periander to make restitution to Corinth. Procles renews the fight with Periander, who fatally wounds his adversary. Periander then stabs himself and with his dying breath declares Corinth free.

Melissa is clearly the moral conscience of Corinth, but Periander ignores her advice and Procles tries to take advantage of her. In the course of the play then, Melissa is verbally slandered and physically attacked, but she still tries to be the intermediary among quarrelsome men, all of whom seem to be ruled by excessive pride. Using the title of the city-state, de Humboldt emphasizes the importance of the democratic government to Corinth, but also she stresses the significance of freedom to its citizens.

TEXT: Readex Microprint of the 1838 printing.

CORNELYS, Margaret (1723–1797). A provincial female actor, Margaret performed on the Yorkshire with her husband John in the 1774–1775 season. They then spent several seasons at Norwich before going to Ireland. BDAA mentions that the "distracted situation" at the Crow-Street Theatre caused Margaret to move to Smock Alley, and it was at this Dublin venue that she acted in the one play she wrote for her own benefit. Her comedy, *The Deceptions*, was performed but once. There is no known publication. Other than one season in Edinburgh, she acted in Ireland, where her daughter made her first appearance at Crow Street 7 March 1791. The following two seasons, Margaret Cornelys (occasionally spelled "Cornellies") acted with her daughter on the Manchester, Liverpool, and Chester circuit. Margaret moved to CG for half a season in 1795, but returned to Dublin for one more season in 1795–96.

Margaret should not be confused with Teresa Imer Cornelys whose dates are exactly the same. Born in Vienna, Teresa was a singer who organized fashionable assemblies and entertainments in London during the 1760s and early 1770s but died in debt. [*BD*, BDAA]

Cortes, Lady Eglantine Wallace. This tragedy was never printed, and the date of its composition is unknown. *BD* suggests that it may be another title for *The Whim* (2: 131), but this seems unlikely.

Cortez; or, The Conquest of Mexico, translated by Elizabeth Helme. This lengthy drama (259 pp.), translated from the German of Joachim Heinrich Campe, was printed in 1799 by Samson Low; a year later there was a Dublin printing by P. Wogan and others, 1800. A new edition, "with the translator's last corrections and improvements," came out in London, published by C. Cradock, W. Joy, and P. Norbury in 1811. The alterations, however, are minor. Events, "related by a father to his children and designed for the instruction of youth," cause the children occasionally to react, but the father's narration is largely a monologue. No professional performance is known.

Organized in sixteen "Dialogues," the piece consists mainly of monologues, chronologically related by the father about the conquest of Mexico by Cortez. When the father describes the clash of the Christian Spanish culture with the Mexican's use of idols in their religion, the father insists on religious toleration: "Never should we permit ourselves the license of ridiculing, even in jest, what a single person among our associates considers as belonging to religion; for what can be more distressing to persons, truly devout, than to see those objects treated with contempt, and turned into ridicule, which they are accustomed to hold in the highest veneration" (134). He then goes on to talk about the human sacrifices of the Mexican "barbarians." Cortez, caught between the Spanish governor in Cuba and the Mexicans, becomes the hero of the father's tale, despite Cortez's several errors in judgment.

Helme's husband William was a schoolmaster in Brentford, where the book was later printed by P. Norbury. Her "dramatic" format involves the youthful readers in the history and geography (there's a map) as they learned about the subjugation of the new world. Although speech prefixes are used, the children speak little, merely reacting to the often grisly tale of Cortez's conquests, or asking for definitions from the omniscient father, who frequently supplies moral lessons for the children. Because of the monologue form, there is no character development, and the drama does not arise from the children's presence, but from the tale being told.

TEXT: Readex Microprint of the 1811 version.

Cottage Dialogues Among the Irish Peasantry, Mary Shackleton Leadbeater. Intended more for reading than for stage performance, *Cottage Dialogues* contains fifty-four, two-person conversations mostly between Rose and Nancy, although other dialogues involve Tim and Jem, Rose and her daughter Betty, Rose and her son Tommy. Published in London by J. Johnson in 1811, it was also printed by Samuel R. Fisher, Jr., in Philadelphia the same year.

Each dialogue has a subject, such as "Benevolence," "Washing," "Housekeeping," "Matrimony," "Manure," and "Cookery." The format has the lazy Nancy asking questions of the clever Rose, who then instructs her in a gentle and positive way. Typical are Nancy's opening gambits: "I wish I had taken your advice," or "I envy you." Rose might begin with "I hope you weren't affronted by the advice I gave you last time." Later, we have dialogues on agriculture methods between Tim and Jem. Once the characters are established, a story begins to emerge. Rose is going to marry Jemmy Whelan, and she hears that Nancy is interested in Tim Cassidy. Nancy says she has married Tim secretly. After the marriages, both couples have children, but when Nancy comes to visit Rose, she always finds the house clean, whereas hers is not. Rose generously shares her recipes and other household hints. Later, Rose goes to help Nancy when Tim is sick. After Tim dies, Nancy, now a widow with six children, begins to drink. In the last dialogue, Nancy is dead, and Rose tells her daughter Betty that Nancy's fault was idleness.

More a novel than the usual drama, *Cottage Dialogues* provides common sense views about everyday living. Traditional lessons emerge: women need to do their household duties well, to stay at home with the family, and to practice domestic frugality. The text is dotted with proverbs that can be easily remembered. Maria Edgeworth, who provided the notes and introduction, says that the story "embraces a wide extent of duties, and for every stage of life from cradle to grave, and inculcates excellent principles, in language happily suited to the people for whose benefit it is designed." Since the notes explain "Hibernian idiom and local customs," the book may anticipate an audience beyond the Irish Peasantry. Clara L. Gandy discusses the various subjects that Leadbeater takes up in the *Dialogues* (*Women and Literature* 3 [1975]: 28–38).

TEXT: Readex Microprint prints Fisher's American edition.

The Cottagers, Anna Ross, later Brunton. Written by Ross at the age of fifteen, this two-act comic opera (featuring sixteen songs) was first printed for the author in 1788 by subscription. The play debuted at the Crow-Street Theatre, Dublin, on 19 May 1789.

Sir Toby Harwin has made a second marriage to the widow Smirk, and they await the arrival of Sir Toby's son, Captain Charles Harwin. Sir Toby also has a daughter, Charlotte, from his first marriage, and the new Lady Harwin, a son, Jonas Smirk, from her previous marriage. Jonas may be drawn from Goldsmith's Tony Lumpkin, though Jonas prefers fashion to horses. Upon meeting his new half-brother, Charles cannot help laughing at Jonas's ridiculous attire. Charlotte plots with her brother to make Jonas think he has a rival for Lotharia, the daughter of Welford, Sir Toby's farm-agent; however, when he goes to visit Welford, Charles is instantly smitten with Lotharia. Upon learning that her brother is enamored with Lotharia, Charlotte plans to disguise herself as a Scottish Captain to act as his rival. She succeeds in provoking Charles into a fight, which Sir Toby stops; he then intercedes to get Lotharia to marry his son. Lady Harwin, however, hoped that Charles would marry the wealthy Lady Fly-away, and she's distraught to find the bridegroom is penniless. No matter for that, Charles says, Lotharia is rich in virtue. The play concludes with Welford announcing that a message has just reached him saying that Lord Donmore has died leaving him in possession of the title and fortune his father "had so cruelly deprived" him of. "Amazing Providence!" exclaims Lotharia, who will now marry Charles as a social equal. The marriage of the good-hearted servants, Reuben and Peggy, will also take place. The snobbish Lady Harwin is mollified by the newfound status of Welford, as well as a possible opportunity that her son, Jonas, may enter fashionable life by marrying Lady Fly-away.

This comic opera is designed as a showcase for Charlotte (probably played by the author), who also acts two other characters in disguise—the Scottish Captain and Reuben's grandmother. Thematically, Lady Harwin's attitude toward the "rustics" is shown to be condescending and wrong-headed, because she only judges people by their wealth and not their virtue. Jonas's fashionable whims (no doubt learned from his mother) are merely ridiculous. Sir Toby is the stout, well-meaning country squire, and Welford gets his just deserts at last. With the songs and bustle, this is an amusing piece, especially considering that it was written by a precocious fifteen-year-old.

TEXT: Readex Microprint.

Count Basil, Joanna Baillie. This five-act tragedy appeared in the first of her *Series of Plays: [on] the Stronger Passions*, published by T. Cadell, Jr., and W. Davies, 1798. It was published as *Basil* in Philadelphia in 1811 by M. Carey. Although Margaret Carhart says that *Basil* was given a professional performance, she doesn't cite the specific date or venue.

Set in Mantua during the sixteenth century when Charles V, the Holy Roman Emperor, defeats Francis I at the Battle of Pavia, the play opens on the citizens of Mantua, anticipating a procession. Count Basil, a general traveling to join the Emperor, arrives with his train in Mantua, where he is delayed when introduced to Victoria, the daughter of the Duke of Mantua, who has been scheming against Charles. She unwittingly assists her father by pleading with Basil to remain in Mantua for several days. To his friend and kinsman, Count Rosinberg, Basil reveals that he had been attracted to Victoria earlier, not knowing who she was. When the Count praises an old soldier who has failed to receive sufficient tribute, the Duke plots to create mutiny within Basil's troops by spreading the rumor that the Count will place them in danger for his own selfish gain. Basil, who has spent the night moping outside Victoria's window, returns to his lodging to discover his men are ready to march with Frederick, their chosen leader. After Basil restores his troops' loyalty, Rosinberg cautions Basil against remaining in Mantua, relaying a warning that he has received from Countess Albini, Victoria's friend and governess. In spite of Rosinberg's exhortation about duty, Basil loses all resolve to leave for Pavia when suddenly summoned by Victoria. Returning from a hunt with Victoria, Basil receives a message that the Imperial Army under Piscaro has beaten the enemy and taken the French King prisoner. The old soldier tries to keep him from committing suicide, but Basil goes into a cave and shoots himself, disgraced by his negligence. Since the Duke of Mantua's scheming against the Emperor has been revealed, Rosinberg compares the Duke's fall with Basil's: "But when a great mind falls, The noble nature of man's gen'rous heart Doth bear him up against the shame of ruin; . . . And they who but admir'd him in his height, His alter'd state lament, and love him fall'n" (191–92).

Much of the play focuses on the power that Victoria exerts over Basil when she asks him to remain with her despite the pending battle. Although her request at first seems frivolous, she later explains to her governess that "there is something strange in this man's love I never met before, and I must test it" (165), as underscored by her use of a mask and her verbal banter. At times, Victoria tries to impose her world—dominated by women and containing idyllic pastoral scenes—upon Basil's commitment as a soldier and her father's political deceit. Nevertheless, Victoria's efforts fail, and her attempt to control Basil is condemned by both Countess Albini and Count Rosinberg: "a short liv'd tyranny that ends at last in hatred and contempt" (163). At the end of the play, Victoria is largely held responsible for Basil's death, and her final words emphasize that her life will become a punishment for her willfulness: "I'll spend my wretched days in humble pray'r for his departed spirit, cold as his grave shall be my earthy bed, as dark my cheerless cell" (190).

TEXT: Readex Microprint of 1812 edition.

FACSIMILE EDITIONS: *Romantic Context: Poetry* reprints the 1798 edition (London: T. Cadell, Jr., and W. Davies). Compiled, with an introduction, by D. H. Reiman (NY: Garland, 1977). *Revolution and Romanticism, 1789–1834* also reprints the 1798 edition, introduced by Jonathan Wordsworth (Rutherford, NJ: Woodstock, 1990).

The Count of Burgundy, translated by Anne Plumptre. Published by R. Phillips in 1798, this translation of Kotzebue's *Der Graf von Burgund* was later adapted by the actor Alexander Pope. His four-act version of Kotzebue, via Plumptre, was produced only once, on the occasion of Pope's benefit night at CG on 12 April 1799. This version was never published and remains in manuscript (Larpent 1249). Genest, however, provides a plot summary of the staged version (7: 435–36), and a plot synopsis also was printed in the *Universal Magazine* (April 1799): 273 (*LS* 5: 2160).

In Plumptre's translation, the play opens at the foot of the Alps in Switzerland during the time of the crusades, where the eighteen-year-old Henry, supposed son of Peter the hermit, is singing narrative songs of battle. Neither is what he appears: Peter is in reality John von Bonstetten, a knight of Burgundy, who rescued Henry after the murder of his father, the Count of Burgundy. Henry has, however, been raised in ignorance of his real heritage until the appearance of Bruno, a pilgrim but also Peter's former servant. In this poor, rural location, Henry has fallen in love with Elizabeth, fifteen-year-old daughter of a down-at-the-heels noble, the Chevalier Cuno von Hallwyl. While Henry and Elizabeth confess their love to one another, Bruno tells Peter that the usurper of Burgundy is dead, and it is time for their return to Arles. Even though Henry does not want to leave Elizabeth, Peter tells him he must go to his real mother who is now living in a convent. Henry swears to love Elizabeth, and she swears not to marry Chevalier Walter von Blonay. The scene shifts to Arles, where the citizens allow Peter to tell how Henry was saved. Henry meets his mother and, on the advice of Peter, asks her blessing to marry Elizabeth. The head of the embassy to Chevalier Hallwyl will be the governor of Arles, Hugo von Werdenberg. Meanwhile, Walter von Blonay has returned and asked for Elizabeth's hand which she cannot give. Her father, however, urges her to marry, but when she refuses he breaks down and weeps. She can do nothing but accept. Just then Hugo's embassy arrives with Henry disguised as a page. He says Henry the Count of Burgundy "requires" Elizabeth as his wife and asks her to hear the suit. Since she doesn't know "her" Henry is now the Count, she says she will keep her word to Walter. When Henry makes himself known, however, she changes her mind, and Walter graciously steps aside. After Cuno blesses them, all shout "Long live the young Count of Burgundy."

The fairy-tale aspects of this story do not always make for effective theatre. Even though Henry and Elizabeth are in love from the beginning, he could not marry her from his humble station. His becoming the Count of Burgundy ranks him far above Elizabeth, but he faithfully returns for her. Walter's suit never stood a chance with Elizabeth; only the emotional blackmail by her father got her to accept Walter, who doesn't rejoice in his good fortune. Elizabeth is mostly a pawn in a high-stakes medieval game of marriage for money and property. That Henry returns for her, against the advice of his elders, is a credit to his commitment and constancy.

MANUSCRIPT of the actor Alexander Pope's version: Larpent 1249.

TEXT: Readex Microprint.

The Counterfeit Bridegroom; or, The Defeated Widow, attributed both to Aphra Behn and Thomas Betterton. Arthur Gewirtz makes a good case for Behn's authorship in his *Restoration Adaptations of Early 17th Century Comedies* (160–63). The five-act comedy was produced at DG in September 1677, though the first performance is likely to have been in the late spring or early summer of 1677 because of the references in both prologue and epilogue to a "vacation" play. An adaptation of Middleton's *No Wit Like a Woman's*, it was printed in 1677 for Langley Curtiss.

Peter Santloe, son of Sir Oliver and Lady Santloe, has married an Englishwoman working in Antwerp where he was searching for his sister and mother. Peter intends to pass Clarina off as his sister, who will be married to his friend Sanders in a mock marriage. When questioned by the recently returned mother, however, Clarina turns out to be the sister who was raised with Peter in his early years. In a second plot, Mr. and Mrs. Hadland try to regain their Kentish properties by an elaborate trick on the Widow of the husband who cheated them. Mrs. Hadland dresses as a man, wins, and marries the Widow, but she puts her brother, Noble, in her place after the wedding, then catches the two of them together. The Widow promises anything so that she won't be exposed and accepts marriage to Noble, who in fact loves her. Once this plot is cleared up, the Widow tells the Santloes that her sister Morley—their old nurse—had exchanged her own daughter Eugenia with Clarina. This revelation allows Sanders to wed Eugenia, and Peter and Clarina to continue as husband and wife.

While some of the minor action of both plots is the shedding of unwanted suitors, the main action focuses on the gaining of proper spouses. Both Mrs. Hadland and her husband use disguises to set up Mrs. Hadland's brother Noble with the Widow, and in doing so they regain their property (possibly lost during the interregnum). While Mrs. Hadland is the title character, Peter is also a possible "counterfeit bridegroom" in marrying Clarina who may be his sister. Unlike Middleton's play where incest causes Bevil much anguish, the possibility of incest causes Peter almost no problem. Naming a character Sir Oliver (recalling Cromwell) in 1677 means he is certainly the butt of many jokes: he is mean-spirited by his willingness to marry his daughter to a (supposed) eunuch to save on expenses of childbirth, and he recounts in a roistering scene events of his early life, where he revels in carousing, chasing maids, and debauching laundresses.

TEXTS: Wing M1983. EEB Reel 642: 23. Readex Microprint.

The Country Coquet; or, Miss in her Breeches, "By a Young Lady." This ballad opera was published on 18 Nov 1755 by an anonymous young woman (*LS* 4: 509). J. Major printed and sold the text, which was advertised "as it may be acted at Drury Lane." There is, however, no known production.

TEXT: Not in Readex Microprint. NUC records copies at Harvard, U of Illinois, Folger Shakespeare Library, and the Huntington.

The Country Inn, Joanna Baillie. First published in her *Miscellaneous Plays* by Longman et al. in 1804, this five-act comedy was not performed.

The play focuses on three couples: Sir John Hazelwood and Miss Martin; Sir John's nephew, Worshipton, and Miss Hannah Clodpate; and the poet Amaryllis and Dolly, a maid. Worshipton is a fashionable gentleman who wishes to marry a wealthy woman in order to support "a groom and valet, a pair of riding horses, and a curricle" (161). When Miss Hannah Clodpate, whom he believes to be Sir Rowland's heiress, arrives at the country inn where he has been staying, Worshipton pursues her until she agrees to elope. After his cocky announcement that they have been secretly wed, Worshipton discovers that his new wife—unattractive, awkward, and slow-witted—has only a small income. In contrast, Amaryllis chooses the inn's maid, Dolly, responding to the "artless charms of a village maid" (275), and discovers that she has just inherited a fortune from her uncle. A figure of moral rectitude and unmarried at forty, Sir John thinks "there is not a woman now existing . . . that would suit me" (161). Almost instantly, however, he becomes attracted to Miss Martin, Hannah's cousin and Lady Goodbody's niece and ward. Annoyed at Lady Goodbody's public efforts to find a wealthy husband for her, Miss Martin treats Sir John curtly, although he overhears her praising him in private. Therefore, he continues to court her until she quietly accepts his marriage proposal, to Lady Goodbody's delight.

With the exception of Lady Goodbody, the women in the play are relatively unimportant. Both Hannah and Dolly are comic stereotypes, and Miss Martin demonstrates character only in her initial rejection of Sir John's suit, which we learn is motivated by her fear that she's the object of his ridicule. The final act is dominated by a comparison of the major male characters and the relative merits of each of their marriages. In *The Country Inn*, humor is generated by misunderstandings that result from class differences, by the foolishness of Worshipton's fashionable behavior, by a servant's obsession with similes, and by very occasional lapses in Sir John's rectitude.

TEXT: Readex Microprint of *Miscellaneous Plays* (2nd ed., 1805): 137–278.

FACSIMILE EDITION: *Romantic Context: Poetry* reprints *Miscellaneous Plays* (London: Longman, Hurst, Rees, and Orme, 1804). Compiled, with an introduction, by D. H. Reiman (NY: Garland, 1977).

The Court Lady; or, The Coquet's Surrender, "by a lady." This five-act comedy by an anonymous woman had only one performance —15 May 1732—at the Haymarket Theatre. *The Coquet's Surrender; or, The Humorous Punster* played for the benefit of the author, now unknown. E. Raynor published the comedy under that title in 1732, but T. Grey reissued the comedy, the title page now reading *The Court Lady; or, The Coquet's Surrender. A Comedy. Written by a Lady.* The running titles remained as they had been in the previous printing—*The Coquet's Surrender; or, The Humorous Punster* (Burling). Evidently a new title page has been substituted, but the old sheets of the play have been used. Both printings are fifty-six pages.

TEXT: Not in Readex Microprint. NUC: Copies of the 1733 printing at LC (Longe Collection 152: 1), Huntington, and Yale.

The Court Legacy, attributed to Delariviere Manley. Printed in 1733 by J. Dormer as being by the author of *The New Atalantis*, this ballad opera was published but not acted. The dedication to "Madam Pultney," wife of William Pulteney, leader of the opposition to Walpole, is signed by Atalia.

There are several plot lines in this play which are underscored by popular ballads, similar to those in *The Beggar's Opera* of 1728. The first has to do with an affair between Lady Fitzhuma and Lord Amorous; another treats Huncamunca's various pending marriages, and in the end she finally marries to Prince Easy; a third plot traces Sir Sidrophel's selling his cure-all medicine; a fourth involves Lord Command's wooing of Miss Question; and a fifth examines Mr. and Mrs. Catchem's paternity suit against Dr. Gregorius. Several scenes in taverns contrast the public views of the government and royalty.

While both Cotton and Pearson comment briefly on this play, neither believes Manley is the author. Cotton notes that it was not mentioned in her will and that the publisher wanted to cash in on the popularity of Manley's *Atalantis* (102). Pearson argues that neither the ballad opera form nor the political content was current before Manley's death in 1724. The play, she says, "deals specifically with events in 1733, especially Walpole's Excise Act [which failed]. It is interesting to note, though, that even nine years after Manley's death the name of her most famous novel was still called upon to help sell another work of political satire" (282).

TEXTS: Readex Microprint. TEC Reel 475: 6.

FACSIMILE EDITION: *Court Intrigue and Scandal II*. Ballad Opera series, vol. 19. Comp. Walter H. Rabsamen (NY: Garland, 1974).

he has fallen in love with Louisa Fairfax, whom he introduces to Lady Diana as his niece. Lady Diana is in love with Cleveland, whom she introduces to the General as her nephew. After much anguish on both sides, the General and Lady Diana agree to tear up their contracts, only to find that Cleveland is to be married to Louisa with the help of Sir Charles Cullender. In the subplot, Captain Herbert had fallen in love with Sophia, the supposed daughter of Farmer Hobson, five years before the play opens. He has gone to India, and during his absence, Sophia Hobson has turned out to be Maria Sydney, the daughter of a gentleman. When Herbert returns from India, he wishes to marry Sophia and sends Corporal Smack in quest of her. But Smack cannot find Sophia Hobson. In the meantime, Herbert falls in love with Maria Sydney. In order to test Herbert, Lady Diana hires the supposed Sophia Hobson for her woman. When Herbert offers his hand to Sophia, she tells him that she is really Maria Sydney and accepts his offer. The General and Lady Diana are invited to both weddings, but do not tie the knot themselves, the General concluding the play by merely asserting that one of life's greatest pleasures is to partake in the joys of others.

Griffiths takes the main plot of her play from Destouches's *L'Amour usé [The old love]*, and she added a subplot, quite "improbable" according to Genest, but no more so than many others of the time. All the names are changed, and a few references to India are added to provide local color. The author took lines from one character in her source and gave them to another; she shortened some scenes and added others, all the while remaining at times so faithful to the original as to translate word for word. But more important, she transformed the ending. In Destouches, the older characters, prompted by Daimon (Cullender's counterpart), forget their infatuation for their "niece" and "nephew," and accept each other in marriage. *Cross Partners* is no match to the French original, which sparkles with wit and quick dialogues. The wonderful scene between the old lovers—each trying to have the other break the marriage promise in order to be free to marry a young partner—has been drastically reduced, and the lively, shrewd servants, Lisette and Frontin, have been entirely eliminated. To use Genest's phrase, *Cross Partners* is indeed "a moderate play."

Getting the right parties married is, of course, the stuff of comedy. In *Cross Partners*, additional humor arises from neither Lady Diana nor the General wanting to honor the longstanding contract. In the other plot, Maria wants to test the depth of Captain Herbert's love, and she does so by challenging his trust and sincerity—both as Miss Sydney and Sophia Hobson. She wants to show Captain Herbert the errors of his inconstancy before she'll agree to marry him. The author makes clear that while gratitude for assistance is necessary, gratitude must not be confused with love. Cleveland is grateful for Lady Diana's financial support of his family, but Maria warns him: "love does not always thrive best in the deep soil of gratitude." Louisa is almost led into a marriage with a man forty years her senior because she is grateful for his aiding her aunt. Sir Charles Cullender seems an harmlessly intrusive character, cheerfully butting in where he is not wanted, and telling tales he is not supposed to repeat. Yet in his generosity to Louisa and Cleveland, he acts the fairy godfather, staking them to £1000 and establishing a firm financial basis for their marriage: all this because he likes to see good people happy.

MANUSCRIPT: Larpent 955.

TEXT: Not in Readex Microprint. We read the play at the Newberry Library, Chicago, IL.

The Cruel Gift; or, The Royal Resentment, Susanna Centlivre. This five-act, "happy-ending" tragedy debuted at DL on 17 December 1716 and was acted six times. One other performance was by royal command on 3 May 1717 to benefit the author, but there was no revival. E. Curl and A. Bettesworth published the play in 1717. The source of Centlivre's only blank-verse tragedy may be found in Dryden's *Fables* (1700), where he poetically rendered Boccaccio's tale of Tancred and Ghismonda. F. P. Lock points out three alterations from Centlivre's source: 1) the happy ending, 2) the added secret of Lorenzo's birth, and 3) the entirely new subplot involving Learchus and

Antimora (105). However, the theatrical tradition comes from earlier heroic drama where characters are forced to choose between love and duty. That Nicholas Rowe wrote the epilogue suggests also the play's connections with his "she" tragedies, which focus on the domestic distresses of the heroines.

Set in Verona, the play treats two pairs of lovers: the King's daughter, Leonora, has secretly married the Lombard General, Lorenzo; and Learchus loves Antimora, Lorenzo's sister. Despite Lorenzo's clandestine marriage, he wants his sister to marry his aide and friend, Cardono, and Learchus's father, Antenor, hopes that Learchus will marry Leonora. To further his political ambitions, Antenor tells the King he has heard Leonora has a secret lover, and the two spy on them and discover the truth. The King is furious and vows to put Lorenzo to death; then he wants Lorenzo's heart delivered to Leonora. Antimora asks Learchus to free her brother: when he will not, she says she will wed Cardono if he can free Lorenzo. Cardono almost succeeds, but is wounded in the attempt to free Lorenzo and thrown into prison. Meanwhile, the citizens revolt, for they love Lorenzo. Learchus appears to carry out the King's wishes: when he delivers the cruel gift (supposedly Lorenzo's heart) to Leonora, she goes mad. After the King has sent Antenor to quell the mob, he finds his distracted daughter and regrets he has ordered Lorenzo's death. Learchus then brings in Lorenzo alive, saying it was the only duty he failed to perform. The King is told by a holy hermit, who married Lorenzo and Leonora, that he was formerly the Duke of Milan, but driven out of office twenty years earlier. He went in holy orders and had his son raised by Alcanor: this son is Lorenzo of a noble line. The King accepts the marriage of Leonora and Lorenzo, and he pronounces Lorenzo his heir apparent. As the play ends, Learchus is given Antimora, and the King hears that since Lorenzo lives the mob has laid down their arms; only Antenor was slain in the disorder.

Cotton believes the tragedy "inane, and the blank verse flat" (144); however, the play surpasses this estimate in several ways. The forcefulness of Leonora's character (played by Anne Oldfield) gives the tragedy backbone: Leonora's refusal of the Tuscan prince, for instance, shows her mastery of language. The main conflict pitting absolute rule and obedience against individual freedom and self-determination causes Frushell to read the play in political—though not allegorical—terms of the Whigs and Tories at the beginning of George the First's reign (*RECTR* n.s. 7.2 [Winter, 1992]: 1–17). While sudden changes by a few characters appear merely to round out the plot, the principles of the main figures in the drama are consistent with the values they espouse. Moreover, the political ambitions of the King and Antenor contrast sharply with the domestic arrangements desired by Leonora and Antimora. At the conclusion, the King somewhat unconvincingly repents and Antenor becomes a victim of his own ambition, whereas Leonora and Antimora gain their ends.

TEXTS: Readex Microprint. TEC Reel 728: 31.
FACSIMILE EDITION: E-CED, with introduction by R. C. Frushell (NY: Garland, 1982).

The Cry, Sarah Fielding and Jane Collier. This "new dramatic fable" examines the place of women and the problems they face in their eighteenth-century world. The dialogues take place in more than forty scenes, involving a number of women and some men. It was published in three volumes by R. and J. Dodsley in 1754. In her Introduction to the facsimile edition, M. A. Schofield does not discusss the probable dual authorship.

In this novel done in dramatic form, the authors intend to entertain and to instruct. Borrowed from the stage are characters, motives of actions, and inward turns of mind. "The nearer things are brought to dramatic representation, the more [readers] are acquainted with the personages and interested in the events of the story" (1: 17). The Prologue establishes the principal speaker Portia, who renders judgment, and the moderator Una (taken from Spenser's *The Fairie Queen*) who maintains truth. Their allegorical assembly, called The Cry, is a cross section of men and women who act as a chorus; they listen to and remark on the events described. More often than not, The Cry adopts traditional male-oriented views, and members feel free to interrupt or to challenge the judgments of the speakers. The story is more important for the dilemmas women face than for its narrative. Most events are related by Portia, who recounts her connections with the Nicanor family, but she tells illustrative tales (not about the Nicanor family) within the larger narrative to engage The Cry and make them examine their inherited opinions. Such differing points of view suggest many options for the reader.

In the Nicanor family the father is a widower whose large fortune has dwindled; he is now dependent on his oldest son, Oliver. The younger twin children are Ferdinand and Cordelia, now grown. Portia makes friends with Cordelia, and here The Cry interrupts, saying Portia should have been more suspicious and reserved. In trying to convince The Cry that her actions were sensible, Portia says she would rather be deceived than to have a limited friendship concocted by reserve. To illustrate her point, Portia tells two stories that support her genuine friendship for Cordelia. In the next scenes, the assembly hears that Portia has fallen for Ferdinand. The Cry is outraged, and it abuses Portia and treats her rudely. Again, Portia digresses from her own story by telling illustrative tales, until Una stops the proceedings for that day.

After Part the Second renders in nondramatic form the history of Nicanor and his family up to the time Portia met them, Part the Third begins with Portia's story of Melantha, who introduced her to the Nicanor family, and who falls in love with the oldest son, Oliver. Although The Cry disapproves of Melantha's involvement, Portia tells how her friend "looked on a lover as one of the necessaries of life" (2: 135). Then Portia assumes the role of Melantha to describe why she shifted her attentions from Oliver to his younger brother, Ferdinand, whom Portia loves. The Cry accuses Portia of being jealous of Melantha and charges her with vanity, but Portia silences The Cry by showing how each individual possesses a perverseness of heart. Melantha wishes to marry Ferdinand merely to triumph over her rival, Portia. To vex Melantha, Oliver tells her of Ferdinand's frolics with women in the country. By now many of The Cry have fallen asleep, and Una dismisses the assembly for the day.

In Part the Fourth, Cylinda becomes the principal narrator. After the death of his wife, Cylinda's father decides to educate her as if she had been a boy: she learns Latin and Greek, reads many philosophical works, and discusses religion with her father. She studies Shaftesbury, but after a discussion with a friend of her father, she sees the fallacy of the *Characteristics*. The death of her father causes Cylinda to throw herself into reading Plato. When she meets Millamour, however, she becomes an Epicurean; he offers to marry her, but she turns him down. Moving to London, Cylinda rejects the high life she finds there. When she meets Nicanor (the father in Portia's tale), who expresses a passion for her, she doesn't wish to marry him, but they live together for five years. Cylinda's agent having absconded with her fortune, Nicanor says he will get the money to free her. Meanwhile, Cylinda tells her friend, Artemisia, of her situation, and Artemisia invites her to Yorkshire to avoid arrest. When Cylinda cannot find Nicanor, she accepts the visit to Yorkshire. Artemisia asks her friend Eustace in London to see what he can find out about Cylinda's finances, and he reports that the agent has been caught and forced to refund all the money. When Eustace comes to Yorkshire, Cylinda falls in love with him, but finds he is married. After Eustace returns to London, Cylinda follows him there only to find out that he has gone abroad with his family to avoid further complications. Considering suicide, Cylinda receives a letter from Eustace, explaining that he cannot leave his wife. Although he cares for her, Eustace urges Cylinda to spend her life trusting God. Una closes the meeting.

In Part the Fifth, Portia continues her story. When Ferdinand plans to leave England, Oliver tries to stop him, but he goes any way. Portia and Melantha react differently on Ferdinand's departure, but Melantha and Oliver blame each other. Oliver falls sick, and Melantha nurses him. When Ferdinand returns, he asks Portia to marry him, but she refuses and retires into the country. Ferdinand, however, finds her and continues his courtship. When Portia flees to Dover, she falls ill, and her servant informs Cordelia that Portia has died. But Portia recovers and writes to Cordelia. Then with Portia's consent, Ferdinand visits and tells his own story with which Portia's part is concluded. Una calls an end to the assembly.

An Epilogue wraps up the loose ends: Portia marries Ferdinand, but their happy marriage is a marked contrast to the troubled marriage of Melantha and Oliver. Cordelia never marries, but lives with Ferdinand and Portia. Cylinda also remains single and lives the rest of her life free from anxious cares. At her death, Ferdinand and Portia lament her passing. Fielding and Collier lose interest in The Cry during the later part of the narrative, and the choral function of The Cry falls away.

FACSIMILE EDITION: With an introduction by M. A. Schofield (Delmar, NY: Scholars' Facsimiles, 1986).

CULLUM, Mrs. (fl.1775). There is no biographical information about Mrs. Cullum, who wrote one drama, entitled *Charlotte; or, One Thousand Seven Hundred and Seventy Three*. Cullum had her play printed by Baker and Galabin in 1775, but there is no known production. [*BD*]

CUTHBERTSON, Miss C[atherine?] (fl. 1793). Cuthbertson wrote only one play, a comedy entitled *Anna*. DL produced the five-act play at the King's Theatre on 25 February 1793. Cuthbertson withdrew the play to "amend" several passages, but the piece was never repeated, nor was it ever printed. The manuscript remains in the Larpent Collection (969). A Catherine Cuthbertson also published a number of novels (FCLE: seven) early in the nineteenth century, from *Romance of the Pyrenees* (1802) to *Sir Ethelbert* (1830). We are not certain that the later novelist wrote the earlier play. [FCLE]

The Cyclopedia, Mrs. Hoper. This three-act farce was performed gratis after a concert. Advertised for one night only, the performance took place at the Haymarket Theatre on 31 March 1748. It was, in fact, later repeated as a lunchtime play and concert on 13 April 1748. There is no evidence of publication.

The Czar of Muscovy, Mary Pix. This five-act tragedy was produced at LIF in March of 1701 and published the same year by B. B. Lintott. Pix's only tragedy in prose, the play was not revived.

Perhaps the visit of Peter the Great to England in 1697 created an interest in Russia and things Russian in the British Isles. By using Moscow as the setting for her drama, Mary Pix may have hoped that this interest would insure the success of her piece. Although her "happy-ending tragedy" didn't cause a great stir on the English stage, it remains one of the few English plays to be set in Russia. The events, however, could take place in any country ruled by a usurping tyrant. Demetrius is said to be the son of the late Czar, but in fact Zueski, the High Steward of Moscow, knows that the real Demetrius was killed in the war. Nevertheless, the false Demetrius is supported by Manzeck, whose daughter Marina (played by Elizabeth Bowman) has just married the false Demetrius when the play opens. In a show of liberality, this Demetrius is willing to grant suits, and Zueski asks clemency for Zarrianna (played by Elizabeth Barry), daughter of Boris, who was killed trying to depose the late czar. Demetrius pardons Zarrianna and instantly lusts after her; so politics give way to passion. Marina, of course, is angry over this turn of events, and she also misses the man she was to marry, Alexander, who was away in the diplomatic service. Zarrianna holds off Demetrius, and Alexander comes disguised as a pilgrim to save Marina. When the information that Demetrius is a usurper gets abroad, the Russian nobles gather their forces to depose him, and in the fifth act Zueski kills him in a sword fight. Manzeck unites Marina and Alexander, and Zueski is crowned the new Czar with the undefiled Zarrianna as his consort.

While both principal women in the play appear at first to be pawns, they show strength and courage. Zarrianna repels Demetrius when he threatens to rape her, and Marina brings Alexander into the offensive against the false ruler. Moreover, Marina and Zarrianna join together to become strong friends rather than rivals. Hume labels the play "a heroic melodrama," whereas Cotton finds it derivative of Fletcher in language and content. While the play could not be called a feminist drama, it does present two strong women who handle demanding situations skillfully under difficult circumstances.

TEXT: Not in Readex Microprint.

FACSIMILE EDITION: E-CED, with introduction by Edna L. Steeves (NY: Garland, 1982).

-D-

DACRE, Barbarina Ogle Wilmot, Lady (1768–1854). The author of *Ina*, which was produced at DL only once—22 April 1815—Dacre also wrote other dramas published in her *Works*, 2 vols., by John Murray in 1821. A children's drama, *Frogs and Bulls*, was written for a private performance in 1834 and played at a fair for the Ophthalmic Hospital in 1838.

The youngest daughter of Hester (Thomas) and Admiral Sir Chaloner Ogle, she was privately educated, learning Italian, and at twenty-one married to an officer of the Guards, Valentine Wilmot. Although they had one daughter, Arabella (b. 1796), they separated, and she spent her time educating her daughter and writing plays. Byron saw the production of *Ida* at DL in 1815, and, perhaps, after that incident he declined to write for production on the English stage. About the episode, Byron commented, "The audience got upon their legs—the damnable pit—and roared, and groaned, and hissed, and whistled. . . . The curtain fell upon unheard actors, and the announcement attempted by Kean for Monday was equally ineffectual" (Byron, *Letters and Journals*, 3: 196). Two years after her marriage in 1819 to Thomas Brand, Baron Dacre, she published her *Dramas, Translations, and Occasional Poems*, which included *Ida*. Dacre's translations from Petrarch and her *Translations from the Italian* (1836) were favorably received. In the latter part of her life, Dacre assisted her daughter by revising and editing two collections of stories, but Arabella's death in 1839 and her increasing deafness made Dacre's last years difficult. [FCLE]

D'AGUILAR, Rose, later Lawrence (fl. 1799–1836). A translator and adaptor of Goethe's *Gotz von Berlichingen*, D'Aguilar published *Gortz* [sic] *of Berlingen* anonymously in 1799. There is no known stage production. In 1802, she translated Gessner's *Works*, and provided a critical introduction. Besides preparing two anthologies of poetry for children, Lawrence (using her married name) published a volume of poetry, including translations from German, Spanish and Italian. She also wrote the memoirs of Felicia Hemans, a long-time friend, in 1836. [FCLE]

The Dame School Holiday, Maria Edgeworth. This three-act play was included in Edgeworth's *Little Plays for Children* published by R. Hunter and Baldwin, Cradock, and Joy in 1827 (a new edition came out in 1834); publication in the United States occurred in 1827 at both Boston and Philadelphia. There is no record of a public performance.

Three children plan a birthday celebration for their father, a clergyman: Cherry and Philip prepare nosegays, and their older brother Edwin has written a play for the occasion. Felix Babberly, recently returned to the village from London, comes by and makes light of the younger children's efforts. When Felix meets Edwin, he disdains his efforts as a playwright because he has been to the London theatre. Nevertheless, the rehearsal goes on under the eye of the school mistress, Dame Deborah. Felix calls at the rehearsal and suggests they give it up. When asked about plays, Felix can't talk about them in any detail, and it is clear that Edwin knows more about drama than the citified Felix, who plans to sabotage the play. Miss Babberly calls on Dame Deborah and condescendingly offers her a shawl that she has purchased in London, but it is refused. Miss Babberly then asks for the use of the benches, but Dame Deborah refuses. Miss Babberly then tries to bribe the school children, first, with the offer of artificial flowers (the children refuse because the flowers have no scent); second, with the offer of an impromptu play and sweetmeats afterwards (this offer is also declined). As Miss Babberly is leaving, she knocks Dame

Deborah's crutch away causing the school mistress to fall. The children wrap the shawl around Miss Babberly to prevent more mischief. Dame Deborah tells the children to release Miss Babberly, who goes off muttering threats. While Cherry, Philip, and Edwin are decorating, Willy Grant (the lead in the "little play") comes to tell Edwin that Felix has pushed him in the river and asks if he will postpone the play. Edwin agrees, telling Willy to forgive Felix, and he reports to the Babberlys that even though the play is canceled they'll need the benches for the dance. Miss Babberly plans to have her father send the bailiff to seize the benches. After the children's first dance, Miss Babberly, Felix, and the bailiff arrive to confiscate the benches. Edwin discovers the debt is seven guineas; he produces four and the fiddler donates three. The Babberlys threaten revenge another time and leave. As the dance continues, Edwin says it's a pity that Felix can't be happy.

The villains in this piece are the immature Babberly children of the rich and powerful landholder; they, of course, should know better, but Edgeworth makes her point by showing that they have been spoiled by their parents and can't always have what they want. Dramatically, the Babberlys are given little motivation in wanting to prevent the school children's innocent entertainment. Still, Edwin takes Christian pity on their spoil-sport attitude, and Dame Deborah counsels kindness in the face of adversity.

TEXT: Not in Readex Microprint. We read the play in the King Collection at the Miami (Ohio) Library.

Daniel, Hannah More. This blank-verse play in seven parts, based on the biblical text taken from the Book of Daniel (Chapter 6), was published in More's *Sacred Dramas* by T. Cadell in 1782. Not intended for the professional stage, the play was meant for the improvement of young ladies. Nevertheless, Tate Wilkinson mentions in *The Wandering Patentee* that two of Hannah More's dramas were altered and presented at Doncaster (195–96). On 12 October 1793, Wilkinson's company performed these adaptations—*Daniel in the Lion's Den* following *Moses in the Bull Rushes*. These sacred dramas were followed by more traditional fare—Frances Brooke's *Rosina* and Henry Fielding's *The Mock Doctor* (*The Yorkshire Stage, 1766–1803*, ed. Linda Fitzsimmons and Arthur W. McDonald, [Metuchen, NJ: Scarecrow, 1989: 710]).

Two Median lords, Pharnaces and Soranus, are angry about Daniel's political ascendancy in Darius's kingdom. Pharnaces complains that Daniel is a "foreigner, a Hebrew, and a slave," who even prays three times a day. These enemies of Daniel plan to subvert him by his piety, and they propose a law to the Babylonian council to reestablish obedience in the empire: "for the space of thirty days, No subject in thy realm shall ought request Of God, or man, except thee, O king!" (215). The penalty for this transgression is to be placed in a "dreadful den of hungry lions." After Darius has put his seal on the law, Pharnaces reminds him that law of the Medes and Persians is irrevocable. Knowing that the law has been passed, Daniel prays at his usual hour and is taken in the midst of his prayer. Darius goes to Daniel to implore his pardon, but Daniel stands before the King with meek respect, asking "why fear death?" In the final scene, Darius and Araspes, a Median lord converted by Daniel, go to the mouth of the den and call for Daniel, who says "Hail! King Darius! The God I serve has shut the lion's mouth To vindicate my innocence" (245). As Daniel is taken from the den, Darius vows punishment of these who urged the unjust law, but Daniel asks that they be spared. Nonetheless, Pharnaces and others are fed to the lions who tear them to bits. After the miraculous saving of Daniel, Darius tells his people that the God of Daniel is Lord alone.

The all-male cast in this reenactment of the Old Testament story is divided between the good characters (Daniel and Araspes) and the bad characters (Pharnaces and Soranus) with King Darius in the middle. Since her readers would have known the outcome, their interest may have been in More's blank verse and its dramatic rendering. While the verse itself is undistinguished, the pattern of its rhythms are very much like those found in the King James Bible.

TEXT: Readex Microprint.

Lauretta is renamed Zilia, and the old man (Paulina's father) becomes Petrowitz. Cowley tightens up the scenes by deleting speeches (though she let stand most of the ones thought "political" in 1792); she adds several songs in order to create a reading text, but at the same time she diminishes stage action in the 1813 edition. Even if the thin plot is much the same, Cowley eliminates the term "Christian" so that the 1813 version appears less controversial.

MANUSCRIPT: Larpent 921.

TEXTS: Readex Microprint of 1793 edition. TEC Reels 4397: 11 (1791, lyrics); 726: 9 (second edition, 1792).

FACSIMILE EDITION: E-CED, with introduction by F. Link (Garland, 1982) reproduces the first edition, 1792.

The Death of Socrates, Elizabeth Harrison. Harrison's only known tragedy was published in her *Miscellanies on Moral and Religious Subjects, in Prose and Verse*, "Printed for the Author," 1756. The subscription list includes Dr. Johnson. According to Davis and Joyce, this one-act play is an adaptation of Plato's *Crito*.

TEXT: Not in Readex Microprint. NUC lists copies at Univs. of Chicago, Johns Hopkins, Ohio State, Illinois, Florida, and Yale, as well as at the Huntington.

The Debauchee; or, The Credulous Cuckold, attributed to Aphra Behn. Based on Richard Brome's *A Mad Couple Well Match'd* (1639), this five-act comedy debuted sometime in February 1677 at DG. It was printed for John Amery later that same year.

Set in London, the comedy opens with Careless (the first title character) bemoaning his disinheritance, but his friend, Saveall, arrives with the news that Sir Oliver Thrivewell, Careless's uncle, is ready to take him back on trial. After Saveall and Careless depart, Watt (Careless's man servant) tries to placate and then to seduce Phebe Gimcrack, Careless's mistress. Before the reinstated nephew and his friend arrive, Lady Thrivewell asks Sir Oliver why he has been so melancholy, and he confesses to having a one-time affair (for 100 guineas) with Alitia Saleware, whose husband runs a shop in the city. Remarkably, she forgives him. When his nephew arrives, Sir Oliver, ironically, encourages Careless to reform, offering to pay his debts and to give him a room in his house. Lady Thrivewell goes to Saleware's shop, gets almost 100 guineas worth of goods, and reminds Alitia that her husband left the money with her earlier, thus taking revenge for Alitia's assignation with Sir Oliver. When Bellamy comes into the shop to leave a letter for Alitia, we learn that he is in reality Clara, Lady Thrivewell's sister, who is acting the role of Lord Loveless's page. She is in love with his lordship and has chosen this disguise as a way to be near him. To forestall Lord Loveless from bedding Alitia, Bellamy woos her. In order to revenge herself on Lady Thrivewell, Alitia tells Bellamy if he can gain Lady Thrivewell's sexual favors, Alitia will sleep with him (her). In an attempt to reform, Careless writes a letter of dismissal to Phebe and a wooing letter to the Widow Crostill, but he mixes up the letters, causing major problems; and while the Widow is willing to forgive him, Phebe thinks he's willing to marry her. Careless's reform is short-lived, however; and he returns home drunk threatening to sleep with any of the female servants, as well as with Lady Thrivewell, but she will have her revenge. Later, when Careless does try to sleep with her, she puts Phebe in her place. In a second substitution, Bellamy tells Alitia that he has enjoyed Lady Thrivewell, but he (she) brings Alitia's husband Tom Saleware to take her place. In the final scene, Careless will accept Phebe, but the Widow Crostill must have Careless, who says he will reform. Mrs. Crostill then offers Phebe £300, and while she won't accept the money, Watt says he will marry Phebe (thus gaining access to the money). Lady Thrivewell brings in Bellamy, now dressed as her sister Clara, to Lord Loveless, and he willingly accepts Clara. Tom Saleware and Alitia are told to return to their shop, but when the wedded couples come in, Tom, the credulous cuckold of the subtitle, calls for a dance.

While Mrs. Crostill's dogged love for Careless strains one's credulity, Careless's final reform is even less likely to convince audiences. Like many events in this play, these last two require a strong willingness to suspend disbelief. Hume remarks that the "intrigue is well managed, the sex interests titillating but really fairly pure" (308). Gewirtz comments that, for a city knight, Sir Oliver is "a surprisingly agreeable figure" (159). While not named in the title or subtitle, Lady Thrivewell is the strongest and most complex character in the comedy: Smith says about her, "the second wife of an older husband, [she] meets with forbearance and tact the problem of her husband's infidelity, resists the advances of a scapegrace nephew of her husband, and then, her reputation slandered by the malice of other characters, clears herself gloriously" (114).

About the attribution, Link says that the play differs very little from the source, but Brome's language is toned down in its crudeness and bawdy. Both internal and external evidence make it probable the play is Behn's. Gewirtz agrees: "*The Debauchee* was ascribed early to Behn, and little in the play speaks against her authorship, while much of it echoes her style" (160).

TEXTS: Wing B4869. EEB Reel 484: 15. Readex Microprint.

The Debt of Honour, Elizabeth Ryves. This comedy, for which Ryves was paid £100 when accepted by DL (c. 1777), was never acted. There is no record of publication.

The Deceiver Deceived, Mary Pix. This five-act comedy was first produced at LIF in November 1697 and published early the following year by R. Basset. The next season, it was acted with the same cast under the title of *The French Beau*; the play was reissued under that title and printed for William Brown in 1699. In the Prologue, Pix says she "shew'd her Play to some, who like true Wits, stole't half away": she had taken the play to the actor George Powell of DL, who returned it to her after plundering most of Pix's play for his musical farce *Imposture Defeated; or, A Trick to Cheat the Devil*, performed at DL (probably in September 1697).

The title character Melito Bondi (performed by Thomas Betterton) plans to deceive his young second wife (Olivia acted by Elizabeth Barry) and daughter (Arianna played by Anne Bracegirdle) by pretending to be blind, but the women organize a counterplot and deceive him. As a Venetian senator, Bondi must take his turn as governor of Dalmatia, but to avoid this expense he feigns blindness and must silently watch Olivia entertain Count Andrea and Arianna carry on an intrigue with Fidelio, an impoverished nobleman. Count Insulls, the stock French fop whom Bondi has planned for his daughter to marry, shows an interest only in clothes and bad poetry, and Arianna wants nothing to do with him. Bondi visits the chapel of St. Sylvester to fake a divine miracle by regaining his sight, and he throws a ball to celebrate his recovery and to enact a swift marriage of Arianna and Count Insulls. Arianna pleads with Bondi's servant Gervatio, who plays a double game with his master, to save her. At the ball, Lucinda, Lady Temptyouth's protégé and a pretended heiress, plays up to Count Insulls, who turns his attention to Lucinda because he wants revenge on Arianna for rejecting him. Gervatio has two informers overhear Count Insulls making treasonous remarks, and they carry him to jail. Gervatio then reports this to Bondi, who blames his wife and wants to poison her. Gervatio arranges for Bondi to overhear his wife and Count Andrea from a balcony, and then he informs the lovers: their chaste remarks convince Bondi he has not been cuckolded. Meanwhile, Lady Temptyouth has Count Insulls freed from prison so he can marry Lucinda who plans to "manage him and his estate" (33). Fake friars from St. Sylvester's rifle Bondi's house, saying he counterfeited blindness and a cure. To protect his money, Bondi sends Gervatio away with his bonds and papers. When Arianna and Fidelio come in married, Gervatio returns and gives them the papers (worth 50,000 crowns) as a dowry from Bondi, who finally acquiesces and vows to reform. His wife, however, can only hope for a speedy widowhood after declaring she would not deceive her husband.

Once the deceit begins, it can be found everywhere in the play, suggesting that Bondi must take the responsibility for starting a dishonorable game that he cannot control, leading to the deceiver being deceived. Through the aid of the clever servant Gervatio, Fidelio and Arianna succeed in marrying with a dowry. On the other hand, the play ends with Olivia, Lady Bondi, stuck with a husband whose reform is unlikely. Even though Count Andrea had courted Olivia before she was compelled to marry Bondi, her situation remains bleak at the end of the play—a consequence of a woman forced to marry against her will.

TEXTS: Wing P2327. EEB Reel 506: 3. Readex Microprint.

FACSIMILE EDITION: E-CED, with introduction by Edna L. Steeves (NY: Garland, 1982).

The Deceptions, Margaret Cornelys. This comedy was first produced at the Crow-Street Theatre, Dublin, 14 March 1781, but it was apparently never published. Davis and Joyce incorrectly name the author as "Teresa Imer CORNELYS." Though they credit Cornelys with appearing in the Dublin production, it is likely that the author—Margaret Cornelys—acted on her benefit night.

De Chatillon; or, The Crusades, Felicia Dorothea Browne Hemans. Written after *The Vespers of Palermo* (1823), this five-act tragedy in blank verse is included in her posthumous *Dramatic Works*, published in Edinburgh by W. Blackwood and in London by Thomas Cadell in 1839. The play was not produced. The unknown editor remarks in a brief introduction that the play was printed from manuscript and that Hemans wished to compress her style, "avoiding that redundancy of poetic diction which had been censured as the prevailing fault" of her earlier play.

Set during the crusades in Palestine, the play deals with two brothers, both French knights, in a holy war against the "Infidels." The father of Rainier and Almer de Chatillon has recently fallen in battle, while Almer the younger brother spent his time wooing his beautiful captive, Moraima. When she asks him not to fight against her brother, Almer refuses to join the crusading Christians, who win the battle without him. In the knights' hall, some want to discredit Almer, but Rainier tells the story of Bertrand, whose son returned from the holy land with an Arabian bride. When the son won't defend the City of the Cross, Bertrand slays his daughter-in-law. Rainier's intent is the same, until he meets Moraima. She stands up to him and says she will die for Almer's life and honor. He is so impressed that he sends her back to her father, but everyone thinks she is dead, including Almer, who again refuses to fight with the Christian knights. The scene shifts to the Saracen camp, where Moraima tells her father, Melech, that the Christians treated her well. Melech, however, has set a price on Rainier's head if he be brought in alive. Rainier's faithful vassal, Gaston, has returned from delivering Moraima, but tells his master that on his way back he was captured by Arabs only to be freed by Almer who has joined them. Disguised as a dervish, Rainier goes to the Arab camp, tries to get his brother to return to the Christians, and is captured. Almer then goes to the knights and tells them of Rainier's plight; finally, they agree to follow them. When they arrive, Almer finds Moraima alive. After Almer accepts Christianity, he dies in his brother's arms. Although Moraima asks her father to save Rainier, he throws himself on the Arabian swords and dies "for the Cross."

The clash of the two cultures and a strong Arabian female are the uncommon features of this play. From Rainier's story of Bertrand, it is pivotal that cultures cannot intermingle, and a bride from a minority culture is a pawn in the hands of the majority culture. Nevertheless, Moraima's willingness to die for Almer's life and honor so affect Rainier that he releases her. Moraima, too, pleads for his life before her father, showing the two cultures partaking in a generous nature. The exotic setting, the Christian sentiments, and the brotherly love—found elsewhere in Hemans's work—are prominent in this play.

TEXT: Readex Microprint of *Dramatic Works* (Edinburgh: W. Blackwood, 1839): 219–270.

The Decision; or, Religion Must Be All, or Is Nothing, Grace Kennedy. Published anonymously in Edinburgh, 1821, Kennedy's religious piece is said to have been written in the form of a dramatic composition by Inglis, as well as by Davis and Joyce. We have been unable to examine a copy. DNB notes that this piece was intended for the young. W. Oliphant published a fourth edition in 1822.

De HUMBOLDT, Charlotte (fl. 1821–1838). The author of *Corinth, a Tragedy, and other Poems* (111 pp.), De Humbolt may have been a Miss Earle (BL Catalogue) when her volume was first published in 1821 by Ellerton and Henderson. An expanded version (188 pp.) under the same title was published by Longman and others in 1838. Davis and Joyce state that the five-act dramatic poem treats the fall of Periander.

De La ROCHE-GUILHEN, Anne (1644–1707). Born in Rouen, France, into a Huguenot family, she died in England. The exact date of her exile to England is not known, as no reliable documents exist. Her latest biographer, Alexandre Calame, suggests that she arrived shortly before the performance of her comic masque, *Rare en tout*, produced at the Hall Theatre at Court, Whitehall (29 May 1677). An order of Charles II requires the musicians "to practice in the theatre at Whitehall at such tymes as Madam Le Roch and Mr. Paisible shall appoint for ye practiceing of such musick as is to be in ye French comedy" (30). Since the work was dedicated to the Duchess of Grafton, the then ten-year-old daughter of Lord Arlington, Calame believes that the French author came as a governess or a French teacher, and that she stayed in London until her death in 1707. This assumption rests on the fact that the Edict of Nantes, which had granted freedom of religion to Protestants, was revoked in 1685, making her return to France unlikely. In fact, the names of Roche-Guilhen and two of her sisters can be found on a list of refugees and other Huguenot victims, who resided in England and received financial assistance.

She wrote a number of novels in French, two of which were translated into English, and she prepared several translations as well. *Rare en tout* remains her only work for the theater. [Not in *BD*. Cotton, Hobby, Nicoll, Pearson, Smith & Cardinale. Biography by A. Calame, *Anne de La Roche-Guilhen: Romancière huguenote, 1644–1707* (1972).]

De Monfort, Joanna Baillie. This five-act tragedy first appeared in *A Series of Plays: [on] the Stronger Passions*, published by T. Cadell, Jr., and W. Davies in 1798. The play was altered for the stage by John Philip Kemble, who took the title role with his sister, Sarah Siddons, playing Jane, the sister of De Monfort. In this version, it was first produced at DL on 29 April 1800 and ran for eight nights. Elizabeth Inchbald printed the play in her *British Theatre* (1808).

To the German village of Amberg, De Monfort comes visiting his former landlord, Jerome, who finds him very much altered. They are interrupted by the arrival of Count Freberg and his lady, who stopped to see him even at the late hour. They ask about Jane De Monfort, who has remained at home, and request that he join in a party the next night. The following morning, De Monfort appears improved until a servant tells him that his countryman Rezenvelt is in town, at which he becomes furious. When Freberg comes, he brings Rezenvelt. After their departure, De Monfort in a soliloquy boils over with hate for Rezenvelt, whom he loathed even as a boy. That evening, while the Frebergs await their guests, a servant announces a "queenly" stranger; it is Jane De Monfort, who will only attend the soiree if she is veiled. While she leaves to prepare, the guests start arriving. In the course of the evening, Rezenvelt talks to the veiled guest, but De Monfort wants her to unveil. When Rezenvelt objects, a fight breaks out which ends in Jane's unveiling. De Monfort rushes into her arms and breaks into tears. Later, De Monfort tells Jane why he has long passionately hated Rezenvelt: Rezenvelt has grown undeservedly rich and has beat him in a duel. Although Jane heard they parted friends, De Monfort still holds a grudge. Jane admonishes him to fight against this passion. Lady Freberg, jealous of Jane, puts it about that Jane has come to gain a reconciliation between De Monfort and Rezenvelt. After the banquet that evening, Rezenvelt tells Freberg the argument from his side. Grimbaldi goes to De Monfort seeking an office in the town government (he cannot ask Rezenvelt whom he has offended). Grimbaldi tells him a rumor is circulating: Jane De Monfort is to marry Rezenvelt. A maddened De Monfort finds Jane walking with Rezenvelt and Lady Freberg while a frightened Grimbaldi sneaks off unnoticed. When the walkers come in, De Monfort rushes at Rezenvelt with a sword, but Rezenvelt disarms him and leaves. Hearing that his enemy is meeting someone in the wood, De Monfort grabs his dagger and follows him. Meanwhile in a gothic chapel on the edge of the wood, monks are conducting a funeral service when one of the lay sisters dashes in, telling of murder. A bloody De Monfort and the murdered corpse of Rezenvelt are brought in, and they are locked in the chapel together. In a self-destructive urge, De Monfort runs his head against a wall, knocking himself unconscious. Jane comes and attempts to comfort De Monfort, but his guilt and self-condemnation will allow him no solace. De Monfort dies in agony and is placed in a bier alongside Rezenvelt, and Jane in a final speech laments her brother's "one dark passion, [his] one dark deed."

In Baillie's brooding tragedy, hate triumphs, and De Monfort's ruinous passion corrupts a community which Jane De Monfort tries to heal. With Sarah Siddons and John Philip Kemble acting opposite one another, the play achieved some success. Paul Ranger notes that Baillie may have made some alterations to *De Monfort* when Edmund Kean was invited to revive the play in the 1820s, and Ranger discusses the gothic elements of the drama (*'Terror and Pity Reign in Every Breast': Gothic Drama in the London Patent Theatres, 1750–1820* [London: Society for Theatre Research, 1991]: 98–103). Joseph Donohue examines the pivotal place of *De Monfort* in its theatrical milieu in his *Dramatic Character in the English Romantic Age* (Princeton: Princeton UP, 1970): 78–83. David P. Watkins investigates social conditions that produce De Monfort's psychological state in his *A Materialist Critique of English Romantic Drama* (Gainesville: U Florida P, 1993): 39–59.

MANUSCRIPT: Larpent 1287.

TEXT: Readex Microprint of 1812 edition.

FACSIMILE EDITIONS: *Romantic Context: Poetry*, compiled, with an introduction, by D. H. Reiman (NY: Garland, 1977) reprints the 1798 edition. *Revolution and Romanticism, 1789–1834*, introduced by Jonathan Wordsworth (Rutherford, NJ: Woodstock, 1990) also reprints the 1798 edition.

CRITICAL EDITION: *Seven Gothic Dramas, 1789–1825*, edited with an introduction by Jeffrey N. Cox (Athens, OH: Ohio UP, 1992): 231–314. Cox adds footnotes showing how the Larpent manuscript differs from the printed text.

DEVERELL, Mary (b. 1737?). First known as a poet, essayist, and writer of sermons, Deverell wrote a drama when in her fifties. *Mary Queen of Scots; An Historical Tragedy, or, Dramatic Poem* (the Preface "To the Candid Reader" is signed from London, 2 Oct. 1792) was published for the author by subscription. It recounts the events of Queen Mary's tragic life that ended with her beheading. This historical subject was popular: John St. John's play with the same name was premiered 21 March 1789 at DL with Sarah Siddons in the title role, and Schiller's *Mary Stuart* was written in 1800. Subscribers to Deverell's play included Hannah More, Mrs. Siddons, John Philip Kemble, Hannah Cowley, and Miss [Elizabeth?] Carter. The tragedy was never produced.

Born into a large family in Gloucestershire, Deverell apparently remained unmarried throughout her life. By 1774, when she published her *Sermons*, Deverell had been accepted in London literary circles. The popularity of the *Sermons* (as shown by several reprints) must have encouraged her further moral views in *Miscellanies in Prose and Verse* (1781), which include poems and essays "particularly calculated for the improvement of younger minds." Several of these pieces were reprinted in Hannah More's *The Ladies' Literary Companion* (1792). Deverell's heroic poem *Theodora and Didymus* (1784) stresses morality through religious fortitude and female strength of character. It may be worth noting that Dr. Johnson subscribed to each of her earlier works, including *Theodora and Didymus*, in the year he died. The end of Deverell's own life, however, is obscure, and the date and place of her death are not known. [DBAWW, FCLE]

A Dialogue in the Elysian Fields between Caesar and Cato, Elizabeth Ryves. This dramatic dialogue in verse was printed in 1784 without a publisher's name. There was no performance. The British Library copy has corrections by the author.

MANUSCRIPT: BL 11632.h.19(3).

TEXT: Not in Readex Microprint.

Dialogues, probably not Sarah Fielding. These dramatic dialogues appear in the second volume of her *Familiar Letters between the Principal Characters in David Simple*. The volumes were printed for the author (by subscription) in 1747 and sold by A. Millar. Fielding herself says the dialogues "were a kind present to the Author by a Friend." Because the dialogues do not appear to be related to the letters, they were merely included along with other pieces to fill out volume two. According to Samuel Johnson, Sarah Fielding solicited them from James Harris, a family friend who also assisted Jane Collier with *The Art of Tormenting* (1753).

"Much Ado," said on a separate title page to have been written in October 1744, is set in a garden by the side of a canal. An old man has been told by his friend that the British ship *Victory* has sunk and all hands have perished. The nieces are told of the disaster, but they don't understand its significance and go off talking about fashion. When the girls discover that their turkey-cock, Veny, has been knocked into the canal, they are upset until their uncle pulls the bird in with a rake. The men go on talking about the lost ship while the girls tend to Veny. The author may have wished to juxtapose the real disaster with the near drowning of the turkey-cock, or to show how age and youth deal with disasters at a distance and nearby.

"Fashion," written in 1746, is set in a mercer's shop. A man and his daughters are dealing with Mr. Prim who claims his dry goods are most fashionable. The father tries to make a point about fabric being in and out of fashion: laws of mathematics don't change; truth doesn't change; and right and wrong don't change. Why then should clothes and dresses change from year to year? Mr. Prim doesn't understand him, and the man leaves the shop. Before the daughters leave, one excuses her father, saying he is often whimsical, and then she takes the silk. Here again, age and youth see the world in a different way, and Mr. Prim, whose job it is to sell materials, can't or won't understand the father's attitude.

TEXT: Not in Readex Microprint.

Diamond Cut Diamond, Lady Eglantine Wallace. Translated from Dumaniant's comedy *La Guerre Ouverte; ou, Ruse contre ruse* (1786), Lady Wallace's two-act version was not acted, though it was published by J. Debrett in 1787. The success of Elizabeth Inchbald's *The Midnight Hour* undercut this version and caused bitter feelings on Lady Wallace's part. *BD* remarks "This piece, which was never acted, is a very indifferent translation of a French drama, called *Guerre Ouverte; ou, Ruse contre Ruse*; which has been made better use of in *The Midnight Hour*, by Mrs. Inchbald" (2: 162). Although the play is not a literal translation, it is a "close adaptation," according to Kinne (199). Lady Wallace's version should not be confused with James Hook's opera *Diamond cut Diamond; or, Venitian Revels* (performed at CG, 23 May 1797).

In contrast with Inchbald's Spanish setting, Lady Wallace's version sets the play in Plymouth, and she gives her characters appropriate English names (such as General Steady). When the Marquis of Dash tells the General he is in love with his niece Lucy, the General gives the Marquis until midnight to take her out of the house successfully, although she has been promised to a brave sea captain. Various schemes fail, and finally Lucy is locked in by her uncle and her clothes are taken away. But with the connivance of the servants, Lucy dresses in male attire, is taken for the Marquis, and pushed out of the house. When Lucy and the Marquis return to tell the General that he has lost, she maliciously concludes that when anyone tries to restrain a woman against her inclination, that person attempts an impossibility.

The farcical contretemps are humorous enough, though most of them are in the original. With Inchbald's greater knowledge of the theatrical conventions of the English stage, her version captured English audiences. Wallace stayed very close to the French original, even

The Disguise, by a woman unknown. This "dramatic novel" was printed for J. Dodsley in 1771.

About this work, *BD* states (the complete text is given): "The Disguise, from which this dramatic novel takes its name, is that of a young man, of the age of nineteen, brought up and educated, without discovery, as a female, until that period. He is addressed by several suitors, and falls in love himself with one of his female friends. The motive for this disguise is a suspicion that the brother of the lady's father had destroyed his former male children as they were born. The story is improbable and ill told, the situations unnatural, and the characters such as are not to be found in real life. The authoress, as a reason for adopting the dramatic form for her novel, says, that epistolary correspondences are grown dull, that narratives were become tedious, and journals heavy; if so, she has not been lucky enough to remove the objections which lie against the usual modes of conducting this species of writing" (2: 165).

TEXT: Not in Readex Microprint. NUC: Copy at U of Illinois.

The Divorce, Lady Dorothea Dubois. The title page to this two-act musical entertainment says it was produced at Mary-le-Bone Gardens in 1771. J. Whele printed the text that same year. *LS*, however, gives only one performance at Mary-le-Bone Gardens as an afterpiece on 27 August 1773 for the benefit of the composer James Hook.

Violante laments her terrible marriage to Don Pedro, who gambles and drinks excessively. This night, however, he has won a thousand guineas, but Violante tells her woman Isabella that he will just lose twice as much tomorrow. After Don Pedro stumbles to bed, the women are visited by Lorenzo. The next morning Violante berates Don Pedro, who cannot understand why she is so disagreeable. Lorenzo, who has been listening at the window, asks Don Pedro if he is willing to give Violante up, and he says he wants a divorce. Violante agrees, and Lorenzo says he wishes to marry her.

Dubois's libretto provides different moods for Hook's music. The stage action is slight, but the quarrels are mildly amusing. This piece appears to be less popular than Dubois's *The Magnet*, first performed in 1771.

TEXT: Readex Microprint.

Don Pedro the Cruel and Don Manuel the Cobbler! or, The Corregidor of Seville!, Caroline Boaden. This comic drama in two acts was first performed at the Surrey Theatre, August 1838. Publication was by J. Duncombe, probably in 1839. A note in the preface indicates that this is "the only edition correctly marked by permission of the prompter's book." The title page also indicates that the play was "adopted from the French," but no specific source is mentioned.

Set in Seville in 1360. While the masses are starving and demanding bread, the rich merchants, Bringas and Guttierez, are making their fortunes by demanding exorbitant prices. The King, known as Don Pedro the Cruel, goes through the streets disguised at night testing the temperature for revolution. On one such evening, Don Pedro overhears the cobbler, Manuel Fraquillo, talking with his apprentice, saying that there would be enough food for everyone if some people were not creating a famine to line their pockets. Later that night, Manuel is shaken from his sleep by officers from the King, who announce that "Don" Manuel has been nominated Corregidor of Seville for twenty-four hours. There is also a caveat: if he cannot succeed in feeding the poor by the end of the day, Manuel will be hanged before the palace gates. Manuel is flustered, but his old friend and lover, Paquita the beggar, tells him how to proceed. Since Bringas and Guttierez have monopolized the corn and locked it away in their granaries, Pedro forces the merchants—on point of death—to produce corn to give to the masses. The King is so impressed with his new popularity that he permanently appoints Manuel as Corregidor, adding a new warning: if one crime goes unpunished, Manuel will be hanged. One evening as Don Pedro makes his rounds in disguise checking out the peace and quiet, he comes upon Herrera (the old Corregidor) wooing Isabella, Bringas's daughter. When Herrera insults him, unaware of who he is, Don Pedro strikes out and slays him, the King escaping (so he thinks) unobserved. Don

Pedro insists that Manuel find the murderer, confident that he will not be discovered. Unable to find the guilty party and terrified that he will be gibbeted, Don Pedro begins to blame people blindly. Once again, however, Paquita comes to his rescue. Since Herrera was a lover who had abused her, Paquita watched him arrange assignations with Isabella. On the night in question, she had not been able to see the face of the murderer, but she did notice an idiosyncrasy in his gait, characteristic of only Don Pedro. Following Paquita's advice, Manuel forces the King to agree to grant him a wish if he successfully catches Herrera's murderer. When Don Pedro is accused of the crime—but quietly, and only in front of the Corregidor—Manuel advises the King to pardon himself. Manuel's single request is to be dismissed as Corregidor. Don Pedro also gives him money, which he chooses over a title, saying he will continue as an amateur cobbler, making shoes for free. Manuel also asks Paquita to be his wife.

Unfamiliar with the source(s) of the drama, we are uncertain how much of the play's verbal cleverness is original with Caroline Boaden. For example, when Don Pedro asks the cobbler if he wishes a title, Manuel responds, "What is the use of clapping a label on an empty bottle?" (21). And later, commenting on the treacherous Don Pedro, Manuel says, "He is as smooth as kid leather this morning" (21). In fact, the dignity of Manuel the cobbler is largely achieved because of his honesty and concise use of language. The role of Paquita is also exceptional. She is both more aggressive and more intelligent than the Corregidor. No wonder Manuel says to her, "you are my good genius" (30).

TEXT: Readex Microprint.

Don Sancho; or, The Student's Whim, Elizabeth Boyd. This odd ballad opera, printed for the author in 1739, was never acted. After twelve pages of front matter including a dedication to Lord North, a prologue addressed to Alexander Pope, and an advertisement thanking Chetwood, the prompter of DL, for giving the play a hearing, the plot begins. Three students at Oxford, on a whim, wish to have the ghosts of Shakespeare and Dryden raised to view. They have asked the help of Don Sancho, a poor nobleman, who says a "charm" and the ghosts rise, speak, and sing airs, telling the present generation to "Goodness practice more than Praise." After they disappear, the scene opens on Minerva's Temple, and the masque that follows stresses Taste and Art, invoking the names, not only of Shakespeare and Dryden, but Gay, Congreve, Addison, Waller, Sheffield, Boyle, and Lansdowne in order to show that Britannia is blessed when the muses smile. Sancho then instructs the students on the importance of books rather than stone monuments.

Even though the motivation of the students is a whim, Boyd's patriotism shines through in praise of the (then) well-known poets and playwrights. In the context of the recent Licensing Act (1737), Boyd's play got a hearing but was not produced at a time when the number of theatres were diminished and there were almost no new plays. Since her prologue was addressed to Pope, the question of taste and tradition is raised. The use of the ballad opera may provide a contrast to Handel's oratorios at the King's Theatre, which he had leased for part of the 1738–39 theatre season.

TEXT: Readex Microprint.

FACSIMILE EDITION: *Magical Transformation and Necromancy*. Ballad Opera series v. 10. Comp. Walter H. Rubsamen (NY: Garland, 1974).

Dorval; or, The Test of Virtue, translation attributed to Elizabeth Griffith. Taken from Diderot's *Le Fils naturel; ou, les Epreuves de la vertu* (1757), this five-act sentimental comedy was not acted on the English stage, but it was printed "for the author [i.e., translator]" by J. Dodsley in 1767.

Whether or not Griffith should be credited with the translation remains a vexed question. In *David Garrick and his French Friends* (1911), Frank Hedgcock used, as evidence for his assertion that Griffith is the translator, a letter from Laurence Sterne to David Garrick (written from Paris on 10 April 1762): the play, Sterne says, was "given me by a lady of talents, to read and conjecture if it would do for you. 'Tis from the plan of Diderot, and possibly half a translation of it. . . . It has too much sentiment in it (at least for me), the speeches too long and savour too much of preaching—this may be a second reason it is not to my taste . . . so I fear it would not do for your stage, and perhaps for the very reason which recommends it to a French one" (152, n. 1; quoted by Kinne, 102–03). Betty Rizzo in *Curtain Calls* does list the play in "Works Cited," though she doesn't discuss it (140), and Susan Staves in DLB 89 does not mention *Dorval.*

In the play itself, Dorval and Rosella have fallen in love with each other despite the fact that Rosella has previously given her heart to Clairville, Dorval's closest friend. Constance, Clairville's sister, realizes that she too loves Dorval, and after reading a letter intended for Rosella, believes that his feelings are reciprocal. Dorval, after much soul-searching (a passionate reminder of his exceptional moral strength), comes to the conclusion that for the sake of virtue, friendship, and honor, he and Rosella must renounce each other, and Rosella reluctantly acquiesces to the sacrifice. Upon the return from America (a long journey fraught with the worst imaginable dangers), old Lysimond, Rosella's father, is discovered to be also Dorval's father. This is a pathetic scene where many tears are shed. The play ends with Lysimond's death, but not before he distributes his painstakingly but honestly acquired wealth, and blesses the union of Rosella and Clairville and that of Dorval and Constance. Not only has virtue triumphed, but it has been rewarded.

Diderot's play is translated literally with some of the characters's names slightly altered (Rosella for Rosalie, Andrew for André, Justina for Justine). In fact, the translator stayed so close to the original that awkward phrases and even outright mistranslations at times mar the text, as Kinne rightly observes (102). Although the *Scots Magazine* (July 1767) found the play "very affecting and sentimental," and Genest (10: 184) asserted that "this is on the whole an interesting play, particularly in the character of Dorval," one has to agree with Sterne: "it has too much sentiment in it, the speeches are too long and savour too much of preaching" (quoted by Kinne, 102). The French must have agreed, for *Le Fils naturel*, published in 1757, was not performed in Paris until 26 September 1771. Although labelled a comedy, it is an illustration of the new *bourgeois drama*, which Diderot expounded in his *Entretiens sur le Fils Naturel [Conversations on Dorval]*, published with the play itself. Its aim was to depict the diverse social conditions, and not the different types of people. For Diderot, then, the key to the work is Dorval's illegitimate status and not his strong attachment to moral values; *bourgeois drama*, as envisioned by Diderot, ended with the eighteenth-century.

TEXT: Readex Microprint, under the title.

The Double Deception; or, The Lovers Perplexed, Elizabeth Richardson. This five-act comedy was produced at DL on 28 April 1779, but it was never printed. The play was acted four times at the end of the 1778–79 season and twice the following seasons (once as a benefit for the author's heirs).

MANUSCRIPT: Larpent 478.

The Double Disguise, Maria Edgeworth. This unpublished play is described by Edgeworth's biographer, Marilyn Butler, as having been written for a family Christmas entertainment in 1786; it features "ordinary people going about their common everyday business." Edgeworth uses characters of middle and lower class origins. The events take place in a common inn on the road between Liverpool and London. The plot uses the standard stage idea of a soldier returning from war: in two different disguises, he tests the faithfulness of his lady. Butler then recounts the constraints Edgeworth came under in the necessity to compose an acceptable part for everyone in the household old enough to learn lines. The author herself took the role of an English servant girl employed in the hostelry where the play was set. "The twelve-year-old Honora, the family's most accomplished actress, was the flighty heroine, Anna her gentle cousin, whose virtue wins the hero in the end." In composing a suitable part for her father, Edgeworth used his abilities as a mimic, for he often entertained his family with impersonations of Irish characters he had met. "The part Maria wrote for him was her first Irish sketch—Justice Cocoa, a Tipperary grocer who had risen in the world and become an enthusiastic officer in the Volunteers" (Butler, *Maria Edgeworth*, 152–53).

MANUSCRIPTS: "The two manuscript copies of the play, with castlist of family actors, are in the Goschen deposit, Bodelian Library, Oxford (Dep. c. 134)" (Butler, 152).

The Double Disguise, Harriet Horncastle Hook. This two-act comic opera was first produced at DL on 8 March 1784, with music by her husband, James Hook. It was published later that month by J. Bell, with a plate of Anna Marie Phillips, who portrayed Emily. Acted thirteen times its first season, *The Double Disguise* remained popular, playing in each of the next four seasons.

The play opens at a London inn where Tinsel (Lord Hartwell's valet) hatches a plot with Sam (his lordship's postilion). Lord Hartwell's uncle has died leaving an estate in Somersetshire—providing Lord Hartwell marries his uncle's goddaughter, Emily, whom his lordship has never seen. Tinsel's idea is to get there first, impersonate Lord Hartwell, and marry the lady. Meanwhile, in Somerset, Emily is concerned about the impending visit because she has taken a fancy to the new steward, Henry, who turns out to be Lord Hartwell in disguise, and he confesses to Emily that he wanted to get to know her before committing himself. If she hadn't been all she is, he tells her, he could have departed "without shocking your delicacy, by letting you suppose I had seen and disapproved" (12). He has managed this ruse through Mr. Sharp, his uncle's attorney, and now he is captivated with her "sweetness of disposition, wit, and accomplishments" (13). The other disguise of the title comes in the second act when Tinsel arrives dressed as Lord Hartwell. Emily's father, Sir Richard, is doubtful because Tinsel looks like none of the family, but Tinsel goes on to woo Rose, Emily's maid, and her maiden aunt, Dorothy, whose head has been turned by reading romantic novels. The critical event occurs when Henry dressed as the real Lord Hartwell enters at the same time as Tinsel, the bogus Lord. Sam and Tinsel are sent away, while Lord Hartwell and Emily are united. Aunt Dorothy leaves with injured pride, but Sir Richard means to bring her around with a dance. There is a final quartet before the curtain falls.

Although Emily is the focus of the arrangement forced on her by her uncle, it is the careful planning of Lord Hartwell that wins the day. The rascally schemes of Tinsel and Sam play off cleverly against the haughty aunt. The Irish maid, Rose, also joins the frolic through her wit and wisdom. The slight plot sets up the commanding male in disguise, who wouldn't injure a lady's situation by refusing her outright.

MANUSCRIPT: Larpent 646.

TEXT: Readex Microprint.

The Double Distress, Mary Pix. This five-act tragedy in blank verse was produced at LIF in March 1701; it was published the same year by R. Wellington and Bernard Lintott. Pix notes, in the Epistle Dedicatory, that she had assistance in her revision of the play. Cotton, Clark, and Pearson point out Pix's adaptation of Beaumont and Fletcher's *A King and No King* alters the perspective from male to female.

Set in Persepolis, the play opens during a war between the Medes and the Persians. Rheusares explains to Darius, the Persian King, that he changed sides from the Medes to the Persians because Astiages, King of the Medes, has become a tyrant. After marrying an Assyrian noble woman and having two children, Astiages began lusting after other women. When the Queen and her offspring died—whether by poison or grief Rheusares doesn't know—Astiages took up with the ambitious Orna, who bore him a child, Tygranes, now the present general of the Medes. Rheusares was imprisoned, and his children held hostages at the Medean court, but his daughter Cytheria (played by Anne Bracegirdle) had her father released. Regardless of the ill-treatment of Rheusares, Cytheria has fallen in love with Tygranes. Darius tells Rheusares that the Persian general Cleomedon has captured Cytheria in the war, and she enters in triumph. But as the captured Medes are paraded across stage, Cytheria steps aside to speak to a prisoner (Tygranes). After the prisoners are sent to the dungeons, Cytheria is comforted by Leamira (played by Ann Barry), but Cytheria asks that the Medean prisoners be released. Darius agrees and gives Cytheria the royal signet to enact the discharge. Cyraxes, a Persian general and Cytheria's brother, has Adrasta follow her to the prison where she urges Tygranes to flee. When Cyraxes discovers what his sister has done, he tells Cytheria that her action has prolonged the war, and he makes her swear never to wed Tygranes; she agrees. Alone with Leamira, Cytheria relates her history: a hermit she visited told her to beware of incest. Leamira divulges her love of Cleomedon to Cytheria, and they go in the temple and ask the high priest to tell their futures: Cytheria is told to shun her brother, whereas it is reported to Leamira that when she marries the Medean Prince wars will cease. Tygranes besieges the castle; Astiages is taken, and Orna commits suicide. In single combat Tygranes fights Cyraxes, but they are stopped by Rheusares, and Tygranes is sent to prison. Meanwhile, Leamira fears Cleomedon is slain and she will have to marry the Medean Prince, Tygranes, for political reasons, so she asks Cytheria to take her place. That way, Cytheria will disappoint both their "rigged Fates" (46). Leamira summons Tygranes, disguised, and provides a priest. Adrasta, however, reports this plan to Rheusares. The next morning her husband leaves before dawn, but he and Cytheria exchange rings. Cyraxes reports that Rheusares's papers reveal that he is not her brother and Cytheria is actually Astiages's daughter from his first marriage. She believes she has committed incest with her half brother, but Cyraxes says he took the place of Tygranes and shows her the exchanged ring. Astiages's other child turns out to be Cleomedon, and now Leamira is willing to marry him as the Medean Prince of the prophecy. Tygranes decides to turn hermit and take up a holy life. Thus the Medes and Persians are united under Leamira and Cleomedon to whom Darius hands over the throne.

The plot turns on Rheusares's secretly bringing up the children from Astiages's first marriage, and this causes the double distress of the title. While Leamira and Cytheria seem to form a friendship, it is Leamira's suggestion that leads to near-incest: Cytheria sleeps with a man she thinks is Tygranes, actually her half brother, only to discover the consummation was with Cyraxes, who is in fact not her brother. Some slight-of-hand with the plot allows Pix to create a happy ending for the two women.

TEXT: Readex Microprint.

FACSIMILE EDITION: E-CED, with introduction by Edna L. Steeves (NY: Garland, 1982).

The Double Mistake, Elizabeth Griffith. This alteration of *Elvira; or, The Worst Not Always True* (performed 1664, published 1667) by George Digby, the Earl of Bristol, was first produced at CG on 9 January 1766. After thirteen performances in its first season, it was presented a fourteenth time "by command of their Majesties." The five-act comedy was not revived. Published by J. Almon, T. Lowndes, S. Bladon, and J. Williams, the play went through three editions in 1766.

Being threatened with a forced marriage, Emily Southerne flees to London where she asks the protection of her cousin Lord Belmont who learns her history: Emily and Sir Charles Somerville had professed love for one another, but in a private interview at Bath a strange man dashed from a closet, and Sir Charles now distrusts her. Although Emily has proclaimed her innocence to Lord Belmont, Sir Charles now plans to go abroad. Lord Belmont takes Emily home to his sisters, Lady Mary and Lady Louisa, as a Miss Lawson. There she also meets Mr. Belmont, a bachelor uncle who is a passionate antiquarian, and Lady Bridget, an aunt who loves to show her erudition by a knowledge of Greek and Latin. In the course of events, we meet the brothers Freeman: the elder is a solid city banker, whereas the younger is a scallywag who wants to marry the romantically inclined Lady Louisa for her money. At the climax in act five, young Freeman makes a midnight visit to persuade Lady Louisa to elope with him. When young Freeman's coach is discovered outside, he is forced to fly. But leaving the house he discovers, to his surprise, Emily. After Emily faints, Sir Charles challenges young Freeman. Lady Louisa then tells the family that young Freeman came to see her, and she severs her relationship with him. Young Freeman is forced to admit he was the man in Emily's closet in Bath, where he was having an intrigue with Emily's maid. Sir Charles is reconciled with

Emily, and her father finally agrees to their marriage.

Bevis finds the play a model of sententious comedy "with its wildly romantic plot, reform motif, middle-class consciousness, sentimental dialogue, trembling sensibilities, and benevolent view of human nature" (1980; 53). Distressed innocence might best describe "poor" Emily, who through no fault of her own suffers for almost the entire play. She is pushed to the very limit of her endurance, and she must even declare her love for Sir Charles in front of everyone. Finally, she repeats her injured innocence, causing Young Freeman to pity her and benevolently tell his story, which clears her name. Since this has been labeled a sentimental comedy, we must assume that young Freeman reforms. Susan Staves ironically notes that Emily articulates "the correct attitude for women": "by nature and by providence design'd, our helpless sex's strength lie in dependance; and where we are so blest to meet with generous natures, our servitude is empire" (DLB 89: 177).

MANUSCRIPT: Larpent 251.

TEXTS: Readex Microprint of the 1766 Dublin edition, printed for A. Leathley (and ten others). TEC Reels 584: 24 (first edition, 1766); 3271: 8 (second edition, corrected, 1766); 4396: 3 (third edition, 1766).

The Double Mistress; or, 'Tis Well 'Tis No More, Delariviere Manley. Although announced for performance in the *Weekly Pacquet* of 20 February 1720, there is no known production according to Burling. This comedy is one of the two plays mentioned in Manley's will, proved in 1724. The text is now presumed lost.

Dramas for the Use of Young Ladies, Mrs. C. Short. This collection includes two three-act plays—*The Fortunate Disappointment* and *Domestic Woe*—intended to be spoken by an all-female cast. According to Davis and Joyce, these pieces were "written for a group of young ladies to promote 'the habit of speaking with grace and propriety.'" Published in 1792 at Birmingham for G. G. J. and J. Robinson and J. Balfour (in London), and for C. Elliott (in Edinburgh), the plays received no public performance. Anna Seward supplied a poetic prologue and epilogue to *The Fortunate Disappointment.*

TEXT: Not in Readex Microprint. NUC: Copy at Harvard.

Dramatic Dialogues, Elizabeth Silthorpe Pinchard. Written "for the use of young persons," Pinchard's plays were not intended for stage performance. Published by Elizabeth Newbery in 1792, the plays follow Madame de Genlis's "Theatre of Education" and show young people improper ways of acting, suggesting corrective measures.

In "The Misfortunes of Anger," Juliet has thrown down her tambour (embroidery) frame and scratched a poor neighbor child (offstage); she has also thrown her doll across the room and squeezed a pet bird to death (on stage). She tells her cousin Paulina she will repent, but later she throws a knife at her brother Charles, who is almost blinded by Juliet's anger (offstage). In the end, Juliet is forgiven by Charles, and Paulina agrees to take Juliet home as a pupil under her moral instruction.

"Sensibility" provides examples of how false sensibility ("enervating and excessive feeling") impedes action: "Isabella fears touching her wounded parrot, but Cecilia, the child of true sensibility, has no such squeamishness" (Bator, *Masterworks* 4:47).

"The Little Trifler" shows how Laura's inability to be punctual causes her and others grief. After she has been late for a carriage ride and left at home, Laura is told that Ruth Saunders, a poor woman, wishes to meet with her. Laura sympathizes with the plight of the Saunders's family and gives to them all she has (a half crown). She then makes an appointment to meet with Mrs. Saunders at six o'clock. Having an opportunity to go for a carriage ride, Laura forgets about the appointment, but her mother meets with Mrs. Saunders. Laura is punished by not being able to visit the Saunders for a fortnight.

"The Little Country Visitor," Rosetta, comes to call on Matilda and Harriet, who make fun of her rural ways, but when Rosetta describes her activities in the country, her hostesses are father meet with Bertha and her mother (the Countess), the Countess promises to help Leopold establish himself. Suddenly, news arrives of Count Lindorf's death, and the Countess reveals that her late husband was killed by his brother; fearing that her male child would suffer the same fate, the Countess exchanged her male child at birth for the daughter of her close friend, Conrade.

"The Wedding Ring." Lady Stanley tests Arthur, the man she wishes to marry. First he is challenged at rapier point; then he discovers that his opponent is a woman, who gives him a choice "twixt two sharp hazards, wedlock or the sword" (61); finally, he agrees to marry her in masks and she disappears from the wedding chamber. In spite of his own doubts, encouraged by his brother Sir Edward's questions, Arthur insists that "I'll trust her still, In all her mystery" (65). Lady Stanley then reappears and they proceed to the wedding breakfast. Although women often assume major roles in Mitford's dramatic scenes, this is the only one in which the woman completely controls the action and her own fate.

"Emily." Amelia has not seen her father since she married against his wishes. Although she and her husband Maurice are poor, they have created a happy domestic life with their son William; her only regret is her separation from her father, Lord Glentham. Meanwhile, by coincidence, William has met a strange gentleman whom he brings home with him. When the gentleman turns out to be Amelia's father, she and her husband plead for forgiveness. Lord Glentham offers to make William his heir and insists that Amelia bear separation from her son in order to receive her father's forgiveness. In this brutally patriarchal tale, Amelia ("Emily" to her father) agrees, and once she submits to her father's will, she is forgiven: "My children, bless ye all! Forgive this trial;—We'll never part again" (105).

"The Painter's Daughter." Colantonio, the painter, has vowed that only a great painter will be permitted to marry his daughter, Laura. Upon discovering such a painter, who has presented a portrait of Laura when she was younger, Colantonio begins to arrange her marriage to Zingaro. Laura insists that she'll marry no one but Angelo, the rich neighbor's son who left Naples ten years ago. With only slight foreshadowing, Zingaro turns out to be this Angelo, who has studied art in Rome, and he wins Laura's hand in marriage.

"Fair Rosamond." Based on a ballad in Percy's *Reliques*, this scene features Rosamond Clifford, mistress of Henry II, as its heroine. While she waits for King Henry to arrive, she recollects their meeting and their years together. When it is Queen Eleanor instead of Henry who appears, Rosamond asks for pity: "Thou art a Queen . . . but still a woman!—Women should be pitiful" (150). When she receives none, she is forced to drink poison just before Henry's arrival. Nonetheless, she makes Henry promise not to kill Eleanor and to make certain that their sons are bred humbly. Rosamond also dies penitent, hoping that her death will expiate their sins, making Henry "Happy and fortunate!" (160).

"Alice." The Great House had stood tenantless, but the heir (Lord Claremont) is arriving. When a stranger named Henry appears to Mrs. Neville and her daughter Alice, the mother relates a story about the heir's grandsire. Mrs. Neville reveals that her husband had inherited the estate, but the entire family was turned out when it was discovered that he was a bastard. When Henry questions Mrs. Neville and Alice about their attitudes toward the current heir, they express no bitterness toward him, saying that he has shown them kindnesses in the past. Eventually, Henry discloses that he is Lord Claremont, and he wishes that Mrs. Neville's son, William, fill his father's seat, restoring the family to their former position.

"Henry Talbot." When Sir Mordaunt visits his friend Talbot, Eleanor explains that her brother is gravely ill from "a settled melancholy" (188). The melancholy dates back to an evening when Lionel Grey, their foster brother, was drowned. Mordaunt discovers that Talbot is exhausted with guilt, and the latter ultimately confesses that he struck Lionel with an oar, sending him overboard, when he discovered that his foster brother was in love with Louisa, the woman to whom Talbot was betrothed. Mordaunt tells Eleanor that Talbot has died a penitent, and he implies that he is romantically interested in her.

"The Siege." The Duchess Bianca is held under siege in Mantua by her cousin Prince Lorenzo. When her wounded General and his wife are returned to her by Lorenzo, Count and Countess D'Osma speak highly of the Prince's many talents and his gentlemanly behavior. When her friend the Countess recommends that she marry her cousin and retain her position, Bianca insists that she would prefer a "happy cottage life" (238) with her maid of honor, Claudia, in exile. Bianca decides to yield her power to Lorenzo's, arguing that she "will no longer sacrifice My faithful subjects in this wasting war" (242). When Prince Lorenzo is revealed to be the talented and gentle Orlando, Bianca decides to accept the Prince's hand in marriage.

"The Bridal Eve." Helen is despondent upon the eve of her marriage to Lord Fitz-Alwyn, because she is in love with Hubert Knowles, the poor but gentle lad with whom she grew up. In the tales that they tell to one another, Helen and Lord Fitz-Alwyn communicate their feelings: she explains why she cannot marry Fitz-Alwyn, and he expresses his resentment when Helen assumes that he is a tyrant. Eventually, Fitz-Alwyn asks the harper who has been singing outside to come in. Because of the heavy foreshadowing, it is no surprise that the harper is Hubert and that Fitz-Alwyn gives Helen to him.

"The Captive." The young Theodore, the rightful king, begs the usurper to the throne of Sicily, Alberto, to allow him to leave his dungeon to live "in some small woodland cottage" (272) in exile. After Alberto refuses, Theodore is rescued by the usurper's daughter, Julia, who arrives at his cell through a secret door. Repeatedly, Julia pleads with him to escape, but Theodore will not do so until Julia agrees to go with him, thereby escaping the marriage her father has arranged with a political ally.

"The Masque of the Seasons." The play begins with actors in the "play" talking just before the masque begins. In the masque itself, each season describes its flowers (fruit, vegetables, etc.) and scenes that are typical of the season are evoked. There are exchanges between the seasons, emphasizing the effect one season has on another.

Many of these one-act scenes are based on other sources (e.g., "Cunigunda's Vow" is influenced by "Mr. Russell's delightful volumes on Germany") or on locations with which Mitford was familiar (e.g., in "Henry Talbot," the Great House is Seymour Court in Marlow). In virtually every drama, pastoral life is alluded to, and characters often seem content with humble lives that are associated with such trappings: shepherds, mountain huts, garden retreats, woodland settings, bowers, embroidery, cottage life and the flowers associated with it. In a number of the scenes, women reject more suitable arrangements to love or marry poorer men. In "Cunigunda's Vow" and "The Painter's Daughter," for instance, we are told that a woman's love is often denigrated because men cannot understand it. While a scene such as "Cunigunda's Vow" has a strong plot, the dramas are often marred by the coincidences used to resolve the action in a single act.

TEXT: Readex Microprint.

Dramatic Scenes from Real Life, Lady Morgan, earlier Sydney Owenson. These two volumes, printed by Saunders and Otley in 1833, include *Manor Sackville*, *The Easter Recess; or, The Tapestry Workers*, and *Temper*. There is no known production of these plays.

Although written in dramatic form (ten scenes, no acts), the content of *Manor Sackville* could have been better handled in a novel. The length of the play, its diverse scenes depicting different classes and religious groups, and its confusingly large cast would make stage production unlikely. Set on the west coast of Northern Ireland, the play opens on Mrs. Quigley and Mr. Galbraith, the housekeeper and estate manager for Manor Sackville, recently acquired by Lord Henry and Lady Emily Sackville. The action is devoted to the locals' efforts to discourage the Sackvilles from spending much time in Ireland. Lady Emily is frivolous, wishing to clothe starving Irish peasants "to give them a picturesque appearance suited to these romantic scenes—like the Swiss or Italian peasantry" (82). More serious-minded and more condescending, Henry wishes to reside in Ireland "to on trial for a month, and he is happy to play Dumb Andy no more.

Noblesse oblige is certainly the lesson being taught in this play. And while the children fall prey to the Brannigans' chicanery, Mrs. Bridgman works to make this a learning experience for them, even though her husband is ready to dismiss the Brannigans and Andy out of hand. Perhaps the most interesting character is Andy himself, who in a moment of crisis must tell the truth. While he doesn't wish to betray the Brannigans, his conscience gets the better of him. This moral dilemma, Levy says, "is a real one, without an easy answer, and it is one of the chief reasons for the play's strength" (127).

MODERN EDITION: Edited with an introduction by J. Levy, *The Gymnasium of the Imagination* (Westport: Greenwood, 1992): 123–160.

The Dupe, Frances Sheridan. This five-act comedy was produced at DL on 10 December 1763 and ran for three nights only. Though Frances Sheridan's biographer and granddaughter, Alicia LeFanu, blamed "the theatrical cabals of a popular actress" (possibly Kitty Clive, who took the role of Mrs. Friendly) for the play's lack of success, the audiences rejected a perceived immorality and hissed at each of the three performances (*LS* 4: 1025–26). *The Dupe* was published with a 1764 imprint by Andrew Millar. Hogan and Beasley mention that the play did so well in print that Millar sent Sheridan £100 "beyond the copyright money" (25).

The title character, Sir John Woodall, has spent his life in debauchery; currently a kept woman, Mrs. Etherdown lives in his London house while he is away in the country. They are in fact married, but Mrs. Etherdown cannot prove it was legal. To bring him to acknowledge the marriage, Mrs. Etherdown pretends to have a son while Sir John is away. Also staying in the house is Sir John's niece, Emily, who learns through Mrs. Friendly (played by Kitty Clive) that her intended, Captain Wellford, has returned on leave from the army; he will send a carriage for her at five. Mrs. Etherdown arranges to have another carriage pick Emily up and take her to a different place where she is awaited by Sharply, a confederate and pretended brother to Mrs. Etherdown, who wants to marry Emily to get Sir John's property. When Rose, Mrs. Etherdown's maid, overhears this plot, she is piqued by jealousy and reports the arrangement to Mr. Friendly and Captain Wellford. They rescue Emily, but Wellford misjudges the situation and blames Emily who will not forgive him. Meanwhile, Sir John returns to find the child and acknowledges his marriage. Moving from a kept mistress to an acknowledged Lady Woodall, Mrs. Etherdown treats Sir John with such effrontery that he regrets his untimely actions. When Friendly reports Mrs. Etherdown's deeds (disclosed by Rose and Sharply in a written confession) to Sir John, he understands he has been a dupe. After Mrs. Etherdown disappears from the house, Sir John says Emily will be his heir. Friendly then brings Wellford in, and Emily finally accepts the Captain's offer of marriage.

While Richard Bevis notes how close the play is to melodrama, he also accuses Sheridan of flat characterization (1980; 53). The creation of Mrs. Friendly as the garrulous gossip, however, seems to repudiate this charge: she is a convincing character—and no doubt memorable when played by Kitty Clive who created the role. Perhaps the play's eighteenth-century audience found too little to care about in most of the characters; they are either wastrels, scoundrels, or rogues. Ann Messenger states "*The Dupe* is not a pleasant play" (DLB 84: 296). While Friendly unravels Mrs. Etherdown's plots, the charge of his possible liaison with her is never answered. Bringing in Sharply and Rose at the end to be forgiven seems unrealistic, and while Rose has been promised marriage to Sharply, he is let off the hook in another unanswered question. Although the lovers make little impression on the spectator, Emily deserves some notice for her spirited refusal to marry a man who, she thinks, does not trust her: "The woman whom you have debased by your mean suspicions, will not, on such terms, condescend to be your wife" (130). Only after she learns that she is no longer penniless, having been named Sir John's heiress, does she agree to receive Wellford.

MANUSCRIPT: Larpent 228.

TEXT: Readex Microprint.

CRITICAL EDITION: Edited with introduction by Robert Hogan and Jerry C. Beasley (Cranberry, NJ: Associated UP, 1984).

The Dutch Lover, Aphra Behn. This five-act comedy was performed at DG on 6 February 1673 and printed for Thomas Dring the same year. There was no revival. Behn's preface shows a playwright angry with the ill-prepared actors and (because the play was a woman's) a prejudiced audience. Behn has adapted Francisco de Las Coveras's novel *The History of Don Fenise* (1651), according to Woodcock (*The English Sappho* 67). Loftis notes resemblances to a pair of Calderon's plays—*No siempre lo peor es cierto* and *Peor está que estaba*, possibly in the Earl of Bristol's translations, *Elvira* and *Worse and Worse* (*The Spanish Plays of Neoclassical England* 146).

In this, her third play, Behn moves from imitating the tragicomic dramas of Beaumont and Fletcher to Spanish intrigue comedy. Four plot lines keep any audience busy because they often converge on each other. Alonzo emerges as the central character, ready to love or fight for honor at the drawing of a sword. He has been brought to Madrid as colonel of the Prince's guards, accompanied by his Spanish friend Lovis. He's in Madrid only a very short time before he meets Euphemia, who has been promised to Haunce van Ezel, the Dutch lover of the title. By assuming Dutch garb, Alonzo acts the Dutch lover and marries Euphemia in the last act. A second plot finds Silvio lusting for his supposed sister Cleonte. However, Silvio turns out to be Roderigo, the son of Count d'Oliverez, who has been brought up by Don Ambrosio with his own children—Cleonte, Hippolyta, and Marcel. When Ambrosio tells Silvio of his real birth, this allows Silvio to marry Cleonte. A third plot involves Marcel and Clarinda. At first, he merely plans to seduce her, but complex events finally lead them to the altar. The fourth plot takes up the deflowered Hippolyta and her lover, Antonio. He has seduced her to get back at her brother Marcel, but Antonio finds he loves her and reforms. In the fifth act they too are wed. Besides all these marriages, Pedro and Dormida reunite, and Haunce along with his servant Gload are tricked into marrying Olinda and Dorice, Euphemia's maids.

In addition to a large cast, the play features mistaken identities, a number of sword fights, and orphans who finally learn their rightful parentage. Link points out the effective use of masques, songs, and dancing in this comedy (40). Pearson believes these masquerades, and the repeated use of such words as "feign," "dissemble," "counterfeit," and "act" point to a world where nothing is what it seems (145). The obscured births also add to such a world. Because of the Spanish setting and sources, the brothers become the keepers of their sisters' honors: Marcel wants to fight Antonio for seducing Hippolyta, and he is ready to kill Silvio when he thinks his "brother" has an assignation with Cleonte. Although Marcel plans to sleep with Clarinda, he recognizes the double standard for men and women before proceeding with his plan, only to be frustrated by Alonzo's being in the way. More important, however, Cleonte helps Clarinda out of her difficult situation even though Cleonte has love problems of her own. This assistance contributes to a recurring pattern of female friendships.

TEXTS: Wing B1726; EEB Reel 445: 32. Readex Microprint.

MODERN EDITIONS: *Works*, ed. Montague Summers (1915; NY: Phaeton, 1967) 1: 215–330; *Selected Writings of the Ingenious Mrs. Aphra Behn*, ed. Robert Phelps (NY: Grove, 1950; NY: Greenwood, 1969): 117–222, based on Summers's text.

-E-

Earl Goodwin, Ann Yearsley. This five-act, historical drama in verse was played at Bath on 3 November 1789, and the title page reports it was performed at the Theatre-Royal Bristol, though no dates are given. G. G. J. and J. Robinson published the play in 1791. Set in 1042, during the time of Edward the Confessor, the drama attempts to rehabilitate the character of Earl Goodwin, whose daughter Editha

In the battle, the Danes appear to be held at a stalemate, so Canute proposes single combat with Edmund to settle the war. Edmund agrees, and in the combat with Canute (described by nobles on both sides), Edmund wins, but both combatants praise the other's strength and skill. Together they decide the English will take the south, west, and Mercia, and the Danes will control the east and northeast. Elgiva, who waits for news of the fight, is lied to by Edrick who says that Edmund is dead. When Edmund does return, Edrick argues with him about the settlement, claiming that Canute has deceived him. When Edmund won't listen, Edrick stabs him. After Cefrid has Edrick taken, Canute makes a healing speech to the Danes and the Anglo-Saxons.

Aptly named for its hero and martyr, *Edmund* shows how the English and Danes come together. Edrick acts the Cain-like figure who murders his brother in order to assume the throne. Edrick's ambition causes him to err in his judgment, but he also knows how to make his treachery work. In the end, however, he overreaches himself and is caught, but not before he murders his brother, who perhaps suffers from being too decent. Of the three women in the play, Elgiva appears most fearful, and for good reason since her husband is always in harm's way. Emma, on the other hand, wants a reconciliation with the Danes so she can reunite with Canute, but not at the expense of her country. Her union with Canute provides a basis for a new British-Danish nation that has been agreed upon by Edmund and Canute. Birtha is frustrated from the outset by her fiancé's treachery, and everything she does to turn Edrick around only drives him further away from her. J. W. Donohue remarks that this tragedy "reveals a more overt 'Romantic' tendency. The play provides a straightforward history of the struggle for political power in Anglo-Saxon times, the King beset by faction within and invasion without; but many of the scenes serve what is evidently the author's more compelling purpose of illuminating the private emotional conditions of her characters" (*Theatre in the Age of Kean* 166).

TEXT: Readex Microprint.

EDWARDS, Anna Maria (fl. 1783–87). Edwards wrote one musical entertainment in two acts, *The Enchantress; or, The Happy Island*, with music by Tommaso Giordani. It was produced at the Capel-Street Theatre, Dublin, 1783. The play was later published in her *Poems on Various Subjects* by H. Colbert in 1787. [Nicoll]

EDWARDS, [Christian?] (fl. 1776–87). Inglis, in *The Dramatic Writers of Scotland* (1868), attributes to Miss Christian Edwards *Otho and Rutha*, which was published in her *Miscellanies, in Prose and Verse* (Edinburgh: printed for the author and sold by C. Elliot, 1776): 137–181. Dr. Johnson, James Boswell, David Hume, and Lord Kames were among the subscribers. Although more a narrative romance in prose than a drama, the piece was revised into a "dramatic tale," with a cast of twenty-four men and women, and printed in both Edinburgh (no publisher credit) and Dublin, by H. Colbert in 1780. Colbert issued another printing in 1787. There is no known performance. Inglis also credits Edwards with a historical ballad, entitled "The Buchanshire Tragedy of Sir James the Ross." [*BD*, Inglis, Tobin]

Edwy and Elgiva, Fanny Burney. This five-act, verse tragedy was produced at DL on 21 March 1795. Although Sarah Siddons was in the cast, the play had only this one presentation on stage. The *Morning Post* of 23 March 1795 commented on the risibility of the production (printed by Hogan in *LS* 5: 1739). Burney acknowledged that the play might not be sufficiently dramatic, but she blamed its stage failure on ill-prepared actors, many of whom did not bother to learn their lines.

The play focuses on the conflict between Edwy (Eadwig), a tenth-century King of the West Saxons, and the monks of England, who refused to acknowledge Edwy's marriage to his kinswoman, Princess Elgiva. When the play opens, Odo (Archbishop of Canterbury) and Dunstan (Abbot of Glastonbury) scheme to prevent the young King's marriage to Elgiva. Edwy tells Elgiva that he has asked Aldhelm—the Bishop of Winchester, his old tutor and ally—to convene the Council expressly to declare his intention to marry. When the Council rebukes Edwy's announcement, since Ecclesiastical Law forbids marriage to a kinswoman, the King grows angry, revealing that he and Elgiva are already married without the consent of either Church or State. In response, the Council agrees to part the lovers. When Dunstan has ruffians abduct Elgiva, Edwy labels him a traitor, asking for his banishment because the Abbot "drain'dst the Coffers, with grasp rapacious, of My credulous Uncle" (44). After Elgiva escapes, Edwy declares that she is Queen; the full Synod reacts, however, by pronouncing her divorced, and Odo recaptures Elgiva and carries her off. Spurred on by the monks, the people rise up and Civil War breaks out, but the King focuses only on his search for his wife. Impetuously, Edwy asks Cerdic (Earl of Mercia) to replace Redwald (Earl of Devon) as head of his Guards, thus encouraging Redwald's defection to Dunstan. Meanwhile, Dunstan's ruffians have stabbed Elgiva in the heart, but before she dies she is briefly reunited with Edwy. After news arrives that his younger brother Edgar has joined forces with Dunstan, Edwy rushes off suicidally before his troops to battle. Discovering that Edwy has found the death he eagerly sought, Aldhelm eulogizes the lovers, insisting that after death "Edwy and Elgiva shall . . . arise to Thrones of permanence, and Crowns immortal!" (82).

Edwy and Elgiva promises justice after death even though it may not prevail in this world. Although apparently triumphant, Dunstan realizes by Act V that he will be punished beyond the grave for the deaths of Elgiva and the King. The play is also preoccupied with Edwy's unfitness to be an earthly King. Repeatedly, the young King courts disaster by his impetuous and irresponsible actions. A feminist response to *Edwy and Elgiva* might be less critical of the King's commitment to personal love and domestic felicity over affairs of the state. Whether Edwy's qualities are tragic flaws or strengths—including his tendency to follow emotion over reason—could be debated; less controversial is the resounding condemnation in the play against the repressive, power-hungry, misogynistic monks. Shocked at Dunstan's condemnation of the institution of marriage and Elgiva the "voluptuous Courtezan" (50), Aldhelm reminds the Abbot that "If woman is our scorn, wedlock our horrour, where dwells the virtue of our [the Monk's] self-denial?" (40).

MANUSCRIPTS: Larpent 1058; New York Public Library, Berg Collection; and Emmanuel College, Cambridge (described by Benkovitz as a later version than the one at the NYPL).

CRITICAL EDITION: Transcribed and edited with an introduction by M. J. Benkovitz (Hamden, CT: Shoe String, 1957).

EGLETON, Jane Gifford (d. 1733?). An actress at LIF from 1717 to 1733, Egleton was the original Lucy Locket in *The Beggar's Opera*. She wrote one two-act ballad opera, *The Maggot*, produced only once, at LIF on her benefit night of 18 April 1732. There is no known printing. Admired as a comic actress, she is said to have been "too much addicted to the bottle" (Davies, *Memoirs of Garrick*). [BDAA (under Gifford), Cotton]

Egmont; or, the Eve of St. Alyne, Jane Porter. This play was offered to Edmund Kean's DL company in 1817, but his fellow actors refused to produce it. The tragedy was neither performed nor published.

The Egyptian Boy, Elizabeth Inchbald. This three-act adaptation commissioned by Harris was proposed for performance at CG on 3 May 1802. During April, Inchbald adapted Louis Caigniez's *Le Jugement de Salomon*, but Harris's delay in the production of her version allowed James Boaden to offer his adaptation, *The Voice of Nature*, based on the same play by Caigniez, for the Haymarket summer season. After the success of Boaden's version which ran twenty performances, Harris set aside Inchbald's adaptation, paying her the contractual price of £105 for her efforts. The recent attribution to Inchbald by Patricia Sigl may be found in a detailed essay, which compares the two versions against the French original (*TN* 43 [1989]: 57–69).

The plot of the "affecting drama" treats Solomon's potential dividing of the child, taken from the old testament story (I Kings 3: 16–28).

MANUSCRIPT: Larpent 1348.

1688. *The Emperor of the Moon* was quite successful with English audiences: Leo Hughes and A. H. Scouten account for more than 130 performances from 1687 to 1749 (42).

Dr. Baliardo, whose sole occupation is to study the moon, believes in the existence of a lunar world, inhabited by superior beings. Thus, he rejects the lovers (Cinthio and Charmante) of his daughter (Elaria) and niece (Bellemante) as unsuitable husbands, for only men of the moon will do. "With so hopelessly silly a guardian, the young ladies have virtually no problem eluding him. So the dramatist needs to devote no attention to the intrigue and can concentrate on the farce episodes" (Hughes and Scouten 44). Assisted by Scaramouch, the doctor's servant, and Harlequin, Cinthio's man, the lovers repeatedly hoodwink the doctor and marry their loves. A second plot, nicely intertwined with the main plot, has Scaramouch and Harlequin vying for the hand of Mopsophil, the governess of the young women.

Aphra Behn's inspiration came from Fatouville's three-act comedy, *Arlequin, Empereur dans la lune*, first produced in Paris in 1684. Although her borrowing amounts to more than "a very barren and thin hint of the plot," she altered and adapted it to the English stage. Gone are the scenes in Italian intermingled with the French, and gone are the original's earthy wordplay and its ribald repartee. Behn retains some of the farcical episodes, but these do not closely follow the original. For example, in the "Scène du desespoir," Harlequin is not instructed to change his voice and gestures as he contemplates ways to end his life, nor does he elaborate on them as hilariously as the French original, and in Behn's adaptation this famous scene loses much of its comic impact. Both plays, however, end in strikingly similar ways: the Emperor of the Moon (in the French, Arlequin, and in Behn, one of the two lovers, disguised as rulers of the lunar world) descends to earth to claim his mistresses—now approved of by Dr. Baliardo. Behn has none other than Kepler and Galileo announce the entrance of the Emperor, lending a pseudo-learned burlesque that is absent in Fatouville's *commedia dell' arte*. Scenic spectacles, a good deal of dancing and singing, and many opportunities for farcical actions give the play a continuing appeal. Link points out how Behn delicately blends "farce, fantasy, pageantry, and romance" to create a "lightness and gaiety which permeate all three acts" (78).

TEXTS: Wing B1727; EEB Reel 203: 4 (1687). Wing B1728; EEB Reel 857: 26 (1688). Readex Microprint of the 1687 edition.

MODERN EDITION: *Works*, ed. Montague Summers (1915; NY: Phaeton, 1967) 2: 383–463.

CRITICAL EDITION: *Ten English Farces*, edited with introduction by Leo Hughes and A. H. Scouten (Austin: U of Texas P, 1948): 39–84.

The Enchanted Island; or, The Freeborn Englishwoman, Mrs. T. Robertson. This musical entertainment—written in 1796—is the only known work by Mrs. T. Robertson (*BD* 1: 775). No known text of the piece exists today.

The Enchantress; or, The Happy Island, Anna Maria Edwards. This musical entertainment in two acts was produced only one night at the Capel-Street Theatre, Dublin, in 1783 with music by Tommaso Giordani. The play was later printed in Edwards's *Poems on Various Subjects* by H. Colbert, Dublin, 1787.

Anna and Selina have fled from their uncle and guardian, Sir Nestor, to an island controlled by an enchantress named Felicia. Anna wishes to avoid a proposed marriage to old Sir Oliver, for she is in love with Edgar. Because Felicia was a friend of Anna's deceased mother, she agrees to help the young women. Meanwhile, Sir Nestor and Sir Oliver have landed on another part of the island. Sir Nestor thinks he'll be a match for the woman, but he is immediately struck dumb. The two men are suddenly transported to a rocky coast, and Sir Nestor hears Felicia say she will never let him go until he sees his faults. Back in the city Edgar and Orlando, Sir Nestor's son, are searching for Anna and Selina; they learn the women are likely to have gone to the island, and that Sir Nestor and Sir Oliver have followed them there. On the island, Felicia tells Fidelia, one of her spirits, that Edgar and Orlando have arrived, but she wants them transported to the Orange Grove that Anna and Selina frequent. The couples meet and embrace, but Sir Nestor's approval must be won. The two old gentlemen are still on the rock, where Sir Oliver believes he should give up his claims on Anna. Fidelia alters the setting to a garden and touches Sir Nestor's lips, allowing him to speak: he realizes he has acted like a fool, and he decides to help those who have suffered by his errors. With that admission, Fidelia touches the scene behind Sir Nestor and discovers Anna with Edgar and Orlando with Selina. As Sir Nestor joins the couples's hands, he asks why Selina fled, and she says that she came with Anna because Sir Nestor had made Anna unhappy. "A rare instance of female friendship truly," he responds, "to prefer another's happiness to your own" (62). After Sir Oliver resigns any pretensions to Anna, Felicia reminds them that all humans have faults, and we must learn to accept those in others. A merry sextet concludes the play.

The stagecraft in this fairy tale allows Edwards to manipulate the set and move characters quickly from one location to another. Not only do the young people gain each other, but the old gentlemen learn a lesson: Sir Oliver is frightened out of his wits, and Sir Nestor finds he is no match for a woman's magic. The Enchantress, Felicia, vows several times that she only uses her power to help, never to hurt. Both Anna and Selina support each other in a true female friendship. The songs (six in the first act and eight in the second act) reinforce the spoken parts. Edwards notes that the last scene of act one in the printed text was omitted to shorten the actual performance.

TEXT: Readex Microprint.

The English Tavern in Berlin, Elizabeth Harlow. This three-act comedy was published by H. Chamberlaine and seven others in Dublin, 1790. *BD* suggests there may have been a 1789 version, published for the author, though we have not seen a copy. The play is not known to have been performed. Genest points out a later drama based on the same subject: John Poole adapted a French story for the English stage in *The Two Pages of Frederick the Great*, 1821 (9: 155–56).

Mr. and Mrs. Conrade, recently married, are opening a new inn, and Lambert arranges for his mother and sister, Jenny, to stay there. Mrs. Lambert tells Jenny that she has lost the family estate at the death of her husband, and she has come to Berlin to petition the King for redress. When Baron Amsdorff finds Lambert waiting to see his mother, he tries to give him money. But Lambert is too proud to take it; they argue and begin to duel before Mrs. Conrade stops them. They say it is just in sport, but they plan to carry on their duel elsewhere. Mrs. Conrade sends a servant to separate them; however, he cannot gain admittance to the King's stables and reports that Lambert came out and jumped on a horse, saying he was on a mission for the King and to send for a surgeon. When Mrs. Lambert hears this she faints, but the Conrades revive her and are willing to vouch for her and her son. The scene shifts to the King's antechamber, where Lambert has just arrived with a letter for the monarch. At this early hour (3 a.m.), he falls asleep. The King finds Lambert, and lets him continue to sleep, while praising his attention to duty and pitying his lax morals. The Baron Amsdorff arrives and tells the King about the quarrel, blaming himself. He also reports that the rumors about Lambert's morals are untrue: the money he is supposed to spend on women is actually sent to his mother. When the Baron explains that she doesn't have a pension, the King sends for the Secretary of War. With the Baron out of the room, the King puts 200 louis d'or in Lambert's pocket and leaves the room. The Baron returns, awakes Lambert, and forgives him. When Lambert looks for the letter he has brought to the King, he finds the 200 louis d'or and thinks the Baron has put them there. They argue, but the King stops them, telling Lambert that he must never disdain a good act: "Gratitude is a far nobler motive than the best intended pride" (51). A page reports that the widow has arrived; Mrs. Lambert, Jenny, and Mr. and Mrs. Conrade enter. The King requests that Jenny accept the Baron as a husband. Mr. Conrade tells the King that he was steward to the General's father, and he has the papers to the Lambert estate. The King promises that justice will be done. A talkative Mr. Conrade invites everyone to drink a health to the king and to toast the young couple at the English Tavern.

BD describes this comedy as "a very ill written piece. Its main character is from an anecdote related of the Great Frederic's rewarding of filial piety of a page of his, to his distressed parent, by putting a rouleau of louis d'ors in his pocket, while he is taking a nap" (2: 198). It is hard to disagree with this assessment: a number of speeches are too long for stage presentation, motivation is seldom developed, and characters tell each other facts that they already know—merely for the benefit of the audience. As, for example, when Mrs. Lambert explains to Jenny why they have come to Berlin. The main value that Harlow espouses is duty to one's sovereign, especially to a benevolent ruler like Frederick the Great. In almost every situation in the play, women must ask men for what they want. The world of the play is very much a man's world.

TEXT: Readex Microprint of Dublin edition of 1790.

The Englishman in Bourdeaux [sic], "Translated by an English Lady now residing in Paris." The publication of this translation of Favart's one-act comedy, *L'Anglois à Bordeaux*, was first printed in Dublin, 1763, and in London for G. Kearsly, 1764. It was not staged in England.

The action of this play takes place in Bordeaux after the French and English have signed the Paris peace treaty ending the Seven-Year War (1756–1763). Brumton, an overly patriotic Englishman, whose ship was sunk by Darmant, still refuses any contact with Darmant, in whose house he resides with his daughter Clarissa, not as prisoners but as revered guests. The Marquise de Floricourt, Darmant's sister, undertakes "to cure [Brumton] of his innate prejudices" against the French. Her brother has fallen in love with Clarissa, and she has fallen for the irascible Englishman. For these reasons and "for the honour" of France, she is determined to succeed. Darmant's discreet generosity and persistent offers of friendship, the Marquise's vivaciousness and spirit, and Sudmer's eloquent pleas for universal brotherhood all combine to overcome Brumton's violently anti-French and antisocial feelings. The play ends with a double marriage in the midst of great rejoicing over the reestablishment of peace between the two nations.

As Kinne states, "the central theme, celebrating the recent peace treaty, shows how love smooths out misunderstandings, removing national prejudices" (89). But it does so in a most unconvincing manner: Brumton's abrupt turnabout is not very believable. Furthermore, both the original and the translation suffer from what Genest calls "want of incident" (10: 181), since the translation is a faithful rendering of the original. In dedicating the piece to Favart, the translator says in her preface that she wanted to give the play "an English dress; a free not a servile one." One striking, if not typical example, is when Clarissa learns she can marry the one she loves. The concise French "Ah! mon père!" becomes "O, Sir, you revive me, you are now a second time my father" (58). The translator also replaced the French ballet and songs with an epilogue extolling the virtues of true universalism.

TEXT: Readex Microprint of the London edition, printed for G. Kearsly, 1764.

Enthusiasm, Joanna Baillie. This three-act comedy was published in the second volume of *Dramas* (Longman, et al., 1836). Like her earlier *Plays on the Passions*, this play was unified by Baillie's commentary on a single passion: enthusiasm, especially as it is employed by Lady Worrymore to ingratiate herself with others. The play was not staged.

Lord Worrymore complains to Lady Shrewdly that his wife no longer attends to what he says; instead, she hangs on to every word spoken by young "coxcombs," especially the poet Clermont. Lady Shrewdly suggests that a trick be played upon her credulity and Blount, a sailor and family friend, agrees to help them. Lord Worrymore writes a speech that is delivered by Blount—masquerading as the great orator Mr. O'Honikin—in front of Lady Worrymore. She is so impressed by O'Honikin's genius that she plans a tribute to O'Honikin and Clermont in the garden before sunset. When the busts of the artists are uncovered, Lady Worrymore discovers that both the speech and sonnet were penned by her husband, and she learns a lesson about evaluating art on its own merit. In a thinly related subplot, Clermont is romantically involved with Miss Frankland, who is preoccupied with the identify of a poor foreigner, a sick German boy named Hugh. She is convinced that Hugh is actually the son of her uncle's (Colonel Frankland's) only daughter, who ran away with an Italian. Clermont helps her verify the boy's identity, and he regains Miss Frankland's respect when he finally rejects Lady Worrymore's flattery and enthusiasm about his poetry.

Miss Frankland and Lady Shrewdly are introduced as positive models for women: thoughtful, unselfish, direct, and full of good sense. Lady Worrymore is a symbol of foolishness, overrefinement, and affectation. As part of the denouement, Colonel Frankland divides his property equitably between his newly discovered grandson and his niece: he offers Miss Frankland "half of my moveable property" (441) as her dowry. Some of the coincidences in the play suggest problems with the plot or character development. Miss Frankland only has to look at Hugh and she knows instantly who he is. Furthermore, the child's identity is established instantly when they discover that his locket contains a lock of the Colonel's hair and a note from the deceased daughter.

TEXT: Readex Microprint of *Dramas* (1836) 2: 321–442.

"EPHELIA" (c. 1640s–1681 or 1682). An unknown poet and playwright of the latter seventeenth century, Ephelia has never been positively identified. That she is the daughter of Katherine Philips ("Orinda") has long been discredited. Based on genealogical evidence, Maureen Mulvihill speculates that Ephelia may be Anne Prowde of Shrewsbury, who became "Joan Phillips" of London. Evidence of Ephelia's only known comedy, *The Pair-Royal of Coxcombs*, which may have been acted at a dancing school in 1678 or 1679, is a prologue, epilogue, and two songs, published in *Female Poems on Several Occasions, Written by Ephelia* (London: James Courtney, 1679), and another edition of 1682—probably posthumous and unauthorized. [Cotton, DBAWW, FCLE, Smith & Cardinale. *Poems by Ephelia*, a facsimile edition, edited with an introduction by Maureen E. Mulvihill, reprints the prologue, epilogue, and two songs from *The Pair-Royal of Coxcombs*.]

Ethelred, Sarah Watts Richardson. Called a "legendary tragic drama," this five-act verse tragedy was printed by Lowndes and Hobbs without a date (c. 1810). There is no record of its being acted. According to Richardson's preface, the subject matter of the play is taken from Madame de Gomez's *La Belle Assemblée*.

Ethelred the Second, King of England, has damaged himself politically by marrying "a lowly maid" and "raising [her] to his throne" (6). In spite of this, Ethelred's uncle, Edgar, has learned to appreciate the King's wife, Ethelgive: "her conduct is revered by all, and she is now the mother of two princes" (12). In Ethelred's absence, Edgar asks the Council Chamber to acknowledge Ethelgive as Queen, and all reluctantly agree. Returning from battle, Ethelred stays with Richard, Duke of Normandy, where he is encouraged to fall in love with Emma, the Princess of Normandy and Richard's sister. After agreeing to make Emma Queen of England, Ethelred returns to England where he tries to dispose quickly of Ethelgive: "One of us must suffer, and why not she? The reasoning is fair: I'll think no more of her, and beauteous Emma shall with her heavenly presence quite dispel each dark and fear-formed vision" (29). Edgar reprimands Ethelred when he pretends to be giving up his wife for the good of the state; and after arriving in England, Emma is distressed to hear that Ethelred has a wife and that she is being sacrificed. Upon hearing of her fate, Ethelgive swoons and is thought to be dead. Although initially delighted, Ethelred begins to feel guilty about his wife's death when he reads a letter she has written to him. When the King tries to postpone her Coronation, Emma grows more assertive, fearing she will be treated like Ethelgive. Emma's demands cause Ethelred to long for his late wife's submissiveness: "Oh, gentle Ethelgive, how did thy meekness conduct itself under much greater injuries!" (70). After he shows remorse, Edgar informs him that his wife is still alive. Angered by the King's hesitation to marry Emma, Richard confronts Ethelred and kills him, even though his sister tries to prevent the murder. Ethelgive dies, too, poisoned by a priest at the altar, an agent of Richard's. Edgar asks Emma to bear the title of Dowager to Ethelred, "the sons of this unhappy Lady [Ethelgive] being acknowledg'd Heirs to the British Throne" (92).

From a feminist perspective, *Ethelred* is most interesting because of the understanding that exists between Ethelgive and Emma. Although the women never meet until the last scene, they cooperate in ways that may be unexpected given their relationships with Ethelred. Before she dies, Ethelgive asks Emma to "Forget, I ask you, when you see my boys, that their unhappy mother was your rival" (91). When Emma pledges to "befriend . . . those tender pledges of your joint affection" (92), readers are not surprised: she earlier despised Ethelred's treatment of his wife and declared "I would not be partner of his throne" (88).

TEXT: Readex Microprint.

Ethwald, in Two Parts, Joanna Baillie. Two five-act tragedies, both of which appeared in A *Series of Plays: [on] the Stronger Passions of the Mind* (Second Series), printed by T. Cadell, Jr., and W. Davies in 1802. Neither play was staged.

Set in England, in the kingdom of Mercia, in the seventh or eighth century. In the first drama, Ethwald rises to power by his prowess on the battlefield, ignoring the wizard's prophecy: "The destruction of his noble line should from the valour of his youngest son in royal warfare spring" (115). When Ethwald captures the British Prince, the King makes him the Earl of Marnieth. At this same time, Ethwald exchanges gifts with Bertha, the woman to whom he is betrothed. In order to rise higher, Ethwald plots with Alwy, described as an "artful adventurer" (110), to have the Prince freed. To ensure the soldiers' loyalty to him, Ethwald shares with them the British booty. Ethelbert, a noble thane who is also a mystic, accuses his friend Ethwald of going to war to satisfy political ambitions. To enable Ethwald to become King, Alwy and Bishop Hexulf plot to burn Ethelbert's castle and to imprison Edward, heir to the throne. The King himself is killed when Ethwald and the rebel chiefs mount a surprise attack on his castle. With secret delight, the King's daughter, Elburga, submits to Ethwald's insistence that they marry. At the end of the first tragedy, Ethwald is wounded by a poor groom, whose family has become homeless because of their loyalty to the King. Apparently at the point of death, Ethwald repents and asks Ethelbert to reinstate Edward as King.

At the beginning of the second tragedy, the reader is surprised to discover that Ethwald has recovered and reneged on his promise to make "brave amends . . . for past offenses" (232). Alwy conspires with Hexulf and Queen Elburga to eliminate their three most powerful foes: Ethelbert, who has become Lord Regent; Selred, Ethwald's brother; and Hereulf, one of the chiefs who fought with Ethwald in the past. Ethwald dreams of uniting all of Britain under his crown, but his military conflicts grow more difficult to win and the continued bloodshed alienates his subjects. After arranging to have Edward killed, Ethwald is haunted by guilt. When Ethelbert and Selred are executed, Hereulf escapes and rallies the other rebel chiefs against the King. Ethwald is deposed and dies defending himself.

Despite Ethwald's miraculous recovery in part two, both plays have merit. Baillie acknowledges that she has been influenced by *Macbeth*, and her protagonist is no less complex psychologically than Shakespeare's. Verbal similarities between names—Ethwald, Edward, Elburga—underscore deeper connections. Elburga, like the man she marries, is motivated by political ambition. Edward, in contrast, functions as Ethwald's alter ego: he is gentle, selfless, and capable of love. Ethwald must kill Edward in part because of what he represents: "His love hath been to me my bosom's sting; His gen'rous trust hath gnaw'd me like a worm" (282). Less important characters but also opposites, Bertha and Elburga are equally doomed by Ethwald's obsessive need to overwhelm all opposition to his will. The figurative language can be powerful, especially when pastoral scenes are contrasted with the devastation of war. Repeated attention is paid to the dislocation and suffering experienced by civilians.

TEXT: Readex Microprint of 1821 edition. Part One—2: 109–237. Part Two—2: 239–360.

FACSIMILE EDITION: *Romantic Context: Poetry* reprints both parts of the 1802 edition (London: T. Cadell, Jr., and W. Davies). Compiled by D. H. Reiman (NY: Garland, 1977).

Eton Montem, Maria Edgeworth. This three-act play was added to a later version of *The Parent's Assistant*, first published in 1796. The play is prefaced with an extract from the *Courier*, May 1799, about a collection of money, "called *Salt*, . . . which forms the purse, to support the Captain of the school in his studies at Cambridge" (115). There is no record of a public performance.

Two students are running for the captaincy of Eton—Wheeler and Talbot. The play opens at the Windmill Inn on Salt Hill, where the landlord and landlady (Mr. and Mrs. Newington) are quarreling about the rooms to be let for Eton Montem, which is to take place the next day. When Wheeler comes in, Mr. Newington wants a debt settled for an injured horse, but he says it was not his fault. A few minutes later, Talbot comes in and settles the debt, thinking the horse was his responsibility. Meanwhile, in the dining room of the inn, Mrs. Talbot shows her daughter, Louisa, a message she has just received: a ship bound for Bombay has gone down with the entire family fortune abroad. Since the landlady has displaced the Talbots from their rooms, Farmer Hearty offers them lodgings. The scene shifts to Etonians arguing about the election of their Captain. Wheeler has told Talbot a lie: Talbot's mother broke her leg and is at a farmhouse in the district; thus Talbot will be unable to canvass for votes, and Wheeler will easily win the election. When Talbot arrives at the farmhouse, he discovers the ruse, but Hearty tells Talbot about the hunting horse that got a sprain by running through his corn. Although Talbot has settled with Mr. Newington about the horse, Hearty thinks he can identify the real culprit. They go to Eton, where Hearty accuses Wheeler of causing the horse an injury and hushing it up. The tide turns, and Talbot wins the captaincy. In the final scene, the Talbots learn that it was not their ship that was wreaked but another.

Although the Talbots suffer many indignities, they succeed in the end. Young Talbot is elected Captain and will be able to go to Cambridge; also, his family has not lost all their money. As is usual in Edgeworth's dramas and tales, those who are good and honest win out, after much adversity, over the evil and vicious. As a play, however, *Eton Montem* suffers from too many plots. Aside from the election, the Talbots lose their room at the Windmill Inn, the feigned story of Mrs. Talbot's broken leg draws her son away from school, and the family suffers the near loss of their fortune. Wheeler, on the other hand, is almost as destitute as Talbot; he must have a friend pay for his special clothing. Moreover, he whines and snivels to try to gain votes, and he treats his opponent unfairly. The clear good-versus-bad characterization is too apparent to create much dramatic interest, and the play dwindles into ineffectual melodrama.

TEXT: Not in Readex Microprint. We read the play in *The Parent's Assistant*, 4th edition (London: J. Johnson, 1804) 6: 115–224, in the King Collection at the Miami (Ohio) Library.

Evening Revels, Mrs. William Barrymore. This "diversion," not listed in Genest, was produced at DL on 10 November 1823, according to Nicoll. Apparently, it was not printed, and no manuscript of the diversion exists in the Larpent Collection.

The Events of a Day, Elizabeth Hull Edmead. The only drama written by Edmead was a five-act drama, *The Events of a Day*, produced at the Theatre Royal, Norwich in 1795. It was not printed.

MANUSCRIPT: Larpent 1100.

Every One Has His Fault, Elizabeth Inchbald. This five-act comedy was first produced at CG on 29 January 1793 and ran thirty-two nights its first season. Published the same year by G. G. J. and J. Robinson, the play ran through eleven printings before 1800.

This enormously popular play treats four different modes of marriage: one between Sir Robert and Lady Ramble has ended in a Scottish divorce; a second between Lady Eleanor and Mr. Irwin suffers because of their poverty; a third between Mr. and Mrs. Placid is strained because of his passivity and her aggressiveness; and a fourth examines the unmarried states of Solus, an old bachelor, and Miss Spinster, an old maid. Into this mix, add Mr. Harmony, a benevolent man who wants everyone to get along together; Lord Norland, the rigid father of Lady Eleanor who has disinherited her for what he considers a foolish marriage; and Edward, the son of Lady Eleanor and Mr. Irwin who was adopted by his grandfather after his parents went off to America with the British army. After a number of contretemps, the Rambles find they cannot get along without each other; Edward with the help of Harmony intercedes with Lord Norland on behalf of his parents and the old tyrant softens into a reconciliation; Harmony helps reunite the Placids; and Solus marries Miss Spinster.

The play exalts "domesticity and sacred motherhood," showing a "sentimental spirit," according to Janet Todd in her discussion of the subject (*Sentimentality: An Introduction* [London: Methuen, 1986]: 48). Paula Backscheider suggests "Inchbald could combine the popular sentimental plot tinged with touches of broad humor with consideration of serious social problems" (xvii). The reverse of this, however, may be the case: sentimental elements carefully blend into the wide comic fabric of the play. In his illuminating essay, Frank Ellis suggests that Inchbald's play "is a sentimental comedy in the process of becoming melodrama" (112). One problem people have with the play results from Mr. Harmony's fabrications of the truth, or—as some believe—outright lies. Excessive compassion does cause Harmony to display "an unbounded affection for [his] fellow creatures." This zeal leads him to flatter people so that they will alter their perceptions toward their antagonists. Harmony's deliberate announcement that Irwin has died may serve two purposes: first, it causes Lord Norland to realize his own complicity in Irwin's offenses; and, second, when Irwin steps on stage he experiences a rebirth in a new relationship with his father-in-law. Nevertheless, Harmony's lies, as Ellis points out, must cause "some ambivalence about sentimentality" (110). While the title states the principal theme of the play, Inchbald could be suggesting that "happiness in marriage may be based on lies and deceptions" (Ellis, 109). Generic considerations of this play have gotten more attention than the treatment of female characters which has largely been ignored. Although Sir Robert treats Lady Ramble in the worst ways, the divorce doesn't improve her situation; indeed, she comes under the control of her guardian Lord Norland. And his lordship's mean-spirited handling of his own daughter's elopement and marriage cause continuing problems for Lady Eleanor. Mrs. Placid is stuck with an unassertive husband, and Miss Spinster marries because of misinformation she has received from her cousin Harmony. These negative treatments of marriage may suggest Inchbald's own perceptions about the not-altogether-happy lives of married women. After her own husband's death, she did not choose to remarry even though she had several opportunities.

MANUSCRIPT: Larpent 967.

TEXT: Readex Microprint.

FACSIMILE EDITION: E-CED, with introduction by Paula R. Backscheider (NY: Garland, 1980).

CRITICAL EDITION: Edited with an accompanying essay by Frank H. Ellis, *Sentimental Comedy: Theory and Practice* (Cambridge: Cambridge UP, 1991): 173–221.

Every Woman in Her Humour, attributed to Catherine Clive. This two-act farce was produced only one time at DL, on the occasion of Clive's benefit on 20 March 1760. Clive took the role of an old maid aunt (Miss Croston), according to *BD* (2: 206). The play was never printed.

Sir Charles Freelove is on his way to see his intended, Harriet Byfield, with his cousin Sir James Freeman. Sir Charles has been out of England for three years, and while he was away Harriet's father, Sir John Byfield, has remarried. Sir Charles explains to Sir James he was nearly married five years earlier to a woman of great fortune; when the woman's father turned out to have no money, he left her, even through they were contracted. At that earlier time, he confesses, he borrowed his cousin's name, since the latter was at Oxford. The scene shifts to the Byfields, where Miss Croston berates Sir John Byfield about his recent marriage to a younger woman. The new Lady Byfield and Harriet have formed a strong friendship, and Lady Byfield speaks frankly with Harriet about her marriage to Sir John: while Lady Byfield feels she cannot love him, she will never injure Sir John. When Sir Charles arrives, Harriet appears ready to marry him, until Lady Byfield enters and finds Sir Charles is the same man who broke his marriage compact with her five years earlier. She tells Harriet, Sir Charles is "one of the most abandoned, obdurate wretches ever," causing Harriet to halt her marriage plans. In front of an assembled party, Lady Byfield orders Sir Charles out of the house, and does the same to Miss Croston. The party congratulate Harriet on her narrow escape.

The plot may have been intended to provide several of the cast with roles in which they excelled, such as clever servants, wily fortune hunters, feckless husbands, and talkative friends. And while some individual scenes do provide situations for cameo appearances, these are at the expense of forwarding the plot. The loose construction does not stress drama as much as it emphasizes farce. Although the plot turns on the discovery of Sir Charles's former falseness to the present Lady Byfield, the denouement of his public exposure shows the enhanced character of Lady Byfield. That Lady Byfield finally stands up to the tart-tongued Miss Croston is another triumph for a second wife. The play refutes the conventional "happy ending" by celebrating Harriet's deliverance from the fortune-hunting Sir Charles. And in another unconventional twist, Lady Byfield gets along well with her stepdaughter rather than acting the traditional stepmother. Lady Byfield's qualifications for a proper relationship are people who "are agreeable, and endeavour to make everybody happy that is in their power." Still, she acts to censure Sir Charles and Miss Croston for their harmful deeds.

MANUSCRIPT: Larpent 174. Readex Microprint of the manuscript.

Everybody to Their Own Liking, Mrs. Green. This farce may have been performed at Bath in 1756. Nicoll provides the only mention that a play by this name was produced. We have been unable to corroborate this production with other sources. Genest doesn't list Bath performances for this year, and the play is not in the Larpent Collection. Apparently the text is lost.

-F-

The Fair Captive, Eliza Haywood. Haywood's first play, a blank-verse tragedy in five-acts, was produced at LIF on 4 March 1721 and published the same year by T. Jauncy and H. Cole. It ran for three nights and was revived once the following season at LIF (16 November 1721) for the author's benefit. In her preface, Haywood says she extensively revised the text from a manuscript, at the request of the manager John Rich, and "there remains not twenty lines of the original." The tragedy by Captain Robert Hurst was announced for a production at LIF on 14 June 1715, but his version was never performed.

The center of Haywood's revised tragedy is Isabella, the fair captive of the title, a Spanish lady who has been seized by the Turks. The Grand Vizier, Mustapha, wishes to make her part of his harem. The play opens when her Spanish lover, Alphonso (not Roderigo as in Pearson), comes to free her. Irene, the wife of the Vizier, becomes aware of her husband's plans; and, disguised as an eunuch, she interrupts Mustapha's attempted rape of Isabella. Mustapha reacts by stabbing his wife, but he later dies by the hands of his janizaries. Only when Mustapha, in a dying speech, declares Isabella's virtue is Alphonso's honor appeased. Being thus reconciled, the Spanish couple is sent back to Spain by Ozmin, the head of the janizaries.

Although Irene acts in her own interest, she is slain, whereas Isabella, who appears passive, lives. She is manipulated by the men in the play, who can only be called hypocritical. Pearson points out the vulnerability of the women in the play, where "male disguise is as limiting as female identity." The context of the play, according to Rudolph, is the old heroic drama: "an exotic setting, distressed beauty, a love/honor conflict, and an ample amount of jealousy, intrigue, deception, disguise, and revenge." Moreover, power and passion divide the characters from each other: only Isabella, who goes to the Vizier to plead for the life of Alphonso against the latter's advice, maintains her virtue and honor.

TEXT: Readex Microprint.

FACSIMILE EDITION: E-CED, with introduction by Valerie Rudolph (NY: Garland, 1983).

The Fair Fugitives, Anna Marie Porter. This musical entertainment was first produced at CG on 16 May 1803, with music by Thomas Busby. The songs were published the same year by T. N. Longman and O. Rees, but the entire play was not printed.

MANUSCRIPT: Larpent 1385.

Fairy Legends; or, The Moon-light Night, Jane M. Scott. Opening at the Sans Pareil Theatre on 7 December 1818, this musical drama played twenty-eight nights with music composed by Nicholson.

MANUSCRIPT: Larpent 2057.

The Faithful General, "A Young Lady." The dedication is signed only with the initials M. N. This tragedy is partly based on Beaumont and Fletcher's *The Loyal Subject* of 1618. It was performed only three times at the Queen's Theatre, opening on 3 January 1706. Because of the direct competition that existed between the two theatre companies, DL mounted the original on 4 January. M. N.'s version was published in 1706 by Richard Wellington.

The new Emperor of the East, Galerius, cashiers Marus, the old and honored general of the Roman forces in Greece, and in his place puts his favorite, the cowardly Lycinius. But when the Thracians attack, Lycinius doesn't know what to do, and Galerius must swallow his pride and ask for Marus's help. With his son, Theodorus, Marus and his troops save the city. Although Galerius has always hated Marus, the new Emperor falls in love with Marus's daughter, Artimesia, who has just returned from studying in Athens: she is famed throughout Greece for her "Beauty, Learning, [and] Vertue" (11). Although she is mildly attracted to him, she will act only on her father's approval. At a banquet for the victors, Galerius —prompted by the scheming Lycinius —reveals that Marus has a private store of treasure. Marus acknowledges the truth of the charge, but he says he is holding it in trust for Galerius because of a promise Marus made to the ruler's deceased father. When Marus will not tell where the treasure is located, Galerius orders him and Theodorus, who also knows the secret, to the rack. In a prison scene, Constantia, Galerius's sister who is betrothed to Theodorus, says she doesn't want to live without him and urges them to a double suicide with the dagger she has brought, but Theodorus cannot strike Constantia. Word arrives that Artimesia has moved Galerius to rescind his order, but Lycinius has carried it out, and Marus is brought in, "mangled and bloody." Lycinius, finding his plot overthrown, stabs himself and in a frenzy "of Blasphemy" expires. Marus blesses everyone —including Galerius —and dies. At this point, Artimesia cannot accept Galerius: she sheds her royal robes and says she "will again be free" (68). She stabs herself twice before Galerius can wrest the dagger from her. Artimesia dies having defended her honor.

Since the play lasted only three nights and was never revived, M. N.'s adaptation of Beaumont and Fletcher's piece cannot be considered a success with audiences. If we can judge by the printed text, however, her version almost doubles the size of the original, forcing necessary cuts for stage presentation. In the Preface, M. N. acknowledges this "prolixity," but she felt that her adaptation was "deform'd and mangled for the Stage" (Advertisement, sig. A4). Hume gives the version only brief notice, calling it "no more than a hideously mangled, sentimentalized recension of Fletcher's *The Loyal Subject*" (476). What M. N. has done, however, is to make "a wholly new play of her Jacobean original," Pearson believes (244). And while there are only two women in the play, they are the focus of M. N.'s version, and it is their active fortitude that contrasts with male cowardice and passivity. Artimesia, the general's daughter, is caught between her family's honor and a ruler who has some allure for her. Because of her education in Athens, Artimesia is able to distinguish between reason and emotion. And she is no coward when she must make a decision: rather than marry the spineless Galerius, she commits suicide in front of him. Even Arthur Colby Sprague, who does not care for the play, points out that the last three scenes owe nothing to the original (*Beaumont and Fletcher on the Restoration Stage* [1926; NY: B. Blom, 1965]: 218–19. What M. N. has done is to recreate and recenter the drama, showing women can be intrepid in matters of state.

TEXT: Readex Microprint.

The Faithful Irishwoman, Catherine Clive. This two-act farce was produced at DL on 18 March 1765 (Clive's benefit night) for the first and only time. Kitty Clive acted the title role. The play, never printed, enlarges and reworks Clive's earlier benefit play, *The Sketch of a Fine Lady's Return from a Rout* (DL, 21 March 1763).

Two female servants open the play by talking about their master and mistress (Sir Jeremy and Lady Jenkins). Lady Jenkins has a passion for gambling, and she has not returned at 7 a.m. from her nightly turn at the tables. They also discuss her ladyship's Irish friend, Mrs. O'Conner, whom everyone seems to like, and the children's governess, whom everyone seems to dislike. Lady Jenkins and Mrs. O'Conner arrive to the noise of the daughters (Nancy and Fanny). When they are quieted down, Sir Jeremy enters and tells English/Irish stories. After Mrs. O'Conner and Sir Jeremy are called away, Lady Jenkins asks for coffee, but falls asleep before it arrives. Meanwhile, Sir Jeremy has received a letter from his banker telling him that Lady Jenkins borrowed £300 by his order, and it has not been repaid. Sir Jeremy storms into Lady Jenkins who is still asleep, takes what money is on the table, and awakens her with questions about the loan. They argue until he is again called away. Lady Jenkins then goes to Mrs. O'Conner, who tells her that she has received a letter telling her that the ship in which she has invested has sunk, though all hands were mercifully saved. But the Captain feels guilty and believes he cannot face her again. (The captain doesn't know that Mrs. O'Conner has gotten a sizable legacy from her uncle.) She sends a letter to her banker to try to find the Captain. Lady Jenkins turns the conversation to her situation: she has taken the £300 and lost it at cards. Just then Sir Jeremy and his lawyer Mr. Nettle appear. He explains the law: if £10 or more is lost, the loser may prosecute the winner for three times the amount. Lady Jenkins then admits she lost £100 at piquet to Mrs. Nettle. He won't believe it and leaves. Mrs. O'Conner is angry with Sir Jeremy for wanting to expose his wife in court, and she gives Lady Jenkins a purse to pay the banker. Mrs. O'Conner is called away to a visitor, who is Captain Truman. She is so cheerful that he thinks she hasn't received his letter, but she is testing his resolve to marry her. Captain Truman confesses he is now a beggar, but she comforts him by telling him the shipwreck was not his fault. He cannot understand how she can bear the loss with such tranquility, and she says that she doesn't want him to go to sea any more; besides she has enough for them both. Mrs. O'Conner then tells him about the legacy from her uncle —£2,000 a year: "My all is in my possession," she sings from *The Beggar's Opera*. This settlement should make them happy for the rest of their lives. They call in the Jenkinses and share their good news with them.

Mrs. O'Conner (played, of course, by Clive herself) is the focal character of the farce: she is good-hearted (even the servants praise her), she has a generous spirit (towards both Lady Jenkins and Captain Truman), and she is a kindly aunt (to her niece Nancy). While she doesn't approve of Lady Jenkins's gambling, she thinks even less of Sir Jeremy's mean spirit. A good deal of stage business pervades the first part of the play but does not contribute to the plot. This suggests some inflation of the text, but Clive may have wished to provide roles for fellow actors who assisted at her benefit night.

MANUSCRIPT: Larpent 247. Readex Microprint of manuscript.

The Faithful Virgins, Elizabeth Polwhele. An unpublished verse tragedy that was probably produced around 1670 at LIF. The known production details of the bloody tragedy are discussed by Milhous and Hume in their Introduction to Polwhele's *The Frolicks* (39–44).

While Merantha and Umira keep watch over the hearse of Philammon, they are visited by Statenor, Umira's brother, who falls in love with Merantha. Statenor plans to have his page, "Floradine," woo her in his stead. Unknown to him, however, "Floradine" is Erasila, Philammon's sister in male costume, who loves Statenor. In another plot, Isabella marries the Duke of Tuscany, after having deserted Cleophon. This event causes Cleophon to confer with two witches, who foretell that he will become the Duke of Tuscany, but he will not gain Isabella. In the midst of the play, a masque provides an allegory on good and evil, before returning to events presaging the tragedy. The Duke is captivated by Umira, who spurns him, so he plans to kidnap her. When Isabella, now the Duchess, discovers the plot, she asks Trasilius to kill Umira, which he does, only to be slain by Cleophon. Statenor slays the Duke, but is fatally wounded. Sickened by these terrible events, Merantha takes her own life. Seeing Statenor dying, Floradine/Erasila commits suicide. Cleophon becomes the Duke of Tuscany and castigates Isabella for her wicked deeds. Even though he continues to love her, Cleophon sends Isabella to a "monastery." And he will have "the faithful virgins" —Umira, Merantha, and Erasila —continually celebrated.

Although written in imitation of Jacobean and later "blood and thunder" tragedy, Polwhele's play emphasizes the faithful virgins, who are in marked contrast to Isabella, who wants to wreak her vengeance on everyone. Some echoes of *Macbeth* emerge in the evil Duke and Duchess, as well as in the witch's prophecy for Cleophon. In one plot, Erasila dresses in male attire, acting a page's part to be near Statenor, the man she loves. The female friendship of Merantha and Umira, Pearson points out, "is the most developed relationship in the play" (138). Although Merantha, Umira, and Erasila die at the end of the play, these faithful virgins will continue to be celebrated. Even though the Duke of Tuscany's lecherous ways cause difficulty for everyone, it is the "affirmative treatment of women," Pearson believes, that raises the play above its generic conventions.

MANUSCRIPT: Bodleian Library MS Rawl. Poet. 195, ff. 49–78.

The Fallen Patriot, Mary O'Brien. It is possible that this five-act comedy played on the Dublin stage, though no actors are named in the Dramatis Personae. William Gilbert printed the play in Dublin without a date on the title page, but most sources agree on 1790 as the publication date.

Sir Richard Greyley becomes "a fallen patriot" when he takes a knighthood and changes his name from O'Greyley. Although he says he has acted to please his wife, he seems quite smug about his new title. He's then censured by his nephew, Freeport, who wishes to marry Greyley's ward Eliza. After his encounter with Greyley, Freeport visits Eliza and confesses his love to her. When Harriot Neville enters, she agrees to help the lovers. Later, Eliza receives a letter saying her uncle whom she thought dead is still alive. Greyley disturbs her by coming to promote his passion and to make her heir to his estate. Stunned by this inappropriate behavior, Eliza chastises him. Greyley tries to pass it off as a jest as Harriot enters. Finding Greyley on his knees to Eliza, Harriot remarks he really is a fallen patriot and laughs at him. After he exits in a huff, Eliza says she will soon tell Harriot everything. She goes to the garden where she finds Freeport who kneels. He is found in this position by Greyley, who calls him "a rising patriot" and swears to put an end to his ambitions. Harriot approaches in time to cast aspersions on Freeport's being a rival to his uncle, who exits. Freeport cannot believe his uncle, a married man, would insult his ward. Harriot responds, "a man that would betray his country is capable of every villainy" (26). Lady Greyley has caught wind of her husband's proposals to Eliza and orders no more talks with Greyley, and then leaves in a passion. Harriot then suggests a retreat for Eliza in the home of a near-relation. As she leaves, Harriot gives a piece of paper to Eliza, and when she is alone Eliza discovers it is a bond for £5,000. After Greyley has urged his nephew to marry Harriot and accept a pension, Freeport says he prefers his honor to riches. A Signor Fernandez (Eliza's uncle Gregory in disguise) comes to Greyley with a bill signed by Gregory, saying they were confined together and he lent Gregory money. Greyley, however, won't pay it because he claims the expense of raising and educating Eliza. Fernandez wants to see Eliza, only to be told she is gone with Harriot: Fernandez says he'll return. Greyley schemes to get Fernandez matched with Eliza, because as a husband Fernandez could reimburse him for her board and education. Meanwhile, Major McCarty, Harriot's intended, arrives, telling her about meeting a Mr. Gregory. Harriot asks McCarty to remain incognito until the next day when she will marry him. Greyley insists on Eliza marrying Fernandez, though Harriot says her uncle provided for her. Upon the arrival of Fernandez, Eliza weeps when he talks about her much-loved Uncle Gregory. Upon Freeport's entrance, Greyley orders him out, but he pleads his love for Eliza. Fernandez approves of the plan when he sees Freeport's rectitude. When Greyley tries to push the visitor out, Fernandez reveals he is Gregory, and he has sent Greyley £50,000 for Eliza. When McCarty comes in, Harriot says she plans to marry him the next day. Eliza returns the bond to Harriot, and Freeport says women surely provide a pattern of virtue to men.

The play examines manners of the Irish nouveau riche, and it is Greyley whose rapacity and promiscuity make him the villain of the piece. He has, of course, gained his money through Gregory's sending allotments for his niece, and Greyley has misused them. The two exemplify the good and bad uncles. That Gregory traps Greyley shows that the tightwad gets what he deserves. The servants' misusing the wrong titles for the nouveau nobility has become an old chestnut by now, but O'Brien uses this means to expose the character of the Greyleys from the outset. While Eliza is the most put-upon figure because of her dependent situation, Harriot has money of her own and uses it generously. The goodwill between Harriot and Eliza is well established before Harriot gives Eliza the bond that sets her free from her lecherous guardian. Their friendship brings out the best in both women. Because she is not economically tied to the Greyleys, Harriot can act as the voice of reason, which she often expresses wryly and wittily.

TEXT: Not in Readex Microprint. TEC Reel 726: 17.

The False Count; or, A New Way to Play an Old Game, Aphra Behn. This five-act comedy was first produced at DG in November 1681, and printed the following year by M. Flesher for Jacob Tonson. The play was probably revived in 1697, possibly in 1705, but definitely in 1715, 1718, and 1730.

Set in Cadiz, the play takes up the actions of Don Carlos to regain the love of Julia, who has been forced to marry old Francisco, and of Antonio to marry Clara, Julia's sister, even though he is promised to Francisco's affected daughter Isabella. The title character, Guiliom, is a chimney sweep, who is recruited by Don Carlos and Antonio to woo the arrogant Isabella as a count. The disguises create a number of amusing mistaken identities, with the audience in on the jokes. Don Carlos acts as Guiliom's man in order to see Julia, and Isabella is charmed with the "Count," merely because of his title. During a pleasure cruise, the group is taken by disguised Turks and carried to Antonio's country estate on the coast, a few miles from Cadiz. Don Carlos, now disguised as the Grand Turk, forces the frightened Francisco to give up his wife. The ruse is discovered when Antonio's father Baltazar arrives, but in the end Antonio marries Clara and Guiliom marries Isabella. After the latter marriage, Guiliom reappears as a chimney sweep to the horrified Isabella. Finally, Francisco relinquishes Julia because of her prior vows with Don Carlos.

An enjoyable farce, *The False Count* provides some amusing parts, including the two servants Guzman and Jacinta, who help their masters —Don Carlos and Julia —reunite. Old Francisco's begging the "Grand Turk" to take his wife is a clever reversal of the old dotard's calling her a "slave" earlier. Pretensions are deflated, as the haughty Isabella finds she has married a chimney sweep. In the end, Julia's forced marriage is effectively canceled.

TEXTS: Wing B1730; EEB Reel 203: 5 (1682). Wing B1731; EEB Reel 1195: 9 (1697). Readex Microprint of 1682 copy.

MODERN EDITIONS: *Works*, ed. Montague Summers (1915; NY: Phaeton, 1967) 3: 95–176; Behn, *Five Plays*, with introduction by Maureen

Duffy (London: Methuen, 1990) reprints Summers's text: 297–377.

The False Friend; or, The Fate of Disobedience, Mary Pix. This five-act tragedy was first produced at LIF in May (*LS*) or June (Hume) 1699 and published the same year by Richard Basset. It was not revived.

When Emilius returns from France to Sardinia with his "Virgin Bride," he asks Appamia (played by Elizabeth Bowman), with whom he was raised, to care for Lovisa (played by Anne Bracegirdle) while he goes to see his father, the Viceroy of the island ruled by the Spaniards. Appamia has long harbored a love for Emilius, and she acts the friend by telling him that she will prepare his father for the news, while Emilius, in disguise, visits his twin sister Adellaida (played by Elizabeth Barry). Appamia knows that Adellaida has secretly married Brisac (alias Don Lopez), who is Lovisa's brother. In her plot of revenge, Appamia uses her suitor, Bucarius, to detain Emilius for questioning as a spy, and to inform Brisac that his sister has dishonored her family. While Emilius is away, Appamia causes Lovisa a disquieting time while she awaits her husband. When the tardy Emilius does return, he has received a challenge to his honor. Since Lovisa is troubled, Emilius tries to calm her. Appamia has prepared a poisoned cordial, which Emilius unknowingly administers before going off to the duel. Brisac appears and fights Emilius; each wounds the other with an "envenomed sword," though neither realize this. They help each other back to Appamia's, where Adellaida arrives. Brisac dies in her arms, and Emilius blames himself for the fatal deed. When Lovisa enters "distracted," he finds her dying and stabs himself; the two die together. The Viceroy tells Appamia that Heaven's mercy will overtake her crimes, for "On Earth thou wilt meet with none" (60). He concludes the play by urging parents not to be too fond of their children and children not to disobey their parents.

In the wake of Jeremy Collier's attack on the immorality of the stage the previous year, Mary Pix nodded toward reformation of the drama with lessons and morals in this tragedy (noted in the prologue). The title describes the failure of one woman's friendships: because Appamia feels jilted by Emilius, she goes on a rampage, striking out at both men and women in her disappointment. Pearson points out that the "active monster" Appamia crushes the "passive saint" Lovisa (174). Cotton believes this is the worst of Pix's plays because it is "a muddle of melodrama and moralizing" (119). The play does have its horrific moments, ending with bodies littering the stage, and the moral is not especially convincing. Nevertheless, Pix may have attempted to create a female Iago, motivated by frustrated love. A number of echoes from *Othello* dot the text: much of the play takes place at night, the setting is on an island in the Mediterranean, several characters are moved by jealousy, and there is a willing dupe named Roderigo. The concern for honor causes Emilius to duel Brisac, though Emilius is concerned for his personal honor, Brisac believes the honor of his family is at stake. The duel, ironically, insures that neither marriage will be consummated. It appears an unusual theatrical arrangement that Elizabeth Bowman is cast as the villain, whereas both Anne Bracegirdle and Elizabeth Barry act passive heroines. Perhaps Pix built into the play different grieving roles for the two leading female actors in Betterton's company.

TEXTS: Wing P2328. EEB Reel 506: 4. Readex Microprint.

FACSIMILE EDITION: E-CED, with introduction by Edna L. Steeves (NY: Garland, 1982).

A Family Legend, Joanna Baillie. Originally titled *The Lady of the Rock*, this five-act tragedy in verse was produced on 29 January 1810 in Edinburgh where it was acted fourteen consecutive nights. Sir Walter Scott, under whose auspices it was produced, wrote the prologue and Henry McKenzie, the author of *The Man of Feeling*, the epilogue. Henry Siddons played John of Lorne and Harriet Siddons played Helen, daughter of Argyll and wife of Maclean. Its successful fourteen-night run prompted the Edinburgh theatre to revive Baillie's earlier success, *De Monfort*. When published in Edinburgh by John Ballantyne in 1810, the foreword explained that the published copy was printed from the original that Baillie had given to the

Edinburgh theatre: "It may suffer, perhaps, from my not having adopted some of the stage abridgments or alterations" (v). There was also an 1810 London edition published by Longman, et al. Although *The Family Legend* was performed at Newcastle and Bath shortly after its premiere, the first London performance did not occur until 29 May 1815 at DL.

During the feast celebrating the birth of a Maclean heir, some of the vassals plot revenge against the mother, the daughter of the rival (Campbell) clan chieftain, the Earl of Argyll. Soon after these disgruntled men of Mull gather in a cavern, where they convince their chief, Maclean, that "coming ills" will overwhelm their clan unless Helen is sent away. Meanwhile, Helen meets with her brother, John of Lorne, who is concerned for his sister's safety. Not long after she assures Lorne of her husband's loyalty, Helen is abducted by the dissidents and left on a large rock midway between the coasts of Mull and Argyll. Just before she is drowned by high tide, Helen is rescued by two fishermen who, fortunately enough, rendezvous with her brother Lorne and Sir Hubert De Grey, a Campbell who has been in love with Helen. Lorne and De Grey restore Helen to her father, who had offered her in marriage to Maclean in order to establish peace between the warring clans. Helen's presence is kept a secret, and when Maclean and his men arrive to express their condolences, they tell false stories about her demise. Determined to revenge only those Mulls who are guilty, Argyll surprises Maclean by seating his daughter next to him. After Helen removes her veil and reveals her husband's duplicity, Lorne fights Maclean, who is mortally wounded. Simultaneously, De Grey arrives having rescued Helen's daughter, who was being held by the mother of one of the dissidents.

It is easy to see why *The Family Legend* was successful in Edinburgh. Its plot is thumping. Many scenes are inherently dramatic, including Helen's veiled entrance to the banquet hall where she is seated next to her husband. Additionally, the play's emphasis on peace instead of war, promoted by the heroine and her masculine counterpart (De Grey), resonates with modern readers. In fact, as the play ends, the Earl of Argyll scorns the waste of war and looks forward to a unified Scotland. Although saved only through the action of men, Helen embodies the values that the play endorses. When advising Argyll, De Grey insists that the Chief "let Helen's wishes [his] measures guide" (99).

TEXTS: Readex Microprint of Ballantyne's second edition of 1810, and of D. Longworth's New York edition, also 1810.

FACSIMILE EDITION: *Romantic Context: Poetry*, reprints 1810 text with an introduction by D. H. Reiman (NY: Garland, 1976).

The Family Picture, by a Lady (Kinne speculates Elizabeth Montagu may be the translator). This five-act sentimental comedy translated from Diderot's *Le Père de Famille* was published by J. Donaldson in 1781. It was not performed on stage.

Kinne remarks that this version "does not suffer from contraction, . . . since it discards many tiresome dissertations and vociferations, yet manages to preserve much of the original spirit" (172). Several of Diderot's characters are omitted.

Two other versions of Diderot's *Le Père de Famille* appeared earlier: *The Father*, possibly translated by Elizabeth Griffith and published in 1770, and Sophia Lee's *The Chapter of Accidents*, an adaptation successfully staged in 1780 and a perennial favorite well into the nineteenth century.

TEXT: Not in Readex Microprint. NUC: Copies at Harvard, U of Georgia, Huntington, and Newberry.

Fashion Displayed, Philippina Burton, later Mrs. Hill. This five-act comedy was acted three nights at the Haymarket Theatre, beginning 27 April 1770. The author played the principal character. Although publication was planned for the spring of 1771, the text of the play was not printed.

Bevis believes this sentimental comedy to be "sententious, studiedly genteel, and totally lacking in any *vis comica*" (1980; 58). He finds Lady Beaufleur's method of handling a roving husband ludicrous: she would merely accept Milord's caprices without question and strive to be attentive. Her plan appears to work almost immediately, but the audience is left wondering if the reform will last.

MANUSCRIPT: Larpent 308.

The Fashionable Friends, attributed to Mary Berry. This five-act comedy was privately acted at Strawberry Hill in 1801, and publicly produced at DL on 22 April 1802 and published that same year by J. Ridgway. The Advertisement to the play mentions "this Comedy, found among the papers of the late Earl of Orford [Horace Walpole], . . . was brought forward at the request of Mr. [Charles] Kemble." Nevertheless, Berry later published the play as hers. Genest notes that the comedy was acted but twice (7: 535–36).

Mr. Lovell (William Barrymore) tells Sir Dudley Dorimant (Charles Kemble) what separate lives he and his wife lead, whereas Sir Dudley is considering marriage to Miss Racket (Dorothy Jordan) but must pretend to woo Mrs. Racket (Jane Pope). Lady Selina (Maria De Camp), who affects "nerves," tells Mrs. Lovell (Mrs. Young) she prefers "the disinterestedness of female friendship." Lady Selina later confesses an interest in Mr. Lovell, making her earlier remarks about women's friendship ironic and showing her to be a hypocrite. Sir Dudley asks Miss Racket to run away with him after an upcoming masquerade, but her mother and guardian, Sir Valentine Vapour (Thomas King), plan to prevent this elopement. While a masquerade provides confusing costumes and mistaken identities, Sir Dudley and Miss Racket leave. Mrs. Lovell regains her husband's affections and is convinced of the insincerity of Lady Selina, who, in disappointment and disgust, decides to go to Naples for her health. Sir Dudley and Miss Racket, having married, return, to the chagrin of her guardians.

The purpose of the comedy is to demonstrate the hollowness of "fashionable" people. Mrs. Lovell is, clearly, the moral center of the play: she is both a good friend and true spouse. With the excellent cast, this comedy should have been more successful, but its satire and "immorality" may have put off the audience.

MANUSCRIPT: Larpent 1344. Readex Microprint of manuscript.

TEXT: Readex Microprint of the third edition, 1802.

The Fatal Falsehood, Hannah More. This five-act verse tragedy was first produced at CG on 6 May 1779 with an Epilogue by Richard Brinsley Sheridan. It was published the same year by T. Cadell. More describes the subject matter in her Prologue as "the humbler scenes of private life . . . a simple scene of domestic woes" (v).

The Earl of Guildford's ward, Julia, is betrothed to his son Rivers. According to her father's stipulation, however, Julia and Rivers cannot marry until he "from the field return'd a conqueror" (4). When the play begins, Orlando, a young Italian count, arrives at the castle to inform the Earl, Julia, and Emmelina (Rivers's sister) that Rivers has been wounded while defending Orlando but that he will be home soon. Initially, Orlando is attracted to Emmelina, who falls in love with him; but the tragic action begins with Orlando's infatuation with Julia. Orlando's behavior is manipulated by an Iago-like character, Bertrand, who is jealous of Rivers and determined to destroy him because if Rivers should die, "his father's lands on me devolve" (24). After Rivers returns a hero, Bertrand plots to create conflict between him and Orlando. When Julia requests that the marriage be postponed for one day, Rivers begins to distrust her, largely because of Bertrand's warnings. Racked with guilt because he is betraying a friend who has saved his life, Orlando wishes to leave England, but Bertrand seduces him into believing that Julia does not want to marry Rivers. Giving Orlando a letter intended for Rivers, Bertrand makes it appear as if she wants to arrange a secret wedding with Orlando. Sent by Bertrand in the direction of the rendezvous, Rivers accidentally wounds a partially hidden Bertrand, thinking he is Orlando. Grief-stricken upon hearing of her brother's death, Emmelina dies. Orlando stabs himself in penance.

The ending —which allows both Rivers and Julia to live —seems contrived; given the arrangements, it is unlikely that Rivers would accidentally stab Bertrand. Bertrand is the only character who seems consistently drawn and has psychological complexity. By the end of the play, Emmelina is reminiscent of Shakespeare's Ophelia, undercutting the strength and shrewdness that she demonstrated earlier, especially when she breaks off a fight between Rivers and Orlando. Julia appears aggressive at times, as when trying to initiate a secret marriage between herself and Rivers, but like the other characters, she is controlled by Bertrand's scheme.

MANUSCRIPT: Larpent 481.

TEXT: Readex Microprint.

The Fatal Friendship, Catharine Trotter. This five-act tragedy in blank verse was first acted in late May or early June 1698 at Lincoln's Inn Fields with strong principal players: Anne Bracegirdle acted Felicia; Elizabeth Barry, Lamira; and Thomas Betterton, Gramont. It was published the same year by Francis Saunders, and while Trotter's name did not appear on the title page, she did sign the dedication to Princess Anne.

Gramont and Felicia married secretly two years before the play begins, and they have a son living elsewhere with a nurse. In the opening scene, Bellgard, Felicia's brother, presses her to marry Count Roquelaure, the father of Gramont. In order to divert her attention from Gramont, Bellgard urges the Count to order his son to marry the widow Lamira, Bellgard's cousin. When Gramont refuses, the Count disowns his son until he obeys. Castalio, who saved Gramont's life in battle, has been wrongfully imprisoned, and Gramont is trying to free him. Leaving the prison, Gramont hears that his infant has been captured by pirates who are likely to demand a ransom. Bellgard arrives and urges Gramont to regain the Count's favor by marrying Lamira; this act will give him the money to buy Castalio's release from prison. Feeling that he has no way out of his financial straits, Gramont commits bigamy and with Lamira's money frees Castalio. When Gramont will not consummate the marriage, Lamira becomes incensed. After Bellgard tells Felicia that Gramont has married Lamira, Felicia confesses that she and Gramont were wedded two years before. In the final act, trying to intercede in a quarrel between Bellgard and Castalio, Gramont accidentally stabs his friend. Finding what he has done, Gramont stabs himself, and both die.

A pathetic tragedy is Hume's classification of the drama, and, like many plays in the period (1697–1703), the audience rejected the tragedy, which was not revived. Nevertheless, Trotter creates strong emotional and moral dilemmas, as well as effective interplay between the characters. Occasional contrived events mar the plot, as when pirates kidnap the son of Gramont and Felicia, which forces Gramont into bigamy with Lamira for financial gain. Pearson demonstrates how such economic imagery undercuts love and human relationships in the play, which she believes is Trotter's best.

TEXTS: Wing C4802. Microfilm EEB Reel 486: 26. Readex Microprint.

MODERN EDITION: *The Female Wits*, ed. Fidelis Morgan (London: Virago, 1981).

FACSIMILE EDITION: *The Plays of Mary Pix and Catharine Trotter*, vol. 2, with introduction by Edna L. Steeves (NY: Garland, 1982).

The Fatal Legacy, Jane Robe. This five-act tragedy, translated and expanded from Racine's *La Thébaïde* (1664), was first produced at LIF on 23 April 1723. There were four performances, one "By Her Royal Highness's Command." Publication was by E. Simon and others in 1723.

This tragedy in free verse takes up the well-known conflict between Polynices and Eteocles, sons of Oedipus, who were given the crown on a rotating basis. When Eteocles refuses to turn it over, a bloody fratricide ensues. Jocasta, their mother, and Antigona, their sister, unable to stop them, are mad with grief; Jocasta has lost two sons, and Antigona has lost two brothers as well as her lover Phocias. The women take their own lives, using the same dagger. Creon, in love with his niece, the proud Antigona, and bitterly jealous of his own son, Phocias, stabs himself to death and expires as his son returns, asking forgiveness for having "caus'd Her [Antigona's] death by feigning thine." Phocias refuses the throne which is now his, for he believes that it should not go to a race so cursed by the gods.

Robe's work is mostly a translation of Racine's *La Thébaïde; ou, les frères ennemis.* The first four acts are the same, except for some minor alterations, such as giving lines to a different character. In the final act, while keeping Racine's addition of Creon's passion for Antigona, Robe alters the ending by having Phocias return unexpectedly and unharmed from battle to witness his father's demise. In Racine, Phocias dies offstage, victim of his love for Antigona, and Creon's death is only hinted at as the curtain falls. Similarly, Jocasta's bloody suicide is given just one line, no death being allowed to take place on stage in classical French theater of the time. Another alteration concerns Creon's behavior: in Robe's version, he relishes the grief he inflicts on Phocias, his own son, and on Antigona. He goes mad when he learns that Antigona will never be his, whereas in Racine he never looses control of his speech or emotions. But whenever the plot line permits it, Robe used Racine's material even in the last act, which, according to Robe's publisher, is supposed to be "entirely new" (p.vii).

The Fatal Legacy was apparently never revived after the April 1723 performances. The publisher attributes the initial lack of success to the play being performed late in the theatrical season, but it is imputable as well to the quality of the translation, which is marred, at times, by gallicisms and awkward paraphrasing of bombastic French verses. But in judging Robe's work, it is worth remembering that *La Thébaïde*, young Racine's first performed work, was, despite its greater success, no masterpiece itself.

TEXT: Readex Microprint.

Fatality, Caroline Boaden. A one-act drama, *Fatality* was produced at the Haymarket Theatre on 1 September 1829 and published in Cumberland's *British Theatre*, vol. 23, without a date. The piece was acted eleven times.

Before the events of the play, we learn that General Loverule disapproved of his son Edward marrying Susanna, a friend since childhood. Therefore, he paired Susanna with Bertrand, a soldier wounded defending his son, and gave them a farm when they married. Years have passed, and the General announces that his son is coming for a visit. Edward has married a woman of high rank —"a marriage of reason," according to his father (15) —but young Loverule is miserable because his wife loves someone else. Although Mrs. Lackbrain tries to prevent him from doing so, Edward declares that he is still in love with Susanna, who has concealed her unhappiness from her kind and loving husband. After condemning his wife for her infidelity, Edward seems unaware of his own hypocrisy. Spying his old friend alone with Susanna at night, Bertrand becomes jealous and shoots Edward. As the play closes, Bertrand is kneeling at General Loverule's feet, insisting "Oh, my benefactor! do not curse me!" (28).

While the treatment of the material is melodramatic and heavy-handed, *Fatality* must have been popular with some audiences. Much of what it says about class seems contradictory. Although the play seems to criticize General Loverule's interference, motivated by class pride and a disdain for "love-matches," it ends with Bertrand begging for the General's forgiveness. Furthermore, Susanna's dissatisfaction with her husband seems to be rooted in his inferior class standing. Susanna's relationship with Mrs. Lackbrain should be noted, because of the good advice the inappropriately named friend gives her. Mrs. Lackbrain is correct when she says, "Though I appear a giddy, perhaps a heartless being! believe me, I am not unworthy of your confidence" (17). Mrs. Lackbrain is the first character to sense the danger that Edward represents, having herself been the target of his attention when she first married. (Mrs. Lackbrain resembles the shrewd Paquita in Boaden's *Don Pedro*.)

MANUSCRIPT: BL Add. Ms. 42896, ff. 341–401.

TEXT: Readex Microprint of the Cumberland version.

The Fate of Corsica; or, The Female Politician, by a "Lady of Quality." Although this five-act comic drama was not produced, it was printed by E. Rayner, 1732. One hundred years later, Genest remarked that the "comedy has considerable merit," but he gives no indication of possible authorship (10: 158).

In this drama, Eliza, an English orphan, plays "the female politician," of the subtitle. Her guardian, Rubarto, wishes to overthrow the existing government of Corsica and to be named Duke. His second scheme is to leave his wife Maria and take up with his ward. Having learned about these plots, Eliza tells herself that "On one Woman's Management depends the Fate of *Corsica*" (22). And manage, she does. Asserting that "Men are bungling Politicians" (56), Eliza—a "Machiavel in Petticoats" (57)—achieves a bloodless revolution. In manipulating several counterplots, she scores a remarkable achievement. As the play ends, Eliza prepares to return to England with Frederick.

Pearson suggests that *The Fate of Corsica* could be a feminized version of Rowe's *Tamberlaine* (247), since the defeat of a tyrant occurs in both. Certainly *Tamberlaine* would have been well known to London audiences since, as A. H. Scouten reports, "all London theatres played [it] on the anniversary of William III's birthday, 4 November" (*LS* 3: lxxxiii). In 1732, however, the anonymous woman author of *The Fate of Corsica* may have intended to satirize the politics of the Walpole government: Rubarto (the tyrannical first minister of state) could represent Walpole; Maria could be Maria Skerret his mistress; and the German Frederick, the Prince of Wales. In such an allegorical satire, Eliza could represent the once and future queen or the English nation, but as the drama's prime character she undercuts traditional gender roles.

TEXT: Readex Microprint.

The Fate of Sparta; or, The Rival Kings, Hannah Cowley. This five-act historical tragedy, based on events from Plutarch, was first produced at DL on 31 January 1788 and published the following month by G. G. J. and J. Robinson. Originally titled *The Siege of Sparta*, the play was performed nine times during its first season. Chelonice was performed by Sarah Siddons, about whom Hannah Cowley wrote in the Dedication: "I wondered such a character [Chelonice] had never been brought on the Stage, to do honour to her sex; —yet I had joy in reflecting, that this was precisely the age in which it ought to be done, for this age boasted a Mrs. Siddons" (v).

The events focus on Chelonice's conflict of loyalty to Sparta, her husband (Cleombrotus), and father (Leonidas). As the play opens, Cleombrotus and his troops prepare to enter defeated Sparta. Before being deposed, Cleombrotus ruled Sparta jointly with Leonidas. Just before he reclaims his crown and Sparta is plundered, Chelonice comes to the soldiers' camp disguised as a priestess, trying to prevent the destruction of her father and her city. In response to her pleas, Cleombrotus agrees to postpone the attack for one more day. Meanwhile, Amphares, the ambitious man responsible for Cleombrotus's fall, convinces Leonidas that Chelonice has been disloyal to her father. When she refuses to prove her loyalty by assisting a plot to murder her husband, Chelonice is taken prisoner and chained. Unaware of Amphares's nature, Cleombrotus allows himself to be tricked into an ambush, where he is supposedly to witness Chelonice's assignation with another man. However, Cleombrotus survives, because Chelonice asks Nicrates to go to the meeting to warn her husband. Nicrates, Amphares's brother, is less fortunate: he is slain when Amphares mistakes his brother for Cleombrotus. Seizing advantage of their leader's absence, Cleombrotus's troops have entered Sparta, but they are forced back by him. After taking refuge in Minerva's Temple, Cleombrotus is attacked by Leonidas, and Chelonice grabs the knife that Cleombrotus uses to defend himself against her father. When her husband is exiled, Chelonice refuses the crown that her father offers her, insisting on banishment with her husband. After Cleombrotus rescues Leonidas from Amphares's attack, the King blesses his daughter as well as Cleombrotus's return to power just before Leonidas dies.

The play is wooden, but contemporary readers —like Hannah Cowley herself —seem to have found Chelonice's role of interest. Although defined completely by her duties to father, husband, and state, she is a strong and consistent character, willing to disregard both males when they request behavior that negates her full range of responsibilities. She also has no difficulty making decisions or initiating action. For example, she goes by herself to request that Sparta not be attacked; she refuses the crown when it is thrust on her by her father; and she urges Cleombrotus to save her father against Amphares.

MANUSCRIPTS: Larpent 791 and 792.

TEXTS: Readex Microprint. TEC Reels 1526: 18; 1639: 20 (Dublin 1788).

FACSIMILE EDITION: E-CED, with introduction by F. Link (NY: Garland, 1982).

The Father, translation attributed to Elizabeth Griffith. *Le Père de Famille* by Diderot is the source of this sentimental comedy. The possible attribution to Griffith comes from her previous translation of Diderot's *Le Fils naturel* into *Dorval; or, The Test of Virtue* (1767), noted on the title page. *The Father* was printed at Lynn for the author in 1770, but sold by W. Whittingham and others in London. Another translation of the same play was done "by a lady," under the title of *The Family Picture* (1781), and Sophia Lee adapted *Le Père de Famille* into the successfully staged drama, *The Chapter of Accidents* (1780).

TEXT: Not in Readex Microprint. NUC: Copies at LC (Longe Collection 155: 5), U of Missouri, and Huntington.

FAUCIT, Harriet Elizabeth [Diddear] (1789–1857). There appears to be some confusion between Harriet and Anne Gaudry Fawcett (1780?–1849), the second Mrs. John Saville Faucit *or* Fawcett, who is credited by Macmillan in the Larpent Catalogue as the author of the play in question. Because Anne Gaudry Fawcett was attached to DL, it seems more likely that Harriet Faucit wrote *Alfred the Great* for a provincial performance. This historical drama in three acts was produced at the Theatre Royal, Norwich on 16 May 1811, probably for the author's benefit. We have no further information about her life. [*BD* Appendix, BDAA for Anne Gaudry Fawcett, Davis & Joyce]

The Feign'd Curtizans; or, A Night's Intrigue, Aphra Behn. This five-act comedy-farce was produced at DG in March 1679 and printed later that year for Jacob Tonson. Behn dedicated the play to Nell Gwyn. In their edition of Downes, Milhous and Hume say there may have been a performance as early as May 1677, titled *The Midnight's Intrigue*. The comedy was performed at Court on 6 March 1681, and it may have been revived in 1696. Twenty years later, a revival took place during the summer of 1716 at LIF; the following season, it played again at LIF.

Disguises, mistakes, and complications make up the plot of this intrigue comedy, which also contains a good deal of farce. The setting in Rome lends an exotic locale. As in *The Rover*, which preceded *The Feign'd Curtizans*, two women are being forced to act against their wishes: Marcella is to marry Octavio, and Cornelia is to enter a convent. They flee to Rome where they disguise themselves as courtesans. Fillamour, the sober lover, had met Marcella earlier and continues to love her. His friend Galliard, like the rover, is interested in pursuing any pretty woman. They are joined by Julio, the brother of Marcella and Cornelia, even though he is contracted to marry Octavio's sister Laura Lucretia. The farce is provided by Petro, who in his various disguises acts as barber, "civility master," pimp, clothing dealer, and fencing instructor to young Sir Signal Buffoon and his tutor Parson Tickletext. The night's intrigues and farcical situations are tangled in various complicated ways, including confused disguises, mistaken identities, near duels, and near losses of virginity. In the last act, Octavio relinquishes Marcella to Fillamour, Laura Lucretia must accept Julio, and Galliard submits to Cornelia.

A number of critics list this comedy as one of Behn's best, though Link has some reservations about the subplot. Ludwig, however, justifies Petro's leading Sir Signal and Tickletext by the nose as "a clever burlesque of the erotic problems of the intrigue plot" (17). Since Tickletext is Sir Signal's tutor, the subject of a proper education arises. The anti-Catholic bias of the play rebounds on Tickletext as a false pastor, one who would mislead youth by his actions. In their own pursuit of an education, Marcella and Cornelia give each other moral support, while gaining a financial independence. The figurative language, as Ludwig points out, is strongly economic: love is a commodity of the market place as well as a risk. But the two women succeed despite their narrow-minded uncle and the problematic trade they have chosen to gain their freedom.

TEXTS: 1st Wing B1732; 2nd Wing B1733; EEB Reel 203: 6. Readex Microprint.

MODERN EDITIONS: *Works*, ed. Montague Summers (1915; NY: Phaeton, 1967) 2: 301–412; Everyman's Library, *Female Playwrights of the Restoration*, edited with introduction by Paddy Lyons and Fidelis Morgan (London: Dent, 1991): 1–101.

CRITICAL EDITION: Edited by Judith K. Ludwig, Diss., Yale, 1976.

The Female Academy, Margaret Cavendish, Duchess of Newcastle. This drama in five acts was printed in her *Playes*, published by John Martyn, James Allestry, and Tho. Dicas in 1662. It was not produced.

Several elderly matrons have set up an academy for wealthy young women, who are "honourably born." Because young men are denied access to this academy, they set up their own nearby. The play seesaws between the two academies and the lectures by selected members of each group. For instance, the women consider topics such as wit and wisdom, proper discourse, truth, friendship, and vanity, whereas the men lecture on their opinions of women. The men believe it is unnatural for women to shut themselves up in their academy; the men think they should be protectors of women; and women have too many humours unless accompanied by men. The women carry on in their high-minded lectures, until the men can stand it no longer and start blowing trumpets when there is a female lecturer speaking. The principal matron comes to the men and asks why they are disturbing the women. The men's main objection is that the women have "incloystered" themselves. The matron explains to the men that the female academy teaches its members "how to be good Wives when they are married," and the women's love will be as strong as the gentlemen's merits, but a man must get permission from a woman's parent to visit.

Cavendish examines the potential of education for women, and she believes a female academy will give a few privileged young women an opportunity to share their views on important qualities such as truth, friendship, and wisdom. Pearson suggests that Cavendish recognizes that women need their own voice, and such an academy is one way to achieve this (128). The series of monologues by the women (and those by the men) do not create much dramatic action, even the men's trumpeting happens offstage. The best classification of this play may be "a drama of ideas"; most of the significant ideas are discussed by the women. All the men seem able to do is to complain that the women are shut away from them, and the men's principal topics are women's behavior and culture.

TEXTS: Wing N868. EEB Reel 502: 11. Readex Microprint.

The Female Dramatist, attributed to Sarah Cheney Gardner. This two-act musical farce was produced at the Haymarket Theatre only on 16 August 1782; it was never printed. *BD* and Peake (in *Memoirs of the Colman Family*, 2: 99, 1841) credit the play to George Colman the Younger. *BD* notes that "the principle character [played by Mrs. Gardner] was borrowed from Mrs. Metaphor, in *Roderic[k] Random*" (2: 235).

Mrs. Melpomene Metaphor writes a large number of plays without getting them produced. As she describes her dramas, one can see why they are not performed: she wishes to bring "Spirit" to the stage, but the dramas are "full of Death and Destruction, Rape, Horror & Homicide." Mrs. Metaphor's plays lack a basic knowledge of technical stage mechanics and a sound critical discernment. In one play she includes a "House on Fire," and another is "ruined by the awkwardness of its actors in a scene calling for 'dead bodies tied to live people'" (Smith & Lawhon 79).

MANUSCRIPTS: Larpent 598 (589 in *LS*). Peake (in *Memoirs of the Colman Family* [1841] 2: 100) reports two autographed manuscripts by George Colman the Younger are held by the Duke of Devonshire.

FIELDING, Sarah (1710–1768). Better known as a novelist, Sarah Fielding often included dramatic dialogues in her prose writings. In the second volume of her *Familiar Letters* (1747), for instance, is a scene entitled "Much

Ado," written as a drama. Her collaboration with Jane Collier on *The Cry: A New Dramatic Fable*, 1754, is an extended dialogue between four women about women's place in the world. *DNB* says Sarah "joined with Miss Collier in *The Cry*," and cites Richardson's *Correspondence* (2: 59–112), which has letters from Richardson to and from Jane Collier and Sarah Fielding. Probably best known for her novel *David Simple*, Fielding led an active literary life writing other novels and translating Xenophon's *Memorabilia*. She died in 1768. [*BD*, BNA, DBAWW, DNB, EBWW, FCLE, OCEL]

FINCH, Anne Kingsmill, Countess of Winchilsea (1661–1720). As "Ardelia," the poetic name she chose for herself, Finch wrote a number of poems and two dramas: *The Triumphs of Love and Innocence* (a tragicomedy, written about 1688) and *Aristomenes; or, The Royal Shepherd* (a tragedy, written about 1690). Neither play was acted, though the latter was published in *Miscellany Poems, on Several Occasions*, published in 1713.

Born into a distinguished family, Anne Kingsmill was orphaned at age three. About her education almost nothing is known. By 1683, she became a maid of honor to Mary of Modena, wife of the future James II. At court she met and, in 1684, married Heneage Finch. Shortly after James II was deposed, they went to live with a nephew at Eastwell, Kent. This enforced retirement allowed Finch's poetry to prosper. When the nephew died in 1712, Heneage Finch succeeded to the title and Anne became the Countess of Winchilsea. The publication of her work not only included the five-act tragedy, but several translations of dramas by Racine and Tasso. She, later, contributed an epilogue to Rowe's *Jane Shore*; it was intended to be spoken on the second night (3 February 1714) by Anne Oldfield, who acted Jane Shore. Lady Winchilsea died in 1720. [*BD*, BNA, Cotton, EBWW, FCLE, Lonsdale; DBAWW and OCEL, under Winchilsea.]

The Fire Goblin and the Three Charcoal Burners, Jane M. Scott. This musical pantomime opened at the Sans Pareil Theatre on 26 December 1818 and played thirty-six nights. Although the pantomime had a large cast, no script for the movements exists.

The First Attempt; or, The Whim of the Moment, Sydney Owenson, later Lady Morgan. A prolific novelist, Owenson wrote this comic opera, which was performed in Dublin, 1807. According to *BD*, it was not printed (2: 240).

First Faults, Marie Therese DeCamp, later Kemble. This five-act comedy was produced at DL on 3 May 1799 on Miss DeCamp's benefit night; it was neither repeated nor printed. William Earle claimed the piece was lifted from his *Natural Faults*, which she denied in a letter to *The Morning Post*, 10 June 1799 (reprinted in *BD* 3: 73, and in Genest 7: 417–19).

MANUSCRIPT: Larpent 1254.

First of April, Caroline Boaden. This two-act farce was first produced at the Haymarket Theatre on 31 August 1830 and acted sixteen times. It was printed singly by J. Cumberland (no. 185), and it is included in his *British Theatre*, vol. 26; neither is dated.

Colonel Airey's aunt has left him £10,000, but her husband, Sir Bumpkin Pedigree, has refused to pay the legacy, claiming there was some informality in the will. Sir Bumpkin arrives at Dover on April 1st, and Airey in disguise shows him the way to the Belford castle, which he assures him is the best inn in the town. Major Belford is a military friend of Airey's, and he and his mother take up the joke; and Clara, with whom Airey is in love, acts as a waitress. They score several jests on Sir Bumpkin by preventing him from eating his dinner and raising his bed off the floor at night. When the bed seems to disappear completely, Sir Bumpkin causes a commotion, which awakens General Belford, who has returned home unexpectedly. In the last scene, Sir Bumpkin is accused of having come to the castle as a spy. In order to extricate himself from the situation, he promises to pay the legacy.

Much of the play's broad humor is generated by Sir Bumpkin Pedigree: "As great a fool as ever breathed! His absurdity is only equalled by his avarice" (11). Possessing inflated ideas about his self-importance, Pedigree expects the rest of the world to see him as he sees himself. The disguises contribute to the verbal irony and there is some clever stage business; still, Genest is correct when he says that "a considerable degree of improbability may be tolerated in a professed farce, but even farce has its limits" (9: 531–32).

MANUSCRIPT: BL Add. Ms. 42903, ff. 367–478.

TEXTS: Readex Microprint of Cumberland editions: (1) *British Theatre*, no. 185; (2) *British Theatre*, vol. 26.

The First of May; or, A Royal Love-Match, Isabel Hill. Described as "a petite comedy in two-acts," this play with songs was produced at CG on 10 October 1829, featuring Charles Kemble as King Edward IV, and performed eleven times. William Kenneth published the play in 1829. The Preface acknowledges Sir Richard Baker's *A Chronicle of the Kings of England* as an influence.

The comedy features three couples and the plots related to their courtship: King Edward IV and Lady Elizabeth Grey; Harry Woodville, Elizabeth's brother, and Katharine Travers; and Roger Oldgrave, Katharine's guardian, and the Widow Jolly, Katharine's aunt. At the beginning of the play, Elizabeth insists that she will not marry her guardian, and when Oldgrave locks her in the house, she escapes to seek assistance from Woodville, the man to whom she is secretly betrothed. Meanwhile, Woodville returns home, shocked to find his sister entertaining King Edward. Encouraged by Edward's banter to think the worst, Woodville disapproves of Elizabeth's relationship with the King; even after discovering that they are to be wed, Woodville continues to object, insisting that the King should not marry one of his subjects. Both Elizabeth and Edward are determined to tease Woodville by revealing his love for Katharine, a woman who is socially inferior. At the same time, Edward plans to teach Elizabeth a lesson about his constancy. When Katharine comes upon Edward before she can find Woodville, the King places her in his rooms, asking her aunt, Widow Jolly, to hint at his impropriety. Edward's game, however, is short lived: Katharine and Elizabeth become friends, enabling Elizabeth to overhear a conversation in which the King shows his hand. Woodville, on the other hand, is successfully fooled. He has heard from an old man (not identified as Oldgrave) that his ward has been waylaid by the King; when Woodville publicly demands that the woman be returned to her guardian, she reveals herself as Katharine. After Oldgrave declares the Widow, whom he has loved for years, his "anchorage" (52), a final jest is played on Jonas, the King's horse-boy, who is told he is discharged from his service, only to discover that he is now Groom of the Chambers. The May day closes with the nuptials over, the Queen crowned, and the King bantering with Widow Jolly.

In Genest's view, "this is a moderate comedy, [but] it is too long, and the author has made it still longer by the addition of some songs" (9: 513). While the songs could have been eliminated after the first three pages, the play does have merit, especially so far as its language is concerned. King Edward's banter is often amusing when he spars with Jonas, Widow Jolly, and Elizabeth. Furthermore, Elizabeth, Katharine Travers, and Widow Jolly are all strong female characters, aggressive and verbally deft in their dealings with men. Additionally, stage business is often well handled, especially when the trick is played on sanctimonious Woodville.

MANUSCRIPT: BL Add. Ms. 42897, ff. 229–256.

TEXT: Readex Microprint.

Fitzormond; or, Cherished Resentment, Frances Burney, niece of Fanny Burney d'Arblay. This three-act verse drama was published in her *Tragic Dramas; chiefly intended for representation in private families: to which is added Aristodemus, a tragedy from the Italian of Vincenzo Monti* (1818). Burney remarks in the preface that she began composing the play at the age of seventeen. It was not publicly performed.

This melodramatic piece alludes to political strife in Ireland but focuses primarily on two men —Charlamont and Fitzormond —who destroy one another. The play begins with Charlamont welcoming the gloom and solitude of the forest in which he walks at night, unaware that his sister (now Lady Fitzormond), whom he has not seen for years, lives in the castle nearby. When they discover one another, Charlamont relates his tale about being sold into slavery at Tunis, but he refuses to tell her about the duel that caused him to flee from Ireland in the first place. She, in return, reveals that their mother died from sorrow over his exile. When he does not want to return to the castle with her, Charlamont is instructed to stay in a hermit's cell, where his sister will return the next day. Lady Fitzormond, delighted that her husband has arrived home after a long absence, brings her brother food. Her pleasure is short lived: Lady Fitzormond and her brother realize to their horror that Lord Fitzormond is Charlamont's bitterest enemy and the man with whom he fought the duel. Late that evening, brother and sister meet in the forest and the entire story is told. When he was Fitzormond's prisoner, Charlamont fell in love with Annabel, Fitzormond's sister. After Annabel helped Charlamont escape, her brother came after them, fighting with Charlamont; the sister was killed when she came between their swords, trying to separate them. Lady Fitzormond counters her brother's narrative by describing the support that Lord Fitzormond gave to her after her mother died. As they talk, Lord Fitzormond bursts upon the scene, encouraged by his retainer to believe that his wife has been unfaithful. Refusing to believe that Charlamont is her brother, Lord Fitzormond attempts to stab his wife; Charlamont retaliates, wounding Lord Fitzormond. When Lady Fitzormond declares, "What was *my* safety, when compar'd with [my husband's]" (43), Lord Fitzormond realizes his mistake, asking for her forgiveness and extending a hand to Charlamont because he saved Lady Fitzormond's life. After her husband's death, Lady Fitzormond is disoriented, her precarious balance restored only when reunited with her young son.

The hatred between Charlamont and Lord Fitzormond is political in nature, but the raw expression of emotion is far more important than character development or motivation. The sisters —Lady Fitzormond and Annabel —have relatively little significance, except as symbols of unconditional loyalty, women willing to die to save those whom they love.

TEXT: Readex Microprint.

The Force of Calumny, translated by Anne Plumptre. Although this translation of Kotzebue's play into a five-act drama was published by R. Phillips in 1799, it was never performed on stage.

The play begins with the sister-in-law, Jenny, making sarcastic comments about the domestic bliss shared by her brother, Syndicus Morland, and his wife, Emilia. Emilia confides that she is expecting a child but wishes to surprise her husband with the news on his birthday. Jenny declares that she respects Emilia, who chose her brother, "a worthy citizen," as a husband rather than become a mistress to the Prince. In exchange, Emilia reveals that Morland's English secretary, Edward Smith, has fallen in love with Jenny. When the master villain —Allbrand, private secretary to the Prime Minister —arrives, he tries to turn Emilia against her husband, alleging that Morland was sexually promiscuous before marriage. After he is unsuccessful, Allbrand toys with Morland, encouraging him to be aggressive with the Prime Minister and to be jealous of his wife's previous association with the Prince. When Allbrand leaves, Edward Smith confesses to Morland that he loves his sister. Smith also explains that he is a wealthy man, but has become Morland's secretary in order to try to win Jenny's heart. In a related subplot, Emilia has been assisting an old and crippled Officer, Captain Ellfield, who has been dismissed from the service for criticisms of the war offered in private conversation. When Allbrand discovers Emilia's connection to the Ellfields, he tries to bribe the old couple to help him arrange an assignation with her at their home; when they refuse, Allbrand informs the Minister that Morland is a traitor, alleging that he plots with Ellfield at his home. In order to stage the meeting between the "traitors," Allbrand encourages Morland to believe that his wife is going to the Ellfield's to meet with the Prince. After witnessing Emilia enter the Ellfield's house, Morland is arrested by the Guards that were waiting for him and charged with treason. After the

Minister's nephew, Scharfeneck, comes to Morland's house to seize his papers, Smith declares his love for Jenny and reveals that he is an English Lord who will attempt Morland's release. After reminding Scharfeneck of a false accusation that he made against a young woman, Smith convinces him that calumny is also involved in the case against Morland. In an interview with the Minister, Smith is forced to reveal his identity to prevent Allbrand from removing Morland's papers, which they discover contain proof that Allbrand's political career was established on a treatise actually written by Morland. Further evidence of Morland's innocence is provided by Mrs. Ellfield, who also reveals that she and her husband were the beneficiaries of Mrs. Morland's generosity. When the truth is revealed by Mrs. Ellfield and Smith to Morland, he throws himself at his wife's feet asking for her forgiveness. Allbrand is thrown in prison, and Jenny declares "Edward, I am yours" (108).

Genest remarks "this is a good play —the dialogue is well written, but some of the scenes might be shortened to advantage —the moral is excellent —Smith observes p. 95 —'the ears of mankind are always open for the reception of slander, but are too often inflexibly closed against all attempts at its refutation.'" (10: 215). The women in the play show much less acceptance of the male slander and give a moral tone to the translation.

TEXT: Readex Microprint.

The Forced Marriage; or, The Jealous Bridegroom, Aphra Behn. This five-act tragicomedy, Behn's first play, opened at LIF on 20 September 1670. It ran six nights and was printed for James Magnus the following year.

When Alcippus is made general of France for his valor on the battlefield, the King asks if he would like anything more. Alcippus states that he desires the hand of Erminia, who —unknown to him —is secretly pledged to Philander, the King's son. Philander is much distressed, as is his sister Princess Galatea, who longs for Alcippus. Erminia pleads with her father, Orgulius, but to no avail, and she is wed to Alcippus. Despite the forced marriage Erminia remains faithful, while Alcippus grows jealous. He fights with Philander, then he strangles Erminia —with his garter —and leaves her for dead. Erminia, however, revives and brings the cast together in a masque, where she shows Alcippus that he must love Galatea and that she must love Philander. Other resolutions round out the happy ending: Aminta and Alcander are reconciled, and the foppish Falatius is joined with Isillia, whom he had jilted.

This "romantic tragi-comedy" (Woodcock, *The English Sappho* 49), in the fashion of Beaumont and Fletcher, is a "mixed play" with virtue being rewarded (Hume 214). Thematically, love vies with duty in the minds of the characters, creating internal and external conflict. Erminia, for instance, will do her duty and marry Alcippus, but she cannot love him. The title stresses a theme that seemed to occupy Behn in many of her plays —that of a woman being forced to marry without her assent or desire. Link praises the structure of the play, Behn's first, in her ability to maintain variety while advancing the central action, but he deplores "the stilted language" and the mixing of prose and verse (29–33). Not previously noted are the large number of family members, especially brothers and sisters, in the play: Philander and Galatea, Cleontius and Isillia, Alcander and Olinda, Pisaro and Aminta. That Alcippus lacks a family connection and remains an outsider may make it easier (though not altogether convincing) for Erminia to cancel her marriage to him. Alcippus's motivation may result from his guilt in attempting to murder Erminia and in deceiving Philander by asking for Erminia. Being aware of these guilty actions of Alcippus, Erminia can more easily change in the denouement. More important, the women in the play eschew common rivalries and show a real concern for one another that goes beyond the royal hierarchy.

TEXTS: Wing B1734; EEB Reel 446: 1 (1671). Wing B1735; EEB Reel 857: 27 (1688). Wing B1736; EEB Reel 857: 28 (1690). Readex Microprint of 1688 edition.

MODERN EDITION: *Works*, ed. Montague Summers (1915; NY: Phaeton, 1967) 3: 281–381.

The Forest Knight; or, The King Bewildered, Jane M. Scott. This two-act burletta opened on 4 February 1813 at the Sans Pareil Theatre and ran thirty-two nights its first season. Michael Parnell composed the music, and Scott performed the role of Richard. Revivals of the play took place in five of the next six seasons.

MANUSCRIPT: Larpent 1757.

The Foresters; A Picture of Rural Manners, translation by Bell Plumptre, the sister of Anne Plumptre, who also translated a number of plays by Kotzebue. Published in 1799 by Vernor and Hood, Bell Plumptre's translation from the German of W. A. Iffland's *Die Jäger* (1785) was rendered into five acts, but it was not staged.

In a home near a forest, the play opens with Matthew, a servant of the head forester Warberger and his wife, telling his fellow servant Rodolph that he is leaving to work for von Zeck, the Amtmann, or Superintendent of Public Works. Matthew holds a grudge against Warberger because his father previously held the post of head forester. We also learn that the Warbergers' son Anthony is in love with Frederica, an orphan brought up by his parents. Frederica has been in a distant town being educated and is to return that day. In the spirit of rising social values, however, Mrs. Warberger wants Anthony to marry Cordelia, the well-to-do daughter of von Zeck. Upon Frederica's arrival, Mr. Warberger proposes a small dinner party and asks Frederica whom she would like to attend. After she proposes the Pastor, Mrs. Warberger suggests the von Zeck family, causing an argument with her husband, who dislikes and distrusts the Superintendent. Cordelia is visiting the newly arrived Frederica when Anthony comes in, embraces Frederica, and ignores Cordelia who is affronted. When the Pastor comes to pay his respects, Frederica and Anthony tell him they wish to marry and ask him to intercede with his parents. Before he broaches the subject, the Pastor requests Mr. Warberger's help for old Frederic, who has lost his place at the von Zeck's in favor of Matthew. The Pastor then proposes the marriage; while Mr. Warberger is lukewarm to the proposition, Mrs. Warberger rejects it because Frederica is of a different religion and has no money. A distraught Anthony leaves the house weeping, only to quarrel with Matthew in a public house. For no apparent reason, Mrs. Warberger changes her mind, approving of Anthony's marriage to Frederica. Meanwhile, the dinner party goes on, but Anthony still has not returned. After dinner Warberger and von Zeck have a private meeting, where von Zeck proposes a bribe to cover costs of his own extravagance, pointing out there are no witnesses. Warberger flatly refuses, and von Zeck threatens that he will not forget this day. Rodolph bursts in to report that Anthony has been accused of stabbing Matthew, and the Pastor informs them that all evidence is against Anthony. Talking privately with von Zeck, the Pastor says that the evidence against Anthony is largely circumstantial, but von Zeck, who will decide the case, turns a deaf ear to him. Even Mrs. Warberger's pleas and her attempted bribe are ignored. In this seemingly disastrous situation, old Frederic arrives and turns himself in, confessing to stabbing Matthew, and the Warberger family praise the Lord.

This melodramatic portrayal of domestic realism focuses on money and manners, but the characters are not very engaging. They frequently argue to no purpose, and the present-day reader cannot help thinking of a soap opera. If Plumptre had been less concerned about a faithful translation and tried to adapt the German text to her English audience, the play might have stood a chance on stage.

TEXT: Readex Microprint.

FORSYTH, Elizabeth (fl. 1784–1789). Nicoll credits Forsyth with the authorship of *The Siege of Quebec*, a pantomime acted at the Royal Grove Theatre, Dublin, on 31 May 1784. A pantomime by this title was previously acted at CG, 14 May 1760. Elizabeth Forsyth may be the author of a five-act, verse tragedy, *The Siege of Quebec; or, The Death of General Wolfe*, printed at Strabane, Ireland, in 1789 by John Bellew, though M. Forsyth signed the dedication to the subscribers, and she described the tragedy as the "first off-spring of my brain." There was apparently a production since a footnote to the Epilogue says that the "Author was present at the representation" (7). No other biographical information has come to light on this dramatist. [Nicoll]

The Fortunate Youth; or, Newmarket Hoax, Jane M. Scott. First performed on 5 January 1818, this farce ran thirty-three times during the season with Scott acting Abraham Gullem.

MANUSCRIPT: Larpent 2005.

Fortune Mends, translated by Fanny Holcroft. This three-act comedy was taken from the Spanish playwright Pedro Calderon de la Barca. There is no indication that this version was acted. It was printed in *The Theatrical Recorder*, vol. 2, no. 8, edited by Thomas Holcroft (London: C. Mercier, 1806): 75–111.

Set in Vienna, the play turns on Flora's visit, in disguise, to a party given by her next-door neighbor and confidante, Laura. Fearing a discovery, Flora tries to put off her intended husband, Licio, who doesn't realize who she is; Carlos objects to Licio's actions, and Licio challenges him to a duel and is killed. In the melee, Flora slips back to her home only to find Carlos asking for a place to hide. Without realizing Carlos has killed Licio, she sends his pursuers on a false trail. When they are gone, she hears the real story of the duel, but she continues to hide him until dark. Flora's father, Don Cesar, vows vengeance on Carlos, but he finds out that Carlos is the son of his old friend the Governor of Brandenberg: he knows he must save the person he hunts down. Carlos, meanwhile, is smitten with Flora, but when she releases him, she says once he is gone, she will be the first to seek his life. Next door, Laura and her lover Arnaldo have just met in the garden, but they are interrupted by Carlos, who says he is being pursued by a jealous husband. They only get him out of the way when Laura's jealous brother Fabio comes out of the house. Laura hides Arnaldo, but she is interrogated by Fabio. On the trail of Carlos, Don Cesar asks for their help in searching the garden, where he finds Arnaldo masked; he then imprisons him in his tower. In another tower room, Carlos has been hidden by Flora's maid, Silvia, without her mistress's knowledge. Carlos hears Don Cesar tell Arnaldo about the friendship with his father. After Silvia tells Flora that she has hidden Carlos in the tower, Flora goes there only to find him fighting Arnaldo, who is subsequently sent away knowing that he has saved Laura's reputation and that Carlos is captured. Laura, however, thinks Arnaldo is still in the tower and comes to see him, but —in a scene marked by mistaken identity —is rebuffed by Flora. After a series of mistakes are cleared up, Carlos asks for Flora's hand, and Arnaldo for Laura's.

Holcroft's translation brings out the swift pace of Calderon's comedy, written in the seventeenth century. The many disguises, sudden quarrels, and frequent misunderstandings are the stuff of this Spanish intrigue comedy, which turns on Flora's decision to hide the unknown man from persecution. One she has committed herself, Flora tests Carlos's honor and commitment. Her success emboldens Laura to circumvent her brother, a stock character who is excessively concerned with family honor. The use of mistaken identity works well without being too confusing.

TEXT: Readex Microprint.

Foscari, Mary Russell Mitford. This five-act tragedy was first produced at CG on 4 November 1826 and published the same year by G. B. Whittaker. It was acted fifteen times, according to Genest (9: 384–85). L'Estrange indicates Mitford received £100 each for the third, ninth, and fifteenth nights (*The Life of Mary Russell Mitford* [NY: Harpers, 1870] 2: 65). According to the Preface, the play is based on a historical narrative in Dr. Moore's *Travels*.

Count Erizzo and his follower Celso try to undermine the old Doge (Foscari) by poisoning his relationship with one of his oldest and most powerful friends, Senator Donato. Donato is encouraged to believe that the Doge regrets his son's betrothal to Camilla, Donato's daughter. At the same time, Count Zeno, another Venetian Senator goes to Foscari with a scroll, warning him to grant the first favor requested of him that morning or "thy very heart shall be rent in twain" (14). Disregarding the warning, the Doge refuses a request from Donato; subsequently, Erizzo tries to foment disorder in the Senate, but the Doge arrives to answer the criticisms. When the Doge's son, young Foscari, arrives a war hero, Erizzo's attempt to depose the Doge is foiled. Knowing that Celso's creditors are after him, Erizzo bribes his friend to kill Donato in a desperate attempt to discredit the Doge. When young Foscari goes to see Camilla, Donato's daughter, her father is killed just as the young man is leaving. Because Donato was stabbed with Foscari's sword, the young man is accused of murder and the Doge must preside over the trial of his own son. After the justices have sentenced him to exile, Camilla insists that she will share Foscari's plight. As they prepare to leave, however, Camilla's brother Cosmo intercedes, forbidding his sister to go: "The laws of Venice give to me a power Absolute as a father's" (73). Goaded on by Erizzo, Cosmo fights with young Foscari, fatally wounding him. Before Foscari dies, Zeno arrives with news that Celso has confessed to Donato's murder. Erizzo is arrested, and Camilla requests that she be buried with Foscari.

This play, much like Mitford's *Dramatic Scenes*, is flawed by a series of unbelievable coincidences, such as the confession of Celso, which is reported just after Foscari is wounded. Nevertheless, the villain Count Erizzo is well realized, and Mitford succeeds in evoking the pleasure he takes in inflicting pain —even when his own role is disclosed. After he is arrested, Erizzo is still swollen with pride: "Not a man of ye But is my tool or victim. I'm your master" (76).

MANUSCRIPT: BL Add Ms. 42880, ff. 341–450.

TEXTS: Readex Microprint of the 1826 edition, and of Cumberland's *British Theatre*, vol. 38, n.d.

FRANCIS, Ann Gittins (1738–1800). The daughter of a clergyman, she grew up with a love of literature and the scriptures. After marriage to a clergyman in Norfolk, Francis wrote a biblical drama in verse based on "The Song of Solomon." Although not acted, the play was published in 1781. *BD* believes the drama to be "a poetical translation from the original Hebrew: with preliminary discourse, and notes historical, critical, and explanatory." It is arranged as "a sacred hymeneal drama, divided into acts and scenes, according to the opinions of Gregory Nazianzen, Harmer, and others" (1: 771). In addition to this drama, Francis published several volumes of poetry. About her life, *BD* says "she was honoured with the friendship and correspondence of many very eminent and learned men; and, although the greater part of her life was passed in domestic retirement, she possessed powers which, if displayed, would have shone conspicuous in the most polished circles. In conversation she evinced great energies of mind, and a pointed wit; but she never suffered the lively sallies of her imagination to lead her either into levity or ill-nature. She died November 7, 1800" (1: 771–72). According to Lonsdale, obituaries especially praised Francis's mental acuteness and her perspicacity. [*BD*, DBAWW, FCLE, Lonsdale]

FRASER, Susan (fl. 1809). Described on the title page as "an Officer's Wife," Fraser includes a verse drama in a volume of poetry, titled *Camillia de Florian and Other Poems*. Davis and Joyce note that the volume of 159 pages contains a dramatic poem, "Comala," adapted from Ossian. The book was printed for the author and sold by J. Dick. We have found no other information about Susan Fraser. [Davis & Joyce, Inglis]

Frederick, Duke of Brunswick-Lunenburgh, Eliza Haywood. First produced at LIF on 4 March 1729, this five-act tragedy in blank verse was acted only three times and printed the same year by W. Mears and J. Brindley. Haywood dedicated the piece to the Prince of Wales, Frederick Lewis, but none of the royal family attended a performance.

The events of the play take place in 1400 immediately after Frederick has been chosen by the Electors as the Emperor of Germany. Count Waldec and Ridolpho, representing the Archbishop of Mentz, are afraid to lose the privileges gained from the previous ruler, and on the instructions of the Archbishop they plan to kill Frederick before he can be crowned. Waldec tells his sister Adelaid, who is still in love with Frederick, that she must consider marrying the Duke of Wirtemberg to recoup the family fortunes. Frederick reports to his faithful princes —Anspach, Anhalt, and Baden —

the problems caused by the Archbishop of Mentz, and Wirtemberg lists the rebel states. Frederick's wife Anna regrets that he must leave the next day to attack the rebels. That night, Ermand, Frederick's cupbearer, is stabbed by Ridolpho, who will only say that he was provoked beyond measure. Since Ridolpho can only be tried by the Archbishop, Frederick banishes him to Mentz. Waldec suggests to Ridolpho that they attack Frederick on the road. Adelaid overhears them and sends a letter to Frederick asking him to come to her apartment. Having been rejected by Adelaid, Wirtemberg enters to take a last farewell; upon Frederick's arrival, Adelaid puts Wirtemberg in a closet to overhear their conversation. Adelaid tells Frederick of the conspiracy. Waldec and Ridolpho rush in to kill Frederick, and Wirtemberg goes to Frederick's aid: Ridolpho is killed and Waldec taken into custody. Frederick, however, has been fatally wounded, and after a brief moralizing speech he dies. Anspach closes the play by saying that Frederick will live in his offspring until the end of time. Thus, Haywood pays tribute to the present Prince of Wales, Frederick Lewis.

Although Frederick is praised for his public virtues, in his private life he has deserted Adelaid to marry Anna, a Saxon Princess. Pearson finds Frederick's attitude toward Adelaid "shifty and self-serving" (243). Still in love with Frederick, Adelaid must make the crucial decision between her brother and the newly elected Emperor. She asks the Spirits to inspire her "with more than manly Courage." While her heroic generosity doesn't save Frederick, Adelaid decides to do what is right. In this flawed tragedy, she is the only one to act on the courage of her convictions.

TEXT: Readex Microprint of 1733 edition.

FACSIMILE EDITION of the 1729 edition: E-CED, with an introduction by Valerie Rudolph (NY: Garland, 1983).

Frogs and Bulls, Brand, Lady Dacre, formerly Barbarina Ogle Wilmot. Described as "a Liliputian Piece in three-acts," this play was "written for a party of children assembled at the Hoo [her home in Hertfordshire], in the winter of 1834, and acted by them" at a house party. Upon its publication by Ridgway in 1838 (fifty copies were printed), the play was dedicated to the use of the Ophthalmic Hospital and performed there at a fair at the Hospital in 1838.

Lady Statley gives Peggy Mudlands, a farm wife, lofty ideas about how she can rise from her situation in life. Peggy becomes angry with her husband when he returns from the fields. When it is discovered that the Statleys have lost their money, they must sell some lands to Farmer Mudlands, who is then reconciled with Peggy. After the sale of the land, Lady Statley offers to help Peggy improve, but Peggy declines.

The class struggle between the elegant but poor aristocracy and the well-off, hard-working farmer provides a democratic lesson for the children who acted the play and those in the audience. Lady Statley's conclusion —people will be happy in every station of life if they make a pleasure of duty —probably isn't ironically intended, though her offer to teach Peggy to improve may be. Peggy wisely rejects the proposed instruction.

TEXT: Not in Readex Microprint. We read the copy in the Lilly Library, Indiana U, Bloomington.

The Frolicks; or, The Lawyer Cheated, Elizabeth Polwhele. This comedy, written about 1671, was not acted. It remained in manuscript until it was transcribed and published by Judith Milhous and Robert Hume in 1977.

In one plot the extravagant rake, Rightwit, is cautioned by his sister Leonora to mend his ways, but he has no notion of reforming —until he meets Clarabell, the daughter of Justice Swallow to whom he is in debt. Swallow wants his daughter to marry a wealthy country knight, Sir Gregory, who has come up to town with his affluent friend, Zany, but the witty Clarabell will have none of these country bumpkins, despite their money. In a second plot, Sir William has come to town with his "country wife," Lady Meanwell, who discovers she likes London better than her rustic life. While she and her sister Faith are squired around town by several gallants, including Lord Courtall and Sir Frances Makelove, Sir William stays at home, while his servant Ralph constantly reminds him that he is likely to be cuckolded. A French bawd, Madame Procreate, provides a place for lovers to meet, but she is also on the lookout for a wealthy, young husband for herself. Rightwit and his friend, Philario, try to gull Sir Gregory and Zany in a tavern, when a young man (Clarabell in disguise) warns Rightwit that Swallow has bailiffs waiting in the street to arrest him for debt. Clarabell suggests Sir Gregory and Zany dress in women's clothes to avoid problems. Once they are out of the tavern in this attire, Rightwit tells a constable to arrest them as whores, and Sir Gregory and Zany are hauled before Justice Swallow, but he lets them go. Swallow then has Rightwit thrown into prison, but Clarabell gets him out by tricking the jailor and locking him in a closet. Rightwit is so taken by Clarabell's cleverness that he proposes marriage, but she says only if he can obtain Swallow's permission. Rightwit then goes in disguise and gets the Justice to tell him how he can wed legally. Swallow says the woman must lead him into the church, and Rightwit asks Swallow to give the bride away. He agrees and causes himself to be the means of contributing to Clarabell marriage (the subtitle). Rightwit also arranges other marriages that take place in masks: Sir Francis marries Faith, thinking she has a fortune; Sir Gregory and Madame Procreate are married; and Zany weds Leonora. After Rightwit has married Clarabell, Justice Swallow even admits he can only acquiesce.

Milhous and Hume point out that this "intrigue comedy" has two principal plots: Sir William acts the "imaginary cuckold," and Rightwit and Clarabell provide the "gay couple" elopement. Pearson points out *The Frolicks* is the earliest "sex comedy" by a woman and stresses Polwhele's use of role reversals: Clarabell dresses in male attire to get Rightwit organized, and the rustics are gulled into dressing like women. As she says, "the play gets a good deal of comic mileage out of its images of unmanly men and manly women" (139). Milhous and Hume argue that "Clarabell belongs to the new breed of heroine —tough, emancipated, and vigorously independent. . . . [she] is really the most vivid and dominant figure in the play" (23). Certainly, she drives the action, and clearly she is the wittiest character on stage.

MANUSCRIPT: Cornell U Lib. MS BD Rare P P77.

CRITICAL EDITION: transcribed and edited with introduction by J. Milhous and R. Hume (Ithaca: Cornell UP, 1977).

From Bad to Worse, translated by Fanny Holcroft. This three-act comedy is taken from the seventeenth-century Spanish playwright Pedro Calderon de la Barca's *Peor está que estaba*, which Aphra Behn also borrows from in her *The Dutch Lover* (1673). There is no indication that Holcroft's version of the play was staged. It was printed in *The Theatrical Recorder*, vol. 1, no. 4, edited by Thomas Holcroft (London: C. Mercier, 1805): 223–269.

The Governor of Gaeta receives a letter from his old friend Don Alonzo in Naples: Alonzo says his niece, Florida, has been recently involved in an affair of honor with a gentleman, causing her to flee Naples independently of her betrothed; would the Governor search for Florida? After the Governor's daughter, Lisarda, has greeted her father, she then tells her woman, Celia, about a masked intrigue with a stranger named Fabio, but Celia reminds Lisarda that her intended is expected daily. They are interrupted by a veiled woman (Florida) who asks Lisarda for protection: she explains that her lover, Don Cesar Ursino, found a man in her garden, fought a duel, and killed him, and she followed Don Cesar to convince him of her innocence. Meanwhile, Don Juan, Lisarda's intended, meets his old acquaintance, Don Cesar, at an inn. The meeting is short, however, for Don Cesar, as Fabio, has an assignation with a veiled lady (Lisarda). But the Governor interrupts the meeting, hauls Don Cesar off to jail, and sends the veiled woman to the care of his daughter Lisarda. Don Juan now arrives at the Governor's to claim his bride, and Lisarda and Celia plan to test the betrothed. Don Juan goes to the prison to visit Don Cesar, who has a note asking him to see the veiled lady, and Don Juan gets permission from the commandant of the prison to let Don Cesar go for the night. Don Cesar meets the veiled Lisarda, and when he is forced to hide because the Governor is coming,

Don Cesar is discovered by Don Juan. Don Cesar convinces Don Juan that he has not been a party to his own dishonor. Meanwhile, Florida has found that Don Cesar is in the country, and she is wild with joy at the prospect of seeing him, but the Governor will not let her go. He goes instead to tell Don Cesar that Don Alonzo has reported that all charges against him have been dropped in Naples, but he must consent to marry Florida. Don Cesar is only too happy to do so. They return to the Governor's house, where Florida unveils and accepts Don Cesar. Don Juan and Lisarda join hands, whereupon Camacho, Don Cesar's servant, says that he denies the proverb that things always go "from bad to worse."

This romantic Spanish intrigue comedy is another of Calderon's fast-action romps. Here, the male lovers are not always discreet, but they are chaste. Still, it is Lisarda who controls the action. She is the clever woman who manipulates her father and the other men by her disguises. This assists her new friend Florida to regain Don Cesar, and it also allows Lisarda to test her intended Don Juan. Holcraft's translation captures the contemporary English idiom: if the plot appeared old fashioned in the early nineteenth century, the language seems quite current.

TEXT: Readex Microprint.

-G-

The Gamester, Susanna Carroll [Centlivre]. This five-act comedy is adapted from J. F. Regnard's *Le Joueur* (1696). According to new evidence, the play was probably first produced at LIF in late December 1704 or early January 1705 (Burling), rather than the February date given in *LS* (2: 88). The play was published by William Turner and William Davis in 1705.

The focal character in this "moral comedy" is Valere, who is torn between his love for Angelica and his addiction to gaming. He swears, once more, to stop gambling, and Angelica forgives him again and presents him with her diamond-studded miniature portrait. This is a token of her love with which he must never part. But his passion for cards takes him back to the gaming table where he is met by Angelica, who has been informed of his relapse. Disguised as a man, Angelica wins all the money, plus the portrait. Shortly afterward, Valere, full of remorse, falls into such despair that even being disinherited by Sir Thomas, his father, becomes unimportant. Shocked by Sir Thomas's cruelty, and moved by a repentant lover, Angelica forgives Valere and agrees to marry him. The subplot involves Lady Wealthy, Angelica's sister and a coquettish widow, who plays with Lovewell's deep attachment to her. She accepts being courted by a ridiculous French marquis whose title is usurped, and even goes so far as to fall for Valere whose vice she encourages with a present of money. But in the end, deeply moved by Lovewell's devotion and generosity, she repents her foolish ways and marries him.

Writing this "reform comedy" (Hume) in a "sentimental-exemplary mode" (Pearson), Centlivre's clear intention was to denounce gaming, which often led to immorality when practiced to excess. As she acknowledges in her unsigned Dedication, she used as her source Regnard's five-act comedy in verse, *Le Joueur*. The part she owns herself "oblig'd to the French" is greater than implied, for at times, she literally translated from the original. But she did make alterations, especially in the ending and in the tone of the work. Her Valere, unlike his French counterpart, does repent, and, consequently, is allowed to marry the one he loves. In Regnard's work, Valère remains an irreclaimable gamester and Angelique marries Dorante the uncle, whom Regnard presents in a more sympathetic light than Centlivre. As Angelica's sister, Lady Wealthy plays a larger role than the Comtesse, and if both are coquettish and foolish, Lady Wealthy is more spiteful in her pursuit of Valere. Furthermore, the noble and patient Lovewell who wins her over has no French counterpart, being entirely created by Centlivre. Assisted by an excellent cast, she succeeded beyond her own expectations. *The Gamester*, one of her four most popular plays, held the stage for many years; in London alone, there were some seventy-five performances through 1756.

TEXTS: Readex Microprint. TEC Reel 578: 7.

FACSIMILE EDITION: E-CED, with introduction by R. C. Frushell (NY: Garland, 1982).

GARDNER, Sarah Cheney (fl. 1763–98). Sarah Cheney made a strong debut in the role of Miss Prue in *Love for Love* on 1 October 1763 at DL, where she performed for two seasons. In the summer of 1765 she went with Foote's company at HAY before going on to CG for the 1765–66 season, after having married William Gardner, a minor actor there. She remained at CG, off and on, for several seasons, acting summers with Foote at HAY.

Her three-act comedy, *The Advertisement; or, A Bold Stroke for a Husband*, was produced with much difficulty at the Haymarket Theatre on 9 August 1777. In her recently discovered manuscript book found at Colyton, Devon, and now privately owned, she describes the problems of this production (F. Grice and A. Clarke, *TN*, 7 [1952–53]: 76–81). Godfrey Greene contrasts Gardner's commentary with reports from various newspapers (*TN* 8 [1953–54]: 6–10). After being away from London for several years, Gardner played in *The Female Dramatist* (attributed to her, but actually by George Colman the younger), produced at the Haymarket Theatre on 16 August 1782. After travels to Ireland, Liverpool, the West Indies, Charleston, and New York, Gardner returned to the London stage in her own one-act prelude, entitled *Mrs. Doggerel in Her Altitudes; or, The Effects of a West Indian Ramble*. Produced at the Haymarket Theatre on 22 April 1795, it was her last public appearance on the London stage. Two plays remain in her manuscript book: *The Loyal Subject*, a comedy in five acts, and *Charity*, a one-act farce.

Isobel Grundy's excellent discussion of Gardner is a thorough investigation of her literary life, discussing the numerous difficulties Gardner had getting her plays produced (*TSWL* 7 [1988]: 7–25). [*BD*, BDAA, DBAWW, DNB, FCLE]

Gaston de Blondeville, Mary Russell Mitford. This romantic drama in three acts, based on the English King Henry III (1207–1272), was apparently not performed. It was published in her *Dramatic Works*, vol. 2 (London: Hurst and Blackett, 1854). Mitford's source was Anne Radcliffe's posthumous romance, *Gaston de Blondeville; or, The Court of Henry III Keeping Festival in Ardenne* (1826).

The two major plots intersect and depend on each other for closure. In the high plot, Lady Isabel is in love with Albert, the lowly King's minstrel, whose birth is mysterious. Against her will, Isabel is being forced into marriage to Gaston Baron de Blondeville, a knight who saved King Henry III's life. In the low plot, two middle-class travellers come to the King asking for justice: Woodreeve, a merchant from Bristowe, asks that the murderer of Reginald de Tolville be punished; and Benjamin comes "to crave remission of this grievous fine" (127) imposed on Jews in England. When Woodreeve tells Henry that Gaston de Blondeville murdered Tolville, his own kinsman, the King insists that the merchant will die unless he proves his charges the following day. Just as Gaston is to wed a despondent Isabel, an apparition of Tolville appears, causing Gaston to swoon. When his attempt to bribe Benjamin does not work, Gaston brutally threatens Benjamin, forcing him to give false testimony in his behalf concerning a gold chain that he wears. At the bridal feast that evening, a mummery appears, acting out the murder of Tolville. Although Gaston tries to ensure that Woodreeve does not survive the night, the merchant appears at the trial the next morning, but his witnesses do not arrive; he demonstrates, nonetheless, that the chain that Gaston wears contains a portrait of Tolville and his wife, proving that the necklace belonged to the deceased knight. Instead of establishing the truth about Gaston, Woodreeve is accused of sorcery, and in desperation, the merchant challenges de Blondeville to battle. Just then, Albert returns with a scroll, confirming that he is Tolville's son; and he fights with Gaston, who loses his sword when the Spectre reappears. Albert fatally wounds Gaston, and Isabel rushes toward her champion.

The play has relatively little to recommend itself beyond the neatness with which the plots are interwoven. The characters are not well developed, the language of little interest, and some details appear superfluous or undeveloped. For example, the scroll is a letter from Tolville's deceased wife, in which she discloses physical characteristics that help identify her son. This information is never used in the play, even though it is essential that Queen Eleanor be able to identify Albert as Tolville's son. The treatment of Benjamin, the Jew, is ambiguous. At the beginning of the play, he is reviled because of his race by a series of characters, but latter on Benjamin refuses Gaston's repeated attempts to bribe him with money: "By the law of Moses, good my Lord, I cannot [tell a falsehood]" (155).

TEXT: Readex Microprint.

GEISWEILER, Maria (fl. 1799–1800). Little is known about this translator, who at the end of the century rendered several German plays into English—*The Noble Lie: A Drama*, Kotzebue's *Die edle Luge*, 1799; *Poverty and Nobleness of Mind*, Kotzebue's *Armuth und Edelsinn*, 1799 (the basis of Prince Hoare's *Signs; or The Daughter*, 1799); *Joanna of Montfaucon: A Drama*, Kotzebue's *Johanna von Montfaucon*, 1799 (the basis of *Joanna* by Richard Cumberland, 1800); *Crime from Ambition*, W. A. Iffland's *Verbrechen aus Ehrsucht*, 1799. The publisher of her translations was C. Geisweiler, possibly father or brother. [*BD*, NCBEL (2: 864)]

The Gentle Shepherd, translated by Margaret Turner. This "Scottish pastoral" is rendered into English by Turner's translation of Allan Ramsey's Scottish text of *The Gentle Shepherd* (1725). Turner's version was printed with Ramsey's text on facing pages by T. Bensley "for the author" in 1790. There is no record of a performance of this version, although various dramatic adaptations of Ramsey's text had been playing in theatres since 1731: *Patie and Peggy; or, The Fair Foundling*, redaction and ballad opera by Theophilus Cibber, played in the 1730s. In the 1740s, theatres performed *Patie and Roger; or, The Gentle Shepherd*, probably a three-act version based on Ramsey's original. In the early 1750s, the play returned to Ramsey's original title. From the later 1750s into the 1770s, two versions, *Patie and Roger* (probably a shortened version) and *The Gentle Shepherd* (the five-act pastoral), were acted at different theatres. In the 1780s and 1790s, a two-act version, adapted by Richard Tickell with music by Thomas Linley Sr., became a popular afterpiece. It was, perhaps, to rescue Ramsey's original from altered states that caused Margaret Turner to provide a translation, not only to preserve the Scottish language of the original, but also to gain a wider reading audience for the work.

This pastoral is set in and around a shepherd's village not far from Edinburgh in May 1660. Patie, the gentle shepherd, loves Peggy (thought to be Glaud's niece), and she reciprocates his love. Roger, on the other hand, cannot win Jenny, and Patie tries to cheer his fellow shepherd up. Peggy encourages Jenny not to disdain Roger because she may regret it; however, Jenny doesn't believe a single life a crime, and besides the shy Roger has never confessed his love for her. Meanwhile, Symon comes to tell Glaud that King Charles is restored and they praise their landlord Sir William Worthy. Expecting to see Sir William soon, they plan a celebration. Bauldy, pledged to Neps, wants to hear his fortune and goes to visit Mause, thought to be a witch; she tells him to return that night after the festivities. In a soliloquy, Mause describes how she saved Peggy who is "daughter to a lord." Elsewhere, Sir William surveys his ruined house (laid waste by Cromwell's forces) and goes to the celebration, disguised as a fortune teller. He relates that Patie will become a squire. In a private meeting with Symon, who has raised Patie, Sir William reveals himself: he is sorry he must remove "Patrick" from his rustic love, but he feels a life at court would be more appropriate and they will leave tomorrow. In the fields, Roger meets Jenny and confesses his love to her; she is concerned about being a prisoner of marriage, but Roger swears his constancy. When they meet Patie and Peggy, they learn of Patie's elevation to squire, but Patie swears undying love for Peggy, and she says she will wait patiently for him. After the festival, Mause gets Madge, Glaud's sister, to join her in playing a trick on Bauldy. When the frightened Bauldy comes to Symon the following morning, he says Mause raised a ghost. Sir William requests her to appear for a trial, and Mause reports that she came to the district after saving Peggy, the child of Sir William's sister, leaving her a foundling at Glaud's door. Sir William then joins the hands of Patie and Peggy, saying he will remain and restore his house with the happy couple. Patie presents Roger, who craves Jenny's hand, and Sir William approves, asking Roger to become his steward.

Turner's reconfiguration of Ramsey's couplets and songs is generally successful, though a bit gentrified. For instance, when Peggy suggests to Jenny that they bathe when the day grows hot, Jenny's response in Ramsey's text is "Daft lassie, when we're naked, what'll ye say, Gif our two herds come bratling down the brae, And see us sae?" In Turner's translation, Jenny retorts "Mad girl! when we're undrest, what will you say, If our two shepherds should come that way?" Many of the lines are exactly the same, but in several instances Turner changes the couplet rimes:

> [Ramsey] Peggy: I darna stay,—ye joker, let me gang,
> Or swear ye'll never tempt to do me wrang.
> [Turner] Peggy: You sly one, let me go—I dare not stay.
> Or swear my innocence you'll ne'er betray.

Turner's English version, thus, provides an understandable rendering of Ramsey's Scots for those south of the border.

TEXT: Readex Microprint.

The Georgian Princess, the Margravine of Anspach. See **The Princess of Georgia**.

Gertrude, Sarah Watts Richardson. This five-act tragedy, published by subscription, was printed, probably in 1810, by C. Lowndes. There is no record of the tragedy's being performed. The "pecuniary Difficulty" noted in the Advertisement resulted from the death of her husband (Joseph R. Richardson) in 1803, and the burning of the Drury Lane Theatre, whose patent her husband shared.

Gertrude Baroness Stibbert discusses her secret with Ursula at the beginning of the play. When the Count and Countess Linckenstein fled Bohemia, they entrusted their infant son to her, and Baron Stibbert became his guardian when the parents died at sea. Later, when the child became gravely ill, Gertrude switched his identify with that of her young son's, fearing her husband's wrath if the rich heir—the source of their wealth—should die. Since the young Count survived, she has been forced to live with guilt and anxiety. The Baroness's emotional state becomes more distracted when a match is proposed between Count Linckenstein and her daughter Clara. Clara too is disturbed, because she loves her brother Henricus, their both being aware that his origin is mysterious. Even though Count Linckenstein loves Wilhelmina, Clara's closest friend, he reluctantly agrees to the match. Gertrude becomes increasingly distressed as Baron Stibbert tries to ensure the match between Clara and Count Linckenstein. This distress is exacerbated because Gertrude's husband has placed her in solitary confinement, believing her objections to her daughter's marriage are motivated by her own romantic interest in Linckenstein. The denouement seems contrived: just before the Countess can commit suicide by taking poison, Father Anselm stops her; he then takes a written note to Baron Stibbert, explaining his true son's identity. Father Anselm also relates that Gertrude, more composed after writing the note, has decided to spend her remaining years in a convent. Henricus announces his wish to marry Clara, and Linckenstein declares his pleasure in gaining a father.

Both the beginning and the conclusion of the play stress that the tragic flaw is Gertrude's fear; as Father Anselm states in the last lines in the play, "Unless the soul is arm'd by FORTITUDE—Her virtues struck upon the Rock of FEAR" (66). Nothing is said in the conclusion about Baron Stibbert's treatment of his wife, nor is his behavior in any way censored, except perhaps in part by his wife's decision to lead a cloistered life. That no direct criticism is made of Stibbert—the cause of his wife's moral timidity—is surprising, because earlier comments by both Clara and Henricus indicate disapproval of the Baron's tyrannical behavior.

TEXT: Readex Microprint.

Il Giorno Felice; or, The Happy Day, Jane M. Scott. This seriocomic opera in two acts was produced at the Sans Pareil Theatre on 24 February 1812. The music was composed by Michael Parnell and James Sanderson. Scott herself took the role of Frederick, the unknown son of the Marquis de Montese. The opera ran for twenty-five nights its first season.

MANUSCRIPT: Larpent 1705.

The Gipsy Girl, Jane M. Scott. This farce opened at the Sans Pareil Theatre on 9 January 1815 and ran twenty-five times its first year. It was revived in the next two seasons. Scott acted the character of Anne. No text of this play has survived.

GOLDSMITH, Mary (fl. 1800–04). Colman the Younger, manager at HAY, submitted a four-act version of Goldsmith's comedy *She Lives; or, The Generous Brother* on 28 Mar 1800 to the Licenser, who approved it in April (Larpent 1284). Apparently a benefit performance at the Haymarket, using Goldsmith's play, had been planned, but we can find no evidence that it took place (no such performance has been mentioned in Genest or *LS*). Later, Goldsmith revised the play, enlarging it to five acts, for a performance at Margate in February 1803 (Larpent 1399); there may also have been a performance at the HAY (*BD*). The following year Goldsmith published a two-volume novel, *Casualties*, and she also completed a two-act musical drama, originally titled *Walcot Castle*; the manuscript (Larpent 1431) was licensed for performance on 25 August 1804, and a production is likely to have taken place shortly afterwards in Margate, under its new title *Angelina*. [*BD*, Nicoll]

The Goldsmith, Fanny Holcroft. Acted twenty-eight times, this melodrama was performed at the Haymarket Theatre, beginning on 23 August 1827. Apparently, it was not printed.

Cardillac, the title character, is devoted to the acquisition of wealth, even so far that he will not scruple about committing murder. His clerk, Oliver, is convinced of his guilt, but for the sake of Cardillac's daughter, Isabella, with whom he is in love, Oliver is loath to accuse Cardillac. When Oliver discovers the secret passage by which Cardillac can enter and leave the house, Cardillac promises to give Isabella to Oliver in hopes of securing his silence. Cardillac decides to assassinate Rosemberg in order to appropriate jewels that are in his custody, but Cardillac is mortally wounded in his attempt. After Oliver assists Cardillac in making his escape into the secret passage, Oliver is apprehended on suspicion of having assaulted Rosemberg. In a dying state, Cardillac enters from the secret passage: he acknowledges his own guilt and Oliver's innocence. Our synopsis follows Genest's remarks (9: 396–397.)

MANUSCRIPT: BL Add. Ms. 42884 (7) ff. 150–182b.

Gonzalvo of Cordova, Lady Dacre, earlier Barbarina Wilmot. This five-act, verse tragedy was published in the first volume of her *Dramas, Translations, and Occasional Poems*, published in 1821 by John Murray. It was not performed. Dacre states in her preface that her source was part of a romance novel, called *Gonzalve de Cordoue*.

The play is set against a background of the wars between the Moors and the Spaniards, near Granada. Almanzor, the son of Moorish ruler Muley Hassan, leads the Moors, and Gonzalvo heads the Spanish forces (when the play opens, he is in Africa). A stranger who will not reveal his name (Gonzalvo) arrives at the Moorish palace having rescued Muley Hassan's daughter, Princess Zelima, from "Ethiopian ruffians" in Africa. Almanzor is suspicious and jealous of the stranger, but Muley Hassan offers him the hand of his daughter—if he can relieve besieged Granada. After the stranger and Almanzor nearly get into a fight, Gonzalvo decides to leave. He has one last tryst with Zelima and reveals his identity. Almanzor sneaks up on them and tries to spur Gonzalvo into a quarrel, but Gonzalvo refuses to fight the brother of Zelima. Back in the Spanish camp, Ferdinand, King of Aragon, greets Gonzalvo as a hero, and Gonzalvo explains that he will attempt to make peace with the Moors, as he has promised Zelima. Before Gonzalvo can meet Almanzor in battle, Gonzalvo's friend, Lara, slays Almanzor. Both Muley Hassan and Zelima blame Gonzalvo for Almanzor's death, and when Gonzalvo is captured he is to be executed. He sees Zelima one last time and informs her that he did not kill her brother. Just as the execution is about to start, Lara bursts in and confesses to killing Almanzor. Zelima says that the spirit of her brother's "generous soul" should prompt mercy. News then arrives that the Spaniards have laid waste to the countryside, but Gonzalvo says that if released, he will "stay their fury." Before he can get to the Spanish forces, however, they break into Granada and capture Zelima and Muley Hassan, the old man being wounded in the fight. Lara saves the day, and Muley revives long enough to commit the wealth of Granada to Gonzalvo.

As the principal woman in the play, Zelima seems pushed around by various men who are politically and militarily powerful, including her own brother. Almanzor's obsessive interest in his sister's romantic life raises a strong suggestion of potential incest, which may be the cause of Almanzor challenging Gonzalvo. In contrast, Gonzalvo treats Zelima with a tender passion. Also, Gonzalvo's several attempts at peace make him appear as an atypical man, who seeks compromises among the warring factions. Writing in the shadow of Joanna Baillie, who is mentioned in the preface, Dacre's verse shows an ability with language that is more poetic than dramatic.

TEXT: Readex Microprint. 1: 1–87.

Gortz of Berlingen, with the Iron Hand, translated by Rose D'Aguilar, later Lawrence. This translation and adaptation of Goethe's historical drama *Götz von Berlichingen* (1771) was printed by J. M'Creery in Liverpool, 1799, and sold by several London booksellers. In her Preface, D'Aguilar notes that she has deleted some lines and changed several names. D'Aguilar's version was never acted. Another translation of Goethe's play by the young Walter Scott was also published in 1799 (by J. Bell): his *Goetz of Berlichingen with the Iron Hand* varies only slightly in its title, but the translated texts are significantly different.

Before the Emperor of the German confederation established the Imperial Chamber to rule on differences among the various kingdoms (1495), private wars abounded. And it is in this setting that *Gortz* takes place. The play with its many scenes tries to achieve the historical sweep of a Shakespearean history play. It opens with two men in a tavern talking about the great warrior Gortz of Berlingen, who then enters and speaks of his previous and coming battles. Adelbert of Falkenhelm is captured by Gortz and taken to his castle, where Falkenhelm falls in love with Maria, Gortz's sister. Although Gortz approves the engagement, Falkenhelm returns to the Court of Bamberg, where he is encouraged to marry Adelaide of Walldorf. He does so, and Gortz—angered by this disloyalty—restarts his war with the Bishop. After many conflicts and much fighting, Gortz is captured and exiled to his castle, but when a peasant rebellion breaks out, the rebels ask Gortz to lead them. Reluctantly he accepts, but with revolutionary zeal they disobey his orders and burn a town, causing Gortz to disassociate himself with them. Later he is captured by the Imperial armies. Falkenhelm is to judge the case, but when Maria begs for Gortz's life, he tears up the order of execution. Exhausted and confined, Gortz dies, speaking the words "Liberty, Liberty!"

The character of Gortz is a larger-than-life portrait of an honest man who loves justice and hates tyranny. He is loyal to his followers and they to him, as the character of Francis Lersen demonstrates. The women in the play take little part in the battles, but Gortz's wife Elizabeth and his sister do provide unflagging emotional support for Gortz. The mutual friendship of Elizabeth and Maria spans the many years in which the events of the drama occur. Adelaide, who married Falkenhelm, manipulates him to remain at Court rather than returning to his castle in the country. When he will not bend to her wishes, she has him poisoned, for which she is executed. The contrasting women, thus, contribute to the factions of justice vs. tyranny. Genest said about Lawrence's translation, *Gortz of Berlingen with the Iron Hand*: "Goethe has probably given a faithful representation of the manners of the 15th century—his play is popular in Germany, but it is not particularly well calculated to please an English reader" (10: 215).

TEXT: Readex Microprint.

The Gotham Election, Susanna Centlivre. This one-act farce in six scenes was not performed during the author's lifetime. The reason, Centlivre says in her Preface, is that "the subject being upon Elections, the Master of the Revels did not care to meddle with it." Publication, with *The Wife Well Managed*, occurred in 1715 for S. Keimer. J. Roberts reissued the two unacted plays in 1715. The 1737 printing by W. Feales was retitled *The Humours of Elections*.

Lady Worthy has quarreled with her husband, Sir James Worthy, over a trifle, and she is determined to have him defeated at the local Gotham elections after his forty years in office. Since women couldn't vote, Lady Worthy canvasses the wives to get them to have their husbands vote for her candidate, Tickup, a womanizing scoundrel, who is reported deeply in debt. It is also hinted that Lady Worthy has more than a political interest in Tickup. All this we learn when Friendly, an agent of Sir Roger Trusty, chats up the local innkeeper, Scoredouble. In addition, the Mayor, with a partiality for France and things French, has a daughter, Lucy, who has £5000 of her own. Later, we see Friendly dressed as a Frenchman going to the mayor, who wants to cheat his daughter out of her money by sending her to a nunnery; Friendly also discovers the Mayor's corrupt actions and his plans to stuff the ballot box. Meanwhile, we see Tickup on the stump making outrageous commitments, but the local Cobbler (Last) and Miller (Tolefree) will not accept his promises. Tickup then stands as godfather to a carpenter's child, but the christening turns into a melee when Lady Worthy starts striking out against people in the party who she believes have made disparaging remarks about her. While the election shouts and scuffles go on, Lucy seeks protection from her father by marrying Friendly. When the Mayor refuses to give his blessing, Lucy reminds him of his plan to cheat her, and he leaves in a huff. In fact we never know who won (Sir James Worthy or Sir Roger Trusty), except we do know that Tickup has lost.

Unquestionably, this farce is a partisan Whig piece, showing the Tories using corrupt electioneering practices. The strong political overtones show a party that promises everything and delivers nothing. The play has a lack of character development and most of the characters are stereotypes, with Centlivre relying on descriptive names and occupations. The six scenes are really vignettes rather than a coherent play, so there is little plot. Pearson notes that the female politician is a striking example of the disorder threatened by Toryism (224), and that Tory principles are shown to destroy the family, for the Tory wife is undutiful, the Tory father autocratic (225). Thus, "within the conventions of farce, *A Gotham Election* explores the consequence of Tory principles within the state and within the family, and urges the oppressed, though within rigidly delineated limits, to use their freedom to choose" (Pearson 225). Genest remarks "this Farce contains a good deal of low humour—but it would have been very improper to have brought it on stage, as it is a strong political Satire on the Tories" (10: 154).

TEXTS: Readex Microprint of 1715 Keimer edition. TEC Reels 369: 1 (Keimer, 1715); 2776: 4 (J. Roberts, 1715); 3400: 14 (as *The Humours of Elections*. W. Feales, 1737).

FACSIMILE EDITION: E-CED, with introduction by R. C. Frushell (NY: Garland, 1982).

The Greek Theatre of Father Brumoy, with translations from Father Brumoy's texts (published in French, 1730) by Charlotte Ramsey Lennox. This three-volume work, published in 1759 by Millar and eight others, contains Lennox's translations of several of the dramas; included in volume one are *Oedipus*, *Electra*, *Philoctetes*, *Hippolitus*, and *Iphigenia in Aulis*. John Boyle, the Earl of Cork and Orrey, wrote the general introduction. Volume two contains translations of *Iphigenia in Tauris* and *Alcestis*, followed by Father Brumoy's "observations"; the remainder of volume two supplies more commentary on plays that are not included in the translation, such as *Prometheus* (by Euripides) and *Antigone* (by Sophocles). Samuel Johnson contributed a "free" translation of the "Discourse on Comedy" in volume three, and various male translators prepared English texts of the comedies—all by Aristophanes. A discussion of Lennox's recruitment of those male contributors can be found in James Gray, *MP* 83 (1985): 142–50. Gray remarks that Lennox "was a scholar of some discernment, who picked her translating team with intelligence as well as care" (144).

TEXT: Not in Readex Microprint. We used the copy at the Lilly Library, Indiana U, Bloomington.

GREEN, Mrs. (fl. 1756). One farce has been attributed to Green (by Nicoll): *Everybody to Their Own Liking*, which he says was produced in Bath in 1756. It was not published and must be presumed lost. Since Jane Hippisley Green (m. 1747) acted at Bath for part of the 1755–56 season (Rosenfeld), our guess is that she may have prepared such a piece for her benefit night. [DNB: Jane Hippisley]

GRIFFITH, Elizabeth [nee Griffith](1727–1793). Griffith became known first on the Irish stage, acting Juliet to Thomas Sheridan's Romeo in 1749. In 1751, she married Richard Griffith, but the failure of his business drove her to the London stage, where she acted at DL under the name of Miss Kennedy. She and her husband put together a novel under the name of *A Series of Genuine Letters between Henry and Frances* (1757, adding to it over the next decade; the 1770 version was six volumes).

After doing some translations, Griffith turned to drama. Her first work in this form, and her only tragedy, was *Amana: A Dramatic Poem*, based on *The Adventurer*, nos. 72 and 73 by John Hawkesworth. Designed to "show the folly of human wishes," the oriental tale was published in 1764, though not produced. The following year saw her first staged drama, a comedy entitled, *The Platonic Wife*. This adaptation of Marmontel's tale "L'Heureux Divorce" was produced at DL on 24 January 1765. Her next comedy *The Double Mistake*, an alteration of *Elvira; or, The Worst was not Always True* by George Digby (possibly acted in 1664, published 1667) was produced at CG on 9 January 1766. Griffith is likely to have translated *Dorval; or, The Test of Virtue* from Diderot's *Le Fils Naturel*; published in 1767, it was never performed. One of her major stage successes, *The School for Rakes*, debuted at DL on 4 February 1769; it was published the same year. Griffith may have translated Diderot's *Le Père de famille* in 1770. When, after working on several novels, Griffith returned to the stage, she prepared a comedy, *A Wife in the Right*, produced at CG on 9 March 1772. Owing to poor acting, it was withdrawn after only one night; publication by subscription followed later in 1772. Her best-known contribution to literary criticism, *The Morality of Shakespeare's Drama Illustrated*, came out in 1775. Although Griffith prepared a stage version of *The Barber of Seville; or, The Useless Precaution*, taken from Beaumarchais, this adaptation was never acted (published in 1776). More translations followed before she wrote her final work for the stage, *The Times*, taken from Goldoni's *Le Bourru Bienfaisant [The Beneficent Bear]*. Produced at DL on 2 December 1779, it was published the following year. In the early 1780s, Griffith and her husband retired to Ireland where he died in 1788 and she in 1793. [*BD*, BDAA, DBAWW, DLB 89 (by S. Staves), DNB, EBWW, FCLE, NCBEL (2: 835). Biography by Dorothy Eshelman, *Elizabeth Griffith*, 1949. Bibliography by Jane E. Norton, *Book Collector* 8 (1959): 418–24. See also Susan Staves on Brandeis Collective, *Eighteenth-Century Women and the Arts*, edited by Frederick M. Keener and Susan E. Lorsch. Westport, CT: Greenwood, 1988: 255–61.]

GRIFFITHS, Miss (fl. 1793). Little is known about this playwright, who may have been the author of one five-act comedy, *Cross Partners*, which was acted at the Haymarket Theatre on 23 August 1792. J. P. Kemble wrote "By Miss Griffiths" in his copy of the published version. Others, including *BD*, have attributed the play to Inchbald. [*BD*]

The Grinding Organ, Maria Edgeworth. A comic drama, originally in two acts, written for an Edgeworth family performance, the play was not intended for the professional stage. When the family and neighbors first acted the play in 1809, it "went off . . . better than I could have expected and seemed to please the spectators," according to the author (*Chosen Letters*, ed. F. V. Barry [Boston: Houghton, 1931]: 159–60). R. Hunter published it in *Little Plays for Children* in 1827. T. H. Lacy's version (1870?) reduces the play to one act, trims several speeches, and cuts three songs from Edgeworth's earlier version.

Farmer Haynes and his wife have three daughters, Bess, Patty, and Lucy; their neighbors in the village are the Widow Ross and her daughter Prissy, relatives of Mrs. Haynes. While the Haynes family live in comparative harmony, the Rosses are discordant, overbearing, and even downright rude. The families learn their cousin Captain Browne (Brown in Lacy's version) plans to retire from the army and return to the village. Accordingly, he sends his belongings to them before he arrives. While the adults sort out Captain Browne's goods, an old man with an organ grinder appears and delights the Haynes children, but Prissy makes fun of the man and his old-fashioned tunes. When the adults return to tea, they argue over who shall keep Captain Browne's china for him, causing Farmer Haynes to bet Mrs. Ross that she cannot keep a civil tongue for half an hour. She almost refuses to take tea because the old organ grinder is present, but she gives in when he offers to sing. His songs, however, nettle Mrs. Ross, and she explodes a few minutes shy of winning the bet. Whereupon the organ grinder reveals himself as their cousin Captain Browne, and he chooses to live with the Haynes: "Indeed," he tells them, "we may always judge of the parents by seeing their children."

Although Mrs. Ross and Prissy are overstated characters, Edgeworth's comic drama urges a democratic treatment of all. The Haynes family, parents and children, may seem too saccharine because of their "proper" values, but good hearts prevail over social hierarchy. As a metaphor, china has come a long way from the late seventeenth century when it was synonymous with sex.

TEXT: Readex Microprint of T. H. Lacy's (1870?) version, titled *The Organ Grinder* and marked for acting.

GUNNING, Elizabeth, later Plunkett (1769–1823). By refusing her father's choice of a suitor, Gunning was forced to leave her home. Supported by her mother (Susannah) and aunt (Margaret Minifie), who both wrote novels, Elizabeth began translating French works and writing novels on her own, beginning with *The Packet* (1794). *The Gipsey Countess* appeared in 1799. After her mother's death in 1800, Gunning came out from under this influence, and changed the direction of her prose.

In 1803, the same year she married Irish Major J. Plunkett, Gunning translated a French tragicomedy, *The Wife with Two Husbands*, based on R. C. Guilbert Pixérécourt's *La Femme à deux maris*. Even though the play was published, it never reached the stage in Gunning's version. *BD* praises the well-drawn characters and the natural incidents, but it believes the speeches are too long for stage presentation. James Cobb's musical drama by the same name was staged at DL on 1 November 1803. There are numerous differences between Gunning's translation and the musical version, according to McMillan. Gunning continued to write for the rest of her life: novels such as *The Exile of Erin* appeared in 1808, and *The Man of Fashion* in 1815; FCLE reports a rejected opera; and there were other translations, though no further dramas. [*BD*, DNB, FCLE; DBAWW under Plunkett]

-H-

H—, Eleanor. (fl. 1803). Author of one drama, *Matilda*, translated from the French of M. Monvel and printed in *The Lady's Magazine*, 1803. The play is based on Inchbald's *Simple Story*, done into French and retranslated by Elenor H—. [*BD*]

Half An Hour After Supper, by "a Lady." This one-act interlude by an anonymous female playwright was first performed at the Haymarket Theatre 25 May 1789 and published by J. Debrett the same year, with the playwright's dedication to George Colman the younger who managed the Haymarket that summer. It was acted eleven times its first season, and it was revived in the following three seasons.

After supper, Mr. Sturdy and his family are being read to by his unmarried sister Miss Tabitha. Although the women are much interested, Sturdy falls asleep. After the family retires, Bentley and Captain Berry arrive with the intent of carrying off Sturdy's daughters, Elizabeth and Sukey, but they are interrupted by Tabitha. They conceal themselves, and then Bentley pretends to be in love with Tabitha. Although Bentley takes her with him, Tabitha leaves him and elopes with Berry.

The intent of this piece is to point out the dangerous consequences when young women read novels (*BD* 2: 276). Curiously, the person most affected by novel reading is Tabitha, who must finish the book before going to bed. But instead of finishing the novel, she seems to have taken part in one, eloping with Captain Berry.

TEXT: Readex Microprint.

The Half-Pay Officer; or, Love and Honor, Jane M. Scott. Opening at the Sans Pareil Theatre on 18 January 1819, this two-act farce ran thirty-two nights with Scott in the role of Miss Fairfax.

MANUSCRIPT: Larpent 2067.

HARDWICKE, Countess of; see Elizabeth Lindsay **YORKE**.

Harlequin Hydaspes; or, The Greshamite, attributed to Isabella Aubert. Though the play had been advertised for 22 May 1719, Christopher Bullock, who was to play the doctor, got arrested, and the play put off until the following week. The burlesque opera in three acts was finally produced at LIF on 27 May 1719. It was not repeated or revived. The preface refers to the writer as male, though this could be a mask. The "mock opera" has long been attributed to "Mrs. Aubert," but recently her authorship has been called into question by William Burling, who found Mr. Aubert identified as the author in several issues (24, 26, and 27 May 1719) of the *Daily Courant* (*RECTR*, 2nd Series, 6 [1991]: 1–16). The play was published by J. Roberts in 1719.

The play is an early harlequinade, the characters transformed from French *commedia dell'arte*, the stock characters altered to suit the English stage. Harlequin and Colombine are the lovers, but this play has a second couple, Scaramouch and Isabella. Often Pantaloon in French works, the blocking figure here is a Doctor of Gresham College, who is constantly prescribing universal medicines to apothecaries and their patients. The Doctor is Colombine's guardian and wants to marry her, but the crafty Harlequin goes in disguise to win Colombine, and after a fight with a stage lion the Doctor is forced to approve of their marriage. Pierrot, the Doctor's factotum, is secretly in love with Colombine, but comes up empty handed as usual.

Avery in *LS* records that "Signora Aubert, lately arrived," sang the role of Mandane in Francesco Mancini's opera *Hydaspes* on 27 August 1715 at the King's Theatre. In the 1718–19 season, she is listed as a singer with the French comedians. The "mock opera" uses songs from *Hydaspes* (and other sources), and the dramatis personae records the operatic characters, such as Artaxerxes. The original was certainly known to Mme. Aubert and presumably her husband. By patching onto the opera a parody of Gresham College (former meeting place of the Royal Society) and medical virtuosos, the author or authors provided a light entertainment.

TEXT: Readex Microprint.

Harlequin Rasselas; or, The Happy Valley, Jane M. Scott. A musical pantomime with a large cast, the play opened on 9 February 1815 and ran for twenty-two nights. The names of the characters suggest the pantomime is loosely based on the novel by Samuel Johnson. No script of the movements is extant.

HARLOW, Elizabeth (fl. 1780–1792). Author of one comedy, *The English Tavern in Berlin*, based on an anecdote where Frederick the Great rewards the filial piety of a page by putting a rouleau of louis d'or in his pocket, while he is taking a nap (*BD* 2: 198). There is no evidence that the play was acted, but it was published for the author in 1789 (Davis and Joyce give London as the place of publication—possibly "for the author"; Readex Microprint gives Dublin, for H. Chamberlaine and others, 1790). [*BD*, Nicoll]

HARRISON, Elizabeth (fl. 1724–56). Best known as a writer of didactic and religious verse, Harrison printed one tragedy, entitled *The Death of Socrates*, in her *Miscellanies on Moral and Religious Subjects, in Prose and Verse*, published by subscription "for the author" in 1756. The subscription lists includes Samuel Johnson and Charlotte Smith. The volume also includes selections by various other persons, signed with initials.

Harrison's first published piece defended John Gay against the critics of *The Captives* (1724). She may be the author of *The Friendly Instructor; or A Companion for Young Ladies, and Young Gentlemen . . . in Dialogues* (1741). Joyce Fullard, writing in DBAWW, points out the popularity of this book, which went into a tenth London edition in 1790. [DBAWW, FCLE, Nicoll]

HARVEY, Margaret (fl. 1814–22). Author of a long poem (1814) and a melodrama, *Raymond de Percy; or, The Tenant of the Tomb* (1822) on the early history of the Percy family. The play was presented at Sutherland in 1822 and published the same year in Bishopswearmouth by G. Garbutt. Harvey ran a boarding school at Bishopswearmouth, where the play may also have been acted. [FCLE asserts that Margaret is probably related to the novelist Jane Harvey (b. 1776), Nicoll]

The Haunted Grove, Lady Dorothea Dubois. According to *BD*, this musical entertainment was produced at the Crow-Street Theatre, Dublin in 1773, but it was never printed (2: 285).

HAYWOOD, Elizabeth "Eliza" Fowler (1693?–1756). Author of novels, poetry, and periodical essays, Eliza Haywood acted in Dublin and London before she was asked by John Rich to adapt a play: her version of *The Fair Captive*, a five-act tragedy, was performed in 1721. An original comedy *A Wife to Be Lett*, with Haywood acting the title character, was produced in 1723. After publishing her *Works* (1724) and a number of novels, Haywood wrote another tragedy, *Frederick, Duke of Brunswick-Lunenburgh* in 1729. She continued acting and joined with William Hatchett to alter Fielding's *Tragedy of Tragedies* to a ballad opera, titled *The Opera of Operas; or Tom Thumb the Great*, in 1733, with music by Thomas Arne. She acted for a while with Fielding's company at the Haymarket Theatre, where she is credited by some critics with her final work for the stage, an adaption of the Renaissance tragedy *Arden of Faversham* (1736), in which she took a major role. After leaving the stage, Haywood carried on a different writing career with a periodical, *The Female Tatler* (1744–46), and a number of novels, the best known being *The History of Miss Betsy Thoughtless* (1751). She died in London in 1756 at the age of sixty-three. [*BD*, BDAA, BNA, Cotton, DBAWW, DNB, EBWW, FCLE, NCBEL (2: 791), OCEL, Pearson. Biography by George F. Whicher, 1915, but Christine Blouch, Diss., U of Michigan, 1991, supplies recently discovered information about Haywood's life. E-CED, with introduction by Valerie Rudolph.]

HELME, Elizabeth (d. 1810). A writer of didactic material, Helme translated two novels, set in dramatic form, from the German of Joachim Heinrich Campe: *Cortez; or, The Conquest of Mexico* and *Pizarro; or, The Conquest of Peru*. Both were published in London (1799) and in Dublin by P. Wogan and others (1800). A revised version of *Cortez* was published in London in 1811 by C. Cradock and W. Joy. Neither play was produced. Before Helme's foray into quasidramatic work, she published *Louisa, or The Cottage on the Moor* in 1787, and she continued to write romantic, gothic, and historical novels (about one a year), all with a strong moral bent. FCLE points out that Helme's daughter, also Elizabeth (later Somerville—d. 1821), not only succeeded her mother as the head of their school in Brentford, but also followed her mother by writing stories for children—the first being *James Manners,*

Little John, and their Dog Bluff (1799). [DBAWW, FCLE, Nicoll]

HEMANS, Felicia Dorothea Browne (1793–1835). Well schooled at home, she learned Latin, modern foreign languages, and drawing. Her first volume of poetry appeared when she was fourteen. After her marriage to Captain Alfred Hemans in 1812, she managed to raise a family and publish a volume of verse almost every year. Far better known for her poetry, Hemans wrote one tragedy that was staged: *The Vespers of Palermo* (1823), but her *Siege of Valencia*, based on the epic of *The Cid* (also 1823), was not acted. A volume of her poetry in 1825, *The Forest Sanctuary, and Other Poems,* has two dramatic poems: "The American Forest Girl" and "Bernard del Carpio." In Mrs. Hemans's posthumous *Works* (published in Edinburgh by W. Blackwood and in London by Thomas Cadell in 1839) are included *De Chatillion; or, The Crusaders*, a five-act tragedy, and *Sebastian of Portugal*, a dramatic fragment in four scenes. Rose D'Aguilar Lawrence wrote a memoir of Hemans in 1836. [DNB, EBWW, FCLE]

Henriquez, Joanna Baillie. Vandenhoff appeared in the five-act tragedy at Drury Lane on 19 March 1836, where the play was a "partial success" (*DNB*). *Henriquez* came out in the first volume of Baillie's *Dramas* (Longman, et al., 1836).

Returning from a campaign against the Moors, Henriquez reads a letter that leads him to believe that his wife Leonora is involved with his close friend, Don Juen. Leonora notes Henriquez's strange behavior, but she is unaware of his misplaced jealousy. At the same time, Alonzo, the King of Castile, arrives, seeking refuge for the night. When Don Juen's murdered body is discovered near Henriquez's castle, it is Antonio who is accused of the murder. In love with Mencia, Leonora's sister, Antonio has been in hiding in the nearby woods. When Don Juen's papers are brought to him, Henriquez discovers a marriage contract between Don Juen and Mencia. After realizing his mistake, Henriquez implores the imprisoned Antonio to try to escape, but the latter insists that Heaven will vindicate him. At the Court of Zamora, Henriquez seeks a private audience with Alonzo before the court "shall sit." He makes the King promise that the murder will be punished. Then, when Antonio is presented, Henriquez declares the man's innocence and his own guilt. Before dying, Henriquez requests a monument for Don Juen and asks to be interred with his friend. At the end of the play, we are told that Diego, Henriquez's steward and the man who triggered the revenge plot, has died in bed.

Baillie's tragedy resembles *Othello*, but the Iago character, Diego, is less important, and he believes that Leonora and Don Juen have betrayed Henriquez. Having jumped to the wrong conclusion, Diego sets the action of the play in motion. The pace of the play is problematic at times, the best example being when Henriquez announces his guilt to the King. The audience is suspended—waiting impatiently to learn his fate—while everyone assembled makes a speech. The women in this play are relatively unimportant: they are pawns controlled by the fates of the men whom they love.

MANUSCRIPT: BL Add. Ms. 42935, ff. 274–314b.

TEXT: Readex Microprint of *Dramas* (1836) 1: 251–370.

HILL, Isabel (1800-1842). Diagnosed with inflammation of the lungs at fifteen, Isabel Hill spent a somewhat retired life with her brother, Benson Earle Hill. Isabel's first play, a five-act tragedy entitled *The Poet's Child*, was published by John Warren in 1820. The play had been offered to CG, but it was rejected on the grounds that it lacked the requisites of an acting tragedy. Isabel went on to publish *Constance*, a prose tale, in 1822, and "Zaphna, or the Amulet," a poem, in 1823.

Although she continued to contribute to periodicals, Hill sent her second dramatic effort, a comedy entitled *The First of May; or, A Royal Love Match*, to Kemble at CG; it was produced at CG, 10 October 1829, and acted eleven (Genest 9: 513) or twelve nights (Benson E. Hill). She published her poetry and stories in *The Gem*, *The Monthly Magazine*, and several juvenile publications during this period of her life. She also translated works by Madame de Stael and Chateaubriand, and her one novel, *Brother Tragedians*, came out in 1834. That same year, two of her plays were performed: *My Own Twin Brother* (EOH) and *West Country Wooing* (HAY). Late in her life, Isabel began a novel focusing on female education, but this work was never completed. A tragedy in five acts, *Brian the Probationer; or, The Red Hand* was published posthumously with a memoir by her brother, published by W. R. Sams, 1842. The play was not staged. [FCLE, Genest, Nicoll]

HOFLAND, Barbara Wreaks Hoole (1770–1844). A writer of many novels and works of moral instruction for children, Hofland printed one set of plays under the title of *Little Dramas for Young People by Mrs. Hoole*, which focused on English history and were "intended to promote among the rising generation an early love of virtue and their country." Although they were published by Longman, Hurst, Rees, and Orme, 1810, they were not publicly performed.

After the death of her husband of only two years in 1798, Hoole began to write, and she produced more than sixty works according to FCLE. In 1808, she married T. C. Hofland, a not-too-successful artist, and supported the two of them with money from her publications. She moved to London in 1811, and expanded her literary production. Shortly after her death in 1844, Thomas Ramsey wrote a biography of Hofland (1849). [DNB, FCLE; see also Mary V. Jackson, *Engines*, 1989.]

HOLCROFT, Frances [Fanny] (1778/83–1844). Daughter of dramatist and radical author Thomas Holcroft, Fanny translated seven plays for her father's journal, *The Theatrical Recorder*, in 1804–05. After Thomas Holcroft's death in 1809, Fanny wrote several novels. Later in her life, she wrote a successful melodrama, *The Goldsmith* (first produced at the Haymarket Theatre on 23 August 1827), which played twenty-eight performances. [FCLE]

HOLFORD, Margaret Wrench (1761?–1834). After publishing several novels, Holford wrote two stage comedies. She prepared *Neither's the Man* for a benefit performance at Chester, probably in November, 1798; it was printed there the following year. Her second play, a five-act comedy entitled *The Way to Win Her*, printed in *The New British Theatre*, 1814, was not produced. [DBAWW (incorrectly lists her death in 1814), DNB (discusses Holford's achievement in the entry on her daughter Margaret Holford Hodson), FCLE]

Holidays at Home, Charlotte Elizabeth Sanders. This novel in dramatic form includes four plays read to the children in the course of the main story: "The Governess" (three acts), "The Giddy Girl; or, Reformation" (two acts), "The Grandmother" (two acts), and "The Errors of Education" (three acts). Within this dramatic novel, the young characters respond emotionally to the plays that their mother reads. Sanders signed the dedication in January 1803, noting "The Grandmother" appeared in *The Children's Magazine* in October 1800. The volume was published by J. Mawman and at York by T. Wilson and R. Spence, 1803.

Through the dramas within the drama, Mrs. Lymington helps promote the moral values of her own children, as well as her nieces and nephews. "The Governess" takes up an educational scheme in the family of Sir Sidney Somerville. Sometime after the death of Lady Somerville, a new governess is to be brought in to teach the children, though the housekeeper, Mrs. Cantwell, tries to turn the children against the new governess before they have even seen her. Mrs. Benhamond, a widow, has left her daughter, Laura, with the Woodley family before she goes to take up her duties as governess. When Mrs. Benhamond arrives at the Somervilles, the children find her a kind and sensitive teacher, so unlike the wicked governess hinted at by Mrs. Cantwell. When their father meets the new governess the next morning, he discovers Mrs. Benhamond is actually the sister he had disowned many years before. He forgives her, takes in his niece Laura, and installs Mrs. Benhamond in the house permanently. Mrs. Cantwell is sacked for disobedience, and the Somerville children take delight in their newly found cousin and aunt (governess).

"The Giddy Girl; or, The Reformation," supposedly written by Mrs. Lymington's nephew Harcourt, focuses on the title character Isabella, who has a habit of blaming others for her mistakes. Isabella has commissioned Robert, a young carpenter, to make a pair of oars so Robert can row Isabella and her sisters about the canals. Being of a lower class, Robert feels compelled to do as he was bid and to make the oars, but his friend William knows the proposal is wrong and urges Robert to explain why to Isabella. When he does, Isabella accepts his argument and learns her lesson; her mother also forgives her for her headstrong actions. In this playlet, the lower-class youths enlighten the upper-class children.

In "The Grandmother," the title character Mrs. Smith provides a social education to correct feuding family members. Set on the Isle of Wight, the play opens with examples of the benevolent acts Mrs. Smith has done for her community, providing aid and comfort to the less fortunate. Her son Frederic has, however, rejected his mother, made a bad marriage, and fallen into dissolute ways. His spoiled children plan to disobey their father and take a moonlight excursion on the ocean, but their uncle, Captain Oliver Smith, who has recently returned from abroad, overhears their plans. Isabella, Captain Smith's daughter, has been raised by her grandmother while he has been abroad; when she is asked by her cousins to go on their moonlight excursion, Isabella refuses and the disobedient children are chastened by her example. Captain Smith urges his mother to reconcile with the Frederic Smith family. We assume a union will be achieved—if the erring Smiths are truly repentant. While the grandmother preaches forgiveness to the converted, we can only speculate that the family of Frederic Smith will return to the family fold and change their ways.

"The Errors of Education" concludes the book, and perhaps the holidays. Read aloud over a winter's evening, the drama deals with the Topaz family of Tunbridge. While their son fancies himself an actor and playwright, their daughter Clementina believes she is the belle of every ball. Their cousin Julia, whose father is away in India, appears the only sensible young person in the family. As Clementina continues to spend money on fashionable clothes, her father is slowly going bankrupt because of her extravagance. The dwindling supply of cash forces the family to let rooms. After the father is taken to prison by the bailiffs, Julia goes to the Colonel, who has taken their rooms, and asks him for help. When they arrive at prison, the Colonel discovers his brother and bails him out of prison. Having found his daughter and near relations, the Colonel decides to retire in England.

Most of the plays involve relations who have lived away for a long time: their return helps remedy problems that have arisen in their absence. The effect of the adult's absence on various children shows the importance of suitable adult guidance. Without this direction, some children have become willful, snobbish, and downright rude. It is Mrs. Lymington's intent to instruct by direct remarks, by object lessons, and by educational stories.

TEXT: Not in Readex Microprint. We read the first edition in the King Collection at the Miami (Ohio) U Library.

HOLT, Jane Wiseman. See Jane **WISEMAN**.

The Homicide, Joanna Baillie. This three-act tragedy was published in the third volume of *Dramas* (Longman, et al., 1836). It was not staged. In the appendix, Baillie includes five pages that could be substituted for the scene on board the ship, which the author says may be suitable only for melodrama.

The play begins with Margaret telling Baron Hartman that Rosella rejects his suit. Rosella has entertained Hartman's attentions to conceal her own engagement to Claudien. To further his own purposes, Kranzberg alerts Hartman to the engagement and to the fact that Rosella is not seriously interested in his proposal. Hartman swears to have his revenge and attacks Claudien, who kills him. As Kranzberg and the officers arrive, Claudien flees. The dagger used to kill Hartman is discovered in the rooms of Van Maurice, Claudien's friend and Rosella's brother. The officers agree to give Van Maurice a day of freedom to prove his innocence. Meanwhile, the ship on which Claudien fled is driven against the rocks. Considered a bad omen by the sailors, Claudien is thrown overboard. Back in Lubeck, Kranzberg (Hartman's heir) moves quickly to prosecute Van Maurice, who refuses to save himself by revealing that Claudien is the murderer. Rosella, on the other hand, wishes to tell the truth to save her brother, but she is silenced by an opiate, administered in response to her brother's instructions. Kranzberg makes it appear as if Van Maurice is attempting to escape from prison in order to ensure that his trial is speedy. Disguised as Father Francis, the returned Claudien comes before the judges to establish Van Maurice's innocence. Only when he removes his disguise and confesses his own guilt, do the judges reconsider the case. Simultaneously, Kranzberg attacks Van Maurice, and Claudien intercedes, eventually wounding both Kranzberg and himself. Claudien dies as Rosella embraces him. The unrelieved tragical events in the play, triggered by Hartman's jealousy and Kranzberg's greed, are balanced by Van Maurice's loyalty to his friend and his confidence that his own innocence will be vindicated. Baillie must have had the biblical Jonah in mind when the impulsive sailors throw Claudien overboard because he has brought bad luck on their ship.

TEXT: Readex Microprint of *Dramas* (1836) 3: 165–278.

HOOK, Harriet Horncastle (d. 1805). She is the author of a popular two-act musical farce, with music by her husband. Used as an afterpiece, *The Double Disguise* was first produced at DL on 8 March 1784 and published the same year by J. Bell. The play was performed in five consecutive seasons. *BD* records her death in Lambeth in 1805. [*BD*]

HOPER, Mrs. [**HOOPER**, Rachael? Harford] (fl. 1742–1760). The daughter of a London cabinet maker, Hoper found it necessary to sell the business after the death of her husband. She then turned to playwriting to provide a livelihood for herself and her son. The author of three plays in three different genres, Hoper staged her tragedy, *The Battle of Poictiers; or The English Prince* at Goodman Fields in 1747. A three-act farce, *The Cyclopedia*, was mounted the following year at the Haymarket. Neither of these plays was printed, but her burlesque in prose and verse, *Queen Tragedy Restored*, produced at the Haymarket on 9 November 1749, was published the same year by W. Owen. According to *The Thespian Dictionary* (1802), she had problems with theatre managers and retired to Enfield where she set up a school with her son. [*BD*, BDAA, Cotton]

Horace, Katherine Philips. Translated from Corneille's *Horace* (1640), this five-act tragedy was presented at Court on 4 February 1668; it opened at the Theatre Royal in Bridges Street on 16 January 1669 and may have run as many as six nights. It was published with only the first four acts translated by Philips in her *Poems* (1667); the play, as completed by Sir John Denham, was included in the 1669 and 1678 editions of her works.

Horace is one of Corneille's four Roman plays and one of his masterpieces. Rome and Alba, at war with one another, are on the eve of a decisive battle, but their respective leaders decide to select three champions from each camp who, through their victory, will decide the outcome of the conflict. The Horatii from Rome and the Curiatii from Alba are chosen. At first, fortune seems to favor the Alban side: two of the Horatii have fallen, and the third, wounded, faces the Curiatii alone. But through a ruse, he separates his enemies, kills each one singly, thus ensuring Rome's victory. Horace, entering Rome as a hero, encounters Camille, his sister, who had betrothed one of the Curiatii. Mad with grief, she breaks out into violent imprecations against her fate and Rome. Horace, incensed at her lack of patriotism, stabs her to death. This horrendous crime leads Horace to be tried and condemned. But after a convincing appeal by his father, Horace is absolved by the king, who ends the play by ordering a sacrifice to the gods and the funerals of Camille and Curiace, which are to take place the following day.

The theme, as in Corneille's previous play, *Le Cid*, is the conflict between duty and love. Duty in the form of total and blind devotion to one's country takes precedence over passion:

Camille pays with her life for not accepting this, and the people, through her father's eloquent appeal, vindicate her assassin.

Death prevented Philips from finishing her translation: she stopped at Act IV, scene 6. The four acts she left behind show the same qualities found in *Pompey*. A careful and faithful translator, she kept Corneille's favorite rhetorical devices, rhymed couplet and strong antithesis, whereas Denham was much freer in his continuation (Souers 229). He also added songs and dances, as Philips had done in *Pompey*, but did not retain the dignified tone she had used in her previous work.

MANUSCRIPT: Folger Shakespeare Lib. MS V.b.231.

TEXTS: Wing P2032: EEB Reel 286: 8 (1664). Wing P2033: EEB Reel 748: 28 (1667). Wing P2034: EEB Reel 772: 3 (1669). Wing P2035: EEB Reel 748: 29 (1678). Readex Microprint of Wing P2033, *Poems* (London: H. Herringman, 1667). [NOTE: The 1991 facsimile in the Scholars' Reprint series of the *Poems* (1667) does *not* include the plays.]

HORNBY, Mary (fl. 1817–20). Author of one tragedy, *The Battle of Waterloo* (Stratman #2408), and one comedy, *The Broken Vow*, Hornby had her tragedy published at Stratford-upon-Avon by B. W. Barnacle, 1819, and her comedy, although printed at Stratford-upon-Avon in 1820, gives no publisher. There is no indication that either play was staged. The BL Catalogue identifies Hornby as the "Keeper of Shakespeare's House," and it credits her with verses and a history about the Bard, printed in 1817; this publication went through five editions by 1820. [Davis & Joyce, Stratman]

Hortensia, Ann Hamilton M'Taggart. This verse drama in five acts, whose heroine Galt found more purely evil than Lady Macbeth, was published anonymously in *The New British Theatre*, ed. John Galt in 1814. There is no evidence that it was produced. The drama was later printed under M'Taggart's name in her *Plays*, published in 1832 by A. J. Valpy.

Beginning literally on a "Dark and Stormy Night" (149), *Hortensia* features a fairy tale plot in which children are made to leave a castle in the middle of the night by order of an evil stepmother who is responsible for their exile. When the children, Leopold and Albertina, eventually return, their stepmother—Hortensia or the Countess de Cronstadt—falsely accuses Leopold of trying to stab her. When Leopold responds to her accusation with "sullen silence" (167), Count de Cronstadt turns his son over to Hortensia for punishment. After Albertina defends Leopold's innocence, both are sent to the dungeon by Hortensia, who indicates to her attendant Ella that she wishes the Count's heirs to be murdered. Soon after this, Hortensia's first husband, Villeroy, who was believed to be killed in the War, reappears and declares his love for Hortensia. Villeroy, too, is imprisoned by Hortensia, but she comes beautifully attired to his cell, declaring her love for him and suggesting that they live happily ever after on Cronstadt's wealth. When he is horrified at her suggestion that the ill Count be eased into an early death, Hortensia believes that Villeroy is rejecting her love, and she declares that she will that night kill both of her husbands: ". . . every wish My heart e'er formed, or by ambition urged, Or hatred, or revenge, will be fulfilled!" (187). Hortensia's will is finally thwarted, however, by a series of coincidences. Villeroy hears the children in an adjoining cell, and he is able to open a hidden door connecting the rooms. Then, Ella confesses Hortensia's plot to kill her husbands to the Count's attendant, Riccardo; since Riccardo happens to have retained the master key, they are able to free the prisoners, who dash to the Count's room to protect him from Hortensia. Villeroy forces the cup of poison from Hortensia's hand, and her machinations are revealed. Instead of remorse after she is exposed, Hortensia announces that she "view[s] ye all with scorn and detestation" (195) before fatally stabbing herself. In the final speeches, the Count acknowledges his weakness and asks the children for forgiveness; and Leopold notes that Hortensia's example should be considered by all "who meditate foul wrongs" (196).

In his remarks on *Hortensia*, Galt emphasizes that the Countess is the only well-developed character. His major criticism of the play is that the author has not "softened the vices of her heroine" (198) by introducing feminine or maternal touches. Galt's second comment ignores Hortensia's repeated declarations that she defines herself in opposition to the softness and tenderness associated with women, and that she believes her power rooted in her defiance of "feminine" behavior. For example, when Ella is moved by Albertina's tears, Hortensia advises her to "subdue such feelings, Or never hope for greatness " (169). Although the play clearly endorses Albertina's "softness," the Countess remains in the reader's mind as an especially powerful female villain with psychological depth. Still, Hortensia's condemnation is absolute.

TEXT: Readex Microprint.

HOUSTON, Lady Eleonora Cathcart (1720–1769). Inglis mentions that the author was married in 1744 to Sir Thomas Houston, who died in 1751. She wrote one comedy, *The Coquettes; or, The Gallant in the Closet*, possibly an adaptation of Thomas Corneille's *Les Engagements du hasard*. Tobin dates the performance at Canongate Theatre, Edinburgh, on 10 February 1759. While *BD* suggests it was presented for three nights, Tobin states that "the play was retired after one performance." The prologue was written by James Boswell, her fourth cousin, who shepherded the play through rehearsals. Inglis notes that Lady Houston is also the author of an unfinished play in manuscript, *In Foro*, which was then (1868) in the library of James Maidment of Edinburgh. [*BD*, Inglis, Nicoll, Tobin]

How Will it End?, Jane West. This five-act comedy was printed in the second volume of her *Poems and Plays*, published by Longman and Rees in 1799. The play may have been staged in a three-act adaptation at Manchester in February 1809 (Larpent 1570).

The play opens with Lord Hazard arguing with Colonel Wilford, when Primary, a marriage broker, comes in. While Hazard considers an arrangement with either Caroline Seymour or Lady Seraphina, Wilford talks with Greville. The scene shifts to Caroline and Constantia, an orphan raised by Mrs. Wilford, who has been the subject of improper advances by Colonel Wilford, Mrs. Wilford's son. Constantia ran away, and Greville took her in as Miss Beverley. Caroline and Constantia greet Lady Seraphina, Caroline's guardian, who has just arrived from Bath. Lady Seraphina tells Mrs. Medium, another marriage broker, she wishes Caroline to marry the nephew of Lord Rusport, and Lady Seraphina takes Lord Rusport to her literary club. Caroline and Constantia plan to trap Colonel Wilford: Caroline explains how she tests her lovers by making life difficult for them. When Lord Rusport arrives, he discovers that Constantia is his daughter. Greville comes to urge Caroline to consider Lord Rusport's nephew, but Caroline honestly tells him that she doesn't wish to lead the nephew on. Having tested Caroline, Greville tells her that he is Lord Rusport's nephew. Lord Hazard is found to be in debt, and Primary and Mrs. Medium are discredited. When Colonel Wilford arrives, Caroline reads his palm, setting up Greville's entrance with Constantia. This confrontation results in the Colonel's repentance, and he is reconciled with Constantia. Lady Seraphina plans to travel, and Lord Rusport concludes the play regretting his libertine behavior, because one never knows "how it will end."

West's sprightly Caroline Seymour provides a strong heroine, who helps Constantia test and reform the would-be rake, Colonel Wilford. Lord Rusport also repents the wicked ways he formerly practiced. Greville, an honest countryman, tests the love of Caroline by concealing the fact that he is Rusport's nephew. Thus, the comedy is strong on testing and reform, and in the end the good characters receive their just deserts.

TEXT: Readex Microprint of *Poems and Plays* (London: T. N. Longman and Rees, 1799) 2: 1–159.

The Hubble-Shue, Christian Carstaires. It seems unlikely that this farce could have been produced, but it was published in Edinburgh (without a publisher's name) probably in 1786. Tobin reprints the brief play in his discussion of Scottish dramatists (71–79).

Throughout the farce, people talk at cross purposes without listening. There is a discussion of the author's poetry that moves on to a wacky dinner party whose participants finally adjourn to the theatre where events end in a wild melee.

Tobin believes the key to solve the play's conundrums may rest in determining the purpose of "the sword brandishing Gustard, whose only function seems to be to frighten the cat" (70).

MODERN EDITION: In Terence Tobin, *Plays by Scots, 1660–1800* (Iowa City: U Iowa P, 1974): 71–79.

Hubert de Vere, Fanny Burney. Written between 1789 and 1791, this five-act tragedy was neither produced nor printed. The manuscript indicates an earlier title was *Cerulia.*

In this "pastoral tragedy," the title character, Hubert de Vere, has been exiled from court for supposed treason to the Isle of Wight, where he falls in love with an orphan, Cerulia. All is well, when unfortunately the greater world invades the island: Geralda, de Vere's old love, comes to tell him how she was forced to marry Glanville, de Vere's rival who is now dead. Responsible for this marriage is de Mowbray, Geralda's uncle and enemy of de Vere, who comes to the island in disguise to keep de Vere from marrying Geralda. De Vere is now torn between Cerulia and Geralda, though the latter encourages him to care for Cerulia. De Vere, nevertheless, wants to explain the situation to Cerulia: when she sees him at Geralda's feet, however, she flees. Cerulia spends the night in a country church yard and has a vision of her death. She laments her lost love (de Vere) and her orphaned and solitary situation. De Mowbray intrudes on her lamentations and confesses to being her father: as Cerulia dies, he believes he has broken her heart. A messenger comes to arrest de Mowbray for his traitorous activity; de Vere's name is cleared, and he is reunited with Geralda.

Adelstein points out the many gothic trappings of the play "with its melodramatic plot, excessive sentimentality, unmotivated villain, and rhetorically swollen lines" (56). In another vein, Joyce Hemlow remarks that the dramatic tale "was suggested by some narrative like Falconer's *Shipwreck*, and meant as an experiment in the wild kind of romantic narrative so popular with the poets of the age" (*UTQ* 19 [1949–50]: 180). In yet a different reading, Margaret Doody shows how the "emotions expressed are almost entirely negative; even love is marked by suspicion and fear, and everyone is both spied upon and alone" (190). In Cerulia ("a feminine power of loving that gets crushed"), Doody finds a biographical equivalent of Burney's anguished feelings at Windsor when she wrote the play.

MANUSCRIPT: New York Public Library, Berg Collection, where two manuscripts exist. Doody describes the earlier one in fragments, "held together by (rather dangerous) old pins"; the later, cleaner "draft consists of five *cahiers*, one for each act" (409).

The Hue and Cry, Elizabeth Inchbald. This two-act farce has as its source in Dumaniant's three-act comedy *La Nuit aux aventures; ou, les Deux Morts vivants* (1787). It was produced at DL only on 11 May 1791 (the benefit night for the actor John Whitfield) and never revived or published. Later, Inchbald's play was adapted by James C. Cross as an opera and produced as *An Escape into Prison* at CG on 13 November 1797 (it ran two nights). According to MacMillan, the texts are substantially the same, except Cross added music by William Reeve, the house composer at CG.

Leonora has slipped away with her cousin, Isabella, to the opera, where she is joined by a gentleman, but they are seen by another cousin, Don Juan. While the two men fight, the women flee. The gentleman then ducks into Leonora's room to escape capture because he thinks he has killed Don Juan. He is the Count Abeville, whom Leonora's father has chosen for her husband. Leonora and her maid, Iris, hide the Count and send the officers to the coach house, where they discover Perroquet, the Count's valet. Iris has a plan to get both master and man out by having them hide in trunks. Just as they appear safe, the officers capture two men in a coach with the trunks on the back and take them to prison. In fact, they have apprehended Don Juan (uninjured) and his man, Fabio. While they are in another room in the jail, the Count and Perroquet emerge from their trunks, and the jailor comes with wine. The Count won't drink and retires, but Perroquet and the jailor drink together. After Fabio comes in, he and Perroquet are whisked off by Iris who has bribed the jailor. The Justice comes to question the prisoners, and the Count calls for his valet. When Don Juan appears, the two are reconciled. After the valets have been released, they tell the story to Leonora, who laughs heartily, and brings in her father. He is pleased at the outcome and gives Leonora to the Count; Don Juan calls for the nuptials in some happier place than prison.

Because each nobleman believes he has killed his opponent, Kinne mentions the "series of comical *méprises* and concealments, climaxed by a meeting in jail of the principals, *éclaircissement*, and wedding bells" (223). Unchanged from the original French text is the setting, Madrid, but the dramatis personae has been partially altered. According to Kinne, "except for the omission of the taciturn Don Lambinos there was no appreciable loss in condensation. Wit was, of course, broader throughout" (223).

Iris, the clever female servant, contrasts with the slow-witted Sanchez, the male servant. Iris masterminds hiding the Count and getting the trunks for master and man. She also plans the escape from jail and has the last lines "Ay, he may now the Hue & Cry deride He has a Habeas Corpus from his Bride" (26).

MANUSCRIPTS: Larpent 900. Readex Microprint of Cross's version in manuscript—Larpent 1184. Inchbald's manuscript transcribed in E-CED, with introduction by Paula R. Backscheider (NY: Garland, 1980).

HUGHES, Anne (fl. 1784–1790). As a poet, Hughes published her *Poems* in 1784. She turned to novels in the latter part of the decade, writing *Zoraida, or Village Annals* (1786), *Caroline; or, The Diversities of Fortune* (1787), and *Henry and Isabella, or A Traite through Life* (1788). Hughes then embarked on writing three closet tragedies in blank verse. These were all printed in her *Moral Dramas*, published by William Lane, 1790. All three works—*Aspacia*, *Constantia*, and *Cordelia*—are named for their heroines. [*BD*, DBAWW, FCLE]

HUMBOLDT, Charlotte de. See Charlotte **De HUMBOLDT**.

The Humourous Lovers, attributed to Margaret Lucas Cavendish, Duchess of Newcastle. This five-act comedy, credited on the title page to her husband, the Duke of Newcastle, was said by Samuel Pepys and other contemporaries to be written by Cavendish. Hume, however, suggests Dryden, Shadwell, or James Shirley may have assisted the Duke. The comedy was first performed at LIF on 28 March 1667 and printed in 1677 for H. Herringman.

The play opens in London, where Courtly meets Colonel Boldman, who is "a despiser of Love." Courtly plans to see his inamorata, Emilia, and asks Boldman to join him. At Emilia's house, Boldman meets Lady Pleasant, who courts him as if she were converting an infidel. When he begins to like her, she reverses the situation and laughs at his efforts at courtship. An old school mistress of Emilia, Mistress Hood (now a matchmaker), brings Dameris for a visit, and the visiting poetaster Sir Anthony Altalk falls for Hood's young pupil, thinking her a great fortune. Courtly asks Altalk to prepare a masque on Boldman, who then pretends madness over Lady Pleasant. Old Furrs, the hypochondriac, agrees to marry Emilia's maid Tatle if only she will keep the mad Boldman away. After Altalk makes marriage arrangements with Hood (for £40), he weds Dameris, only to find out that she is an illegitimate child of old Furrs, who then gives Dameris £2,000 to smooth matters over. After Boldman comes to his senses, Lady Pleasant accepts him, and Emilia agrees to marry Courtly.

In a play where almost everyone ends up being married, it is likely that the title refers to "humourous" as amusing, rather than suggesting the use of "humours" characters. Colonel Boldman and Lady Pleasant act the "gay couple" in this comedy, according to John Harrington Smith (55–57). Emilia and Courtly do not suit Smith's definition of a "gay couple" who begin as antagonists and develop a love relationship over the course of the play; they are in love from the very outset, and even though they trade some contrary couplets, they act like committed lovers.

TEXTS: Wing N883. EEB Reel 393: 18. Readex Microprint.

MANUSCRIPT: BL ms. Harley 7367, article I.

Huniades; or, The Siege of Belgrade, Hannah Brand. This five-act, historical tragedy was first produced in Norwich, 7 April 1791. It was performed in London at the King's Theatre by the DL company on 18 January 1792, where it lasted only one night. It was then altered and retitled *Agmunda*. It played only one more night under its new title at the same theatre on 2 February 1792. (James Cobb's popular comic opera *The Siege of Belgrade*, which opened 1 January 1791 at DL, may have suggested the subtitle.) It was collected in Brand's *Poems and Plays*, published at Norwich by Beatniffe and Payne, 1798.

When Belgrade is besieged by the Turks, the town suffers reduced circumstances. Mahomet offers to make peace if Princess Agmunda, sister of the young king, will marry him. The Regent Huniades (played by Kemble), who is also the Princess's guardian, fights the Turks at sea; his son, Corvinus, declares his love for Agmunda, encouraging her to marry him before she can be forced to marry Mahomet. Although horrified at the thought of marriage to "a Turk! a murderer! An Infidel!" (47), Agmunda resists marriage to Corvinus, since she has sworn to Huniades that she would never marry his son. After counsel from the monk Campestran, however, she is secretly wed to Corvinus. Mistakenly thinking that Huniades's fleet is in flames, the Council pressures the Princess to save Belgrave by marrying Mahomet, but Agmunda refuses to do so, finally admitting she is already married. Through the treachery of her uncle, Count Cilley, who wishes to become regent, Agmunda is carried to the Turkish camp where she again rejects Mahomet. Told that Corvinus is dead and Belgrade overwhelmed, Agmunda is compelled to marry Mahomet to save her people. After the offstage marriage between acts, Huniades defeats the Turks. When news arrives that his troops are being slaughtered, Mahomet leaves to try to keep them from retreating. Upon instructions given to Mahomet's minister Mustapha, Agmunda is poisoned when the Sultan's ring is returned without him. After Huniades and Corvinus enter, Agmunda dies, realizing how cruelly she has been deceived by Mahomet. Word arrives that Count Cilley has been slain; and although Corvinus wishes to commit suicide, Huniades convinces him to live to care for his wounded father, to revenge Agmunda's death, and to assume political responsibilities.

The central character, Princess Agmunda, boldly refuses Mahomet's proposal of marriage, scolding him to his face as a "base, dishonourable, treacherous, coward!" (93). Similarly, she initially refuses Corvinus's proposal, and she accuses Count Cilley of being a traitor in front of the Lords' Council. Although her arguments successfully counter those made by powerful men, Agmunda never questions Huniades's authority, especially as it concerns the vow he extracted from her. After breaking the vow when she marries Corvinus, Agmunda believes that everything that happens to her subsequently is the direct result of her disloyalty to her guardian. Apart from the character Agmunda, the play has little to recommend it. Some incidents in *Huniades* seem superfluous: for example, Campestran girds Corvinus with a sword that is supposed to bestow miraculous power, but the sword is never used.

MANUSCRIPTS: Larpent 896. Readex Microprint of this manuscript. As *Agmunda*: Larpent 932.

TEXT: Readex Microprint of 1798 *Poems and Plays*, as *Huniades*.

-I-

I., P. (fl. 1786). This unknown dramatist left only her initials in the preface of her volume of *Dramatic Pieces*, 3 vols., published by J. Marshall, c. 1786 (NUC) or c. 1788 (BL). The plays were published in America by Abel Morse in New Haven, 1791 (Readex Microprint). The plays include "The Good Daughter-in-Law" and "The Good Mother-in-Law," vol. 1; "The Maternal Sister" and "The Reformation," vol. 2; "The Contract" and "The Triumph of Reason," vol. 3. The plays, all in three acts, are "calculated to exemplify the mode of conduct which will render young ladies both amiable and happy, when their school education is completed." None was professionally staged. [Davis & Joyce]

Ibrahim, The Thirteenth Emperour of the Turks, Mary Pix. The first play written by Mary Pix, *Ibrahim* is a five-act tragedy, which made its debut at DL in May or June of 1696 and was published the same year by John Harding and Richard Wilkin. In her preface, Pix notes that Ibrahim was historically the twelfth emperor. The tragedy was revived several times—in 1702, 1704, possibly 1709, and 1715. On the latter occasion (her benefit night), Jane Rogers, who originated the role of Morena, introduced her daughter in the same role.

Ibrahim, the Sultan of Turkey, lives a lascivious and degenerate life; an early example of this occurs when he chooses one of twenty virgins he will "enjoy" that night. His Vizier and his principal mistress, Sheker Para, easily manipulate Ibrahim, and this causes discord in the kingdom, as bemoaned by the Mufti, a religious leader, and Mustapha, the head of the janizaries: the army is ignored and merchant ships are plundered. Sheker has a passion for Amurat, Mustapha's son, who leads the Turkish troops, but he has ignored her interest because he is in love with Morena, the daughter of the Mufti. Not to be denied, Sheker appeals directly to Amurat; unsuccessful in her explicit approach, she has Achmet spy upon him to discover her rival. Meanwhile, the Mufti and Mustapha have accepted the mutual love of Amurat and Morena, and they allow them to be contracted. Achmet, disguised as a mute, discovers the situation and reports it to Sheker, who schemes with the Vizier to take revenge on the Mufti, Mustapha, Amurat, and Morena. Going to Ibrahim, Sheker and the Vizier kindle his interest in Morena with a delectable description. He goes at once to the Mufti and asks to see his daughter, but the Mufti pleads that she is unsuitable for the Sultan, owing to her learning in philosophy, history, and the arts. Ibrahim presses for her appearance, but when Morena arrives, she rejects him because of her prior contract. Ibrahim, however, will not take no for an answer, causing Morena to grab his "naked Scimitar" and run it across her hands. Even with her bleeding hands, Morena is led away to Ibrahim's bed, as he gloats how he will "Rifle her sweets, till sense is fully cloy'd; Then take my turn to scorn what I've enjoy'd" (25). In the next scene, the distracted Morena is returned to her father, who tells Amurat what has occurred, and a full-blown rebellion ensues. Solyman, Amurat's friend, fights with Ibrahim and both are fatally wounded. Sheker boasts how she has been the cause of the rape, but to avoid punishment she stabs herself. Morena takes poison and dies in Amurat's arms. The distracted Amurat then takes his own life, leaving the distraught fathers, Mufti and Mustapha, to carry on the business of state.

Clark labels the play a "historical tragedy" and quotes a seventeenth-century account of the actual Sultan Ibrahim (230-32). Hume believes "Amurat and Morena give the play a considerable pathetic interest" (423). Not withstanding the blood bath on stage, *Ibrahim* does have power to move an audience, largely through the strength of Morena. She is not the "passive saint" that Pearson claims (174), for she actively argues her case with Ibrahim. When he will not listen to her, she purposely slices her hands with his scimitar, and she must be forcibly subdued and dragged to Ibrahim's bed. Later, she describes the rape by saying "I have been in Hell!" (27). Finally she feels that she has no choice but to make an offering of herself. Unlike most men in the drama of this age, Amurat feels no compunction about marrying a woman who has been sexually abused. When she mentions her "pollution," he says "Thy Virgin Mind was pure!" (40). The structure of the play focuses our attention on the villainous characters in the opening act; this contrasts with the upright love of Morena and Amurat. The evil plotting of the villains leads to Morena's rape, followed by the rebellion against the heinous crime they have committed. But the feckless Ibrahim is killed early in act five leaving us to anticipate the outcome of the virtuous characters. Pix also sets up contrasting inner scenes: early in the play, we see

Young Men and Old Women, 1792. She retired from acting in 1789. Aside from her success as a dramatist, Inchbald wrote two successful novels—*A Simple Story* (1791) and *Art and Nature* (1796).

Late in her career as a dramatist, Inchbald took up the vogue for Kotzebue, adapting *Lovers' Vows* in 1798 and *The Wise Man of the East* in 1799. After she stopped writing for the stage, Inchbald was asked to provide critical prefaces for *The British Theatre* in twenty-five volumes, published by Longman, 1806-08. This editorial work was followed by her selecting plays for a *Collection of Farces* in seven volumes (1809) and *The Modern Theatre* in ten volumes (1811). Inchbald was a clever businesswoman and invested money from her writings: upon her death in 1821, Inchbald's estate was valued at more than £6000.

Love and marriage recur in Inchbald's dramas, but she showed a great concern about social problems of her day. Sentimentality impinges on many of her dramas but does not overwhelm them. One of the reasons for her extraordinary achievement as a female playwright and critic is her performer's knowledge of theatre practices: brilliant stagecraft is evident even when reading Inchbald's plays. A few of her comic characterizations, such as Mr. Harmony, have passed into the language. [*BD*, BDAA, BNA, DBAWW, DLB 89 (by Patricia Sigl), DNB, EBWW, FCLE, NCBEL (2: 842-44), OCEL, Scouten (by G. Kelly). On the mss., see Patricia Sigl, "The Elizabeth Inchbald Papers," *N&Q* ns 29 [227] (1982): 220-24, where she notes the Folger holds nine of Inchbald's diaries and Harvard has the mss. of *Animal Magnetism* and *I'll Tell You What*. An early biography was written by James Boaden (1833), a more recent one by Roger Manvell, *Elizabeth Inchbald, A Biographical Study* (Lanham, MA: UP of America, 1987). Patricia Sigl is currently preparing a critical study of Inchbald's drama. Bibliography by G. Louis Joughin in *Texas Studies in English* 14 (1934): 59-74. E-CED series, 2 vols., ed. P. Backscheider, 1980. Inchbald's critical stance may be assessed in her collections of plays and farces, in 42 vols., 1806-11; see discussion by K. M. Rogers in *Curtain Calls*. Performance dates were established by Hogan in *LS*.]

Incle and Yarico, attributed to Mrs. Weddell. This three-act verse tragedy is founded on Sir Richard Steele's story in *Spectator*, no. 11. Intended for CG, the play was found unacceptable, and the tragedy was published by T. Cooper in 1742. A "friend" supplied a "Preface: or, A General View of Dramatic Poetry, Particularly applied to this Play," which refers to the author as "he." George Colman the younger wrote a successful opera with the same title, first acted at the Haymarket Theatre, 4 August 1787. Lonsdale included a poem by Frances Seymour on the same subject, written about 1726 (106-09).

Incle is shipwrecked on the African coast. While he thinks of the wrongs he has done Violetta in England, he meets Yarico, a Princess who protects him from capture. At the tribal court, Satamamo asks for Yarico's hand in marriage, but she wants to put it off "for six short moons" (20). When Yarico returns to her "retirement," she decides that if Incle leaves, she plans to go with him: a boat from a ship comes, Yarico joins Incle and they depart. Seeing that Yarico has gone, Satamamo jumps into the sea and is dashed against the rocks. Upon arrival in Jamaica, Incle sells Yarico, now pregnant, into slavery. He says he can't marry her and demean his name. Yarico is purchased by a planter, whose son, Amyntor, has an honest concern for Yarico's plight. She is unused to work and bemoans what Incle has done to her. Amyntor wishes to marry Yarico himself, but she has a very strong aversion to men because of Incle's ill-treatment of her. Since she has rejected him, Amyntor pleads with Incle to take Yarico back without repayment. Meanwhile Honorius, visiting Jamaica, hears the story of Yarico, and in turn tells the merchant of his former love Violetta, who was seduced and betrayed by a neighbor youth. Amyntor comes to Incle and tells that Yarico died in premature childbirth; a remorseful Incle goes to see the body. When the two arrive at the merchant's, Incle gets in a fight with Honorius, who fatally wounds him, revenging "*two* Murders by *one* Wound" (69).

Little contemporary interest was raised by this early antislavery tragedy, perhaps because it was not staged. The authors of FCLE remark that Weddell "blunts the stark racial opposition of Richard Steele's story" (1143). It took thirty-five more years before the English theatre would present—in Colman's opera—such a message, but by then Wilburforce and his antislavery forces were becoming organized, though it would not be until 1807 that the English passed laws abolishing slavery altogether. The main interest in this play, however, must be the character of Yarico, who saves Incle only to be sold into slavery by her faithless lover. While in Africa, she fed him, protected him from her tribe, and loved him. Yet the difference of race causes Incle to refuse to marry Yarico; in doing so, he justifies his views on the grounds of religious training. In her situation, Yarico has no recourse but to accept the position she has been forced into, but she does not go willingly; while her spirited defense (51-52) does not move Incle, it could have moved a theatre audience.

TEXT: Readex Microprint.

Inez de Castro, Mary Russell Mitford. Planned as early as 1827 when Mitford sent a synopsis to her friend the Reverend William Harness, this five-act tragedy was finished by 1828. The title page of Dicks' Standard Plays states that the first production took place on 12 April 1841 at the City of London Theatre; G. B. Whittaker published the play in 1842. The tragedy can also be found in her *Dramatic Works* in 2 vols., published by Hurst and Blackett, 1854. Mitford wrote to Charles Kemble in 1828 putting off any performance by CG, but it is not clear what other causes delayed the production. Other playwrights who have dramatized the same story are Catharine Trotter (*Agnes de Castro*, published 1696) and Barbarina Wilmot, later Lady Dacre (*Ina*, published 1815).

Set in Portugal, the play presents a triangle of love: Pedro is the Prince whose father, King Alphonso, wishes to unite the kingdoms of Castile and Portugal through Pedro's marriage with Constance, the sister of Philip of Castile. However, he loves Constance's companion, Inez de Castro. The two women have different interests, as shown in the second act where Constance has proved herself a proficient hunter by killing three deer. Inez, on the other hand, presents a soft heart and regrets seeing anything killed. She publicly divulges her love for Pedro when it is reported that he may have been thrown from his horse. King Alphonso urges Pedro's marriage to Constance only to have Inez and Pedro admit that they are already married. Because of an old law stating that any commoner who marries the kingdom's heir is subject to execution, Inez must be put to death. Pedro's dispute with his father comes to nothing and the sentence on Inez is passed. After Pedro has organized a revolt and Constance pleads for Inez, the King relents. In prison, however, Inez stabs herself with a dagger just before Pedro rushes in with a reprieve.

Several women dramatists, as well as Aphra Behn's novel, have taken up the plight of Agnes (Inez or Ina) de Castro. Mitford's tragedy focuses on the force of the obsolete law and on King Alphonso's stubborn refusal to grant the ill-fated Inez mercy—until the last minute. It is a more unified play than Trotter's *Agnes de Castro*, which emphasizes political and sexual warfare in its several subplots. Wilmot's *Ina* shifts the tale to medieval England, but ends it happily with a reconciliation between father, son, and daughter-in-law. The weakness of Mitford's tragedy comes in the final act, when Manuel the King's old minister tries to get the imprisoned Inez to marry him, forcing her to suicide. Manuel suffers no punishment for persecuting Inez.

The strength of Mitford's heroine derives from her ability to defend herself verbally under assault, yet she is willing to accept punishment by Portugal's laws even though she is herself a Spanish citizen. While Inez is a well-developed character, Constance—by way of contrast—has few lines and appears a pawn in national alliances: she is the "haughty sister," whereas Inez is the "melting beauty."

MANUSCRIPT: BL Add. Ms. 42909, ff. 188-239 (in the Lord Chamberlain's Plays, February to April 1831).

TEXT: Readex Microprint of Dicks' Standard Plays, no. 672, n.d.

The Inflexible Captive, Hannah More. This five-act verse tragedy was published by S. Farley, Bristol, 1774. There was one performance at Bath (18 April 1775), and it was also played at Bristol and at Exeter. More's biographer, M. G. James, notes that "As early as 1775 Garrick had decided to try out her classical drama, *The Inflexible Captive*, in the provinces [Bath], where Garrick provided the epilogue" (32). It was licensed to be performed at DL (*LS* 4: 1889 for 2 May 1775), but it was not staged in London, owing to More's own objections that there was too little action. M. G. James explains that the play is a free translation of Metastasio's *Attilio Regolo.* Genest says "many speeches in this T[ragedy] are well written, but on the whole it is a very dull play—it was acted at Bristol" (10: 189).

The play begins with Attilia, daughter of Marcus Attilius Regulus, bemoaning the fact that her father has been a prisoner of the Carthaginians for the past five years. Barce, a Carthaginian slave owned by Attilia's brother, announces that Regulus is finally returning to Rome, accompanied by the African Ambassador, Hamilcar, who is also Barce's lover. When he addresses the Roman Senators at the Temple of Bellona, Regulus explains that he is still a captive, who has agreed to relay his captors' peace proposals, which involve the exchange of Carthaginian captives (including Barce) for Regulus. But Regulus sternly instructs Rome to reject the Carthaginian proposals: he argues that he is too old to serve his country, and the young Carthaginians who would be released are "her chief bulworks" (19). The Senators are shocked at his words, aware that Regulus has promised to return to Carthage, and he looks forward to horrible death if this peace mission fails. The rest of the plot consists of a series of attempts to keep Regulus in Rome. The old rival of Regulus, Manlius, now the Consul of Rome, is touched by the hero's courage; Manlius offers to exert his influence to convince the Senate to approve the exchange of prisoners. Barce encourages Attilia to go to the Senate and speak individually to the Senators, encouraging the prisoner swap. Regulus's son Publius speaks openly in the Senate and tries to talk his father into sparing himself. Attilia's lover, Licinius, who is also a Roman Tribune, uses his influence with the people, who rise up in anger that Regulus should return to Carthage as a prisoner. Eventually the crowds even try to block Regulus's path so that he cannot leave on the ship bound for Africa. Even the Carthaginian Ambassador, Hamilcar, responding to Publius's decision to free Barce, offers to let Regulus escape from his guards. With each entreaty, however, Regulus remains inflexible, insisting that his death is a triumph and the only way he can maintain Rome's honor. Late in Act IV, Regulus acknowledges that he has family as well as state responsibilities: "I recollect I am a *father*! My Publius! My Attilia!" (52). These duties are quickly transferred to Manlius, who agrees to function as guardian, and after a long speech about honor and sacrifice, Regulus leaves for Carthage.

M. G. James offers an accurate summary of *The Inflexible Captive*: "Through five long, immobile acts [Regulus] harangued his countrymen in dignified and sententious declamation to refuse the terms proposed by the enemy, and returned to Carthage, apostrophizing glory and honour, to suffer a horrible death" (32). Regulus's inflexibility is celebrated in the play: eventually even his son and daughter recognize his sacrifice as appropriate and emulate his behavior. Attilia's last minute conversion, however, is not very believable. The play abounds in patronizing comments about the weakness of women, Regulus advising his daughter to "set a bright example of submission, Worthy a Roman's daughter" (73). Carthaginians of either sex are seen as inherently inferior, and Regulus's first response to Hamilcar's offer to help him escape is "Abhorr'd barbarian!" (66). Despite repeated references to her as a barbarian, Barce seems to have more courage than Attilia. Readers might well applaud Barce's assessment of Roman nobility:

> This love of glory's the disease of Rome;
> It makes her mad, it is a wild delirium,
> An universal and contagious frenzy;
> It preys on all, it spares nor sex nor age
> (76).

MANUSCRIPT: Although it was licensed, the play is *not* in the Larpent Collection.

TEXT: Readex Microprint of 1774 Bristol edition.

The Innocent Mistress, Mary Pix. Although early critics said this five-act comedy was taken in part from Etherege's *The Man of Mode; or, Sir Fopling Flutter*, there seems little correlation between the two. Betterton's company produced the comedy at LIF in late June 1697; it was printed the same year by J. Orme for R. Basset and F. Cogan.

Sir Charles Beauclair (played by Betterton), a younger brother, has been "marri'd by his Friends to a Rich ill-favoured Widow," but he is in love with "Bellinda" (played by Elizabeth Barry), who was being driven to a forced marriage in the country and fled to London where she took the name of Mariamne. Because she fell in love with Sir Charles before she knew he was married, they carry on a platonic relationship; thus, she is the "innocent mistress" of the title. Beaumont, another moral force in the play, is in love with Arabella, a ward of Barnaby Cheatall, brother to Lady Beauclair. Sir Francis Wildlove, a roving male, serves as a direct contrast to Beaumont. Miss Beauclair (played by Anne Bracegirdle), niece to Sir Charles, who is attracted to Wildlove, plans to tame his wild ways. In St. James's Park, Miss Beauclair spots Wildlove, goes to him in a mask, and suggests he practice speaking love to his mistress. Bellinda encounters Beaumont at Beauclair's, and he encourages her to return to her distraught father in the country. At Lockett's, Wildlove meets Mrs. Flywife, but they are interrupted by Miss Beauclair, who enters in man's clothes. When Wildlove is called away, Mrs. Flywife gives her a ring in pledge. Wildlove returns to find them gone. Miss Beauclair is still in disguise when Wildlove arrives at the Beauclair's and discovers her real identity. Bellinda tells Beaumont she must leave Sir Charles forever, and she pleads with Sir Charles not to follow her: she must go to her father's house. They both part in painful adieux. Wildlove hears Miss Beauclair is married to Spendall and wishes to see him. Thinking Spendall has married Miss Beauclair, Wildlove comes in angrily, but Miss Beauclair says he has been misinformed. At this, Wildlove confesses his love for her. Beaumont and Arabella arrive and announce their engagement. When Flywife follows his wife in, he is recognized as Lady Beauclair's first husband. Sir Charles quickly stops Bellinda, before her departure, and tells her of Lady Beauclair's earlier marriage. They will now be free to wed.

Readers of this play may find all the names beginning with Beau confusing, but it would not be so on stage with the different costumes and speaking voices of the characters. A woman testing a man is nothing new, but Miss Beauclair's use of a male disguise succeeds admirably. Pix's central preoccupation is the effect that male injustice has on women and the actions the women take. Mariamne, for instance, must run away and become Bellinda because her father is forcing her into an unwanted marriage. Arabella, a ward, is cheated of her rights and her money, even to the point of being locked up. Mrs. Flywife must go to Jamaica to find an eligible man, but in fact the man she finds is fleeing from his wife. Hume classifies the plot as exemplary, but he fulminates against its "preachy righteousness." Pearson, on the other hand, praises Sir Charles's androgyny and his virtue. Both he and "Bellinda" don't just speak in homilies, they act morally.

TEXTS: Wing P2330. EEB Reel 506: 6. Readex Microprint.

MODERN EDITION: *The Female Wits*, ed. Fidelis Morgan (London: Virago, 1981): 263-328.

FACSIMILE EDITION: E-CED, with introduction by Edna L. Steeves (NY: Garland, 1982).

The Inscription; or, Indian Hunters, Jane M. Scott. This two-act "Melo-Dramatic Romance, or Naval Burletta" opened at the Sans Pareil Theatre on 28 February 1814. It ran fourteen nights its first season. Scott played Sidney Nelson, a Midshipman.

MANUSCRIPT: Larpent 1804.

The Intrigues of a Morning; or, An Hour in Paris, Eliza Parsons. William Lane published Parson's two-act farce, an abridgement of Molière's *Monsieur de Pourceaugnac* (1669), in 1792. The first performance occurred on 18 April 1792 at CG as an afterpiece (the main piece was Inchbald's *Child of Nature*) for the benefit night of Isabella Mattocks, who took the role of the clever servant Nerina. Charlotte Chapman played Julia, and William Macready acted Erastus. The farce was replayed a month later (17 May 1792) at a benefit night for Thomas Hull, but it was not revived. Parsons, even with an adapted text, points out the evils of forced marriage, and she provided Isabella Mattocks with a role (including two quick change disguises) that was a tour de force.

The play opens with Nerina upset at having to prevent her mistress, Julia, from being forced to marry a country booby against her will by her miserly father Closefist. Nerina promises that Julia will not marry Squire Lubberly and that she will help her to gain her beau Erastus. To arrange this, she enlists the aid of Carlos, Erastus's man, who meets the outlandishly dressed Squire Lubberly and directs him to the house of Erastus. Two physicians are there and have been told to give the squire a diagnosis and a cure, but he runs away from them. Nerina and Julia, meanwhile, try to dissuade Closefist from forcing his daughter to marry the rich bumpkin. When he won't listen, Nerina dresses up as a discarded lover of Lubberly and returns just about the same time the physicians arrive looking for the Squire, who they claim is mad, and demand payment from Closefist. Lubberly, searching for Closefist's house, sees Carlos, who suggests the squire will succeed with the daughter who "is no better than she should be" (25). Upon Closefist's entrance, Lubberly tries to back out of the marriage, while at the same time being hounded by bogus creditors. Carlos reappears as a peasant with a woman and children, claiming they are the Squire's wife and family. Julia and Erastus arrive to find that Closefist is glad of an escape and presents Julia as a wife for Erastus. Nerina has the last word and sends Lubberly back to the country.

In her adaptation of Molière's *Monsieur de Pourceaugnac*, a three-act comedy-ballet first produced for Louis XIV in September 1669, Parsons omitted the dances and songs which open and close the French piece, and, while keeping the main plot line, she shortened it to two acts. The events still take place in Paris, and M. de Pourceaugnac, now Squire Lubberly, remains a gentleman from Limoges, who nevertheless refers to Lombardy as his native province. But more significantly, Parsons modified some of the characters: her Julia weeps and begs her cruel father to change his mind, whereas her French counterpart plays the dutiful daughter since she knows that her acquiescence is part of a scheme to ensure her marriage to Erastus. The English Nerina is much more violent verbally and even physically as her hot temper leads her to cuff Julia's father when he offers to marry her, a scene not to be found in the original. The latter's miserly character is accentuated as well: not only does the country bumpkin's wealth attract him as it did Molière's Oronte, but he is shown carefully studying a map of his future son-in-law's forests, which leads Julia to accuse him of having "a heart made of oak."

Although she sometimes translates Molière's lines verbatim and retains some of his farcical scenes, such as Lubberly's meeting the bogus children he has never set eyes on, Parsons has altered the original. She drops Molière's stinging and hilarious attacks on doctors, nearly eliminating their presence on stage. She also deletes the crude sexual allusions made by secondary characters. The result mixes farce with serious comedy.

Robin Riley Fast, writing in DBAWW, stresses the moral tone of Eliza Parsons's novels: this same tone can be seen in the play she adapted, which decries forced marriage, but allows the daughter to maintain a tolerable relationship with her miserly father. After the father has seen the errors of his unreasonable insistence on her marriage with a rich country booby, he allows his daughter her choice in marriage.

MANUSCRIPT: Larpent 943.

TEXT: Readex Microprint.

The Irishwoman, Lady Olivia Clarke. Clarke's one five-act comedy, *The*

Irishwoman, was produced at the Crow-Street Theatre in Dublin, 1819 and printed the same year in both Dublin and London by H. Colburn, who also published the novels of her sister Sydney Owenson, Lady Morgan.

TEXT: Not in Readex Microprint. NUC: Copies at the Univs. of California, Berkeley, and Michigan.

ISDELL, Sarah (fl. 1805-25). Isdell began her writing career by publishing anonymously a novel entitled *Vale of Louisiana, an American Tale* (1805); this was followed by *The Irish Recluse; or, A Breakfast at the Rotunda*, published with her name in 1809. In her first work for the stage, Isdell wrote a successful comedy, entitled *The Poor Gentlewoman*, which was produced at the Crow-Street Theatre in Dublin on 4 March 1811. A comic opera, *The Cavern*, was performed at the Hawkins-Street Theatre in Dublin (1825) with music by Sir John Stevenson. Apparently neither of her plays was published. [*BD* Appendix, FCLE, Nicoll]

The Island of Slaves, attributed to Catherine Clive. This afterpiece in two acts, translated from Marivaux's *L'Ile des Esclaves* (1725), was acted only one time on 26 March 1761 at DL for Clive's benefit night. In EBWW, Frushell determines that the play is not Clive's.

When four Athenian travelers find themselves shipwrecked on an imaginary island, they discover that social conditions have been reversed. Kinne points out "two excellent scenes": in one the maid gives a detailed account of her mistress's faults; in the other the man and maid parody the affected manners of the *beau monde*. After taking a course in humanism based upon Utopian rather than revolutionary ideals, they are allowed to return home.

The translation is intelligibly rendered, making little deviation from the original. Kinne believes, however, a "paucity of incident" may have caused the piece to fail (80-81).

MANUSCRIPT: Larpent 190.

-J-

Jephthah's Daughter, Ann Wilson. This poetic drama, published in 1783 by W. Flexney, was not staged. Lonsdale notes this is not the Anne Wilson who published the poem *Teisa* (Newcastle, 1778).

Readers of this piece will gain a better grasp of Wilson's achievement by reading its Biblical source (Judges 11:1-12:7), for she expands forty-seven verses into a full-scale drama. Before the play, Jephthah has made a rash vow to God: if he defeats the Ammonites, he will make a burnt offering of "whatsoever cometh forth from the doors of my house to meet me" (Judges 11:31, KJV). Jephthah is victorious; when he returns home, his daughter and only child "came out to meet him with timbrels and with dances" (Judges 11:34). She acquiesces to the predicament in which her father has placed her, asking only to spend two months alone "up and down upon the mountains [to] bewail my virginity" with her women friends (Judges 11:37). When the play opens Jephthah's daughter, Jemima, is finishing her two months away from Gilead with her virgin attendants. Upon her return to Gilead, she has accepted the situation and is ready to sacrifice herself. Just then a messenger comes to Jephthah's house, reporting that the Ephraimites are planning an attack. Jephthah asks Ebineezer, one of the elders, to care for Jemima when he goes to battle. Alone with Jemima, Ebineezer makes indecent proposals to her, and she twice refuses him before he starts to struggle with her. At that point, Ibzan, a young captain of the army, breaks in and stops the rape. After Ebineezer is taken off, Ibzan explains that he sensed Jemima was in danger and left the battle field to rescue her. The virgins return and with Ibzan they sing. Having defeated the Ephraimites, Jephthah tells Adonikim, a captain in his forces, about his personal history, how he came to make the rash vow to God, and what the present situation is for Jemima.

Julian, Mary Russell Mitford. Originally titled *The Melfi*, this five-act tragedy was first produced 15 March 1823 at CG and acted eight times, featuring William Charles Macready in the title role. Nicoll reports that Mitford "received only £200" from CG for the play. *Julian* was published in 1823 by G. and W. B. Whitaker and collected in her *Dramatic Works*, published by Hurst and Blackett, 1854. In the preface to the play, Mitford acknowledges both Euripides's *Orestes* and Sophocles's *Electra* as influences. Within the play, the Duke of Melfi and Julian compare their plights, respectively, to those of King Laius (*Oedipus*) and Antigone.

Set in and around Messina, the play begins with Prince Julian waking from a mysterious illness, attended by his wife Annabel and Alfonso, the young King of Sicily who is disguised as the page Theodore. Julian awakens to the fear that he has killed his own father, the Duke of Melfi and Regent of the kingdom, while trying to rescue his cousin Alfonso from an assassination plot engineered by Julian's own father. Julian is relieved when news arrives that Melfi was only wounded. Aware that the young page must be Alfonso, the Duke orders his son to take Theodore with him to Madrid, but Julian disobeys. After Julian halts his father's coronation by announcing that Alfonso is still alive, Count D'Alba—a powerful nobleman who is in love with Annabel—charges both Melfi and Julian with treason. Banished after insisting that he is guilty, Julian comes upon his father in weakened condition, who blesses both his son and Alfonso before dying. Although too young to assume political power, Alfonso demonstrates nobility by pardoning Melfi because he is his kinsman. Meanwhile, Annabel is being held in a tower against her will by D'Alba, who threatens to have Julian killed if she does not agree to marry him. After refusing to be his bride, Annabel hangs her rosary on the casement of the Gothic window, and it is seen by Julian when he comes to rescue her from D'Alba. When murderers sent by the Count come to the tower, Annabel rushes in front of her husband, receiving the fatal wound intended for him. Although wounded himself, Julian confronts D'Alba and shows him Annabel's dead body. Alfonso arrives and orders the guards to seize D'Alba. When Julian dies, the young King declares "I am left in the wide world Alone. My Julian!" (81).

Genest pronounces the play a tolerable tragedy (9: 201-02). According to Josephine Donovan in EBWW, Mitford's drama received "much sexist criticism" (329) when first performed, and this may account for the plea in the Epilogue (written by T. A. Talfourd):

> Methinks our Author's sex you shrewdly guess—
> "It is a Lady's Drama"—frankly, "yes."
> Yet let no censure on her daring fall. (82)

Tension in the play is generated by Julian's anguish as he chooses between love for his father and duty to his cousin and to the State. Those characters (Julian, Alfonso, Annabel) who honor their responsibilities to family and to State contrast the villains (Melfi, D'Alba) who pursue more personal ambition.

MANUSCRIPT: Larpent 2341.

TEXTS: Readex Microprint of the first and second editions, 1823, and Cumberland's *British Theatre*, vol. 32, n.d.

-K-

Kate of Aberdeen, attributed to Mary Darby Robinson. This comic opera may have been written as early as 1787. *BD* speculates: "We have heard that Mrs. Robinson also wrote a comic opera called *Kate of Aberdeen*" (1: 787). It was not printed, and there is no known performance. From February to May 1787, BDAA reports that Robinson acted in Edinburgh, and the title may have been intended to appeal to Scotch audiences. Robinson might have put such a musical entertainment together for a benefit night while in Edinburgh, as she had earlier prepared *The Lucky Escape* for her benefit night at DL in 1778.

The *Morning Post* (10 January 1794) reported that Sheridan had adopted "a bantling of Mrs. Robinson's" for DL, and identified it "as an opera, entitled *Kate of Aberdeen*" While the *Oracle* urged the production of Robinson's opera, Kemble became more recalcitrant. Finally, the *Oracle* declared on 30 March 1793 "Mrs. Robinson has wholly withdrawn her promising Opera" (Lucyle Werkmeister, *A Newspaper History of England, 1792-1793* [Lincoln: U of Nebraska P, 1967] 95, 316).

Kathleen O'Neil, Mary Devens Balfour. This three-act piece, described on the title page as "A Grand National Melo Drame," was produced at the Belfast Theatre on 9 February 1814 in Belfast. It was printed in Belfast by Archbold and Dugan in 1814.

The heir to Clan Colman disguises himself as a minstrel and comes to O'Neil Castle having heard of Kathleen O'Neil's virtues. He observes the request for Kathleen's hand by the Scot M'Donnel, who is rejected. M'Donnel vows revenge, and with the help of the sinister Ferdarra, who knows a secret passage into the castle, he kidnaps Kathleen while her father is away dispensing justice. Clan Colman suspects Ferdarra and goes to the cell where the so-called monk resides. He rescues Kathleen, and with the help of O'Neil's men captures Ferdarra. While Ferdarra is being tried by O'Neil, M'Donnel rushes in, accuses Ferdarra of betraying him, and in a scuffle stabs Ferdarra. O'Neil tells the Scot he must leave Ireland immediately. O'Neil and his followers return to the castle for an evening of festivities celebrating the betrothal of Clan Colman and Kathleen O'Neil.

About the protagonist and play, FCLE remarks: "This Kathleen, a famous deer-slayer combining boldness with 'all the timidity of my sex,' is abducted (and rescued) only by suitors. The Celtic colour extends to a comic subplot, with songs" (53). Beyond this view, however, readers may observe the firm actions and strong linguistic ability of Kathleen that keep her from being a passive heroine. Her father has sworn she will never be a sacrifice to a political union, and he accepts Kathleen's refusal of M'Donnel, couched in these terms: "I would not to be the empress of the world accept your hand" (13). As observed by Colman, Kathleen knows what she wants (and what she does not want) and her virtues are apparent in her kindness to others.

TEXT: Readex Microprint.

KEMBLE, Elizabeth Satchell [Mrs. Stephen] (1762?-1841). Daughter of an instrument maker, John Satchell, Elizabeth made her theatrical debut as Polly in *The Beggar's Opera*, 21 September 1780 at CG, where she took singing and acting roles until 1784. She married Stephen Kemble in 1783, and the couple acted in Manchester in the 1784-85 season. It was there that Elizabeth wrote a two-act pastoral farce with music, *Philander and Rose; or, The Bridal Day*, which was produced, probably for her benefit, 25 April 1785 (Larpent 689). The songs were printed in Manchester the same year. She performed with her husband in Edinburgh from 1786-87 before they were employed by Colman at HAY for the summer season. For almost a decade, the couple spent summers acting in London at the HAY and winters in Edinburgh, where Elizabeth acted and Stephen managed various theatres through 1800. Elizabeth made her "first, and only" appearance at DL on 20 October 1800 as Ophelia (*Hamlet*) and Cowslip (*The Agreeable Surprise*). Little is known about Elizabeth after she retired from the stage: Stephen died in 1822, and Elizabeth survived until 1841. She died near Durham, where she is buried in the cathedral. [DBAA, DNB]

KEMBLE, Marie Therese DeCamp (1775-1836). A well-known actress (born in Vienna) whose career spanned more than four decades, Kemble began her early days on stage as a dancer at several venues. Later at DL, she occasionally acted children's characters. The death of her father when she was twelve caused Miss DeCamp to work industriously on improving her general studies, but especially languages and singing. Her performance as Macheath in *The Beggar's Opera* during the summer season brought her much attention as an actor and singer.

She wrote several humorous plays; Kemble's first comedy, *First Faults* (in five acts), was claimed by one William Earle to be lifted from a play of his, but she denied this in a letter to *The Morning Post* on 10 June 1799. She married Charles Kemble in 1806, against the wishes of his family. Two interludes are ascribed to her: *Personation; or, Family Taken In* (1805) and *The Day After the Wedding; or, The Wife's First Lesson* (1808). She is also credited with two other comedies—*Match-making; or, 'Tis a Wise Child that Knows its own Father* (1808) and *Smiles and Tears; or, The Widow's Stratagem* (1815). She returned to the stage briefly in 1829 to play the nurse to her daughter, Frances Anne (Fanny), Kemble's Juliet. Fanny went on to have a distinguished career as an actress and abolitionist. [BDAA, DNB, FCLE]

KENNEDY, Grace (1782-1825). Born in rural Scotland, Kennedy moved with her pious parents to Edinburgh where she was brought up. From her religious background and her interest in children's education, she wrote a number of religious tales, *Father Clement* (1823) being the best known; it went through twelve editions by 1858. According to Davis and Joyce, Kennedy wrote two volumes in dramatic form, *The Decision; or, Religion Must Be All, or Is Nothing* and *Profession Not Principle; or, The Name of Christian is not Christianity*, both published in Edinburgh, 1821. Neither was acted. Kennedy's best-known stories for children are "Anna Ross" and "Jessy Allan, the Lame Girl." *Dunallan*, her longest narrative, appeared in 1824, and Kennedy has also been credited with a number of other religious writings. W. Oliphant published a collected edition of her *Works* in 1827; here a brief biography appears as a foreword. [Davis & Joyce, DNB]

KILLIGREW, Anne (1660-85). Although born to the Royal Chaplain, Anne had theatrical connections through her uncles and cousin. She was one of the Maids of Honor to Mary of Modena along with Anne Finch. After she died of smallpox, her father had her poems printed, prefaced by Dryden's "Ode" praising her poetry, painting, and virtuous life. Included in this collection of Anne's poetry are three "Pastoral Dialogues." This posthumous volume of her *Poems* was published by S. Lowndes in 1686. [Cotton, DBAWW, DNB, EBWW, FCLE, Hobby]

The Knapsack, Maria Edgeworth. The only drama included in her *Moral Tales* (1801), *The Knapsack*, consisting of eight scenes in two acts, may have been written in 1799 or 1800.

Set in Sweden, this piece begins with a mother and her two children (Kate and Ulrich) waiting for their father to return from a war with Finland. In the course of events, the children find a purse which they take to their godmother Ulrica, who is housekeeper to Count Helmaar. This honest act sets up a reunion with their father, who has saved the Count's life in the war.

A lack of conflict makes this moral drama a little too moral—even preachy. The one bit of tension in the play is when a knapsack is brought to the children's mother, who believes her husband has been killed in the war.

FACSIMILE EDITIONS: Reprints of the Longford edition (1893) of Edgeworth's *Tales and Novels* (Hildersheim: Georg Olms, 1969) and (NY: AMS, 1967) 1: 411-438. "The Feminist Controversy in England, 1788-1810" series reprints the 1802 text, with an introduction by Gina Luria (NY: Garland, 1974) 3: 237-279.

-L-

The Labyrinth; or, The Fatal Embarrassment, attributed to Agnes Stratford. This five-act tragedy, taken from Thomas Corneille's *Ariane*, was printed by R. Marchbank in Dublin, 1795, and "sold for the benefit of Miss Agnes Stratford, sister of the late Rev. Thomas Stratford." There is no record of this tragedy's having been acted. An unknown editor wrote in the Preface: "The subject of the present piece is taken from a tragedy wrote by Corneille. The author has adopted the same characters and attended the like management as to incident and fable. . . . He [sic] has made the rest his own. . . . 'Altered from Corneille by A[gnes] S[tratford]'."

According to D. F. Canfield (Fisher), the Rev. Dr. Thomas Stratford held the Rectorship of Gallstow, County Westmeath, Ireland, where he may have lived with his sister (261). He wrote an unacted play, *Darius* (Readex Microprint of the manuscript, 1784). He also wrote and produced *Lord Russel* (performed four nights at DL beginning 20 August 1784, but not published for ten years, c. 1794). It appears that his sister was responsible for printing *Lord Russel* by subscription: "London. For Agner [sic] Stratford."

TEXT: Not in Readex Microprint. NUC lists copies at Harvard, U of Michigan, and Huntington.

The Lady Contemplation, Margaret Lucas Cavendish, Duchess of Newcastle. This drama, in two parts, was printed in her *Playes*, published in 1662 by John Martyn, James Allestry, and Tho. Dicas. There was no performance.

Using three parallel plots, Cavendish explores the title character's triumph of imagination over reality; Lady Ward's corrective measures with her errant fiancé, and Poor Virtue's emphasis on moral rectitude as a guide to life. Examining each plot individually, readers may observe Lady Contemplation's life of the mind in the imaginative stories she formulates and tells to Lady Visitant. She is contrasted with Lady Conversation, who talks more but with less mental acumen. At the beginning, Lady Ward is actually the ward of Lord Courtship, whose deceased father wished them to marry. Lord Courtship, however, rejects his father's wishes and carries on with several women; in order to train Lady Ward in their future marriage, he will do exactly as he pleases. Finally, she refuses to be a "bawd" by delivering letters of assignation to Lady Amorous. When he threatens her, she says his licentiousness and cruelty belie his noble characteristics. After he realizes how badly he has treated her, he feels guilty and reforms. Now she can accept him in marriage. In the third story line, Lady Virtue's father has died and she is suddenly penniless. She takes a servant's position at Roger Farmer's house and tends his sheep. She is wooed by Lord Title, Sir Effeminate Lovely, and Sir Golden Riches, only to have the men change their views of her as a "country wench." Mall Mean-bred, who gives in to the money offered by Sir Golden Riches, acts as a foil to Virtue. Lord Title changes his ways, discovers Poor Virtue's background, and asks her to marry him. The play concludes implausibly with five weddings taking place at the City Hall.

While characters do not overlap in the plots—except at the end—similar thematic ideas emerge in all three story lines. For instance, Lady Ward emphasizes virtue over vice, correcting her erring fiancé Lord Courtship; Poor Virtue protects herself with her pronouncements on morality; and Lady Contemplation stresses sound reason over bestiality. Several men alter their dubious behavior after encountering women's virtue, and readers can also observe several members of the nobility learning a higher morality. The Marquis of Newcastle supplied several scenes of the play—those dealing with Mall Mean-bred and other "low" characters. His treatment of the lower orders deviates from a theme Cavendish frequently includes—"blood will tell." This is particularly evident when Lord Title reflects that Poor Virtue may be an illegitimate daughter of a noble father. He then learns that Poor Virtue is actually Lady Virtue, whose parents were Lord Morality and Lady Piety. Cavendish seems to believe that well-bred and titled characters will usually act in a high-minded way, though some nobles, all too frequently men, need to have that lesson brought home when they forget their gentility.

TEXTS: Wing N868. EEB Reel 502: 11. Readex Microprint.

LATTER, Mary (1722?-1777). Born in Henley upon Thames, Latter settled in Reading after the death of her father. She published some satiric verse in 1740, but her first book was *Miscellaneous Works, in Prose and Verse* in 1759, published by subscription.

Early in 1761, John Rich considered staging her play and assisted her publication of *A Miscellaneous Poetical Essay*. But when Rich died, Latter's hopes of seeing her play produced died with him because it was rejected by the succeeding managers. She then printed her one five-act verse tragedy, *The Siege of Jerusalem By Titus Vespasian*, in *Miscellaneous Works*, published by C. Bathurst, 1763. Later the tragedy was produced at Reading in 1768 for a community benefit. Her last work before her death in Reading was an essay, entitled *Pro and Con, or the Opinionists*, 1771. [*BD*, DBAWW, DNB, Lonsdale]

Lausus and Lydia with Madam Bonso's Three Strings to her Bow; or, Three Bows to her String!!!, Sarah Lawrence, written under the pseudonym A. B. C. Published by W. Earle in 1806 (vii + 78 pp.), this comedy may have a source in a French play titled *Lausus et Lydia*, published in Lyon, 1787.

TEXT: Not in Readex Microprint.

LAWRENCE, Rose D'Aguilar. See **D'AGUILAR**, Rose.

LAWRENCE, Sarah (fl. 1806-1844). Under the pseudonym of A. B. C., Lawrence wrote *Lausus and Lydia with Madam Bonso's Three Strings to her Bow; or, Three Bows to her String!!!*, published by W. Earle in 1806. A French play, titled *Lausus et Lydia* (Lyon, 1787) may be a source. Lawrence also wrote poetry and prepared anthologies. [Davis & Joyce, NUC]

LEADBEATER, Mary Shackleton (1758-1826). The daughter of an Irish schoolmaster, she lived all of her life in Ireland. In 1791, she married William Leadbeater, a farmer, and began raising a family as well as operating a local post office in County Kildare. She wrote some anecdotes for the improvement of children, published 1794. In 1808, Leadbeater published her *Poems*, and in 1811 came *Cottage Dialogues Among the Irish Peasantry*, which follows the lives of the sensible Rose and the lackadaisical Nancy through their frequent discussions. Maria Edgeworth contributed the introduction and notes. *The Landlord's Friend* followed in 1813. With her mother she wrote *Tales for Cottagers* in 1814; the volume adds a dramatized lesson, *Honesty is the Best Policy*. During the 1820s, Leadbeater edited her mother's memoirs and her parents' letters, and published lives of cottagers and lives of Irish Quakers. In the last year of her life, *The Pedlars* was published. [Clara L. Gandy, *Women and Literature* 3 (1975), FCLE]

LEAPOR, Mary (1722-1746). Born to a gardener and a maid servant, Leapor learned to read and write but had very little other formal education. She composed verses as a child, but after a while her parents tried to stop her writing. She, nevertheless, continued to compose verse, using Pope and Dryden as her models. While she is referred to as Mrs. Mary Leapor, she never married. The author of one blank-verse tragedy, *The Unhappy Father* (c. 1745), Leapor had apparently sent her play to a gentleman in London. When it was sent back, the botched manuscript prompted her poem, "Upon her Play being returned to her, stained with Claret." Leapor died of measles in 1746 before she could see her work in print. Her dying wish to have her poems published for the benefit of her father was achieved in 1748 when the first volume of her poetry, edited by Issac Hawkins Browne, appeared as *Poems Upon Several Occasions*. The second volume, also published by subscription, contains *The Unhappy Father*, scenes from a projected play, as well as additional poems. J. Roberts published volume two in 1751. George Colman and Bonnel Thornton reprinted 120 pages of her poetry in *Poems by Eminent Ladies* (1755). [*BD*, Cotton, DBAWW, DNB, EBWW, FCLE (cites a PhD thesis by Richard Greene, Oxford, 1989), Lonsdale. Some biographical information may be found in Edmund Blunden, "A Northamptonshire Poetess: Mary Leapor," *Journal of the Northamptonshire Natural History Society* 28 (June 1936): 59-74.]

LEE, Harriet (1757-1851). Younger sister of Sophia Lee, and daughter of thespians, Harriet Lee published an epistolary novel, *The Errors of Innocence*, in 1786. The first of her three plays, written over a period of almost forty years, was a comedy, *The New Peerage; or, Our Eyes May Deceive Us*, successfully staged at DL in 1787 (nine nights, but not revived). Later, she began to write with Sophia *The Canterbury Tales*, which continued into the next century. In 1798, she published a closet drama, *The Mysterious Marriage; or, The Heirship of Roselva*. Before her last play in 1825, she assisted Sophia in running a school at Bath. Harriet's final work for the stage was a melodrama, *The Three Strangers*, a dramatization of her tale *Kruitzner*. She lived into her nineties.

[*BD*, DBAWW, DNB, FCLE, NCBEL (3: 742), OCEL]

LEE, Sophia (1750-1824). Upon the death of her mother in 1770, Sophia took charge of the family, trying to keep her quarrelsome father out of disputes. Her first play was an enormous success: this comedy, *The Chapter of Accidents*, 1780, played every season until the turn of the century. She turned to a novel, *The Recess*, 1783-85, to help finance the school which she ran with her sister at Bath. Her tragedy, *Almeyda; Queen of Granada*, based in part on Shirley's *The Cardinal*, 1796, was less successful than her earlier play; it was acted only five times. Her second comedy, *The Assignation* (1807), was condemned after a brief run, and she wrote for the theatre no more. She collaborated with her sister on *The Canterbury Tales*, and she wrote other tales and novels under her own name, but *The Chapter of Accidents* remained her most popular work in her lifetime. [*BD*, DBAWW, DNB, EBWW, FCLE, NCBEL (2: 1007; 3: 742), OCEL]

LEFANU, Alicia Sheridan (1754-1817). The daughter of the dramatist and novelist, Frances Sheridan, and the sister of the dramatist and theatre manager R. B. Sheridan, Alicia LeFanu wrote one comedy, *Prejudice; or, Modern Sentiment*. It was first produced by the DL company at the Lyceum Theatre 11 April 1812 and acted twenty-seven times. Shortly after the opening, LeFanu requested that the title be changed to *The Sons of Erin; or, Modern Sentiments*, but apparently it reverted to its original title later in the run. Publication by J. Ridgway was under the second title in 1812. Alicia, her daughter, prepared a biography of Frances Sheridan in 1824. [DNB (under Philip Lefanu)]

LENNOX, Charlotte Ramsey (1729?-1804). The daughter of an army officer, she grew up in New York state. Sometime in her teens she was sent to England, where in 1747 she published *Poems on Several Occasions* and married Alexander Lennox, a shiftless printer. She acted in and around London from 1748 to 1750; her last known performance took place on 22 February 1750, when she played Almeria, the title role, in Congreve's *The Mourning Bride* at the Haymarket for her benefit. The following year, Samuel Johnson organized an all-night party to celebrate her first novel, *The Life of Harriot Stuart*. Johnson remained a friend and supporter all of his life. Lennox's best-known and best-selling novel, *The Female Quixote*, appeared in 1752 with a dedication by Johnson; it was favorably reviewed by Fielding in the *Covent-Garden Journal*. A play on this subject attributed to Lennox, *Angelica; or, Quixote in Petticoats*, is not in fact by her, but only dramatizes a portion of her novel. In the advertisement following the dedication, the unknown male author acknowledges that the entirety is taken from "the ingenious Mrs. Lennox." Her *Shakespear Illustrated* in two volumes came out in 1753 with a third volume the following year; it is one of the earliest critical examinations of his sources.

After a number of translations from the French, she prepared her first drama, a romantic pastoral entitled *Philaster*. Although it was rejected for the stage by Garrick, Lennox published the play in 1757, again with a dedication by Johnson. The following year, she published another novel, *Henrietta*, which she would later use as the basis for her drama *The Sisters*. In 1759, Lennox headed a team, including Johnson, to translate *The Greek Theatre of Father Brumoy*: her own contributions were translations of *Oedipus*, *Electra*, and *Philoctetes*. Through the 1760s, Lennox continued to write novels and to prepare translations, as well as to edit a monthly, *The Lady's Museum* (1760-61). When Lennox's play *The Sisters* appeared on the CG stage in February 1769, with a prologue by George Colman the Elder and an epilogue by Goldsmith, the comedy was, according to her contemporary Benjamin Victor, "so ill treated by the Audience the first Night, that the Authoress had Spirit enough to withdraw it from the Theatre." Two printings of the play were called for in March. At Garrick's suggestion, Lennox adapted the Renaissance comedy *Eastward Hoe!* by Jonson, Chapman, and Marston, and it was successfully staged at DL in November 1775, running seven nights. While she continued to write novels sporadically, Lennox didn't enter the field of drama again. According to Duncan Isles, she began to receive financial support from the Royal Literary Fund in 1792, and this assistance continued until her death in January 1804, when as a pauper she was buried in an unmarked grave.

Constantly troubled by financial worries and an unsupportive husband, Lennox's life does not appear to have been an easy one. She seldom stayed long at one lodging as her addresses on her letters indicate. Her daughter was born when Lennox was 36, her son when she was 42, and most of this time she was the family's sole breadwinner. While she is best known as a novelist, Lennox retained her connections with the stage after working as an actress. She not only prepared translations of drama, but she also adapted and wrote her own dramas, which may be more important for their influence than for their own success. [*BD*, BDAA, BNA, DBAWW, DNB, FCLE, Lonsdale, NCBEL (2: 848), OCEL. Small contains a primary bibliography.]

A Lesson for Lovers, by a Lady. Davis and Joyce list this three-act farce written by an anonymous woman, published with another farce in three acts, *The Conjurer*, in 1823 by S. Gosnell. We have been unable to locate the drama.

James Thomas Goderham Rodwell's *The Young Widow; or, A Lesson for Lovers* (published by John Miller, 1824) uses her main title as a subtitle for his play (performed at the Adelphi on 1 November 1824). NUC lists "*Lessons for lovers, in several poems*, by a hypochondriac, an unhappy young lady, and an elderly gentlewoman of considerable experience," published by Hurst, Chance in 1829.

TEXT: Not in Readex Microprint.

LEWIS, Mary G. (fl. 1823–1825?). Simpkin and Marshall published Lewis's poetic works in a volume that contained a long poem with a drama in *Zelinda, a poem, and Cardiff Castle, a Dramatic-Historic Sketch* (1823). Lewis may have translated or adapted *Ambition*, from the French of Scribe, published by T. Cadell, 1825. We have been unable to verify if this version is drama or prose fiction. Lewis earlier published a novel entitled *Gwenllean* (1823). [Davis & Joyce, NUC]

Lie upon Lie; or, Two Spanish Valets, Jane M. Scott. See **The Two Spanish Valets; or, Lie upon Lie**.

Like Father, Like Son; or, The Mistaken Brothers, Aphra Behn. Although this comedy was likely to have been produced at DG in March 1682, only the prologue and epilogue were printed. The play was probably an adaptation of Thomas Randolph's *The Jealous Lovers*.

TEXTS: Prologue and Epilogue only: Wing B1759. EEB Reel 1396: 13.

Little Dramas for Young People by Mrs. Hoole, Barbara Wreaks Hoole Hofland. Longman, Hurst, Rees, and Orme published these historical dramas in 1810. The Preface is signed from a boarding school in Harrogate (20 October 1809) where presumably Hoole was teaching. The four blank-verse tragedies, published with notes, were "intended to promote among the rising generation an early love of virtue and their country." None was professionally performed.

These four short dramas are arranged chronologically by the historical events that prompted them: "The Death of Henry II at the Nunnery of Fontervrault" (1135), "The Flight of Queen Margaret and her Son, after the Battle of Hexham" (1461), "The Death of

Lady Jane Grey" (1554), and "The Fortitude of Lady Rachel Russel" (1683). With the exception of the first piece, each drama focuses on a female protagonist who faces difficult circumstances. Amid threats of physical violence, Queen Margaret of Anjou must flee England with her son; Lady Jane Grey receives a sentence of death for supposedly usurping the throne; and Lady Rachel Russel must support her husband, who is condemned to death for political reasons. She not only assists Lord Russel, but she also helps their three children through the ordeal.

While the title page suggests the intended readers are adolescents and young people, Hoole makes clear in her preface that the dramatic sketches are gender specific—"for the use of a seminary of young ladies" (v). In each drama, courage, fortitude, and strength of character are called for, and the playlets show women dealing with matters of state in a personal way. In the dramas, Hoole centers on crucial moments in the lives of her subjects, and her notes to the plays (about a quarter of the book) supply additional details "from the best historians" and underscore the moral lessons for young readers.

TEXT: Not in Readex Microprint. We read the copy in the Main Library at Indiana U, Bloomington.

The Little Family, Charlotte Elizabeth Sanders. As the title page to this novel in dramatic form explains, Sanders wrote it "for the amusement and instruction of young persons." The volume, which includes several dramas within the main story line, was first printed in 1797, according to *BD* (2: 373). J. Mawman, the publisher, brought out a "second edition" in 1800, though it was probably a reprinting.

In the central story, Madame de St. Claire and her three children go from Paris to the family chateau in Switzerland. Their adventures along the way provide learning experiences for the children; they are taught information about the solar system, but mostly they learn about proper modes of behavior. Once settled in the chateau, the children (whose father is in the West Indies) begin to appreciate nature, learning about the indigenous plants, the rural Swiss, and natural phenomena. The interaction among the three children (Clara, Henry, and Emmiline) reveals lessons in handling relocation (Clara wishes she were back in Paris), dealing with sibling rivalries (Henry calls Clara names), and coping with overblown views of their own egos (Henry is put in his place for acting like a "know-it-all"). Scattered through the events in the lives of the de St. Claire family are poems and stories told or read by their mother. Included are three dramas within the text of the story—"The Bird's Nest" (one act), "The Little Gamester" (two acts), and "The Foundling of Savoy" (three acts). In "The Bird's Nest," the mother teaches the children lessons about cruelty to animals and kindness to an impoverished family. "The Little Gamester" argues that those who practice gambling become dissolute. "The Foundling of Savoy" shows the value of being industrious—and lucky. Rose, the title character, has been brought up by the poor Joanna, whose friend de Jonville sends her monthly stipends. De Jonville suggests a companion to Madame de St. Pierre in her sorrow, and he brings Rose. During the meeting, Rose is found with a picture of her real mother about her neck: it is Madame de St. Pierre. The St. Pierres behold in Rose their real daughter, whose loss has created their sorrow. A celebration follows, and Joanna is invited with Rose to live in the chateau of the de St. Pierres.

Madame de St. Claire gives her children moral instruction through lessons and by her interpretation of events that occur. When their carriage breaks down, they are put up by a poor cottager (Albert de Livré) for the three days. During this time, de Livré tells them his history: his son drove the family business into debt by gaming and excessive spending. Solvency is achieved only by the help of a generous friend, but the affliction of poverty causes the death of his son, daughter-in-law, four grandchildren, and—finally —his wife. The de St. Claires are so moved that they share their goods and money with him, and de Livré emerges as an important character in the story. Helping the humble poor, then, becomes a recurring theme. Most of this training is done by the mother, who shapes the children's values, urging the concept of noblesse oblige. At the same time, the humble and working classes learn to be satisfied with their station in life. Many of the good deeds done in the story result in tears of compassion or joy, underscoring the strong sentimentality in the tale.

TEXT: Not in Readex Microprint. We read the second edition of 1800, published by J. Mawman in the King Collection at Miami (Ohio) U.

The Little French Lawyer, Ursula Agnes Booth. This two-act farce is based on the play by John Fletcher and Philip Massinger (*LS*), though the title page credits Beaumont and Fletcher. The only known performance of Booth's adaptation occurred at CG on 27 April 1778; the play was mounted as an afterpiece on the benefit night for the actor John Quick, who played the title role. J. Bell published the play without the author's name the same year.

Dupre tells his friend, Mellefont, he is angry because the woman he loves, Lamira, is marrying an old sea captain, Champernel. Dupre confronts the couple at the church door after the wedding. Champernel's nephew, Verdone, and Lamira's brother, Beaupre, agree to duel with them at the vineyard. Lamira asks her woman Agnes to bring Dupre to her, and she sends him to the west part of Paris, away from the vineyard, supposedly to defend her reputation. At the vineyard, Mellefont can't understand why Dupre has not arrived for the duel, but when La Writ, the little French lawyer, comes along, Mellefont enlists his aid. In fact, La Writ disarms both Beaupre and Verdone. Returning to the city, La Writ encounters Dupre. They start to fight, but Mellefont arrives in time to stop them, and Dupre vows revenge on Lamira for duping him. Back at Champernel's, the old man is angry that Verdone survived in infamy, but Lamira explains that she sent Dupre on a fool's errand. When Champernel becomes upset with Lamira, she tells him: "if you value my esteem, and wish to keep me constant, let trust and confidence in you beget and cherish it. Unnecessary jealousies make more women frail, than all baits else laid to entrap their virtue" (21). In the next scene, we meet Sampson, the nephew of Lamira's father, Judge Vertaign. Talking with his clients, Sampson finds that La Writ has given up his legal calling to become a swordsman and fighter. La Writ wishes to challenge Vertaign and asks Mellefont to deliver the summons. Since Mellefont cannot talk La Writ out of this, he takes it to Vertaign, who says he will enlist his nephew Sampson to undertake the duel for him, but he asks Mellefont to manage the fight so there are no wounds. While La Writ and Sampson prepare at the duelling grounds, Mellefont absconds with their swords and doublets, and the shivering combatants become friends. When Vertaign arrives with Champernel, he argues with La Writ and knocks him down. Champernel then beats La Writ until the little French lawyer agrees to take up his legal affairs again. Just as this is resolved, a servant comes with a message for Champernel: ruffians have carried off Lamira and Villeta, his niece. The two are rescued by Dupre and Mellefont, who arranged for the ruffians to carry the women off. Lamira appreciates what Dupre has done, and he says he will ever be her protector. When Champernel and Vertaign arrive, Lamira says she owes her safety to Dupre, and Villeta tells them that she has agreed to marry Mellefont. La Writ says he is wiser now and will be a lawyer again, and Sampson says he's learned from his friend. Champernel asks them all to rejoice that past enemies have become present friends.

One unusual feature of the play is that Lamira does not give in to Dupre's entreaties, as might have happened in a Restoration comedy. Although she has recently married, Lamira still maintains her freedom to do what she believes is necessary, and she convinces Champernel that she deserves his confidence. The instance of a woman marrying one man while maintaining a friendship with another man is rather atypical in dramas of this time.

TEXT: Readex Microprint.

The Little Hermit; or, The Rural Adventure, Sarah Kirby Trimmer. This drama for children in three acts is said to have been printed in *The Juvenile Magazine*, published by J. Marshall, in 1788 (unverified). It was not professionally staged.

TEXT: *The Juvenile Magazine*, 1788.

Little Plays for Children, Maria Edgeworth. This collection, published in *Parent's Assistant*, vol. 8, by R. Hunter and Baldwin, Cradock, and Joy in 1827, contains *The Grinding Organ*, *Dumb Andy*, and *The Dame School Holiday*. Edgeworth intended the plays for private presentations. There are separate entries for each play.

The London 'Prentice, attributed to Catherine Clive. Frushell in EBWW believes Clive was not the author, and D'Fesch who composed the music probably supplied the libretto. The operetta was staged at DL for Clive's benefit night on 23 March 1754. The prompter Richard Cross remarked "Farce dull & hiss'd at ye End" (*LS* 4: 416).

The Lord of the Castle, Jane M. Scott. This two-act melodramatic romance opened the season at the Sans Pareil Theatre on 13 October 1817. It was performed forty-three times its first season and revived the following year. According to Franklin Case, the title was later changed to *The Castle of Alberti; or, The Sacred Oath* (*Adelphi* 24). Jane Scott's name does not appear on the manuscript in the Larpent Collection.

MANUSCRIPT: Larpent 1989.

The Lost Lover; or, The Jealous Husband, Delariviere Manley. This five-act comedy, Manley's first play, was probably produced in March 1696 at DL and published the same year by R. Bentley and others. "By Mrs. Manley" is printed on the title page.

Wilmore, a young rake, is engaged to marry a rich, old woman, Lady Younglove, while his widowed father (Sir Rustick Goodheart) has Lady Younglove's approval to marry her wealthy daughter, Marina. Wilmore, however, wants to marry Marina, and he must get around several obstacles: first, he must get the assistance of his former mistress, Belira; next, he must get the approval of Lady Younglove, his present fiancée, who controls Marina's fortune of £12,000; then, he must deal with his father's anger at being displaced. With the help of his friend Wildman, he sets up Sir Amorous Courtall with Lady Younglove, but Belira does not give in so easily and gets the better of Wilmore when he first pleads with her in act four. When their second dialogue occurs in the final act, Lady Younglove overhears them, causing Belira to leave in a rage. Her absence and Sir Amorous's advances to Lady Younglove allow Marina to choose Wilmore, with whom, she says, she will not think herself unhappy. Sir Rustick leaves in a huff. In the subplot, Wildman tries several ways to gain the affection of Olivia, whose father has forced her to marry Smyrna, an old but rich merchant. Olivia finally tells Wildman that she forbids "any more pursuit whatever"; he accepts this and turns immediately to the poet Orinda.

Manley says in her Preface that she had only been to the theatre twice in six years. Despite her unfamiliarity with the stage, she uses ideas found in earlier plays as well as reversing some well-used situations. For instance, the motif of a father and son wishing to marry the same woman appears occasionally in Restoration drama, whereas Olivia's rejecting an affair with Wildman is a change from earlier comedy; Belira is a stronger cast-off mistress than those previously seen in Restoration comedies. For a useful essay of how Belira's position as a deserted mistress is different from the earlier patterns, see Candace Brook Katz's discussion (*RECTR* 16 [1977]: 27–39). Other critics have noted Manley's muddy plotting and problems with motivation (Payne in DLB and Cotton). Still, the characters might have been enough of a departure, causing the audiences to reject the play: Manley complains in the Preface that it did not last three days, and "the bare Name of being a Women's Play damned it beyond its own want of merit."

TEXTS: Wing M435. EEB Reel 36: 6. Readex Microprint.

Love and Fashion, Fanny Burney. Written between 1798 and 1799, this five-act comedy was accepted by Thomas Harris, Manager of CG, for a production in the 1799–1800 season with an offer of £400, but it was never staged.

Because of her father's objections, Fanny withdrew the play, though she may have anticipated a performance at some later time.

When the Exbury family falls into poverty through the recklessness of the elder son, Hilaria Dalton (Lord Exbury's ward) must move to the country with the family. She becomes divided between her love for Valentine, Lord Exbury's younger son, and more fashionable (and affluent) prospects for marriage. Burney chronicles the moral progress of her heroine: Hilaria is at first fascinated by the attractions of the town, but in the course of the play, she learns how hollow these superficial attractions are. Ultimately, she finds acceptance in the pleasures of country life. Burney includes a subplot which exploits gothic drama, such as Matthew Lewis's popular *Castle Spectre* (1797): in *Love and Fashion*, a ghost supposedly haunts the country house; however, Burney turns ghostly terror into farce.

Joyce Hemlow says that the characters often remind the reader of *As You Like It* since they are torn between love and fashion. Positive and wholesome values are set against the "Slaves of Fashion," where "stereotyped stage characters are indicted for their extravagance and callousness or insensibility." Ultimately, Hemlow concludes that "the characterization is thin and hackneyed," the plot obvious, and the play's "solution and much of its conduct mawkish" (*UTQ* 19 [1949–50]: 186–87). In her edition of *A Busy Day*, Tara G. Wallace refers to this play as the most sentimental of Burney's comedies (158). Judy Simons, on the other hand, argues that the sentimentalism is not "allowed to dominate and the dialogue frequently has a Wildean brittleness and cynicism." Moreover, realism undercuts emotional exaggeration (131).

MANUSCRIPT: New York Public Library, Berg Collection. The holograph manuscript is 235 pages, according to Doody, who believes this was probably the copy that Harris saw (418).

Love and Law, Maria Edgeworth. First published in her collection of *Comic Dramas, in three acts*, 1817, this play should not be confused with John Till Allingham's *Love and Law*, acted with the title *Transformations; or, Love and Law*, 1810. *Love and Law* is one of three plays in Edgeworth's collection of *Comic Dramas*, printed for R. Hunter and Baldwin, Cradock, and Joy. From her own list of publications, Edgeworth recorded that she received £300 by her publishers for these plays (Butler 492). The play was not publicly performed.

Near the Irish towns of Ballynavogue and Ballynascraw, the Rooneys and the M'Brides are engaged in a feud, which is being encouraged by Gerald O'Blaney, the crooked (and near-bankrupt) local distiller, who wants to marry Honor M'Bride for her money. Honor, however, despises "his vile proposhals," for she is in love with Randal Rooney. The title, then, refers to the love that Honor M'Bride pursues and the legal wrangling that follows when the Rooneys file suit against the M'Brides over a piece of bog land. The Justice of the Peace is Mr. Carver; his wife and her waiting-maid Bloomsbury are helping to prepare Honor for service in the Carver family. Because of the revelations in the final act—a courtroom scene—the Rooneys and M'Brides are brought together when O'Blaney plots against them both. At the conclusion, the Carvers invite all the litigants for a wedding supper honoring Randal Rooney and Honor M'Bride.

Butler points out that two characters in the play are copied from real life: Catty Rooney, a genuine Irish character, and the magistrate, who like her father is the moral arbiter of justice (249, 247). How much more of the plot relies on Edgeworth's Irish experiences is unclear. Possibly very little, because the comedy treats a number of stock figures from earlier drama—the talkative, opinionated old woman (Catty Rooney), the miser (the elder M'Bride), the scoundrelly businessman (O'Blaney), and the two young lovers (Randal and Honor). The conflict among the characters gives rise to a plot which leads to the third-act trial.

TEXTS: Readex Microprint of *Comic Dramas, in three acts*, 1817 and Readex Microprint of the 2nd ed., corrected, 1817.

FACSIMILE EDITIONS: Two reprints of the 1893 Longford edition of Edgeworth's *Tales and Novels* are, first, the duodecimo size (Hildesheim: Georg Olms, 1969) 8: 127–185, and second, the quarto size (NY: AMS, 1967) 1: 411–438.

Love at a Loss; or, Most Votes Carry It, Catharine Trotter. This five-act comedy premiered at DL on 23 November 1700. Although published the following year by William Turner, *Love at a Loss* dissatisfied Trotter, who revised the play, retitling it *The Honourable Deceivers; or, All Right at the Last*. The revision, however, was neither printed nor performed, and it must be presumed lost. Trotter's single comedy may have displayed too much morality or an excess of social satire to be successful; it was not revived.

Set in France, the play features three women who have to deal with potential problems posed by their suitors before marrying. (1) Lucilia (played by Anne Oldfield) is to marry Phillabell the next day, but she is concerned that some indiscreet letters she sent Cleon (played by Colley Cibber) will be made public. (2) Lesbia loved Grandfoy, but she believed he was false to her. In the height of her resentment against him, she met Beaumine, fell in love with him, and signed a contract ("with our Blood") to marry, once his mother died, since she opposed the match. They consummated their engagement, then, rather than a marriage. She has now learned Grandfoy wasn't false, and she loves him instead of the roving Beaumine. (3) Miranda, "a Gay Coquette," is contracted to Constant, a stolid lover whom she persists in teasing. While the play has minimal action, it has much talk about ineffectiveness of both love and marriage: lovers seem either cynical or hypocritical —sometimes both; and marriage is a poor substitute for the single life. Beaumine, for example, likes "the Squeaking of a Fiddle, better than the Squalling of Brats." Perhaps the most important intrigue that takes place is when Lesbia is visiting Miranda, and Beaumine comes. To let Lesbia hear Beaumine's faithless remarks, Miranda places her in a closet. But when Constant comes, Lesbia leaps out to defend Miranda, who then agrees to marry Constant. Later, Cleon gives up Lucilia's letters allowing her to unite with Phillabell. After Grandfoy and Beaumine almost draw swords over Lesbia, she can't make up her mind which to take, and Miranda suggests Lesbia put it to a vote of those present. Although Grandfoy loses, he agrees to be friends with the couple. Beaumine, now reformed, takes Lesbia and concludes the play with moral couplets.

"Love is always at a loss in the play," according to Sophia Blaydes (DLB 84: 325). The characters appear to be playing at love, with only Constant taking it seriously. But love is most at a loss when Lesbia is unable to decide on which suitor to take, bringing out the literal meaning of the phrase "at a loss," as "puzzled" or "unable to decide." That the characters vote for Beaumine merely reconfirms that they have voted their emotions and their pocket books. Beaumine is after all one of them, and his weak reformation suggests that cynicism and hypocrisy win in the end. Still, Lesbia learns the truth about Beaumine and retrieves her precontracted lover, largely through the cooperation she and Miranda exhibit.

TEXT: Readex Microprint.

MODERN EDITION: Edited with introduction by Kendall in *Love and Thunder* (London: Methuen, 1988): 63–112.

FACSIMILE EDITION: E-CED, *The Plays of Mary Pix and Catharine Trotter*, vol. 2, with introduction by Edna L. Steeves (NY: Garland, 1982).

Love at a Venture, Susanna Carroll [Centlivre]. This comedy, adapted from Thomas Corneille's *Le Galand Doublé* (1660), was first produced in 1706 at the New Theatre, Bath, where Centlivre probably acted in the play. It was printed the same year in London for John Chantry—"by the author of *The Gamester*." During Centlivre's lifetime, there was no London performance. Centlivre had offered the play to DL, but Colley Cibber rejected it. Later, Cibber's *The Double Gallant* (Queens, 1 November 1707) showed many similarities to Centlivre's play—"plagiarized" some said—though Corneille's comedy could have been Cibber's main source.

Bellair arrives from the continent and immediately becomes involved in several intrigues: disguised as Colonel Revel he woos Beliza, and as Constant he woos Camilla.

Problems arise because the women are cousins and dwell together. When Bellair arrives to visit Camilla, whom he has saved from a fall into the Thames, he also encounters Beliza. Bellair puts on his best assurance and tries to talk his way out of a situation that will cause him to lose both women. Both are suspicious, and demand his presence at the same time. He outdoes himself with the clever contrivance of having the Colonel hauled off to jail, and immediately showing up as Constant. While Beliza is skeptical, Camilla accepts him. Unbeknownst to Camilla or Bellair, their fathers have planned for them to marry each other, thus further complicating the plot before its resolution. In a related story line, Sir William had been saved from ruffians in Spain by Bellair, and he assists Bellair in his plots—until he learns that Bellair has been wooing Beliza, his inamorata. Adding a strain on their relationship is Bellair's attempt to seduce Sir William's sister, who is married to an old valetudinarian, Sir Paul Cautious. Bellair convinces Sir William that he was ignorant of the relationships and apologizes to his friend. An unimaginative minor character, Wou'dbe, apes Sir William's dress, and proposes several silly projects, before he is shamed into returning to the country.

Lock details Centlivre's alterations of Thomas Corneille's text; couplets are changed into prose: "Centlivre is less interested in verbal wit than in stage action" (57). Though Sir William, the serious lover, "is largely Centlivre's creation," the servants (Robin, Patch, and Flora) are less consequential in her version. While Corneille has no subplot, Centlivre adds one with the characters of Sir Paul and Lady Cautious, highlighting problems of a forced May-December marriage. The character of Wou'dbe (no source in Corneille) serves as a double in his imitation of Sir William's sartorial nicety. Bellair differs from his French counterpart, Fernand, in being more lively and less sententious.

The adaptation is more like a Restoration comedy than any of Centlivre's plays, for it shows the rake in full flight, but even libertinism has its limits in a less flamboyant age. The use of doubles in Centlivre's plot forces the audience to consider how one person may act many roles. Not only does Bellair have several identities, but in one scene we hear Sir William speaking first like Lady Cautious and then in Bellair's voice. Wou'dbe is a pale imitation of Sir William, dressing exactly like him and at one point being mistaken for him. While Camilla is passive, Beliza is active—physically and linguistically. And Beliza will not be fooled by Bellair's impersonations, nor will she accept Sir William until she is quite ready. As a comedy of intrigue, *Love at a Venture* comes close to Aphra Behn's technique.

TEXTS: Readex Microprint. TEC Reel 578: 6.

FACSIMILE EDITION: E-CED, with introduction by R. C. Frushell (NY: Garland, 1982).

Love, Honor, and Obey, Jane M. Scott. This two-act farce opened at the Sans Pareil Theatre on 7 December 1812 with music by Michael Parnell. The play ran thirty times its first season and was revived in five of the next six seasons. Scott adapted the play from Patrat's *L'Heureuse Erreur* and took the role of the Countess.

MANUSCRIPT: Larpent 1746.

Love in a Convent, the Margravine of Anspach, formerly Baroness Elizabeth Berkeley Craven. This comedy was produced privately at Brandenburgh House in July 1805 (*BD* 2: 386). There is no record that the play was published, and the text is apparently lost.

Love in the City, Jane M. Scott. This farce, "founded on *The Romp* and written into verse by Miss Scott," opened at the Sans Pareil Theatre on 8 March 1813 with Scott in the role of Priscilla Tomboy. After five performances its first season, it was revived the next year and in the seasons of 1816–17 and 1817–18. No text of the farce is extant.

Love Rewarded, the Margravine of Anspach, formerly Baroness Elizabeth Berkeley Craven. This pastoral may have been acted in 1799. Nicoll and NCBEL assert it was printed in both English and Italian, but we have not located a copy of the printed text.

TEXT: Not in Readex Microprint.

Love's Adventures, Margaret Lucas Cavendish, Duchess of Newcastle. This drama in two parts was printed in her *Playes*, published by John Martyn, James Allestry, and Tho. Dicas in 1662. There was no performance.

Three separate plots are intermixed in the drama, and Cavendish jumps from one to another with only a break for a new scene. Each of these plots follows love's adventures. The principal tale is the quest of Lady Orphant for Lord Singularity. The play opens with Singularity telling his father that he doesn't wish to marry, even though his father had wanted him to marry the young Lady Orphant. After the death of both fathers, Lady Orphant decides to follow Lord Singularity to Venice where he has been made General of their army. With Foster Trusty, she travels to Venice and, disguising herself in male attire, she becomes the General's page under the name of Affectionata. She survives calumny from other servants, accusations of being a spy, and a war with the Turks in which she saves the General's life. By now the General, still ignorant of her gender, has made her the sole heir to his name and estate. Affectionata's fame grows, and the Venetians promote her to Lieutenant General and invite her to participate in the Council of War. When the General decides to retire, he and Affectionata are asked to visit the Pope in Rome, where she disputes with the Cardinals. Even though she is offered a sainthood or post as a Cardinal, she prefers to stay with the General, Lord Singularity. Upon their return to England, his lordship wants Affectionata to marry and suggests the woman his father wanted him to marry as being about the right age. When he can't find her, Lady Orphant goes to visit Foster Trusty and Nurse Fondly; they explain that since she had disappeared they are accused of murdering her. At their trial, Lady Orphant appears as herself in female dress setting them free, but Lord Singularity recognizes his Affectionata and offers her marriage, which occurs in the final act of the second part.

In a second plot, Lady Bashful's father has died and her woman, Mrs. Reformer, attempts to help her become less bashful. Among her visitors (Lady Wagtail, Lady Amorous, Sir Humphry Bold, and Sir Timothy Compliment) is Sir Serious Dumb, who says nothing, but is so struck by Lady Bashful that he begins to correspond with her. She doesn't encourage him, but he is willing to be her servant. When the same visitors come at a later time, Sir Humphry speaks disparagingly of Sir Serious, who boxes his ear. Sir Humphry draws his sword, forcing Sir Serious to do likewise, but Lady Bashful steps between them to stop the fight. She asks Sir Serious for his sword, and when he has given it to her Sir Humphry charges him. Lady Bashful knocks the sword from Sir Humphry's hand and steps on it, castigating him for attacking an unarmed man. She then gives herself to Sir Serious. After the visitors have left, he speaks for the first time—his vow of remaining silent having expired. Sir Serious demonstrates that he is an appropriate match for the thoughtful and intelligent Lady Bashful.

The third plot might be called the education of Lady Ignorant. Married to Sir Peaceable Studious, Lady Ignorant can't see why he spends all his time with his books; she would like to go into society. He agrees to take her into society, suggesting that she may not like it as well as she thinks. Gambling takes money away from household needs, she doesn't like wine, and malicious women (Lady Wagtail and Lady Amorous) take Sir Peaceable away from her company. When the couple return home after a series of incidents, Lady Ignorant apologizes to her husband, who says he only went into society because he loved her so well.

The juxtaposition of each plot comments on the other in effective ways. Lady Orphant goes to war as Affectionata and proves strong in battle, even saving Lord Singularity's life. Lady Bashful not only defeats Sir Humphry, but she protects Sir Serious. Often parallel phrases are used to link the different plots: for example, Affectionata states she won't carry a letter to the General's mistress "for the whole world" (38). Her remark is complemented by Mrs. Reformer telling Lady Wagtail that she

Pastor are instrumental in ensuring that the nobleman who is responsible must recognize what he has done and make full restitution, including a public wedding to the woman whose shame was publicly exposed.

MANUSCRIPT: Larpent 1226.

TEXT: Readex Microprint.

FACSIMILE EDITIONS: E-CED, reprints 1798 edition with introduction by Paula R. Backscheider (NY: Garland, 1980); *Revolution and Romanticism, 1789–1834* reprints the 1798 edition, introduced by Jonathan Wordsworth (Rutherford, NJ: Woodstock, 1990).

The Lowland Romp, Jane M. Scott. This two-act comic operetta set in Scotland opened at the Sans Pareil Theatre on 27 December 1810 with music by Sanderson and Winslow. It ran fifty-nine times in its first season and was revived in each of the next four seasons.

MANUSCRIPT: Larpent 1648.

The Loyal Subject, Sarah Cheney Gardner. Available only in Gardner's manuscript book, this five-act comedy is described as "feeble, derivative, and mindlessly misogynistic [using foolish female stereotypes]" by Isobel Grundy (*TSWL* 7 [1988]: 15). F. Grice and A. Clarke credit the play "with some literary merit" (*TN* 7 (1953): 77). It was neither performed nor printed.

MANUSCRIPT: The Colyton Ms., described by Grundy, is privately owned.

Lucius, the First Christian King of Britain, Delariviere Manley. First produced on 11 May 1717 at DL, where it was acted three times. This five-act tragedy was published the same year by J. Barber. It is dedicated to Sir Richard Steele who supplied the prologue. In the preface Manley praises the acting of Barton Booth who played Lucius and of Anne Oldfield who played Rosalinda. The tragedy was given one final time as a benefit for Manley at DL on 27 April 1720, when Oldfield, rather than Mrs. Horton, spoke the original epilogue by Matthew Prior, as noted by Richard B. Kline (*RECTR* 14 [1975]: 53–58).

After being victorious in battle, the pagan Lucius finds that he has fallen in love with the captive Christian Queen Rosalinda. Lucius's father (the usurping King Vortimer) is opposed to Christians, but he now lusts after Rosalinda. Princess Emmelin loves Lucius and plots with Arminius, Prince of Albany, to win the conqueror. Matters are further complicated because Arminius's sister, Sylvius, also loves Lucius. While Queen Rosalinda is lamenting her situation, Lucius comes to tell her of his conversion to Christianity and his love for her; they are married. When he hears they have wed, Arminius lies to Lucius about the "faithless" Queen. Lucius asks for proof of these charges, and Arminius produces a forged letter supposedly from Rosalinda. Lucius curses the Queen and retreats to a forest, feeling he has been duped by a woman's falsehood. Meanwhile, upon hearing that Lucius has departed, Vortimer attempts to rape the Queen. When she calls for help, Lucius returns to save her. Only then do he and the Queen sort out the lies that have been told. Sylvius enters, having been stabbed by Vortimer, and she dies telling them that Vortimer has sentenced them to die: the Queen is to be raped by the "deathsman" (the King acting this part) while Lucius looks on. Arminius goes to Lucius in prison and tells him he'll provide a sword if Lucius will kill the ravisher. Arminius plans to let the two fight it out; then he will kill the victor, gaining Queen and crown. Lucius stabs Vortimer and is attacked by Arminius, who is also killed by Lucius. The Prince of Cambria (Lucius's uncle) says Vortimer is not Lucius's father; Lucius is the son of the rightful king. Having avenged his real father, Lucius now asks the people to praise heaven, saying, "I have pass'd the threat'ned Storms of Fate, Aveng'd my Parents, and preserv'd my Wife" (54).

In their introduction, Armisted and Davis focus on the political implications and on Manley's reconciliation with Steele. In the play, we see Rosalinda's Christian goodness surrounded by lying, cheating, and evil. Her strength and fortitude in the face of ever-present danger finally moves Lucius to choose a correct course, and villainy is defeated.

TEXTS: Readex Microprint. TEC Reel 484: 4.
FACSIMILE EDITION: Augustan Reprint Society, with introduction by Jack M. Armisted and Debbie K. Davis (LA: Clark Library, 1989).

The Luckey Chance; or, An Alderman's Bargain, Aphra Behn. This five-act comedy was produced at DL in April 1686 and printed the following year for W. Canning. Performances in 1697 and 1718 are noted in *LS*. Behn's preface is important because she asks to be judged not by her sex, but by her achievement—and on an equal footing with men. Paula Backscheider, in *Spectacular Politics* (Baltimore: Johns Hopkins P, 1993), discusses another matter Behn raises in the preface: "the vexing issue" of women's language (83).

As the play opens, Bellmour, after a duel in which he killed a man, returns surreptitiously from abroad. Having been contracted with Leticia earlier, Bellmour finds she is now going to marry Sir Feeble Fainwou'd. His friend Gayman tells him that Leticia only agreed to the marriage because of her near destitution and because she heard Bellmour died at the Hague. They intercept a letter to Sir Feeble, saying that his nephew, Francis Fainwou'd, is coming to England. Bellmour takes his cue and passes himself off as Francis, in hopes he can stop the consummation of the marriage; he also discovers he has been pardoned for the duel. Gayman, meanwhile, is living in extreme poverty after spending all his money on gifts for Julia, now married to Sir Cautious Fulbank. When Bredwell, Sir Cautious's apprentice, tells Julia of Gayman's plight, she sends him, anonymously, £500 she's taken from her husband's counting house. With the money comes a summons for Gayman to a cryptic assignation that night. While Bellmour gets Sir Feeble out of his house with a feigned message from Sir Cautious about "some damnable plot" in the City, Gayman is led to a masque, prepared by Julia, at Fulbank's house. Not knowing where he is, Gayman believes the meeting has been arranged by an old female benefactor. With Sir Feeble's arrival, the only way to get Gayman out of the house is to pretend he is a ghost. Alarmed and frightened, Sir Feeble returns home just in time to prevent Bellmour and Leticia from escaping. The next day, after drinking with his cronies, Sir Cautious gambles with Gayman, wagering a night with his wife against £300 and losing. Delivered to Julia's room in a chest, Gayman takes Sir Cautious's place. Bellmour, attempting to prevent Sir Feeble from his marriage consummation that same night, pretends to be a ghost. Sir Feeble is so frightened he locks himself in a closet, while Bellmour and Leticia flee to the protection of Julia, who readily agrees. But Julia, angry at being made a bargain of, vows to separate from Sir Cautious and rails at Gayman for violating her honor. Sir Feeble then arrives, feeling scared and guilty for reporting Bellmour dead. When Bellmour and Leticia present themselves, Sir Feeble asks forgiveness and retires with Sir Cautious who gives up Julia to Gayman, after Julia says she has proved Gayman's constancy.

Well-plotted and witty, Behn's "comedy of intrigue," as she calls her play in the preface, exhibits a combination of serious concerns for marital love, an abundance of good humor, and farcical inventiveness. Link finds *The Luckey Chance* "a falling off" from Behn's best work (75), whereas Woodcock ranks it "among the really outstanding comedies of the Restoration" (175). While Cotton praises the play for its substantial "attack on arranged marriages" (63), Pearson finds it shows "a decided darkening of her vision of society and especially of the options available for women" (166). Given these various views of the play, one might examine what Behn has done in overturning existing hegemony. Money is power for the old aldermen. All the rest of the characters seem in some way dependent on the largess flowing from their coffers. Julia and Leticia marry to avoid poverty, but their hearts are not committed. Gayman lives on the edge of indigence, and Bellmour is little better off: Gayman will take money for favors, and Bellmour acts Sir Feeble's nephew. Once the destined couples have triumphed over greed and lust through love and persistence, the aldermen are willing to share their fortunes: Sir Feeble bestows jewels on Leticia, and Sir Cautious bequeaths his estate, after he dies, to Bellmour. The reordering of the world of the play forces the characters to see their community differently. The aldermen give up their power and ultimately surrender their money to a new generation as it takes the reigns of self-government.

TEXTS: Wing B1744. EEB Reel 1195: 10. Readex Microprint.

MODERN EDITIONS: Behn, *Works*, ed. Montague Summers (1915; NY: Phaeton, 1967) 3: 177–279. *Restoration Comedy*, ed. A. Norman Jeffares (London: Folio Society, 1974) 3: 1–104. *The Female Wits*, ed. Fidelis Morgan (London: Virago, 1981): 73–143. Acting text, ed. Fidelis Morgan (London: Methuen, 1984). Behn, *Five Plays*, with introduction by Maureen Duffy (London: Methuen, 1990), reprints Summers's edition (1–99). *The Other Eighteenth Century: English Women of Letters 1660–1800*, edited by Robert W. Uphaus and Gretchen M. Foster (East Lansing, MI: Colleagues P, 1991), reprints Summers's edition (62–137).

CRITICAL EDITIONS: Edited by Jean A. Coakley, Diss., Miami (Ohio) U, 1981. Satire and Sense series, edited with introduction by Jean A. Coakley (NY: Garland, 1987).

The Lucky Escape, Mary Darby Robinson. This two-act farce with a pastiche of music played as an afterpiece on Robinson's benefit night at DL on 30 April 1778, with the songs printed the same year "for the author." The mainpiece was *Macbeth*, in which Robinson made her first appearance in the role of Lady Macbeth.

Before the play begins, Venture has received an introduction to Sir Toby Stedfast's country house from the lawyer Trickwell. His intention is to marry Sir Toby's daughter, Maria, for her money. Maria, who opens the play with a love ballad, has an amorous interest in Edwin, a country swain. Maria's friend, Letitia, enters with the news that Venture has arrived. Though Edwin thinks his hopes are at an end, Letitia resolves to help him. When Sir Toby introduces Maria to Venture, she is indifferent to him, privately telling him to leave his "detestable solicitations." Letitia, however, mentions to Venture that he has a rival, with whom Maria intends to elope, and she suggests a challenge. While Venture won't fight, Letitia tells him to give her a suit of his clothes and she'll fight a duel. After he agrees, Letitia explains her scheme to Maria and Edwin; then she leaves Venture's clothes for Edwin in the greenhouse. That night, Edwin acts Venture, but he is interrupted by Venture himself. Edwin finally tells the truth to Sir Toby, and Letitia produces a letter from Venture to Trickwell spelling out his real purpose. Sir Toby throws Venture out and gives Maria's hand to Edwin.

The linchpin to this slight but clever afterpiece is Letitia, who schemes to get Maria off the hook with Venture while at the same time helping Edwin. Though Venture is unwilling to duel, Letitia says she will do so. Moreover, by getting Venture to give her a suit of his clothes, she discovers the letter that exposes his rascally intentions.

MANUSCRIPT: Larpent 447. Readex microprint of manuscript.

TEXT: Readex Microprint of songs only.

-M-

MACAULEY, Elizabeth Wright (1785/86?–1837). Apparently connected to the stage for much of her life, Macauley contributed only one dramatization when she adapted Sir Walter Scott's *Marmion; or, The Battle of Flodden Field*. Macauley's version, *Marmion: A Melo-Drama*, was published in a second edition at Cork by John Connor in 1811. Notes in this printing indicate the melodrama, originally performed in Dublin, encountered a great deal of criticism. The text was changed from the Dublin performance for presentation in Cork. Macauley includes both original and altered scenes in the second edition printed at Cork. In her preface, Macauley states that *Marmion* is her first and last theatrical effort. Perhaps her problems in the Dublin theatres caused her to write *A Pamphlet on the Difficulties and Dangers of a Theatrical Life* (Dublin, 1810).

Macauley went on to publish, often at her own expense, *Poetical Effusions* (1812), *Theatrical Revolution* (1819), *Tales of Drama* (1822), a poem *Mary Stuart* (1823), and *Facts Against Falsehood* (1824), dealing with her problems relating to the stage in London. She brought out her *Autobiographical Memoirs* in 1834, and prepared an expanded version the following year. [Davis & Joyce give her name as Macaulay, NUC]

MACCARTHY, Charlotte (fl. 1745–1767). Scant information is available about her early life in Ireland, except that her father was a gentleman and both parents were deceased by the time of her first known work, *The Fair Moralist, Or Love and Virtue*, 1745, with an expanded edition in 1746. She published *News from Parnassus, or Political Advice from the Nine Muses*, in Dublin, 1757. Her one dramatic dialogue, *The Author and Bookseller*, appeared in 1765, "Printed for the Author." *BD* says about the dialogue: "This was merely designated as an introduction to proposals for printing a book, entitled 'Justice and Reason faithful guides to Truth. A Treatise under thirty-seven heads.'" *Justice and Reason, Faithful Guides to Truth* did appear in 1767. Judith Stanton notes *Celia; or, The Perjured Lover* (1749) has been attributed to MacCarthy in her listing in *Curtain Calls* (348); although a play by this title by Charles Johnson was performed at DL in 1732 (published 1733), we find no evidence that MacCarthy contributed to this play. [FCLE]

M'TAGGART, Ann Hamilton (c. 1753–1834). After the death of her mother, when Ann was ten, she went to live in Exeter with an aunt and uncle to whom she read aloud a great deal. When she rejoined her father in London, she wrote and painted. During her travels in Europe, 1788–89, M'Taggart maintained a journal and started writing plays. She offered at least two plays to John Philip Kemble, who did not respond.

It wasn't until 1814 that M'Taggart's plays were issued in John Galt's *The New British Theatre*; these included *Theodora*, *A Search after Perfection*, *Villario*, and *Hortensia*. Although another play in the collection, *Manoeuvering*, may be by M'Taggart, it does not appear in the 1832 collected *Plays*. *Theodora*, based on a French work by Baculard d'Arnaud, has wrongly been attributed to Sophia Burrell because of similar titles. *A Search after Perfection* has also been mistakenly ascribed to Burrell. This comedy in five acts may base its characters on real life situations (M'Taggart is likely Mrs. Rational). Originally titled *The School for Mothers; or, A Search After Perfection*, the play makes light of then current educational theories popularized by Hannah More and others. *Hortensia*, a verse drama in five acts, has a heroine Galt found more purely evil than Lady Macbeth.

About ten years later, other dramas by M'Taggart appeared—*Constantia*, a tragedy in five acts that was based on a story by Madame de Genlis, and *Valville; or, The Prejudices of Past Times*, a verse drama in five acts. Published by subscription, the plays were printed by M. A. Nattali, 1824. All of her dramatic writings were collected in *Plays*, published in two volumes by A. J. Valpy in 1832. We find no evidence that any of her plays was ever staged. She published her *Memoirs* in 1830, as written by "a Gentlewoman of the Old School." [FCLE]

The Magic Pipe; or, Dancing Mad, Jane M. Scott. This musical pantomime was first performed at the Sans Pareil Theatre on 3 December 1810 and ran seventy-six times its first season. Harlequin and Columbine head the large cast. Although no plot or plan for movement has survived, Scott's father appears to have designed falling snow and other effects for the pantomime.

The Magicians; or, The Enchanted Bird, Jane M. Scott. Opening at the Sans Pareil Theatre on 23 December 1813, this comic pantomime with music was performed fifty-three times its first season. Included in the cast of twelve, Scott played the Sylph. No script for the actions in this pantomime is extant.

The Maggot, Jane Gifford Egleton. This two-act ballad opera was only performed on her benefit night of 18 April 1732 at LIF. The play was not printed, and the text is apparently lost.

The Magistrate, Jane M. Scott. This musical entertainment first played at the Sans Pareil Theatre on 15 February 1808 and ran thirty-six nights. James Sanderson provided the music, and Scott acted the role of Edward. The piece was revived in the next four seasons. No libretto or score of the music has survived.

The Magnet, Lady Dorothea Dubois. This popular entertainment, with music by Samuel J. Arnold, opened at Mary-le-Bone Gardens on 27 June 1771. There were twenty-three performances in its first summer season. T. Becket published the libretto in 1771. It was revived the next three summer seasons at the same venue.

A triangle of characters form the main action of the piece, which begins with Claudius breaking his arranged engagement to Clara because he is pursuing Honoria. Clara blames Honoria for the broken engagement, whereas Claudius believes love is the magnet that will bring him to Honoria. After an incident of mistaken identity, Clara relinquishes Claudius, but she also claims Honoria as her friend.

The slender libretto provides a vehicle for Dubois's verse set to music; consequently, there is little action. The conclusion of the piece brings together two warring females in friendship.

TEXT: Readex Microprint.

Malcolm, Miss R. Roberts. This five-act historical tragedy in blank verse was printed "for the author" in 1779, but the play was not staged. The events depicted in Roberts's tragedy follow the death of Macbeth. Malcolm and Macduff originate from the same characters drawn by Shakespeare in *Macbeth*.

Malcolm has been put on the throne by Macduff, in place of the usurper (Macbeth), and he must deal with the Norwegians who now want peace. A larger problem, however, is to fight William the Conqueror and put Edgar, who is in exile in Scotland, on the English throne. In addition to problems of state, there are romantic entanglements: Malcolm wants to marry Margaret, Edgar's sister; both Edgar and Douglas have a romantic interest in Mariora, Macduff's daughter, as does the Norwegian commander, Hasmond; but Macduff wants Mariora to wed Malcolm. Malcolm asks Edgar for Margaret's hand and is accepted, but when Douglas requests Mariora's hand, Macduff refuses. He and fate are against it. As preparations for the war against William and the Normans continue, Macduff speaks to Mariora, who would like to marry Edgar; Macduff agrees, but wants to get Malcolm's approval. At the same time, Douglas wants Malcolm to help him win Mariora by pleading with Macduff. After Mariora and Edgar concur on marriage, the Norwegian Hasmond plans to take Mariora against her will and disguises himself as a porter to gain entrance at Macduff's house. As Mariora is reading Ovid, Hasmond advances on her, saying "You must, you shall be mine" (63). Macduff and Douglas arrive in time to save her, but Hasmond wounds Mariora before Douglas stabs him to death. Unaware of the earlier events, Margaret urges Malcolm to support Edgar's wish to marry Mariora, but he says she is not his to give and he's pledged to help Douglas in his love of Mariora. Margaret then releases Malcolm from his vow of marriage. In another scene, Edgar has a vision of King Edward prophesying to him that he will have no children, but his sister Margaret will be the mother of kings. Moreover, he will not fight the Normans, and William will rule England. The denouement occurs in a room of state where Mariora publicly thanks Douglas for saving her from Hasmond, and the Norwegians are placated. It is then discovered that Mariora is Douglas's sister, who was saved from Macbeth's slaughter. Macduff turns over his office to Douglas and Mariora, allowing Douglas to give Mariora to Edgar. He also asks Margaret to accept Malcolm. Edgar then tells of his vision and says that a daughter of Malcolm and Margaret will marry William. Macduff speaks the final lines about the future kingdom.

In the feudal world of the play, women are pawns in a high stakes game of statecraft; they can exercise little free will of their own, and love is out of the question. Nevertheless, Margaret has enough fortitude to release Malcolm from their marriage vows when he will not support Edgar's attachment to Mariora. Roberts desires to fit her play between the imaginary work of Shakespeare and actual history, and it takes Edgar's dream vision to wedge the play between myth and reality.

TEXT: Readex Microprint.

Malek Adhel, the Champion of the Crescent, Frances Burney, niece of Fanny Burney d'Arblay. This three-act verse drama was adapted from "the celebrated Crusade-Romance of *Mathilde* by Madame Cottin." It was printed in *Tragic Dramas: chiefly intended for representation in Private Families: to which is added Aristodemus, a tragedy from the Italian of Vincenzo Monti*, published for the author in 1818. Public performance was not intended.

The events of the drama take place in Palestine, near Cesarea, at the time of the third Crusade. Lusignan, king of Jerusalem, dethroned by the Saracens, and Malek Adhel, governor of Cesarea and brother of Saladin, sultan of Egypt, have both fallen in love with Matilda, sister of Richard Coeur de Lion. Before taking her final vows as a nun, Matilda decides to accompany her brother to the Holy Land. Fearing that Lusignan will marry Matilda, but believing his city safe from Christian attacks, Malek leaves his post to retrieve her from the convent where she resides. But the crafty Lusignan launches an attack; as the Saracens are winning, Malek is taken prisoner. Matilda, who despite her sincere vows has fallen for the handsome and generous Moslem, begs for his life, because she cannot bear the thought that he will die a pagan. Lusignan feigns to assent, but bribes Demas, his squire, to kill Malek, should he be unable to do so himself. Lusignan is then called to meet with the other Christian princes who are eager to know the fate of Malek, whom they esteem very highly. Anselm, the archbishop of Tyre, visits Malek in prison and arranges his escape as a means of repaying Malek for his past generosity. Knowing full well that a freed Malek will fight against the Christian army, as the governor of Cesarea reminds him, Anselm releases Malek anyway. He believes his act is not his own but God's, and he admonishes Malek to convert and to forget Matilda. Before the decisive battle between the Christians and the Moslem army led by Malek, his brother Saladin forgives him for his reckless act. On the battle field, Lusignan searches for Malek, his hated rival. Both fight heroically, and a seriously wounded Malek succeeds over his foe. After Lusignan dies, Demas stabs Malek, leaving him for dead. Anselm and Matilda arrive to find Malek "cover'd with wounds, extended on the dust," hardly breathing. Matilda implores the archbishop to pray for the Infidel's conversion, which occurs as Malek kisses the crucifix held to his lips. Anselm unites the two lovers in holy matrimony, as Malek expires, bidding his young bride farewell "but for a season," since they will be reunited in Heaven. The play ends as Matilda contemplates the "cold, livid corpse." Informed of his brother's conversion and marriage, Saladin permits Matilda to take the body to the convent, that "last retreat Of grief eternal, soon to be [her] tomb" (110).

Despite the historical and geographical setting of her piece, Burney focuses more on the depiction of ill-fated love than on Christianity triumphing over Islam, since her Saracen characters are as noble and admirable as the Christian princes. In fact, the only character who demonstrates no chivalric qualities is the treacherous and vengeful Lusignan. Furthermore, the high esteem in which Malek is held renders his conversion almost perfunctory. From the beginning, Malek practices Christian virtues. What precipitates the tragedy is not the clash of two antagonistic religions, but Lusignan's hatred of his more fortunate rival.

As indicated on the title page, Francis Burney adapted Madame Cottin's lengthy novel. She reduced the eight hundred pages of the original to a mere three-act drama, not an insignificant feat in itself. Even though Madame Cottin's heroine is an imaginary figure, Burney disregarded the many details of her source except Matilda's fateful love for Malek. This gives her drama intensity and unity, if not verisimilitude, a quality also lacking in the original. Burney's Matilda becomes the most engrossing character of the drama: she is unexpectedly thrown into a world she was never supposed to experience; here, she discovers human love and human frailty. Her faith, intense and sincere, does not guard her against the grief caused by the earthly loss of Malek. To Saladin who asks her if she really was his slain brother's bride, she answers with simple words full of strongly felt regrets: "Oh, Heaven! I was,—I was! Alas! I am no longer."

TEXT: Readex Microprint.

The Man's Bewitched; or, The Devil to do about Her, Susanna Centlivre. This five-act comedy is partly based on Regnard's *Les Folies amoureuses* (1704) and on Hauteroche's *Le Deuil* (1672). It was produced at the Queen's Theater, also known as the New Theatre in the Haymarket, on 12 December 1709 and ran for only three nights. Publication of the play was advertised in the *Daily Courant* of 28 December 1709 as printed for Bernard Lintott (Burling), though the quarto is without a date.

The comedy boasts three plots, two of which are from French sources, the third from Centlivre's pen. The first plot centers around Captain Constant who is in love with Belinda, the "supposed daughter" of Trusty, his father's steward. Penniless, he decides to trick Trusty into giving him the rent money owed his father by spreading the rumor that his father is dead. He arrives in Peterborough with his servant, both in mourning dress. His scheme works well until his father appears in person in the village, where people take him for an incarnation of the devil, at times appearing as a dog as big as an ox, and they flee from him, horrified. At the prompting of Lovely, who pleads for his friend in the name of love, the father forgives his son. The fact that Belinda turns out to be a rich noble orphan, and not the mere daughter of the steward, helps the reconciliation between father and son. Centlivre borrowed most elements from a one-act comedy in rhymed couplets entitled *Le Deuil [The Mourning]* by Hauteroche (some say Thomas Corneille collaborated, but the printed edition contains Hauteroche's name with a dedication to André-Girard Le Camus). Centlivre changed the names and switched some characters around, but the only true alteration resides in the discovery that Belinda is an orphan of noble origins, not a very significant addition after all, since, in the original, Captain Constant was already of a higher condition than the woman he loved.

In the second plot, Faithful, "a gentleman of fortune," is in love with Laura, who, alas, is closely observed by her old guardian, Sir David Watchum, whom she hates, and who wants to marry her. Laura, with the help of servants, pretends to be raving mad, at one moment appearing as an old woman who, in her youth, bore fourteen boys, at another as an army chief in need of recruits to wage a bloody war. Sir David concludes she has been bewitched and consents to hire an exorcist who, in order to cure her, transfers her spell to Faithful, hence the title of the play. In the ensuing confusion, the two young lovers escape and get married. All the farcical elements—the old guardian's incongruous passion, his obsessive behavior, his unwittingly bringing the young lover into his own home, and the mad scenes—come from Regnard's three-act comedy, *Les Folies amoureuses*. The ending of this plot, despite the additions of the characters from the other episodes, remains the same: Sir David, tricked by youth and love, is left cursing while every one rejoices.

The third pair of lovers consists of Maria, "a gentlewoman of fortune," and Lovely, a friend of Captain Constant. Maria, whose parents object to the match, does not want to marry him "without a portion," but given Lovely's disposition, this insistence is quite unconvincing, and the poor Lovely wonders if he "must dangle after [her] two or three years longer" (65). Trusty removes all Maria's imaginary obstacles by offering either to reconcile her to her father, or to give her "a portion" himself.

The Man's Bewitched suffers from lack of unity, its three plots being too loosely connected, and from lack of a common tone, at times a comedy, at times a farce. Nevertheless, the play offers some good scenes, such as the one between Faithful's servant and the old guardian: the former deftly avoids answering any questions, while the latter doggedly pursues inquiries about his unwanted presence in the house. Another interest lies in Belinda's view of marriage, which she does not imagine as the blissful state so often hinted at in most comedies, but as a condition fraught with tears and hardships. To Maria, she suggests: "Let us marry whilst we are young, that we may be able to bear it [marriage and its sources of grief] with the better courage" (31). *The Man's Bewitched*, one of Centlivre's least successful plays because of its many disparate elements, is, as Lock states, "neither an effective farce nor a good comedy" (78).

TEXTS: Readex Microprint. TEC Reel 576: 23.

FACSIMILE EDITION: E-CED, with introduction by R. C. Frushell (NY: Garland, 1982).

MANLEY, Delariviere (1663? [1667? 1672?]–1724). A good deal of confusion exists not only about when Manley's birth took place, but where: did it occur on the isles of Jersey or Guernsey, between the Channel Islands and England, or was she born in Holland with a Dutch mother? Details of Manley's early life are equally vexing: was she educated at home, did she spend time in France, both or neither? For details of Manley's formative years, critics have relied on her fictionalized autobiography, *The Adventures of Rivella* (1714), which is no guarantee of accuracy. It is a fact, however, that she married her cousin, John, and had a child by him. But the union turned out to be bigamous (he was already married). After leaving him, Manley stayed for a time with the Duchess of Cleveland. When a quarrel ended their relationship, Manley spent more than a year in Exeter, where she began writing plays.

Manley's first play, a five-act comedy titled *The Lost Lover; or, The Jealous Husband*, came out at DL in March 1696. This was quickly followed by the five-act tragedy *The Royal Mischief*, produced at LIF within two months. Even though both plays were published, Manley didn't try another play for more than ten years. Her five-act tragedy, *Almyna; or, The Arabian Vow*, appeared at the Queen's Theatre in December 1706.

Between writing dramas, Manley penned her best-known works, *The Secret History of Queen Zarah* (1705) and *The Secret Memoirs . . . From the New Atalantis* (1709), which scandalized the court of Queen Anne, especially the Duchess of Marlborough. These two, as well as her *Memoirs of Europe* (1710) and *Adventures of Rivella* (1714), fit the genre of *roman à clef*. And even though she was briefly imprisoned, Manley continued to provide lifelike detail about court society. During this time she probably edited *The Female Tatler*, and later Manley assisted Jonathan Swift with *The Examiner*, an anti-Whig newspaper, for several years.

It was more than ten years after *Almyna* that Manley returned to writing for the stage. Her last theatrical production, a five-act tragedy entitled *Lucius, the First Christian King of Britain*, played at DL in 1717. A work entitled *The Double Mistress; or, 'Tis Well 'Tis No More* was announced for performance in 1720, but no production took place, and the manuscript is presumed lost.

The last published piece during Manley's lifetime consisted of seven brief novels collected under the title *The Power of Love*. Although some stories came from a Renaissance text by William Painter, Manley augmented the collection with additional tales. Manley died in 1724 and was buried in the church of St. Benet's, Paul's Wharf. *The Court Legacy* (1733), a ballad opera advertised as by the author of *The Atalantis*, calls attention to Manley's scandalous work merely as a way to sell the publication. Although the ballad opera (never staged) may have been based on her work, it cannot be credited to her.

Manley's contribution to the theatre has been dimmed by her success as novelist. Like Aphra Behn, she defended Tory principles while vilifying the Whigs in her plays. Payne stresses the significance of choice for women in Manley's dramas: "women who seek to govern their own lives rather than allowing themselves to be passively bartered among men make her work particularly vital today" (DLB 80: 136). Although Manley's plays show the consequences of governance and societal order, women end tragically when they subvert these issues. According to Payne, this calls "into question the very order she depicts" (80: 136).

[*BD*, BNA, Cotton, DABWW, DLB 80 (by L. R. Payne), DNB, EBWW, FCLE, Hume, Morgan, OCEL, Revels, Smith & Cardinale. Patricia Koster provides fresh biographical information in *ECLife* 3 (1977): 106–11. The attack on Pix, Manley, and Trotter in *The Female Wits* (produced DL, Sept. 1696; published 1704) is available in an Augustan Reprint Facsimile edition. Constance Clark's *Three Augustan Women Playwrights* furnishes a biocritical discussion of Manley and her works, with those of Pix and Trotter, 1986.]

Manoeuvering, attributed to Maria Edgeworth because the source of the drama is Edgeworth's novel with the same title. First printed in *The New British Theatre* (London: for Henry Colburn, 1814), the author of this play is unknown. With no precise evidence, the comedy has been ascribed to Ann Hamilton M'Taggart because several of her dramas are included in *The New British Theatre*. John Galt, editor of the collection, indicates the author is female when he comments that he hopes the author will "invent a subject [more] suitable to *her* own genius" in his note on the play (our emphasis). The five-act comedy was not staged. Until more information appears, the female adaptor of this comedy will remain a mystery.

The comedy is set at the neighboring country houses of the Beaumonts and the Walsinghams, where Mrs. Beaumont, a widow with two grown children, plans intrigues to make "proper" marriages for her son and daughter. Her near-relation, Mr. Walsingham, a widower, also with a son and daughter, considers Mrs. Beaumont "a Machiavel in petticoats." In the neighborhood live Sir Archer Uppingham, who has expectations of inheriting the Wentworth estate and an earldom, and his sister Matilda. The wealthy Mr. Pemberton, who is related to both the Beaumonts and the Walsinghams, has recently returned from Jamaica and is coming for a visit to the Beaumonts, and Mrs. Beaumont hopes to manage his stay so that her family—rather than the Walsinghams—will inherit his property. If Mrs. Beaumont gets her way, her son will marry Matilda Uppingham, and her daughter will wed Sir Archer, but young Beaumont wants to marry Eliza Walsingham, and Amanda Beaumont plans to wed Captain Walsingham, who has just returned from sea. Amanda's candid plans go astray when she learns that Captain Walsingham will bring with him Donna Clara, a Spanish lady; nevertheless, she turns down an offer from Sir Archer. Amanda is mortified further when Donna Clara, arriving by mistake at the Beaumonts, thinks Amanda is the Captain's sister. Meanwhile, the Captain hears that Amanda will marry Sir Archer and prepares to return to sea. When Mrs. Beaumont learns her son has been accepted by Eliza Walsingham, she feels all her schemes have been in vain. She then hopes to marry Sir Archer herself. With the help of Captain Walsingham, Captain Lightbody and Twigg (two minor characters) rescue Donna Clara from a bailiff, bringing about the denouement. Donna Clara is actually English. Many years ago on a voyage to the West Indies, she was captured by the Spaniards. She asked a relative to ransom her, but he reported her dead and had her shut up in a convent. That relative was one Wentworth, who is now dying and wishes to make restitution: Clara Wentworth will inherit the Wentworth estate, leaving Sir Archer and Matilda nearly destitute. They also learn that Sir Archer sent the bailiff, but he's forgiven by Clara and the company at Pemberton's urging. Mrs. Beaumont reveals she has married Sir Archer with Twigg as a witness; Archer will now have to live on her fortune. Amanda accepts Captain Walsingham, and young Beaumont and Eliza Walsingham unite.

Although the unnaturally happy ending gets in the way, the comedy has its witty moments. The title comes from Amanda's remark "So without deception, without manoeuvering, I thought I had gained the heart of Walsingham." Thus, manoeuvering suggests the various deceptions that occur in the play, but above all the several self-deceptions. As the play closes, Pemberton remarks that they should not try to regulate the future. That Mrs. Beaumont fails in her attempts to orchestrate everyone's life points out that self-regulation wins out over domination. Contrary to her mother's plans, Amanda Beaumont shows a good deal of grit in refusing "a good match" with Sir Archer, who turns out to be a scoundrel.

TEXT: Readex Microprint.

Manor Sackville, Sydney Owenson, Lady Morgan. See **Dramatic Scenes from Real Life**.

Marcelia; or, The Treacherous Friend, Frances Boothby. This tragicomedy was probably first performed by the King's Company at the Bridges-Street Theatre sometime in 1669: Van Lennep (*LS*) suggests August, whereas Hume says early 1669. The play was licensed 9 October 1669, entered in the *Term Catalogues* in November, 1669, and printed for Will. Cademan, 1670. No cast list is given. A five-act tragicomedy in prose and rhymed couplets, *Marcelia* has multiple plots which are characteristic of the period: the main plot deals with romantic affairs of state, whereas a comic subplot contrasts the cowardly acts in the high plot. A slight third plot connects near the end of the play with the comic plot.

Marcelia (set in France) turns upon Melinet's betrayal of his friend Lotharicus to gain Marcelia for the King. Even though Melinet is a favorite of the king, he has failed to gain a place at court. The King's mistress Calinda, meanwhile, feels the King has lost interest in her. Indeed he has, for he asks Melinet to discover if Marcelia, Melinet's virtuous cousin, plans to marry Lotharicus. Knowing she is, Melinet asks Lotharicus to use his interest to help him to meet Arcasia, and Lotharicus sends a note arranging an assignation in the garden that night. When Melinet arrives at Marcelia's, they walk in the garden where they see Lotharicus and Arcasia. Marcelia thinks Lotharicus has another lover and believes him unfaithful. The following night, Melinet takes Marcelia to the court masque, where Lotharicus watches the King courting Marcelia. After the masque, Lotharicus tells Melinet his plan to leave the kingdom, and Melinet has his servant DuPrette follow Lotharicus. At Lyons, Lotharicus meets Marcelia's brother, Euryalus, and tells him of Marcelia's supposed ambitions with the King. Meanwhile, Marcelia laments that she must accept the King but cannot give her love. Melinet's servant, DuPrette, and three villains stab Lotharicus and leave him for dead. DuPrette falls out with the villains, who kill him, but before he dies, he is found by Euryalus to whom he gives a letter. Melinet hears that Lotharicus is dead, but fears Euryalus, who returns to tell Marcelia of Melinet's plot. The King and Melinet discuss Lotharicus's death. But Lotharicus, whose wounds were not fatal, returns in disguise to take his revenge. When he finds Melinet, they duel, but the fight is broken up and reported to the King. Since Melinet was wounded, the King demands to see Lotharicus. Meanwhile, Euryalus tells Marcelia that Lotharicus is alive and has wounded Melinet. They agree to go to the King and plead Lotharicus's case. In the final scene, the King sees Lotharicus, who gives him Melinet's letter to DuPrette ordering the murder. Melinet is arrested, and Marcelia must choose between Lotharicus and the King, saying "neither must be mine." Out of honor, the King gives Marcelia to Lotharicus and returns to Calinda, who graciously accepts him.

The low plot features Moriphanus, "a proud, silly, rich fellow," and his servant, Graculus: Moriphanus, an early "man of mode," wants to have a phalanx of servants in different attire, and Graculus makes fun of him in asides, but undertakes to train young beggars to be footboys. When Moriphanus sees his new family of servants, he wishes to attend the King's birthday masque. Although he is admitted, Moriphanus is the subject of much ridicule. Later, when Arcasia is in a garden with Perilla, a rich widow, Moriphanus arrives. Their conference is observed by Lucidore, who argues with Moriphanus over the widow Perilla. When Moriphanus declines to fight, Graculus upbraids Moriphanus for his refusal. Perilla rejects Moriphanus's suit, but she shows a willingness to accept Lucidore. A very slight third plot is not much more than an extended joke: Lucidore's long-sought-after mistress turns out to be a pile of gold. Then late in the play, suiting the action to the jest, he woos the rich

is a trap door), but Marplot crawls up the chimney, thinking that is Ravelin's means of escape. Meanwhile, Dona Perriera tells her duenna that she expects the Englishman, and Charles arrives. As they adjourn to the next room, Marplot falls down the chimney. Cursing him, Charles gets away by a rope ladder, but Marplot is discovered by Don Perriera, who has the house searched. A frightened Marplot gives money to Margaritta, Dona Perriera's maid, and escapes. Back on the street, Marplot sees Charles and Ravelin go into a house where Ravelin's French mistress Mademoiselle Joneton lives. Just as Marplot decides he'll knock on the door, he encounters a young gentleman, Isabinda in disguise, asking for Charles. Despite Marplot's attempt to be wily, she discovers Charles's lodgings. After she has gone, Marplot receives a letter for an Englishman, opens it, and reads that the receiver is a villain. Lopez begins to beat Marplot, but is rescued by Charles and Ravelin, leaving Mademoiselle Joneton's. They are joined by the young gentleman (Isabinda), and she gives the papers to Charles. Since Charles and Ravelin both have assignations, Marplot is frustrated because he can't follow both at once, but he decides to follow Charles in a visit to Dona Perriera, who thinks her husband is out of town. Marplot hears Lopez and Don Perriera plotting and goes to warn Charles. Not sure of the house, he pitches his rope ladder and intrudes on Ravelin and another French woman, Marton. The interruption causes Ravelin to discover Marton and Mademoiselle Joneton are sisters, but Marplot insists on Ravelin's helping Charles. At the same time, Isabinda bribes the two priests sent to confess Charles and Dona Perriera before Don Perriera and Lopez kill them. Putting on a priest's collar and gown, Isabinda and the other priest enter. Isabinda has Charles put on the clerical outfit and leave with the other priest. The priest announces to Don Perriera that there are only women in the room. Don Perriera goes to them and apologizes to his wife. In the final scene, Isabinda reveals herself to Charles who asks her forgiveness. Mademoiselle Joneton agrees to marry Ravelin, and Marplot calls for a dance. Isabinda concludes the play in a speech about regaining and keeping a husband's love.

Most commentators dismiss *Marplot* as an unsuccessful sequel: Lock points out the major problem of the play, saying it's an easy-going comedy through four acts, while act five turns into a serious melodrama. The morality of the final act clashes with the loose escapades of the rest of the play. Moreover, Marplot does not seem the same genial busybody of the previous play; he is a nuisance without any redeeming attributes. The setting in Lisbon provides a contrast with English attitudes: Lopez's jealous concern with honor makes him a meddler in Don Perriera's family. He becomes an angry Portuguese Marplot with sword in hand ready to fight rather than to live affably with his neighbors. The reconciliation of Don Perriera and his wife may succeed, but it doesn't seem convincing. It is Isabinda who gives a moral tone to the play: after she saves her husband, she forgives him. Nevertheless, she insists on a woman's patience, modesty, and meekness as ways to overcome male vice.

TEXTS: Readex Microprint. TEC Reel 476: 26.

FACSIMILE EDITION: E-CED, with introduction by R. C. Frushell (NY: Garland, 1982).

The Married Man, Elizabeth Inchbald. Based on Philippe Néricault-Destouches's *Le Philosophe marié; ou, Le Mari honteux de l'être* (1727), Inchbald's three-act adaptation of this comedy was first performed on 15 July 1789 at the Haymarket and published the same year by G. G. J. and J. Robinson. Eight performances were given its first season. Elizabeth Kemble played the role of Lady Classick and Stephen Kemble acted Mr. Tradewell Classick.

Sir John Classick, a self-proclaimed philosopher adamantly against matrimony, keeps secret his marriage to the virtuous and loving Matilda for fear of being derided by acquaintances and friends. Matilda pleads with him to make it public, for she is now courted by Lord Lovemore who believes her to be single, but Sir John will not listen. Even the threat of his rich uncle Tradewell to disinherit him, should he not accept the wife he has chosen for him, has no effect. Only his loving father, whose well-being depends on Tradewell's generosity, manages to secure an admission from Sir John. Tradewell is eventually won over by Matilda's willingness to sacrifice her own happiness in order to insure her husband's inheritance. The play ends on the admission by a chastised Sir John that he had usurped the title of philosopher. To which his father responds: "no title is more honourable than that of a Married Man" (63).

Inchbald followed closely the plot of Destouches's sentimental domestic drama, but she made substantial cuts, reducing the five-act original to three acts. She shortened the dialogues between Matilda and her jealous sister, Emily, and the battle of wits, setting the proud Emily against Dorimont, whose love she refuses on the grounds that he has no title and no fortune. Inchbald also eliminates most of the subplot involving Lord Lovemore, who, in the French original, ends up marrying the woman the uncle planned for his nephew. Thus, Inchbald's adaptation tightens up the longer work and centers it on the title character. For comical effects, she relied, as Destouches had done, on the foibles of the hero: his paralyzed vanity that renders him incapable of shaking off "the idle fear of the world" concerning his marriage, and the numerous misunderstandings that arise from it. Inchbald dropped the verse form, the characters' French names, and the lengthy original title. Beyond the altered title and the missing elegant verses lies a successful prose adaptation, perfect in length "for the short evenings and the warm weather of the Haymarket season" (*The Critical Review* 68 [August, 1789]: 157; quoted in Kinne 210).

MANUSCRIPT: Larpent 838.

TEXT: Readex Microprint.

FACSIMILE EDITION: E-CED, with an introduction by Paula R. Backscheider (NY: Garland, 1980).

MARSHALL, Jean (fl. 1766–1788). After publishing two novels (*The History of Miss Clarinda Cathcart, and Miss Fanny Renton* (1766) and *The History of Alice Montague* (1767), Marshall turned to drama with *Sir Harry Gaylove; or, Comedy in Embryo* (Edinburgh, 1772). The many problems she encountered in her unsuccessful attempts to get the play performed are described in the preface. Ultimately, she decided to publish her play by subscription. In her later years, Marshall published *A Series of Letters* in Edinburgh, 1788. Of her early or her last years, nothing appears to have been recorded. [DBAWW, DNB, FCLE]

MARTIN, Mrs. (fl. 1823). Known only for this single drama in three acts, Mrs. Martin wrote *Reparation; or, The Savoyards*, which was published in 1823 by John Nichols and Son. We have been unable to identify her first name. [Davis & Joyce]

The Martyr, Joanna Baillie. This religious drama in three acts was first published by Longman et al. in 1826. In 1836 it was reprinted in volume one of *Dramas*. Sir Alexander Johnston, Chief Justice of Ceylon, asked for permission to have *The Martyr* translated into Cingalese, "being desirous of raising the minds of the inhabitants of that island, and of eradicating their vices"(*DNB*).

Both major plots are quickly introduced. The first involves the betrothal of Cordenius Maro, heroic officer of the Imperial Guard, to Portia, daughter of the Senator Sulpicius. The second plot focuses on the persecution of the Christians and the growing popularity of the sect as they bravely assume martyrdom. These plots first intersect when the betrothal between Maro and Portia is delayed in order to punish the defiant Nazarenes. As he watches the procession of martyrs, Maro is impressed by their courage, and when another military hero, Sylvius, asks him to go to the catacombs, Maro reluctantly agrees. It is here that Maro is converted, and he hears about the recent imprisonment of Ethocles, a Grecian who has converted many to Christianity. Soon after this, Sulpicius formally offers his daughter in marriage, and although he enthusiastically responds, the Senator guesses that Maro has converted to Christianity. When Sylvius is summonsed to Nero's palace, Maro goes in his place, emphasizing that he is willing to give up his life for Ethocles's. In an unsuccessful attempt to convert Nero, Maro speaks at length about Christianity, and the soldier is condemned to public execution. Disgusted by Nero's tyrannical behavior, Orceres, a Parthian Prince, begins to listen to Maro's message. On his way to his execution, Maro is cheered by the crowd. Before being fed to the lions, however, Maro is pierced through the heart with an arrow by Orceres, who thinks Maro deserves a "death more worthy of a Roman" (76).

In her preface, Baillie admits the major problem with *The Martyr*: "I need scarcely observe to the reader that the subject of this piece is too sacred, and therefore unfit for the stage" (xvi). The didacticism is overwhelming: the long passages of religious ecstasy, containing some impressive use of extended metaphor, are too abstract and not sufficiently rooted in character or action. This is especially true when Cordenius Maro first meets with the Christians and is converted. Furthermore, the two major plots are related, but they have a jarring effect when joined: it is almost as if the plot from a romantic comedy had accidentally been inserted into a religious tragedy.

TEXTS: Readex Microprint of the 1826 edition and Readex Microprint of *Dramas* (1836) 1: 371–464.

Mary Queen of Scots, Mary Deverell. Printed for the author in 1792, this five act drama in blank verse was published by subscription. Classified as a historical tragedy, Deverell's only drama was not performed.

The action begins with several noble lords planning to force Mary to abdicate the Scottish throne in favor of her son James. When Murray the Regent reports this to her, she says they will regret this action. Later, in Glasgow, the nobles learn that Mary has escaped to Galloway where we see her after the defeat of her forces at Langside. In despair, she plans to take refuge with her cousin Elizabeth in England. Lord Herries tells Mary that since she is the presumptive heir Elizabeth will take umbrage at her coming. Mary, however, insists upon her decision. At Whitehall, Elizabeth discusses Mary's arrival with her Prime Minister Sir William Cecil, who suggests Mary be confined to Bolton Castle. Elizabeth, then, tells the Duke of Norfolk to meet with the Scottish lairds. He does so, but returns to Mary at Bolton and woos her. At Court, Elizabeth rejects the suits of Spain and France for Mary's release. When Norfolk comes to ask for Mary's hand, he is taken to the Tower. After the Archbishop of Ross reports this to Mary, he too is arrested. Walsingham recounts to Elizabeth the insurrection against her; however, the regicides have been arrested. Mary is tried for treason at Fotheringay Castle and puts up a spirited defense. Elizabeth realizes if Mary doesn't give up her crown, Elizabeth must forfeit hers: "the Protestant Religion must fall, if Mary lives" (99), and she signs Mary's death warrant. After the sentence is delivered, Mary has a final scene with her household, and in the morning she's taken to the block.

Since Deverell's text runs to 116 pages, it would be much too long for stage representation. Moreover, her characters tend to speak in lengthy periods. The strength of the drama comes from Deverell's ability to capture the crucial scenes in Mary's life and to make Mary a heroic figure.

TEXT: Readex Microprint.

Mary, the Maid of the Inn; or, The Bough of Yew, Jane M. Scott. First performed at the Sans Pareil Theatre on 27 December 1809, this two-act melodrama ran forty-three times its first season and was revived in three later seasons. Brokaw and McHugh mention that this "Gothic verse melodrama derived from Southey's poem," though Scott has "complicated Southey's plot, and her surprise revelations at the denouement softened his stark version" (*Adelphi* 9).

MANUSCRIPT: Larpent 1605.

The Massacre, Elizabeth Inchbald. Written in 1792, the play was withdrawn because its subject was thought too "disagreeable" (Boaden, I, 303). A few copies of the 1792 printing exist (one is reported to be in the Library of Congress). *The Massacre* was included in the *Memoirs of Mrs. Inchbald*, edited by James Boaden (1833). It is an adaptation from L. S. Mercier's *Jean Hennuyer, Evêque de Lisieux*, printed in 1772.

In a small town near Paris, Tricastin and his daughter-in-law await anxiously Eusèbe's return from Paris. They learn from him that a brutal massacre has just taken place. Fearing that the fury will spread, Eusèbe wants to stay and protect his family, but he reluctantly accepts his family's desire to leave for England. Before departing, however, he is arrested by his enemies, his sole crime being that he does not think as they do. But the judge, an equitable and virtuous man, refuses to condemn a peaceable citizen who has become a victim of fanaticism. Outside the court, despite Eusèbe's wife's heroic efforts to shield her children, they are slain by the mob. The tragedy ends with the judge's claim that it is necessary "to extend charity EVEN TO OUR ENEMIES," as "the bier is carried off in slow procession" with father and husband following as mourners (capitals in the original, 31).

Through a series of tableaux, the tragedy depicts the horrors perpetrated by fanaticism upon innocent victims. As a commentary on the Reign of Terror gripping France, Inchbald explains clearly in her advertisement: "The story of this play is founded upon circumstances, which have been related as *facts* [referring to the St. Bartholomew's Massacre of the Protestants in Paris, 1572]; and which the unhappy state of a neighbouring nation does but too powerfully give reason to credit" (vi). *The Massacre* is a free adaptation of Mercier's historical drama *Jean Hennuyer, Bishop of Lisieux*. The plot remains basically the same, but Inchbald eliminated all references to historical figures or events and to the Catholic-Protestant conflict of 16th-century France. The change of focus, reflected in the new title, may also be seen in the characters: the heroic bishop of Lisieux, who defends the protestants in the name of Christian charity, becomes Glandeve, the just and compassionate judge who defends virtuous citizens in the name of that same Christian charity, though he plays a lesser role. If both plays end with a procession, Mercier's is exultant and fraternal, led as it is by the victorious bishop, whereas Inchbald's is tragic as the main characters follow mournfully the bier where the slain mother and children lay.

TEXT: *Memoirs of Mrs. Inchbald*, edited by James Boaden (1833), 1: 355–80.

FACSIMILE EDITION: E-CED, with introduction by Paula R. Backscheider (NY: Garland, 1980), reprints the text in the *Memoirs*.

The Match, Joanna Baillie. This three-act comedy was published in volume three of Baillie's *Dramas* (Longman, et al., 1836). The play was not staged.

The plot involves two matches. The more important one is between two difficult people: the suspicious Sir Cameron Kunliffe and the indecisive Latitia Vane (32 years old). Of their match, the author confides: "If they are together, two people may lead an uneasy life, to be sure; but it will, in all probability, save four from being in the like condition" (377). The older couple is contrasted by an ideal, younger match: Cameron and Latitia are distrustful and calculating while Franklin and Emma (Latitia's niece) are sincere in their affection and direct in the expression of it. The only obstacle to marital bliss for the second couple is the lack of sufficient funds. The play's action is unified toward one goal: the older couple must recognize their faults before marrying. To achieve this end, Baillie has Cameron falsely accuse Franklin of asking Lawry (Latitia's nephew) to steal the key to his iron box; and she has Latitia insist that Dr. Crany, a phrenologist, examine Cameron's skull ("an organ of destruction," according to Crany [431]). Wearing oversized women's clothing as a disguise, Cameron exposes the doctor as a fraud, but the end of the play focuses, instead, on appropriate punishments for the couple. Because she cannot make her own decisions, Latitia agrees to obey Cameron's decree, which is that they should marry in the morning before eleven. Cameron is publicly chided for his distrustfulness: "You have been oftener cheated and duped by your own supposed knowledge and your distrust of mankind, than the veriest flaxen-headed simpleton in the parish" (473). After both are sufficiently humbled and agree to marry, Cameron gives Franklin the financial support that will enable Franklin and Emma to marry.

There are clever lines throughout the play, but none of the characters has much depth. This is especially true of Latitia, who is not even allowed to grow as a result of her punishment. Cameron's chastisement forces him to see the error of his ways, whereas Latitia's encourages her to be still more indecisive, in effect turning over her ability to make decisions to Brightly, a male friend of Cameron's who prescribes the punishments, and to her future husband.

TEXT: Readex Microprint of *Dramas* (1836) 3: 369–495.

Match-making; or, 'Tis a Wise Child that Knows its own Father, attributed to Marie Therese DeCamp Kemble. Genest believes Kemble to be the author of this comedy, which was first produced at CG on 24 May 1808. About the production, Genest remarks: "Match Making is attributed to Mrs. C. Kemble—it was not acted a 2d time" (8: 94). Apparently, it was never printed. A manuscript version does not appear in the Larpent Collection.

Matilda, Eleanor H—. According to *BD*, this drama, published in *The Lady's Magazine* in 1803, was translated from the French of M. Monvel, who converted Inchbald's *Simple Story* into a play. There is no known production of the play. Two tragedies (by Francklin, 1775, and Delap, 1803) share the same title.

TEXT: In *The Lady's Magazine*, 1803; this publication ran from 1770–1818, but we have been unable to examine this particular year.

The Matrimonial Trouble, Margaret Lucas Cavendish, Duchess of Newcastle. This drama in two parts was printed in her *Playes*, published by John Martyn, James Allestry, and Tho. Dicas in 1662. The title page of part one says the play is a "Comedy," whereas part two is labeled a "Come-tragedy."

The author has ten plots running simultaneously in this play, unusual even for Cavendish. The title suggests the theme central to the various mini-dramas, and most of them continue from part one through part two. The play opens with Sir Francis Inconstant leaving Mistress Forsaken, vowing not to abandon her. Later, when she hears that he is planning to marry in another country, she follows him, taking a male costume and calling herself Monsieur Disguise. She arrives just after Sir Francis's wedding to the daughter of Sir James Hearty and delivers a note that Mistress Forsaken is dead. Sir Francis is so melancholy he cannot enter into the wedding festivities and takes to his bed. Disguise is asked to stay and participate, which she does. The marriage of the Inconstants goes from bad to worse; Lady Inconstant is sick with love, but is not beloved. She even offers herself to Disguise, because she would have her husband dead. Lady Inconstant tries to poison his broth, but he has overheard this plot and forces her to drink the poisoned broth. After she is dead, he blames Disguise and they duel. Each fatally wounds the other, but before they both expire she reveals herself to him, and with mutual forgiveness they die together in the last scene.

Dramatizing less spectacular marital predicaments, "Cavendish depicts the vulnerability of women within marriage," according to Pearson: "Occasionally the women are at fault—Lady Wanton cuckolds her husband—but more often the men are to blame" (131). When Sir Henry Sage accuses his young wife of being false, Lady Chastity feels grievously wronged: "True Love never makes doubts" (462). He must ask for her forgiveness. Sir Timothy Spendall drinks, whores, and gambles his family into debt, leaving Lady Poverty and their children indigent; friends help, providing she never sees Spendall again, which suits her. Sir Edward Courtly is unfaithful to Lady Jealousie and thinks it his right to do so, but he expects her to be faithful to him. Other marriages flounder because of class differences: Lord Widower plans to marry his deceased wife's maid, until dissuaded by his daughter, Lady Sprightly, and Sir John Dotard marries his kitchen maid Briget Greasie. Unsuitable temperaments cause Sir Humphrey and Lady Disagree to argue over trifles. They are reunited, but in a banquet for their friends the pair begin throwing dishes at each other. Lady Hypocondria [sic] is constantly in fear of her health and of her husband's well being. After many of her anxieties, he asks her to be more discreet, but when he is wounded in a duel, she stifles her reaction so much that he thinks she doesn't love him. During his recovery, he is attacked by the man who wounded him in the duel; Lady Hypocondria coolly grabs the pistol and shoots the miscreant. By way of contrast, Cavendish introduces several scenes with Lady Single, who is not sure she wants to marry. Finally, no marriage is without problems: each requires the pair to work out social and sexual relations.

While Nancy Cotton calls Cavendish's plays "structurally incoherent" (46), the plays have a unity of their own. *Matrimonial Trouble*, for instance, hews to a broad theme, and by having the tales running at the same time, events in one story line juxtapose those in the previous and following tale. While the placement of the scenes—ninety in the two parts of this play—may seem capricious, they are more carefully arranged than may at first appear. Ideas are contrasted, themes are echoed, and situations paralleled. As is usual in Cavendish's plays, a good deal of commentary is supplied by servants, who often see what their masters and mistresses overlook. This lengthy drama also shows how large households with a cadre of servants might run, depending on the temperament of master and mistress: some of course run effectively, while others do not. Remedies for sicknesses are called for, details about cosmetics are discussed, and home remedies are given. As a drama of domestic activities, Cavendish's play treats problems particular to the seventeenth century, as well as the timeless problems of marital interaction.

TEXTS: Wing N868. EEB Reel 502: 11. Readex Microprint.

Matrimony; or, The Sleep Walker, attributed to Frances Abington. This unpublished comic afterpiece was prepared for her benefit at CG on 27 April 1798. Based on *Le Somnambule* (1739) by Antoine de Ferriol, Comte de Pont-de-Veyle, the play was not printed.

Kinne notes that this version owes little "to either Lady Craven or to Pont-de-Veyle. Sir Harry Somnus, who sleeps in church and elsewhere, is the only connecting link. Lady Compound [acted by Abington], who considers it bad form to be seen too often with her husband, suggests [a French earlier play] *Le Préjugé à la mode* in reverse" (214).

MANUSCRIPT: Larpent 1209, without Abington's name.

Maximian, Lady Sophia Raymond Burrell. This five-act tragedy in verse, adapted from Thomas Corneille's *Maximian* (1662), was printed in 1800 by Luke Hansard. There is no record of the tragedy having been staged.

Maximian takes place in imperial Rome, at the time of Constantine's reign. Maximian, a trusted advisor, plans the murder of the very emperor to whom he recently gave his daughter's hand, despite having previously betrothed her to her lover, Severius, who returns from his victorious conquest of Gaul and learns the fateful news. Driven by mad ambition, Maximian does not hesitate to sacrifice his daughter, Faustina, another time by accusing her of instigating a conspiracy. Through clever self-accusations and crafty manipulation of others' senses of honor, as well as through sentimental attachments, Maximian manages to remain in favor for most of the play. He is finally unmasked by the dying Severius, who has stayed faithful to his sovereign despite his profound resentment. The tragedy ends with Maximian stabbing himself, for death is preferable to not fulfilling his ambition.

Burrell's *Maximian*, translated more than a century after the publication of Corneille's *Maximian*, does not read like the original. The translation is not literal, which according to Burrell would have been "too formal," but it is a loose adaptation, despite the presence of a few verbatim renditions of short passages taken from the original. Burrell deemed it necessary to add "more bustle and variety" to the events, such as meetings of the conspirators, Severius's harangue of the rebellious crowd, or Severius's assassination. Thus, events recounted, as the seventeenth-century rules of French drama would require, are made in Burrell's version to take place on stage. This structural change severely altered the unity of

Harry, she can then show it to Belvil and embarrass him for not taking her love seriously. Even after all her coquetry, Miss Loveless demonstrates some spirit by dispatching the fortune-hunting Lord Mackgrinnon.

MANUSCRIPT: Larpent 525.

TEXT: Readex Microprint.

Minna Von Barnhelm, translated by Fanny Holcroft. This five-act comedy is translated from the German of G. E. Lessing, originally published in 1767. Holcroft's translation was published in *The Theatrical Recorder*, vol. 1, no. 10, edited by Thomas Holcroft (London: C. Mercier, 1805): 215–259. There is no record of this translation being performed.

Disbanded from the army, Major von Tellheim goes to live with his servant Justin in a small hotel, but when a paying client arrives he is turned out of his large room and placed in a smaller one. The widow of a former soldier under his command comes to the hotel to pay her husband's debt, but the Major tells the widow her husband owed him nothing, and he offers to be a second father to her son. After the widow leaves, he tears up the old soldier's note. To clear himself with the landlord, the Major offers a ring in pledge. Meanwhile, the lady who displaced the Major is none other than his former inamorata from Saxony, Baroness Minna von Barnhelm. When the landlord comes to register Minna and her maid Fanny, he shows them the ring he has received in pledge from the Major. Minna asks for the ring temporarily and demands to see the Major. When he comes, he is quite reticent: he cannot continue their relationship because he is a beggar and a cripple, stripped of his rank and injured in his honor. Later, when he is offered money by his old sergeant, Werner, the Major refuses, though Werner calls this an "ill-judged pride." Finally, the Major says if he needs money, he'll apply to Werner, who then helps Fanny by setting up a meeting between Minna and the Major. Swallowing his pride, the Major asks Werner for money to regain the ring from the landlord, for a matching ring is worn by Minna. In the meantime, Minna knows that the Major has spurned her because he is poor and she is a rich heiress, but if she were disinherited he would help her. At their meeting, she then tells the Major of her (feigned) unhappy situation, and he rallies and offers her the ring, which she refuses. Even when the Major's honor is cleared and his rank restored, she tells him: "Your wife must be rich, of unsullied reputation, not a penniless Saxon girl," and throws some of his own words back at him. Upon the arrival of Minna's uncle, however, she knows her story won't hold up, and accepts the Major.

Minna's clever manipulation of her stubborn lover forces him to see that she loves him for himself and not for worldly possessions. Even with a little deception, Minna demonstrates a strong spirit to achieve what she wants. Still, the Major's pride deserves to be humbled. He is clearly a good man who has the allegiance of his former soldiers, but his concern for his honor seems excessive. Minna, of course, is able to see through these concerns and to turn the tables on him. In conversations with her maid Fanny, Minna also shows herself to be understanding as well as witty.

TEXT: Readex Microprint.

The Minstrel; or, The Heir of Arundel, Jane West. This five-act tragedy was printed in her *Poems and Plays*, vol. 4 (London: T. N. Longman and O. Rees, 1805). It was not staged.

At Arundel Castle, a minstrel has appeared, the only survivor of a ship wreck. Alicia, the daughter of Rodolph, is told by Father Anselm that her father may have done evil deeds to win the castle and the earldom. Rodolph's greatest enemy appears to be de Courcy, and he kidnaps Matilda de Courcy and brings her to the castle. Trying to comfort Matilda, Alicia tells her about the minstrel. When he comes and sings, Matilda puts on her veil, but she faints at the words of the song. As she's being carried out, the veil comes off and the minstrel cries "Matilda, *my* Matilda." The minstrel then tells Alicia that he is Fitzalan and gives her a ring to take to Matilda. Meanwhile, Rodolph is carousing with his knights, but he has Matilda brought to him privately. His intent is to test her with the jewels he took from the de Courcy castle; she refuses them, but when he is about to throw a lock of braided hair into the fire she objects, saying it is from her dead sister. He wants to marry her to consolidate his false claim with her family's actual right to Arundel Castle, but she refuses. When Father Anselm speaks to the minstrel in prison, Fitzalan says he is actually Edmund, the rightful heir of Arundel. In the final scene, Rodolph stabs at a woman he thinks is Matilda, but it is his own daughter, Alicia, whom he kills. Edmund and his friends capture Rodolph, prevent him from committing suicide, and send him to Father Anselm. Edmund finally rules as the rightful heir of Arundel.

West, in her last published play, dramatizes events in a medieval world where there are clear distinctions between good and evil. From the action emerges the rightful heir of Arundel who overcomes the usurping Earl, Rodolph, whose generous daughter turns out to be the victim of her father's foul schemes. Even Rodolph's retainers will not fight for him once he is proved to be a usurper. Matilda, who spends most of the play imprisoned in the castle, shows a defiance in rejecting Rodolph's offer of marriage. But the world West has recreated is one of feudal quarrels, marriage for political advantage, and heavy-handed knights—in short, a male-dominated world where women have little influence.

TEXT: Not in Readex Microprint. We read the copy at the Newberry Library, Chicago, IL.

MINTON, Anne (b. 1785). She may have been the daughter of a Mr. Minton who had a brief appearance at the HAY in 1797, but she herself performed at Sadler's Wells in the summer season of 1795. Minton later acted in the summer season of 1800 at Birmingham, where she presumably met and married Charles Justin Macartney. In the next decade she acted at various venues, including the Royal Circus (1804, 1807, 1808), Sadler's Wells (1804–05 season), and the Sans Pareil Theatre (1807–08 season).

Minton's adaptation of Eliza Haywood's 1723 play, *The Comedy of A Wife to be Lett; or, The Miser Cured . . . Compressed into Two Acts*, may have been intended for a benefit performance, though we can find no evidence that it was staged; Genest records no performance. A. Seale printed Minton's shortened version in 1802. [BDAA]

Miss Scott's Entertainment, Jane M. Scott. This title refers to a collection of three plays, produced forty times at the Sans Pareil Theatre from 17 November 1806 until 10 January 1807. Apparently the scripts for these three entertainments—*The Rout*, *Tempest Terrific* and *The Vision in the Holy Land; or, Geoffrey of Bouillon's Dream*—have been lost. None is listed in the Larpent Collection under this title, nor under the individual play titles.

MITFORD, Mary Russell (1787–1855). Although born into an affluent family, Mitford spent much of her life in impecunious circumstances owing to her father's gambling. She was educated at home until she won a lottery allowing her to attend a Chelsea school for "ladies," where she gained a knowledge of French, Italian, and Latin. Mitford, who remained single all her life, first published poetry, three volumes from 1810 to 1813. Nearly destitute by 1820, her family moved near Reading, to Three Mile Cross, which became the basis of her series of prose pieces *Our Village* (five volumes published from 1824 to 1832).

To save her family from poverty, Mitford turned to historical drama. Her first tragedy, *Julian*, was produced in 1823 with William Charles Macready in the title role. Another tragedy, *Foscari*, performed to large audiences in 1826. Mitford's *Dramatic Scenes* were published in 1827 without performance. One of her most popular tragedies, *Rienzi*, was played thirty-four times in the 1828–29 season. *Charles I* was produced in 1834, followed by an opera, *Sadak and Kalasrade; or, The Waters of Oblivion*, in 1835. Her next tragedy, *Inez de Castro*, appeared in 1841. She published in 1854 her collected *Dramatic Works*, which included two dramas not performed: *Otto of Wittelsbach* and *Gaston de Blondville*.

Aside from her dramatic efforts, Mitford continued to write rural tales in the vein of *Our Village*, which she described as "not one connected story, but a series of sketches of country manners, scenery, and character, with some story intermixed, and connected by unity of locality and of purpose"; these later works included *Belford Regis* (1834), *Country Stories* (1837), and *Atherton* (1854). To make ends meet, she undertook hackwork to support her family. Her own failing health and her father's death in 1842 reduced her literary efforts, though she continued to correspond with Elizabeth Barrett (Browning) and other important literary figures. Further financial problems obliged Mitford to move to Shallowfield, also near Reading, late in life; in this quiet village she died in 1855.

[DNB, EBWW, FCLE, NCBEL (3: 748–49), Nicoll, OCEL. Biography by V. Watson, 1949.]

Modern Sentiment. See **The Sons of Erin; or, Modern Sentiment**.

A Mogul Tale; or, The Descent of the Balloon. Elizabeth Inchbald. Her first play, a two-act farce, began at the HAY on 6 July 1784 and was acted ten times its initial season. The manager, George Colman, the elder, paid Inchbald 100 guineas for the use of the farce, in which Inchbald took the role of Irene. The popular farce played in almost every season until the end of the century. An unauthorized printing "for the booksellers, 1788" appeared in Dublin that year; it was the first publication of the play.

Dr. Pedant has taken Fanny and Johnny Atkins—cobblers from Wapping—for a balloon ride, and as the play opens they drop into the Mogul's seraglio. The eunuchs take them to see the Mogul, who has compassion on them, but he also wants to observe how they act in this new location. He has the doctor seized and threatened with execution; Fanny is placed in the harem; and Johnny is plied with liquor and tempted by the women of the seraglio. After several women of the seraglio, including Fanny, parade before Johnny, he chooses Fanny. Then they undergo a mock trial and are threatened with execution, but the compassionate Mogul sets them free. As they leave, the doctor says he will explain this generosity of conduct in the Mogul's Tale that he intends to publish, giving an account of their travel by air balloon.

Much of the humor arises from the contrast between England and the near-eastern country of the Mogul. The Doctor has hired Fanny and Johnny to fly in his balloon by offering them £5, and the language of each shows a class difference. Female characters in the farce are under the control of the men: the Mogul and his eunuchs rule the women of the harem, and Fanny lets Johnny take charge of situations. Moreover, Fanny seems frightened about everything in this strange land.

MANUSCRIPT: Larpent 661.

TEXTS: Readex Microprint (London: F. Powell, 1796). TEC Reel 504: 2 (1788 Dublin edition).

FACSIMILE EDITION: E-CED: (Dublin: Booksellers, 1788), with introduction by Paula R. Backscheider (NY: Garland, 1980).

MONTAGU, Elizabeth Robinson (1720–1800). The eldest daughter of prosperous parents, Elizabeth was schooled with her sister Sarah Scott (later a well-known novelist) in Cambridge. Dr. Conyers Middleton, their step-grandfather, supervised an education devoted to wide reading in English, French, and classical literature. At the age of 22, Elizabeth married Edward Montagu, who was twenty-eight years older. The couple got on well together: she visited his various estates and collieries with him, and at home they entertained literary and intellectual discussion with a wide circle of friends.

Besides her extensive correspondence, Elizabeth Montagu contributed (anonymously) three dialogues to Lord Lyttelton's *Dialogues of the Dead* (1760) and prepared an essay in defense of Shakespeare, responding to Voltaire's disparagement of the Bard (1769). She cared for her husband through a long illness before his death in 1775. Elizabeth not only inherited a good deal, but she continued to manage her husband's various property holdings. In 1781, she had Montagu house built on Portman Square with decorations by Angelica Kauffman. She asked "Capability" Brown to improve the grounds at her

Sandleford estate in Berkshire. Still, she may have had time to do some further literary work.

It is Kinne's assertion—although he provides no evidence and no other commentator supports the claim—that Montagu may have translated Diderot's *Le Père de Famille*, published anonymously in 1781. She did know French well, and she certainly had a strong dramatic judgment to render a convincing version of Diderot's sentimental comedy. Because she had many close female friends and correspondents, Montagu's nephew published four volumes of her witty and frank letters after her death in 1800 (1809, 1813). [DBAWW, EBWW, FCLE]

MONTAGU, Lady Mary Pierpont Wortley (1689–1762). Lady Mary had a great interest in the drama: she attended rehearsals of Addison's *Cato* (1713) before its first performance and made suggestions to the playwright, which were incorporated into the text. Her nephew, Henry Fielding, came to her with his first play, *Love in Several Masques* (produced 1728), and again she made recommendations that were accepted. Her own work for the theatre is a translation and adaptation of a Marivaux comedy that had been produced by a French Company at the Haymarket in 1734. *Simplicity: A Comedy* adapts Marivaux's *Le Jeu de l'Amour et du Hazard; ou, Maître et Valet* for the English stage, though this version was never produced. A modern text of the play has been edited by R. Halsband & I. Grundy (Oxford: Clarendon, 1977), from Harrowby ms. 80.160–187 at Sandon Hall, Stafford. [BNA, DBAWW, DNB, EBWW, FCLE, Lonsdale, OCEL. Biography by R. Halsband, 1957. Letters, ed R. Halsband, 1965–66.]

MORE, Hannah (1745–1833). The fourth of five daughters to a schoolmaster father, More grew up near Bristol where she assisted her sisters in running a successful school. Gifted in languages, she learned Latin, French, Italian, and Spanish. A broken engagement to a local landowner caused More to go to London in 1773: her family connections and her intelligent conversation moved her into a society that included David Garrick and his wife. Having begun a theatrical interest in Bristol, she reached a wider audience in London.

It is unlikely that More's first drama, *The Search after Happiness*, subtitled "A Pastoral Drama for Young Ladies," was staged professionally, but it was printed at Bristol, 1773, and in London by 1778, if not before. A later version published in 1796 has some alterations. Her next play, a classical tragedy, *The Inflexible Captive*, gained recognition first as a closet drama, published in Bristol in 1774. It was then produced the following year in Exeter and Bath. The first London production was licensed to be played at DL on 2 May 1775, but it was never performed, owing to her misgivings about its dramatic qualities. Not deterred, however, More wished to prove herself to Garrick and worked very hard on her new drama *Percy*, which became a hit in the 1777–78 season, being acted nineteen times. In addition, the publication of *Percy* brought More £150: 4,000 copies had been sold by March 1778. *The Fatal Falsehood*, More's final play to be performed professionally, was produced in 1779. After Garrick's death, More seemed to lose interest in drama, though she did publish several biblical plays in *Sacred Dramas*, 1782. Intended for reading in schools, the collection includes *Belshazzar*, *Daniel*, *David and Goliath*, and *Moses in the Bulrushes*. Two additional dramas, *Reflections of King Hezekiah in His Sickness* and *Village Politics*, were included in her *Works* of 1801, where she denounced attending plays as inappropriate entertainment.

Having given up the theatre, More turned to poetry and polemic for much of the rest of her life. She contributed works to the abolitionist cause, censured English reform in the face of the French Revolution, and attacked the works of Thomas Paine and Mary Wollstonecraft. More's unquestioning adherence to authority made her the darling of conservatives and the despised of radicals. She continued, too, with more educational materials in her series of *Cheap Repository Tracts*. Some of these *Tracts* use some dramatic dialogues, especially between two people with opposite points of view, such as portions of "Mr. Fantom," "The History of Mr. Bragwell," "Parley the Painter," and "The Two Shoemakers." Her only novel, *Coelebs in Search of a Wife* (1809), describes the attributes she believed requisite in an ideal wife. In her eightieth year, she assembled selections from her earlier work in *The Spirit of Prayer* (1825). Having made more than £30,000 on her writings, More died at Clifton in 1833.

Writing in EBWW, Mary Ferguson Pharr points out how More's living in two eras caused a schism in her audience: "Toward the close of her life she was a celebrated anachronism, refusing to accept the fundamental social and philosophical changes that accompanied Romanticism. To the last she defended what, in effect, was already gone" (335). Once More became active in the Sunday school movement, she rejected dramatic performances and roundly condemned the theatre. [*BD*, BNA, DBAWW, EBWW, FCLE, Lonsdale, NCBEL (2: 1598–99), OCEL. Biographies by M. A. Hopkins, 1947, and by M. G. Jones, 1952. C. L. Shaver establishes 10 May 1773 as the publication date of *The Search after Happiness* in *MLN* 62 (1947): 343.]

More Ways Than One, Hannah Cowley. This five-act comedy, originally titled *New Ways to Catch Hearts*, was first produced at CG on 6 December 1783 and published the following year by T. Evans. Cowley dedicated the play to her husband, who had recently departed for India. Although the play had fifteen performances in its first season, only limited revivals occurred in London, 1789 (chosen by Anne Brunton for her benefit night—*LS*), and in Bath, 1784 and 1812 (Genest).

Two greedy old men are the blocking figures of the comedy: Evergreen wishes to marry—for her dowry—Arabella Melville, a country girl who is the ward of Doctor Feelove. Miss Archer, Evergreen's own worldly ward, banters him about his May-December marriage, but he tells her he will keep Arabella locked up (shades of *The Country Wife*), which Miss Archer will of course do her best to subvert. Feelove, an incompetent society doctor, desires the marriage to give Evergreen as small a dowry as possible while taking the largest part for himself. Two young men, Bellair and Carlton, aspire to marry Arabella and Miss Archer. Their methods of courting the young women suggest the title: Bellair feigns sickness so that Arabella will nurse him back to health and thereby fall in love; Carlton, in another way, feigns a nonchalance toward Miss Archer, because other men who have admired her in the past have been unsuccessful. One of the more comic situations occurs when Bellair takes Arabella away from Dr. Feelove's house and leaves her in the protection of Evergreen. Several caricatures provide some humor: the language of David, Evergreen's Welsh servant, causes others confusion; Sir Marvel Mushroom, a newly minted knight, tries to act learned, but he seems always to get his facts hopelessly muddled. Miss Archer assists Arabella in escaping and in helping her marry Bellair. She also reconciles with Carlton and agrees to marry him. While Evergreen and Feelove quarrel over their bungling, Miss Archer tries to bring harmony in her final speech.

The women in this comedy are not treated especially well by Cowley: Miss Archer appears sprightly when she first appears, but becomes more passive as Carlton treats her indifferently. Gagen remarks that in the end "one cannot help feeling that Miss Archer deserves better" (DLB 89: 97). While Arabella exhibits honest country feelings—speaking her mind to Evergreen, for instance—she becomes the object of the old men's wrangle over her money, not an inconsiderable £30,000 a year. By becoming an object over which men quarrel, Arabella is marginalized as a person. A minor character, Miss Juvenile cannot spell correctly and must have a man correct her spelling and put her poetry in the newspaper for her.

Link points out that while "satire on medical quackery and avarice abounds, . . . the play lacks the wit and charm of Cowley at her best" (xxxiii–xxxiv). In Cowley's 1813 *Works*, Feelove becomes Barkwell and his servant's name is changed to Pound. Evergreen's age is sixty-five; it's sixty in the 1784 printing. Although the plot in the 1813 version remains the same, Cowley made a number of minor changes in the dialogue, cutting some and adding to others. Several stage directions are added to the reading text of 1813.

MANUSCRIPT: Larpent 640.

TEXTS: Readex Microprint of 1784 Dublin edition. TEC Reels 590: 18 (1784 London); 4827: 6 (1784 Dublin).

FACSIMILE EDITION: E-CED, of the 1784 London edition, with introduction by F. Link (NY: Garland, 1982).

MORGAN, Lady. See Sydeny **OWENSON**.

Moses in the Bulrushes, Hannah More. Published in her *Sacred Dramas* in 1782 by T. Cadell, this play is based on the biblical text in Exodus (2:1–10. KJV). Not intended for the professional stage, the play was meant for the improvement of young ladies. Nevertheless, Tate Wilkinson mentions in *The Wandering Patentee* that two of Hannah More's dramas were altered and presented at Doncaster (195–96). On 12 October 1793, Wilkinson's company performed these adaptations—*Daniel in the Lion's Den* following *Moses in the Bull Rushes*. These sacred dramas were followed by more traditional fare—Frances Brooke's *Rosina* and Henry Fielding's *The Mock Doctor* (*The Yorkshire Stage, 1766–1803*, ed. Linda Fitzsimmons and Arthur W. McDonald, [Metuchen, NJ: Scarecrow, 1989: 710]).

Pharaoh, the King of Egypt, has decreed that male children of Hebrew mothers must be put to death. Jochebed fearing for her newborn child tells her daughter Miriam that she has built an ark and plans to put the child in the Nile to save him. Although Miriam is apprehensive, Jochebed has put her faith in God, "whose promise never yet has failed." Miriam agrees to take the ark to the riverside and wait at a distance. Having put the ark in the river, Miriam sings a psalm, but she withdraws when some women comes. The Egyptian Princess plans to rest on the bank with her attendant Melita. Seeing a "chest" at the edge of the river, the Princess sends Melita, who investigates and reports there is a child in the vessel. The Princess wants a Hebrew woman to attend the baby and finds Miriam nearby. Miriam suggests the baby's mother care for the child. The Princess decides to have the child raised as her son; he shall be trained by Egyptian sages; and she will name him Moses because she has "drawn him from the perilous flood." When Jochebed goes to the river and finds the baby gone, Miriam comes with the news that he is alive, saved by the Princess, who wishes Jochebed to care for the child. Jochebed rejoices that she may raise him with virtue, and both praise God for His deliverance of the child.

Based on only a few verses of biblical text, the play develops the strength of a mother dealing with a threat to her child. In More's play, we see Jochebed's personal commitment and trust in God, not detailed in the scriptures. The poetry shows More's knowledge of the scriptures, as she uses other parts of the Bible to support her poetic lines.

TEXTS: Readex Microprint; *The Gymnasium of the Imagination: A Collection of Children's Plays in English, 1780–1860*, introduced and edited by Jonathan Levy (Westport, CT: Greenwood, 1992): 55–75.

Mother White Cap; or, Hey up the Chimney, Jane M. Scott. This comic pantomime with music by James Sanderson was first performed at the Sans Pareil Theatre on 27 February 1809 and ran sixty-four nights. Harlequin, Columbine, and Pantaloon encounter Mother White Cap in this pantomime. No plot or plan for the staging has survived.

Mrs. Doggrell in Her Altitudes; or, Strange Effects of a West Indian Ramble, Sarah Cheney Gardner. This one-act prelude was produced at the Haymarket Theatre on 22 April 1795; the piece may have been written as early as 1782 (Smith & Lawhon 168). The play was not printed and remains only in manuscript.

Mrs. Doggrell, like the playwright, has recently returned from the West Indies and is obsessed with bizarre theatrical notions. Freeman, a friend from former times, visits her "in her altitudes," where she dreams of her own success "in the celestial flame of inspiration." In her ravings, however, Mrs. Doggrell mentions her gratitude to the theatrical public. Freeman questions her about her plans and is dismayed to learn that she wants to dispense

TEXT: Readex Microprint of the Dublin edition, 1798.

Nature's Three Daughters: Beauty, Love, and Wit, Margaret Lucas Cavendish, Duchess of Newcastle. A drama in two parts, printed in her *Playes*, published by John Martyn, James Allestry, and Tho. Dicas in 1662, but not produced.

While the destiny of the three daughters happens to be the central plot in the two continuous parts of the play, Cavendish includes other story lines for contrast. For instance, the Esperances are a married couple who argue over petty matters (the clothes she wears), but go on to more serious controversies (jealousy and inconstancy). The other plot lines relate to the lives of the three daughters: for example, Phantasie is in love with Mademoiselle Bon until he sees Nature's beautiful daughter, La Belle. He curses his situation because his love for La Belle is not returned, while he can only pity Mademoiselle Bon. Later, he picks a fight and duels Heroick over La Belle, even though Heroick has never seen her. Almost fatally wounded, Phantasie is nursed back to health by Mademoiselle Bon, who remains constant; he finally offers her marriage. One daughter, Amor, immediately loves Nobilissimo and going against custom tells him so. He responds positively and lives up to his name by acting nobly, curtailing jealousies, and allaying fears. Over the course of the play, he demonstrates generosity, as well as an abiding and sensible love for Amor. Late in the play, Nobilissimo introduces his brother, Heroick, to La Belle, and they agree to marry. The third daughter, Grand Esprit, believes marriage is the "tomb of wit," and she chooses to lead a single life. Grand Esprit lectures to large public audiences about broad issues that affect both women and men. Her first discourse treats the subject of an Almighty Being, and over the two parts of the play she examines love, vice, beauty, and finally, when her two sisters marry, gives a discourse on matrimonial love to the bridal guests.

Courtship, marriage, and nonmarriage keep coming up in the two parts of the play, and Cavendish continually raises questions about these topics. What are the expectations of those who plan to marry (the daughters and their suitors)? What causes problems for those already married (the Esperances)? How does one deal with unrequited love (Phantasie and Mademoiselle Bon)? These questions often overlap in the various plot lines. And the chorus of commentators on these affairs (Spightful, Malicious, and Detractor) have a corrective voice in Tell-truth. It is curious that in a play focussing on the daughters, the mother (Nature) never appears to give direction or advice. The drama, finally, presents issues that readers versed in modern psychology should find challenging.

TEXTS: Wing N868. EEB Reel 502: 11. Readex Microprint.

Necromancer; or, The Golden Key, Jane M. Scott. This musical pantomime opened at the Sans Pareil Theatre on 11 December 1809 with music by James Sanderson. The popular piece ran eighty-four nights during its first season and was revived the following year. No plan for staging this pantomime now exists.

Neither's the Man, Margaret Holford. This five-act comedy was licensed by the Lord Chamberlain on 3 November 1798. It was produced at Chester probably later in 1798 and printed in Chester by W. Minshull, and in London for G. Sael, both dated 1799.

Sir Charles Mortimer confesses that he has fallen in love with Miss Emma Mansfield, whose Guardian has requested that she choose between two eligible bachelors that he has selected, Lord Filligree and Mordecai. Since Charles misrepresented himself as a poor soldier when he earlier made Miss Mansfield's acquaintance, he must continue to appear as such despite his recent new title and large estate. In a related subplot, Miss Maria Hastings comes to Miss Mansfield to complain of her treatment by Widow Freelove. Desperately in need of assistance after her uncle's sudden death, Maria is taken advantage of by Widow Freelove, who was in league with a young gentleman—named Charles Mortimer—who wished to seduce her. An outraged Miss Mansfield arranges an appointment between

Sir Charles Mortimer and Miss Hastings, only to discover that the young woman was mistreated by a distant cousin of Sir Charles. Although it is clear earlier that Miss Mansfield will marry Sir Charles, the remainder of the plot focuses on her torment of the other two suitors and her punishment of Maria Hastings's abusers. In a not particularly amusing scene, Miss Mansfield disguises herself as a fortune teller and gains information from Mordecai and Filligree that she uses against them when rejecting their suits. More effective is the ironic manner in which Miss Mansfield responds to Sir Charles's attentions, signaling her matrimonial decision. The strongest scene occurs at the end of the play when both Widow Freelove and Charles Mortimer (the poor cousin) are publicly humiliated. Miss Hastings's future is ensured when her beloved Mr. Piercy arrives, reporting that the will of her late uncle has been finally discovered and she is his sole heir.

Miss Mansfield aggressively pursues the groom of her choice, even though she believes until the end of the play that he is a poor soldier. Furthermore, by herself she engineers the exposure of two people who have tried to take advantage of a financially dependent woman's virtue. Less impressive are the racial jokes about the suitor Mordecai's cheapness (16, 53), his litigiousness (75), his foreign accent, and his swarthy complexion (25). Miss Mansfield shares the general prejudice against him which is based entirely on racial stereotyping: for example, when teasing her uncle, Miss Mansfield says (using his accent) that "to prove myself a proper helpmate for my dear little Mordecai, I did not neglect to exshact mosht exhorbitant interesht for my monish" (60). Although Jewish characters are often treated negatively in the plays we have read, Holford's characterization of Mordecai—he given only one name—is especially disturbing.

MANUSCRIPT: Larpent 1231. Readex microprint of manuscript.

TEXT: Readex Microprint of 1799 text printed for G. Sael.

The New Peerage; or, Our Eyes May Deceive Us, Harriet Lee. This five-act comedy opened at DL on 10 November 1787 and ran nine nights, but it was not revived. G. G. J. and J. Robinson printed the text the same year. The play is dedicated to Thomas King who took the role of Mr. Vandercrab.

Returning from their travels abroad, Charles Vandercrab and Lord Melville decide to change places. They believe they can accomplish this because Melville is to stay with a guardian he has never met, and Charles has been raised in Holland the last fourteen years, and he thinks his father will not know him. This exchange will give Charles a title with which to woo Lady Charlotte Courtley, and Melville will be in the same house with Miss Harley, his inamorata. Within twenty-four hours of Melville's arrival at his supposed father's, the wealthy merchant Vandercrab becomes disgusted that his supposed son acts like a fashionable dandy. Charles, disguised as Lord Melville, passes himself off without difficulty on his supposed guardian, Sir John Lovelace, described as a "beau and virtuoso . . . of threescore" (3). Trying to pass himself off to Lady Charlotte, however, Charles is rebuffed because she realizes who he really is. When one of Charles's friends from Holland arrives, he makes it known to Vandercrab that Lord Melville is not his son, and Melville says he will make his room a prison, giving Charles time with Lady Charlotte. Miss Harley offers to help Melville escape; when he says he will only leave with her, she is offended and goes to Lady Charlotte for protection. Instead of Lady Charlotte, however, she meets Sir John who professes love for her. After he steps out, Charles enters and says he will take her to Lady Charlotte, who tells Miss Harley of the exchange Charles and Melville have made. In the final scene, the complications are unraveled: Vandercrab is reunited with his son, and Lady Charlotte agrees to marry Charles because she has tested him enough. Miss Harley accepts Lord Melville.

Most of the early complaints about the play by *BD* and Genest focus on the improbabilities of the plot, yet both comment on its lively dialogue. Part of this sprightly conversation is given to Vandercrab, the merchant banker, but Lady Charlotte has a number of clever thor to receive a benefit night. The play, now evidently lost, was never printed.

Nobody, Mary Darby Robinson. This two-act farce was first performed at DL on 29 November 1794. It lasted but three nights and was not printed. DBAA notes the play satirized "fashionable female gamesters" (13: 37). A clack, made up of the women so derided, organized to condemn the play.

MANUSCRIPT: Larpent 1046.

NOOTH, Charlotte (fl. 1807–16). Described as the daughter of a successful London surgeon, Nooth wrote one five-act verse drama, *Clara; or, The Nuns of Charity*, printed in her *Original Poems, and a Play*, published by Longman, Hurst, Rees, Orme, and Brown, 1815. There is no indication that the play was staged. The following year, she completed a novel, *Eglantine, or The Family Fortescue*, praised in FCLE for its domestic humor and social satire. Other details of her life are wanting. [FCLE, Stratman #4724]

The Northern Heiress; or, The Humours of York, Mary Davys. This five-act comedy premiered at LIF on 27 April 1716 and ran for three nights. Later the same year, in the preface published with the play by A. Bettesworth, J. Browne, and W. Mears, Davys comments on some slight disturbances in the audience on the first night.

The action centers on two couples—the heiress Isabella and Gamont, whose sister Louisa is courted by Welby. But "the humours of York," from the subtitle, emerge from a variety of rural characters and customs. Staying in York with her aunt Lady Ample, Isabella, with the assistance of her maid Liddy, pretends to have lost her fortune in order to test the sincerity of Gamont. Perhaps the most rollicking of the humours characters is Lady Greasy, whose daughter Dolly receives the attentions of Captain Tinsel, a half-pay officer, whom she finally marries. As the widow of a tallow chandler, Lady Greasy runs a business and tries to run the lives of those with whom she has contact. Other stock characters involved in the Yorkshire life of the play are Sir Loobily Joddrel (a drunken horseman), Lady Swish (a brewer's wife), Lady Cordivant (a glover's wife), Sir Jeffrey Heavey (a country knight), and Bareface (a fop). As the couples come together in the last act, Bareface is tricked into marrying Isabella's maid Liddy, and Lady Greasy agrees to accept Liddy's new spouse Bareface into the tallow business.

The economics of the play interest Pearson because many of the women have some financial stability and are not dependent on men for money. Cotton underscores the domesticity and the "country realism" that emerges from the text. J. H. Smith finds Isabella assuming the role of the "difficult lady" when she reports that her fortune is lost, and Loftis (*Comedy and Society from Congreve to Fielding*) briefly mentions the humorous portrayals of rustic customs and character types. W. H. McBurney mentions Davys's references from earlier playwrights—Congreve, Etherege, and Farquhar (*PMLA* 74 [1959]: 348–55). In addition, we note the linguistic variations in the characters, their use and misuse of language.

TEXT: Readex Microprint.

CRITICAL EDITION: Text from *Works* (1725), edited with introduction by Donald H. Stefanson, Diss., U of Iowa, 1971.

Nourjahad, the Margravine of Anspach, formerly Baroness Elizabeth Berkeley Craven. This drama was produced privately in 1803 at Brandenburgh House. The idea for the play was drawn from Frances Sheridan's oriental tale, *The History of the Nourjahad* (1767). The play was not performed publicly nor was it printed.

-O-

The Oaks; or, The Beauties of Canterbury, Mrs. Burgess. This five-act comedy with a number of songs is thought to have been produced in Canterbury in 1779. It was printed there in 1780 by Simmons and Kirkby, but the play never reached the London stage. Although Genest calls this "an indifferent comedy" (10: 193), he remarks that Issac Pocock borrowed the character of Faddle from Burgess's play to use in his *For England Ho!* (acted 15 December 1813 at CG).

When Colonel Bloom arrives in Canterbury, he asks his landlord about the city, and he is told that, aside from the "old-fashioned cathedral," there is a "genteel walk" called the Oaks, "frequented by ladies in a morning" (1–2). Because the landlord also points out that fine women may be among the beauties of Canterbury, Bloom wishes to find out for himself. Bloom meets his old friend Brown, who informs him about Isabella: she escaped a forced marriage overseas, but Brown does not know when she will return to England. Unknown to them, she has in fact just arrived at Canterbury, but she is destitute, hoping for the assistance of Providence. Meanwhile, Misses Worden and Sprightly have seen the Colonel walking in the Oaks with a Mr. Johnson, and they have set their caps for the men, who are equally interested in them. Miss Worden, however, has an old aunt, also Miss Worden, who rules the house where the young Miss Worden lives with her father, and the young Miss Worden is not aware that her fortune provides a living for her father and her aunt. The Wordens and Miss Sprightly go to an assembly where the young women have the opportunity to dance with their beaus. But the next day as Bloom visits Miss Worden, the elder Miss Worden enters and, to avoid suspicion, Miss Worden tells her aunt Bloom is asking her help to woo the aunt. The confusion of the Miss Wordens continues until Mr. Worden signs a paper permitting "Miss Worden" to marry Colonel Bloom. The Colonel uses the permission to marry the young Miss Worden; he also finds that Isabella has been employed as a lady's maid, so he is able to bring her and Brown together. Johnson marries Miss Sprightly, and the self-deceived aunt leaves in a huff, having given Miss Worden back her fortune.

The younger Miss Worden knows she wants to marry Bloom, but she tests him by shifting him to her aunt to see how he will handle the change. In the process, Bloom must act a ballad singer and a fortune teller to arrange for Miss Worden to retrieve her fortune. Although the aunt deceives herself about Bloom, she is culpable because she has usurped her niece's fortune. Another dupe is Faddle, a relation of the Wordens, who thinks he is marrying a Countess, but she turns out to be the former French governess to Bloom's sister and only marries Faddle for a settlement. While a number of details and transitions are unclear in Burgess's comedy, she must be commended for an impressive first play.

TEXT: Readex Microprint.

O'BRIEN, Mary (fl. 1785–90). An Irish writer who spent some time in London, O'Brien wrote two plays: a comic opera entitled *The Temple of Virtue*, undated, and a comedy in five acts, *The Fallen Patriot*, printed by William Gilbert, Dublin, 1790. *The Temple of Virtue* exists in the British Library manuscript collection (Cat. #91 of mss.), according to R. W. Babcock, *PMLA* 52 (1937): 907–08. O'Brien's comic vein extended to poetry in her *The Pious Incendiaries, or Fanaticism Display'd* (1785) and *The Political Monitor, or The Regent's Friend* (1790). [DBAWW, FCLE, Nicoll]

The Ode Rejected, Ann Yearsley. According to *BD* (2: 282), this comedy was advertised but not printed. There is no known text.

Old City Manners, Charlotte Ramsey Lennox. Based on the earlier comedy, *Eastward Ho* (1605) by Jonson, Chapman, and Marston, Lennox's adaptation was first produced at DL on 9 November 1775; there were seven performances that season. Publication by T. Beckett took place the same year.

Touchstone, a goldsmith, has two apprentices—Quicksilver and Golding—who are the opposite of each other: Quicksilver likes to act the beau, whereas Golding works hard and learns his craft. Touchstone's daughters share similar traits to the young men: Gertrude loves fashion and desperately wants to marry a nobleman, whereas Mildred embraces her father's recommendation and marries Golding. Quicksilver has arranged for Gertrude to marry

Arne, about half of them collected in *The Most Celebrated Aires in The Opera of Tom Thumb* (printed by Benjamin Cooke, [1733]). The theatre revolt caused DL to commission a new set of airs written by J. F. Lampe (now lost). This version was performed with some of the original cast (7 November 1733) to counter the rebels who were performing with Arne's music at HAY. The DL version ran only three nights.

When Tom Thumb returns from war, he brings a captive giant, the "fair Glumdalca," and in recompense for his service the King bestows his daughter, the Princess Huncamunca. The Queen, enamored of Tom, objects to the match, causing a quarrel between the King and Queen. To complicate matters, Lord Grizzle, a courtier, is in love with Huncamunca; to take revenge on Tom, Grizzle gets Huncamunca to agree to marry him privately. While he goes for a license, Tom waits on the Princess, who tells him she is promised to another. Glumdalca enters at this crisis and the two rivals argue, but Tom gives his preference for Huncamunca. As Glumdalca leaves full of fury, the King throws himself in her way as a lover. Tom marries Huncamunca, and when Grizzle returns she says she will marry him too. Meanwhile, the ghost of Gaffer Thumb appears to Arthur, who foretold Grizzle's rebellion, and the kingdom finds he has brought a force against them. As Tom marches to defend the kingdom, Merlin tells him of his begetting. The armies fight, and Grizzle slays Glumdalca before he is slain by Tom. As the King rejoices, a messenger brings word that Tom has been devoured by a huge red cow, causing much killing to follow. But the scene of destruction is transformed by Merlin's magic, and Tom is restored, just as all the others are returned to life. Tom rejoins Huncamunca, and Grizzle offers marriage to Glumdalca.

The text is mostly Fielding's clever burlesque on heroic tragedy, but Haywood and Hatchet add a revised ending similar to *The Beggar's Opera*. Most of the play's parody is a response to tragic excess and Italian opera. Tom's song (Air 10), for example, begins "I'll hug, I'll eat her up with love" (19). The contrast of physical stature of the small male hero with the "giantesses" adds to the humor of the piece.

TEXT: Readex Microprint.

FACSIMILE EDITION: E-CED, with introduction by V. Rudolph (NY: Garland, 1983), reprints the text (London: William Rayner, 1733) and the music, *The Most Celebrated Aires in The Opera of Tom Thumb* (London: Benjamin Cooke, [1733]), which is in an appendix.

OPIE, Amelia Alderson (1769–1853). Better known as a novelist, Opie, in one of her early literary productions, wrote a tragedy, entitled *Adelaide*. Performed at Plumptre's Private Theatre, Norwich, 1791, no copy of the text of the play seems to have survived, and it was not printed. Several of her stories were dramatized: *Father and Daughter* provided a source for Marie Therese Kemble's five-act comedy *Smiles and Tears; or, The Widow's Stratagem* (performed 1815); *Love and Duty* a source for Issac Pocock's two-act entertainment *Twenty Years Ago!* (performed 1810); and *The Ruffian Boy* a source for Thomas Dibdin's two-act melodrama of the same name (printed by Cumberland without a date). Opie gave up writing when she joined the Society of Friends in 1825. Except for a volume of poems on departed friends and relatives (1833), she devoted the rest of her life to "good works." [*BD*, BNA, DBAWW, DNB, EBWW, FCLE, OCEL. Biographies by C. L. Brightwell, 1854 (rpt. 1975); M. E. Macgregor, 1933, with bibliography; and J. M. Wilson, 1937.]

The Oracle, Susannah Maria Cibber. This adaptation from *L'Oracle* by Germain-François P. de Saint Foix (1740) was first produced as an afterpiece at CG on 17 March 1752 for Susannah Cibber's benefit night, with the author in the role of Cinthia. J. Roberts printed the play for R. Dodsley the same year. Issac Bickerstaffe turned the piece into a popular opera, *Daphne and Amintor* (debuted at DL, 8 October 1765).

The Fairy Queen tests Cinthia's love for her son Oberon by forcing him to remain silent with Cinthia, whom she has stolen at birth and raised to believe that she and the Fairy Queen are the only two creatures capable of "speech, thought, and understanding." By declaring her love to the supposedly "machine-like" Oberon, Cinthia transforms him into a speaking and feeling human being, thus fulfilling the oracle's prophecy which required, as a condition for his happiness, that he be loved by a young princess who would believe him to be deaf, dumb, and insensible.

Combining classical myth with contemporary wit about beaus, the piece provides a showcase for its principal actors. The Fairy Queen manages the youngsters with her wise—and somewhat cynical—council, which must have gotten sure laughs from the somewhat cynical audience.

Susannah Cibber said in the "Advertisement" that she was "so struck with the novelty of the subject and the simplicity and delicacy of the sentiments [that] she could not resist attempting a Translation" of St. Foix's *L'Oracle*. His one-act comedy in prose had played twenty-two nights when it was produced in Paris in 1740, and it may have been seen by Cibber. Except for the change of the three characters' names and slight alteration in their speeches, Cibber translated the French piece faithfully, word for word, which led her into a few mistranslations. One significant addition is a new stanza appended to St. Foix's "Divertissement," where Cibber expresses her view that the true oracle is the audience itself.

MANUSCRIPT: Larpent 94.

TEXT: Readex Microprint of the 1763 edition.

FACSIMILE EDITION: E-CED, with introduction by D. Mann (NY: Garland, 1981).

The Organ Grinder, Maria Edgeworth. See her title, **The Grinding Organ**.

Orra, Joanna Baillie. First published in *A Series of Plays: [on] the Stronger Passions* (third series), this five-act tragedy was published by Longman, Hurst, Rees, Orme, and Brown in 1812. It was not staged.

Set in Switzerland in the late fourteenth century, the play begins with Hughobert's displeasure that Orra has no interest in marrying his son, Glottenbal, the man to whom she is betrothed. Alarmed by the attention being paid to her by Theobald, a nobleman of reduced fortune, Hughobert gives Orra the ultimatum that she must agree to marry Glottenbal soon or be sent to Brunier's castle in the Black Forest, supposedly haunted by the ghost of the hunter knight. Because of Orra's highly superstitious nature, Hughobert is convinced that a sojourn there will drive Orra into marriage. Rudigere, a bastard relative of Hughobert's, agrees to accompany Orra to Brunier's castle, motivated by his own determination to seduce and marry Orra himself. The night that Orra and Rudigere arrive, they are disturbed at midnight by the sounds of a hunting party, unaware that the visitation is an attempt by local outlaws to scare them away from Brunier's castle. Orra, disgusted by Rudigere's declarations of love, declares "Off, fiend! let snakes and vipers cling to me, So thou dost keep aloof" (51). While Orra is tortured by her fear of the living dead and her abhorrence to Rudigere, Theobald has discovered the outlaws, who happen to be headed by Franko, who is really Albert, a childhood friend of Theobald. Because Franko knows of a secret passage into Orra's room, Theobald plots to rescue Orra. When he sends a message to her, she must burn it to keep it from Rudigere; therefore, she is distraught when a man dressed in black as a huntsman comes into her room that night. Theobald and Franko remove Orra from the castle just before Hughobert arrives, furious after discovering that Rudigere has betrayed himself and Glottenbal. As they are struggling to bind him, Rudigere frees one of his hands, stabbing himself and, soon after, Glottenbal. The real horror at the end of the play is reserved for Orra's appearance. Although disoriented, Orra still possesses both dignity and strength. As the play ends, the final speeches are Orra's, as she forces Theobald and Hughobert to move back, protecting them from "the living and the dead, [which] together are . . . In horrid neighbourship" (99).

Orra, according to Baillie's preface, is about "the dominion of Superstitious Fear; and that particular species of it (the fear of ghosts, or the returning dead), which is so universal and inherent in our nature" (iv). But Orra's strength, instead of fear, stands out most in the reader's mind. It is first demonstrated when she refuses to marry Glottenbal, a wise decision given the relish with which he contemplates Orra's mental torture. She is similarly bold in her rejection and condemnation of Rudigere at Brunier. In fact, she is clear-minded from the beginning of the play about the potential of abuse in marriage; as Orra tells Hartman when he promotes Theobald as a suitor, "I must consign myself With all my lands and rights into the hands Of some proud man, and say, 'Take all, I pray, And do me in return the grace and favour To be my master.' ...Well I know In such a partnership, the share of power Allotted to the wife" (22–23). Orra's social conscience extends to her commitment to "Improve the low condition of my peasants, And cherish them in peace" (23). While he acknowledges that "the very distant sound of war" (24) excites men, Theobald also exhibits the fairness that Orra espouses, and especially when he encourages others to treat her with sympathy and dignity at the end of the play.

TEXT: Readex Microprint of 1821 edition. 3: 1–100.

FACSIMILE EDITION: *Romantic Context: Poetry* reprints the 1812 edition (London: Longman, Hurst, Rees, Orme, and Brown). Compiled by D. H. Reiman (NY: Garland, 1977).

Otho and Rutha, Miss [Christian] Edwards. This drama was first published by subscription in her *Miscellanies, in Prose and Verse* in Edinburgh (printed for the author, sold by C. Elliot, 1776): 137–181. Dr. Johnson, James Boswell, David Hume, and Lord Kames were among the subscribers. The first version, in two parts, combines a dramatic tale with a narrative romance in prose. According to Tobin, the play opens with the hero confessing to Rutha that he abandoned Sabina when their dwelling was attacked; Sabina fled with the children. "Rutha preaches patience in coping with life's difficulties" (60). The consolation helps Otho cope with his situation until he is reunited with Sabina. In the second part, not in dramatic form, Otho narrates his life history.

Davis and Joyce indicate that Edwards revised both segments into a dramatic tale, with twenty-four speaking parts. *Otho and Rutha* was published at Edinburgh for the author, and at Dublin by H. Colbert in 1780. Colbert prepared a "third edition" in 1787. There is no known performance. *BD* finds it "impossible to commend this production."

TEXT: Not in Readex Microprint.

Otto of Wittelsbach, Mary Russell Mitford. This five-act tragedy was planned by Mitford as early as 1828, when she wrote her friend, the Reverend William Harness, that she wished to write about "a man under the ban of the Empire and succored by his daughter" (*The Life of Mary Russell Mitford* [NY: Harper, 1870] 2: 82). At the death of her mother in 1830, Mitford still had not finished the play. It is not until 1837 that she remarks in a letter to Elizabeth Barrett that she has completed the drama. There is no record of the play's having been acted. It was published in Mitford's *Dramatic Works*, 2 vols., by Hurst and Blackett in 1854.

Set in Germany in the early thirteenth century, the play begins with news that Otto of Wittelsbach has defeated Duke Leopold of Brunswick. Although he has offered Otto his daughter Adela, the Emperor Philip of Suabia distrusts the courageous warrior who has placed "the Imperial crown on [his] brow, . . . and held it there" (215). Because he complains to Philip when knightly codes are violated or when nobles waste the general revenues, Otto is considered by the courtiers "dangerous to us and to the State" (185). Otto antagonizes Count Calheim, the Ambassador for Leopold, when he scornfully refuses Calheim's request to marry his daughter Ida, who is in love with the knight Sir Isidore. Seeking revenge, Calheim arranges a marriage between the defeated Leopold and the Emperor's daughter Adela, promising the arrangement will ensure Leopold's loyalty. When Otto is summoned to defend the Bavarian border, Isidore warns him that Philip plans to marry Adela to Leopold while Wittelsbach is gone. Because he cannot believe that Philip would repay his support in this way, Otto tries to prove Isidore wrong. In a scene that has dramatic impact, Otto is gradually compelled to see what he cannot believe: he is being sacrificed out of political necessity, and Adela is being forced to marry Leopold. When Otto unsheathes his sword to stop the wedding ceremony, Philip rushes forward and is accidentally killed by Otto. To revenge the death, Count Calheim follows Otto to his castle, but he and his son Ulric escape to prevent further bloodshed. Meanwhile, Leopold has been crowned Emperor of Suabia. Although Ida goes to the Diet to defend her father, a cruel Ban is cited that punishes not only Otto but the entire family: his castle is razed, his wealth confiscated, his land forfeited. Under penalty of death, no one can assist a member of the family. Continuing to pursue Otto and Ulric, Calheim tries to punish the few who offer them food. Even as they seek shelter in a cave in the wilderness, waiting to rendezvous with Ida, one of Calheim's men pursues them. Returning with his frail son to the ruins of his castle in Wittelsbach, Otto is overwhelmed with grief when Ulric dies. In a final attempt to marry Ida, Calheim offers Otto and his daughter sanctuary if Ida marries him. In an ironic gesture, Otto says that he is acting as an agent of the State when he stabs and kills Calheim, who has violated the law he swore to execute. Otto then kills himself.

While never performed, *Otto* features lead characters who are well drawn and their behavior effectively motivated. The protagonist is a substantial figure who is as human as he is idealistic. Soon after Philip's death, Otto tries to justify the killing, telling himself "'Twas the All-Righteous Power that served My arm to smite him" (216); however, he soon acknowledges that his honor is tarnished. While Adela and Ida are less important than Otto and lack the psychological depth given to Calheim, both exhibit boldness. Adela decides to enter a convent rather than have Otto and Leopold fight over her; Ida goes by herself to the Diet to defend the family honor, and she enlists assistance for her father and brother as they wander the countryside.

TEXT: Readex Microprint of *The Dramatic Works of Mary Russell Mitford*, vol. 2 (London: Hurst and Blackett, 1854).

Ourselves, Marianne Chambers. A five-act comedy performed by the DL company at the Lyceum on 2 Mar 1811 and acted sixteen times. It was printed the same year by J. Barker.

Sir John Rainsford, who has had nothing to do with women for fifteen years, suddenly finds he has been appointed co-guardian to a young Irish woman who has inherited a fortune. When Fitzaubin comes to London, he tells Sir John that his recently deceased uncle has left him nothing: the money has gone to Sir John's ward. Sir Sydney Beaufort agrees to assist Fitzaubin's attempt to marry the ward, Octavia, and gain the fortune Fitzaubin believes rightfully his. But when Sir Sydney calls on his sister, Miss Beaufort, it is clear to him that Fitzaubin is attached to her. After a carriage overturns in front of Miss Beaufort's house, the O'Shanauhans, Mr. Darlington, and Octavia come in. O'Shanauhan is the other coguardian bringing Octavia to London, and Darlington, his wife's son from a previous marriage, who hopes to marry the ward. Meanwhile, Miss Beaufort cares for Octavia who relates her story: she was raised in a clergyman's family and never knew who her parents were. When Sir Sydney arrives, he is smitten by Octavia, who leaves a few minutes later and asks for Fitzaubin's protection from Darlington. At Fitzaubin's, Octavia meets an "Unknown Lady," who turns out to be her mother. When Miss Beaufort and Sir Sydney pay a call, she's jealous, and he is revealed to be the man who betrayed Octavia in Ireland. Sir Sydney claims that he was too proud to make her his wife earlier. In the final act, the "Unknown Lady" is proved to be the wife of Sir John, who deserted her, but they reconcile their differences. Since Octavia has found her father, she forfeits the inheritance to Fitzaubin, who proposes to Miss Beaufort. Sir Sydney is accepted by Octavia.

The great concern with "ourselves" is the overriding thematic element in the play, shown by Mrs. O'Shanauhan's remark "We must be taking care of Ourselves." This self-concern drives the action of the play. Sir Sydney had been too proud to offer marriage to Octavia in Ireland. Sir John had been so self-absorbed that he deserted his wife. Mrs. O'Shanauhan wants her son to marry a fortune by any means.

In Chambers's creatively plotted comedy, Octavia seems to be the outsider, suggested by her Irish background. When she learns who her parents are and finds Sir Sydney's pride humbled, Octavia can then integrate herself into a new (London) society.

MANUSCRIPT: Larpent 1663.

TEXT: Readex Microprint.

Owen, Prince of Powys; or, Welsh Feuds, Jane Porter. This five-act tragedy was first acted at DL on 28 January 1822 with Edmund Kean in the cast (perhaps in the title role). It was acted only three nights, according to Genest (9: 146). The play was not published.

MANUSCRIPT: Larpent 2271, under its original title *Henry the First; or, The British and Norman Feuds*.

OWENSON, Sydney, later Lady Morgan (1776–1859). Born into a theatrical family, Owenson became a novelist after her father went broke as an actor manager. It was only after her popular Anglo-Irish novel, *The Wild Irish Girl* (1806), that Owenson wrote a comic opera, *The First Attempt; or, The Whim of the Moment*. To get it performed, she hired the theatre and paid the conductor of the orchestra. Performed at Smock Alley, Dublin, in 1807, the play apparently was not published. More than twenty years later, as Lady Morgan (m. 1812), she wrote several plays, published by Saunders and Otley in 1833, under the title *Dramatic Scenes from Real Life*; these included *Manor Sackville*, *The Easter Recess; or, The Tapestry Workers*, and *Temper*. None of these plays was produced. Lady Morgan's success as a novelist enabled her to live as a professional woman writer, but she wrote no more dramas. Many biographical details of her writing and travels are contained in her letters to her sister, Lady Olivia Clarke, who also wrote one play. [*BD*, DNB, EBWW, FCLE (under Morgan), NCBEL (3, 754–55), OCEL. Biographies by L. Stevenson, 1936; Mary Campbell, 1988.]

-P-

The Pair-Royal of Coxcombs, "Ephelia." Traditionally thought to have been acted at a dancing school in the late 1670s. Mulvihill, however, suggests a performance in the early to mid-1670s. On the basis of the Prologue, the play was not written for the patent theatres, for Ephelia says that "they must fawn, that write for a Third day. She scornes such Baseness." In the first song, "Begone fond Love," the singer stresses duty over love; in the second, "Come quickly Death," the singer wants to die because she has been scorned by her swain. Taken together, little can be learned about the plot. The Epilogue says the poet is at the mercy of the gentlemen in the audience, telling them "if you'l Clap the Play, and Praise the Rime, She'l do as much for you another time."

TEXTS: Wing P2030; EEB Reel 645: 16 (1679). Wing P2031; EEB Reel 1211: 6 (1682). The Prologue to *The Pair-Royal of Coxcombs* is printed in *Kissing the Rod: An Anthology of Seventeenth-Century Women's Verse* (1988; NY: Noonday, 1989): 275–276.

FACSIMILE EDITION of *Poems by Ephelia* (1679 edition) includes the Prologue, two songs, and Epilogue; Edited, with introduction by Maureen E. Mulvihill (Delmar, NY: Scholars' Facsimiles, 1992): 16–21.

PARSONS, Mrs. Eliza Phelp (1748–1811). Better known for her novels, Eliza Parsons did write one two-act farce for the theatre, *The Intrigues of a Morning* (1792). The daughter of a Plymouth wine merchant, she married Parsons, a turpentine distiller of Stonehouse, by whom she had eight children. After her husband's business failed, the family moved to London, but his worsening financial situation and death encouraged Mrs. Parsons to take up the pen to support her family. *The History of Miss Meredith* (2 vols., 1790) and *The Errors of Education* (2 vols., 1792) had already been published when she wrote her play in 1792.

She went on to publish by 1807 more than a dozen novels, including some Gothic thrillers mentioned by Jane Austen in *Northanger Abbey* as favorites of Catherine Moreland. [*BD*, DNB, FCLE]

Pastoral Dialogues, Anne Killigrew. These three pastoral dialogues are included in her *Poems* (1686), printed by Samuel Lowndes.

The first dialogue (11–13) between Dorinda and Alexis contrasts earthly and heavenly love, "dazling Objects which we cannot know." In the second dialogue (57–62), Amintor professes his love to Alinda, who tests Amintor's resolve. If Alinda could love, it would be Amintor, but it is enough that she has listened to him. The third dialogue (63–67) involves male and female shepherds: the females have come to listen to Melibaeus recite one of his songs, "Sage Precepts cloath'd in flowing Eloquence." The group invites Almira and Alcimedon, who usually shun serious discourse, to join them, and they do. Melibaeus will take up the theme "of love take heed": most males make love their pastime, but when a female gives her heart, then he vanishes like clouds before the wind. His narrative examines Rodanthe, whose beauty outshone her heart, and Alcander, the foremost of swains. After he wooed and won her, Rodanthe thought him true, but Alcander goes on and makes "Mad Love else-where." Rodanthe drooped like a withered flower and remained constant. So, Melibaeus concludes, when you love, you put your peace in your lover's power, and reason stands aloof. Maids should not let amorous passions govern their hearts. While Almira likes the song, Alcimedon tells Melibaeus that he's old and spoils the pleasure of others. The female shepherds all support Almira, and Melibaeus says his song is meant for both sexes and all should develop a noble mind. They all leave at sunset.

In the pastoral convention, these dialogues generally warn female swains about roving shepherds. In the last, more lengthy one, however, Melibaeus tries to provide a balance between the sexes. Killigrew's couplets are typical of the late Restoration pastoral lyrics, which often find their way into the drama of the period through song and masque as part of the play.

TEXT: Wing K442. EEB Reel 189: 7.

FACSIMILE EDITION: With introduction by Richard Morton (Gainesville, FL: Scholars' Facsimiles, 1967).

Pedrarias, Lady Dacre, earlier Barbarina Ogle Wilmot. This play appears in the first volume of her *Dramas, Translations, and Other Poems*, published in 1821 by John Murray. It was not performed.

Set in Panama and in the surrounding mountains, the play begins as the Indians are preparing to sacrifice Alphonso, the son of Pedrarias, the governor of the Isthmus of Darian. The sacrifice has been postponed several times: a young Indian woman of high birth, Amazilla, sympathizes with the Spaniard Alphonso, as does Capana, the Indian cacique or chief. Thelasco urges Capana to execute Alphonso, because if he escaped, he could reveal the location of the Indian's retreat to the Spaniards. Although his father Pedrarias has killed many Indians, Capana finally refuses to execute him, because Alphonso reminds Capana of his own son Houaco, who was killed or lost two years ago. In return, Alphonso promises never to reveal the Indians' location, a promise that he keeps when he is reunited with his father in Panama. Enraged at his son's loyalty to the Indians, Pedrarias banishes Alphonso, hoping that he will lead the Spaniards to the Indians. He allows an Indian slave to accompany his son in exile, not realizing that the slave is Houaco, Capana's lost son. When they confess their true identities, Houaco and Alphonso become fast friends, but their friendship is destroyed when they encounter Amazilla. Although earlier betrothed to Houaco, Amazilla now declares her love for Alphonso, causing Houaco to distrust the Spaniard. When he tries to strike Alphonso while he is sleeping, Houaco is overwhelmed by his friend's Christian goodness: "The virtues *I* have prized are savage Nature's—*Thine* are from Heaven" (185). Arriving at the Indian retreat, Alphonso and Houaco discover the Spaniards chasing the Indians; Houaco overwhelms Pedrarias, but refuses to kill him for his son's sake. Eventually,

the same masque. Pearson, however, points out several parallels (212). The play thus fails as a unified work, and Centlivre never attempted another tragicomedy. As to the influence of Regnard's *Le Divorce*, it could not be more tenuous. Limited to the comical subplot, it consists solely of the notion of a mismatched couple (an old man and a young woman), having become tired of each other. In Regnard's *commedia dell' arte* play, infidelity has no part, and his comedy ends with Judge Hymen granting a separation in favor of the young wife.

TEXTS: Wing C1671. Readex Microprint. EEB Reel 449: 15.

FACSIMILE EDITION: E-CED, with introduction by R.C. Frushell (NY: Garland, 1982).

PARTIAL TEXT: Subplot, *The Adventures of Venice*, edited with introduction by Kendall in *Love and Thunder* (London: Methuen, 1988): 17–29.

The Perplex'd Lovers, Susanna Centlivre. This five-act comedy was first produced at DL on 19 January 1712 and printed the same year for Owen Lloyd, William Lewis, John Graves, and Tho. Harbin. The play ran only three nights.

This "cloak-and-dagger comedy" (Cotton 141) revolves around two sets of lovers. Constantia loves Colonel Bastion, but her plans to marry him are opposed by her father, Sir Roger Merryman, who wants her to marry Lord Richlove because of his title, and by Belvill, her brother, who wants her to marry his friend, Sir Philip Gaylove. This dual opposition is at the core of the plot since Lord Richlove will pursue her to the point of almost raping her several times. Bastion's need to meet Constantia in secrecy and defend her will force him to hide either in a closet, behind a mask, or in a peddlar's pack and draw his sword in order to rescue her. Camilla, Constantia's cousin and confidante, loves Belvill, but she does not want to acknowledge it; her lies are intended to help Constantia make Belvill suspicious and feed his jealous nature. They quarrel fiercely, but in the end they are reconciled. Belvill relents in his opposition to Bastion when he unexpectedly receives a letter from Sir Philip asking to be forgiven for having concealed the fact that he is already married. The father also relents when he learns that Lord Richlove has several times tried to ravish his daughter. While Camilla accepts Belvill, Constantia is finally allowed to marry the man of her choice, Colonel Bastion.

The comedy relies on inopportune encounters, crude disguises, providential events such as the arrival of Sir Philip's letter, and on mistaken identities fostered by the characters' inability to see, the play taking place mostly at night. Constantia manages to mistake three other men for her lover—Lord Richlove, his valet Le Front, and her brother. Despite a few amusing scenes, "*The Perplex'd Lovers* is certainly one of Centlivre's weakest plays" (Lock 89). In her Preface, she herself acknowledges that having "four Acts in the Dark" caused an "Absurdity" which she resolves not to repeat in the future. Notwithstanding this admission, she claims that the play's failure stemmed from political considerations surrounding her epilogue deemed Whiggish for praising the Duke of Marlborough. Concerning the origin of the play, she contends that "most of the Plot [is] from a Spanish play," but no one has been able to identify the work. According to Bowyer, none of her other so-called Spanish plays came directly from Spanish sources, "nor, probably, did this one" (148). As to any French influence, there is very little, if any. The opening scene where Bastion refuses to pay his servant his long overdue wages is faintly reminiscent of Centlivre's own opening scene in *The Platonick Lady*, a more likely source than a similar scene in Regnard's *Attendez-moi sous l'orme* which she had loosely adapted in her 1706 play.

TEXT: Readex Microprint.

FACSIMILE EDITION: E-CED, with introduction by R. C. Frushell (NY: Garland, 1982).

Personation; or, Fairly Taken In, Marie Therese DeCamp Kemble. This one-act afterpiece was first produced at DL on 29 April 1805 for John Bannister's benefit night; he took the role of Lord Harry, and DeCamp acted Lady Julia. The play is based on Dieulafoy's *Défiance et Malice*.

Lord Henry fancies himself a philosopher, who wants to learn if a three-year absence has changed the sentiments of his intended bride, his cousin Lady Julia. He returns under the guise of his old servant, La Roche. But Julia has been informed of the stratagem and vows to see that "the biter will be bit." She fashions a stratagem of her own that mirrors Henry's: she will, when necessary, assume her old French governess's identity and garb. Her feigned indifference at hearing of Henry's simulated accident, which has prevented him from coming in person, and her readiness to leave for a ball send poor Henry in despair and rage. She returns immediately as her governess, clad in a heavy cloak that hides her youth. She reveals to "La Roche" that her "mistress" expects a visit from her lover that very night. Henry's jealousy knows no bounds, and later—as he waits in the dark, in the woods, as instructed—he hears Julia lamenting his violent temper which forces her, she claims, to accept a certain Eastdale's hand. Upon hearing a sound that she "identifies" as coming from Eastdale, she throws herself at her unsuspecting cousin, and out of feigned honesty, feels she must inform "Eastdale" that, although she is ready to marry him, she had, until then, loved her cousin, Lord Henry. A marriage contract is then signed, and, as Julia swiftly resumes her disguise, a horrified Henry is made to believe he has just married the French governess, "that infernal old hag." The misunderstanding is cleared as Julia sheds, one by one, her borrowed pieces of clothing, and reveals herself as Julia, "a truthful cousin that should never be doubted," as she tells a repentant but joyful Henry.

This short play is taken directly from Dieulafoy's one-act play, *Défiance et Malice* (1801). The two plots are essentially the same, and at times Kemble translated parts of the dialogue closely. But this close rendering is rare, for Kemble made a number of alterations. She changed the characters' names, all the while giving the two assumed servants a distinctive speech: the French governess retaining words or phrases from her native tongue and La Roche using a definitely low-class accent. Kemble also eliminated Dieulafoy's rhymed couplets and long, sententious speeches on men and women. Kemble's interlude is thus a pleasant one which, despite its intrinsic comedy, had to rely entirely on acting, as Genest rightly stated (7: 650), since it revolves around only two characters who at times assume the roles and identity of four.

By discovering Lord Henry's scheme, Lady Julia can test his resolve to marry her, and at the same time she can demonstrate how foolish his jealousy is.

MANUSCRIPT: Larpent 1447.

TEXTS: Readex Microprint of Cumberland's *British Theatre*, vol. 32, n.d., and of Fisher's *Standard Farces* (Philadelphia: Turner & Fisher, n.d.).

The Peruvian, by a lady. This anonymous, three-act comic opera debuted at CG on 18 March 1786. The play's principal source, according to the advertisement in the text, is based on Marmontel's tale of *Coralie; ou, L'Amitié à l'Épreuve*. Although Hogan in *LS* gives Charles Favart and Claude de Voisenon's *L'Amitié à l'Épreuve* as the source, this is a dramatized version of Marmontel, with songs. The comic opera was performed six times and printed by J. Bell in 1786, going through three printings in its first year. It is worth noting that the role of Blandford was taken by a female actor, Margaret Kennedy. The music, composed chiefly by James Hook, was published separately under the title of *The Fair Peruvian* by S. A. and P. Thompson the same year.

The main plot centers on the struggle between love and friendship, as exemplified by Belville's moral dilemma. Before departing from England on another voyage, Blandford places Coraly, the young Peruvian girl whom he rescued from Spanish conquerors, under the care of Belville, his closest friend, and Clara, Belville's sister. As Blandford feared, Belville falls in love with the beautiful, naive Coraly. But Belville feels he must check his passion, as he considers her engaged to her benefactor, Blandford. Torn between his love and his loyalty to his trusted and trusting friend, he opts for friendship and honor, to Coraly's despair, since she also has fallen in love with him. Blandford returns, but on the eve of his marriage to the young Peruvian, he cannot fail but notice the deeply-altered state of Belville and that of his bride-to-be. He immediately understands the cause of their wretched condition and relinquishes Coraly's hand, since he would be unable to make her happy. As he gives her to Belville, he reassures him that their friendship remains unaltered. The opera ends with the chorus hailing friendship, that "delightful power," which, according to Belville, "lends its bright'ning gleams" when man is "most depriv'd of peace and rest."

The playwright, as she acknowledges, took the main plot from one of Marmontel's moral tales, entitled *L'Amitié à l'Épreuve*. Coraly is no longer an orphan girl from India where Blandford was serving his country, but a young Peruvian; her father, in both cases, dies in Blandford's arms as he entrusts her to his care. Most of the details in the story, and much about Coraly's education and her refusal to adopt the insincere code of Europe's social behavior, have been omitted; she, nevertheless, remains a strong voice for the rights of the heart over conventions. What is left is at times a close rendering of the original: for example, the author, forgetting that her heroine is no longer from India, has her, on the eve of an unwanted marriage, lamenting over her fate which she considers worse than that of the Indian widow who must follow her husband in death.

Further departing from her French source, the author adds a subplot centered on Clara and her love for Captain Frankly, a love that is never really threatened despite her guardian's desire to marry her to someone else. Frankly manages to get her hand by passing himself off as the intended groom who, upon his arrival, is taken for a mere impostor. The latter, having never before set eyes on Clara, relinquishes her without any difficulty.

According to *The Critical Review* (61 [April 1786]: 285), Hook's ballad tunes helped to furnish an agreeable entertainment, although the piece did not "rise to any great excellence." In a similar vein, *The London Chronicle* (59 [March 1786]: 268) found the dialogue easy and elegant rather than animated and witty, adding that the new subplot was "of a common kind." W. C. Oulton, in his *History of the Theatres of London* (1792), states that the opera was indebted to Elizabeth Billington, who acted the role of Coraly. Whether he meant praise for her talent in acting the principal role, or whether she is the author of the play is unclear. That *The Peruvian* ran through three printed editions the year it was produced indicates its favor among the public of the time. It was not, however, revived on stage.

MANUSCRIPT: Larpent 727.

TEXT: Readex Microprint.

La-Peyrouse, translated by Anne Plumptre. This two-act drama of Kotzebue's *La Perouse* was denied a license because the play deals with bigamy (Conolly 125–26). Plumptre's translation was published in 1799 by R. Phillips.

As the play begins, La-Peyrouse sees a boat on the horizon and contemplates being rescued from his island. The sole survivor of a shipwreck eight years ago, La-Peyrouse was saved by Malvina, who has become his companion and mother of their son Charles. Before long, a European woman named Adelaide arrives and greets Malvina, explaining that she is looking for a Frenchman, a husband whose "thirst after fame tore [him] from my arms" (5). Driven by love to find him, Adelaide has fitted out two ships and risked dangers at sea. When La-Peyrouse enters, he is tortured because he loves both women, both have sacrificed for him, and he has children by both. After telling Adelaide how Malvina saved his life—giving up her father and brothers to live with him—La-Peyrouse is forgiven by his wife, but he is forced by her to choose between them. Each argues why her claim on La-Peyrouse's affections is superior, but this competition ceases when he declares he will commit suicide. Although repeatedly called a "savage" by Adelaide, Malvina proves the more civilized of the two women. While Adelaide hates Malvina and eventually wishes for her death, Malvina is unable to hate and she saves Adelaide when she almost eats poisoned fruit: even Adelaide recognizes that the other woman's heart is "nobler than mine" (26). After La-Peyrouse prays for a disinterested party to resolve the domestic conflict, Adelaide's brother Clairville arrives with news that a revolution has occurred—no doubt a reference to the French Revolution. Since anarchy rules at home, Clairville proposes that they all stay on the island together and begin a new colony. The tension between the two women disappears when Malvina suggests that they be sisters. Adelaide proposes that they think of La-Peyrouse as a brother: "by day we will make but one family, at night we will separate" (33–34), the women living together in a separate hut. Everyone rejoices, Clairville toasting "The Paradise of Innocence" (34).

Two women quarrelling over one man sets up the triangle in this short piece. What is unusual, however, is that the two women become friends in this island utopia, choosing to form one large family.

MANUSCRIPT: Larpent 1313.

TEXT: Readex Microprint.

The Petticoat Government, Ann Yearsley. According to *BD* (2: 282), this farce was advertised but not printed. There is no known text.

The Phantom, Joanna Baillie. This two-act musical drama was published in the second volume of her *Dramas* in 1836 (Longman, et al.). It was not performed.

The Phantom begins with a highland wedding, where talk turns to the long-planned match between the chief's son, Malcolm, and the Glasgow Provost's daughter, Alice. It soon becomes clear, however, that Malcolm is in love with Emma Graham, Alice's friend in Glasgow. The chief Dunarden is also concerned that his son's generosity will exhaust their financial resources. After Alice and her brother Claude arrive for a visit with Malcolm and his sister, Marian, a letter arrives from Emma Graham, describing the contagion that has overwhelmed Glasgow. That night in her room Marian is visited by the ghost of Emma, who reveals that she has hidden a paper away. Returning to Glasgow, the young people pass by Emma's funeral procession. Although disappointed that Malcolm does not reciprocate Alice's love, the Provost consoles himself with the thought that she will marry a prosperous merchant and remain close to her father in Glasgow. At Emma's grave that night, Malcolm meets Claude, who reveals that he too loved Emma. As they fight over who loved her most, a messenger arrives, instructing them to go to Emma's room. There the assembled family and friends find a marriage contract between the deceased and a young man, Basil Gordon, who has contracted Emma's illness. As the play ends, the bell tolls for Basil Gordon, whose relationship with Emma was kept a secret because he was Catholic.

The women in *The Phantom* control the action to a large degree. Even beyond the grave, Emma Graham reconciles two families and prepares the way for the marriage between Alice and Malcolm. Emma, Alice, and Marian all demonstrate a kind of maturity that makes friendship possible in spite of circumstances that might result in jealousy or estrangement. In contrast, the relationship between Malcolm and Claude quickly deteriorates as a result of their rivalry over a dead woman. The question of genre is unresolved because in the midst of a tragic situation the songs are distracting. Finally, the issue of whether or not Alice and Malcolm will marry is never completely answered.

TEXT: Readex Microprint of *Dramas* (1836) 2: 215–319.

Philander, Charlotte Ramsey Lennox. This pastoral drama in poetry, containing three short acts, was not performed. Two printings occurred in 1758: one in London by A. Millar, the other in Dublin by Richard Smith. Lennox's source, as she says in her dedication to Viscount Charlemont, is *Pastor Fido* (by Guardi), and it contains two songs "by another hand" (vi); Small suggests Giuseppe Baretti, who had earlier written an ode in praise of Lennox's work (162).

Sylvia has been promised to Philander, son of Montano, a priest of Apollo, by her parents, but Sylvia prefers her freedom to marriage. She says Philander was her parents' choice, not hers. Philander lapses into a melancholy state, and his friend Thrisis tries to cheer him, even in the face of hopeless love. Montano reports that Apollo has decreed Sylvia must either marry or die. When Philander goes to tell Sylvia, he finds her being attacked by a satyr, and he drives the beast away. Still, she will not accede to his wishes and accepts death instead. At the temple of Apollo, Sylvia is about to be slain when Philander offers himself in her place. Sylvia is moved by Philander's love and asks that she die in lieu of her admirer. Apollo comes from the heavens and permits both to live. Philander feels "restored to life," and Sylvia lauds the "truest passion, that e'er warm'd A virgin-breast" (48).

One possible reading of the pastoral is to see Sylvia as wishing to lead her own life without the impediment of men. Her friend Nerina urges her to follow convention and marry. After Sylvia's refusal of marriage, the god Apollo forces her to marry or be sacrificed, and she prefers the latter, even after Philander saves her from a wicked satyr. Finally, Philander offers himself as a sacrifice, changing Sylvia's attitude toward the swain. But it takes a *deus ex machina* to force an alteration in Sylvia's views. Perhaps Charlotte Lennox felt her writing and publishing beset by male manipulation and wished she could dispense with masculine interference.

TEXT: Readex Microprint of London edition, 1758.

Philander and Rose; or, The Bridal Day, Elizabeth Satchell Kemble. The only known play by Elizabeth Kemble (a provincial actor with her husband, Stephen George Kemble) was this two-act pastoral farce with music, produced at Manchester in 1785. The songs were printed in Manchester, 1785, but without the text of the play.

MANUSCRIPT: Larpent 689.

Philip the Second, translated by Fanny Holcroft. This tragedy in five acts is taken from the Italian of [Count Vittorio] Alfieri. It was printed in *The Theatrical Recorder*, vol. 1, no. 2, edited by Thomas Holcroft (London: C. Mercier, 1805): 81–116. There is no indication that this translation was staged. Holcroft notes that she worked with two versions by Alfieri, possibly one published in Siena in 1783, and the other in Paris, 1787–89.

Isabella has recently married Philip, who is much older and who has a son Carlos nearer her age. When the play opens, Isabella declares in a soliloquy that she is in love with Carlos, but when he enters she says they must not see each other again. Philip, meanwhile, wants Isabella watched, and he charges Carlos with disloyalty to the crown and suggests that his son would improve if he spent more time with his stepmother. Carlos, then, goes to warn Isabella of Philip's machinations. Shortly thereafter, Philip charges Carlos with criminal behavior and with attempting to murder him; other charges are that Carlos is negotiating with the French, and that Carlos has given up the faith. After all of these trumped up charges, Philip absolves Carlos. But later when they argue, Philip plans to have Carlos thrown in a dungeon; just then Isabella enters and is told Carlos plotted against her life too. She learns that Carlos is now charged with treason and that Philip hates his son because he possesses all the good qualities that Philip doesn't have. Nevertheless, Isabella attends Carlos in prison where Philip finds her. Philip then accuses them of an illicit affair, but both declare their innocence. When Philip's henchman, Gomez, comes with a sword, Carlos grabs it and kills himself. Philip offers Isabella a poison bowl, then dashes it to the ground, saying he wants her to live with him, but she seizes the sword and stabs herself. Philip has had his revenge, he tells Gomez, who is now responsible for cleaning up the evil deeds to preserve Philip's honor.

No poetic justice prevails in the tragedy: it shows a grim portrait of tyranny in which the tyrant lives to do more cruel deeds. Carlos is scarcely the ambitious man his father portrays, Philip merely wants to eliminate him so that he can have all of Isabella's attention. Isabella, the only woman in the play, has the strength to stab herself rather than live with such an evil man as Philip. Although Isabella makes a strong defense of herself and her honest dealings with Carlos, Philip is determined to control her thoughts as well as her actions: Isabella's suicide denies Philip's wishes. Although Holcroft's straightforward translation does not always plumb Philip's motivation, it was the first she contributed to her father's theatrical enterprise.

TEXT: Readex Microprint.

PHILIPS, Katherine Fowler ["The Matchless Orinda"] (1632–1664). Born in London to a middle-class family, Katherine Fowler attended Mrs. Salmon's academy for girls and acquired a penchant for post-Shakespearean drama and cavalier verse. After the death of her father, she went to Wales with her mother, who had remarried. At age 16, Katherine herself married Colonel James Philips. During the chaotic civil wars, Katherine strove to find a peaceful alternative through her poetry. Taking the name of Orinda, she addressed poems to friends by using pseudonyms.

Better known as a poet, Philips translated two of Pierre Corneille's tragedies—*Pompey* and *Horace*. The first, written while on a visit to Dublin, was produced there at the Theatre Royal, Smock Alley, on 10 February 1663. It was first published in Dublin and later that same year in London (EEB 89.37 and Readex Microprint). Back in Wales, she began a translation of *Horace*. Uncompleted at her death in 1664, the tragedy was produced posthumously (with the last act by Sir John Denham) for a performance at Court on 4 February 1668. Publicly, *Horace* was first performed at Bridges-Street Theatre on 16 January 1669 and probably five more nights during the remainder of the season. Both dramas were published with her *Poems* in 1667, *Horace* in Philips's unfinished version. The *Poems* of 1669 contains both plays with the completion of *Horace* by Denham. [*BD*, BNA, Cotton, DBAWW, DNB, EBWW, FCLE, Hobby, Hume, Morgan, OCEL, Pearson. Biographies by P. W. Souers, 1931; Elaine Hobby, 1988; Patrick Thomas, 1988. *Poems* "unauthorized," 1664 (Wing P2032; EEB Reel 286: 8). *Poems . . . To which is added Monsieur Corneille's Pompey & Horace, Tragedies*, 1667 (Wing P2033; EEB Reel 748: 28); 1669 (Wing P2034; EEB Reel 772: 3); 1678 (Wing P2035; EEB Reel 748: 29). Readex Microprint of Wing P2033, *Poems* (London: H. Herringman, 1667). Volume 3 of Philips's *Works* contains critical editions of both dramas and other translations, edited with commentary by G. Greer and R. Little (Stump Cross, Essex: Stump Cross, 1993). The recent facsimile in the Scholars' Reprint series of the *Poems* (1667) *omits* the plays.]

PHILLIPS, Joan. See "**EPHELIA**."

Le Philosophe Moderne, Baroness Elizabeth Berkeley Craven, afterward the Margravine of Anspach. There is no record of this three-act comedy being acted, through it was printed in French, in 1790 (with no publisher's name on the title page). A German version, *Der Moderne Philosoph*, was translated by J. J. C. von Reck from the French and also published in 1790.

TEXT: Not in Readex Microprint.

A Piece of a Play, Margaret Lucas Cavendish, Duchess of Newcastle. This fragment of a play, which she intended for *The Blazing World*, was printed in *Plays, Never Before Printed*, published by A. Maxwell, 1668.

This beast fable opens with Sir Puppy Dogman asking Monsieur Ass, Head of the Company of Mode Wits, about the various kinds of wit, which Ass defines. The scene shifts to Lady Eagle, Lady Sparrow, Lady Woodcock, and other "Ladies," who are discussing Lady Phoenix, whom no one has ever seen. Lady Leverit's maid Dormouse says she has served Lady Phoenix who is of a studious nature, leads a retired life, and cares not what the world says. In company, she is civil, kind, bountiful, charitable, and humble, but she is severe on those who are rude. Later, Lord Bearman and Sir Puppy try to make love to Lady Monkey, but neither is fashionable enough for her. They return fashionably attired and quarrel over Lady Monkey, planning a duel, but Lady Monkey stops this folly. In another amorous design, Sir Politick Fox-man plans to woo Lady Leverit and asks advice from Worm-man, who suggests he write in prose not verse. Lady Leverit sends a note saying she'll hear his suit. After his visit, Sir Politick observes her entertaining Monsieur Satyr. When Worm-man asks why he didn't fight Satyr, Sir Politick answers that great and subtle politicians are never valiant. In the last portion of the fragment, Lady Leverit wants to know Lady Monkey's views about choosing a husband. Contrary to Lady Monkey's recommendation (Sir Puppy), Lady Leverit chooses Monsieur Ass, who arrives and offers to take them to a "Mode" play of which he is the author. "Mode plays," he tells them, "are all Rhime and no Reason, or all Action and no Wit." And they all leave together.

Cavendish satirizes the various modes current in the 1660s. Several kinds of wit are defined. Then, many characters comment on Lady Phoenix, whom none of them has ever met. Finally, Dormouse, her former maid, gives her a good character. Types of wooing are examined, including the proper verbal style, the latest fashions, the use of letters, and the best way to court a married woman. All methods should be in the latest mode, and the use of animal names supports the satire.

TEXTS: Wing N867. EEB Reel 674: 2. Readex Microprint.

PILKINGTON, Laetitia Van Lewen (1706?–1750). Mostly remembered for her "scandalous" *Memoirs* (3 vols., 1748–54), Pilkington was encouraged to learn by her father and dissuaded in this pursuit by her mother, so as not to hurt her eyes. In 1725, she married a poor minister, Matthew Pilkington, with whom she had several children. On the basis of trumped-up charges, he divorced her in 1738, and she went to live in London, where she tried to make a living by her pen. During this time, she wrote one farce and part of a tragedy. Her burlesque play, *The Turkish Court; or, The London 'Prentice* was produced at the Little Theatre in Capel Street, Dublin, in 1748 (*BD*); for unknown reasons, however, it was never printed. The first act of her tragedy, *The Roman Father*, is printed in the second volume of the *Memoirs* (1749). [*BD*, BNA, Cotton, DBAWW, DNB, EBWW, FCLE, Lonsdale. Forthcoming biography by A. C. Elias, Jr.]

PINCHARD, Elizabeth Sibthorpe (fl. 1791–1823). Author of several educational tracts for the young, often written in dramatic form, Pinchard's works were published by Elizabeth Newbery in the 1790s. After *The Blind Child, or Anecdotes of the Wyndham Family* (1791), she wrote *Dramatic Dialogues for the Use of Young Persons* in 1792, which was followed by *The Two Cousins, A Moral Story* in 1794. Pinchard lived with her husband, John P. Pinchard, a practicing lawyer, in Taunton; they had five children. She began writing novels for adults in 1814, when she published *Mystery and Confidence*; this was followed by *The Ward of Delamere* in 1815. *Family Affection, A Tale for Youth*, published in Taunton, followed in 1816 and *The Young Countess* in 1823.

The Blind Child was her first excursion into dramatic novels for young people. This work also opens up a concern for people now referred to as sight impaired. Lessons and morals are prominent in *Dramatic Dialogues*, with each title suggesting the subject; these dramas include 1) "The Misfortunes of Anger," in two parts; 2) "Sensibility," in two parts; 3) "The Little Trifler"; 4) "The Little Country Visitor"; 5) "The Distrest Family"; 6) "The Village Wedding"; and "The Mockingbird's Nest." Aside from their publication in England, Pinchard's works ("by a Lady" or "by the author of The Blind Child") were enormously popular in the United States. [FCLE; Mary V. Jackson, *Engines of Instruction, Mischief, and Magic: Children's Literature in England from its Beginnings to 1839* (Lincoln: U of Nebraska P, 1989)]

PIX, Mary Griffith (1666–1709). One of the triumvirate of female playwrights who brought plays on stage in the theatrical season of 1695–96. Her first play, the tragedy of *Ibrahim, the Thirteenth Emperour of the Turks*, and a farce entitled *The Spanish Wives* were both produced in the late spring and summer of 1696. The following year saw two more comedies—*The Innocent Mistress* and *The Deceiver Deceived.* Pix next wrote two tragedies—*Queen Catharine; or, The Ruines of Love* (1698) and *The False Friend; or, The Fate of Disobedience* (1699). Because her next play, *The Beau Defeated; or, The Lucky Younger Brother* (1700), was not signed, it has sometimes been ascribed to others, but she did acknowledge *The Double Distress*, a comedy produced in March 1701; that same month also saw a production of a tragedy in prose, *The Czar of Muscovy*. It was two years before Pix prepared a new play. Considered by L. R. Payne to be one of her "brightest comedies," *The Different Widows; or, Intrigue All-a-Mode* provides a striking contrast between two widowed sisters. The tragedy, *Zelmane; or, The Corinthian Queen* (produced 1704), is usually attributed to Pix, though the dedicatory epistle in the 1705 edition says it is based on an unfinished manuscript by William Montfort. Another tragedy, *The Conquest of Spain*, was produced in May 1705 and attributed to Pix by John Downes in *Roscius Anglicanus*. Her last play was *The Adventures in Madrid*, a farce produced in 1706. [*BD*, Cotton, DBAWW, DLB 80 (by L. R. Payne), DNB, EBWW, FCLE, Hume, Morgan, NCBEL (2: 797–98), Revels, Smith & Cardinale. E-CED series, ed. E. Steeves. Constance Clark provides bio-critical material on Pix in her *Three Augustan Women Playwrights* (1986), which includes Manley and Trotter.]

Pizarro. The Spaniards in Peru; or The Death of Rolla, translated by Anne Plumptre. The text of the second edition of *The Spaniards in Peru; or, The Death of Rolla* is exactly the same as her translation of Kotzebue in the first edition except the title page has been changed, presumably to capitalize on the success of R. B. Sheridan's drama, titled *Pizarro* (produced DL, 24 May 1799). R. Phillips published this second edition of Plumptre's translation in 1799, with *Pizarro* appearing twice on the title page.

For a detailed discussion of the play, see *The Spaniards in Peru; or, The Death of Rolla*.

TEXT: Readex Microprint, second edition, under the name of Anne Plumptre, 1799.

Pizarro; or, The Conquest of Peru, translated by Elizabeth Helme. This historical novel, framed as a drama, was translated from Joachim Henrich Campe's *Die Entdeckung von Amerika* and published in Dublin by P. Wogan and six others, 1800. There is no known production.

The form of this document begins in a prose description of the children asking their father about the conquest of Peru. The speech prefixes indicate that the children (who are given no individuality either by traits or language)—Charles, Henry, Ferdinand, Charlotte, Mathias, Frederic, Nicholas, John, Theodore, and Theophilus—ask questions, prompting "The Father" to tell them the tale of Pizarro and how he conquered Peru. In addition to their questions, the children react to the story, which is told in sixteen dialogues over the course of sixteen days. The Father interrupts his monologues to interrogate the children to see if they have understood and have learned the moral precepts of the narrative. Another method of instruction occurs when the Father explains theology, geography, and other topics as they come up in the narrative. He relies on such phrases as "you will recall," "you doubtless recollect," and "you'll remember" to remind the children of prior events in the tale. The title, probably chosen by the publishers, imitates Sheridan's recent stage success of the previous year.

Pizarro ravaged Peru in a merciless way: although he was a strong commander, his greed and ambition overrode his military talents. The history the Father tells involves ruthless men and underdeveloped natives who cannot cope with modern European firearms. Pillage and plunder, especially of gold, jewels, and precious metals, are the Spaniards' methods of enriching themselves without a concern for the natives. The internecine strife between native factions assists Pizarro's conquest, but later the Spanish fall out over their booty. The Father balances a respect for Pizarro's daring with an acknowledgment that most of what the conqueror did was downright wicked.

Almost no woman figures in the story, though Philipillo, the corrupt translator of the Spaniards, wants permission to marry an Inca who is a Virgin of the Sun. Her name has not survived. The Father's history treats men, deeds of daring-do, and events and adventures in distant lands—no women need apply. Besides the Mother, Charlotte (among the ten children) is the only other female auditor.

TEXT: Readex Microprint.

The Platonick Lady, Susanna Carroll [Centlivre]. This five-act comedy, based in part on Regnard's *Attendez-moi sous l'orme* (1694), was produced at the Queen's Theater on 25 November 1706 and printed for James Knapton and Egbert Singer the same year (*Daily Courant* 9 December 1706) with 1707 on the title page (Burling). The comedy ran only four nights despite a strong cast that included Thomas Betterton (as Sir Thomas), Anne Bracegirdle (as his platonic niece), Anne Oldfield (as Isabella), Barton Booth (as Sir Charles), Robert Wilks (as Captain Beaumont), and Colley Cibber (as Sharper).

This comedy of intrigue revolves around two pairs of contrasting lovers. Lucinda, the title character, believes herself in love with the rakish Belvil, a young man of unknown origin, who saved her and her uncle, Sir Thomas, from a robbery. Sir Thomas, who believes he knows of Belvil's parentage, asks him not to marry Lucinda without his permission. The contracted lovers, Isabella and Sir Charles Richley, actively dislike one another, and he pursues Lucinda. Isabella had in fact fallen in love with Belvil after meeting him in France five years earlier, but her hasty departure prevented them from maintaining contact. Now that her flame is rekindled, Isabella tries to win Belvil back through several outlandish schemes and disguises. Belvil, prompted by Sir Thomas, courts Mrs. Dowdy, whose late husband was Lucinda's family steward, in order to recover documents showing that Lucinda and Belvil are siblings, who were defrauded of their fortune by the unscrupulous Dowdy. Meanwhile, Isabella employs a number of clever disguises to regain Belvil, but she remains unsuccessful until it is discovered that Belvil is Lucinda's brother, thus freeing Belvil for Isabella, and allowing Lucinda to marry Sir Charles.

Although it is commonly said that *The Platonick Lady* is based on Regnard's comedy, *Attendez-moi sous l'orme*, the two plots have almost nothing in common. Dorante, a handsome officer, in search of a rich wife, disturbs the peace of a small village by successfully courting Agathe who, despite being contracted to Colin, a local peasant, falls for him. Lisette, a friend of Agathe and Pasquin, Dorante's witty servant, plot to ridicule and expose the fortune seeker. Agathe regains her senses and marries the plain but trustworthy patois-speaking Colin while Dorante rides off, proffering idle threats against the whole village. Centlivre borrowed a few features from Regnard: her opening scene, for example, is lifted from his work, at times translated literally. Equipage and Pasquin, faithful servants of eight years, but "weary of being well beaten, and ill fed" ("las d'estre bien battu and mal nourry"), ask for their long overdue wages, but are given a mere receipt in return. Pasquin's remarks about clothes designed to hide women's defects and excerpts from a French book on coiffures designed for the same effect are used by Centlivre, but in a different context (III.1).

The lack of unity in *The Platonick Lady*'s several plots probably caused the play's failure, according to F. P. Lock. Still, he praises "Centlivre's evocations of the disreputable substratum of fashionable life" (60–61). Lock also singles out Sir Thomas "as Centlivre's only sympathetically conceived father and authority figure" (61). Pearson focuses her attention on Isabella as the active woman, whereas Lucinda is passive; she also praises Isabella's tour de force in her language and disguises (219–220). Angry about the unjust criticism her play received, Centlivre, in her unsigned Dedication, appeals "To all the Generous Encouragers of Female Ingenuity" for a fair hearing without regard to gender. Any play known to be by a woman "flags in the Opinion of those that extoll'd it before, and the Bookseller falls in his Price, with this Reason only, *It is a Woman's*" (sig. A2, emphasis in the original).

TEXTS: Readex Microprint. TEC Reel 484: 15.

FACSIMILE EDITION: E-CED, with introduction by R. C. Frushell (NY: Garland, 1982).

The Platonic Wife, Elizabeth Griffith. An adaptation of Marmontel's moral tale *L'Heureux Divorce*, this five-act comedy opened at DL on 24 January 1765, but it was not well received. It was altered and improved for production on the five following nights, but there was no revival. The publication by W. Johnson and others coincided with the author's benefit on 26 January 1765. A Dublin edition was also published in 1765. Gordon Ruesch has discovered some substantive variations between the manuscript and the printed text and discusses them in his essay, "On Editing Elizabeth Griffith's *The Platonic Wife*" (Keener & Lorsch 263–68).

Lord Frankland's young bride is outraged by the absence of romantic, passionate love on her husband's part. Now estranged from him, she throws herself into society, searching for the perfect lover, and she is quickly disappointed. Her first lover refuses to enter into "the Platonic system" that she offers him, for he has no time for such nonsense. Her second lover, although he fought a duel for her, reveals himself, putting "self-love" before true passion. Realizing that no man equals her loving, dependable, if unromantic, husband, she sets aside her chimerical notions of love found in novels and seeks a reconciliation, which Lord Frankland is happy to accept.

Griffith intended to expose "the error of a delicate and elevated mind unacquainted with the manners of real life, or the general frame of the human heart" (Advertisement). She found this theme in Marmontel's *L'Heureux Divorce*, and certainly did more than get "the hint of this Piece," as she claims, for her plot is basically Marmontel's, down to the episode of the portrait depicting a repentant wife, bathed in tears. But Griffith felt "obliged to contrive an entire under-plot," involving the unsuccessful attempts by Clarinda to take revenge on the heroine for having married the man she wanted for herself. Unfortunately, tiresome and awkward French phrases used by Lady Frankland's French maid, as well as by one of her admirers, mar the play. The exaggerated language is often too precieux, and the subplot occasionally unconvincing. *The Critical Review* refused to "censor" Griffith's comedy "as it is wrote by a lady" (19 [1765]: 153). Victor believed its lack of success was owing to the hasty stage handling of the portrait "upon which the interesting Part of the Fable was to turn" (*The History of the Theatres of London and Dublin*, 3: 59–62). This comedy might be labeled a "cautionary tale" because of what Lady Frankland experiences in the play.

MANUSCRIPT: Larpent 244.

TEXTS: Readex Microprint. TEC Reels 3876: 10 (London, 1765); 583: 6 (Dublin, 1765).

Playes, Margaret Cavendish, Duchess of Newcastle. Published in 1662 by John Martyn, James Allestry, and Tho. Dicas, the closet dramas included are *Love's Adventures, 2 parts*; *The Several Wits*; *Youth's Glory and Death's Banquet, 2 parts*; *The Lady Contemplation, 2 parts*; *Wits Cabal, 2 parts*; *The Unnatural Tragedy*; *The Public Wooing*; *The Matrimonial Trouble, 2 parts*; *Nature's Three Daughters: Beauty, Love, and Wit, 2 parts*; *The Religious*; *The Comical Hash*; *Bell in Campo, 2 parts*; *The Apocriphal Ladies*; and *The Female Academy*. None of these plays was performed.

Plays, Never Before Printed, Margaret Cavendish, Duchess of Newcastle. A. Maxwell printed these five closet dramas in 1668; they include *The Bridals*, *The Convent of Pleasure*, *A Piece of a Play* (intended to be included in her prose work *The Blazing World*), *The Presence*, and *The Sociable Companions; or, The Female Wits*. No performance of any of the plays has been attempted.

PLOWDEN, Dorothea (d. 1827). Author of one comic opera with music by S. J. Arnold. Plowden's *Virginia* was produced at DL on 30 October 1800. According to Genest (7: 496–97), it was damned the first night because there are so many improbabilities. In Plowden's preface to the published version (London: J. Barker, 1800), she claims the manager (John Philip Kemble) mutilated the play and caused it to fail. Her detractors said that the angry preface was merely a stratagem to promote the sale of the book text of the play. She did not write another dramatic work. [DNB (under Francis Plowden)]

PLUMPTRE, Anne (1760–1818). Apparently educated at home with her sister, Bell,

Anne (sometimes Anna) had a strong grounding in modern foreign languages. Her mother, a schoolmaster's daughter, and her father, President of Queen's College, Cambridge, brought them up in Norwich and Cambridgeshire. Anne's ability in languages, especially German, materially assisted her translations of the dramas of Kotzebue. Her translations helped make that playwright a staple on the English stage. Among the plays that Plumptre translated by Kotzebue were *The Widow and the Riding Horse; or, The Paradox*, *The Count of Burgundy*, *La-Peyrouse*, *The Virgin of the Sun*, *The Spaniards in Peru; or, The Death of Rolla* (the basis of R. B. Sheridan's *Pizarro*), *The Force of Calumny*, and *The Natural Son* (the original English version of *Lover's Vows*, though Inchbald's rendition was preferred because of its stageability). The translations of these plays were all published in 1798 and 1799. In addition to translating drama, Anne wrote novels, travel books, and biographical sketches. [*BD*, DBAWW, DNB, FCLE, NCBEL (2: 864)]

PLUMPTRE, Bell, or Annabella, sister of Anne (1761–1838). Like her sister Anne, Bell translated from the German. Her English version of William Augustus Iffland's *Der Jäger* became *The Foresters; a Picture of Rural Manners*, a five-act play, printed for Vernor and Hood in 1799. There is no record of a production of this translation. Bell Plumptre is said to have translated *The Guardian Angel* from Kotzebue, though the 1802 version does not bear her name. Early in the nineteenth century, she wrote *Stories for Children* and *Domestic Management; or, The Healthful Cookery Book* (1804). She later joined her sister in writing *Tales of Wonder, of Humour, and of Sentiments* (1818). [*BD*, DNB (under Anne Plumptre), FCLE, Lonsdale]

PLUNKETT, Elizabeth. See **GUNNING**, Elizabeth.

The Poet's Child, Isabel Hill. John Warren published this five-act tragedy in 1820. Although Hill offered the play to CG, Charles Kemble, the manager, felt it would not be effective on stage and rejected the manuscript. On the advice of her brother, Benson Earle Hill, to whom the play is dedicated, she consented to have the play printed.

Set in Rome and its environs during Roman times, the drama opens on an argument between Pierro and his married daughter, Clyte, who pleads for her husband's reinstatement to the family. Pierro has information from his nephew, Lartius, that her husband, the poet Phoenix, continues to consort with other women and to keep disreputable company. Meanwhile, Marcia, daughter to Clyte and Phoenix, wishes to know her father whose name has been banned from the house. Marcia loves and wishes to marry her cousin Eugenius, but she feels it would be a disgrace since she doesn't know who her father is. Having returned from war, Eugenius cannot understand her attitude, and he tells her about the Noble Hermit who took care of him when he was wounded in the conflict. Eugenius knows that the hermit is Marcia's father: although he has been forbidden to tell her, he narrates the story of the man who became the Hermit when he was slandered in Rome, concluding by saying that man is your father. Marcia agrees to marry Eugenius now that she knows the identity of her father, but she insists on meeting him. After the pair receive permission to go visit a ruin, they go instead to the Hermitage. Because Marcia is tired, Eugenius has her stay with a peasant woman while he goes on, promising to return for her. These plans are overheard by Lartius. Following a talk with the peasant woman, Marcia is eager to meet her father and goes to him, though he says he is only Phoenix's friend. On the road, Eugenius meets Lartius, who has the young man taken by two ruffians. Lartius then sends one of the ruffians to get Marcia. Phoenix and his servant Volscius stop the abduction of Marcia, free Eugenius, and capture Lartius and the ruffians. Lartius, fatally wounded in the scuffle by Phoenix, curses his rival and dies. Eugenius takes Marcia and returns to Pierro to plead for Phoenix, who waits outside. After a long night of Eugenius speaking for Phoenix, Pierro sees that he has been wrong in believing Lartius's slanders against his son-in-law. Pierro receives

Phoenix and plans a banquet to reinstate him amongst the Roman nobles. Without Clyte's knowledge, Phoenix enters with Pierro's blessing, giving her quite a shock. Phoenix gives Marcia to Eugenius and buries the past, for truth has overcome slander.

While the author calls the play "a tragedy," it ends happily. The slanderer, Lartius, has been found out and has died for his crimes at the hand of his victim, and Phoenix has been restored to his wife and daughter. Phoenix's goodness attested to by Clyte, a harper, the peasant woman, and Marcia's nurse cannot move Pierro who remains convinced that Lartius, his own nephew, must be right about his son-in-law. Clyte, however, persists in supporting Phoenix. The stern Roman father Pierro finally admits his error in accepting the slanderous reports submitted by Lartius, who was motivated by greed for a legacy from Pierro and by lust for Clyte. Once Phoenix is rehabilitated in Pierro's eyes, the old Roman orchestrates the arrival of Phoenix for Clyte and arranges the marriage of Eugenius and Marcia. His making a public spectacle of these surprises seems to be intended to startle the women in the play, for by astounding them he appears as if he himself were suddenly responsible for truth emerging from slander.

TEXT: Readex Microprint.

The Poison Tree; or, Harlequin in Java, Jane M. Scott. This large-cast pantomime with fifty-eight roles and fifteen scenes opened 18 November 1811 and ran sixty-five successive performances that season. Although no staging plan for the pantomime appears to have survived, Frank McHugh describes the action as a patriotic celebration of the British conquest of Franco-Dutch forces in Java earlier that year. The spectacle included a bridal procession, an incidental ballet, and several views of Asiatic plants, including the poison tree (*Adelphi* 13).

POLWHELE, Elizabeth (1651?–1691). Possibly the daughter of Theophilus Polwhele and his first wife (m. May 1650). Polwhele was the author of several plays early in her life. Later, she married a dissenting clergyman, Stephen Lobb, and had five children. Elizabeth died in 1691.

This playwright of the Restoration era was virtually unknown until her manuscript of *The Frolicks* (1671) was transcribed and published by Judith Milhous and Robert Hume in 1977. In the preface to the manuscript, Polwhele mentions another play entitled *Elysium*, about which little is known since no manuscript or printed version survives (Milhous & Hume 58). An earlier tragedy, *The Faithful Virgins*, was likely to have been produced at LIF about 1670. It still exists in manuscript at the Bodleian Library, Oxford. Her comedy, *The Frolicks; or, The Lawyer Cheated*, has an extensive introduction by Milhous and Hume. [Cotton, DBAWW, FCLE, Hobby]

Pompey, translated by Katherine Philips. This tragedy, a translation of Pierre Corneille's *La Mort de Pompée* (1643), was first produced at the Theatre Royal, Smock Alley, Dublin, 10 February 1663. It may also have been performed in London during the late Spring of 1663 (*LS* 1: 64), though Curtis Price argues against a London performance (*TN* 33 [1979]: 61–66). Publication of the tragedy was that same year, in Dublin for Samuel Dancer, and in London for J. Crooke.

Pompée, the last of Corneille's four Roman dramas, takes place after the bloody and heroic battle of Pharsala (48 B.C.). Viewed by later critics as one of Corneille's least successful tragedies, it was well received by his contemporaries. Caesar has defeated Pompey, who seeks refuge at the Egyptian court of Ptolemey. Prompted by his scheming counselor Photin and by his own desire to secure the victor's favors, Ptolemey has Pompey treacherously assassinated, outraging Caesar. What follows is a web of intrigues and uprisings, ending in the death of the Egyptian advisors and in Ptolemey's drowning after a fierce battle. Thus, Cleopatra, who loves Caesar more out of ambition than anything else, finds herself the sole inheritor of the crown of Egypt that her father had entrusted to both herself and her brother, Ptolemey. Cornelia, Pompey's indomitable widow, warns Caesar of Ptolemey's plot to kill him out of her deep sense of honor and not because she had forgiven him her husband's death. Finding herself partially avenged, Cornelia vows to pursue Caesar openly until his death. The play ends on the preparations for Cleopatra's coronation and Pompey's public funeral. The true hero of the play is Pompey who, with his admirable widow, embodies moral integrity in a world led by corruption and unbridled ambition. His moral stature stands constantly in sharp contrast to the other characters' dark motives and sordid actions.

Twenty years after its opening in Paris, the tragedy was faithfully translated by Katherine Philips. Her version was first performed in Dublin, where she was staying at the time. The play met with extraordinary applause with its gorgeous costumes and splendid settings, despite what Souers calls its lack of "poetical quality" (204). Five hundred copies were quickly printed and sold. The elaborate production partly accounts for this reception, but credit must be given to the quality of the translation. As Souers shows, she remained very close to the sense of the original, while keeping to a couplet-for-couplet rendition and maintaining, as much as possible, the balanced constructions so characteristic of Corneille's rhetoric. Philips's fidelity stems from her belief that a translator is like a painter making a copy. She strongly criticized *Pompey the Great*, another translation that was staged a few months later (October 1663) in London, for the numerous liberties taken by her rivals, Waller, Buckhurst, and Sedley. Her only alteration resides in the added songs that punctuate each act and the dances incorporated after acts I, III, and V. She wanted "to lengthen the Play," but while doing so, she imparted her own verses with the heroic tone, so characteristic of the original work.

In the aftermath of the English civil wars, Corneille's play seems an appropriate one for Philips to choose. Caesar's attempted reconciliation and magnanimous treatment of the defeated side must have been what Philips wished for from Charles II since her husband actively supported Cromwell. The result was, in Patrick Thomas's words, "a remarkable achievement" (Cardiff: U of Wales P, 1988): 41. Philips may also have been gratified with the implicit morality that Pompey stood for—even in defeat and death. Cornelia, too, serves as a continuing reminder to keep these moral principles alive.

MANUSCRIPTS: (1) Folger Shakespeare Lib. MS V.b.231. (2) National Lib. of Wales MS 21867B.

TEXTS: Wing C6317; EEB Reel 89: 3 (London: J. Crooke, 1663). Wing C6318; [No EEB Microfilm yet.] (Dublin: printed by J. Crooke for Samuel Dancer, 1663). Readex Microprint of Wing C6317 (1663). Wing P2033; EEB Reel 748: 28 (1667); Wing P2034; EEB Reel 772: 3 (1669). Wing P2035: EEB Reel 748: 29 (1678). Readex Microprint of Wing P2033, *Poems* (London: H. Herringman, 1667). [NOTE: The recent facsimile in the Scholars' Reprint series of the *Poems* (1667) omits the plays.]

CRITICAL EDITION: Philips's *Collected Works*, vol. 3, ed. G. Greer and R. Little (Stump Cross, Essex: Stump Cross, 1993): 1–91.

The Poor Gentlewoman, Sarah Isdell. A comedy produced at the Crow-Street Theatre, Dublin on 4 March 1811. *BD* (appendix) says the play was acted "with great success. The heroine of this piece was a female *Goldfinch*; and the satire is directed against those ladies who, laying aside all the delicacy and softness of their sex, only wish to rival the heroes of the Four-in-Hand Club. We know not whether it has been printed, or not." There is no record of the play's being published.

POPE, Jane (1744?–1818). Growing up in the vicinity of Covent Garden, Pope appears to have been stage struck from an early age. After playing a few children's roles, she performed several parts at DL in the 1759–60 season, and during her apprenticeship formed a strong friendship with Kitty Clive, which lasted until Clive's death in 1785. Her stage career lasted fifty-two years, allowing her to play a wide range of characters. Having been the original Lady Flutter in Frances Sheridan's *The Discovery* (1763), Pope trimmed the plot to a two-act comedy, focusing on the feuding, newly married couple, and she performed it for her benefit night on 21 April 1767 at DL. *The Young Couple* was an afterpiece to Wycherley's *The Plain Dealer* (Pope playing Olivia). Pope's version did not enter the repertoire.

She performed with Garrick's company until a dispute over her salary caused her to go to Ireland for the 1775–76 season. According to BDAA, it was probably Kitty Clive who intervened on Pope's behalf, for she was back at DL the following season and remained there until 1807, where she created a number of well-known characters, such as Mrs. Candour in *The School for Scandal*. BDAA points out that her last original character was the Dowager Lady Morelove in Sophia Lee's *The Assignation* on 28 January 1807. She left the stage at the end of the following season and lived comfortably, thanks to prudent investments, until her death in 1818. [*BD*, BDAA, DNB, Nicoll]

PORTER, Anna Maria (1780–1832). Like her older sister Jane, Anna Maria was educated in Edinburgh and later moved to London, where she published her first work, *Artless Tales*, in 1793 at the age of thirteen. Best known for her historical and sentimental romance novels, Anna Maria also wrote a single play, a musical piece titled *The Fair Fugitives*. The performance took place at CG on 16 May 1803. Although the songs were published, as *Airs, Duets, and Choruses*, the full text has apparently not survived. Her novels tend to foreground individuals set against a large backdrop of European history and locales. Late in her life she entered into several collaborations with her sister Jane. [*BD*, DNB, EBWW, FCLE, NCBEL (3: 757), OCEL]

PORTER, Jane (1776–1850). Educated in Edinburgh, Jane is the sister of Anna Maria Porter, Sir Robert Ker Porter, and Dr. William Porter. Her first historical romance, *Thaddeus of Warsaw* (1803), became a great success largely owing to her sympathy with the Polish cause during the time of Napoleonic wars. Porter's five-volume story of William Wallace, *The Scottish Chiefs* (1810), also won acclaim by incorporating history and legend. A three-volume novel about the Stuart clan, *The Pastor's Fireside* (1815), was less successful, and for a while she turned to drama.

Porter completed three plays between 1817 and 1822. *Egmont; or, the Eve of St. Alyne*, her first play, was offered to Edmund Kean whose fellow actors refused to produce it; the play was never printed. Her next two dramas, however, did reach the stage. *Switzerland* was performed at DL on 15 February 1819 with Kean leading the cast, but it failed after one night. *Owen Prince of Powys; or, Welsh Feuds* played, again at DL, on 28 January 1822, but this tragedy was acted only three nights. The two plays that were staged were considered "lamentable failures," and neither was published.

After her encounter with the stage, Porter returned to her novels, a particular blend of history and imagination. With her sister, she also published *Tales Round a Winter Hearth* (1826) and *The Field of Forty Footsteps* (1828). After the death of Anna Maria from typhus in 1830, Porter's literary production fell off. During Porter's visit to her brother in St. Petersburg (1842), he died. Even though she received honors from abroad, Porter continued to live in financial difficulty until her death in 1850. [DNB, EBWW, FCLE, NCBEL (3:757), OCEL]

Poverty and Nobleness of Mind, translated by Maria Geisweiler. This transcription of Kotzebue's *Armuth und Edelsinn* was published in 1799 by C. Geisweiler. The three-act drama was not acted under Geisweiler's name, but the same play became the basis of Prince Hoare's *Sighs! or, The Daughter*, produced at the Haymarket Theatre on 30 July 1799.

Peter Plum is a man of business, who can scarcely speak a word without bringing money into the conversation. After the morning post has arrived, Stopsel, his clerk, says he has received a letter telling him of his father's death and of a large legacy. This allows Stopsel to offer marriage to Louisa, the supposed daughter of Plum's housekeeper, Mrs. Rose; despite Plum's urging, however, Louisa will not accept Stopsel. She prefers Plum's poor lodger, Cederstrom, from Sweden. In the same post, Plum has heard from an old university friend,

nor the Princess is aware that they are intended for each other, they try to get out of their state obligations. Under Nainda's guidance they are finally brought together, but not before the evil Iskouriah threatens the Prince. When he pulls a dagger, Nainda consigns him to the underworld. Nainda then urges Darakardin to maintain a permanent passion for Hlydia, while the Princess is warned to avoid indifference and inconstancy in marriage.

As a musical fairy tale, the Margravine's piece functions like a masque: music, dancing, and spectacle are more important than plot or language. That the female fairy also acts the governess to Hlydia is important, because Nainda teaches continuing mutual love between the couple, whereas Iskouriah, who covets power and freedom from control, causes tyranny to be added "to power, avarice to Wealth, Deceit to Love, Plunder to War" (3). Nainda organizes events so that after the couple falls in love they must be absent from one another for a while. In this case absence makes each heart grow fonder and more committed.

MANUSCRIPT: Larpent 1251. Readex Microprint of manuscript.

Profession Is Not Principle; or, The Name of Christian Is Not Christianity, Grace Kennedy. Published anonymously in Edinburgh, 1821, Kennedy's religious piece is written in the form of a dramatic composition according to Inglis, as well as Davis & Joyce. We have not seen a copy. DNB notes that this went through eight editions by 1855.

PROWDE, Anne; see "**EPHELIA**."

The Prude, Elizabeth Ryves. This three-act comic opera is set in 1558 at the end of Queen Mary's reign and the beginning of Elizabeth's; it was not performed. It was printed for Ryves in her *Poems on Several Occasions* and sold by J. Dodsley, 1777.

A love plot of two couples develops despite the blocking figure of the prude, Grizilda, aunt to Clementina. Sir William Sandby shows how gullible this intriguing old woman is by flattering her into an assignation so his friend the Earl of Lewington can visit Clementina, whom her aunt plans to send to a convent. Sir William discovers that Grizilda is in league with Father Dominick to gain the estate of Don Pedro, Grizilda's brother. Upon Don Pedro's return, the information is given to him, and he plans to have Father Dominick unfrocked; Grizilda leaves in a huff. The Earl is united with Clementina, and Sir William wins Jenny, who turns out to be the Earl's long lost sister. Thirty-five songs, incorporated into the libretto, are set to airs from old tunes. *BD* remarks that the "dialogue is chaste and animated; the incidents are simple, yet interesting; and some of the airs have considerable merit" (3: 185).

Using gender, class, and religious stereotypes, Ryves concocts an easy-going divertissement in the tradition of the comic ballad opera. By assuming that all older, unmarried women are intriguers, she creates the title character who acts the prude in public while scheming in private. Class is important to Sir William, who can't bring himself to marry the rustic Jenny until she turns out to be the sister of his friend the Earl. The anti-Catholic, Protestant views of priests having liaisons with nuns and other women is confirmed by Father Dominick's various manipulations. One character who breaks out of a stereotype is the Spanish diplomat, Don Pedro, who regrets his excessive religious zeal in trying to force Clementina into a convent. When shown the plots that have gone on behind his back, he makes amends by allowing his daughter to marry the Earl. Another admirable character, Mrs. Wilson, has raised Jenny on the request of her mother who was shipwrecked on a trip abroad, and Mrs. Wilson is pleased to deliver Jenny to her brother, the Earl.

FACSIMILE EDITION: Ballad Opera series, "Historical and Patriotic Subjects," vol. 2. Comp. Walter H. Rabsamen (NY: Garland, 1974).

The Public Wooing, Margaret Lucas Cavendish, Duchess of Newcastle. The drama was included in her *Playes*, published in 1662 by John Martyn, James Allestry, and Tho. Dicas. Called a "comedy" in the epilogue, the play was not staged. The text includes a few scenes by Cavendish's husband, the Marquis of Newcastle.

The controlling plot, as given in the title, is the public wooing of Prudence Sage by all sorts of eligible suitors: orations are made by various admirers, including a soldier, a country gentleman, a divine, a lawyer, a courtier, a citizen, and a farmer. Setting up a public event will, she thinks, protect her and curb unruly passions in men. Prudence, then, judges whether or not she finds suitors acceptable and explains why all are unacceptable, until a "strange wooer" comes to plead his case. He is described as a man with "a wooden Leg, a patch on his Eye, and Crook-back'd, unhandsome snarled Hair, and plain poor Cloaths on" (393). But he successfully woos Prudence's soul, and when she accepts the shocked audience goes away "holding up their hands as at a wonder" (396). After the marriage ceremony and before the bedding ritual, the bridegroom removes his eye patch, snarled periwig, and fake wooden leg to reveal himself as a very handsome man. We learn through the chorus of two gentlemen conversing that the bridegroom had previously led the army of the great Mogul, had been called another Julius Caesar, and is the Prince of Grandy. At this point a chorus of several young maids who had disdained the marriage, now become envious of Prudence. The only other sustained plot finds Sir Thomas Letgo unable to bolster an interest in his fiancée Lady Mute, because she says so little and everyone thinks her a fool. Sir William Holdfast, however, taking time to talk with and listen to her, finds Lady Mute sensible and virtuous; and he wishes she were not engaged. Later, Letgo, who spends much of his time gambling and losing, makes a wager with Holdfast, staking Lady Mute against £15,000. When he loses, Lady Mute speaks because she feels she has been set at liberty. In the end, Holdfast and Lady Mute are quietly married.

Like several of Cavendish's plays, this one has a fairy-tale structure, reinforced by Mistress Trifle's fable of the King's three daughters who are allowed to marry, but they must choose whether they want their husbands to be men during the day and beasts at night, or the reverse. The first two daughters want men during the day and beasts at night, but the youngest chooses to have a husband who was a beast during the day, "and a man at nights: for, said she, I will please my self, not caring what the World thinks or says" (412). Once Prudence has chosen the "strange wooer," he turns out to be a handsome prince. In the secondary plot, Letgo will not encourage his fiancée, and he loses Lady Mute to Holdfast who appreciates her virtue and dignity.

TEXTS: Wing N868. EEB Reel 502: 11. Readex Microprint.

Puss in Boots, the Margravine of Anspach, formerly Baroness Elizabeth Berkeley Craven. This pantomime was produced privately at Brandenburgh House in early June of 1799. There is no evidence that the play was printed.

PYE, Jael-Henrietta Mendez (1737?–1782). Pye wrote one farce, titled *The Capricious Lady*. It was produced at DL on 10 May 1771 as an afterpiece to Arthur Murphy's *Zenobia*, but it was never printed. The manuscript (Larpent 323) is in the Readex Microprint collection. [*BD* (some misinformation), DBAWW, FCLE]

-Q-

Queen Catharine; or, The Ruines of Love, Mary Pix. This five-act historical tragedy was first produced at LIF in June of 1698 and published for William Turner and Richard Basset the same year. Catharine Trotter supplied the epilogue. Elizabeth Barry took the title role; Anne Bracegirdle acted the Queen's ward Isabella; and Thomas Betterton played Owen Tudor. Even with a fine cast the tragedy met with little success and was not revived.

During the War of the Roses and following the death of Henry VI, the house of York hopes to win back the throne from the Lancasters. Edward IV claims the title, but must defeat the forces of Queen Catharine. He is also angry with the Queen, who earlier spurned his advances in favor of Owen Tudor. Edward expresses his objections to Clarence's desire to marry Isabella, the ward of the Queen. The villain of the piece is Gloucester (later Richard III) who plans to use Clarence's love of Isabella for his own ignoble ends. Meanwhile in Ludlow Castle, Catharine plans a clandestine meeting with Owen Tudor. She also warns Isabella about Clarence. Sir James Thyrrold comes to woo Isabella, but she has no interest in his "sawcy passion"; after she leaves, he plans to undermine her love for Clarence, who prefers love to war and awaits Isabella in a grove outside the castle. Her "divided Soul" is torn between her love for him and her duty to the Queen; finally, she agrees to meet Clarence at midnight and fly with him to France because she has a key to a secret entrance to a castle. Gloucester fabricates a story to make Clarence suspect Isabella's constancy. When Owen Tudor arrives at the secret entrance, Isabella admits him and leaves the key with one of Gloucester's henchmen. Gloucester gets the key to the secret entrance and gives it to Edward, who plans to trap Tudor. Clarence receives a feigned letter in which Isabella is characterized as Sir James Thyrrold's "plighted wife," and this is reinforced when Thyrrold orders Clarence away. Inside the castle, the Queen and Tudor are the example of the loving couple, but suddenly they are confronted by Edward and Gloucester who have gotten in the secret entrance. The Queen pleads for Tudor, but when he flies at them Gloucester stabs him dead and sends Isabella off with Thyrrold. Edward claims victory. At the castle Thyrrold forces Isabella to marry him and threatens her if she doesn't consummate the marriage. Clarence enters and Isabella is wounded in the scuffle: Thyrrold flees, and Isabella tells Clarence they were both betrayed and dies. Clarence wishes a Roman death and is about to fall on his sword when Warwick stops him. Catharine goes mad over Tudor's death, but when her children are brought to her she remembers Tudor's last wish that she should live for them. She'll retire to a monastery. Edward concludes the play hoping for justice throughout the kingdom.

Trying to follow Shakespeare in writing a historical play, Pix set the time between *3 Henry VI* and *Richard III*, in the mid 1470s. While the play relies on historical figures, actions and events are largely made up for Betterton's LIF acting company and their strengths. The relationships of the historical characters, however, are muddy: when Henry is mentioned, for instance, the audience isn't clear whether it's Henry V or Henry VI. The play has gotten little appreciative notice by recent critics: Pearson notes how men manipulate the passive women. Cotton dismisses the tragedy because "the play reduces the War of the Roses to a quarrel over thwarted love" (115), and Hume calls it "an historical tearjerker" (451). However, Clark notes that Herbert Carter found this play to be the best one written by a woman in the Restoration (263, referring to "Three Women Dramatists of the Restoration" in *Bookman's Journal* 13 [1925]: 97).

TEXTS: Wing P2331. EEB Reel 1099: 3. Readex Microprint.

FACSIMILE EDITION: E-CED, with introduction by Edna L. Steeves (NY: Garland, 1982).

Queen Tragedy Restored, Mrs. Hoper. This allegorical burlesque was produced at the Haymarket only two nights, 9 and 11 November 1749, and printed the same year by W. Owen. Mrs. Hoper acted the Queen, and the second night was for the benefit of the author.

The play attempts to show, according to Smith and Lawhon, that the stage can be restored to its former greatness (166). In her current state, Queen Tragedy is suffering from too much bombast. Her physicians, Dr. Doleful and Dr. Drollery, recommend cures by opposite methods, but they finally agree on a mixture of half tragedy and half comedy. A play-within-a-play from Virgil's "Dido and Aeneas" is then given, but it only succeeds in putting the Queen to sleep. At the conclusion, Shakespeare rises and the Queen recovers.

Genest remarks that, although he finds the piece "indifferent, there are 3 or 4 very good observations in it" (10: 175). Smith & Lawhon point out that Elizabeth Boyd's *Don Sancho* (1739) anticipates Hoper's burlesque, especially in the framing of the play-within-a-play and the return of Shakespeare to the stage (167).

TEXT: Readex Microprint.

Quite Correct, Caroline Boaden. This three-act comedy was produced at the Haymarket Theatre on 29 July 1825. It is founded on a French piece, called *The Slanderer*. While it was acted forty-eight times, the comedy was never printed. Genest (9: 315) says Boaden "added Liston's character [Grojan, a hotel-keeper] and made other alterations." The comedy, shortened to two acts, was revived at HAY on 1 July 1830 and ran for thirty-six performances; J. Reeve took the role of Grojan, since Liston had retired (Genest 9: 528).

MANUSCRIPT: BL Add. Ms. 42874, ff. 651–690b.

-R-

RAINSFORD, Mrs. (fl. 1794). The author of one musical farce, Rainsford is not otherwise known. Her play, *The Speechless Wife* (produced at CG on 22 May 1794), was based on Matthew Prior's poem "The Ladle." The dramatization was condemned the first night and never printed. Rainsford's foray into the theatre now exists only in manuscript, Larpent 1025. [*LS*]

Rambles Farther: a Continuation of Rural Walks, Charlotte Turner Smith. This novel in dialogues written in dramatic form for young people follows Smith's earlier *Rural Walks* (1795). T. Cadell and Davies published the sequel in 1796; a Dublin edition of the sequel came out the same year, printed by P. Wogan and six others. Smith's preface is dated 16 May 1796.

In this dramatic novel, Mrs. Woodfield instructs her two daughters and other young people. All the lessons have a clear moral. In this sequel to the previous *Rural Walks*, the extended family goes from the country to the city, and the children profit by comparisons of urban and rural settings. The structure, typical of books for the young, moves from home in the country to a larger world and back again to the rural home.

Contrasts frequently demonstrate lessons, which Mrs. Woodfield is quick to point out. The frequent quotations of poetry encourage the young to memorize verses to fix an event firmly in their mind. In her biography of Smith, Florence Hilbish cites the importance of public life in these episodes. Comparing *Rambles Farther* to the earlier *Rural Walks*, she notes that a commentary in the *Critical Review* found the chapters "noticeably inferior in spontaneity and dialogue, but not in didacticism" (185). An evaluation in the *Monthly Review*, however, believed the two volumes could stand together.

TEXT: Not in Readex Microprint. We read the 1796 Dublin edition in the King Collection of the Miami (Ohio) U Library.

Rare en Tout, Anne de La Roche-Guilhen. A comic masque in French performed at the Hall Theatre at the Whitehall Court on 29 May 1677. *Rare en Tout* was published the same year in French by Jacques Magnes and Richard Bentley.

The setting to *Rare en Tout* shows an exterior scene of Whitehall in the background, and a prelude begins with an extended (four-page) prologue. In the play itself, Europe, followed by the nations of the continent, implores the Thames (a nymph) to intercede with the King of England and encourage him to impose peace in time of war. The comedy itself is composed of three acts in verse with two interludes made up of songs and ballets. The thin plot has Rare-en-Tout following the singer Climène, whom he loves, to England where he falls under the charms of Isabelle, an English singer. Finette, Isabelle's maid, accepts favorably the declarations of love made to her by La Treille, Rare-en-Tout's servant, until she learns of his master's betrayal of Climène. Then Finette rejects La Treille for not informing her, saying that she and her mistress will, in fact, soon marry better suitors. Neither master nor servant seems much upset by the news, because the latter is promised gold and the former considers infidelity a guiding principle, believing no woman can resist him. So Rare-en-tout goes immediately on further amorous conquests. In the epilogue, set in a pastoral decor, Love addresses the ladies and calls upon shepherds and satyrs to close the performance with more singing and dancing.

This masque appears to have no other ambition than to provide a pleasing aesthetic experience. Despite one or two remarks against arrogant masters, the combination of music, dance, scene, and verses are principally designed for the enjoyment of the court, but especially for Charles II on his birthday. Elenore Boswell quotes John Verney's eye-witness account of the performance, which he claims was "most pitifully done" (122). Pearson notes the reversal of social roles prominent in the play: "the servant rebukes the master, the valet insists on his essential equality with the gentleman" (137).

TEXT: Wing L448. EEB Reel 109: 14. Not in Readex Microprint.

Raykisnah the Outcast; or, The Hollow Tree, Jane M. Scott. This three-act spectacle was first performed at the Sans Pareil Theatre on 22 November 1813 and ran thirty-three nights. Scott took the role of Luxima, and George W. Reeve composed the music.

MANUSCRIPT: Larpent 1784.

Raymond de Percy; or, The Tenant of the Tomb, Margaret Harvey. Described as "a romantic Melo Drame," this three-act play was produced in Sutherland in April 1822 and published the same year by G. Garbutt in Bishopswearmouth. Although a cast list appears in the printed version, Nicoll believes the play may have also been presented at Harvey's boarding school in Bishopswearmouth, Durham. Harvey notes in the dedication to Mrs. Coutts and her preface that this is her "first dramatic effort" (iii, v).

Set at Alnwick Castle, Northumberland, and at Castle Angus, on the Tweed River, the play includes Scottish music. The events take place at the time of the crusades, probably the twelfth century. After the Earl of Northumberland has welcomed Sir Conrade de Valmonte to a banquet, a bugle sounds announcing the arrival of the Earl's son, Raymond de Percy. When de Percy sees Conrade, he calls him a villain and demands he leave, contrary to the dictates of hospitality. De Percy has no time to explain himself for just then Gwynilda, his intended, enters. During the preparation of a toast, Kenrick, Conrade's henchman, slips in and pours a phial into de Percy's goblet. After a song by the harper Duncan, de Percy feels ill and is carried to his chamber. In his own supposedly haunted castle, Conrade awaits Kenrick, who comes to report that the deed has been done. After de Percy's burial, Gwynilda kneels by his grave when Conrade accosts her, only to have a voice speak from the tomb: "Villain forbear!" Conrade faints, allowing Gwynilda to flee. Conrade later tells Kenrick, who warns him away from the tomb. Heedless of this advice, Conrade goes back and cries "come forth, thou tenant of the tomb" (26), and a specter rises, causing Conrade to flee. After he tells this story to Kenrick, the specter comes and takes Kenrick below through a trap door, causing Conrade to faint. The final act occurs two years later, when a repentant Conrade confesses to a speechless Hermit, who is actually Kenrick in disguise. Northumberland has planned a tournament to celebrate the return of some warriors from the crusades. When an unknown knight enters the lists, he is challenged by a knight with a red cross on his arm. This knight just back from the crusades defeats the stranger, who turns out to be Conrade, and declares he is Raymond de Percy. Kenrick confesses he gave de Percy an opiate, not poison, and he carries the fatally wounded Conrade from the field. Now de Percy can wed Gwynilda. In a second plot, Lord Hubert de Umfranville plans to marry his cousin Bertha de Umfranville, but his father, the Earl of Angus, objects. Duncan the harper assists Bertha to escape from the castle of her uncle, Hubert's father the Earl of Angus. Duncan takes Bertha, disguised as a highland boy, to Northumberland's Castle Alnwick where she has a reunion with Gwynilda. Upon Hubert's return from the crusade a marriage will take place after the tournament on Alnwick's fields.

Coincidence and unbelievable occurrences mar this gothic drama, but Harvey's play includes popular strains of theatre in the early 1820s. In addition to the gothic stage sets, the Scottish trappings point to the wide interest in Sir Walter Scott, whose novels were often dramatized. The music, as noted on the title page, is also Scots: indeed, bagpipes offstage herald the approaching tournament. Harvey arranges her horrific scenes to be followed by comic ones that involve a fool (Motley), a dwarf (Goliah), and a housekeeper (Ursula), who speaks in malapropisms. This juxtaposition of comedy and terror sets up contrasts in the extremes of fear and laughter. While they are not on stage a great deal, both aristocratic women demonstrate bravery in the face of oppressive men: Gwynilda fights off Conrade in the graveyard, and Bertha in a male disguise flees from her uncle.

TEXT: Readex Microprint.

Rayner, Joanna Baillie. This five-act tragedy first appeared in her *Miscellaneous Plays* of 1804. It was not acted.

Set in Germany, the play begins with the dissipated Count Zaterloo reveling with his followers. Zaterloo suggests a new addition to their party: Rayner, who is despondent because the villain Hubert has deprived him of his inheritance. Desirous of this fortune, Zaterloo plays on Rayner's anger, encouraging him to kill Hubert as he leaves town with his treasure. At first Rayner recoils, insisting "there's a law above all human bonds . . . and says, 'do thou no murder'" (15). Meanwhile, the woman to whom Rayner is betrothed, Elizabeth, has been abandoned by the friend with whom she lived and is coming to meet him. Insisting that Rayner join them, Count Zaterloo and his band go into the woods to intercept Hubert's carriage. Separated from the others in a wild storm, Rayner seeks shelter in a cave of a hermit, who confesses he is a murderer and deeply repentant. Just as he is ready to repudiate Zaterloo, Rayner hears a shot, and leaving the cave, Rayner is captured by some of the men traveling with Hubert. After he is condemned to death and led away from court, Hubert comes upon Elizabeth, who faints upon realizing his fate. As he awaits his execution, Rayner is befriended by an old general, Hardibrand, who served with and was a close friend to Rayner's father. Thinking of Rayner as his own son, Hardibrand goes to the Governor in his behalf, but he is not successful. Elizabeth is steadfast in her love for Rayner, declaring that she would be willing to live with him in prison, making "a little parlour of thy cell" (86). Meanwhile, Countess Zaterloo has discovered the whereabouts of her son; learning that he is wounded and an outlaw, she disguises herself and goes to nurse him. After Zaterloo has confessed that he is the murderer to his mother, Elizabeth arrives begging the Countess to notify the Governor and thereby prevent an innocent man's death. Countess Zaterloo refuses to do so, but later reconsiders when Zaterloo is dying. Just before Rayner goes to his execution, Ohio—an African prince who became a slave and was abandoned at the prison when he became ill—tries to steal the prisoner's cloak because he is cold. Rayner treats him kindly and gives him the cloak. Growing in stature as he awaits his execution, Rayner goes to the gallows with dignity; but he is saved by Ohio, who has sawed across the main prop of the scaffold, causing the platform to fall when the executioner steps upon it. A messenger then arrives with the Governor's pardon, declaring that Rayner is guiltless of the crime. Hardibrand declares that Ohio is indeed a prince, and he makes Rayner his heir.

According to her preface of *Miscellaneous Plays*, Baillie wrote *Rayner* "many years ago, when I was not very old, and still younger from my ignorance of every thing regarding literature than from my years" (xi). Nevertheless, the play is typical of the concern in Baillie's dramas for stable domestic situations, rooted perhaps in the financial dependence she, her mother, and sister experienced for the decade after her father's death. Rayner, denied the inheritance he anticipated, must let his servant go and is unable to pay for his housing. Elizabeth, too, goes to Rayner, no longer having a place to live. Other characters seem similarly displaced: Ohio has been taken into slavery and abandoned when ill; Count Zaterloo dismisses his mother's care until he is an outlaw

Humour leave her small chair? Forced into an undesirable marriage, she will have no choice but to run to her "Neighbor's bed" (554). These parallels encourage readers to consider the two marriages of each plot: a forced marriage versus a voluntary marrying for love.

TEXTS: Wing N868. EEB Reel 502: 11. Readex Microprint.

Reparation; or, The Savoyards, Mrs. Martin. This three-act drama was printed by John Nichols and Son in 1823. There is no indication in Genest that it was acted, and there is no manuscript in the Larpent Collection to indicate a performance.

Set in the Savoy countryside between Geneva and Turin, the play opens on Belton, a young Englishman dwelling in the area with his old servant Frank. The lengthy first act provides the background of Belton and his friend, Lord Rivers, both of whom seem to live only for pleasure: current women friends include Viola and the Marchioness Lusigni (who never appears on stage). Belton speaks of a past interest in Claudine, while Rivers has a present interest in Justine who has recently left him. Belton tells how he betrayed Claudine, and he wishes to make reparation to her; Rivers wants to find Justine and hopes that Madame Felix will assist his search. Little Ben reports to Belton that Claude, Claudine in disguise, is sick and Belton goes with him to aid her. Claude tells Belton that Claudine is no more: because he is Claudine's cousin, Claude knows her story. Belton asks Claude and Ben to live with him. Through Madame Felix, Rivers has discovered that Claudine and Justine are one in the same, and he decides to help, if he can locate her. Meanwhile Claude tells Belton Claudine's story: finding herself pregnant, Claudine confessed to her father, who threw her out. Nannette, Claudine's sister, took her to a pious priest who admitted Claudine to his house where she gave birth to Ben. When she felt she couldn't stay longer, Claudine traveled with Claude to find Madame Felix, who then introduced her to Rivers. The English lord pursued her "ungenerously." Claude says that when Claudine was no more, he took responsibility for Ben. Claude also relates that Claudine forgave Belton's "error of thoughtless youth" and asked him to care for Ben, his son. Two more events complicate the plot: Viola, Belton's former lover, has hired an assassin to murder him, and Claudine's father and sister are seeking Madame Felix. Just as the assassin prepares to kill Belton, Claude leaps in front of Belton and is stabbed. A surgeon arrives to tend the wounded Claude, who—believing the injury is fatal—confesses to Belton that she is Claudine. When the surgeon assures Belton that Claudine will live, Belton wishes to marry Claudine, but she will only accept him if her father blesses her. Just then, Nannette enters with their father, and in a tableau the three Savoyards end the play together once again.

While the main title suggests a theme of making amends for having done wrong, the subtitle reminds us of the country people of Savoy to whom redress is due: Claudine, her father Simon, and her sister Nannette. The dissolute Englishmen have come to their country with seduction in mind, and the simple country folk cause them to adjust their sophisticated views. It is not enough for Belton to marry the woman he has wronged, but she must receive her father's blessing. While Belton regrets his betrayal of Claudine, she takes the responsibility and does something to rectify his disloyalty. Questions still remain: why does the woman feel she must satisfy male authority (father and seducer)? Is it significant that Claudine must gain Belton's confidence by cross-dressing? And isn't Claudine at the end of the play taking the traditional role of the forgiving woman? Because most of the dissolute characters arouse little interest, readers may feel grateful for Claude/Claudine's appearance in the second act. Her excessive nobility, however, plainly reinforces what was to become the Victorian norm: "suffer and be silent."

TEXT: Readex Microprint.

The Revenge; or, A Match in Newgate, attributed to Aphra Behn. Based on Marston's *The Dutch Courtesan*, the five-act comedy was probably produced at DG in June 1680 and printed later that year for W. Cademan. While several early commentators attribute the play to Thomas Betterton (*BD*), others (Langbaine and Genest), as well as most recent critics (Hume, Link, Gewirtz), believe the comedy to have most of Behn's hallmarks.

Wellman, the rover of the play, has seduced Corina (played by Elizabeth Barry), but he intends to marry Marinda, whose sister, Diana, would like to marry Friendly—if he only showed a little more spirit. Wellman introduces Friendly to Corina, and Friendly falls for her instantly. But before Corina will accept him, she wants Friendly to kill Wellman. The companions plan to trick Corina with a fatal duel; however, Wellman has Friendly arrested, then rescues him at the last moment in Newgate prison. After Friendly's involvement in several scrapes, Diana proposes marriage to him in Newgate. Marinda accepts Wellman, who passes Corina off to Sir John Empty as his only sister. The subplot takes up the duping of Dashit, a vintner, by Trickwell, who believes Dashit has bilked him out of his estate. The two plots are brought together in the last act as Wellman forces Trickwell to marry Mrs. Dunwell, a bawd. The final scene in Newgate includes a digression where Shamrock's wife admits to a robbery she did not commit in order to hang with her husband.

Wellman's treatment of Corina is evidence of the double standard in action: men simply have a greater degree of sexual freedom than women. Nevertheless, Wellman changes by the end of the play: he takes care that Corina is provided for by marrying her as his "only sister" to Sir John Empty, telling her aside "nor will I ever undeceive him" (62). The treatment of the deflowered woman differs greatly from Behn's source, where she is whipped. Audience sympathy for Corina grows after she is angry enough to have Wellman murdered. As the compassionately treated whore, Corina is related to others in Behn comedies such as Angellica Bianca (*Rover I*), La Nuche (*Rover II*), and Diana (*The City Heiress*), as Clifford Gewirtz notes (165).

TEXTS: Wing B2084. EEB Reel 14: 4. Readex Microprint.

CRITICAL EDITION: An old-spelling text with an introduction edited by Douglas R. Butler, who argues convincingly for Behn's authorship. Diss., Penn. State, 1982.

The Revolution of Sweden, Catharine Trotter. This five-act, historical tragedy in blank verse premiered at the Queen's Theatre on 11 February 1706 and ran for six nights (Downes 102; Hume and Milhous in their notes say only four performances). Although the play was not revived, it was published by James Knapton and George Strahan the same year (*Daily Courant*, 18 March 1706—Burling). In 1703, Trotter sought assistance from Congreve, whose suggestions seem to have assisted her in shaping the play. The cast included Thomas Betterton as Count Arwide and Elizabeth Barry as Constantia.

Gustavus, with the popular support of loyal Swedes, attempts to drive the Danes from his country. As the play opens, Gustavus has managed to escape the Danes, but he feels it important to send the peasants in his army back to harvest their crops. While he is discussing the next move with his lieutenant Erici, Christina (in men's clothing) comes to join his forces, taking the name of her nephew Fredage. Gustavus tells Fredage that Christina saved his life: she learned that her husband, Beron, planned to betray Gustavus, and she helped him escape. Since that time she has been a fugitive from her husband and the Danes. Gustavus sends a conciliatory letter to the Archbishop of Upsal urging him to join the loyal Swedes, but he is so angered by this that he goes on the attack. The Archbishop's troops run into Count Arwide's troops, and when they try to retreat Gustavus routs them. Even in defeat, the Archbishop's diminished force captures Constantia, Arwide's wife, as well as Fredage. Discovering his wife has been taken hostage, Arwide goes to the Viceroy and offers to take her place, even though Constantia is willing to die for the Swedish cause. The Viceroy and Beron separate Arwide and Constantia. A critical event takes place offstage: Beron proposes terms to Arwide, and he agrees. But the articles he signs are wholly different. Meanwhile, the Viceroy lusts after Constantia and shows her the false articles Arwide signed, promising to assist the Danes and leaving her a hostage. After the Lubeck fleet has blocked the port of Stockholm, Gustavus will permit the Danes to leave, if they release their prisoners. The Archbishop urges this, and the Viceroy finally accepts, even though it means he will lose Constantia. Beron and Fredage will rejoin the Swedes. Constantia arrives at the camp before her husband and demands to see Gustavus. Having seen the false articles Arwide signed, Constantia warns Gustavus that Arwide has acted treacherously. Nevertheless, she asks his pardon. Gustavus wants to find Arwide honest, but treats him coolly when he arrives and asks for Beron's pardon. Arwide can't understand why he's shunned, but he suspects Beron, who in fact plans more mischief. At the senate, Gustavus is named Administrator, but a charge is brought against Arwide. Fredage, wounded by Beron, says Arwide signed the false articles and swoons. Arwide is condemned to death, even though Constantia pleads for him. Just as Arwide is being taken out, Fredage revives and declares Arwide innocent and Beron—her husband—guilty of substituting false articles. After Fredage (Christina) dies, Beron is sentenced to death, and Arwide, now freed, unites with Constantia. Gustavus makes a final speech about the duty of a monarch to his subjects.

The decision almost every major character in the play must make is for either public or private good. Because Christina believes Beron's betrayal of the Swedish is wrong, she disguises herself in order to join the Swedish campaign. Her dying words free the patriot Arwide and condemn Beron. Constantia feels impelled to tell Gustavus her suspicions about Arwide. Even the Viceroy would rather keep Constantia than retreat to Denmark. Cotton stresses that "each wife is the superior of her husband" (106), and she believes the depiction of heroic women creates a strong play. Although well-crafted, the play did not succeed on stage. Burling notes that "after 1701 Trotter consciously moved in the direction of 'soft' tragedy, which featured tests of fidelity and courage and a resolution stressing the inevitable triumph of love" (*Curtain Calls* 317). Posing another point of view, Blaydes declares "Trotter's heroes are women who place honor and courage above romantic or married love" (DLB 84: 330).

TEXT: Readex Microprint.

FACSIMILE EDITION: *The Plays of Mary Pix and Catharine Trotter*, vol. 2, with introduction by Edna L. Steeves (NY: Garland, 1982).

RICHARDSON, Elizabeth (d. 1779). The author of one five-act comedy, Richardson died in the same year of its production. *The Double Deception; or, Lovers Perplexed* was first produced at DL on 28 April 1779, but it was never printed, though the manuscript is in the Larpent Collection (478). There were four performances at the end of the 1778–79 season. Two performances were given the following season (one as a benefit for the author's heirs). [*BD*]

RICHARDSON, Sarah Watts (d. 1823/24). After the death of her husband, Joseph, Richardson turned to writing to support herself and her family. She wrote two tragedies that were published by subscription, but neither was acted. *Ethelred* and *Gertrude* have no date on the title pages, but they came out around 1809 or 1810. [DNB (under Joseph Richardson), FCLE (gives her maiden name as Fawcett)]

Rienzi, Mary Russell Mitford. This five-act tragedy was first produced at DL on 9 October 1828 and published the same year by J. Cumberland. The play was acted thirty-four times its first season, according to Genest (9: 454–55). Mitford received £400 for the production and the book version sold well (8,000 copies in its first two months). In her Preface, Mitford says that the play is based on Gibbon (*History of the Decline and Fall of the Roman Empire*) and on the second volume of *L'Abbé de Sade's Mémoires pour écrire la Vie de Pétrarque*.

Rienzi begins with exposition, revealing the Roman citizens' hatred for the noblemen who rule the city, "plundering and killing the peaceful citizens" (13). Risen from modest birth, Cola di Rienzi leads the people in a revolt, motivated largely by his idealistic view of ancient Rome and his desire to revenge his younger brother's murder. In a related (Juliet and Romeo) subplot, Rienzi's daughter, Claudia, is in love with Angelo Colonna, the son of the head of one of the two rival noble families. Aware of Angelo's love for justice, Rienzi enlists the young Colonna's support for the rebellion. Alberti, Captain of the Guard and an old friend of Rienzi's, also lends his support. When Savelli, a lord of the Colonna faction, warns Stephen Colonna (Angelo's father) that Rienzi is leading a rebellion, the threat is not taken seriously, since all attention is focused on the rival Ursini house. With unqualified support from the people, Rienzi easily overwhelms Rome and is hailed as the Tribune, refusing the title of Consul or Emperor. Instead of feeling joy at her father's success, Claudia laments the change in her status, fearing "the hot barons, . . . the fickle people, And the inconstancy of power" (34). Dissatisfaction with the Tribune grows after Martin Ursini is condemned to death. Although he argues that he doles out equal justice for citizen and nobleman alike, Rienzi makes repeated references to his brother's murder by the Ursinis. When the houses of Ursini and Colonna unite to plot his overthrow on the day of his daughter's bridal banquet, Rienzi is forewarned and forces the noblemen to take a vow of loyalty before pardoning them. Impressed by the Tribune's mercy, Angelo calls Rienzi his "father," but Angelo later severs ties with Rienzi when he seems increasingly ambitious and tyrannical. When the Colonnas and Ursinis plan an uprising, Angelo plays a leading role in the revolt; although their forces are pushed back, the people of Rome are tired of fighting and the Tribune is faltering. Having killed Stephen Colonna and Ursini in battle, Rienzi has taken Angelo prisoner. When he refuses to submit his will, insisting that the Tribune has "levelled to the earth the pride Of my old princely race" (58), Angelo is sentenced to death. Although Claudia successfully begs for his life, Rienzi's pardon arrives too late, and Angelo is executed. In the final scene, Savelli joined by citizens advances against Rienzi, who recognizes too late that he has forgotten his idealism: "Oh, had I laid All earthly passion, pride, and pomp, and power, . . . and hot lust of rule, Like sacrificial fruits, upon the altar of Liberty" (64). After the people pierce his body through with swords, Claudia throws herself on his body and bleeds to death.

Although set in Rome in the fourteenth century, *Rienzi* demonstrates the extent to which the French Revolution influenced early nineteenth-century writers. It is easy to see why the play was popular. The character of Rienzi combines cynicism and idealism; and even minor characters such as Lady Colonna are well defined and psychologically convincing. Mitford has crafted the plot carefully and she generates a good deal of suspense, especially at the bridal banquet.

TEXT: Readex Microprint.

The Rival Widows; or, Fair Libertine, Elizabeth Cooper. This five-act comedy had its debut at CG on 22 February 1735 and was printed the same year by T. Woodward. It ran for six nights with the author taking the role of Lady Bellair on her benefit nights, 27 February and 6 March. In the preface, Cooper stresses the play's "Regularity and Decorum" while she preserves the unities. She also points out that in her first play she has created a heroine "capable of thinking for herself, and acting on the Principles of Nature and Truth" (v).

The play opens with Sir William Freelove arguing with Modern about how they can best foster the development of young men. Freelove gives his son only a pittance, whereas Modern provides a generous income for his nephew. Young Freelove has a strong affection for the impoverished widow, Lady Bellair, and Young Modern has an interest in another widow, Lady Lurcher, because she is rich—even though he thinks her a prude. These two widowed cousins engage in a not-always-friendly rivalry. In much of the play, Lady Bellair tests Young Freelove to see if he will be a suitable husband. On the other hand, Lady Lurcher schemes to gain Young Freelove for herself, thus the play's title. To complicate matters, Freelove wants his son to marry the wealthy Lady Lurcher and to give up the penurious Lady Bellair, whereas Young Modern wants to marry Lady Bellair merely to sleep with her. When Lady Lurcher is discovered to hold a deed in trust for her cousin for £10,000, her plots and schemes crumble, clearing the way for Young Freelove to marry Lady Bellair. Lady Lurcher leaves in disgrace, and Young Modern's hypocritical actions cause him to be rejected by his uncle, who would disinherit him except for Lady Bellair's plea of generosity toward a young man who may change his ways. Thus, Lady Bellair is, as the epilogue notes, "but a Libertine in Name" (124).

Although the play lacks action and comes across as excessively prolix, it emphasizes the importance of a woman testing a man before marriage to see what sort of husband he will be. Lady Bellair has several trials that Young Freelove must pass before she agrees to marry him: a proviso scene in Act III, Scene 12 works very much like the similar scene in *The Way of the World* by Congreve, whose work provided the epigraph, "This was an Off'ring to the Sex designed," that Cooper choose for the title page. A subtheme included in the play, the proper education of young men, comes through the text by showing that generosity and not miserliness is an important characteristic to be learned. In the end, virtue triumphs over vice with a vengeance in the discrediting of Lady Lurcher and the rejection of Young Modern, and in the likely marriage of Young Freelove to Lady Bellair.

TEXT: Readex Microprint.

The Robbers, translation attributed to the Margravine of Anspach, formerly Baroness Elizabeth Berkeley Craven. NCBEL credits her son with the translation (2: 863). This five-act tragedy, translated and altered from Schiller's first drama (1782), was produced privately at Brandenburgh House in 1798 and printed the following year by W. Wigstead and M. Hooper. The translator also supplied the prologue and epilogue.

Set in the sixteenth century, *The Robbers* deals with two brothers who have rejected their father's court for different reasons. Karl Moor has escaped to a Bohemian forest where he has become leader of a band of robbers who steal from the wealthy and give to the poor. In order to ingratiate himself, Franz recounts Karl's acts to their father. While contemplating a return home, Karl receives a letter from Franz falsely telling Karl that he has been disinherited. Anxious to acquire his legacy, Franz tells his father that Karl has died in order to hasten the old man's death. Franz also attempts to gain the regard of Amalia, Karl's beloved. When Karl does return, he finds Franz has taken over his father's estate and rules like a tyrant. Karl believes himself responsible for his father's death, until he learns that Franz has imprisoned their father, leaving him to starve. With Karl as their leader, the robber band sets the fortress ablaze. During the onslaught, a frightened Franz commits suicide. When Karl's father realizes Karl commanded the attack, he dies. Amalia, who still loves Karl, finds he has committed himself unalterably to the robbers by oath, and she entreats that he kill her. He does as she asks, but then turns himself over to the authorities of justice.

TEXT: Not in Readex Microprint. TEC Reel 4963: 9.

ROBE, Jane (fl. 1723). Author of one five-act tragedy, entitled *The Fatal Legacy*, Robe translated Racine's *La Thébaïde* and added an additional act. The play was produced at LIF on 23 April 1723, running four nights (once by royal command). FCLE reports that Robe received over £40 for her benefit. E. Simon, J. Roberts, and A. Dodd printed the tragedy the same year. [*BD*, FCLE]

ROBERTS, Miss R. (1730?–1788). Better known as a poet and sermon writer, Roberts wrote one historical tragedy in blank verse with Malcolm and MacDuff acting the same characters as in *Macbeth*. *Malcolm* was not acted, but it was printed for the author in 1779. [*BD*, DBAWW, FCLE]

ROBERTSON, Mrs. T. (fl. 1796). Little is known about this one-time playwright who wrote a single musical entertainment that was said (by *BD*) to have been acted at Wisbeach in 1796. *The Enchanted Island; or, The Freeborn Englishwoman* was not printed. The play should not be confused with a ballet by the same first title (acted 20 June 1804 at HAY). [*BD*]

ROBERTSON, Mrs. (fl. 1800). Author of a romantic (perhaps gothic) drama, Robertson wrote only one play, *Ellinda; or, The Abbey of St. Aubert*, which was produced at Newark in 1800 but never printed. Davis & Joyce note that she was a member of the Newark acting company. Because Mary Darby Robinson wrote a novel by the same name (BDAA 13: 37), could this be a dramatization based on Robinson's novel? [*BD*]

ROBINSON, Mary Darby, "Perdita." (1758–1800). Born in Bristol to a sea captain and his wife, Mary attended a school run by the five sisters of Hannah More and later went to schools in London. She secretly married Thomas Robinson, a solicitor's clerk, in 1774, but shortly after the birth of their daughter her husband went to debtors' prison where Mary joined him. Subsequently, with Garrick's coaching, Robinson made her debut at DL as Juliet on 10 December 1776 and performed several roles until the birth of her second daughter in the spring. In the fall of 1777, she became a regular member of the DL company.

Learning by her association with the stage, Robinson wrote her first drama the following spring: *The Lucky Escape*, a farce with a pastiche of music, was performed as an afterpiece for her benefit night on 30 May 1778; she had taken the role of Lady Macbeth in the main piece. She acted in the 1778–80 seasons at DL, while "Thomas Robinson sank lower, financially and morally" (BDAA 13: 33). Mary gained the attention of several noblemen who wished to "take her into their protection"; after her appearance as Perdita in *The Winter's Tale*, the Prince of Wales made advances, which led to an affair that lasted more than a year. Robinson did return to the stage at CG where she created the role of Victoria in Hannah Cowley's *Bold Stroke for a Husband* (25 March 1783). On a trip to Europe, she contracted rheumatic fever which would plague her for the rest of her life. In an effort to recoup her finances, Robinson acted for a few months in early 1787 at the Edinburgh theatre, where she may have written a farce with music, *Kate of Aberdeen*. This play has been attributed to her by *BD*, though the authors claim not to have seen it. Robinson turned to poetry and other writing while she tried to regain her health: in 1792, she completed a novel, *Vancenza, or The Dangers of Credulity*, and the following year a second volume of poems. She also returned to the drama: her satiric farce *Nobody* was produced at DL on 29 November 1794; it played only three nights and was never published. In addition, she wrote a tragedy, *The Sicilian Lover*, in 1796; though it was published, no performance occurred.

In her last year, Robinson wrote *Ellinda, or the Abbey of St. Aubert*, another volume of poetry, a translation, and a Christmas tale in verse. After her death in December 1800, her daughter, Maria Elizabeth, edited her mother's *Memoirs* (1801) and her posthumous *Poetical Works* (1806). [*BD*, BDAA, BNA, DBAWW, DNB, EBWW, FCLE, Lonsdale. Biography M. Steen, 1937.]

ROCHE-GUILHEN, Anne de La. See **De La ROCHE-GUILHEN**.

The Roman Father, Laetitia Pilkington. Only the first act of this tragedy was printed; it appears in the second volume of her *Memoirs* (1749). Pilkington says that the personal opposition of Thomas Sheridan, manager of the Smock Alley Theatre in Dublin, stopped her from completing the play. It is perhaps worth noting that William Whitehead's play by the same title, but on a different subject, premiered 24 February 1750 at DL.

The Patrician tyrant Appius Claudius tells Clodius of his infatuation with the Plebeian Virginia, and the latter informs him of her engagement and imminent marriage to Iccilius. Clodius undertakes to help facilitate Appius's cause: Clodius sends a messenger to Virginius's father and to Iccilius that they are to report for urgent military duty, thus getting them out of the way for Appius Claudius's evil plans. Here, the fragment ends.

Pilkington took for the subject of her tragedy the often dramatized tale of Appius and Virginia (first recorded in Livy), where her father Virginius kills the despotic Appius, who has raped his daughter.

TEXT: *Memoirs of Mrs. Laetitia Pilkington*, vol. 2 (Dublin and London: R. Griffiths, 1749): 319 [mispaged 219] – 340.

FACSIMILE EDITION: *Swiftiana*, vol. 18 (NY: Garland, 1975).

Romiero, Joanna Baillie. This five-act tragedy was published in her collected *Dramas* in 1836 by Longman, et al. There is no record of a performance.

The play is set in the castle of Romiero during the fourteenth century when Peter the Cruel was King of Castile. Among the shipwrecked sailors who seek refuge in the castle is Sebastian, the father of Donna Zorada, wife of Don Romiero. Sebastian has fled the country when his plot to depose the unjust King was discovered, and he warns Zorada not to inform her husband of his presence, since Romiero has sworn to the King to turn the traitors in. When Romiero reveals to his wife that he indeed made such a promise, believing his father-in-law out of the country, Zorada decides to keep Sebastian's presence a secret, a decision which inadvertently prompts Romiero's jealousy of his wife. When Zorada absents herself from her husband's presence, and Don Guzman (Romiero's friend) overhears a woman speaking with Maurice late at night, Romiero becomes increasingly jealous, convinced that his wife intends to run away with Maurice. When Romiero discovers that Maurice is trying to run away with Beatrice—not Zorada—his jealousy subsides until he discovers a picture of his wife in a basket of delicacies intended for Sebastian. Meanwhile, Sebastian himself has been hidden in an old abandoned chapel in the woods, and a servant informs Romiero that a woman resembling Zorada has been observed going into the woods at night. Determined to catch his wife with her lover, Romiero goes into the woods and becomes insane when he discovers Zorada and her nurse with an unidentified man. As Romiero comes toward them, Zorada tries to force her father to flee, but he returns to protect her against her husband. Accidentally, Romiero stabs Zorada while pursuing Sebastian. As she is dying, Zorada forgives her husband. Out of blind despair, Romiero baits Sebastian into fighting; after he is fatally wounded, Romiero asks for forgiveness and requests that Guzman aid Sebastian's escape.

Marlon B. Ross (DLB 93: 12) notes that Baillie's *De Monfort* is not as "ambitious nor as accomplished" as *Romiero* and several of her other late tragedies. According to an article she wrote in *Fraser's Magazine* (Dec. 1836), Baillie wished to "internalize the psychology of jealousy, rather than granting so much influence to a seemingly unmotivated villain like Iago" (DLB: 93: 12). In this and other respects, the author succeeded admirably. Although Romiero explains that his jealousy is the result of his loving too passionately, there is considerable evidence in the text that his negative attitude toward women may be a more deeply rooted cause. For example, when speaking to Beatrice, he says that "*well* [the condition of wellness or health] was banish'd from the world When woman come to it" (96). And slightly later he adds, "It makes me sick To think of what you [women] seem and what you are" (97). This attitude has apparently been held for some time: his servant Pietro reports that Romiero's mother was exasperated when she would encourage him to marry and "he'd speak Of women, even the fairest and the best, With such sharp taunts" (22). While he seems to love his wife, he is distrustful at best of her gender. Zorada, too, has psychological depth, and she is courageous and wise in her decision to aid her father without informing her husband. She, her nurse, and Beatrice help one another work around Romiero's difficult behavior. Even less important characters such as Beatrice and Guzman are developed sufficiently to serve as contrasts to the lead roles: for example, as Romiero goes increasingly mad in the woods, Guzman tries to control his emotions with appeals to rationality and sane behavior.

TEXT: Readex Microprint of *Dramas* (1836) 1: 1–119.

Rosamond, translated by Fanny Holcroft. This five-act historical tragedy is rendered from the German of [Christian Felix] Weisse

(1642–1702). Printed in *The Theatrical Recorder*, vol. 2, no. 12, edited by Thomas Holcroft (London: C. Mercier, 1806): 359–397, the play was not produced.

With the help of Helmige, Rosamond has murdered her husband, King Alboin, but the two found it necessary to flee Lombardy. They are sheltered in Ravenna in the palace of Longinus, where the action takes place. Longinus has granted them protection for the sake of Albissvintha, Rosamond's daughter by Alboin. Albissvintha wants her mother to confirm she had no part in the murder of her father, but Rosamond tells Albissvintha that she took revenge because Alboin killed her father, though in war. Rosamond also orders Albissvintha to stay away from Longinus, for in a soliloquy Rosamond expresses lustful interest in Ravenna's ruler. This presents a problem for Albissvintha because she loves Longinus, yet she tells him that if he is offered her hand, Longinus must refuse. To win friendship with Longinus, Helmige urges the ruler to marry Albissvintha. When Longinus demurs, this feeds Rosamond's view that Longinus loves her. Accordingly, Rosamond plots the murder of Helmige and tries to enlist the help of Albissvintha, who is at first ready to take revenge. After a talk with Longinus, however, she tries to dissuade her mother from murdering Helmige. But Rosamond has prepared the poison, and she has a dagger if the poison fails. When Helmige drinks, he realizes what has happened; he grabs a dagger and forces Rosamond to drink poison also. They are nearly dead when Albissvintha and Longinus find them, and asking her daughter for one last embrace, Rosamond stabs her. The wound is slight, however, and Albissvintha lives. Longinus concludes the play saying that illicit love caused tragedy.

Weisse's original in verse features only four characters. Holcroft translates the play into prose, and she manages to maintain the tension between the characters quite well. As the instigator of all the crimes, Rosamond is wickedness incarnate: she has convinced Helmige to murder Alboin; and she later presses her daughter to take revenge for Alboin's sake and kill Helmige. Pairing the depraved Rosamond with her better-natured daughter provides two contrasting women. Albissvintha avoids being pulled into her mother's plot to kill Helmige, thanks to Longinus who convinces Albissvintha that even a revenge murder is wrong. Rosamond, on the other hand, has no compunction about killing anyone who stands in her way, and in this she outdoes Lady Macbeth.

TEXT: Readex Microprint.

The Rose, the Thistle, and the Shamrock, Maria Edgeworth. Printed in her volume of *Comic Dramas, in three acts*, published by R. Hunter et al., in 1817, the play was not produced professionally.

Set in the Irish village of Bannow, the play turns on who will manage the new inn. The interrelationship between the English, the Scotch, and the Irish begins with Sir William Hamden, who, with his servant Gilbert, has come to visit his niece Clara O'Hara, who has become the new owner of the inn. The present manager is the boozy Christy Gallagher, who has let the inn run down so badly that he can scarcely quarter the Scottish troops who have come. The drum major of the Scottish regiment is Andrew Hope, whose brother told him of the generosity of the old innkeeping family, the widow Larken and her two children, Mabel and Owen. The bashful Gilbert can only woo Mabel by giving her an English rose and an Irish shamrock. It appears that Christy will win the right to manage the inn because he sent a poem with his petition to Clara, and she has written across the bottom "granted the poet's petition." But the lazy Christy merely copied a poem written by Owen, so Owen and the Larkens, now including the bashful Gilbert, will run the inn, to be called "Rose, Thistle, and Shamrock."

The rather thin plot is overwhelmed by an assortment of nationalistic characters, as well as poetry, dance, and song celebrating each of the three kingdoms. Butler, in her biography of Edgeworth, says that Edgeworth took the character of Christy Gallagher from real life, whereas the others are stock stage figures of turn-of-the-century drama.

TEXTS: Readex Microprint of *Comic dramas, in Three Acts*, 1817, and of the second edition, 1817.

FACSIMILE EDITION: The 1893 Longford edition of Edgeworth's *Novels and Tales* has been reprinted by two presses: AMS (1967) and Georg Olms (1969).

Rosina, Frances Brooke. This popular comic opera in two acts is founded on the biblical story of Ruth, but largely adapted from Charles Simon Favart's *Les Moissonneurs* (1768). Produced at CG on 31 December 1782, with music by W. Shield, the opera scored a great success with audiences, being acted thirty-nine times the first season; it held the stage well into the nineteenth century. Genest notes an earlier English translation, *The Reapers*, published in 1770, but not performed (6: 266–67). Lorraine McMullen, Brooke's biographer, believes Brooke used Favart's French text rather than the English translation. T. Cadell published Brooke's version in 1783; by 1796 it had gone through fourteen editions.

Set in the countryside at harvest time, this pastoral opera centers on Rosina, a beautiful, destitute, but virtuous orphan who devotes her youth and energy to ensure the survival of her beloved adopted mother. Necessity made a gleaner out of her, but Belville, the land-owning squire, has noticed in Rosina a dignity and decorum incommensurate with her low status. Captain Belville, the squire's libertine brother, who lusts after Rosina, tries to seduce her with money and goes so far as having her kidnapped. But his attempts fail, and the reticent Rosina, who turns out to come from a very fine family, marries the man she did not dare love openly: Belville, the generous but very paternalistic landholder, has shown throughout the piece a concern for the lowly reapers. Songs and dialogues alternate until the happy ending.

The stimulus for this work comes from Favart's *Les Moissonneurs [The Reapers]*. In fact, Brooke retained most of the plot, including the purse episode where money is left on a bench to seduce Rosina, and the abduction scheme where Captain Belville slips into the poor women's humble cottage. Both pieces end happily as the reapers dance and offer flowers to the happy couples, but minor changes are introduced, such as part of the abduction taking place by way of a skiff, the French stepmother becoming an adopted mother, the omission of the comical three gossips, or the addition of two unimportant characters William and Phoebe who marry as well at the end. Although she preserved Favart's stage directions (in fact, she translated them word for word), Brooke did alter the mood of the piece by toning down the sentimental and moralistic message of Favart. She also condensed the work from three acts to two acts, while retaining parts of Favart's dialogue ("Quiconque offense ce qu'il aime est indigne de l'obtenir" becomes under Brooke's pen "Whoever offends the object of his love is unworthy of obtaining her" [42]). Although the family relationship of the two men who woo Rosina has been altered —uncle and nephew become brothers—it is hard to see Brooke's piece as a source of "heightened suspense," suggested by Kinne (176), since their rivalry is short-lived. Brooke's alterations from her source appear to have suited British audiences, who made the opera a great success well into the nineteenth-century.

Despite Rosina's spirited personality, it is her newly discovered social status, as the daughter of deceased Colonel Martin, that allows Belville to accept her. Without the disclosure of this class distinction, Rosina could have ended being seduced and abandoned by Captain Belville. Crass realism seldom seriously mars comic operas, however; and in an age that asked for sentiment and sensitivity, Brooke provided the right balance of tuneful pathos and high-flown moralizing.

MANUSCRIPT: Larpent 612. Readex Microprint of manuscript.

TEXT: Readex Microprint of 1782 edition. Readex Microprint of Dick's edition, vol. 12, 1872.

ROSS, Anna, later Anna Brunton (b. 1773). The child of actors, Anna Ross saw her comic opera, *The Cottagers*, printed by subscription in 1788 and later produced at the Crow-Street Theatre, Dublin, on 19 May 1789. Writing in the preface to her one play, the fifteen-year-old

Ross describes herself as a "forward little scribbler." Her alter ego may be represented in *The Cottagers* by the inventive Charlotte Harwin, who loves disguises and dressing up. Though her play was never performed in London, she herself acted in one performance on the London stage at CG on 16 May 1788, when she took the role of Sylvia in *Cymon* for the benefit night of her mother, Mrs. Brown, and her stepfather, Mr. J. Brown. She later played on the Edinburgh stage in 1792, and married the younger John Brunton (1775–1849) later that year. She acted at Norwich from 1794 to 1800, and acted in her husband's company at Brighton in 1809. The Bruntons had several children, but there is no information as to the length of Anna Ross Brunton's life. According to FCLE, she is not related to the novelist, Mary Balfour Brunton (1778–1818). [*BD*, BDAA]

The Roundheads; or, The Good Old Cause, Aphra Behn. This five-act comedy is based, in part, on John Tatham's *The Rump* of 1660. Probably produced at DG in December 1681, *The Roundheads* was printed the following year for D. Brown, T. Benskin, and H. Rhodes.

After the death of Cromwell and the resignation of his son Richard, the "Rump Parliament" governed England late in 1659 and early in 1660. Behn sets her play during this turbulent period before the return of Charles II. It is at once a play of political and sexual intrigue. Freeman and Loveless are Royalists, often referred to as "Heroicks," who are trying to get back their sequestered lands from the Commonwealth. While waiting on the slow-moving bureaucracy to act on their cases, these Cavaliers have preoccupied themselves with two Puritan ladies: Freeman loves Lady Desbro; Loveless woos Lady Lambert. Lady Desbro feels herself wedded to Freeman because her husband had acquired Freeman's lands during the interregnum and they are not legally married. Lady Lambert's husband may be named Protector, or King, and she is sufficiently vain about the possibility. The play moves from political intrigue to sexual adventure: as Lords Lambert and Desbro embroil themselves in political maneuvering and matters of state, their wives arrange assignations, hide their gallants, and make the most of their husbands' absences. As the events unfold, the governing of the state gets worse and falls apart when the Commonwealth Council hears that General Monk and his army are marching from Scotland. This leads to quarrels within the Council, where Lord Lambert is remanded to the Tower, and Lord Desbro dies of fright. Freeman and Loveless save their ladies from being attacked by the angry pro-Royalist mobs, and in the last scene several of the former Commonwealth leaders are reduced to rejoining the common people.

The play mingles politics, seduction, and comedy; it includes ahistorical events with real characters; and it clearly opts for the Tory/Royalist side (Behn's own persuasion) against the Puritan leaders of the Commonwealth. Audiences can find some sympathy for Lady Desbro's position, for she has Royalist views while living with a Puritan husband. But it is more difficult to appreciate Lady Lambert's vanity: she does after all want to be Queen. Loveless, however, declares his love for her despite her place in the Commonwealth hierarchy. Link mentions the "farcical exaggeration" of the Commonwealth Council and finds the play "farcical propaganda" (68–69). In Behn's later play, *The Widow Ranter*, there are similar jokes at the expense of self-serving committee meetings, featuring pointless remarks and stupid actions. For Hume, the play is "boisterous but hopelessly disjointed" (358); and Woodcock can scarcely find anything good to say about the play, "as political satire, it is in the worst taste" (153). Elizabeth Bennett Kubek finds lots to praise about the play and provides a detailed comparison with Behn's source John Tatham's *The Rump* (*Restoration* 17 [1993]: 88–103). Finally, Susan J. Owen puts the play in the context of the Exclusion Crisis (1678–1683) in her discussion of that topic (*Restoration* 18 [1994]: 37–47).

TEXTS: Wing B1761; EEB Reel 54: 6 (1682). Wing B1762; EEB Reel 1396: 14 (1698). Readex Microprint of the 1682 edition.

MODERN EDITION: *Works*, ed. Montague Summers (1915; NY: Phaeton, 1967) 1: 331–425.

The Rout, Jane M. Scott. This one-woman show, an entertainment, was presented by Scott for the first time on 17 November 1806; that season Scott gave forty-two performances, each "advertised to run forty-five minutes." No text of the entertainment survives.

The Rover; or, The Banish't Cavaliers, Aphra Behn. The most popular of Behn's comedies, this five-act play was produced at DG on 24 March 1677, with Thomas Betterton as Belvile, Mary Betterton as Florinda, William Smith as Willmore, Elizabeth Barry as Hellena, Anne Quin as Angelica, and Cave Underhill as Blunt. The play was printed for John Amery in 1677. In *Aphra Behn: An Annotated Bibliography* (1986), Mary Ann O'Donnell points out that *The Rover* was reprinted seven times in the eighteenth century, showing its continuing popularity. Behn also adapted Thomas Killigrew's *Thomaso; or, The Wanderer* (1654, never acted). Arthur Gewirtz compares Killigrew's closet drama to Behn's theatrical success in his *Restoration Adaptations of Early 17th Century Comedies* (Washington, DC: UP of America, 1982): 94–100.

In Spain, Belvile had rescued Pedro and his sister, Florinda, who has fallen in love with the English colonel. Set in Spanish Naples during Carnival season, the first scene reveals Hellena, who is bound for a convent, and Florinda, who will be forced to marry Vincentio, a rich old man, or Antonio, the viceroy's son. When the young women masquerade as gypsies, they see the cavaliers—Belvile, Blunt, Frederick, and Willmore, the rover. Florinda makes an assignation with Belvile, Willmore banters with Hellena, and Blunt makes a date with Lucetta, a courtesan. The cavaliers hear about the famous courtesan, Angelica Bianca, and they observe Pedro and Antonio fighting over her. After the Spaniards depart, Angelica invites Willmore in, falls in love, and lavishes her favors on him. Later, in different disguises, Florinda, Hellena, and Valeria step aside to observe the cavaliers. After Willmore leaves Angelica, Hellena comes forward and makes him swear never to see Angelica again. Florinda arranges a meeting with Belvile. That evening, Blunt arrives at his assignation with Lucetta, but going into her bedroom, Blunt falls down a trap door. Her cohorts take his money and jewels. Blunt emerges from a sewer and curses Lucetta and himself for being such a fool. The same evening, a drunken Willmore makes amorous advances to Florinda without realizing who she is. This causes a rift between him and Belvile. Several disguises and a number of quarrels later, Florinda accepts Belvile with Pedro's approval, but when they get to church, Willmore again blunders by giving away the disguised Belvile. Hellena comes, disguised in men's clothes, and argues with Angelica about Willmore. Florinda escapes only to be pursued by Willmore. To avoid him, she ducks into a house that happens to be Belvile's. Seeking revenge, Blunt is about to rape her, when Belvile enters and saves her. While Belvile and Florinda are being married, Angelica comes in and threatens Willmore with a pistol, but she ultimately leaves, giving Willmore his life. Hellena and Willmore finally agree to an unconventional marriage.

Hellena and Florinda set the tone of this very theatrical comedy in the opening scene: they decide what they wish in their future husbands, though not how they will achieve their goals. The conflicts they encounter, and the various kinds of love developed are central to the action. The brave but stolid Belvile and the serious Florinda (who avoids a forced marriage) are romantic lovers; they differ markedly from Willmore and Hellena, the witty couple. Love as a commercial transaction can be seen in Blunt's assignation with Lucetta, and in Pedro and Antonio's fighting over Angelica. Yet Angelica gives up her economic interest by freely offering herself to Willmore. His later rejection of her leads to a last melodramatic scene where Angelica gains our sympathy as the wronged woman. Moreover, she shows her "contempt" by threatening to shoot Willmore and then by walking out on him.

TEXTS: Wing B1763; EEB Reel 446: 3 (1677). Wing B1764; EEB Reel 1627: 9 (1697). Readex Microprint of the 1677 edition.

MODERN EDITIONS: Behn, *Works*, ed. Montague Summers (1915; NY: Phaeton, 1967) 1: 1–107. *Restoration Comedy*, ed. A.

Norman Jeffares (London: Folio Society, 1974) 2: 227–331. Acting text adapted by John Barton (London: Methuen, 1987). Behn, *Five Plays*, introduction by Maureen Duffy (London: Methuen, 1990), reprints Summers's text: 101–204.

CRITICAL EDITIONS: Edited with introduction by Frederick Link (Lincoln: U Nebraska P, 1967); edited with introduction by Anne Russell (Peterborough, Ont., CAN: Broadview, 1994).

The Row of Ballynavogue; or, The Lily of Lismore, Jane M. Scott. This two-act farce opened on 27 November 1817 at the Sans Pareil Theatre and ran thirty-seven times its first season. McMillan notes that the licenser's copy had the title, *Ballynavogue; or, The Lilly [sic] of Lismore*, and had some deletions.

MANUSCRIPT: Larpent 1994.

The Royal Mischief, Delariviere Manley. This five-act tragedy was first produced at LIF in April or May 1696 and printed the same year for R. Bentley, F. Saunders, and J. Knapton. It was acted six nights by an exceptional cast: Thomas Betterton (Osman), Elizabeth Barry (Homais), Ann Bracegirdle (Bassima), William Bowman (Levan Dadian), and Elizabeth Bowman (Selima). Jean Chardin's *Travels to Persia* (1686) is Manley's immediate source, but hovering in the background are the heroic dramas of Dryden and the bloody revenge tragedies of the 1670s, such as Behn's *Abdelazer*.

Set in and around the Castle of Phasia in Libardian, the tragedy examines a pervasive evil radiated by the Princess, Homais. Like the libardine plant (*aconitum* or wolf's-bane), Homais poisons the aristocracy. Recently married to the Prince of Libardian (the elderly and impotent "protector"), the Princess spreads her lust with the aid of Acmat, her trusty eunuch. Her first suitor, Osman, now the Chief Visier, has married the Prince's sister Selima. Osman's brother, Ismael, was Homais's first lover, and Acmat comes to enlist Ismael's help in securing the Prince's nephew for Homais. They convince Levan Dadian to visit the Princess, since the Prince is knocked out by an opiate draft. Bassima, Levan's wife, has been cool to him, and he is delighted by the prospect of seeing Homais. During this tryst, Osman—overheard by Selima—woos Bassima. Homais tries to get Ismael to kill the Prince, and he agrees—if she will go to bed with him again. Selima, meanwhile, charges Osman with duplicity, and he says only that Bassima is innocent. The Prince knowing of Homais's villainy has her seized: his plan is to have her killed, but incredibly she talks him out of the execution. Bassima is poisoned by Acmat, and as she is dying Osman tries to make love to her. When she expires, Osman is dragged away and shot from a cannon; Selima goes mad from grief. As Homais tells Levan that they have conquered, the Prince rushes in and stabs her. Levan falls on his sword, leaving only the Prince.

The blood and gore are precipitated by Homais whose lust knows no bounds. Other than Homais, the characters develop little: it is her lust, or "royal Mischief," that affects the entire kingdom. Married to the jealous Prince of Libardian, she has a former paramour procure Levan Dadian, the Prince's nephew, for her. Lust and, ultimately, death abound: the play concludes with the Prince the only person alive on stage. The "notorious" detail, usually recalled about the tragedy, is a report of the death of Osman, who is shot from a cannon, "his carcass shattering in a thousand pieces." Then, we hear of his faithful widow Selima "gathering the smoaking Relicks of her Lord." With a drama that seems to thrive on excess, it is not surprising that a parody was staged only a few months after *The Royal Mischief* opened. Nevertheless, the play was popular with contemporary audiences; a "succès de scandale" is Fidelis Morgan's term.

TEXTS: Wing M436. EEB Reel 36: 7. Readex Microprint.

MODERN EDITION: *The Female Wits*, ed. Fidelis Morgan, (London: Virago, 1981): 209–61.

The Runaway, Hannah Cowley. This five-act comedy was produced at DL on 15 February 1776 and printed the same year for the author. Originally called *The Cantabs; or, The College Vacation*, the altered title was suggested by Garrick. Cowley also dedicated the publication to Garrick, who supplied the epilogue and supervised the production. Sarah Siddons originated the title role in her first year at DL. The comedy had a successful run of seventeen nights its first season and continued to be staged for the next fifteen years.

When George Hargrave returns from Cambridge for the summer, he finds his widowed father interested in Lady Dinah, who has £40,000. In fact, Hargrave senior wishes his son to marry Lady Dinah, and this confusion produces many of the contretemps in the play, such as when George goes to discuss with Lady Dinah her marriage with his father. Harriet, George's sister, admires one of his college friends, Sir Charles Seymour, though George hints that Seymour may have another inamorata. Bella, the lively cousin of George and Harriet, joins them in the garden, where Lady Dinah holds forth on the ancients, while Hargrave talks about his horses and hounds. Mr. Drummond, George's godfather, arrives and explains that Emily has run away to avoid a forced marriage; he has taken her under his protection, but since he is single, he asks Hargrave to allow her to stay in his house without giving her family name. The coincidence is that George had previously met Emily at a masquerade and fallen in love with her. After Sir Charles arrives, Lady Dinah observes George's partiality to Emily and offers her maid, Susan, £200 if she can drive Emily from the house. Susan concocts a scheme with Jarvis, another servant, to assert that Emily was once a strolling player with him. Asked about this allegation, Emily stoutly rejects the charge. Upon Major Morley being announced, Emily admits he is her uncle. Although Morley forces Emily to leave, George follows and snatches Emily from him, causing Morley to return to the Hargrave house. However, Emily requests George to conduct her to her uncle. Drummond prevails upon Morley to allow the couple to marry, and Sir Charles asks for Harriet's hand. The deceptions of Lady Dinah are uncovered, and she leaves in disgrace. Bella has heard that her lover has returned to England; thus, the happy group anticipates three weddings.

Genest offered qualified praise for the comedy: "Cowley afterwards wrote other plays that were more successful than the Runaway, but she perhaps never wrote a better" (5: 490). Even with problems that beset a new playwright—undeveloped situations, use of stock characters, and scenes that don't forward the plot, Cowley did indeed capture the essence of a country house comedy. In his introduction, Link recognizes how Cowley has arranged contrasting pairs with George and his cousin Bella providing the wit, Sir Charles and Harriet supplying the sentiment. Drummond maintains a voice of reason throughout. When others become acrimonious, he maintains a calm demeanor; and when others are avaricious, he represents a spirit of generosity. Link argues that the comedy is well constructed because of the intertwining of the three principal plot lines: George and Emily's uncertain marital expectations; Sir Charles and Harriet's misunderstandings, created by George and Bella; and the exposure of Lady Dinah's schemes, her pretentiousness, and the contretemps over who is to marry her—Hargrave or his son—when in fact neither wants that honor. Cowley had some second thoughts about the language of the play and made several alterations in her *Works*, published posthumously in 1813, though the plot remains the same.

MANUSCRIPT: Larpent 402, includes Garrick's alterations.

TEXTS: Readex Microprint. TEC Reels 1494: 1 (probably a piracy [1776]); 2953: 8 (first, 1776); 576: 18 (second, 1776); 4364: 10 (new edition for I. Dodsley and others, 1776).

FACSIMILE EDITION: E-CED, with introduction by F. Link (NY: Garland, 1982).

Rural Walks, Charlotte Turner Smith. A novel in dialogues written in dramatic form for young people in which lessons are taught by the highly capable mother. Published by T. Cadell, Jr., and W. Davies; a Dublin publication appeared the same year by P. Wogan and eleven others. The preface, dated 19 November 1794, records that Smith intended the moral lessons for her youngest daughter Harriet aged twelve. This work is one of several pieces Smith prepared for children and adolescents. A sequel, *Rambles Farther: a Continuation of Rural Walks*, was published by Cadell and Davies in 1796.

The events in the dramatic novel take place over a calendar year from January to December: Mrs. Woodfield, a widow who lives "about sixty miles from London," agrees to rear her thirteen-year-old niece with her own daughters. The somewhat spoiled niece, Caroline Cecil, has suffered the recent death of her mother, and she has nowhere to go since her father, Mrs. Woodfield's brother, must rejoin his regiment abroad. Many of Mrs. Woodfield's instructional monologues occur on the walks in the neighborhood, where she provides some factual material about flowers and gardens followed by moralistic lessons. Elizabeth and Henrietta Woodfield have a strong moral education and slowly Caroline learns from their actions, as well as from her aunt. They assist their poor and sick neighbors, learn from bad and good examples of diverse villagers, and gain an appreciation of poetry from Mrs. Woodfield. Every chapter concludes with verses from Cowper, Thomson, Anna Seward, Burns, Hannah More, or other poets writing about nature. Toward the end of the year, they learn that Colonel Cecil has been injured and will be returning to England. The events close on the longest night of the year with the family—including the Colonel—assembled together, reciting verses and telling stories.

A number of subjects to be taken up by romantic poets are considered in the dialogues: the beauty of nature and what it teaches, the lesson of man's inhumanity to man, and the appearance of crippled beggars and ruined monasteries. Mrs. Woodfield (her name is well chosen) teaches by her words and actions. She also becomes a model to the girls, showing courage and tolerance in raising young girls as a single parent.

TEXT: Not in Readex Microprint. We read the 1795 Dublin edition in the King Collection of the Miami (Ohio) U Library.

Rural Visitors; or, Singularity, Jane M. Scott. A musical piece, with recitation, acted first by the author at the Sans Pareil Theatre on 12 January 1807. It ran four nights and was revived the following season. J. W. Donohue reprints a playbill from a pre-Easter 1807 performance of this play in his *Theatre in the Age of Kean* (1975). No text is extant of the musical numbers.

RYVES, Elizabeth (1750–1797). She describes herself in a letter to David Garrick (10 June 1770) as "the Daughter of an Officer who left me an Orphan at 8 years old at his decease." Ryves's letter, quoted in notes to Garrick's response, asks him to produce a play of hers—*The Tragedy of Adelaide* (No. 595 in *The Letters of David Garrick*, ed. D. M. Little and G. M. Kahrl [Cambridge: Harvard UP, 1963] 2: 699–700). He refused and the play is no longer extant.

In addition to her early dramatic aspirations, which include four plays, Ryves was also known as a poet and novelist. A ballad opera, *The Prude*, and a masque, *The Triumph of Hymen*, are both printed in her *Poems on Several Occasions*, 1777. For her comedy, *The Debt of Honour*, Ryves was paid £100 when accepted by DL, but it was never produced. A dramatic dialogue in poetry, *Dialogue in the Elysian Fields between Caesar and Cato* appears to have been published in 1784; the manuscript, which has corrections by the author, is at the BL [11632.h.19 (3)].

In the 1780s, Ryves wrote several published poems for various occasions: odes addressed to Lord Melton (1787) and the Reverend Mr. Mason (1780), an epistle to John Cavendish (1784), and a satire on the Warren Hastings trial—the *Hastiniad* (1785). Her one novel, *The Hermit of Snowden*, came out in 1790. Ryves also translated M. De la Croix's lectures into *The Review of Constitutions of the Principal States of Europe and the United States of America* (1792). [*BD*, DBAWW, DNB, FCLE]

-S-

Sacred Dramas, Hannah More. Printed 1782 by T. Cadell, the volume includes *Moses in the Bulrushes* (11–44); *David and Goliath* (45–124); *Belshazzar* (125–189); *Daniel* (191–253). Added in later editions was *Reflections of King Hezekiah in his Sickness*, which appears in volume 2 of her *Works* (1801): 259–70. More had these plays from the Old Testament acted by school children before their publication in 1782. The dramas were enormously popular to judge by the number of editions (16th in 1810, 24th in 1829), with printings in New York (1794), Boston (1811), and Edinburgh (1825).

In all these plays, More hewed closely to the biblical texts, not allowing herself "to invent circumstances," as she remarks in her preface. Because two plays have epigraphs from Racine, More must have wished her dramas to follow the success of his biblical plays in French schools. Two of More's plays (*Moses* and *Daniel*) were altered for performance by Tate Wilkinson's company in Doncaster, though audiences in Hull objected to putting biblical characters on stage, and further performances were canceled.

TEXTS: Readex Microprint (plays by their titles) of 1782 edition; Readex Microprint of *Reflections of King Hezekiah in his Sickness* from volume 2 of More's *Works*, 1801.

FACSIMILE EDITION: 1782 text (Bern, Switzerland: Herbert Lang, 1973).

The Sacrifice, Susanna Centlivre. Although announced for performance in the *Weekly Pacquet* of 20 Feb. 1720, it was unperformed according to Burling. No known text is extant. The mention of such a title may refer to Centlivre's *The Artifice* (1722). Or, perhaps, the title may have been altered.

Sadak and Kalasrade; or, The Waters of Oblivion, Mary Russell Mitford. Work on this romantic opera in two acts was begun late in 1831, but production did not happen until 20 April 1835 at the Lyceum Theatre; the libretto was published the same year by S. G. Fairbrother. The music was composed by Charles Parker. Genest records an "Asiatick Spectacle," *Sadak and Kalastrade; or, The Waters of Oblivion*, that was first performed at CG on 11 April 1814 (Kalastrade spelled with a "t"). This piece, said to be "in the Tales of the Genii," was "acted 33 times," but was "not printed" (8: 424). In her Preface, Mitford mentions no specific Eastern tale as her source.

As the opera begins, Kalasrade rejoices in the garden that her husband Sadak, the Commander of the Persian army, is returning victorious from war. The Caliph of Persia—Amurath—has however chosen this moment to kidnap Kalasrade after firing on her palace, burning it to the ground. Acting against his will, the Captain of the Caliph's Guard, Azim, brings Kalasrade to Amurath and the Grand Vizier, Achmet, who also plot the downfall of Sadak. After encouraging his soldiers to return home to their families, Sadak discovers his wife's abduction and goes to rescue her at the Caliph's palace. Meanwhile, Amurath presses his attentions on Kalasrade; in order to delay his advances, she requests that he gather untasted the Waters of Oblivion, as she is advised to do by the chorus of Good Spirits. Suddenly, having "dared a thousand deaths" (16), Sadak appears before Amurath, who agrees to release his wife if he can bring back the Waters of Oblivion. On his trip, Sadak's boat sinks and he is the only person to make it to the Enchanted Island. Encouraged by the chorus of Good Spirits—and taunted by Evil ones — Sadak advances: plucking the magic fruit; taking his sword to break the rock apart, exposing the magic fountain; placing the fruit next to the serpent who guards the waters in order to placate it; and ignoring the Nymph of the Fountain's encouragement to taste the water before he draws it. When he succeeds, the Nymph is released from "thrice 300 years" (27) of captivity, and she and Sadak are borne away in a balloon-like vehicle to return to Persia. Just as Kalasrade contemplates suicide to avoid marriage to Amurath, Sadak descends with the Waters of Oblivion. Recalling that "fortunate for Persia and for love Would be the draught" (31), Amurath drinks the water and dies immediately. While the balloon ascends, the setting is changed to the Garden of Kalasrade's Palace, where all the choruses celebrate Sadak's heroic return.

According to the preface, *Sadak and Kalasrade* is based on an old tale by the same name. The major alterations are that the children in the tale have been omitted; the events have been condensed; and the Good and Evil Spirits and the scene on the Enchanted Island are original with Mitford. The fairy-tale opera provides lavish staging with an oriental flavor. While the musical extravaganza may delight the eye, the text seems bland without these embellishments

TEXT: Readex Microprint.

SANDERS, Charlotte Elizabeth (fl. 1787–1814). As a writer for children, Sanders published an anthology of her own work for young readers, entitled *The Little Family* (1797). Besides her poetry and prose, the volume contained several dramas, including *The Little Gamester* and *The Bird's Nest*. Another work for children in dramatic form, *Holidays at Home, Written for the Amusement of Young Persons*, was published in 1803 (Microprint of NY edition of 1810). [*BD* (under title), DBAWW]

The School for Friends, Marianne Chambers. This comedy in five acts was first produced at DL on 10 December 1805 and published the same year by Barker and Son. Genest mentions that this popular comedy was acted twenty-five times (7: 702–03).

The play opens with a woman in distress: Mrs. Hamilton, living under an assumed name in a lodging house, cannot pay her overdue rent; she has been abandoned with a child by an unfaithful husband who no longer pays her quarterly allowance. A contrasting scene follows: Sir Edward Epworth (Mrs. Hamilton's husband) and Lady Courtland, the woman he is apparently living with, are playing chess when Lord Belmour arrives and tries to remind Sir Edward of his moral responsibilities, but Sir Edward is in debt because of his gambling. Meanwhile Mrs. Hamilton refuses to press her case against her husband; Lord Belmour, however, insists on buying her jewels for much more than they are worth. In a related plot, an impoverished gentleman who has been out of England for twenty years, Hardy, meets Felix Mordant, a member of parliament. Hardy hopes his niece will receive him as a family member, and Mordant agrees to help him. Lady Courtland insists Sir Edward approach his uncle for money, and he blames her for enticing him into gambling. When he arrives, Mordant reveals that Sir Edward's estate is mortgaged to Lady Courtland, and he scolds her. Sir Edward is then arrested for debt, and Mrs. Hamilton has him freed—anonymously. Mordant discovers that Lady Courtland forged a document to stop the allowance of Sir Edward's wife, and he uses this information to force Lady Courtland to return Sir Edward's estate to him. Meanwhile Lord Belmour takes Sir Edward in disguise to witness Mrs. Hamilton's suffering; Sir Edward reveals himself to her, and she accepts her erring husband's apologies. Mrs. Hamilton is also reunited with Hardy, her uncle, who announces that he is in fact rich and that she is no longer impoverished.

In this drama, the prodigal husband returns to his wife as a result of her steadfastness and moral strength. She assumes that good will happen to those who wait; however, she does act to free her husband from debtors' prison. Much of the comedy comes from mistaken identities: Hardy, for instance, thinks Lady Courtland is Sir Edward's wife, while Lady Courtland thinks he is Sir Edward's uncle Mordant; and both think the other insane. A minor character, Daw, a Quaker watchmaker, acts the moral representative of the middle-class. While Genest describes the play as "tolerable," he does complain about the plausibility of Lady Courtland's committing forgery for the mere £80 allowance. What he calls a "forced incident" may ask for too much realism in this redemptive comedy (7: 702–03).

MANUSCRIPT: No manuscript exists in the Larpent Collection.

TEXT: Readex Microprint of the 6th edition, 1806.

A School for Greybeards; or, The Mourning Bride, Hannah Cowley. Taken from Aphra Behn's *The Lucky Chance* (performed 1686) and considerably chastened, Cowley's five-act comedy opened at DL on 25 November 1786. It was published the same day by G. G. J. and J. Robinson. There were nine performances its first season, but it did not survive as a repertoire piece.

While the plot of the comedy owes much to Aphra Behn, its language is greatly altered to reflect that of the late eighteenth century. Set in Portugal, rather than London, the play opens with Henry, banished from the country for fighting a duel, learning that Antonia, his contracted wife, is to marry old Gasper that night. Julio, Gasper's nephew in Madrid, reported this to Henry, who now plans to act Julio at Gasper's house. When Alexis, an old husband with a young wife, arrives at Gasper's, he warns his host of such a marriage, and he also suggests that Gasper's son, Octavio, marry his daughter, Viola. Alexis relates this potential match to his wife, Seraphina, and she meets Octavio instead of Viola. She even tells him that the moment "Alexis consents to my being yours, I'll yield you my hand" (23). Meanwhile, in the garden Henry's friend Sebastian woos Viola against Alexis's wishes. He quickly leaves when Alexis shows up and asks what Viola thought of Octavio, causing confusion on both sides. As her husband exits muttering, Seraphina explains the situation to Viola, recommending that Viola meet with Sebastian while she entertains Octavio. At Gasper's, the old man explains to Julio (Henry) how he got Antonia to accept him: he showed her a piece of paper saying that Henry was dead, and as she was a woman of no fortune who was beset with suitors, he stepped in. Henry, as Julio, asks what would happen if the real Henry showed up; Gasper has taken care of that by buying Henry's pardon which is to be delivered tomorrow. Henry then goes to the garden where he meets Antonia. As they vow their love, Gasper and Alexis enter the garden. Some fast talking gets them off the hook, and Gasper leaves with Antonia. Alexis thinks Julio's "joke" has earned him a ring; and while Julio can't accept it, he will hold the ring in trust and return it to Alexis. That night before the wedding, Julio uses the ring to get Gasper to go to Alexis because of a plot—"all Lisbon may be fired" (54). Grudgingly, Gasper takes the ring to Alexis only to find out there is no city-wide alarm. When he returns, Henry and Antonia are just about to elope. At Alexis's, Octavio has arranged for the pretended Viola to steal out of the house, but she insists she be accompanied by a lady (Viola veiled), who is to be dropped off at Sebastian's. Moreover, she wants to go to Antonia and put herself under her protection. In the last act, Viola has married Sebastian; Henry has his pardon directly from the Queen and claims Antonia by right of prior contract. Seraphina tells Octavio that she hoodwinked him to assist the lovers and asks forgiveness, and Octavio obliges with good humor. Alexis says to Gasper: "You have lost a young wife, and I have found one" (74). Knowing that he tried to trick Antonia, Gasper accepts the situation.

Seraphina is more lively than her predecessor in Behn's play: her use of language always seems to flummox Alexis, who prides himself on his "sagacity." She remarks that her husband is a "gudgeon, there's no credit in deceiving him" (48). Because of the predicament she is in, Antonia appears passive, but when she is caught with Henry in the garden and in trying to elope with him, she thinks of excuses quickly and gets them out of the compromising circumstances. Unlike Julia in Behn's *The Luckey Chance*, Seraphina says she will remain with her husband while he has confidence in her, and this allows her to be the guardian of her own honor.

When Cowley revised the play for her *Works*, posthumously published in 1813, she shortened the play by trimming a number of speeches and by cutting others extensively. Perhaps responding to audience reaction or reviews, she eliminated any phrase with a hint of bawdy language. The Epilogue, tailored for Elizabeth Farren (Seraphina in the 1786 production), has been reduced and Farren's name deleted.

MANUSCRIPT: Larpent 748.

TEXTS: Readex Microprint. TEC Reels 4397: 10; 2264: 2 (Dublin 1787).

FACSIMILE EDITION: E-CED, with introduction F. Link (NY: Garland, 1982).

The School for Rakes, Elizabeth Griffith. An adaptation of Beaumarchais's *Eugénie* (1767), this five-act comedy opened at DL on 4 February 1769 and was acted twelve times its first season. T. Becket and P. A. DeHondt published the play during its initial run.

Lord Eustace, a young libertine, fraudulently and secretly marries Harriet in order to seduce her. Rumors about his impending marriage to an heiress, Lady Ann, reach Harriet who beseeches him to make their union public. He refuses to do so and manages to pass the rumors as mere newspaper gossip. However, when irrefutable proof not only confirm the rumors but reveal the sham ceremony he repents and offers to marry Harriet, who is expecting his child and whom he truly loves. Now it is Harriet, so deeply wounded in her honor and her love, who refuses such an union, despite her persistent passion for him. But her father, to whom she had confessed her horrible "crime" and who had wanted to avenge the family's honor by challenging the seducer to a duel, now gives her away summarily ("Take her; she is, and shall be yours"), for, says he, "the man who sincerely repents of error, is farther removed from vice, than one who has ne'er been guilty" (90).

The main theme of the *School for Rakes*, as of many other domestic, bourgeois dramas, is the triumph of innocence and virtue brought about by the villain's sudden conversion. The specific plot here comes from Beaumarchais's five-act "serious drama" entitled *Eugénie*. Griffith followed the French original rather closely, especially when dealing with Harriet/Eugénie, as she readily acknowledged: "as the situation of Harriet would not admit any change, I have not attempted to deviate from the gentle, and interesting Eugenie of Monsieur Beaumarchais" (Advertisement 4). Griffith, however, added the character of Frampton, himself a former rake, who prompts his friend, Lord Eustace, to marry Harriet and undo the harm he inflicted upon this virtuous woman. Since his influence on the plot and on the hero's repentance is negligible, Griffith must have introduced him mainly "to lengthen the performance" (Letter to Garrick, 18 July 1768). Griffith made the adaptation truly English first by changing Beaumarchais's French names and setting into English ones; second by introducing references to British phenomena such as the freedom of the press ("the very *Magna Carta* of freedom" 27), unknown in the France of Ancien Regime; and third by having characters refer to British works such as Salmon's *Geography* or Collins's *Peerage*. According to Kinne, Griffith chastens and brightens the more somber French drama in her treatment of "abandoned innocence" (109). *The Monthly Review* remarked that the play produced "higher pleasure than laughter can bring" (40 [February 1769]: 153–56), which may explain why Griffith's adaptation held the stage for seven years.

MANUSCRIPT: No manuscript exists in the Larpent Collection.

TEXT: Readex Microprint. TEC Reels 726: 18 (London, 1769); 3570: 6 (2nd ed., London, 1769); 3602: 1 (Dublin, 1769).

The School of Eloquence, Hannah Cowley. This one-act interlude appeared as an afterpiece at DL on 4 April 1780. It was acted only one night and never printed. *The Morning Advertiser* (5 April 1780) gives a plot synopsis (*LS* 5: 328). Referring to *BD*, Genest remarks "it was intended to ridicule the number of debating societies, which at this time were opened, and frequented" (6: 132).

MANUSCRIPT: Larpent 515.

SCOTT, Jane M. (fl. 1806–30). An actress and playwright of the early nineteenth-century, Scott wrote more than fifty plays, many of them operas, burlettas, and pantomimes. All were performed at the Sans Pareil Theatre, which her father had built for her. Beginning in November 1806 with three brief plays, the young writer directed and acted in a number of dramas. Among those credited to her in the Larpent Collection are *Rural Visitors; or, Singularity* (1807), *The Bashaw; or, Adventure of*

was composed, and the fragment was not staged.

Sebastian, King of Portugal, returns to his country after being detained as prisoner in Africa. Although his friend Gonzalez warns him to proceed cautiously and to expect changes, Sebastian is horrified to discover that Philip II of Spain has seized the country. As he walks anonymously in the streets of Lisbon, he discovers that he himself—his rashness and imperialism—is blamed for the Spanish occupation. Going to a close friend, Sylveira, for support, Sebastian is bitterly disappointed. Not only is his friend preparing to entertain the Spanish lords, but Sylveira responds to Sebastian's fond memories of their friendship with coldness, telling him he no longer has a place in the country. Sebastian concludes that he has "live[d] An age of wisdom in an hour" (217).

This one-act fragment has relatively little to offer, other than the contrast between Sebastian's initial enthusiasm and love of his country and his gradual awakening to his political status. Gonzalez's warnings serve to foreshadow those changes that Sebastian confronts. Another friend, Zamor a young Arab, accompanies Sebastian and Gonzalez when they return to Portugal, but Zamor has little function in the plot, and it seems that Hemans may have forgotten about him.

TEXT: Readex Microprint of *Dramatic Works* (Edinburgh: W. Blackwood, 1839): 199–220.

The Second Marriage, Joanna Baillie. This five-act comedy appeared in *A Series of Plays: [on] the Stronger Passions of the Mind* (Second Series), printed by Cadell and Davies in 1802. There is no known production.

While the two parts of *Ethwald* (the other plays in this volume that focus on ambition) trace a warrior's determination to become king, Seabright's ambitions in *The Second Marriage* are more modest. After the death of his first wife, he marries Lady Sarah for her family connections to gain a seat in Parliament. When he is elected and an office with a modest income is made available, Seabright is still not satisfied. As Baillie says in her preface to the volume, "Ambition alone [among the passions] acquires strength from gratification, and after having gained one object, still sees another rise before it, to which it as eagerly pushes on . . ." ("To the Reader" ix). In an attempt to become instantly wealthy, he schemes with Sir Crafty Supplecoat, investing all of his resources in rock salt. When the investment fails, Lady Sarah leaves him and goes to live with her brother, Lord Allcrest, who wishes to have nothing to do with his brother-in-law's financial ruin.

Among the play's preachy messages, two are heard most frequently: there is some good in everyone; and "what a charm there is in doing good! it can give dignity to the meanest condition" (477). Seabright's brother-in-law from his first marriage, the benevolent clergyman Beaumont, is instrumental in achieving domestic harmony for Seabright and his poor children. Beaumont goes to Seabright in his darkest moment, and he arranges for Seabright's first wife's uncle, Morgan, to live with the family and give them financial support. Further, there are hints that Seabright's long-suffering daughter, Sophia, will marry Beaumont's son, William; and that Lady Sarah, while living apart from the family, will invite the children to visit her on occasion. One of the subplots involves the servants' resentment of Lady Sarah and their attempt to frighten her by appearing as ghosts. This effort fails, however, and the subplot adds little to the play, other than to emphasize that Robert is a faithful old retainer.

TEXT: Readex Microprint of second edition, 1802.

FACSIMILE EDITION: *Romantic Context: Poetry* reprints the 1802 edition (London: T. Cadell, Jr., and W. Davies). Compiled by D. H. Reiman (NY: Garland, 1977).

The Second Part of The Rover, Aphra Behn. This five-act comedy was produced at DG in January 1681 and printed that same year for Jacob Tonson. Following Behn's earlier hit, *The Rover*, 1677, the comedy principally takes up the further escapades of Willmore, the title character. Again, Killigrew's *Thomaso* is the source, but the distance between the two *Rover* plays, according to Gewirtz, "is so great that we seem to be listening to Mrs. Behn's own voice" (*Restoration Adaptations of Early 17th Century Comedies* [Washington, DC: UP of America, 1982]: 104).

Willmore, having won Helena at Naples in the first play, has lost her at sea before the second *Rover* opens. In this play the banished cavaliers turn up in Madrid without Belvile, now married to Florinda. Ned Blunt, who shared the adventures in the first part, is the only other continuing character besides Willmore. Joined by Fetherfool, Shift, Hunt, and Harlequin, Willmore remains as amorous as ever. His friend, the English Ambassador's nephew Bellmond, is engaged to Ariadne but has fallen for La Nuche, a beautiful courtesan. It is Willmore, however, who begins to woo La Nuche almost immediately upon his arrival. Ignored by Bellmond, Ariadne puts on a male disguise and follows the inconstant Willmore through much of the play. This disguise is one of many: Willmore acts a mountebank doctor with his servant as Harlequin in order to dupe Blunt and Fetherfool into marrying a dwarf and a giantess. The intrigues come so fast and so often that the plots overlap with confusing frequency. Willmore finally convinces La Nuche to go away with him without matrimony, for true love will overcome poverty and will go beyond social institutions. Ariadne returns to Bellmond but only under conditions of love within marriage.

Link praises this "very carefully constructed" intrigue-comedy, pointing out the many deceptions (63), but he feels that the farcical elements distract from the main plot. Hume also says that the total effect of combining "serious themes with wild farce is a little dizzying" (353). Gewirtz provides a strong discussion of the play's altered value system: true love is the highest good and wins out over money. "The romanticism of *The Second Part of the Rover*," he explains, "is atypical in the Behn canon, as it is in the body of Restoration comedy" (106). Rothstein and Kavenick contrast the two plays: the 1677 *Rover* is Carolean comedy, whereas the 1681 *Rover* shows a decreasing social cohesion (*The Designs of Carolean Comedy* 189). Dramaturgically, the fights and near-fights (there are eight of them) push the play along at a brisk pace, but the brawling also serves to move characters off the stage in order to get on to the next scene. While both *Rover* plays feature Willmore, Behn's handling of the courtesan who appears in each, Angelica and La Nuche, is very different.

TEXTS: Wing B1765. EEB Reel 446: 4. Readex Microprint.

MODERN EDITION: *Works*, ed. Montague Summers (1915; NY: Phaeton, 1967) 1: 109–213.

Second Thoughts are Best, Hannah Cowley. Originally titled *The World as It Goes; or, A Party at Montpellier* and performed at CG on 24 February 1781, the play was revised under this new title and produced at CG on 24 March 1781, but the revised version was played only once; it was not printed. Genest says that *The World* was "disapproved of" and *Second Thoughts* "again disapproved of and finally withdrawn" (6: 192–93). While the original version is in the Larpent Collection (548), no version of the revised five-act comedy is known to exist.

The Self-Rival, Mary Davys. The information printed on the play's half-title page expresses Davys's frustration about having the play rejected: "A Comedy As it should have been Acted at the Theatre-Royal In *Drury-Lane*," but no details explaining why the play was not performed by the triumvirate at DL have been found. Mary Davys published this comedy in her *Works* of 1725, printed by H. Woodfall for the author.

The title character, Colonel Bellamont, assumes a second role, that of his uncle Lord Pastall, in order to woo Maria. Having learned of his trick, Maria willingly accepts the supposed uncle. In a second instance of self-rivalry in the play, Emilia, a gentlewoman, acts the maid to Maria in order to gain the hand of Maria's brother, Frederick. Three humours characters enliven the plot. There are the contrasting "old Maids": Lady Camphire Lovebane (described in the Dramatis Personae as "An Affected Old Maid") is a stereotypical unmarried older woman, whereas Mrs. Fallow ("A good-natur'd old Maid") is cheerful and good humored. The misogynist Verjuice ("A

Cross Old Batchelor"), who quarrels with each of them, ends up duped by both.

The young women, Maria and Emilia, control their suitors by their wit and sagacity. They must also deal with Maria's father, Sir Ephraim Purchase: Maria says she will accept his recommendation for a husband, and Emilia rejects him as a potential marriage partner in favor of his son. Marriage with someone of a similar age is stressed several times during the play, and this view is supported by Mrs. Fallow, who still prefers to remain single at her age and to live a productive and useful life.

TEXT: Readex Microprint.

CRITICAL EDITION: Edited with introduction by Donald H. Stefanson, Diss., U of Iowa, 1971.

The Separation, Joanna Baillie. This five-act tragedy was first printed in her collected *Dramas*, published by Longman, et al, 1836. Written as early as 1819, the tragedy was considered for production in Edinburgh during the 1819–20 season. It was eventually produced at CG on 25 February 1836, with Charles Kemble as Garcio and Helen Faucit as Lady Margaret. The uneven reception of the play is discussed by Baillie's biographer, M. S. Carhart (159–64).

The play begins with Baldwin, an Italian Count's faithful servant, raving on his death bed. There is speculation that Baldwin helped Count Garcio murder Ulrico, Garcio' brother-in-law, enabling him to marry Ulrico's sister Margaret and gain his property. Returning home from his campaign with the Moors, Garcio receives a hesitant greeting from the Countess, who is still disturbed by Baldwin's dying words. Observing her behavior, Rovani, the Count's friend, assumes that she is attracted to the Marquis of Tortona, who has unexpectedly arrived. When Garcio confronts his wife, Margaret asks her husband to deny what Baldwin has confessed. Garcio tells her the story of her brother's death, acknowledging his guilt. Following a hermit's counsel, the Count leaves his wife and child to live a quiet life of self-denial. This exile is disturbed when Tortona presses his attention on Margaret and attacks the castle with three thousand men. Rovani attempts to defend her, but he stubbornly refuses to send for the necessary reinforcements. Tortona's troops are driven back only when Garcio (disguised as the Hermit) rallies his men. Although he slays Tortona, Garcio too is mortally wounded. Before her husband dies, Margaret forgives him and criticizes her own "cruel unrelenting sternness" (105) toward her husband.

Margaret is one of Baillie's more aggressive female protagonists. Her role is not as important as Garcio's, but she does much to advance the action. Garcio confesses his guilt only in response to her questions; Garcio seeks out the Hermit only after she has declared they cannot live together, saying she will go to a cloistered cell. Additionally, Margaret rejects Tortona's advances; and when he attacks the castle, she risks her life by going to the walls where the troops are fighting to cheer her soldiers.

MANUSCRIPT: BL Add. Ms. 42934, ff. 770–816.

TEXT: Readex Microprint of *Dramas* (1836) 2: 1–106.

SERRES, Olivia Wilmot (1772–1834). Brought up by a father who was a painter, Serres married a painter and became recognized as the landscape painter to the Prince of Wales in 1806. After separating from her husband in 1804, Serres wrote a three-act opera (never staged), *The Castle of Avola*; it was included in her collection of poems, *Flights of Fancy* (1805). In that same year Serres also wrote a sentimental novel, *St. Julian* (1805). After the death of her uncle, Dr. James Wilmot, she published a memoir about him (1813), pronouncing him—incorrectly—to be the author of the Junius letters. Later, Serres declared herself the daughter of the Duke of Cumberland, brother to George III, by a secret marriage, and she spent most of the remainder of her life trying to authenticate this claim. After she was buried in the churchyard of St. James Piccadilly, her daughter, Lavinia took up the cause. Finally in 1866, the Serres documents were judged to be forgeries.

[*BD*, DNB, FCLE. Biography by M. L. Pendered and J. Mallet, 1939.]

The Several Wits, Margaret Lucas Cavendish, Duchess of Newcastle. This comedy appears in her *Playes*, published in 1662 by John Martyn, James Allestry, and Tho. Dicas. The play was not acted.

In this multiple-plot drama, Cavendish explores wit and its involvement with love. Mademoiselle Caprisia acts a witty lover who refuses Monsieur Importunate, who can't keep up with her clever remarks and quick repartee. Caprisia's mother tries to reign in her daughter's tongue. When Caprisia abruptly dismisses Monsieur Generosity, her mother shames her for rudeness and advocates that Caprisia be modest, civil, and courteous. Alone, Caprisia weighs her faults and decides to change her ways. When Generosity comes back, she thinks he intends to laugh at her, but he insists he's ready to marry her. She responds: "I shall not refuse you" (119).

A second plot line takes up Mademoiselle Volante's wit in her love affair: after talking to a grave matron who stresses she should look for title and wealth, Volante believes valor, wisdom, and honesty are better guides; she would rather be praised for her virtue than her wit. After a visit by Monsieur Discretion, Volante feels she has appeared foolish before him. With Doctor Freedom's encouragement, she overcomes a lack of confidence, and the two appear on their way to matrimony.

Mademoiselle Doltche, a third witty woman, hears that Monsieur Nobilissimo wishes to be her suitor. She feels that she possesses little beauty, riches, or wit to recommend herself, but she believes she does possess virtue. And virtue has the greatest appeal to Nobilissimo: Doltche tells him she would rather be honored for her merit than her birth, breeding, and wealth; for her virtue rather than her beauty. He continues unequivocal in his vows, and he expects hell to take his soul if he ever forsakes her. In the last act, we hear they are to wed.

Finally, there is Mademoiselle Solid whose chief concern is the soul, "the supream part of life" (83). Monsieur Profession woos Solid to no avail, but it is Monsieur Perfection who wins her heart when he praises her soul, and they are to marry at the end of the play.

Wit and love predominate in this drama, though all the women find reason important in a potential mate. In her prologue, Cavendish lists four categories of wit: 1) wise wit is fresh, pure, and clear; 2) wild wit is often foul and filthy; 3) "cholerick" wit is rough and salty; and 4) humble wit is smooth and straight. It does not appear that each of the four protagonists is meant to represent a particular kind of wit, rather certain kinds of wit come into play at different times depending on circumstances and events. Each protagonist uses wit and vivacity to determine if she wants to marry or remain single: all determine that they want compatible husbands for a long marriage. One of the principal characteristics each looks for in a would-be husband is virtue, which includes truth, honesty, and wisdom. In this way, the women in *The Several Wits* succeed. Although post-marriage problems occur in other plays by Cavendish, she calls *The Several Wits* a comedy, perhaps because of the marital accords in the final act.

TEXTS: Wing N868. EEB Reel 502: 11. Readex Microprint.

She Lives; or, The Generous Brother, Mary Goldsmith. *BD* indicates that a version of this comedy may have been performed at the Haymarket Theatre on 7 March 1803. Two manuscript versions of the play exist—one in four acts (Larpent 1284), one in five acts (Larpent 1399). The comedy was not printed, and Genest provides no information about the play or performance. Colman, the younger, submitted an application for the four-act version on 28 March 1800; the Lord Chamberlain approved the play for performance at the Haymarket in April 1800 for a benefit night, though not during the regular summer season, according to Macmillan. Thomas Vaughan provided both prologue and epilogue. For whatever reasons, no performance seems to have occurred during the Haymarket season. It was probably the five-act version of Goldsmith's play (Larpent 1399) that was performed in February 1803 at Margate; this same five-act version was likely dramatized in March at the Haymarket. Macmillan notes that the revision seems to be the same plot as

Larpent 1284: the new version "adds one scene [act?]"; he also points out that the manuscript alters the names of characters, but no other changes appear to be substantive.

Sir George and Lady Sinclair have lived in the Scottish Highlands for most of their marriage. They have traveled to London via Bath to arrange a marriage for their daughter Clementina with the affluent but elderly Lord Seymour. Over the years, Sir George has been quite irresponsible: he has arranged for others to care for his brother's daughter after the death of her mother, and he has also been living on the money of his ward, Frederick Percy, now an Ensign in the army. When the play begins, Sir George is going to meet his brother, Mr. Sinclair, who is returning from Bengal. At the same time Clementina openly objects to marrying someone old enough to be her grandfather; for this opposition, Lady Sinclair threatens to put Clementina in a nunnery. After Clementina refuses Lord Seymour, he benevolently recommends his nephew Colonel Alfred Hubert. Clementina, however, has long loved Sir George's ward, young Percy. Although Colonel Hubert makes his addresses to Clementina, he himself is in love with Eliza, and in fact has had two children by her; he is relieved when Clementina turns him down. Into this mix comes Frederick Percy, back in town with his regiment. As the generous brother, Sinclair proposes to Sir George that he provide the money belonging to Percy that Sir George had squandered. Sinclair then welcomes Percy and learns from him that Colonel Hubert must be married, since Percy saw the Colonel leaving a house with a woman and child at the window. Sinclair further learns that the Colonel's uncle, Lord Seymour, knows nothing of his nephew's arrangements. By testing the various lovers' commitments to their intended spouses, Sinclair discovers Eliza is his own daughter, reconciles Lord Seymour with his nephew, and bestows a dowry upon Eliza when she marries the Colonel. Sinclair is also generous with Percy and Clementina, and Sir George apologizes for his irresponsible behavior.

The problematic situations in this comedy turn on men fathering children before they marry the mothers. Many years before, Sinclair has gotten his inamorata with child before they can marry. When she dies in childbirth, Sinclair, who is going to India, asks his brother to care for the child. Sir George wishes his own child to inherit and finds someone else to raise Eliza, sending word to Sinclair that the child had died. Currently, Colonel Hubert and Eliza have had two children together, but they are not married, owing to the presumed objections of his wealthy uncle. This leaves Eliza in a vulnerable position until she can marry Hubert. In the drama, things turn out favorably: marriages can now take place, and Sinclair, the rich uncle, showers money on the newlyweds. After having been manipulated by the nobility (Sir George, Lady Sinclair, and Lord Seymour), the young people in the play are rescued by the merchant class (Mr. Sinclair). While Goldsmith raises issues about the predicament of unmarried women with children during this period, she provides little in the way of practical solutions.

MANUSCRIPTS: Larpent 1284 (four-act version). Readex Microprint of this manuscript. Larpent 1399 (five-act version).

She Ventures and He Wins, "Ariadne." This five-act comedy, written by a young woman calling herself "Ariadne," was produced at LIF, early in September 1695, but shortly thereafter LIF was closed. Maximillian E. Novak believes that the closing may have been caused by the sexual reversals of several roles ("The Closing of Lincoln's Inn Fields in 1695," *RECTR* 14 [1975]: 51–52). Elizabeth Barry played the faithful wife Urania, Anne Bracegirdle acted Charlot, who dresses as a male to test Lovewell, and Dogget dresses as a woman in his role of the lecherous Squire Wouldbe. *She Ventures* was printed for Hen. Rhodes, J. Harris, and Sam. Briscoe in 1695, though dated 1696 (*London Gazette*, No. 3122, 10–14 Oct 1695).

Charlot, an heiress dressed in men's clothes, wants to discover if Lovewell, an impecunious younger man, loves her or her money. She plans a series of elaborate tests for him: she first has him wooed by a rich woman and, later, has it reported that she (Charlot) is untruthful and unfaithful. Finally, she has him arrested and imprisoned. Once Charlot has proved his fidelity, she is willing to accept Lovewell. The subplot also involves a number of tests. Squire Wouldbe wishes to bed Urania who is married to Freeman: she anticipates him by informing her husband and by pretending to be interested. In fact, she plots his downfall, much as Mistresses Page and Ford dupe Falstaff. At first, dressed as a woman, he hides in a cistern and is soaked, then he dives into a vat of feathers, and finally he hides in a chimney. After everyone has had a good laugh at Wouldbe's expense, Urania reads him a moral lecture and sends him back to his shrewish wife, Dowdy.

One undercurrent in this comedy is a serious concern about sincerity. It is first represented by Sir Charles Frankford and Juliana, a very sober couple, and then by Sir Charles's sister, Charlot, who tests the sincerity of Lovewell. Once she has tested him in several situations and proved his steadfastness, she *knows* he is sincere. A parallel from the previous season at LIF is Angelica (Congreve's *Love for Love*), who similarly exercises tests for her gallant. Ariadne demonstrates one answer to the perennial question of "What do women want most?" by showing her female protagonist's desire to verify a male's sincerity.

TEXTS: Wing S3054. EEB Reel 511: 43. Readex Microprint.

MODERN EDITION: Everyman's Library, *Female Playwrights of the Restoration*, edited with introduction by Paddy Lyons and Fidelis Morgan (London: Dent, 1991): 103–159.

SHERIDAN, Elizabeth [Betsy] Hume Crawford, later Mrs. Henry Lefanu (1758–1837). Daughter of Frances Sheridan and sister of Richard Brinsley Sheridan, Elizabeth married Henry Lefanu in 1789. She is the author of one farce, *The Ambiguous Lover*. *BD* reports the play was produced at the Crow-Street Theatre in Dublin, 1781, but it was never printed. [DNB (under Philip Lefanu)]

SHERIDAN, Frances Chamberlaine (1724–1766). Born in Dublin and educated with the help of her brothers, Frances Chamberlaine married Thomas Sheridan, the actor-manager of Dublin's Smock Alley, in 1747. In the midst of raising a family, the Sheridans moved to London in 1754, where Thomas was engaged at CG for a season. Francis began writing for publication in 1759 at the encouragement of Samuel Richardson. Her *Memoirs of Miss Sidney Bidulph* (1761), published anonymously, sold well. Her principal contributions to the theatre, two comedies, were produced in 1763: *The Discovery* (opened at DL, 3 February 1763) and *The Dupe* (opened at DL, 10 December 1763). In the former, her husband played the feckless Lord Medway, and David Garrick spoke the prologue and took the comic role of Sir Anthony Branville. Although *The Discovery* was a great hit at the boxoffice, *The Dupe* lasted only three nights. Financial difficulties and health problems caused the family to relocate to Blois, France, the following year. Here, Frances wrote a third comedy, *A Journey to Bath*, which she sent to Garrick, who refused it because he objected to the characters and plot. Unfortunately, only three acts of her play have survived. During this period, she also completed a sequel to *The Memoirs of Miss Sidney Bidulph.* While staying in Blois, Frances had fainting fits and died in September 1766 at the age of forty-two. Burial took place in a protestant cemetery outside of Blois. Posthumous publications of prose fiction include *Eugenia and Adelaide*, *The History of Nourjahad*, and her sequel to *The Memoirs of Sidney Bidulph*. [*BD*, BNA, DBAWW, DLB 84 (by Ann Messenger), DNB, EBWW, FCLE, NCBEL (2: 858–59), OCEL. Bibliography by Norma H. H. Russell, *Book Collector* 13 (1964): 196–205. A critical edition of her *Plays*, edited by Robert Hogan and Jerry C. Beasley (Cranberry, NJ: Associated UP, 1984), includes a brief biographical account.]

SHORT, Mrs. C. (fl. 1792). Author of *Dramas for Young Ladies*, published in Birmingham by G. G. J. and J. Robinson, J. Balfour, and C. Elliott in 1792, Short is not otherwise known. It appears she kept a school and wrote these plays for her students. The text includes two three-act dramas—*Domestic Woe* and *The Fortunate Disappointment*. The latter has a prologue and an epilogue written by Anna Seward. Davis & Joyce say that the plays were "written for a group of young ladies to promote 'the habit of speaking with grace and propriety.'" [Davis & Joyce; no information in FCLE, DBAWW, EBWW; no Microprints.]

The Sicilian Lover, Mary Darby Robinson. Printed for the author by Hookham and Carpenter in 1796, this five-act verse tragedy did not reach the stage.

In sixteenth-century Lombardy, the Marquis of Valmont insists that his daughter, Honoria, marry Albert, the only son of the Milanese Prince Montalva. Honoria has no interest in Albert, and she does not wish to "sell her freedom." In a late medieval tournament, Albert shows his prowess by winning against three foes, but he is defeated by a knight who is unknown except to Honoria. She recognizes Alferenzi, a noble Sicilian, who then presents his scarf to her. After the tournament games, Honoria confides to Agnes, her companion, that several months earlier she met Alferenzi in Tuscany where they professed vows to each other. Alferenzi had asked Valmont for Honoria's hand but the imperious Marquis refused his offer. Honoria wishes her deceased mother could guide her, when Agnes hints that her father has been accused of her mother's death. Albert comes in person to ask for Honoria's hand, but she declares she will never marry him. He goes away threatening to take revenge on Alferenzi. When the Sicilian lover repeats his request to marry Honoria, Valmont insists she will wed Albert the next day. That night Honoria sends Agnes as an emissary to Alferenzi, but Valmont overhears her plan and goes to kill the hated rival. Without realizing it, he kills Albert, who has been lurking outside the castle seeking his own revenge on Alferenzi. The injured Valmont flees the castle with Honoria, leaving Alferenzi's bloody scarf with which Honoria bound her father's wound. Alferenzi, believing that Valmont has murdered Honoria, launches a search. Valmont hides Honoria in a cave while he goes to find food. Upon his return, he encounters Alferenzi, who challenges him to a duel, but Honoria halts their combat. Exhausted, Valmont asks Honoria to restore his lands to his wronged brother, Leonardo, and dies. Alferenzi urges Honoria to recover her strength at a hermit's cottage where he will follow her. Meanwhile Montalva, believing Alferenzi has killed Albert, tries to locate him in the hills and stops to rest at the same hermit's hut. When Alferenzi arrives, Montalva learns Valmont killed Albert, and the hermit exclaims: "my brother!" This is the Leonardo whom Valmont defrauded of his lands. The last act occurs near a convent where Honoria has planned to reside, feeling that Alferenzi bore a responsibility for her father's death. As she tells the abbess her story, Honoria discovers this is her mother, who was repudiated by Valmont many years before. In his search for Honoria, Alferenzi is attacked by robbers, and while he overcomes them he is fatally wounded. He goes to the convent chapel for help only to find Honoria lying in a bier (she apparently died from fatigue and an unfulfilled passion for her Sicilian lover). Alferenzi asks to be buried with Honoria and dies.

Genest remarks that "this is a moderate tragedy by Mrs. Robinson, formerly of DL—the language is sometimes very good, but in general rather florid and fanciful than natural—the plot is not well managed" (10: 204). Indeed, the plot does suffer from several highly improbable coincidences—Leonardo as the hermit, and the abbess as Honoria's mother. It is likely that Robinson wanted the tragedy to turn on the many gothic elements she included: southern European Catholicism, ghosts, night scenes, thunder and lightning, bandits, caves, a hermit, revenge motifs, and a proud villain of remarkably devious capacities. But it is Valmont's forced marriage of Honoria to Albert that leads to the tragedy, which has been brewing ever since Valmont's early deceit of his brother and his offensive repudiation of his wife. One recurring theme contrasts hope, frequently mentioned by several characters, with fear. Honoria is perhaps the most hopeful, and she dismisses her fears by assuming virtue will protect her. She also demonstrates mental strength in her refusal to marry Albert and in her service to her father. After insisting on her rights, Honoria exhibits physical strength by making her way to the convent alone.

TEXT: Readex Microprint.

The Siege, Joanna Baillie. This five-act comedy was first published in *A Series of Plays: [on] the Stronger Passions* (third series) by Longman, et al. in 1812. It was not performed. The name of Antonio is incorrectly given as "Antoni*a*" in the castlist.

Set in "a castle, on the French confines of Germany," the play begins as Walter tries to convince his brother, Baron Baurchel, that the Countess Valdemere is merely flattering him, more intent on his extravagant gifts than she is on his love. Walter laments that the money spent on wooing the Countess rightfully belongs to the Baron's ward and male heir, Antonio, whose suit to Livia is being ignored because of Count Valdemere's (the Countess's son's) attentions. Dismissed as the cynic he is, Walter goes to his friend, Dartz, who has a military commission, for assistance. Dartz informs Walter that while Valdemere may be bold in love, he is cowardly in military action. Therefore, Dartz hatches a plan to ensure Valdemere's failure with Livia, taking advantage of a friendly regiment that is stationed nearby the castle and the knowledge that Valdemere has seduced his page's sister, Nina. To vindicate the Countess, the Baron goes with Hovelberg, a jewel merchant, who has been asked to meet with her at the castle. The Baron in disguise is horrified to hear the Countess and even her maid make jokes at his expense. Meanwhile, further incidents occur that add to her son's, Count Valdemere's, uneasiness: learning he is superstitious, both the page (through Nina's letter) and Dartz (disguised as a fortune teller) predict his early demise. As everyone meets that evening in Livia's Grotto, decorated for the occasion as a sea-nymph's hall, the Baron informs Valdemere that the enemy is nearby and the local regiment fakes an attack on the castle. When placed in charge, Valdemere proves indecisive and cowardly, fleeing to hide in a vault after declaring that he is ill. When a real foe is sighted, Antonio leads the regiment in defense of the castle. Toward the end of the battle, the Baron, Walter, and Livia go to the vault disguised in military dress. Thinking that the enemy has seized him, Valdemere further disgraces himself as a coward. At this point, Antonio arrives, successful in running off the enemy, and he treats Valdemere generously, suggesting that everyone has fearful moments. Admiring his fairness, Livia helps Antonio declare his love for her. Told that this embarrassing incident will be forgotten if he marries Nina, Valdemere readily agrees. As the matches are made, Countess Valdemere makes a final angry entrance, leaving in a rage after renouncing her son.

Although not performed, there is much clever stage business in *The Siege*. Early in the play, the Countess flirts with the Baron while his brother Walter provides a running commentary on their dialogue. Later Count Valdemere tries to woo Livia by repeating Antonio's own comments about her painting, and he is arrogant enough to use Antonio's own words as he speaks to her in front of his rival. Other scenes that would play well include the Countess's ridicule of the Baron in front of his (disguised) face and the Count's cowardice—twice revealed—before the assembled group. In addition to situational comedy, language adds amusement: for example, when the Count appears paralyzed after being asked to provide military leadership, Walter says, "Thought and consideration become a good Commander, with some spice of activity into the bargain" (243). Finally, there is a satisfying range of comic characters. While the Countess and her son—pretentious and greedy to spend money that others provide—warrant the most criticism, the foibles of more positive characters, such as Antonio's timidity in front of Livia and Walter's cynicism, are not ignored.

TEXT: Readex Microprint of 1821 edition. 3: 173–265.

FACSIMILE EDITION: *Romantic Context: Poetry* reprints the 1812 edition (London: Longman, Hurst, Rees, Orme, and Brown). Compiled by D. H. Reiman (NY: Garland, 1977).

The Siege of Jerusalem, Mary Eleanor Lyon Bowes, Countess of Strathmore. This five-act tragedy in verse was published privately in 1774; it was not produced. According to Ralph Arnold, her biographer, Lady Strathmore received little encouragement from her husband, yet she wrote her only published literary work in 1769. She titled this verse drama in five acts and twenty-five scenes *The Siege of Jerusalem.*

The tragedy, set in Jerusalem and nearby camps and woods, includes "star-crossed lovers, women disguised as men, mistaken identities, forewarnings of death, mourning vows, conversions to christianity, suicides, and cravings for 'some convent's gloom.'" Unrequited love is a recurring theme:

> The too short moments spent with Tancred fled
> On downy wings, but left a sting behind,
> Which I attempted not to pluck, or if I did,
> 'Twas with a hand so fearful, that the gentle touch,
> Did only force it further in.—'Twas like
> The tooth of timorous dove who tries
> To draw the dart the hunter had infix'd,
> But wanting strength, does now enlarge the wound,
> Making it wider gape, and bleed the more.

(quoted in *The Unhappy Countess and her Grandson John Bowes* [1957; London: Constable, 1987] 29–30).

Arnold takes the moral from the concluding lines of the drama: "Lord Strathmore's lack of interest in culture and in the arts was a cross which [Lady Strathmore] had to bear" (30),

> In Saladin's sad doom we tremble at thy wrath
> And view in him an instance of this truth—
> Nor strength nor treasures to th'unjust avail,
> For soon or late bright virtue must prevail.

TEXT: Not in Readex Microprint.

The Siege of Jerusalem by Titus Vespasian, Mary Latter. This five-act, verse tragedy, Latter's only drama, was first printed by C. Bathurst, probably in 1763. John Rich, who was assisting Latter in revising the text for the stage, died in November 1761 before the play could be readied for production; the subsequent management rejected the drama, as did David Garrick later. The only known production took place in Reading for a benefit (though not for Latter) sometime during 1768. The text is based on historical events that occurred in A. D. 70 when Titus Vespasian conquered Jerusalem.

While the defenders of Jerusalem feel ready to withstand an attack from the Romans, they have also launched a program of misinformation, telling the Hebrews that Romans will treat them cruelly if they flee the city. In fact, the Hebrews seem split by various factions who mete out punishment to opposing groups. In the Roman camp, Titus can't understand why the Hebrews won't accept his generous terms of surrender; only sixty Jews have asked for Roman protection. Flavius-Josephus, described as "an Honourable *Jew* in the Roman camp," goes to John and Simon, the Hebrew leaders, to try to arrange a peace, but they reject his offer. Matters are complicated because Flavius's wife, Eliza, is held in a Jerusalem prison where she is wooed by Simon. Speaking to her friend, Drusilla, Eliza fears Flavius is dead, and when Simon comes she must fend off his unwelcome advances. Flavius, with the help of his friend Malachias, goes in disguise to see Eliza in prison. After Flavius considers that she may be false to him, he discovers his error and exonerates Eliza. Malachias comes to report that Jephtha, a Hebrew officer, has been captured because he wants to surrender to the Romans. Jephtha's being put into prison has made security tight, so Malachias will take Eliza and Drusilla to a subterranean cell that is unknown to Simon. Meanwhile, the Hebrews drive off a Roman attack, but Titus rallies his forces, describes the plan of attack, and gives a rousing speech to his troops, who win the battle and capture Jerusalem. Flavius finds Eliza and Drusilla who have fled the prison. Titus and his followers are praised by a grand concert, and Titus makes a victorious speech, saying that justice now rules in Jerusalem.

While the battle of the Hebrews and Romans is being fought, the situation of Eliza and Flavius provides the audience with an affecting subplot. Held against her will, Eliza remains a faithful wife even though wooed by Simon, one of the Hebrew leaders. He offers her freedom and love, but she prefers prison and her husband, who acts as an peacemaker for the Romans to try to prevent the destruction of Jerusalem. When he goes to see Eliza in prison, Flavius is anything but a peacemaker: upon scant evidence, he suspects her of a liaison with Simon and draws his sword against her. His conflict between a duty to make peace and his concern for his wife goes back to the same struggle of love and honor, central to the heroic plays of a century earlier. Eliza's faithfulness to Flavius is without question, reinforcing her honor in a traditional role that emphasizes women's chastity and virtue. By way of contrast, the friendship of Eliza and Drusilla, which helps each support the other, is perhaps more important since they are the only two women in the cast.

TEXT: Readex Microprint of the undated edition [1763?], printed for C. Bathurst.

The Siege of Pevensey, Fanny Burney. This historical drama was written between 1789 and 1791 when Burney served as Second Keeper of the Robes in the royal household at Windsor. It was not printed or produced and remains in manuscript.

In a period of early English history, William and Robert, two brothers, claim the throne. Robert has seized the castle of Pevensey, and William attacks the stronghold, where Adela, the daughter of the Duke of Chester, is held prisoner and falls in love with De Belesme, son of the ruler of the castle. He urges Adela to marry him, and she agrees to do so even without her father's permission. Before they can wed, Chester comes disguised, and he is upset because she has agreed without his consent. With the aid of De Belesme, father and daughter escape. Later, De Belesme is captured, and Chester is believed to be disloyal and sentenced to death. If Adela will marry the loathed knight De Warrenne, Chester will be pardoned, but he prefers death rather than forcing his daughter to wed. Adela does not want to be responsible for her father's death. She, therefore, requests a compromise: she will enter a convent, and William will receive her dowry. Instead of this unhappy ending, Burney brings about a sudden peace, which allows De Belesme to marry Adela with her father's blessing.

Before the happy ending, however, Adela must make a crucial decision which will decide her fate: whether to marry De Warrenne, whom she hates, or to let her father die. Adela's proposal of a compromise shows that women often can see a middle course where men frequently cling to extremes. Adelstein praises the drama because the conflicts arise from the siege "and from the interaction of the characters rather than the machinations of a diabolical villain" (87). He also notes that the action in *The Siege of Pevensey* is sustained, whereas it is unequally distributed in *Edwy and Elgiva*. While both Adelstein and Doody point out the centrality of the father-daughter relationship in the drama, Doody considers the psychological impact on Fanny Burney, who would like to see her own father in the character of the freedom-loving Chester. The various motifs of imprisonment suggest to Doody that Burney must have felt a prisoner at Windsor.

MANUSCRIPT: New York Public Library, Berg Collection.

The Siege of Quebec; or, The Death of General Wolfe, Elizabeth Forsyth. This five-act tragedy may be the same play performed at Cork on 30 August 1792 (Clark 1965; 345). At least two pantomimes bear the title *The Siege of Quebec*. The first took place at CG on 14 May 1760. Another pantomime masque by this title was acted once at the Royal Grove Theatre (said by Nicoll to be Astley's equestrian establishment near Westminster Bridge, London) on 31 May 1784. Published at Strabane, Ireland, by J. Bellew in 1789, Forsyth's tragedy did not play in London.

The play begins in England, where Amelia's false friend, Clara, shows her a letter "proving" that General Wolfe has taken a Canadian lover. Although she tells Clara that Heaven will punish those who tell falsehoods, Amelia has lingering doubts, which are removed only by Wolfe's mother's insistence that the reports are untrue. Jealous because Wolfe loves

Amelia and not herself, Clara has also forged a letter to Wolfe about Amelia's "perfidy." Meanwhile in Canada, Wolfe, recovered from a serious illness, leads the attack on Quebec. Upon receiving the forged letter, the General denounces Amelia as a "fair deceiver" (23), and he refocuses his attention on the coming battle and his duty to country and King George. Although his troops are successful, General Wolfe dies from a wound—but not before witnessing the French defeat.

The two plots—the siege of Quebec and the love relationship between Wolfe and Amelia—are not well integrated, and the romance seems trivial in comparison to the triumph of battle. Nationalism is the play's central theme, and even the French General Montcalm acknowledges British superiority:

> The meanest peasant in the British isle
> Harbours a courage matchless:
> They tower above all human obstacles,
> And look on death, as on a midnight dream (26).

At their moment of defeat and shortly before he dies, Montcalm agrees that the French will be treated decently by their British foes:

> ...my only consolation [is]
> They'll not propose dishonorable terms.
> With my expiring breath I'll own
> They're honorable, valiant, and humane (45).

An unabashed tribute to General Wolfe and to Great Britain, this play has relatively little to recommend it. At the end of the play, self-sacrificing Amelia goes mad and dies, apparently, of a broken heart; a wretched Clara confesses; and Mrs. Wolfe lives on to build a monument in her son's memory.

TEXT: Readex Microprint.

The Siege of Sinope, Frances Brooke. Based on Giusseppi Sarti's opera *Mitridate a Sinope*, Brooke's five-act verse tragedy debuted at CG on 31 January 1781 and played ten nights during the season. T. Cadell printed the tragedy in 1781. Mary Ann Yates originated the role of Thamyris, the Queen of Pontus, the only female character; Yates also spoke the Epilogue, contributed by Brooke's long-time friend and playwright, Arthur Murphy. Brooke and Yates had managed the operatic season at the King's Theatre together during the previous decade.

The play begins with two rival Generals, Artabanes and Artaxias, celebrating peace between Pontus and Cappadocia. This peace, however, is undermined by Athridates, King of Cappadocia, who continues to plot against Pharnaces, King of Pontus. Athridates is overwhelmed by his desire for revenge against Pontus: Pharnaces has married his daughter Thamyris against his will; and Pharnaces's father (Mithridates) drove Athridates from his throne and caused the death of his son in battle with Pontus. While pretending to forgive Pharnaces and Thamyris, who is now Queen of Pontus, Athridates awaits support from Roman troops to mount a surprise attack against his enemies. After the attack begins, Pharnaces and Thamyris are briefly reunited; fearing the worst, the King makes her swear to kill both herself and their young son Eumenes if he is slain in battle and they are taken captive. Reluctantly, Thamyris agrees. After Pharnaces leaves, Athridates rushes to take the palace and punish his disloyal daughter. When the Queen will not reveal where she has hidden her son, her father has her followed. After discovering that Thamyris goes to the Tomb of Mithridates, Athridates vows to have the monument levelled; in order to prevent this disaster, Thamyris confesses that Eumenes is hidden within the Tomb, and the child is taken away by the King. Ultimately, Athridates decides to forgive his daughter if she is willing to break her ties to Pharnaces. When Thamyris refuses to be disloyal to Pharnaces, Athridates threatens to kill Eumenes. Arriving via a secret passage to the palace, Pharnaces comes to free his wife from her oath because he anticipates military success; still, he is angry at his wife when he discovers that his son is now a captive. On her own, Thamyris obtains her son's freedom and asks the High Priest to hide him in Themis's temple. Just when Athridates finds Thamyris and threatens to defy the temple's sanctity to locate Eumenes, news arrives that the Romans have fled and Pontus has won the battle. After this, Pharnaces enters the temple, and as he tries to kill Athridates, Thamyris intercedes. Refusing the forgiveness that Thamyris encourages Pharnaces to extend, Athridates stabs himself and repents his desire for revenge just before dying.

According to Lorraine McMullen, Brooke's biographer, the play received mixed reviews. Yet the role of Queen Thamyris is noteworthy and was perhaps enhanced as a tribute by the author to her colleague Mary Ann Yates. Early in the play, the Queen's intelligence and capability are emphasized: she is said to "more than share" (8) her husband's power. Although her responsibilities as a queen, a mother, a wife, and a daughter come into conflict, Thamyris responds courageously and boldly in the face of false accusations by her father and her husband that she has been disloyal and cowardly. Not only does she initiate some of the most important action, including the rescue of her son, but Thamyris dominates the play as its moral center.

MANUSCRIPT: Larpent 545.

TEXT: Readex Microprint.

The Siege of Valencia, Felicia Dorothea Browne Hemans. This verse tragedy, described as "a dramatic poem of nine scenes based on the epic of The Cid," was not acted. Hemans included the drama in her volume entitled *The Last Constantine, with Other Poems*, published by John Murray in 1823.

Led by Abdullah, the Moors have surrounded the city of Valencia, whose forces are commanded by Gonzalez. The Moors have captured Alphonso and Carlos, the young sons of Gonzalez and Elmira, and they will release them only if Gonzalez surrenders the city. Despite Elmira's appeal to free the boys, Gonzalez, who is a descendant of the Cid, refuses. In disguise, Elmira goes to Abdullah to implore him to return the children; he tells her she needs to convince Gonzalez to give up the city. Ximena, the daughter of Gonzalez and Elmira, ignited by poetry about her ancestors, endeavors to rally the beleaguered Spaniards. Ximena's patriotic speeches stir the multitude, and they prepare to fight. Below the walls, Abdullah brings the boys and asks if Gonzalez will surrender. When Gonzalez refuses, Abdullah pronounces their execution. Suddenly, Ximena and her troops arrive singing the Cid's battle song; Hernandez, the priest, urges them to rescue the young boys, but it is too late. The scene shifts to a church where Elmira laments over her lost boys and is discovered by her wounded daughter. Ximena is near death, and when the trumpet of Castile sounds, she dies. Gonzalez, himself fatally injured, arrives to find Ximena dead. A messenger reports the Moors are gathered for an assault. After Gonzalez praises Ximena's courage, he goes to the ramparts. Hernandez reports that the Spanish are losing the battle until he sees the Castilians coming to engage the Moors. The Castilians subdue their enemy, and Gonzalez lives just long enough to hear the Spaniards have won. Gonzalez's body is carried to the tomb of the Cids, followed by Elmira.

Hemans places so much emphasis on the poetry that no clear narrative emerges. Too many of the events take place offstage: for instance, Ximena's leading the Spaniards into battle and Elmira's arrangement with Abdullah to try and regain the children. The family of Gonzalez and Elmira are at the heart of the play: Elmira takes what action she can to retrieve the boys, and Gonzalez watches the slaughter of his sons for which he must assume a terrible responsibility. One strength of the drama originates from Hemans's understanding of mothers and children. This also leads to the theme of family unity. When her brothers are in trouble, Ximena becomes a female warrior, rallying the tired Spanish forces and leading them to fight the Moors. Hemans's poetry raises two prominent issues: the first continuing metaphor, which provides contrasts with the family, is the frequent consideration of loneliness, being alone, and isolation: the situation of the city being surrounded and isolated persists throughout the tragedy, and some characters express this, as when the priest says "Death knows no companions" (126). A second metaphor is the forgiveness requested by several characters in the face of death. Gonzalez tells Elmira that he asks Heaven "to record th' exchange Of our tired hearts' forgiveness" (227). In her discussion of the drama, which she clearly admires, Anne K. Mellor argues for the importance of maternal love in the private sphere, contrasting with heroic exploits in the public arena. When the two clash, however, "the public sphere takes control of the private, [and] both realms are destroyed" (*Romanticism and Gender* [NY: Routledge, 1993] 135–41).

TEXT: Readex Microprint.

The Silver Tankard; or, The Point at Portsmouth, Baroness Elizabeth Berkeley Craven, later the Margravine of Anspach. This two-act, musical entertainment was first produced at the Haymarket on 18 July 1781 with new music provided by Arnold, Giordani, and the author; T. Cadell printed the songs, which could be purchased at the theatre. Six performances were given during the summer season; the musical was not revived.

A retired sailor called Old Rosemary has two daughters, Nancy and Sally, and runs an ale house near the point in Portsmouth. Sally had been engaged to Tom Splicem, but because Tom is said to have died, Sally has taken up with Ensign Williams. Ben Mainstay, Old Rosemary's nephew, and Tom Reefem come on a mission for Splicem, who is still alive, to determine if Sally continues to love him. Although Sally now has other interests, Nancy can still sing the song Splicem taught her several years before, and it is clear that she fancies him. When Old Rosemary asks Williams if he'll marry Sally, the Ensign says he cannot marry a woman without a dower. If Old Rosemary provides a dowry of £500, he will have nothing left for Nancy. Tom is willing to marry Sally, but he can offer no dowry. At this crux, Nancy produces her grandmother's legacy—a silver tankard—as her own dowry and offers it to Tom, who says if Ensign Williams marries Sally, he will take Nancy. Old Rosemary blesses both couples, and the following day there will be two weddings.

Although the manuscript has as its main title *The Point at Portsmouth* with *The Silver Tankard* written in above (as if it were an afterthought), the more appropriate main title appears to be *The Silver Tankard* because the vessel is a visual symbol of Nancy's love for Tom Splicem. The tankard reminds us of the ale house at the point in Portsmouth, but its silver qualities also convince Tom that Nancy will endow their marriage with steadfastness and generosity. The sibling rivalry at the beginning of the play transforms into sisterly friendship in the last act, as Sally and Nancy become willing to assist one another.

MANUSCRIPT: Larpent 564. Readex Microprint of manuscript.

Simplicity, Lady Mary Wortley Montagu. The only known play by the poet, diarist, and letter writer is a three-act comedy, a free translation and adaptation of Marivaux's *Le Jeu de l'amour et du hasard; ou, Arlequin maître et valet*. First staged and printed in Paris, 1730, Marivaux's version was performed when a French company visited London during the 1734–1735 season; it was first produced at the Haymarket Theatre on 31 October 1734 and played three other times that season. In the introduction to the play, printed for the first time in 1977, Robert Halsband remarks "It is likely that Lady Mary saw the play, read it, and then made her translation. Whether or not she hoped to see her version produced on the stage—not, of course under her own name—we do not know. The manuscript remained among her papers, unnoticed by previous editors, biographers, and even the cataloguer for Sotheby's in 1928" (315). Halsband also notes that Montagu's version falls between a literal translation and a free adaptation with the setting and names changed. "In rough proportions," Halsband continues, "about a quarter of her play is a literal translation of Marivaux, about half is a free translation, and about a quarter is original" (315). The real change lies in tone and style: Lady Mary's "robust, practical English" replaces Marivaux's subtle, sentimental style.

The play opens at the English country house of Sir John Hearty, who has arranged for Gaymore, an eligible suitor, to visit with the expectation that his daughter Bellinda might marry him. Bellinda tells her maid Lucy that she doesn't want to marry a man she has never seen. Her father, Sir John, suggests that she change roles with Lucy to investigate Gaymore's character from the maid's perspective. After the women go to change costumes, Sir John reads a letter from Gaymore's father: his son will be acting the servant William, and William will act the master. The humor follows from the participants' not knowing of the double exchange. The real Lucy falls for the real William, whereas Gaymore, as William, falls for Bellinda, acting her maid. When Gaymore as the servant William tells Bellinda, as Lucy, that he is the real Gaymore, she can then manipulate the situation to test his love. And in the end, the lovers are united within their social classes: Bellinda with Gaymore, Lucy with William.

This amusing comedy shows a potential rupture in class distinctions, but the threat is in name only because Sir John Hearty knows about the double exchange. For the actors, however, having to switch roles frequently during the performance (from man to master or mistress to maid) could be challenging. Humor is generated because the audience/readers are in on the joke, and they can enjoy watching the characters cope with the changing roles. While Marivaux's title might be literally translated *The Game of Love and Chance*, Lady Mary titled her adaptation *Simplicity*. Halsband in his *MP* essay believes she wanted to stress "freedom from artifice," because "love was more serious than a game of chance" (20). Barbara Darby suggests that Lady Mary's title urges that arranged marriages be replaced with "a sensible union of compatible minds" (39). Since simplicity implies a lack of complication, the title could also have an ironic intent: nothing is simple in a comedy where extensive role-playing forces everyone to act duplicitously. Perhaps Lady Mary believes that if marital arrangements are to be made, they can be made more easily.

A more detailed discussion of the play by Halsband may be found in his essay "The First English Version of Marivaux" [*MP* 79 (1981): 16–23]. Barbara Darby considers the feminist aspects of Lady Mary's adaptation in her discussion "Love, Chance and the Arranged Marriage: Lady Mary Rewrites Marivaux" (*RECTR* 2nd Series 9:2 [1994]: 26–44).

MANUSCRIPT: Harrowby MS. 80. 160–87 at Sandon Hall, Stafford.

CRITICAL EDITION: Lady Mary Wortley Montagu, *Essays and Poems and "Simplicity, A Comedy"*, edited by Robert Halsband and Isobel Grundy (Oxford: Clarendon, 1977): 313–379.

Sir Harry Gaylove; or, Comedy in Embryo, Jean Marshall. This five-act comedy was printed for the author, whose name doesn't appear, in Edinburgh by A. Kincaid and W. Creech, 1772. Although Marshall submitted the play to Dagg at CG, Garrick at DL, and Foote at the HAY, none of them was willing to produce it. After the play was refused by Digges at the Edinburgh theater, Marshall reluctantly decided to publish it by subscription. Subscribers include James Boswell, Dr. Beattie, Wes Digges, David Hume, Lord Lyttleton, Adam Smith, and many Scots.

At age 25, Bellmour has squandered his money and been disinherited by his uncle. Worst of all is his banishment from his inamorata Ophelia by her father. Sir Harry Gaylove tries to cheer Bellmour up and gives him a purse of money. They discuss possible career choices, and Bellmour, who has sketched out a comedy about "a wild fellow reclaimed," decides to turn playwright. Sir Harry says he can help because his uncle has an interest with the managers. Meanwhile Mr. Godfrey, Ophelia's father, wants her to entertain a marriage proposal from the wealthy Bobby Leeson, but while he talks of fortune and beauty, she insists on reciprocal affection. Ultimately, Ophelia wants a man with more sense than wit and one who places honesty above disguise. When Ophelia goes to Chelsea for advice from her Aunt Heartfree, she is "rescued" from a carriage accident by one Lecky, who takes her to Lord Evergreen, the uncle of Sir Harry. While Lord Evergreen, who plans to seduce Ophelia, keeps her a captive in his house, Bellmour comes to ask about his play. Seeing Ophelia a virtual prisoner, he attempts to free her, but is tossed out by Evergreen's footmen, who then have him arrested. Lady Harriet learns of Ophelia's imprisonment and asks Sir Harry to help. He gets Ophelia away from his lecherous uncle, bails Bellmour out of prison, and takes Ophelia to her distraught parents. After Sir Harry describes Bellmour's effort to save Ophelia, the Godfreys are so grateful that they relent and let her marry him. For Sir Harry's part in aiding the distressed Ophelia, Lady Harriet accepts him.

The young women in this play know what they want. Ophelia Godfrey is determined to have a man with whom she shares a mutual affection. Lady Harriet would like to find higher qualities in Sir Harry than that of a gadfly. Being held against her will, Ophelia learns about malevolence first hand, but Lady Harriet rallies to help her out of the predicament. As the title character, Sir Harry assists all parties while demonstrating his good qualities which convince Lady Harriet to marry him. Although this comedy has some problems of a first-time playwright (unclear continuity, as when Ophelia goes to Chelsea), it has merit as a clever comedy with a good deal of humor. The contrast of freedom and imprisonment works effectively as an underlying metaphor for the action of the play.

TEXT: Readex Microprint.

Sir Patient Fancy, Aphra Behn. This five-act comedy was produced at DG on 17 January 1678 and printed later that year for Richard and Jacob Tonson. The farcical intrigue of the play succeeds with most modern critics, but whether or not it flourished in its own day has been questioned. In her combative preface, Behn demands vindication against the charge "That [the play] was Baudy" and that the women in the audience disliked the play. She also states that others objected to the play because it was by a woman, "who is forced to write for Bread and not ashamed to owne it" (7). Another question has arisen about the performance: who acted Lady Knowell? Several critics (Van Lennep and Link) believe it was Ann Quin because she performed in some of Behn's earlier plays, and because Nell Gwyn had retired from the stage in 1670–71. Others (Woodcock and Goreau) argue for Nell Gwyn because a contemporary engraving shows her in that role (no documentation) and Behn dedicated her next play, *The Feign'd Curtizans*, to Gwyn. All agree, however, that Tony Leigh, as the title character, and James Nokes, as Sir Credulous Easy, seem to have created much hilarity in their roles.

The opening scene with Lucretia, the daughter of Lady Knowell, and Isabella, the daughter of Sir Patient Fancy, has been praised by Link for its well-managed exposition. From them, we learn that Lucretia is in love with Leander, Sir Patient's nephew, and Isabella is in love with Lodwick, Lucretia's brother; their remarks characterize Sir Credulous, Lady Knowell, Sir Patient, and Lucia (Lady Fancy); and this exchange sets a tone while asserting themes of "arranged marriages, foppery, pedantry, and the battle of the sexes" (Link 54). Despite Lucretia's avowed love for Leander, Lady Knowell professes an interest in Leander, having designed that her daughter should marry Sir Credulous Easy. When Sir Patient discovers his wife with her lover, Wittmore, Lucia passes the young man off as Mr. Fainlove, a suitor for Isabella. Mistaken assignations cause humorous incidents in the night, setting up wonderfully farcical situations, such as Wittmore trying to get out of Lucia's bedroom after Sir Patient, who has been drinking to calm his nerves, sits on the bed Wittmore is hiding under. Thanks to a lot of conniving and manipulation, Isabella marries Lodwick and Lucretia wins Leander. Lucia will leave her husband and return to Wittmore, but Sir Patient will start a new life as a gallant and give up doctors and religion.

In her preface, Behn mentioned one source: Molière's *Le Malade imaginaire*, though twentieth-century critics have cited several other derivations. Yet Behn has reshaped her borrowings into a unified English comic drama. Sir Patient is not merely Argan copied from Molière; and while he is a hypochondriac, he is also a Whig, a Puritan, and an alderman who has married a young wife, but he is neither contemptuous nor pathetic, as Link points out (55). Even though Sir Patient is stubborn, he can be shrewd. He provides an effective contrast to the gullible Devonshire knight, Sir Credulous; and although Sir Credulous knows dogs and horses, he flounders in London society and emerges as the comic butt of the play.

Lady Knowell, the "learned lady," may be a pedant, but she is well treated by Behn, in contrast to the usual satiric figure of the *femmes savantes*; and in the end Lady Knowell assists her daughter by testing Leander's affection for Lucretia. Once again Behn turns to various kinds of marriages that fail: those entered into for mercenary reasons, those that are forced, and those where the pair are incompatible. These bad unions contrast with marriage for love, desired and achieved by Lucretia and Isabella.

TEXTS: Wing B1766. EEB Reel 203: 7. Readex Microprint.

MODERN EDITION: *Works*, ed. Montague Summers (1915; NY: Phaeton, 1967) 4: 1–116; *The Meridian Anthology of Restoration and Eighteenth-Century Plays by Women*, ed. Katharine M. Rogers (NY: Penguin-Meridian, 1994): 19–130.

The Sister, Charlotte Ramsey Lennox. Adapted from her own novel, *Henrietta*, this five-act comedy was performed only one night at CG on 18 February 1769 before being withdrawn. Lennox said that the audience came to the theatre prejudiced against the play. Still, two English editions were published that year by J. Dodsley and T. Davies. A Dublin edition, printed by P. & W. Wilson, also came out in 1769. Burgoyne's *The Heiress*, produced at DL on 14 January 1784, draws upon Lennox's play.

Assumed names cause most of the confusion in this sentimental comedy. Harriet Courteney took the name of Miss D'Arcy when she fled the home of her Roman Catholic aunt and went to stay with Miss Autumn, who lives with her stepmother at Windsor. Harriet's brother Mr. Courteney, who is acting as a tutor to Lord Clairville, has come with his pupil from France, and they have taken the names of Freeman and Belmour. Incognito, they wish to see the woman whom Lord Clairville's father, the Earl of Belmont, has chosen for his son's bride. The young lord does not approve of his father's choice; instead he falls in love with Miss D'Arcy (Harriet). When Courteney tries to prevent their engagement, he discovers that Harriet is the sister he hasn't seen for many years. He wants her to keep her identity a secret because he feels he would be accused of influencing Clairville to marry Harriet, penniless as she is. Moreover, he gets Harriet to agree to leave with him the next day. Now everyone believes that Courteney has fallen in love with Miss D'Arcy, and Clairville challenges Courteney to a duel. They meet offstage: Clairville misses, apparently on purpose, and Courteney discharges his pistol in the air. Lord Belmont arrives and blames Courteney for misleading his son, but Clairville exonerates Courteney. Lord Belmont then recommends Harriet for Clairville's wife, and he further urges Miss Autumn to take Courteney, showing Lady Autumn that she was self-deluded in thinking herself the object of Courteney's passion.

It may seem strange that Lord Belmont suddenly changes his mind and selects Harriet as his son's bride, but his explanation is that Harriet is "a truly virtuous woman! She who would sacrifice her fortune to her conscience; would subject her inclinations to her duty; who could despise riches, and triumph over love; she brings you in herself a treasure more valuable than both the Indies" (72). Lord Belmont discovers Harriet's strength in almost no time. Moreover, the audience has long realized that Harriet's decisions would be more effective than those of her brother Courteney. She wants to make their identity known, whereas he wants it kept secret for the flimsiest of reasons. Had they followed her idea, much unnecessary grief would have been saved. From the first act, we know that Harriet is more sensible than the affected Miss Autumn, who ends up with Courteney. "The sister," Harriet, is the title character for good reason: she displays more good sense than any other of the characters. Unfortunately, it takes Lord Belmont, who appears late in the play, to open everyone else's eyes to her reason and virtue.

MANUSCRIPT: Larpent 291.

TEXT: Readex Microprint.

The Sketch of a Fine Lady's Return from a Rout, Catherine Clive. Written for her benefit night at DL, this three-scene farce had only one performance—on 21 March 1763 as an afterpiece. The *Theatrical Review* (1 April 1763) "damns the writing and the performance on all counts," according to *LS* (4: 985). The play was not published.

Two clerks discuss their master and mistress, Sir Jeremy and Lady Jenkings, as the play begins. Lady Jenkings's maid, Jane, joins them, asking if her mistress has returned. Because Lady Jenkings has a passion for gambling, Jane has been forced to wait up all night, and it is now seven in the morning. Jane also condemns the French governess, whom she dislikes. When she finally arrives, Lady Jenkings goes directly to her dressing room, where she verbally abuses Jane. The noise of the daughters (Nancy and Fanny) puts her even more out of sorts, and she sends them away. After Lady Jenkings has asked for coffee, she begins to reckon her gains and losses but falls asleep while doing so. In Sir Jeremy's apartment, he receives a letter from his banker telling him that Lady Jenkings borrowed £300 by his order, and it has not been paid. After he has sent for his lawyer, Sir Jeremy storms into Lady Jenkings's bedroom, takes what money is on the table, and awakens her with questions about the £300. They are arguing over the money left on the table when the lawyer Mr. Nettle arrives. He explains the law: if £10 or more is lost, the loser may prosecute the winner for three times the amount. Lady Jenkings then confesses she lost £100 at piquet to Mrs. Nettle, and according to the law Nettle owes her £300. After the disgruntled lawyer leaves, Lady Jenkings vows not to play cards again for any sums that would make her husband blush or give her uneasiness.

Lady Jenkings's gambling creates a problem for the family, but she manages to escape the financial embarrassment this time. Neither of the Jenkings holds much interest for an audience: they are snobbish about Sir Jeremy's recent knighthood, and Lady Jenkings has even dismissed a servant for failing to use "your ladyship." Sir Jeremy appears easygoing until it comes to money, which brings out his greed.

MANUSCRIPT: Larpent 220. Readex Microprint of manuscript.

The Sleepwalker, Baroness Elizabeth Berkeley Craven, later the Margravine of Anspach. This two-act comedy, adapted from *Le Somnambule* by Antoine de Ferriol, Comte de Pont-de-Veyle (1739), was performed for charity in a private production at Newbury, March 1778. The play was printed at Strawberry Hill for T. Kirgate the same year.

As its title indicates, this short comedy focuses on a young somnambulist who fears that if his strange illness were known, his imminent marriage to Lady Bellmour would be ruined. Exhausted by a long journey, he decides upon arriving to lie down and rest. As feared, his ailment takes over and makes him act inappropriately. Unaware that he is clad in his nightgown in broad daylight, and believing himself to be at a ball, he takes his bride-to-be and her mother for masks and makes fun of them. Outraged, the mother breaks the marriage promise, to the delight of her daughter, who loves Frontless and is loved by him. Seeing that their love is reciprocal, the somnambulist gracefully bows out of the marriage. The play ends with his servant reminding him that he is not the first man to lose a wife while fast asleep. This flimsy comedy demands to be acted out, since so much depends on gestures and actions provided by the players.

The Sleepwalker follows closely Pont-de-Veyle's *Le Somnambule*: it is in fact a faithful, but not a slavish, translation, even though Craven, at times, lengthens or shortens parts of a scene, or introduces minor changes which, in no way, affect the plot. These changes affect the setting—now an English country house; the names of characters—now English and more picturesque; and the origins of the title character—no longer one of the richest bankers of Bordeaux, but just the son of a rich merchant. Slightly more significant, Craven spells out the motive for the ill-suited marriage (money for one spouse, social connections for the other), but the interest of this play lies elsewhere: for example, in the potential comedy of the episode of somnambulism or in the hilarious inability of the gardener to understand or pronounce the word *somnambule* in the original or the word *somnambulator*, the fanciful Latin equivalent Craven uses.

According to Kinne (152), Craven's replacement of Thibaut's French jargon with the Dutch gardener's broken English provides a marked improvement, but in fact both represent a surefire source of comedy. Nicoll also finds the gardener's character effective, and he believes the somnambulist Mr. Devasthouse to be "pictured with some considerable skill" (3: 177). But since Craven has mainly translated the text, the credit goes to the original author, Pont- de-Veyle.

TEXT: Readex Microprint.

Smiles and Tears; or, The Widow's Stratagem, Marie Therese DeCamp Kemble. Originally titled *The Law-Suit*, this five-act comedy was first produced at CG on 12 December 1815, with the author in her first appearance in three years taking the role of Lady Emily Gerald, a young, rich widow. Acted nine times its first season, the comedy was printed by J. Miller (1815); its text is partly based on Amelia Opie's novel *The Father and Daughter* (1801).

Delaval, Lord Glenthorn's son, is distressed by debt and threatened with scandal. To help recuperate his losses, he desires to marry Lady Emily Gerald, a wealthy widow to whom Sir Henry Chomley is also attracted. Lady Emily, however, is attracted to O'Donalon, described by Stanley, Lady Emily's uncle, as a "hotheaded Irishman." Stanley encourages her interest in Delaval, a man he believes to be honorable, but Stanley learns that Delaval took advantage of Miss Cecil Fitzharding, making her a mother at eighteen and leaving her friendless and destitute. This has caused her father to become mentally deranged, and he is confined to a mental institution. When he escapes, she finds him and asks only to care for him. In a law suit, Sir Harry has attempted to deprive Mrs. Belmore of her estate. In her widow's stratagem, Lady Emily arranges an interview between Mrs. Belmore and Sir Henry, who have never seen one another. They fall in love and join hands at the end. The conclusion also finds Delaval remorseful over his treatment of Cecil, and although they are not reconciled Cecil does give him their son to raise, while she cares for her father who has recovered his wits. Lady Emily is united with O'Donalon.

Small bits of wisdom in the play come from Mrs. Jefferies, who waits on Lady Emily. On second marriages, she remarks, "she's a fool that tries it a second time." On freedom and confinement in marriage, she comments "a husband is still a master; give me freedom I say." On women's silence, she says, "if one is denied the satisfaction of talking, one ought at least to be placed upon the secret service list, and be handsomely rewarded for one's silence." Lady Emily, too, has her share of bons mots: when Stanley discourages her from offering comfort to a fallen woman, Cecil, she responds, "Is there any situation, my dear Sir, that puts one person above the obligation of succoring another in distress?" The two disparate plots do not blend particularly well, but they may illustrate Kemble's main title.

MANUSCRIPT: Larpent 1889.

TEXT: Readex Microprint.

SMITH, Charlotte Turner (1749–1806). Born in London, Charlotte was raised by an aunt after the death of her mother. Upon the remarriage of her father, Charlotte's aunt quickly organized a marriage in 1765 for her young niece to Benjamin Smith, son of a director of the East India Company. The marriage became difficult because she had to raise a large family (she had twelve children) and because her husband managed money poorly, running them into debtors' prison. In order to provide a subsistence for her family, Charlotte published a volume of elegiac sonnets, which proved successful (eleven editions to 1851), but the family situation continued in straightened circumstances. Living in France for a while, she translated into English *Manon Lescault* and *Les Causes Célèbres*, but upon her return she separated from her husband and began to write novels. Writing almost a novel a year until the end of the century, Charlotte managed to subsist. *Emmeline, The Orphan of the Castle* (1788) was followed by four more novels before her best known work, *The Old Manor House*, in 1793.

Two novels for young people, *Rural Walks* (1795) and *Rambles Further, a continuation of*

Rural Walks (1796), done in dialogues, may have prompted her to write for the stage in her fiftieth year. Her five-act comedy, *What is She?*, was produced at CG on 27 April 1799 and published in London the same year by T. N. Longman and O. Rees, and in Dublin by A. George Folingsby. Moving frequently in her later years, Charlotte died in Tilford, near Farnham in Surrey, and was buried at Stoke church, near Guildford. [*BD*, BNA, DBAWW, DNB, EBWW, FCLE. Biographies by F. Hilbish (Diss., U of Penn, 1941) and a forthcoming one by Judith Stanton; on correspondence, see R. P. Turner, Diss., U of So. Cal, 1966.]

The Sociable Companions; or, The Female Wits, Margaret Lucas Cavendish, Duchess of Newcastle. This comedy was printed in her *Plays, Never before Printed*, by A. Maxwell in 1668. There was no production.

The comedy treats ways in which the disbanded Cavaliers try to reintegrate themselves into English society after the Cromwellian era. But like most plays by Cavendish, relationships between men and women create the central events. The play opens after the Restoration; the Cavaliers have lost their estates, exhausted their funds, and have no trades to return to. The female wits, of the second title, are the sisters of the returning soldiers, and the women suggest that they marry wealthy men who did not go to war to reestablish themselves and their brothers. They group themselves together as the sociable companions and collectively work to help the women achieve their goal of "good and rich husbands." Get-all (a usurer), Plead-all (a lawyer), and Cure-all (a physician) all wish to marry the old widow, Lady Riches. So the companions set Dick Traveler up with her while they arrange to dupe each of the rich men. They organize a mock trial for Get-all, charging him with getting Peg Valourosa, sister to the disbanded Captain Valour, with child by imagination. Since Get-all has never been to Spiritual Court, the ruse works. By the time Peg explains the hoax to him, Get-all has fallen in love and gladly agrees to marry. To deal with Plead-all, Jane Fullwit disguises herself as "Jack Clerk." Will Fullwit then charges Plead-all with keeping his sister in man's clothes. The lawyer says if the charges can be proved, he will marry the woman. Jane enters in feminine dress, and Plead-all accedes to the marriage. After Cure-all has learned that the rich, old widow just married, Anne Sencible arrives and explains she is lovesick for him. As if on cue, Anne's brother, Harry, pops in the room, and, finding them alone, draws his sword, but Cure-all asks Harry's consent to marry Anne. In the subplot, Prudence Save-all interviews various young marriageable suitors, but because most are vain and avaricious she finds them all wanting: "They consider my wealth before my person" (68). When an older man wishes to wed Prudence, however, he offers her all of his substance instead of expecting a dowry. Because of his wisdom and experience, she agrees and publicly defends her choice.

The duping of gullible men, so popular in Restoration comedy, emerges as a device for Cavendish to show how the female wits operate. After the women have hauled their brothers out of taverns, they get the Cavaliers to assist in achieving their goals. Thus, women who have been inactive during the war now institute a social offensive. As a well-organized unit, the sociable companions—both female and male—actively pursue the women's plans. To achieve their ends, Jane Fullwit disguises herself as a male clerk, and Harry Sencible dresses as a chambermaid. Their success is the outcome of working together. As Plead-all is forced to acknowledge: "Faith, I find that the Cavaliers are the best deceivers" (82). Besides the prominence of economics in the women's actions, legal proceedings, real and feigned, provide a structure for the comedy.

TEXTS: Wing N867. EEB Reel 674: 2. Readex Microprint.

The Song of Solomon, translated by Ann Gittins Francis. This transformation of biblical verses into dramatic form is the only recorded drama by Francis, published in 1781 but never acted. *BD* describes the play as "A poetical translation from the original Hebrew: with preliminary discourse, and notes historical, critical, and explanatory." Francis arranges the

Song of Solomon "as a sacred hymeneal drama, divided into acts and scenes, according to the opinions of Gregory Nazianzen, Harmer, and others" (1: 771). In DBAWW, Gillian Beer says the speeches are divided "between Solomon and two women, the Spouse and the Jewish Queen (Solomon's new and old loves)" (132). Francis uses this triangle to show emotions and to provide motives for the characters's actions. The verse is at the same time "stately and voluptuous": Francis, thus, extols marital love while insinuating an allegorical eroticism, and she strengthens the drama by supplying an appropriate cultural setting.

TEXT: Not in Readex Microprint.

The Sons of Erin; or, Modern Sentiments, Alicia Sheridan LeFanu. Her only play, a five-act comedy, was first produced by the DL players at the Lyceum Theatre on 11 April 1812 and published the same year. Originally titled *Prejudice; or, Modern Sentiment*, the play proved quite popular, being acted twenty-seven times. It was printed by J. Ridgway, 1812. In the Advertisement that begins the play, LeFanu explains that "the principal object of the author in the following Comedy was to do away [with] any lingering prejudice that may still exist in England against the people of Ireland" (iii). The only difference between the first and second editions is the ordering of the epilogues, one spoken by Lady Ann and the other by Mrs. Rivers.

After the death of Mrs. Rivers, the family has greatly changed: Mr. Rivers has remarried a younger wife who affects airs of refinement; and Rivers's daughter Emily has married and run off with Fitz-Edward, an Irishman whom the family has never seen and who has gotten himself in pecuniary difficulties by his extravagance. Rivers's son, Captain Rivers, is courting Lady Ann. Set in London at the Rivers's house, the play begins with the arrival of Mr. Oddley, the crotchety brother of the late Mrs. Rivers. The plot is further generated by the arrival of Lady Ann, who introduces the family to Melville, a man who acts as an amanuensis to Miss Ruth Rivers but who is in fact Fitz-Edward, Emily's husband. Lady Ann hopes that the family will accept him if they can move beyond their prejudice of the Irish. The Rivers family becomes so dependent on Fitz-Edward that this is exactly what happens. Miss Ruth (Mr. Rivers's sister) wishes to marry him herself; and Mrs. Rivers avoids a foolish liaison with Sir Frederick after Fitz-Edward illustrates the man's callous attitude toward women. Even the antimatrimonial Oddley achieves sympathy for Emily and a begrudging respect for the Irish because of Emily's dignity when she arrives late in the play. In addition to proving that she is "capable of friendship" to Fitz-Edward (32), Lady Ann teaches Captain Rivers a lesson about jealousy.

Sons of Erin is as preoccupied with gender issues as it is with Irish prejudice. Although ultimately ridiculed for her shallow knowledge, Miss Ruth Rivers is "a lady of science" who believes women are "capable of the highest attainments, who can become astronomers, metaphysicians, logicians, chemists..." (25). Lady Ann, like Miss Ruth, distrusts marriage because of the degrading effect it has on women. Forced by her father to marry at sixteen, Lady Ann experienced "six years of bondage" before freeing herself. Lady Ann removes any apprehensions that Emily has about her husband's faithfulness, and she encourages the more timid woman to greater strength and determination. Most unusual about this play is the friendship between a male and female character, who we discover are not only relatives but have been in love with each other in the past.

MANUSCRIPT: Larpent 1714.

TEXT: Readex Microprint of third edition, 1812.

The South Briton, by a lady. First performed at Smock Alley Theatre, Dublin, on 24 January 1774, this five-act comedy was published in Dublin by G. Allen the same month. The only London performance occurred at CG on 12 April 1774 for Mary Bulkley's benefit. J. Williams published the play the same year in London, but lists the Dublin cast.

The anonymous playwright mentions in the dedication that the comedy is her first dramatic effort. Even as a novice, she is quite inventive, for the play bristles with plot lines. The main action, however, turns on the title character, Mowbray, who has just returned from the continent when the play opens. The recipient of two legacies, Mowbray lavishes money everywhere and falls in love wherever he pleases, usually with seduction in mind. He has no interest in abiding by his parents' wishes—expressed in their wills—that he marry Miss Audley, and instead he pursues Henrietta Egerton, whose brother loves Miss Audley. Henrietta displays an indifference, even a dislike for Mowbray, whose friend Leslie tells him frankly he is wrong to purse Henrietta. Learning Henrietta has come to town, Miss Audley sends her friend £200 anonymously, fearing she may be in financial straits. Captain Egerton believes the money represents an inducement from Mowbray, and the two men nearly fight over the matter before Leslie reconciles them. Miss Audley asks Henrietta to accompany her to a masquerade, and because they wear similar costumes, Henrietta is kidnapped instead of Miss Audley. Mowbray comes to the rescue. This worthy act demonstrates a change in his character; having discovered Mowbray's transformation, Henrietta accepts his offer of marriage.

Another plot line takes up Captain Egerton who, along with his sister, suffers from a lack of money. The situation even forces the Captain to sell his commission, but the investment house where he placed his money fails. Their uncle fortuitously—and coincidentally—comes from the country to lodge in London at Mrs. Ornel's, where they are staying. Old Egerton holds the inheritance that Captain Egerton should have received. Without realizing who they are, Old Egerton becomes quite absorbed with the brother and sister, and when he learns their identity he is delighted. Along with Sir Terence, Miss Audley's Irish uncle, Old Egerton urges Miss Audley to marry his nephew.

Additional plot lines—seldom developed—take up Issacher, a Jewish broker and moneylender, and his wife Maria; a romance between Miss Audley's maid Jenny and Mowbray's valet Strap; and the devoted assistance of the old Scotch soldier McPherson, who served in the regiment of Mowbray's father. All these characters and situations are stereotypical, but making Issacher a villain because of his race and profession is particularly offensive. Leslie, a Scotsman and half-pay officer, talks sense to both Mowbray and Captain Egerton. His voice of reason from the North accompanies that of Sir Terence O'Shaughnesy from the West of Ireland. Old Egerton is the fox-hunting squire who appears out of place in London, and there is the retired Admiral Swivel who speaks a nautical lingo when he appears in the last two acts. Most of these characters never break out of their occupational or national stereotypes. The only ostensible justification for their inclusion comes in the last nationalistic scene where the English, Scottish, and Irish combine to make the great British empire. Readers shouldn't overlook the theme of women's friendships, which emerges when Miss Audley anonymously sends Henrietta £200, and continues through the remainder of the play. At the conclusion, however, the men, particularly Mowbray and Old Egerton, have all the lines as if they were entirely responsible for the various changes of heart that have occurred.

TEXT: Readex Microprint of the 1774 London printing.

The Spaniards in Peru; or The Death of Rolla, translation by Anne Plumptre. This rendition of Kotzebue's *Die Spanier in Peru oder Rollas Tod* became the basis of R. B. Sheridan's *Pizarro* (produced DL, 24 May 1799). Although the DL account book records that she was paid £25 for her translation (*LS* 5: 2178), Plumptre appears to have been paid £50 (£25 each paid on 6 and 13 May 1799 [BL Add. MS. 29710, f. 139]), according to Sheridan's letter (#362) to Richard Phillips, the publisher (*Letters of R. B. Sheridan*, ed. Cecil Price, 2: 115–16). R. Phillips published Plumptre's translation of the five-act tragedy in 1799. Except for the title page, the second edition is identical. The events of this play follow those dramatized in *The Virgin of the Sun*, which Plumptre also translated from Kotzebue in 1799.

Before the events of the play, Alonzo has defected from Pizarro's Spanish forces because of their cruel treatment of the Peruvians; he has married Cora, and they now have a child. Alonzo and Rolla, an Inca who maintains a virtuous love for Cora, now lead the Peruvian militia. Opening at the Spanish camp, the play introduces Elvira, Pizarro's mistress, speaking with the General's secretary, Valverde. Pizarro arrives and eyes them suspiciously, but he turns his attention to Alonzo's servant, Diego, who has just been captured. From Diego, Pizarro learns that the Peruvians will have a religious festival and plans to attack during these ceremonies. When the scene shifts, Alonzo, Cora, and their child are enjoying a pastoral moment out of doors; Rolla comes to suggest that Cora go to the mountains with the child, but she wishes to stay. As the religious ceremony gets underway, a scout reports the Spanish are advancing. In the battle, the Peruvians triumph, thanks to Rolla's exhorting his troops to rally, but Alonzo is captured. Pizarro intends to have him executed the following morning, despite Elvira's urging for mercy. That night Rolla, disguised as a monk, slips into Alonzo's tent; Alonzo reluctantly accepts the monk's habit and escapes, while Rolla awaits execution. When she finds Rolla instead of Alonzo, Elvira entreats Rolla to kill Pizarro. Although he feigns interest, Rolla will not kill Pizarro, who then sets his opponent free. Meanwhile, having returned to the Peruvian camp, Alonzo searches for Cora, who is in the forest with her child. When she hears Alonzo's voice, she leaves the child to search for her husband. But while she is gone, two Spanish soldiers find the child and take him with them to their camp. Cora is distraught when she cannot find the baby. Rolla, leaving the Spanish camp, is stopped and bound over to Pizarro, who has him freed, when two soldiers come in with the child of Cora and Alonzo. Recognizing the baby, Rolla grabs him and escapes, but not before he has been shot. In the last scene, he returns the child to Cora and dies.

Plumptre's translation is a straightforward rendering of Kotzebue's German text, though she does note some minor alterations in the preface. A more major change occurred in making Valverde a secretary, rather than a priest, as he is in the original. The most important modification, however, is the rejuvenation of Elvira's character from a camp follower to a high-minded woman, who now deserves "compassion and admiration" (v). R. B. Sheridan's alterations of Plumptre's translation for his successful stage version are discussed at length in Joseph W. Donohue, Jr., *Dramatic Character in the English Romantic Age* (Princeton: Princeton UP, 1970): 125–156.

Although Elvira's fate at the end of the play is uncertain, she forces Pizarro to reconsider his actions, and while he doesn't always follow her advice, she compels him to consider a different point of view. By way of contrast, Cora, as wife and mother, is pushed from one emotional extreme to another: first, her husband is taken prisoner; she, then, unfairly blames Rolla; finally, she runs off to try to find Alonzo, leaving her child unprotected. The loss of the child creates a trauma almost too much for Cora. Clearly, the hero is Rolla, "a heathen" more noble than the vicious Spaniards. And the term heroism comes in for a good deal of examination, by words in Elvira's discussions with Pizarro, and by deeds in Rolla's rallying his troops and in his freeing the child from the Spanish. The consideration of heroism also brings up the central question of the play: what does it mean to be a man? Pizarro constantly refers to Alonzo as "boy," whereas he considers himself a man. Elvira says that if Pizarro were a real man he would be more magnanimous. Thus the play stresses that masculinity embodies generosity, as well as fortitude; it involves virtue, as well as strength. Notably, manliness comprises characteristics of androgyny.

TEXT: Readex Microprint, under the name of Anne Plumptre, 1799.

The Spanish Wives, Mary Pix. This popular three-act farce was first produced at DG in August 1696 and printed the same year for R. Wellington. Based on a translation of Gabriel de Bremond's novel *The Pilgrim* (1680), also the source of the subplot in Dryden's *The Spanish Friar* (1681), Pix's farce is more invention than adaptation. Paula L. Barbour compares the three works in her critical edition (24–44). Perhaps taking her cue from Hume (418), Constance Clark gives details of Pix's debt to Aphra Behn in this play (254). The farce was revived in 1699, 1703, possibly 1714, and 1726; W. S. Clark points out a performance at Smock Alley, Dublin, in the 1707–1708 season (1955; 124).

Tittup and Elenora are the Spanish wives who are both married to older men. The wife of the easy-going Governor of Barcelona, Tittup contemplates an affair with an Englishman, Colonel Peregrine. When the plans are discovered by the Governor, she repents and gives up the Colonel; her husband forgives her. Elenora, on the other hand, has been pledged to Count Camillus, but her family forces her to marry the jealous Marquis of Moncada. He spends the play worrying that he will be made a cuckold, and Camillus schemes to remove Elenora to a monastery until a Cardinal can provide an edict of divorce.

While Hume finds the play "wishy-washy stuff" (418) and Cotton labels it "a sentimentalized intrigue comedy," Kendall says it is "a model of what a feminist farce is" (34). Much of the farcical humor is supplied by the contrast between the Governor and the Marquis: the Governor encourages his wife's freedom, whereas the Marquis keeps his wife continually locked up. Unable to meet each other because of the Marquis's jealousy, the wives intrigue in different ways. Tittup has an affectionate relationship with the Governor, but she is also sexually attracted to the young Colonel. Elenora's maid, Orada, acts as if she sides with her master, even though she works tirelessly for her mistress. Hidewell, one of the Count's retainers, adds to the laughter by his disguises and his country accent. The Count's other retainer, Friar Andrew, is a figure of ridicule, providing low comic humor and supporting anti-Catholic attitudes.

TEXTS: Wing P2332. EEB Reel 396: 7. Readex Microprint.

CRITICAL EDITION: Edited by Paula L. Barbour, Diss., Yale, 1975.

MODERN EDITION: With introduction by Kendall in *Love and Thunder* (London: Methuen, 1988): 29–62; *The Meridian Anthology of Restoration and Eighteenth-Century Plays by Women*, ed. Katharine M. Rogers (NY: Penguin-Meridian, 1994): 130–184.

FACSIMILE EDITION: E-CED, with introduction by Edna L. Steeves (NY: Garland, 1982).

Spectrology of Ghosts, Jane M. Scott. This entertainment was given forty-three times at the San Pareil Theatre in its first season. The piece, perhaps a magic lantern show narrated by Scott, opened on 12 January 1807. No text is extant.

The Speechless Wife, Mrs. Rainsford. This two-act musical farce, produced at CG on 22 May 1794, was attributed to Rainsford by the *Morning Herald*, 9 May 1794. The music was composed by S. Webbe. The *London Gazette*, 23 May 1794, credits "A Lady" but provides no name. *BD* comments that the play was based on Prior's poem "The Ladle," and that it was condemned the first night. Genest notes that a similar tale was previously dramatized by Miles Peter Andrews in *Belphegor*, produced at DL on 16 March 1778 (7: 167–68). Rainsford's play was not printed.

Prior found the source for his poem in Ovid's tale of Baucis and Philemon. Mercury and Jupiter stop for a night at a farmer's cottage where they are fed. In return the gods grant the farmer and his wife three wishes, and she immediately wishes for a ladle for their silver dish. Her husband is angry at what he considers a foolish desire, and he wishes the ladle in her ass. No sooner said than done, and the two join in the last wish to ease her of her pain and "get the Ladle out again."

The stereotypical greedy farm wife makes this farce another misogynistic treatment of women.

MANUSCRIPT: Larpent 1025.

The Spoiled Child, attributed to Dorothy Jordan [Dorothy Bland]. This popular two-act farce was first produced at DL, 22 March 1790, on Jordan's benefit night. The afterpiece followed Jordan's first appearance as Letitia Hardy in Hannah Cowley's *The Belle's Stratagem*. An unauthorized Dublin printing of *The Spoiled Child* came out in 1799; it was later printed for Jordan's benefit in 1805. The play has also been ascribed to Issac Bickerstaffe, Richard Ford, Prince Hoare, and Elizabeth Inchbald.

Little Pickle's father has indulged him terribly, and the child is always into mischief. To correct the situation, Miss Pickle persuades her brother to say that Little Pickle is not his son, but the son of Margery, who had nursed him. However, Little Pickle, in cahoots with Margery, acts her son in disguise, and he helps foil Miss Pickle's attempt to elope with the poet Tagg. At the end of the play, Little Pickle's father forgives him, and Little Pickle promises to be good.

Genest says that "this farce is poor stuff" (6: 591), but Dorothy Jordan, who played Little Pickle, made it popular by her acting. The play requires Little Pickle (Jordan) to assume several roles using various disguises. Whether she wrote the play or not, the farcical actions clearly showcase Jordan's talents.

MANUSCRIPT: Larpent 862.

TEXT: Readex Microprint, under Bickerstaffe.

STARKE, Mariana (1762?–1838). Born to Mary and Richard Starke, a governor in Madras, Mariana selected elements from her life in India to develop in two plays: *The Sword of Peace; or, A Voyage of Love*, a comedy, and *The Widow of Malabar*, a tragedy. Produced at HAY in 1788, the comedy was followed by an adaptation of a French play, *The Widow of Malabar*, privately produced at Mary Champion de Crespigny's theatre in 1790. A third drama, *The British Orphan*, was also performed privately at Crespigny's theatre in 1790 or 1791 (the manuscript is now lost). Another imaginative work from this period is a long poem, *The Poor Soldier; An American Tale, founded on a recent fact* (1789), which details the misfortunes of Charles Short, a South Carolina loyalist. Traveling through Europe during the next several years, Starke published her *Letters* from 1792 to 1798; these combine a narrative with practical travel tips. Also in 1800, Starke published her last play, *The Tournament*, taken from "the celebrated German drama, entitled *Agnes Bernauer*"; it was not performed.

In 1811, while living at Exmouth, Starke translated the poetry of Carlo Maria Maggi and published it with some of her own verse. Following the expansion of her *Letters*, Starke returned to guide-book materials in her *Travels*, after revisiting France, Italy, and Switzerland (1820). These books advising travelers where to stay, what to see, and how to get around became the prototypes for the well-known Baedeker travel series much later in the nineteenth century. Starke died in Milan during her later travels. [*BD*, DBAWW, DNB, FCLE, OCEL (under John Murray)]

The Statue Feast, Baroness Elizabeth Berkeley Craven. later the Margravine of Anspach. Altered from Molière's *Dom Juan; ou, le Festin de pierre* (1665), this drama was privately produced at Benham House in 1782. It was not published, and no manuscript appears to be extant.

Kinne quotes *The London Chronicle* (52 [1 August 1782]: 163): "The theatre was made in the wood behind Benham House, the trees formed a canopy, and the darkness and stillness of the night were favourable to the lights and the dresses. The play was Molière's Statue Feast, but much altered, and cut into two acts. Lady Craven has with taste, lessened Don Juan's villainy into mildness, and instead of permitting the horrible catastrophe at the end of the fifth act, has caused the statue to be found the brother of Elvira, who assisted her in her plot of terrifying her inconstant husband in his pursuits" (162–63). Kinne adds that "the hostess's attractive, three-year-old child played the role of Don Juan's son, and when the little fellow was presented to his father by the statue he "embraced his theatrical [parent] with much grace" (163).

The Stolen Heiress; or, The Salamanca Doctor Outplotted, Susanna Carroll [Centlivre]. Although the title page proclaims the play is a comedy, the double-plot structure imitates tragicomedy. The source of the five-act drama is Thomas May's *The Heir* (1620) and possibly the anonymous play *The Heiress*

(1669), according to Burling. First produced as *The Heiress* at LIF on 31 December 1702, it was printed anonymously for William Turner and John Nutt early the following year. The subplot later served as the basis for Hannah Cowley's *Who's the Dupe?* (DL, 10 April 1779).

Set in Sicily, the play opens with Gravello, father of Lucasia and Eugenio, pretending his daughter has become his heir by having it erroneously reported that his son has died in Rome. This, he believes, will bring wealthy suitors to woo Lucasia (performed by Elizabeth Barry). Eugenio arrives in Sicily having heard the rumor, and he disguises himself to find out why the false report has been circulated. He goes to his father's house with a letter saying Eugenio lives, and since no one has been told, Gravello invites Eugenio, disguised as Irus, to stay. Eugenio has also learned that his father has arranged with Count Pirro, the Governor's nephew, to marry Lucasia, even though she loves Palante. Irus represents himself to be a poor poet with a grudge against Eugenio, and Pirro offers him a contract to poison Eugenio so Lucasia will actually be Gravello's heir. Lucasia pleads with her father to no avail, and she decides to run off with Palante. They meet and wed clandestinely, but as they prepare to flee, Gravello apprehends them; Palante goes to prison where the sentence is death without reprieve for unlawfully marrying an heiress. Lucasia makes a valiant plea for Palante's life to the Governor, but the only way he'll spare Palante's life is if she marries Pirro. At the Governor's house, Euphenes (Palante's father) begs for mercy to no avail, until Irus takes off his disguise, divulges his father's chicanery, and reveals Pirro's contract to poison Eugenio. The Governor banishes Pirro, and Lucasia unites with Palante.

In a parallel plot, Gravello's brother Larich demands his daughter, Lavinia, marry Sancho, a scholar from Salamanca; but Lavinia longs to marry the penniless Francisco. When Sancho arrives, he meets Francisco, whom he has known in Spain. Francisco convinces Sancho that his father-in-law-to-be really wants a son-in-law learned in the ways of men. Taking the clue, Sancho acts a worldly wise role, whereas Francisco appears in Sancho's scholarly guise. The ruse appears to succeed, but Sancho unknowingly reveals the impersonation. As the forced marriage seems imminent, Lavinia pretends she's with child. Francisco arrives, stating that he loves Lavinia for herself, not for Larich's wealth. Larich grumbles that they can starve together. In the final scene, Lavinia informs her father that she is not pregnant, and Larich also learns that Francisco has received an inheritance from his uncle. Sancho is left with his man, Tristram, in the midst of the general merry making.

Centlivre integrates the parallel plots well: the scene where Lucasia pleads with the Governor for Palante's life precedes the scene in which Lavinia implores her father not to make her marry Sancho. Here and elsewhere in the play, each plot comments on the other. Clearly, Lucasia's situation is the more serious of the two, and her contention with the governor carries the stronger language. The lighter subplot provides some comic relief as Lavinia and Francisco outmaneuver Sancho. Thus, the theme of parental tyranny dominates both plots, as Lock points out (40); and he provides a comparison with Centlivre's source in Thomas May's earlier play. Contrasting a potentially tragic plot with a comedy of intrigue allows Centlivre to comment on the possible disaster of forced marriage. While Lavinia wittily assists Francisco in handling her father, Lucasia moves the audience to side with her against an unfortunate law. When Pirro's fortune-hunting motives reveal his ugly character, Lucasia is vindicated; and the Governor says he will attempt to get the law annulled.

TEXT: Readex Microprint without name or date on the title page.

FACSIMILE EDITION: E-CED, with introduction by R. C. Frushell (NY: Garland, 1982).

Stratagems; or, The Lost Treasure, Jane M. Scott. This two-act melodrama opened at the Sans Pareil Theatre on 4 March 1816 with Scott in the role of Yamira. After fifteen performances its first year, there were revivals in two later seasons.

MANUSCRIPT: Larpent 1913.

STRATFORD, Agnes (fl. 1794–95). Possibly the translator or adaptor of a tragedy, *The Labyrinth; or, Fatal Embarrassment*, taken from Thomas Corneille's *Ariane*, printed for the author in Dublin, 1795. There is no record of the play having been acted. She is the sister of The Rev. Dr. Thomas Stratford, author of several plays, and he may have had a hand in the tragedy, published posthumously for her benefit. [*BD*]

STRATHMORE, Countess of. See **BOWES**, Mary Eleanor.

The Stripling, Joanna Baillie. This five-act tragedy was published in the second volume of her *Dramas* in 1836 (Longman, et al.). It was never staged.

Mr. Arden has been accused of forgery, and his wife reluctantly asks for assistance from an old suitor, Mr. Robinair. Unbeknownst to Mrs. Arden, Robinair has ensnared her husband in debt and unwise business practices. Robinair plans to offer damning testimony against Mr. Arden to revenge "all the insults I have endured from that proud woman [Mrs. Arden]" (134). Most of all Robinair is motivated by his desire to gain control over Mrs. Arden, whom he will treat "nobly" once her husband is in jail and she submits to his "power" (138). When she goes to see him, Robinair insists that Mrs. Arden join him in his rooms in Chelsea that night, a proposition that she repeats to her husband unaware that her son is present. Determined to revenge both father and mother, young Arden goes to Chelsea instead and kills Robinair with his gun, accidentally leaving his hat behind. When the hat is discovered, the boy is accused of the murder, and a skirmish ensues when they come to arrest the youth. Young Arden is wounded and reveals that his death is the punishment he has prayed for. The play ends with the father cursing himself for his "vanity and extravagance" which caused his son's death.

The tragedy initially focuses on the fall of an unwise middle-class father, who has been manipulated by another shrewder, more malevolent male. Described in elevated and noble terms, the son not only sacrifices himself but he is also conscious of the implications of his actions. Although more practical (but also more believable) than her son, Mrs. Arden is superior to her husband: she is shrewder in her assessment of others and stronger in her opposition to Robinair.

TEXT: Readex Microprint of *Dramas* (1836) 2: 107–214.

Successful Cruize; or, Nobody Coming to Woo, Jane M. Scott. This musical entertainment, said to be a continuation of *The Fisherman's Daughter* by Gabriel Giroux, opened at the Sans Pareil Theatre on 14 November 1807 with music by James Sanderson. Scott created the role of Jennette. The piece ran seventy-six times, but no script of the dramatic portion remains.

Such Things Are. Elizabeth Inchbald. This five-act comedy-drama was first produced at CG on 10 February 1787 and published the same year by G. G. J. and J. Robinson but dated 1788. There were twenty-two performances the first season, and the drama held the stage for several years.

Set in Sumatra, the play treats the colonial interaction with the natives. Sir Luke and Lady Tremor represent the socially-minded British colonials; Lord Flint, an Englishman who has been raised in Sumatra, now works for the Sultan; Twineall is a recently-arrived colonial; Haswell, a wise, older colonial, is interested in prison reform. In order to ingratiate himself with the Tremors, Twineall asks a departing colonial about the Tremors, but he is given wrong information. When Twineall acts on the misinformation, comic misunderstandings result. Haswell seeks information about the prisons, where he meets a son and his sick father, as well as a female prisoner, who keeps expecting a ransom even after fifteen years in prison. Haswell goes to the Sultan to plead for the prisoners. The Sultan, who claims to be a Christian, has been merciless since the death of his European wife at the hands of rebels. Haswell persists and asks for a test case: free six prisoners and observe the results. Both Sir Luke and Lady Tremor are angry with Twineall, and with Lord Flint they have

Twineall arrested for speaking disparagingly of the Sultan. Haswell, at the prison, meets Twineall, who regrets his foolish behavior. With Haswell's aid Twineall is freed. Haswell then speaks with the female prisoner and learns that she is the wife whom the Sultan thought dead. Haswell reunites the Sultan with his wife, and the Sultan plans to adopt Haswell's prison reforms. The sick father has his lands restored, and the play closes with many tributes to Haswell.

Inchbald says that she modeled Haswell on the real-life reformer John Howard, and his central place in the drama stresses the importance of morality in the play. Haswell's humanitarian instincts suggest how British colonial policy could benefit from sympathetic reformers. With England in the midst of the trial of Warren Hastings, the governor-general of India, perhaps "such things" described in the title are the terrible conditions in the colonies, and one way to deal with such tyranny is through kindly treatment and sympathy.

MANUSCRIPT: Larpent 761.

TEXTS: Readex Microprint. TEC Reel 1526: 27.

MODERN EDITION: *The Meridian Anthology of Restoration and Eighteenth-Century Plays by Women*, ed. Katharine M. Rogers (NY: Penguin-Meridian, 1994): 489–558.

FACSIMILE EDITION: E-CED, with introduction by Paula R. Backscheider (NY: Garland, 1980).

The Summer House, Jane M. Scott. This one-act comic opera with music composed by Mr. Lawrence opened at the Sans Pareil Theatre on 16 February 1815. It ran five times its first season and was revived in the following two years. Scott performed Jemima.

MANUSCRIPT: Larpent 1847.

Susanna; or, Innocence Preserved, Elizabeth Tollet. This libretto for a musical drama, published posthumously by her nephew, appears in Tollet's *Poems on Several Occasions* (London: John Clarke, 1755). Although some musical markings (D. C. for Da Capo) exist in the text, no music or composer is mentioned. Because no date of composition is given for Tollet's work, we cannot know its relation to Handel's oratorio *Susanna* (first performed 10 February 1749 at CG), though it may pre-date Handel's work. According to Paul Henry Lang (*George Frideric Handel* [London: Faber, 1966]: 475), Handel's librettist is unknown.

Based on the biblical story in the Apocrypha, Tollet's drama retells the story of Susanna and the Elders. Set in Babylon, where the Jews are in captivity, two of the elders watch Susanna bathing. She discovers them spying, and they want her to submit to them. When she refuses, they report that a youth was with her, assuming their word will be believed before hers. Wed to Joachim who won't believe the elders, Susanna would still rather die than have her name besmirched. With much lamenting, she is about to be led away to die. Daniel, however, asks the elders, "What tree the lawless Love conceal'd?" The first elder names "a drooping Mastick" tree, but the second one says the tree was a "stately Holm." Caught lying, the elders are "both destin'd to be slain." Daniel commends Susanna's virtue and returns her to Joachim, and the couple sing praises to him "Who vindicated the Chaste and True." A grand chorus concludes the musical drama celebrating the "Author of connubial Love."

This archetypical tale treats the perennial problem of a woman's word against a man's. In Tollet's version, the elders have tribal status, though they are not judges. Caught as voyeurs and rejected by Susanna, the elders make up a story that they are sure will be accepted. For a while they are believed, putting Susanna in a terrible situation. Acting with cunning wisdom, however, Daniel overturns their lie and saves Susanna. Mostly in rimed couplets, Tollet's libretto brings out Susanna's virtue and has the two lecherous elders punished.

TEXT: Readex Microprint.

Switzerland, attributed by the DNB to Jane Porter. This tragedy was acted only once at DL on 15 February 1819 with Edmund Kean as the principal character (Genest 8: 683). It was not printed.

MANUSCRIPT: Lost; only the Prologue exists as Larpent 2075.

The Sword of Peace; or, A Voyage of Love, Mariana Starke. A five-act comedy first produced at the Haymarket Theatre on 9 August 1788 and acted six times its first season. HAY revived the play the following summer (four performances). J. Debrett published the play in 1789, and there was a Dublin printing in 1790. *BD* prints Starke's defense of the play.

The drama is set in India on the coast of Coromandel. In England, before the play opens, Edwards and Eliza Moreton had wished to marry, but his father—a baronet—thought he'd prevent the match by sending Edwards to India. Louisa, Eliza's cousin, joins her on the voyage to India, because her father, Eliza's uncle, charged his daughter and niece to go to India to "receive their fortunes," a phrase that keeps recurring. When he learns that Eliza and Louisa are going to India, Sir Thomas Clairville requests that they retrieve his son's sword and provides them with £5000, his son's legacy, to procure the sword. All of these plot strands come out after the play opens upon Eliza and Louisa having arrived in India. They first learn that at Clairville's death, he gave his sword to Lieutenant Dormer. They are prepared to offer the full £5000 for the sword, but the Resident tells them Dormer is poor and would probably accept 500 rupees, but Eliza and Louisa believe they should give Dormer the full amount. When Dormer finds Sir Thomas wants the sword as a remembrance of Clairville for his family, he agrees to give it to Eliza and Louisa to take back to England. But on no condition will Dormer accept any money for the sword. In the meantime, Eliza discovers her old suitor Edwards, who happens to be a friend of Dormer and the merchant David Northcote. Finding that Eliza rejects his suit, the Resident and his ally, Supple, try to force Eliza's hand by having Edwards imprisoned. Eliza gets the bail only to find out that Dormer and Northcote had gotten Edwards released. Pursued by the Resident at her lodgings, Eliza moves with Louisa to the home of Northcote and his wife. A ship arrives with news naming Northcote the Resident, and his first act is to cashier Supple. Dormer, who had faithfully helped the women, is given by Eliza to Louisa. Having word that his father has died in England, Edwards asks Eliza for her hand and she accepts. In a subplot, Jeffreys, servant to Eliza and Louisa, purchases the freedom of Caesar, a slave, and helps him learn English ways. Caesar assists the plot by putting Eliza and Louisa in touch with Mazinghi Douza, who lends them money to free Edwards from prison.

Starke displays an insider's knowledge of Anglo-Indian culture, especially in her descriptions of the scenes. She also shows the lack of interaction between the Indians and the English, shades of *A Passage to India* many years later. The Resident and Supple are among the English who only want to profit by their presence in India, whereas Jeffreys, a servant, illustrates the humanity of the English freeing an indentured slave. Eliza is the more sprightly of the women with Louisa being shy and modest. Eliza is not about to accept the status quo described by the old Resident, and she adventurously strikes out on her own to achieve her goals.

TEXT: Readex Microprint of the Dublin edition, printed for the Booksellers in 1790.

-T-

Temper, Lady Morgan, earlier Sydney Owenson. See **Dramatic Scenes from Real Life**.

Tempest Terrific, Jane M. Scott. This entertainment played forty times at the Sans Pareil Theatre in its opening season, beginning 17 November 1806. The text of the entertainment has not survived.

The Temple of Virtue, Mary O'Brien. No production date of this comic opera has been identified. If it was performed, the venue is likely to have been one of the Dublin theatres. There appears to be no printed text of the play.

MANUSCRIPT: R. W. Babcock notes that the opera is in BL Catalogue #91 of manuscripts (*PMLA* 52 [1937]: 907–08).

Theodora, Ann Hamilton M'Taggart. This five-act drama in verse first appeared in John Galt's *New British Theatre*, 1814. Reprinted in M'Taggart's *Plays*, A. J. Valpy published the work in 1832. *Theodora* has been confused with a play by the same title written by Lady Sophia Burrell (published 1800). In his afterward, Galt notes that the drama had been in the hands of the players for fifteen years.

Before the drama begins, the Duke of Longueville has raised his daughter, Theodora, with his adoptive son, Beaufort. The Duke intends for Theodora and Beaufort to marry, but disobeying her father, Theodora has married Doricourt instead. The Duke disowns Theodora, but Beaufort remains friends with her and Doricourt, who quickly runs his family into poverty. Theodora has given birth to a child, while Doricourt ignores her and has taken a mistress. When the play opens, Theodora pours out her grief to her companion, Clara, who has just returned from a visit to her home: Theodora feels she must endure a parent's curse and a husband's hatred. Doricourt comes in to say he must leave on business, and Theodora reminds him of Beaufort's visit. He insists that she must see Beaufort and departs. When Beaufort comes, Theodora refuses his financial assistance and implores him to see her no more. In agony about her decision, Beaufort agrees and starts to leave, when Doricourt rushes in and stabs him. The servants call for officers, who take Doricourt to prison. Later, Clara reports that she met a funeral procession and heard the mourners whisper Beaufort's name; she also saw the Duke, which caused her to return. After the Duke comes to Theodora and discloses his plan to get revenge, Theodora goes to see Doricourt in prison. He wants her help, for only she can save him. The next morning before the trial, Doricourt learns his mistress has been unfaithful to him. After the Judge opens the trial, the case features a long speech by the Duke condemning Doricourt. The prisoner is about to be taken away when Theodora appears and pleads for Doricourt, who is set free and immediately repudiates Theodora. Before she can speak to him, Doricourt goes to get revenge on his mistress. Doricourt's servant soon brings word that his master has been stabbed by the mistress's lover. A dying Doricourt is brought in; he has at last become a convert to Theodora's virtue. The Duke brings in Beaufort, who is pale but not dead: he feigned the funeral. Before he dies, Doricourt praises Beaufort, bids him care for his child, and dies repentant.

Galt, in his afterword, calls the play a "pathetic tragedy," one that arouses pity, sorrow, and compassion. Early dramas of this classification go back more than one hundred years to Otway and Rowe. In this genre, the emphasis is on the suffering woman, who suffers distress after distress, causing much affliction in the audience. Yet Theodora seems more a self-inflicted martyr. To make one mistake is human; early in the play Theodora condemns herself saying "what little wisdom I have shown" (292), but to persist in error (assuming guilt to free Doricourt) seems the height of folly. Perhaps, M'Taggart wished to draw a distinction between men's revenge and women's forgiveness, surely one strong theme of the play. Concluding the play with the coincidence of Beaufort's reappearance weakens the dramatic structure, and the improbability fragments the climactic tension.

TEXT: Readex Microprint.

Theodora; or, The Spanish Daughter, Lady Sophia Raymond Burrell. This verse tragedy in five acts was printed by Luke Hansard and sold by Leigh and Sotheby in 1800. It was not staged. Burrell dedicated the play (by permission) to Georgiana, the Duchess of Devonshire, who is mentioned in the prologue.

Before the play begins, Theodora had loved Alphonso from her youth, but her father, Don Guzman, prohibited them from marrying and made Theodora take an oath never to give her hand to Alphonso. Because of the interdict, Alphonso sought his fortune at sea, but after a dreadful storm, no word arrives from his vessel. When the play opens, Theodora mourns the sixth anniversary of Alphonso's departure. Her father, now heavily in debt, is taken away by his creditor Don Garcia. To free Guzman, Theodora sends Carlos, the family steward, to

Garcia with her jewels and a message that the remainder will be paid upon the return of her cousin, Antonio. In Tunis, meanwhile, Antonio finds Alphonso alive, pays a ransom for him to the ruler, and tells him about Theodora's grief and Guzman's debts. While they return to Spain, Theodora learns that Garcia will not release Guzman. Carlos urges her to wait for Antonio's arrival, but she insists on seeing Garcia. When he discovers the beautiful petitioner, Garcia will grant the release of Guzman only if she will marry him. After much anguish, Theodora agrees. Shortly after the marriage, Guzman dies, and Antonio returns with Alphonso. Carlos reports Theodora's situation to Antonio. A melancholy Theodora broods about the loss of her father and her present predicament, and while she says she respects Garcia, her coldness disturbs him. When Antonio tells Alphonso of Theodora's marriage to Garcia, he believes her "faithless," saying "I dare not wish To punish her (perfidious as she is) With my reproaches" (62). Aware of Alphonso's views, Antonio goes to see Theodora. Garcia's jealousy grows because he thinks Theodora loves Antonio. In the private meeting, Antonio quietly reveals that Alphonso lives and gives her the ring she gave Alphonso before his departure to sea. Theodora faints and her woman Elvira takes her out. After Antonio has left, Garcia finds the ring, increasing his jealousy. To trap the assumed lovers, Garcia says he must go to Madrid, but he remains to spy on Theodora, who wants to say goodby to Alphonso and asks Antonio to arrange a meeting. Alphonso, however, has gone, and Antonio with Carlos goes to tell Theodora. Knowing about the meeting, a masked Garcia ambushes Antonio who kills him in a scuffle. Thinking all is lost, Theodora plans to throw herself into the sea but is stopped by Alphonso. Elvira comes to tell them Garcia confessed to his crimes before he died and sends the ring to Theodora as proof. In this concluding turn of events, Theodora sees the hand of Providence.

Burrell handles the plot deftly, until the final act where the happy ending is arranged rather than resulting from the events. Theodora must face many difficulties caused by uncaring men, yet she maintains her fortitude in the initial loss of Alphonso, the imprisonment and death of her father, and an unacceptable marriage. Elvira, her faithful companion, supports Theodora in her adversity as confidante and friend. Under so much stress, however, Theodora sees no way out of her dilemma, and in the final scene she prepares to jump into the sea only to be prevented by Alphonso. The importance of the sea provides unifying imagery, representing an ever-present threat to Theodora.

TEXT: Readex Microprint.

Theodorick, King of Denmark, "A Young Gentlewoman." Published in Dublin in 1752 by James Esdall, this tragedy (104 pp.) gives no indication of the "Young Gentlewoman" who is the playwright, nor is there any indication that the tragedy was produced. Genest says the play was never staged, and remarks "it is a poor play, but not a very bad one" (10: 177). According to *BD* (3: 330), the plot is built on the novel *Ildegerte* (the full title is *Ildegerte, Queen of Norway; or, Heroic Love*; the author is Eustache Lenoble; and the novel, written in French in 1694, was translated into English in 1721). [Stratman #6302]

TEXT: Not in Readex Microprint. NUC lists copies at the Library of Congress, Huntington, and U of Michigan.

THOMAS, Elizabeth Frances Amherst (1716–1779). This pastoral is the only known dramatic work by Thomas, identified in BL as the wife of the Rector of Notgrove, perhaps to distinguish her from the poet Elizabeth Thomas (1675–1731). The *Dramatick Pastoral* was produced at Gloucester in 1762, "occasioned by the collection at Gloucester on the Coronation day, for·portioning young women of virtuous character." On the title page, the playwright's name is given as "A Lady." The play (16 pp.) was printed in Gloucester by R. Raikes, 1762. [FCLE]

The Three Crumps; or, Crooked Brothers of Damascus, Jane M. Scott. This two-act farce opened at the Sans Pareil Theatre on 5

February 1818 and ran for sixteen nights. Scott created the role of Nerina.

MANUSCRIPT: Larpent 2005.

The Three Strangers, Harriet Lee. A dramatization of Lee's tale of "Kruitzner" from *The Canterbury Tales* (5 vols., 1797–1805; two tales contributed by her sister Sophia), this five-act melodrama was produced at CG on 10 December 1825 and published the following year by Longman, Rees, Orme, Brown, and Green. Lee's advertisement in the printed version indicates that Byron founded his tragedy *Werner* (published 1821, but not acted) on the same tale, "even to adopt much of the language." She also mentions that her play had been written many years before, and that after Lord Byron did her the honor to choose the tale of Kruitzner for the subject of his tragedy, "it became necessary to make her Play known, or incur the imputation of its being thought a subsequent attempt." For this reason, she offered it in November 1822 to CG. *The Three Strangers* was accepted and planned for February 1823, but it was "postponed wholly at her own desire." Lee published the acting version of the play.

Before the melodrama opens, Count Siegendorf had banished his son for reasons that the play only hints at—the son's unapproved marriage. Taking the name Kruitzner, the son has a family of his own. In an effort of reconciliation, the Count willingly raised his grandson, Conrad, from the age of twelve. At twenty, Conrad has left the estate of his grandfather to travel. Meanwhile, Kruitzner, his wife Josephine, and young son live in poverty, but the recent death of Count Siegendorf makes them want to return to the family estate except that Kruitzner has fallen ill. The Intendant (steward) of the absent Margrave allows the family to stay in the recently vacated apartments of the Countess de Roslach, close to the palace. When the play opens, many of these details emerge through a conversation between Mrs. Weilburg, wife of the postmaster, and Idenstein, a local lawyer. We subsequently learn that Baron Stralenheim has been rescued from a carriage, overturned in a flooded river, by Conrad and a mysterious Hungarian. These three strangers to the village are invited by the Intendant to stay at the Margrave's palace, where the Baron gives the Intendant orders for a messenger to take a letter to a military garrison some distance away. During the night, Kruitzner goes by a secret passage to the palace and discovers that his bitter enemy, the Baron, has written to the Commandant of the garrison demanding Kruitzner's capture. In haste, Kruitzner grabs a rouleau of gold and flees. Reappearing at his apartment, Kruitzner explains to Josephine what he has done. Conrad interrupts, asking for a room to accommodate the Hungarian, who will not stay at the palace, and discovers his parents, who tell him his grandfather has died. After a brief reunion, the family learns the Hungarian is suspected of the theft of the rouleau and agrees to provide a room for him. Kruitzner arranges to flee the village and return to his deceased father's estate. As they are about to leave, they find the Hungarian gone. Conrad reports the Baron is dead, and the Hungarian again suspected. The final act occurs at the estate of Count Siegendorf, formerly Kruitzner. Conrad seems quite downcast, and his mother fears he is jealous of his father's inheritance. When the Hungarian arrives, he blames Conrad for the murder of the Baron. When Siegendorf demands his proof and his name, the Hungarian says he is the Count de Roslach, and he saw the murder from the secret passage. After Conrad delivers his sword to de Roslach, Siegendorf takes responsibility for having degraded and undone himself and his son.

When Lee dramatized her story, many of the relationships and motives got lost, making the play difficult to follow. The character of Conrad seems to change after his discovery that the Baron is a family enemy. Honor and class cause most of the problems. If Kruitzner's marriage is indeed the basis of the banishment by his father, one reason may be Josephine's lack of aristocratic standing. Kruitzner's loss of place and honor has made him indecisive and quarrelsome. His treatment of Josephine makes one wonder why she would want stay with him: he makes snippy remarks and veiled innuendos about women, and when Conrad gives him a sabre, Kruitzner says it is "the weapon of a man" (62). Still, he seems to be aware of his shortcomings, for when she says she is willing to think for him, he responds "would thou hadst always done so" (35). It is, perhaps, her fortitude that has kept the family going through the penurious existence.

TEXT: Readex Microprint.

The Times, Elizabeth Griffith. Taken from Goldoni's *Le Bourru bienfaisant [The Beneficent Bear]* (1771), Griffith's five-act comedy was produced at DL on 2 December 1779. It was performed nine times that season, and published in 1780 by Fielding and Walker, et al.

Woodley and Lady Mary have, in four years of living extravagantly, dissipated most of their fortune. Out of love for his wife, Woodley conceals from her their financial distress. His uncle, quick-tempered Sir William, not only violently disapproves of his conduct but also dislikes intensely Lady Mary, for he holds her responsible for his nephew's foolishness. These violent feelings hide a generous man who is easily won over when he realizes that Lady Mary is willing to retire to the country and live modestly. A capital scene, the fashionable rout with its wild card game, reveals to Lady Mary their financial ruin as well as the role played in it by Mr. and Mrs. Bromley, two knaves whom she had believed to be friends. The play ends well: Sir William gives his own London house to Lady Mary as a winter residence, and Louisa, Woodley's sister, will marry young captain Mountfort, and not the generous, but much older Belford whom her uncle wanted.

Griffith adapted Carlo Goldoni's first comedy written in French, *Le Bourru bienfaisant*, published in 1771. From it, she took the character of Géronte/Sir William, an irascible, ill-tempered but good-hearted man who momentarily threatens the happiness of those he loves through his uncontrollable outbursts of anger. But she turned Goldoni's comedy of character into a satire of contemporary mores, hence the English title so different from the original. To do so, Griffith added Mr. and Mrs. Bromley, a thoroughly dishonest and immoral couple who live off credulous friends, such as Lady Mary and her husband, whom they discard after fleecing them. She also added the crucial rout scene in the last act that unveils the unscrupulous conduct of the Bromleys and the heartless behavior of Lady Mary's other guests, who merrily go on playing and gossiping even while witnessing her profound distress. This episode, in particular, constitutes a harsh denunciation of a dissolute society, totally absent in Goldoni. Although Griffith's adaptation was not unanimously applauded by the critics, it does contain, besides the card-game episode already noted, some excellent scenes, such as those in the third act where the beneficent bear constantly interrupts; this results in fragmentary pieces of information that lead to comical misunderstandings and exchanges. *The General Advertiser* reported that Griffith's comedy "has a considerable share of merit, and holds out a useful lesson to a thoughtless dissipated age" (qtd. in Eshleman 98).

MANUSCRIPT: Larpent 499. Readex Microprint of manuscript.

TEXTS: Readex Microprint. TEC Reel 3876: 11.

Tit for Tat; or, The Comedy and Tragedy of War, Charlotte Cibber Charke. This may have been a puppet show, or an afterpiece, produced at James Street, 16 March 1743. The text has never been printed. This is not the same play as Henry Woodward's *Tit for Tat; or, One Dish of His Own Chocolate* (performed at DL 18 March 1749) or Colman, the younger's *Tit for Tat* (performed 29 August 1786).

To Marry or Not to Marry, Elizabeth Inchbald. This five-act comedy, Inchbald's last play, opened at CG on 16 February 1805 and was acted seventeen times its first season. The comedy was printed the same year for Longman, Hurst, Rees, and Orme. Inchbald included *To Marry* in her collection *British Theatre* (1808).

Before the play opens Sir Oswin Mortland has prosecuted Lavensforth, forcing him out of England. Lavensforth has left his daughter, Hester, to be raised by the Ashdale family, but they force her into a marriage contract with

Willowear. The play begins on the day of the wedding, but Hester flees to Sarah Mortland, Oswin's sister and a woman she knows only slightly, asking for protection. When Sarah submits the case to her brother, he allows Hester to stay. Only later does Oswin find out that Hester is the daughter of the hated Lavensforth. Willowear comes to reclaim his bride, but his friend Oswin says that Hester will stay under his care until he can determine the best course of action. He suggests Willowear seek another bride, recommending Lady Susan Courtly. Even though he is a confirmed bachelor, Oswin slowly falls in love with Hester, until Lavensforth returns from Africa with his black servant, Amos. With revenge against Oswin foremost in his mind, Lavensforth vows to assassinate his old foe and sends Amos to find out where Oswin is. Amos discharges his gun injuring Oswin, who is brought to Lavensforth's cottage. As a host, Lavensforth cannot bring himself to stab Oswin. When Hester tells her father of Oswin's protection and generosity, Lavensforth gives up his revenge plot and permits Hester to marry Oswin. Forgiveness is extended to Amos. Perhaps because of this reconciliation, Lady Susan accepts Willowear.

More a melodrama than a comedy, *To Marry or Not to Marry* does consider aspects of marriage, though the play is more about hate and forgiveness. An assumption exists among the characters that marriage is something most people should do: Oswin concludes the play, saying that "every man" who loves should marry. In her comments on the drama, Inchbald accuses herself of lacking wit and humor. And while she has avoided farcical incidents, persons speaking in dialect, and songs, the characters "are all justly drawn, but not with sufficient force for high dramatic effect" ("Remarks," *British Theatre* 4). One unusual feature of the play is the presence of a prominent black character, Amos, who has attached himself to Lavensforth during his travels and calls "his master" his only friend. In fact, the reverse seems also to be true; Amos is Lavensforth's only friend.

MANUSCRIPT: Larpent 1438.

TEXT: Readex Microprint.

FACSIMILE EDITION: E-CED, with introduction by Paula R. Backscheider (NY: Garland, 1980).

TOLLET, Elizabeth (1694–1754). Her father, a Commissioner of the Navy, under William III and Queen Anne, provided her with a fine education. Her first collection of poems appeared anonymously in 1724. She was particularly adept at translating the Psalms, and a volume of these biblical songs came out in 1730. After her death, her nephew included her one dramatic piece, a libretto for an oratorio entitled *Susanna; or, Innocence Preserved*, in his posthumous publication of Tollet's *Poems on Several Occasions*, 1755. [*BD*, DNB, FCLE]

The Ton; or, Follies of Fashion, Lady Wallace. This five-act comedy first played on 8 April 1788 at CG and ran for three nights. It was not revived. T. Hookham published the play the same year with speeches cut in the stage version marked with double quotes. In her discursive preface, Lady Wallace disparages those who railed against the play before it was performed, inferring that those who complained feared their own vices would be satirized. The "Ton" of the title refers to a group of rich, fashionable aristocrats who are literally "high rollers," being addicted to gambling, and who have loose morals.

The principal plot takes up the progress of Lord Raymond's marriage to Fanny, a wealthy young woman bred in the City, whose mother comes from the minor nobility but whose father is a tradesman. Lady Raymond objects to her husband's gambling and his formerly keeping a mistress, which she finds out only later in the play. To deal with his gambling debts, she goes to Ben Levy, a Jewish money lender, and gives him her diamonds to pay off her husband's loans—upon the promise of secrecy. She also arranges a meeting, under the name of Mrs. Tender (another character in the play), with her husband's castoff mistress, Clara. Lord Boulton and Captain Daffodil, hidden in either side of the clothes press, overhear the conversation. Clara had married a school friend of Raymond's, who gambled away their money and had to take a job in India where he died. In this situation, a penniless Clara gave in to Raymond. Because of his marriage, however, she refused to continue the arrangement. Lady Raymond, as Mrs. Tender, gives her 100 guineas, and promises to continue the stipend annually. When they hear footsteps on the stairs, Lady Raymond goes to one side of the clothes press where she finds Boulton. When Raymond enters, he discovers Clara and Boulton, and inside the clothes press Daffodil on one side and his wife on the other. Clara speaks up for Lady Raymond, who says nothing. Raymond asks, "What still silent—not once attempt a vindication?" Before leaving, she answers, "And dare you suspect my honor? had you, My Lord, been as careful of your own, I had not been forced to this concealment" (78). It isn't long before a repentant Raymond comes to ask his wife's forgiveness, which she generously gives. A weaker second plot exposes another erring man. Lord Ormond and Lady Clairville are to be married, when he suddenly calls off the marriage. Lady Clairville believes Ormond may be in debt and sends him £20,000. The situation Ormond cannot explain to Lady Clairville is that he has seduced Raymond's young sister, Julia, and feels compelled to marry her. Later Julia, who never appears on stage, sends word that she has (conveniently for Ormond) decided to enter a convent, but Julia wants Ormond to tell Lady Clairville. He can only bring himself to confess during a masquerade when both are in costume—she is a vestal and he a black domino. Once she has heard the story, Lady Clairville unselfishly forgives Ormond's libertine behavior, and they agree to marry.

Too often, Lady Wallace creates scenes where the Ton stand around making jokes, which only exposes their shallowness. Tobin believes this causes too much focus "on dialogue at the expense of incident" (184). Aside from the excessive dialogue, the characters are largely cast as moral or amoral. While the two plots are intermixed, the resolution of Ormond's knavery without Julia on stage may strike audiences as farfetched. Readers who know Sheridan's *The School for Scandal* will recognize several parallels, especially between Wallace's clothes-press scene (IV.3) and Sheridan's screen scene. One interesting aspect of the play is that Lady Raymond from the City has greater virtue than any of the licentious Ton, who dwell in the West End. Because Lady Raymond exercises her virtue to good purpose, she develops as a character. While Lady Clairville is generous and forbearing, her character is established from the beginning of the comedy. Appearance and reality gain in thematic importance over the course of the play, proving that what one sees is not necessarily the truth.

MANUSCRIPT: Larpent 801.

TEXT: Readex Microprint.

The Tournament, Mariana Starke. Adapted from J. A. von Toerring und Kronsfeld's *Agnes Bernauer*, this historical tragedy—founded on actual events that took place in Bavaria about 1435—was printed in 1800 for R. Phillips, but it was not staged. Although FCLE claims a public performance occurred, no evidence corroborates this, and no dramatis personae appears in the printed text. The drama is listed by Genest under "plays printed, but not acted."

As the play opens, Albert, the heir apparent to the Bavarian throne, has married Agnes, even though she is an orphan of low birth. He's concerned about the reaction of his father, who had planned for Albert to marry Elizabeth of Wirtemberg. After the wedding, Albert learns that "Elizabeth has chosen for herself" (7). When Count Eberhard, "Straubing's despotic Viceroy," arrives, he informs Albert of a summons to a tournament to honor Thorring, a kinsman. The Viceroy, a rival for Agnes's love, goads Albert into accepting the challenge. Upon his arrival at Ratisbon, Albert learns he is barred from the games because of "vicious morals." When Albert asks who accuses him, his father announces he is his accuser: Albert must quit Agnes or leave the lists. Albert breaks his lance, and the Ruler disowns his son. Albert declares that it's Agnes or war. After Albert departs, Thorring says he'll go to Albert and reason with him. Before Albert returns to his castle, the Viceroy tells Agnes that Albert has renounced her. To back up this lie, the Viceroy woos Agnes, calling Albert faithless. She will not believe him, but he says if she tells Albert of his visit, he'll kill the Prince. Bugles announce Albert's arrival: he embraces Agnes, but she feels responsible for his exclusion from the throne. Thorring comes with a letter offering a reunion, but Albert must disband his troops. If Albert will go see his father, Thorring will stay as a hostage. With Albert gone, the Viceroy—in a nearby woods—prepares to storm the castle. Thorring, meanwhile, requests an audience with Agnes and discovers by a portrait she wears that she is his daughter. She throws herself into his arms, where the Viceroy in his assault on the castle finds her. Seeing Thorring as a rival, the Viceroy attacks him while a henchman takes Agnes off to prison. Incarcerated and bound with fetters, Agnes receives the Viceroy, who removes her chains and asks her to flee with him. She objects, saying that Thorring is her father and her marriage to Albert legal. When the Viceroy rejects this, she manages to get his sword and force him from her cell. Agnes contemplates suicide, but before she can act officers enter and take her to a trial where—despite her spirited defense—she is found guilty. The next morning, as Agnes is taken to a bridge over the Danube, Albert rides in and saves her. The Viceroy must meet the fate he would have dealt to Agnes (being thrown into the swiftly moving river). The Ruler arrives with Thorring, who though fatally wounded reconciles Agnes with Albert's father. After Thorring's death, Albert urges his kinsman's faults be forgotten and his virtues recorded. A weeping Agnes concludes the play: "innocence is the peculiar care of Heaven" (64).

Genest remarks that although there are improbabilities, "it is an interesting tragedy" (10: 220). Perhaps he was referring to Starke's handling of Agnes, who as the only woman in the drama presents several strengths. Although she feels guilty for having been the cause of Albert's disinheritance, she is willing to enter a convent so that he may assume the right of succession. Each time the Viceroy tries to get her to leave Albert, Agnes repudiates these attempts to make her a kept woman. In her trial, Agnes argues convincingly, only to be found guilty through the Viceroy's political machinations. Imprisoned, Agnes disarms the Viceroy and keeps him at bay. Starke's title, contrasting with the German *Agnes Bernauer*, seems to place less emphasis on Agnes and more on the less important medieval aspects of the drama.

TEXT: Readex Microprint.

The Town Before You, Hannah Cowley. This five-act comedy first appeared at CG on 6 December 1794. T. N. Longman published it the following year. Although there were ten performances during the season, the play was not revived. In her preface, Cowley regrets that the comedy she printed was the one the "Public have chosen," rather "than the Comedy which I intended," indicating that two scenes (between Tippy and his Landlady and between Tippy and the Bailiff) were not part of her original design. Originally titled *The Town as It Is*, the comedy ended Cowley's career as a dramatist.

The play opens on Fancourt, who reveals himself as an educated but loutish husband who has squandered his and his second wife's money, and the two of them argue over the relative merits of the rich and the poor. Although Sir Robert Floyer has sent £20 to relieve their finances, Fancourt has no interest in helping others. Sir Robert, a Welsh knight, has come to London with his daughter, Georgina, who has become fascinated with Lady Horatia Horton, a sculptor. While Georgina is smitten with Conway, Lady Horatia loves Sidney Asgill, who is employed by his uncle in the City. When Asgill learns that the family business has gone broke, he resolves to give up Lady Horatia, donates his small stock to his uncle, and determines to go to sea. His uncle, Sir Simon, has several interviews with Lady Horatia, and while he disapproves of her being a sculptor, he sees that she loves his nephew. Asgill is found at Portsmouth, returns to London, and unites with Lady Horatia. The play ends with an ostentatious patriotic exhortation.

In the subplot, Fancourt and his friend Tippy, who bears a resemblance to Lord Beechgrove, design a scheme to bilk Sir Robert out of £1000. But the two have darker intentions: with the help of Tippy's sister Jenny, who is Georgina's maid, they want to marry the rich heiress off to Tippy. Mrs. Fancourt gets wind of their conspiracy, and disguised as a Savoyard she performs fortune telling, shrewdly warning Georgina of danger. After constables arrest the two miscreants, Mrs. Fancourt learns that Tippy—disguised as a parson—performed her marriage to Fancourt, thus invalidating their vows. Georgina accepts the grateful Mrs. Fancourt as the mother she never knew, the sister she never had, and the friend she has always wanted. Conway and Georgina are destined to marry.

As evidenced by her final revisions to the play (posthumously published in 1813), Cowley shows a dissatisfaction with the comedy in its performance and subsequent publication. She deletes many inconsequential plot details (the scenes involving Mrs. Bullrush and Buckram, which she objected to in the first edition); she makes relationships clearer, especially between Fancourt and Tippy, named Brisk in the final version; she metes out punishments to the con artists—Fancourt and Brisk—rather than letting them get off scot free at the end of the stage version; and when Asgill goes to sea in the final version, he goes as an officer, not "before the mast" as in the first edition. There are enough changes, in fact, that the version published posthumously seems to be a much-altered play that presents a forceful moral emphasis.

While the plots suffer from implausibility because of the testing motif exercised by Sir Simon, the characterization and dialogue exhibit strength and vivacity. Cowley takes stock characters, such as the Welsh servant Humphrey and gullible master Sir Robert, and creates individuality through their language and actions. The interplay between the business-oriented City and the fashionable Westminster shows Cowley's ability to write appropriate dialogue and to form interactions that reveal the prejudices, as well as the values, of each group. Finally, when Lady Horatia's preoccupation with Asgill displaces her artistic vitality, "neither she nor anyone else protests" Lady Horatia's giving up her art, as Jean Gagen points out (DLB 89: 103). Gagen also recognizes that "the play has generous doses of moralistic sentimentalism, with decency and goodness given a full representation along with villainy, which has comic as well as serious dimensions" (DLB 89: 102).

MANUSCRIPT: Larpent 1045, titled *The Town as It Is*.

TEXTS: Readex Microprint. TEC Reels 4478: 7; 4550: 20 (second edition, 1795).

FACSIMILE EDITION: E-CED, with introduction by F. Link (NY: Garland, 1982).

The Town Fopp; or, Sir Timothy Tawdrey, Aphra Behn. Partly based on George Wilkins's *The Miseries of Enforced Marriage* (acted 1605, printed 1607 and 1637), this five-act comedy was produced at DG early in September 1676. It was printed for James Magnes and Rich. Bentley the following year. The play was probably revived in the 1698–99 season.

Bellmour and Celinda have secretly exchanged vows to marry, but his uncle Lord Plotwell forces Bellmour to marry his cousin Diana. If this weren't complication enough, Bellmour has been asked by Celinda's brother, Friendlove, to help him renew his suit to Diana, and Sir Timothy Tawdrey has been chosen by Celinda's parents as a potential match. During the wedding party, Celinda arrives dressed as a boy: when her angry brother starts to draw his sword, she protects Bellmour, who after the party won't consummate the marriage with Diana. The next morning Sir Timothy comes to sing a bawdy song under the bridal window, Bellmour runs him off, and the angry Diana asks for the protection of Celinda, still in male attire. Celinda takes her home where Friendlove woos her. Meanwhile, Bellmour is so angry at himself for his perjury toward Celinda that in madness he goes drinking and gambling with Sir Timothy, whose mistress Betty Flauntit attaches herself to him. Bellmour's brother Charles rescues him, but Lord Plotwell is furious because of Bellmour's libertine actions and because Diana has written asking for a divorce. The four lovers finally meet: Bellmour reunites with Celinda and Diana claims Friendlove. With some urging Plotwell changes his attitude. Sir Timothy thinks he has used a false preacher to marry Phillis, Bellmour's sister, but he discovers that a real clergyman performed the marriage. Despite this, Sir Timothy plans to continue keeping Betty Flauntit.

In this play Behn returns to one of her favorite themes—forced marriage—only this time a man is forced to marry causing difficulties for all concerned. Pearson says that the brothel scenes reinforce the "symbolic equivalence between forced marriage and prostitution" (161). To sort out the problems of the forced marriage, the characters use disguises, mistake identities, and brandish swords. Cotton mentions that while the play is not sentimental, we see the real suffering of the principal characters. Hume classifies the play as somewhere between an Italian intrigue comedy and a London sex comedy. Gewirtz points out that in the melodramatic action the sympathetic heroes have their libertine attitudes undercut. Link notes a balance between the virtuous men and women that is contrasted by Sir Timothy's continued licentious actions. Leaving Phillis with Sir Timothy may be realistic, but it abandons her in an untenable marriage. In contrast with Behn's source, the principal women are active in bringing about solutions to their awkward situations: Celinda dresses as a boy, and Diana asks for a divorce. Both of these self-initiated actions help resolve their problems.

TEXTS: Wing B1769; EEB Reel 446: 5 (1677). Wing B1770; EEB Reel 1454: 7 (1699). Readex Microprint of 1677 edition.

MODERN EDITION: *Works*, ed. Montague Summers (1915; NY: Phaeton, 1967) 3: 1–94.

Tragic Dramas, Frances Burney, niece of Fanny Burney, Mrs. D'Arbley. Burney's volume, *Tragic Dramas; chiefly intended for representation in Private Families: to which is added Aristodemus, a tragedy from the Italian of Vincenzo Monti*, included her own *Fitzormond; or, Cherished Resentment* (a three-act verse drama) and *Malek Adhel, the Champion of the Crescent* (a three-act verse drama, adapted from *Mathilde* by Madame Cottin), as well as the translation of Monti's five-act tragedy. The collection was printed for the author in 1818 by Thomas Davidson. There are no known public performances of these tragedies.

TEXT: Readex Microprint.

TRIMMER, Sarah Kirby (1741–1810). Born and educated in Ipswich, Sarah went with her parents in 1755 to London, where she met Dr. Johnson, Hogarth, Reynolds, and Gainsborough. In 1762, Sarah married James Trimmer of Brentford, where she raised and educated her twelve children (six daughters and six sons). Encouraged to provide methods she used to educate her children, Trimmer wrote *Easy Introduction to the Knowledge of Nature* (1782). Out of this grew Trimmer's *Sacred History* (1782–84) in several volumes. Through her efforts a Sunday school opened in Brentford, and Queen Charlotte conferred with Trimmer about promoting and managing Sunday schools. From the outcome of the meeting, Trimmer wrote *The Oeconomy of Charity* (1786); that year she also published her *Fabulous Histories*, encouraging kindness to animals.

Even with her commitment to education, Trimmer managed to write one (didactic) play, *The Little Hermit*, printed in *The Juvenile Magazine*, 1788. She later published several books under the aegis of the Society for Promoting Christian Knowledge. From 1802 to 1806, she produced a periodical, *The Guardian of Education*, which analyzed writing for children and books on education. Trimmer died at Brentford in 1810, survived by nine children. [*BD*, DBAWW, DNB, EBWW, FCLE, OCEL. An anonymous biography, *Some Account of the Life and Writings of Mrs. Trimmer* (1814), includes some of her diaries and prayers.]

A Trip to Bath, Frances Sheridan. See **A Journey to Bath**.

The Triumph of Hymen, Elizabeth Ryves. A masque printed in her *Poems on Several Occasions*, printed for the author in 1777 and sold by J. Dodsley. The play was never performed.

TEXT: Not in Readex Microprint. NUC lists a copy at Princeton and a microfilm at Iowa.

The Triumphs of Love and Innocence, Anne Finch, Countess of Winchilsea. Written about 1688, this tragicomedy was not acted. It was published in her *Miscellany Poems, on Several Occasions*, printed "for J. B.," 1713.

Set on the isle of Rhodes, *The Triumphs of Love and Innocence* focuses on the Queen of Cyprus, who has been deposed and exiled from Cyprus. She must rely on the Master of Rhodes as her protector. When the Cypriot General Lauredan arrives, he pretends to continue his support of the usurper, but in fact he wants to restore the Queen, whom he loves. And while she reciprocates this love, the political problems make it difficult for them to unite. A second plot involves Blanfort, who also loves the queen, and Marina, whom he has jilted. Marina, disguised as a page, now serves the Master. Rivalto, the villain of the piece, loves Marina; but being refused by her, he exposes her disguise in order to disgrace the Master and to make Marina look as if she has had an illicit assignation with the Master. The comic subplot brings the villainy to light, as Capriccio helps capture Rivalto. Finally, the Master's innocence is reestablished, Lauredan and the Queen are engaged, Marina accepts Blanfort, and Rivalto is banished from Rhodes.

Probably written between 1688–1691, *Love and Innocence* was, according to Finch's editor Myra Reynolds, an experiment "to see whether she could carry through such an attempt." As a first play, "it is a surprisingly well-knit piece of work. Of the characterization less can be said. Innocence is too innocent, virtue too virtuous, villainy too villainous. There is no shading." Although the comic subplot is not particularly humorous, Finch does combine it with the main plot. The representation of women shows them manipulated by the male power figures. Both women are wronged: the Queen politically, Marina romantically. While the Queen can only wait for Lauredan or the Master to act, Marina rejects the oppressive love of Rivalto. Why she insists on her extravagant devotion to Blanfort is hard to determine. Still Marina believes that steadfast love is her only option, thus making her a pathetic character. Although she is finally rewarded with Blanfort, the reader has a hard time accepting this stoic devotion.

MANUSCRIPT: Folger Shakespeare Lib. MS N.b.3.

TEXT: Readex Microprint.

CRITICAL EDITION: *The Poems of Anne Countess of Winchelsea*, edited with introduction by Myra Reynolds (Chicago: U of Chicago P, 1903): 271–336.

TROTTER, Catharine, later Cockburn (1679–1749). Although she grew up in penurious circumstances after the death of her father (a navy Captain) in 1684, Trotter gained an education in languages (French and Latin), much of it self-taught. She published a prose romance, *Olinda's Adventures*, when she was fourteen and moved on to writing plays. Her first play, a dramatization of Aphra Behn's novel *Agnes de Castro*, was staged at DL in 1695 and published the following year. Although identified as one of the female wits, with Delariviere Manley and Mary Pix, she knew and corresponded with Wycherley, Congreve, and Farquhar. Over the next decade, she wrote more plays, mostly tragedies; her popular success came in *The Fatal Friendship* (LIF, 1698). Trotters's one comedy, *Love at a Loss; or, Most Votes Carry It,* was produced at DL, 1700 and published 1701. She revised it under the title of *The Honourable Deceivers; or, All Right at the Last*, but the revision was never printed and is now lost. She returned to tragedy for her last two plays: *The Unhappy Penitent* (1701) and *The Revolution of Sweden* (HAY, 1706). Her philosophical turn of mind can be seen in *A Defence of Mr. Locke's Essay of Humane Understanding* (1702) and in *A Discourse Concerning a Guide in Controversies* (1707).

After her marriage in 1708 to the Rev. Patrick Cockburn, she turned to raising four children. With the marriage, she later explained, "I bid adieu to the muses, and so wholly gave myself up to the cares of a family, and the education of my children, that I scarce knew, whether there was any such thing as books, plays, or poems stirring in Great Britain" (Birch xl). After her children grew up, Trotter returned to writing philosophical, moral, and theological treatises. Just two years before her death, Trotter published *Remarks upon the Principles and Reasonings of Dr. Rutherforth's Essay . . . in Vindication of the late Dr. Samuel Clarke*. When Trotter died in

1749, four months after her husband, she was buried at Long Horsley in Northumberland, his last curacy. Her *Works* in two volumes were edited after her death by the Rev. Thomas Birch in 1751, but he omitted four of her five plays—*The Fatal Friendship* only being considered worthy of inclusion.

Trotter wrote for the theatre in a decade of wrangling between the playhouses (LIF and DL), and her best-known plays are moralizing tragedies contrasting love and honor. She put morality on stage at a time when Collier blasted the theatres for their profaneness. While her plays did not succeed in reforming the stage, they hinted at a direction the theatres would go in the coming decades. Even with fine casts (Elizabeth Barry, Anne Bracegirdle, Anne Oldfield, and Thomas Betterton), her tragedies seldom caught on with theatre audiences, and none of the plays went into the repertoire. [*BD*, BNA, Cotton, DBAWW, DLB 84 (by S. B. Blaydes), DNB, FCLE, Hume, Morgan, NCBEL (2: 802), OCEL (under Cockburn), Pearson, Revels. Biography by Thomas Birch, 1751. E-CED series, ed. E. Steeves. Constance Clark provides a bio-critical discussion in *Three Augustan Women Playwrights* (1986).]

The Tryal, Joanna Baillie. This comedy was first published in her *Series of Plays: [on] the Stronger Passions* by Cadell and Davies in 1798. It was not performed.

Set in Bath, the play begins with two cousins—Agnes and Mariane—asking their uncle and guardian, Mr. Withrington, to play along with their scheme. Agnes, a wealthy heiress, is tired of the men of fashion who are attracted to her money; therefore, she wishes to change identities with her "portionless" cousin, Mariane, who consents to the idea in order to exact revenge from the snobbish men who ignore her because she has no money. Mariane has already committed herself to marry Edward, Withrington's favorite nephew, and Agnes is attracted to a man with a sensible countenance and unfashionable dress, Mr. Harwood. The play consists of a series of trials that Mariane makes Harwood undergo in order to test his love. At first, he succeeds by resisting Mariane's attempts to flirt with him: he has eyes only for Agnes. Then when her uncle doubts that Harwood loves her, Agnes tests the depth of his commitment by pretending to be both extravagant and ill tempered. Although everyone from whom he seeks advice warns against marrying such a woman, Harwood remains constant in his love for Agnes. Finally, when Withrington fears that Harwood's love for her suggests that he is mentally unbalanced, Agnes agrees to a final test after noting that her uncle's distrust "injures" (277) her. With this test, Agnes leads Harwood to believe that she slandered Lady Fade intentionally, and he demonstrates his moral rectitude and soundness of mind by trying to break off the relationship with Agnes. While Agnes tests Harwood, Mariane has great fun revealing the superficiality and falseness of both Sir Loftus Prettyman and Mr. Opal, going so far as to threaten a lawsuit against Opal when he flees from the relationship after discovering that Mariane is not the heiress. Trying to defend himself, Opal declares, "Upon honour, madam, we men of fashion don't expect to be called to an account for every foolish thing we say" (295). The comedy ends with Withrington promising to provide Mariane and Edward with a small fortune, and with Agnes's suggestion that Harwood will continue to practice law, achieving distinction as "the poor man's advocate" (299).

Agnes and Mariane cooperate skillfully to ensure that each succeeds at the marriage of her choice; in fact, almost all of the action is initiated and controlled by them. *The Tryal* introduces but never addresses the lack of confidence Mr. Withrington sees missing in Agnes: Agnes simply accepts the challenge and proves him wrong when Harwood falls in love with her. While the play lacks some of the cleverness with language demonstrated in Baillie's comedy *The Siege*, Agnes is a memorable female protagonist, one who refuses to allow circumstances to be dictated to her.

TEXT: Readex Microprint of 1812 edition.

FACSIMILE EDITIONS: *Romantic Context: Poetry* reprints the 1798 edition (London: T. Cadell, Jr., and W. Davies). Compiled, with an introduction, by D. H. Reiman (NY: Garland,

1977). *Revolution and Romanticism, 1789–1834* reprints the 1798 edition, introduced by Jonathan Wordsworth (Rutherford, NJ: Woodstock, 1990).

The Turkish Court; or, The London 'Prentice, Laetitia Pilkington. This burlesque play was said to have been produced at the Capel-Street Theatre, Dublin, 1748, though for unknown reasons it was never printed.

TURNER, Margaret (fl. 1790). Known only for her English rendering of Allen Ramsey's pastoral drama, Turner published *The Gentle Shepherd* in 1790 with parallel texts—English and Scottish. There is no record that the translation was performed. [*BD*]

The Two Cousins, Elizabeth Silthorpe Pinchard. This novel written in dramatic form is the third such work she wrote in the 1790s. Elizabeth Newbery published the volume in 1794. It was often reprinted in America. The title page announces the theme: "the necessity of moderation and justice to the attainment of happiness."

Mrs. Leyster, a widow, lives with her only daughter, Constantia, in Hampshire. Constantia has just turned twelve at the beginning of the story; her mother acts as her teacher in reading, writing, and drawing, but masters in French and dancing come to her several times weekly. When the story opens, Mrs. Leyster and Constantia are going to assist the poor on a frosty winter day. They are discussing Alicia, Constantia's cousin who lives in London, and her problems there, when they discover an infant and her mother almost frozen to death. They take them back to their house with the aid of two servants. The doctor is sent for and the two survive the incident. As the woman (Mrs. Thomson) and her child (Jenny) improve, Mrs. Leyster learns their story. Mary Thomson, a widow of five months, was on her way to stay with her sister in Portsmouth, but learning the job she was to take fell through, she was returning to her parish when the snow came. Mrs. Leyster says she will verify Mary Thomson's story, as "common prudence requires," but in the meantime she and her daughter will stay with them. While awaiting a reply, Mrs. Leyster and Constantia visit Mr. and Mrs. Selwyn and their daughter Maria. Here the contrast of parental education shows that the Selwyns have spoiled Maria, the results being made obvious when Constantia attempts to play with the spoiled child. On the way home, Mrs. Leyster explains to Constantia that happiness depends on ourselves rather than on outward circumstances. When the positive reply about Mary Thomson comes from her parish, Mrs. Leyster arranges for her to keep a little school for reading and to set up a small shop. Mrs. Leyster will advance her the money, to be repaid in five years. In the meantime, Constantia offers to teach Jenny, but Mrs. Leyster asks what Jenny can do with her education: "the notion of equality is an absurd, and unnatural notion" (76). She disapproves of teaching servants to write because it makes them idle and less useful. Still, it is important that Jenny can provide for herself, and she must learn the principles of religion.

After Mary Thomson and Jenny are settled in another house, Mrs. Leyster receives a letter from her sister, saying that the system of education that Mrs. Leyster argued against has indeed been shown to be erroneous. Because Alicia has exceeded her allowance, Mrs. Woodford wants to send her to the country. The question "will you take her?" causes Mrs. Leyster some anguish, but she agrees. The remainder of the book takes up the education of Alicia, who arrives a week later smoldering with "sullen pride." There are clear contrasts between city and country educations, but Constantia helps to bring her cousin around. They visit the Thomsons, practice drawing, and do French lessons. Much is made of the reading Alicia does, and—not incidentally—she reads Pinchard's *Dramatic Dialogues*, especially "The Little Country Visitor," which causes her to burst into tears. Finally, Alicia admits how absurd she's been, and Mrs. Leyster tells her a story, stressing the importance of paying one's bills promptly, which also shows how the economics of trade work. Alicia even confesses that the visit, which she dreaded, has proved the happiest of her life, and she asks if she can stay another six months.

Her mother agrees, if the Leysters will come to London when Alicia's visit is over. On the final page, Mrs. Leyster states "Justice and moderation are the securest means of obtaining true happiness" (144).

Mrs. Leyster's kindness, prudence, and morality assist the young people in overcoming their difficulties. First, she practices prudent generosity with Mary Thomson and her child; then, she trains Alicia and Constantia in the "proper way" of conduct. Providing a model may be the most effective method of education, but the negative examples of the Selwyns is another. Since they merely spoil their child, Maria acts willfully and has no concern for others. And civility toward others is a strong tenant in Mrs. Leyster's system of education. It must be observed, however, that Mrs. Leyster's plans are based on a uncompromising hierarchial class structure in which democracy or meritocracy has no place. And while Mrs. Leyster may be reacting negatively to the French Revolution, mentioned in a footnote, people have their place in her socially structured world.

TEXT: Not in Readex Microprint. We read the first edition in the Ball Collection of the Lilly Library, Indiana U, Bloomington.

The Two Guardians, Maria Edgeworth. This three-act play appears in her *Comic Dramas*, printed in 1817 by R. Hunter, Baldwin, Craddock, and Joy. It was not produced.

Set in London, the play opens on two crafty servants who work for the wealthy Courtington family. Popkin and Blagrave try to figure out how to "educate" the young St. Albans, a guest of the family from the West Indies. They know that in the will of St. Albans's father, the young lad is assigned two guardians—Lord Courtington and Mr. Onslow. The children of the Courtington family—Juliana and Beauchamp—are spoiled and do not want to take lessons from their private tutors. Juliana would rather dance, while Beauchamp is only interested in horses. Juliana will not even see to the payment of her harp lessons given by the widow Beauchamp, a poor relation. St. Albans, meanwhile, explains to his black servant Quaco the freedoms of England, and he gives Quaco a purse of money. After the widow Beauchamp has waited for her pittance, she turns to leave, and Quaco puts the purse in her basket. Above stairs, Mr. Onslow arrives to talk to Mrs. St. Albans about the guardianship: Lady Courtington suggests that the lad spend the winter with them in London and the summer with Onslow in the country, but Onslow rejects the plan, saying that if he is to be the guardian he wants complete charge year round. When Beauchamp challenges St. Albans to a horse race, the West Indian lad takes a spill and injures his shoulder. Both families go to him in a humble cottage, the home of the widow Beauchamp. There St. Albans learns the horse he had ridden was fixed by Blagrave, and the widow returns Quaco's purse showing that Juliana has been false. In the end, St. Albans selects Onslow as his friend, guide, and guardian.

Given Maria Edgeworth's interest in the education of the young, it is not surprising that education is central to this play. The laxness of training at the Courtington's results in Juliana's being a young snob who will neither apply herself nor treat her teachers well, and in Beauchamp's using the servants to cheat a guest and being a false friend to St. Albans. Although the play is too didactic for wide acceptance on the public stage, it shows how Edgeworth planned to educate children by having them read or act out dramas. *The Two Guardians* and other of her plays provide both positive (Onslow) and negative models (the Courtingtons). Because young Beauchamp Courtington spends his time with grooms and servants, he picks up their bad morals. That Lord and Lady Courtington have not seen to the proper education of their children makes them suspect as guardians. Lord Courtington, who never appears on stage, is a bad model, because he is at Newmarket wagering on horses. Anne K. Mellor points out how Quaco becomes "the voice of innocent virtue in the play," as well as a "moral exemplar" (*Romanticism and Gender* [NY: Routledge, 1993]: 80).

TEXT: Readex Microprint of first and second editions of 1817.

Two Misers of Smyrna; or, Mufti's Tomb, Jane M. Scott. After opening on 8 March 1810, the farce ran for ten nights; it was revived the following three seasons. No text of the play is extant.

Two Spanish Valets; or, Lie upon Lie, Jane M. Scott. This two-act farce opened at the Sans Pareil Theatre on 2 November 1818. The title was reversed from the manuscript, where it appears as *Lie upon Lie; or, The Two Spanish Valets*. The play was performed forty-two times its first season with Scott in the role of Francetta.

MANUSCRIPT: Larpent 2051.

-U-

The Unhappy Father, Mary Leapor. Written about 1745, Leapor's only play, a five-act verse tragedy entitled *The Unhappy Father*, was printed posthumously in the second volume of her *Poems Upon Several Occasions*, published in 1751. There is no evidence that the play was acted.

Dycarbas, the title character, has two sons, one married daughter, a son-in-law, and a ward: all live together in a country house. The sons, Polonius and Lycander, prepare to leave home; Polonius, the elder, has a position overseas, while Lycander goes north to manage an estate that will soon be his own. Problems arise in the first act, for both sons are in love with Terentia, the ward of Dycarbas. Although Terentia loves Polonius, Lycander still woos her, even though she has no romantic interest in him. Aware that his permission for Polonius to marry Terentia has caused divisions in the family, Dycarbas regrets he has one happy son while the other mourns. Eustathius, Dycarbas's son-in-law, often becomes angry over trifles, and Dycarbas councils Emilia to reason her husband out of his rages. On the day of the sons' departure, Leonardo, Eustathius's cousin and former rival for Emilia, stops by bent on revenge. Upon his departure, Leonardo bribes Eustathius's servant, Plynus, to give his master a glove containing a forged letter from Emilia arranging an assignation in a nearby grove with Leonardo. Meanwhile, Lycander urges Emilia to bring Terentia to a grove so he may bid her farewell. Terentia does not want to go to Lycander, but with Emilia's urging she finally agrees. Although Eustathius can scarcely contain his rage over the forged letter, he warns Emilia about walking in the evening. When Emilia arrives in the grove, she has lost Terentia, but her husband has followed her. Upon Lycander's appearance, Eustathius, thinking it's Leonardo, jumps out and stabs Emilia, who dies almost immediately. Lycander hits him, and Eustathius repents his mad jealousy, but claims Emilia was false and shows the letter. From Plynus they learn that Leonardo's letter was forged, and Lycander chases the villain. Plynus is dragged off by Eustathius, who returns to regret the way he acted toward his father-in-law before he dies. Lycander brings back Leonardo, both having been wounded fighting each other. Dycarbas urges Leonardo to repent, but he flaunts his revenge before he dies. Lycander bids Terentia farewell and dies. Terentia does what she can to comfort her guardian, saying they will be mourners together. Dycarbas tells his servant, Paulus, to fetch Polonius back from the ship, while Terentia blames herself for being the cause of the deaths. When Paulus returns, he must report that Polonius and his servant, Timnus, have been devoured by a shark. Dycarbas reels from the "deadly Blow" and dies. Feeling all is lost, Terentia prepares to take poison. Only then do Timnus and Polonius arrive, having been saved from the shark. Terentia and Polonius decide to be mourners together.

Leapor has carefully prepared for the crucial scene in the grove so that all the characters arrive for good reasons. Without realizing that her husband has received a forged letter, Emilia has some complicity for entreating Terentia to meet Lycander. Mad with jealousy, Eustathius acts without thinking, while Lycander reacts to the stabbing, knocking his brother-in-law down. When Lycander brings the villain back, Dycarbas is taunted by the re-

Bebbemeah and the black slave. Callapia kills the black slave, but Munzuffer won't believe Bebbemeah's plea of innocence, even though Chousera supports her. Bebbemeah's maid, Sardeah, warns her of Callapia's plot to poison her, and Bebbemeah flees with Sardeah. When Callapia and Cemat argue over the spoils, she plans to poison him. Chousera rejects Cemat's incestuous lust, and he stabs her, but he has been poisoned by Callapia. In his death throes, he tells Callapia's evil schemes to Munzuffer. In prison, the ghosts of Cemat and Pechai come to Callapia, and when a priest goes to comfort her, she goes mad and slays him. Munzuffer finds Bebbemeah, and they are reconciled. They go to Callapia's cell, where she stabs herself.

Hume calls the play "a bloodbath" and Milhous labels it "a villainess tragedy." As "a showpiece for Mrs. Barry, [and by] LIF's standards," Milhous continues, "the production was elaborate, but the play was apparently not very well received" (107). *The Unnatural Mother* comes at a time, Hume points out, when bloody tragedies were often performed, perhaps to display the histrionics of both Elizabeth Barry and Anne Bracegirdle. Unnatural family relationships, however, show the seamy underside of the frequent humorous family situations usually found in comedy. What this tragedy demonstrates is how lust can be an all-consuming passion, and, when this is the situation, destruction is pervasive.

TEXTS: Wing U87. EEB Reel 1076: 21. Readex Microprint.

The Unnatural Tragedy, Margaret Lucas Cavendish, Duchess of Newcastle. The tragedy was included in her *Playes*, printed in 1662 by John Martyn, James Allestry, and Tho. Dicas. It was never performed.

The unnaturalness can be found in one plot line of the tragedy where Monsieur Frere lusts after his married sister, Madam Soeur. She feels trapped because he threatens suicide if she will not lie with him, and at the same time she doesn't want to dishonor her family and keeps his passion a secret. Madam Soeur does everything to repulse her brother, but he finally forces her against her will. After he has raped her, Monsieur Frere kills Madam Soeur and himself. Another plot with tragic consequences, though less unnatural, is the ill treatment of Madam Bonit by her husband Malateste. When Madam Bonit dies, largely as a result of neglect and abuse, Malateste marries one of the Sociable Virgins he calls a "free spirit" (347). Malateste's new wife treats her husband much as he treated his previous wife: she finds fault with his house and demands a London residence; she sacks a servant, a "lusty Wench" her husband has been chasing; and she spends freely and stays out as late as she wishes. He becomes "sick, even to death," regretting how he treated his previous wife and wishing to be buried in the same tomb with her. The third plot focuses on the Sociable Virgins, "a company of young Ladies that meet every day to discourse and talk, to examine, censure, and judge of every body, and of every thing" (328). Women's education, women's literary and spoken language, and women's history are several of the topics they consider. One of their number chooses to wed Malateste: after the wedding, it is she who controls that marriage, having explained the importance of control in the discussions of the Sociable Virgins.

Selfishness and solipsism cause many of the problems in two of the plot lines: Monsieur Frere cares only about cohabiting with his sister; Malateste neglects his wife, concerned only for his own pleasures; and the second Madam Malateste has little use for her husband because she has another life to lead. And in Cavendish's poetic justice, Malateste gets what he deserves for mistreating his first wife. Madam Soeur, however, falls victim to her lecherous brother, and the horrendous result is surely a tragedy. The Sociable Virgins may be included in the drama to point out the importance of giving women a greater stake in the educational, political, and marital hierarchy. That women have no access to public affairs and lack power is in itself, Cavendish construes, unnatural and, perhaps, even a tragedy. Once the first virgin has married Malateste, the Sociable Virgins have no more discussions, and we observe the new Madam Malateste in action. Because she is denied any place in the hierarchy, she disregards her husband and carves out her own position.

TEXTS: Wing N868. EEB Reel 502: 11. Readex Microprint.

Ulthona the Sorceress, Jane M. Scott. 14 November 1807 was the opening night of this entertainment; it was performed seventy-six times this season. Scott acted the title role with music by Mathias von Holst. No text of the play has come down to us.

-V-

Valville; or, The Prejudices of Past Times, Ann Hamilton M'Taggart. This five-act drama in verse was published in 1824 by M. A. Nattali. It is based on Baculard d'Arnaud's anecdote entitled *Valmiers*, published in 1779 in *Les Epreuves du sentiment* (1764–1780).

The events of the drama take place in the time of Louis XII. Before dying, a father arranged the marriages of his sons: Liancourt to Adelaide, Valville to Leonora. Because he desires instead to marry Leonora, who has encouraged his attention, Liancourt seeks revenge against his brother. Although his father when dying asked him to "look on Valville as [his] brother" (112), Liancourt tries to disinherit his brother and subject him to public scorn by revealing that Valville was adopted, an infant abandoned at his parents' door. Valville decries the "laws, made by blind prejudice, in barbarous ages" (115) that deny his position. In response to this revelation, Leonora breaks off her engagement to Valville, but Adelaide responds more kindly. Adelaide is torn between her own love for Valville and a sense of loyalty to Leonora—in spite of her friend's rejection of his suit. (Valville reciprocates Adelaide's love, but they do not communicate their feelings.) Desiring a quick death, Valville goes to the walls of Orleans, where an army is encamped awaiting an impending battle. Instead of "an honourable death," however, Valville performs valiantly and saves the King's life. He then seeks out Baldwin so that the devoted servant can tell Adelaide of his success. Valville's biological mother ("a woman of good air but meanly dressed" 146) materializes and relates the story of how her husband, Count de Villeroy, was falsely accused of murder. Valville was given away so that he would never have to bear his family's shame. After asking Adelaide to care for his mother, Valville goes to the King to seek his assistance in restoring his father's title and forfeited estates. Meanwhile, learning of Valville's success with the King, Leonora has reconsidered her rejection of Valville. Unable to witness a marriage between Leonora and Valville, Adelaide makes preparations to enter a convent. Just as the ceremony begins for Adelaide's initiation as a nun, an officer from the King interrupts the service: the King has pardoned Villeroy and restored his land. Valville and his real father arrive, and in response to Leonora's protestations of love, Valville rebukes her and declares his love for Adelaide, who agrees to marry him. In his closing speech, Count de Villeroy condemns Liancourt, who would use "ungenerous means" to "gain his purposes" (200).

M'Taggart based her drama entirely on Baculard d'Arnaud's *Valmiers*. She retained the plot: the revelation of Valmiers/Valville's obscure birth by a jealous friend/brother; his consequent rejection by the haughty, highly class-conscious Madame Lormesson/Leonora; his heroism in battle and his saving the King's life; the restoration of his honor and title; and his marrying the generous, self-sacrificing Mlle Ermanci/Adelaide. However, she made some modifications, such as the location of the battle and the identity of some of the characters. More importantly, she ended her work with Valville's plan to marry Adelaide, whereas Baculard d'Arnaud has his hero marry, become the father of two children, leading a most exemplary life much admired by the king who, tired of his courtiers' hypocrisy, wants nothing more than become his friend. But, in the end, these two works belonging to different genres exude the same sentimentality and morality.

Valville contains social statements about class prejudice that are underscored by the denouement. Even Leonora acknowledges that "The violence of passion and of prejudice has been my ruin" (198). Nevertheless, the play fails to combat the roots of true class prejudice: Valville's goodness and lack of prejudice cannot be ascribed to a humble birth; although his parents are in reduced circumstances, they are the Count and Countess de Villeroy, and their full social privileges are restored by a grateful King by the end of the play.

TEXT: Not in Readex Microprint.

The Vespers of Palermo, Felicia Dorothea Browne Hemans. Originally titled *Prodica; or, The Vespers of Palermo*, this five-act tragedy was produced at CG on 12 December 1823. Genest says it was withdrawn for alteration, but acted only this once (9: 251–52). It was published by John Murray in 1823.

The play begins with peasants complaining about the yoke of France oppressing them since the Provençals conquered Palermo. In the castle, Vittoria—who had been engaged to marry the slain Sicilian King Conradin—is pressured to marry the French Viceroy, Eribert, but she refuses. As Eribert contemplates a marriage to Vittoria, which would expand the area under his control, the disguised Count di Procida plots an attack against the Provençals, unaware that his son Raimond is in love with Eribert's sister, Constance. When Vittoria and Raimond attend one the dissidents' councils, Raimond is horrified that his father's supporters wish to massacre all the French in Palermo, and he leaves determined to save Constance. Vittoria agrees to say that she will wed Eribert, so that the attack could take place on a festival day—just as the Vesper bell summons them to the ceremony. As Raimond warns Constance to meet him when she hears the vesper bell, the traitor Alberti reveals the plot to De Couci, who tries to warn Eribert who ignores the messenger. As the disguised Sicilians begin to attack at the sound of the bell, Eribert is wounded. Refusing to leave her brother while he is alive, Constance is finally forced by Raimond into hiding at Anselmo's hermitage. Accused of being an informer because of his relationship with Constance, Raimond is brought in chains before his father's tribunal, where he refuses to discuss his guilt or innocence, appealing instead to God's authority. Although Constance comes before the tribunal offering to give her life in exchange for Raimond's, her proposal is refused and she is allowed to leave with Anselmo who finds a place for her to live with the Sisters of Mercy. Raimond's execution is postponed because the Provençals are at the gates of Palermo, and Vittoria has him freed so that he can prove himself by rallying the Sicilians fleeing from the French. Raimond succeeds in pushing back the Provençals, but he and Vittoria are mortally wounded. Attended by Constance and the Sisters of Mercy, Raimond dies; his father throws himself on his body asking for forgiveness.

Characters in *The Vespers of Palermo* are well developed, and even fairly minor ones, such as Montalba, a dissident whose entire family was killed, are rendered vividly. While this play and *Sebastian of Portugal* focus on royalty, peasants or "citizens" appear, voicing their sentiments. *Vespers* and *Sebastian* deal with similar ideas—the occupation of another country, the deposed leaders' desires to regain control of their countries—but their conclusions and tones are entirely different.

MANUSCRIPT: Larpent 2375.

TEXT: Readex Microprint.

FACSIMILE EDITION: A reprint of the 1823 edition, with an introduction by D. H. Reiman (NY: Garland, 1978).

The Village Maid, written by a Young Lady. This three-act comic opera was published by subscription and printed by William Innes for "the authoress" in 1792. There is no indication that the author submitted the play to either the London theatres or those in the provinces. *LS* has no record of the opera being staged.

Emmeline, the title character, lives with her mother, Danvers, on the estate of Lord Ormond. His youngest son, Henry, has an interest in Emmeline, but Danvers explains to Henry that he shouldn't woo the young woman because they are of different classes. When he returns from abroad to visit Lord Ormond, Sir

William Hargrave is melancholy because his wife and daughter were lost in a shipwreck many years ago. In the course of the action, he discovers that his wife and daughter survived the wreck, and they are living under the name of Danvers; Emmeline is his own daughter. This discovery paves the way for Henry to marry Emmeline. In a subplot, Lord Frederick, Lord Ormond's oldest son, is in love with Lady Caroline. While they live in the same house, a tension exists between them. Lady Harriet, Lord Ormond's daughter, plots with Caroline to test Frederick, whom she really loves. Emmeline dresses as Sir Harry Wilding and woos Caroline. This angers Frederick so much that he challenges the supposed Sir Harry to a duel. Harriet loads the pistols with blanks: the duel ends with Frederick declaring his love for Caroline, and a good laugh for the others. Rustics, Colin and Phoebe, provide duets and country dances, though everyone of the cast does some singing, usually at inappropriate moments.

The women in this piece move the action along with their imaginative schemes. Harriet's clever dialogue contrasts with the various sets of lovers, who are either irritable or moonstruck. The other characters seldom rise above stereotypes. Genest remarks, "this opera, in 3 long acts, was written by a Young Lady—it is very far from a bad piece" (10: 200).

TEXT: Readex Microprint.

Village Politics, Hannah More. Using the pseudonym of "Will Chip, a Cockney Carpenter," More addresses "all the mechanics, journeymen, and labourers in Great Britian" on the importance of maintaining the existing order of things. Printed in the first volume of her *Works* (321–48), publication was by T. Cadell, Jr., and W. Davies in 1801, though the piece was first printed in 1792 in response to the French Revolution and to Thomas Paine's *The Rights of Man*. There was no performance.

Jack Anvil, the blacksmith, finds Tom Hod, a mason, in a grouchy mood about English government, having just read Paine's *The Rights of Man*. Tom wants liberty, equality, a new constitution, and a general reform. But Jack takes his democratic aspirations apart by insisting that the English have as much liberty as they need, all English citizens are treated the same under law, and the present constitution serves them well. In contrast, the French are free to rob and kill because there is no law; their democracy means government by a thousand tyrants. It soon becomes clear that Tom hasn't grasped the difficult concepts in Paine's tract, and Jack leads him around to the conclusion that life in England is better than Tom thought at first. Jack concludes by quoting the parson's Sunday sermon: "Study to be quiet, work with your own hands, and mind your own business" (348).

This piece had an extraordinary reception, according to M. G. Jones, More's biographer, and it illustrates More's cardinal principle (echoing Edmund Burke): there is "a divine purpose immanent in the existing order of things" (134). In More's "attempt to stem the torrent of French Jacobinism," as Jones notes, the scales of the argument "are heavily weighted against" Tom, the mason (136–37, 135). Using simple parables, Jack, who does most of the talking, makes Tom see the error of his acceptance of Paine's ideas. That Tom fails to put up a very strong counterargument didn't appear to trouble most readers who agreed with More.

TEXT: Readex Microprint.

FACSIMILE EDITION: "Revolution and Romanticism, 1789–1834" series, with introduction by Jonathan Wordsworth (NY: Woodstock, 1995).

Villario, Ann Hamilton M'Taggart (wrongly ascribed to Lady Sophia Burrell). According to John Galt, the editor of *New British Theatre*, the female author of *Villario* also wrote *Theodora*, published in the same volumes in 1814 by A. J. Valpy. Confusion of authorship arose since Burrell had earlier written a play titled *Theodora* (1800). In his afterward, Galt mentions that the five-act drama had been sent fifteen years before to Kemble, who never returned it to the author. While Galt may have overstated the lapse of time (John Philip Kemble became the actor-manager of CG in the fall of 1803), Kemble was seldom punctilious in dealing with playwrights. *Villario* was collected in M'Taggart's *Plays*, printed in 1832 by A. J. Valpy.

Villario harbors many secrets: his wife (Honoria) and son (Bertram) died eighteen years prior to the events of the drama. The King of Dalmatia has charged Villario to rear his daughter, the Princess Eugenia, in a castle on the shore of the Adriatic Sea. Now grown, Eugenia prepares to meet her father for the first time. Eugenia regrets having to leave her best friend, Villario's daughter Constance, and to give up the quiet life of the castle for Court; she must also bid adieu to her male friend, Beraldus, even though it's clear she cares for this noble forester, whom she has often met in a nearby grove. Eugenia wants to take Constance to the Court with her, but Villario refuses. Richly dressed for the King's arrival, Eugenia and Constance confront Villario, who is angry that his daughter wears royal robes. Eugenia says it was her idea, and presses Villario to permit Constance to go to Court with her. He again refuses and informs Eugenia that he expects Anselmo, who's to be Eugenia's husband. When Anselmo arrives, however, he assumes Constance to be the Princess. Villario disabuses Anselmo of this idea and orders Constance to be locked in a tower until the next day. When the King arrives, he joins the hands of Eugenia and Anselmo, and all go off to the banquet. Meanwhile, Anselmo's servant Frederick has arrived, but he tells Beraldus he does not wish to see Villario yet. Alberto asks Anselmo to meet Villario, who questions Anselmo about his parents: Anselmo only knew his mother and was raised in Algiers, where they were taken by pirates and sold to the Dey. His mother died two years later, and the Dey provided protection until fate took him to Palestine where he entered the service of the King of Dalmatia. He has a picture of his mother which he will show to Villario when his friend brings it. After the Princess has Constance freed from the tower, it is clear that Anselmo and Constance are in love, though neither wishes to injure Eugenia. When he sees the King, Villario raises questions about Anselmo: what if I were his father? The King could accept that, but Villario wishes to postpone the wedding. Anselmo brings Constance to Eugenia, but now Constance refuses the offer to go to Court. When the nuptial day arrives, the King enters with his retinue, and he asks Villario to give him his daughter: thus, Constance would become Queen. She declines graciously, preferring to stay in the castle with her father. Anselmo shows the picture to Villario: it is Honoria. In anguish, Villario cries out, stop the rites: "they are incestuous" (184), and Villario reveals he switched Eugenia and Constance at birth. His wife objected and he ordered her killed. Frederick, who was to be the assassin, comes forward to explain he could not perform the order, arranging instead that Honoria and Bertram be protected by the Dey of Algiers, who made Frederick young Bertram's servant after his mother's death. Now destined to marry Anselmo, Constance solicits forgiveness for all and requests that Eugenia be allowed to marry Beraldus. Constance has the last word: "vice must ne'er usurp Dominion over virtue" (188).

The elements of mystery and surprise work effectively in this drama; portions of prior events and earlier relationships are revealed in fragmentary ways until the final revolutions in the last scene. M'Taggart uses storms, thunder, lightning, and rough seas to support the atmosphere of the events on stage and what they portend. Every time Villario appears on stage, he exhibits turmoil in his words and actions, which reminds the audience of unresolved mysteries. M'Taggart has not entirely gotten around improbability (too many coincidences occur in *Theodora*), but most of the events in *Villario* are plausible. The characterization of Eugenia and Constance provides a convincing contrast between the two. Eugenia prefers life in the country where her reticence and timidity will be less noticed. Constance, on the other hand, puts forth bright and witty remarks that pepper anyone within range. Constance's exceptional commitment to Eugenia forces her to give up any pretensions to Anselmo, until she discovers she is in fact the Princess. The sisterly relationship between the two forges a strong friendship at the heart of the play.

TEXT: Readex Microprint.

The Virgin of the Sun, translated by Anne Plumptre. This five-act rendering of Kotzebue's *Die Sonnenjungfrau* was published in 1799 by R. Phillips. The events in this play precede those in *The Spaniards in Peru; or, The Death of Rolla*. Frederick Reynolds's three-act operatic version, based on Plumptre's translation, was staged at CG on 31 January 1812 and acted thirty-three times. Later, Plumptre's translation was condensed and produced in Norwich, probably during June 1815.

Before the play begins, Rolla, the general of the Peruvian forces, fell in love with Cora, but she became a Virgin of the Sun which prohibited her from marrying. When the play opens, Rolla tells his uncle, the High Priest of the Sun, that the deprivation of Cora has frustrated him, and that he will shun public life by living in a cave. Alonzo, who left Pizarro because of the cruelty his commander inflicted on the native population, has joined the Peruvians, saved the life of the King of Quito, and fallen in love with Cora, who loves him in return. Rolla discovers their love, which he sanctions, because Cora's fulfillment is uppermost in his mind. He counsels the pair to flee to the other side of the mountains; but upon her reappearance at the Temple of the Sun, Cora is taken prisoner when she declares her love for Alonzo. The High Priestess denounces Cora to the King, who determines that the Priests of the Sun must pass judgment not only on her and Alonzo, but upon her family. While the High Priest pleads for mercy, Xaira and the other priests pass a sentence of death. Rolla, meanwhile, has organized his former troops; to force the King to relent, he storms the temple. The King says that mercy cannot be compelled by pressure, and Cora intercedes with Rolla, urging him to lay down his arms and to accept the King's rule. Rolla accedes to her judgment. The King, after some thought, frees Alonzo, Cora, and her family, and he then abolishes the inhumane law.

Without some abridgement, the play would be difficult to stage: there are too many long monologues and too little action. While the exotic location and elaborate scenic designs could appeal to audiences, the static nature of the play would not. As a kind of "noble savage," Cora sees that she has done nothing wrong in loving Alonzo, and Cora, the title character, drives the plot toward more humane treatment for all. The High Priest supports her views, and realizing that all humans are imperfect, he argues for mercy instead of adherence to the rigid law. The King comes to understand the importance of forgiveness and compassion, in marked contrast to the injustice and cruelty practiced by Pizarro and his Spaniards. The King is convinced, moreover, by Cora's willingness to take the blame and to die when she explains in open proceedings to Rolla that force cannot be used when mercy is required. Even though she appears naive, Cora presents strength in virtue and high-mindedness.

MANUSCRIPT: Larpent 1868 of Reynolds's operatic version.

TEXT: Readex Microprint of the 5th edition, 1799.

Virginia, Frances Brooke. After both Garrick and Rich rejected the manuscript because each had recently produced a play on the same subject, Brooke decided to print her five-act tragedy in blank verse "for the author" (sold by A. Millar) in 1756. Brooke used as her source Livy's *Early History of Rome* which described events that happened about 450 B.C.

While the centurion Lucius Virginius is away fighting for Rome, his only daughter Virginia has become the object of lust by Appius, the Roman tyrant. When he is unable to seduce her, Appius plots to have Virginia declared a slave, and not Virginius's daughter at all. Appius then demands Virginia's return, but Virginia's fiancé and uncle insist that the ruling be postponed until Virginius can be present. Even though Appius tries to have the centurion arrested, Virginius arrives to hear the verdict go against Virginia; but before she can be taken away, Virginius stabs her. An insurrection follows, and Appius and his followers are overthrown. After being jailed, Appius commits suicide.

Brooke makes a number of significant changes in her version of the story; most of these alterations occur in the development of the characterization of Virginia. Before judgment is passed, for instance, Virginia knows it is her decision to kill herself if the verdict goes against her. "In *Virginia*, courage rather than chastity is Virginia's foremost virtue," according to Lorraine McMillan (35). By adding another character not in her source, Brooke underscores the importance of female friendships. Icilia is the sister of Virginia's fiancé, and ironically enough it is Virginia who supports Icilia through the trial. As Virginia is dying, she urges Icilia to live and help her brother take revenge against Appius. Although the *Critical Review* of April 1756 noted that too often actions take place offstage and have to be reported, it praised Brooke's morality and poetry in this, her first printed, drama.

TEXT: Not in Readex Microprint.

Virginia, Dorothea Plowden. This three-act comic opera, with music by S. J. Arnold, was produced at DL on 30 October 1800. J. Barker published the text in 1800. Plowden's preface discusses the many difficulties she encountered in the play's acceptance by the manager, the rehearsals, the players, and the mangling of the text.

Set in Virginia, during the time of James I, this musical entertainment stresses spectacle over plot and stereotypes over characterization. On his way to the colonies, Captain Beauclerc has rescued a Spaniard, Don Alphonso, and a Dutchman, who stubbornly refuses to give his name. Shortly after their arrival, his chief passenger Lord Delaware shows a romantic interest in Gertrude, the President's daughter. Delaware, however, had earlier been forced to marry an older woman for her money in order to support a dying parent, though he doesn't want this known. Even though Gertrude claims to love him, Delaware cannot pursue her because of his dilemma. When Lady Delaware arrives from England, she finds not one husband but two, for the Dutchman turns out to be her first husband, who she thought was lost at sea. This leaves Lord Delaware free to marry Gertrude. The natives—Manteo and his daughter Benowee—put in brief appearances to provide local color, and one scene of pageantry occurs at Pawhatan's court.

Genest notes that the opera was damned the first night, and he has a negative reaction to the introduction of songs in such an absurd manner (7: 496–97). It is true that songs often materialize for no dramatic necessity. While realism is not a primary concern in musical comedies, playwrights need to be mindful of dramatic conventions and pay some attention to continuity in plot details that unite the piece. The play may work as musical entertainment, but as a drama it's pretty silly. There are so many characters that some of them get lost (e.g., Blanche and Sir William drop out about halfway through); and the several marriage plots never get developed (Matilda and Alphonso, Captain Beauclerc and Jennet). One must sympathize with the many problems that Plowden describes in her prologue; the weak play appears to have gotten no help from the manager or the actors. Gertrude almost becomes a fully realized character. She rejects her father's choice for a husband, finds her admirer is married, and—to leave the colonies—dresses as a sailor. Lord Delaware's character also has identifiable problems. Beyond these two, however, the author exercises little character development: most are cardboard figures or stereotypes often found in musical comedies.

MANUSCRIPT: Larpent 1303.

TEXT: Readex Microprint.

The Vision in the Holy Land; or, Godfrey of Bouillon's Dream, Jane M. Scott. Acted in the Sans Pareil Theatre's first year of operation, the spectacle opened on 17 November 1806 and was performed forty times that season. Although no text of the piece exists, Richard Altick describes the spectacle as "representing, apparently in the air, an ancient grand battle in shadow, in which several thousand figures, armed in the costume of their time, are seen engaged" (217; quoted by Brokaw and McHugh in *Adelphi* 3).

The Vizier's Son and the Merchant's Daughter, Jane M. Scott. This comic operetta opened at the Sans Pareil Theatre on 16 December 1811 and ran sixty-two nights. A possible second title appears on the cover of the application: "*or the Ugly Woman or Maid of Bagdad*." Michael Parnell composed the music.

MANUSCRIPT: Larpent 1697.

A Voyage up the Thames, attributed to Mrs. Weddell. FCLE mentions that the work has also been ascribed to Thomas Bryan Richards. "Ironically dedicated to the impresario Heidegger, it is a travel burlesque (up-river to Eton instead of abroad), stringing heterogenous material (like a fan-letter from a rejected author to himself) on the thread of an all-male party of London types observing local color" (1143). There is no evidence that the play (ESTC calls it a "comic novella") was acted, though it was published in 1738, and sold by J. Roberts.

TEXT: Not in Readex Microprint. TEC Reel 2583: 4.

-W-

Walcot Castle. See **Angelina**.

WALLACE, Eglantine Maxwell, Lady (d. 1803). A native of Scotland, she was the youngest daughter of Sir William Maxwell and a sister of the Duchess of Gordon. Married in 1770 to Thomas Dunlop, later Sir James Wallace, she was after several years divorced, "by the laws of Scotland," because of alleged ill treatment. About the divorce, *BD* remarks, "We must suppose that the court which pronounced the sentence was satisfied with the truth of the case. It stands on record, however, that the lady herself could be carried above *concert* pitch; for sometime after, a woman, who had been recommended to her Ladyship from principles of humanity, and to whom she afforded asylum at her house in St. James Place, charged her with an assault before Mr. Bond, at the office in Bow Street. Her Ladyship, by direction of the magistrate, compounded the matter; but was so angry, that she declared, whenever an opportunity offered, she would go to France, and reside there during the remainder of her days" (l. 733).

The writer of several tracts and four dramas, Lady Wallace translated her first comedy, *Diamond Cut Diamond*, taken from a popular French comedy, *La Guerre ouverte; or, Ruse contre ruse*, and published it in 1787. Because of the success of Elizabeth Inchbald's *The Midnight Hour*, taken from the same play, Lady Wallace's translation was not acted. Her second comedy, *The Ton; or, Follies of Fashion*, was produced at CG on 8 April 1788, but it ran for only three nights. Another comedy, *The Whim*, was prohibited by the royal licenser: published at Margate in 1795, the play contains an angry preface about the prohibition. L. W. Conolly suggests the censorship of the play may have been because several speeches commented unfavorably on the aristocracy. A tragedy, *Cortes*, was never printed. True to her word, Lady Wallace went to Paris for most of the rest of her life, though she died in Munich in 1803. [*BD*, DBAWW, DNB, FCLE, Inglis]

The Ward of the Castle, Miss Burke. This two-act comic opera debuted at CG on 24 October 1793 with music by Tommaso Giordani. T. Cadell printed the songs, which were sold at the theatre the three nights the piece was performed. The text of the opera has remained in manuscript.

When Bertram returns from battle with the enemies of Duke of Albarosia, the Duke congratulates him and provides him a place to stay in a court outside of his castle, where he has mewed up his ward, Matilda. Bertram has given the Duke an offer of peace from his adversaries, and an emissary will come at seven, the time the Duke usually meets his ward. Matilda and her maid, Jacquenetta, a voracious reader of romance fiction, discuss their situation and the Duke's jealousy; Matilda wishes Bertram would return to save her. The Duke's arrival is signaled by the undoing of several locks. He tells her he plans to marry her the next day and pledges his sincerity with a ring. After he is gone, Bertram's squire Geoffrey, a former carpenter, arrives, having tunneled his way into the castle. Bertram enters and embraces Matilda. After she has given him the

Duke's ring, he has a plan to deceive the Duke: Matilda will dress up as his Turkish bride, and they'll get the Duke to give her to Bertram. As it turns out, Geoffrey and Bertram return by the secret passage to their building, and the Duke comes. When he sees the ring on Bertram's hand, he becomes suspicious. The Duke flies to the tower, only to find Matilda has the ring, returned via the passage. Coming back to Bertram's, the Duke finds a Turkish lady, who's to marry Bertram. Again the Duke is suspicious and runs back to the tower, where he finds Matilda asleep; even though Jacquenetta asks him not to wake her, he does. Upon his return, the Duke finds the nuptials going forward, and convinced that the Turkish lady is not Matilda, he gives her in marriage. As Bertram and his bride leave, they tell the Duke he has given away Matilda in marriage, and before he can stop them, they sail away with Geoffrey and Jacquenetta.

This musical farce satirizes the popular gothic drama of the 1790s and makes use of the same sets. An older guardian (the Duke) keeps a young female ward pent up in a tower until he can marry her—only to have his plans exploded by a young lover. Another well-worn component of the plot is the use of a will made by the young woman's deceased father, requiring the guardian to give her hand in marriage. Despite the stock plot devices, the play comes off cleverly as the resourceful young people dupe the aged guardian. The sassy servant Jacquenetta, who is so fond of reading novels of romantic intrigue, finds herself involved in an episode that could be taken from one of these novels, using the same elements of subterranean passages and trap doors. The lady in distress, Matilda the Countess of Vergy, must act the role of a Turkish woman that she feels unprepared to execute, but she succeeds in foiling her guardian and in marrying the man she loves.

MANUSCRIPT: Larpent 992. Readex Microprint of manuscript.

The Wavering Nymph; or, Mad Amyntas, possibly adapted by Aphra Behn. *Amyntas; or, The Impossible Dowry*, a play originally by Thomas Randolph (now lost), may have been adapted for the 1683–84 season. A possible performance is cited in *LS* (I. 323), altered from Thomas Randolph's play. Two songs from the play are printed in Behn's *Poems Upon Several Occasions*, 1684. Milhous and Hume say there is no evidence that Behn adapted this "lost" play, which was more likely a revival of Randolph's *Amyntas* (*HLB* 31 [1983]: 5–39).

TEXT: Two songs from the play. Wing B1757. EEB Reel 525: 2.

The Way to Win Her, Margaret Wrench Holford. This five-act comedy appeared in *New British Theatre*, printed by A. J. Valpy in 1814. According to John Galt, the editor of the collection, the play was not offered to the theatre managers.

Set in Regency London, the play opens on Lady Emma and her husband, Danvers, at breakfast. They've both been gambling the night before, and she confesses she lost £500 to Sir Harry Enville, while he brags he lost £5,000. When the mail comes, Danvers receives a letter from Cecilia Howard cutting off their relations and another from her husband challenging him to a duel. On his way out he drops the letter from Cecilia, which Emma reads, remarking that the affair parallels hers with Sir Harry. Unconcerned with the news, Emma goes to visit her young cousin, Julia, who lives with her Aunt Deborah in Grosvenor Square, where Emma will have a chance to meet Harry. Aunt Deborah, a learned lady, dotes on the ancients and constantly recalls classical instances for contemporary occurrences. A disguised Harry calls on Deborah as the famous German polymath, Count Muffendorf, and offers to teach Julia, who instantly spots his disguise. Julia has been forced into a marriage with a man she scarcely knows—St. Evremont—and shortly after the wedding he departed for the war; consequently, Julia hates her husband. When Emma comes, she suggests Harry and Julia join her in a visit to an auction. In the auction rooms, Julia overhears a kindly man with an eye patch assisting a poor woman with two children. And Julia is even more impressed when that gentleman purchases a cabinet that belongs to another woman and returns the cabinet to her possession. The gentleman with the eye patch rescues Julia from some offending rogues and takes her to her Aunt Deborah. Although the audience learns that the gentleman is St. Evremont, he goes by the name of Von Crump, who acts as an intercessor for St. Evremont, in an attempt to determine what Julia requires to reunite. Julia becomes enamored of Von Crump's benevolence, and the two plots intertwine when St. Evremont assists Cecilia Howard and her infant daughter, taking them to Julia for protection. Hate turns to love when Julia discovers that Von Crump is actually St. Evremont. He brings the repentant Danvers and Howard together after Emma has broken up their near duel. Julia regrets her mistaken actions toward St. Evremont; Cecilia forgives her husband; and Danvers and Emma renew their vows.

The several mistakes about how people appear and their actual underlying natures force a number of difficult reconsiderations. Several characters reveal better traits than they show at first. Over the course of the play, because of the transformed actions of various characters, benevolence emerges as the principal theme. As the "Her" of the title, Julia's forthright reactions to pretense dismiss the social concerns of the more sophisticated set. Yet she must learn about real generosity through observing the actions of disguised St. Evremont to confront her own hatred. Her ingenuous actions, however, reveal a spirited protagonist, who for all her naiveté is capable of learning and growing.

TEXT: Readex Microprint.

WEDDELL, Mrs. (fl. 1737–1742). Possibly the author of three plays that were published anonymously, Weddell has left few biographical traces to follow. Nicoll credits Mrs. Weddell with two plays: *The City Farce* (1737) and *Incle and Yarico* (1742, by the author of *The City Farce*). With only Nicoll's unsupported evidence of female authorship, Pearson omits Weddell from her discussion, relegating her to an endnote. Even though Cotton treats these two plays, Pearson rejects Weddell for other reasons: contemporary references allude to no woman writers of this name; the writer of these plays is referred to as male (though as Pearson points out this is not conclusive); and "s/he appears in neither DNB or DBAWW" (284). FCLE not only credits Weddell with the two plays noted above, but a third play, *A Voyage Up the Thames*, possibly written by Weddell in 1738, is mentioned. The attribution comes from its mention on the title page of *Incle and Yarico*. [Cotton, FCLE, Pearson]

The Wedding Day, Elizabeth Inchbald. This two-act comic drama was first produced at DL on 1 November 1794 as an afterpiece. Printed the same year for G. G. J. and J. Robinson, it was acted nineteen times its first season and became a staple of the repertory.

The wedding day of the title unites Sir Adam Contest in a second marriage (his wife thought drowned in a shipwreck fifteen years before) with an eighteen-year-old Lady Contest. He has married for youth, she for money. Arriving in London the same day is Tom Contest, Sir Adam's adult son, just back from abroad with the intention of marrying Lady Autumn, an older widow. Mrs. Hamford, whom Lady Autumn met in her travels, is actually the first Lady Contest, who survived the shipwreck and goes under an assumed name to visit the new Lady Contest. Although she explains who she is, she can't face Sir Adam immediately. The new Lady Contest then tells Sir Adam that his first wife is alive and in London. When Tom Contest arrives with his intended Lady Autumn, she turns out to be the mother of the second Lady Contest. As Sir Adam and his first wife reunite, she tells Tom and Lady Autumn that in their "plans of wedlock [they] have both been in the wrong." Sir Adam will settle a dowry on the second Lady Contest, who is now freed from her marriage.

The genre of this work raises the question: is it a comedy (title page of the first edition), a farce (so called by Hogan in *LS*), or a drama (title page in Inchbald's *Collection of Farces and other Afterpieces*, 1809)? The play has some misunderstandings, but there is less stage business than farces usually have. Although the second Lady Contest has symbolically lost her wedding ring, there is not the hue and cry after it that one would expect in a farce. While the play does have its comic moments, humor is not central to the action. Perhaps, the play could be classified as a serious comic drama. A second question grows out of the first: why is the closure of the piece so problematic? If Tom's parents are back together again, and his mother discourages him from marrying an older woman, three people remain in unresolved situations—Tom, Lady Autumn, and her daughter. Paula Backscheider calls attention to the wedding as a fulfillment of the ambitions of both Sir Adam and the second Lady Contest, but shortly after the wedding they quarrel, find themselves disappointed, and their motives exposed: that their marriage dissolves is, perhaps, a resolution that may have pleased contemporary audiences.

MANUSCRIPT: Larpent 1044.

TEXT: Readex Microprint.

FACSIMILE EDITION: E-CED, the 1794 edition with introduction by Paula R. Backscheider (NY: Garland, 1980). The 1809 version in *A Collection of Farces and Other Afterpieces*, selected by Mrs. Inchbald (NY: Benjamin Blom, 1970).

West Country Wooing, Isabel Hill. This monodrama, acted and sung by Harriet Waylett, was approved by the Lord Chamberlain under "Songs for the Theatre Royal, Haymarket," sometime between June and September 1834.

MANUSCRIPT: Add. MS. 42927 (12) ff. 358–365b.

WEST, Jane Iliffe (1758–1852). Born in London, but brought up in Northamptonshire, West seems to have been largely self-educated. It was probably in 1782 that she married Thomas West, a yeoman farmer. They had three sons. Even as a young mother, West continued to write poetry, novels, and plays. Her first tragedy, *Edmund Surnamed Ironside* appeared in her *Miscellaneous Poems*, printed in York, 1791. Eight years later, her *Poems and Plays* (2 vols.) included *Adela* (a tragedy) and *How Will it End?* (a comedy). *The Minstrel; or, The Heir of Arundel*, another tragedy, was printed in her *Poems and Plays* (vols. 3 & 4), 1805. Although none of her plays was acted, her four dramas were collected in *Poems and Plays* (2 vols., 1799; 2 vols. 1805). West wrote a number of novels from *The Advantages of Education; or, The History of Maria Williams* (1793) to *Ringrove; or, Old-Fashioned Notions* (1827). Under the name of Mrs. Prudentia Homespun, she narrated several novels through the personae of an elderly spinster, for example *The Sorrows of Selfishness* (1802). Pamela Lloyd reports that West's papers were left to a grandson, but their whereabouts are now unknown (*N&Q* ns 31 [229] (1984): 469–70). [*BD*, BNA, DBAWW, DNB, EBWW, FCLE, Lonsdale, NCBEL (3: 772)]

Whackham and Windham; or, The Wrangling Lawyers, Jane M. Scott. A comic burletta in two acts, this piece was opened at the Sans Pareil Theatre on 24 January 1814 and ran thirty-seven nights its first season. It was revived the following season for twenty-five performances. Originally titled *Broad Grins; or, Whackham and Windham, The Wrangling Lawyers*, it was described on a playbill, for 8 March 1814, as a "Broad Farcical Comick Burletta" (Donohue). Frank McHugh believes this may be Scott's "most original and successful comedy" (*Adelphi* 17), and the burletta even won praise from *The Theatrical Inquisitor* (February 1814: 128).

MANUSCRIPT: Larpent 1798.

WHARTON, Lady Anne Lee (1659–1685). Poet and playwright, Anne Wharton could not get her only tragedy, *Love's Martyr; or, Witt Above Crownes*, acted or even published: the Stationer's Register has a warning against publishing the play, 3 February 1686. It is in manuscript (Add. Ms. 28693) at the British Library.

Orphaned at birth, Anne was brought up by her grandmother, the mother of John Wilmot, the Earl of Rochester. Married at the age of fourteen, Anne had the misfortune of marrying a rake, Thomas Wharton. After the death of her uncle who had encouraged her poetic muse, she felt even more isolated. Abandoned by her husband, she died, attended by her grandmother. [*BD*, Cotton, DBAWW, DNB, EBWW, FCLE]

What is She?, Charlotte Turner Smith. This five-act comedy was first produced at CG on 27 April 1799 and ran six nights. The play was published the same year by T. N. Longman and O. Rees, but portions omitted in performance (III.4 and part of V.2) were retained in the printed edition. *What is She?* is incorporated in Inchbald's *Modern Theatre*, vol. 10 (1811). Smith's authorship of the play was questioned even by her biographer Florence Hilbish, but Hogan points out that on the benefit night (1 May 1799) Smith is named in the CG account book (5: 2168).

Set in Carnarvonshire, Wales, the play spans two days. Mrs. Derville has rented a small farm from Lord Orton, who has taken a disguise as Belford because he is in love with Mrs. Derville and believes she is higher born than she lets on. Orton's sister, Lady Zepherine, described as a votary to whatever is fashionable, comes to visit Mrs. Derville and decides to return in the guise of Lord Orton. Right away, Mrs. Derville recognizes Zepherine, who (as Lord Orton) asks if Bewley is not a rival. Mrs. Derville tells the would-be Lord Orton that Zepherine may lose Bewley by her folly. Meanwhile, Bewley is in the neighborhood meeting with Ap-Griffin to extend the mortgage on the family farm. Bewley's uncle is supposed to send a casket of jewels to recoup the mortgage. After Zepherine leaves, Sir Caustic Oldstyle is brought in from a minor carriage mishap and kindly treated by Mrs. Derville. Period, Oldstyle's travelling companion, meets his uncle, Ap-Griffin, who asks his nephew to get an evaluation on a cask of jewels (they have come for Bewley, and Ap-Griffin has appropriated them). When Period asks Oldstyle to estimate the worth of the jewels, Sir Caustic recognizes them and knows the real owner, and Period reports that the person who gave him the jewels will be at the party that night. Period then goes to act Lord Orton at Mrs. Derville's with Belford (the real Lord Orton) eavesdropping, but Mrs. Derville discovers Belford and he shamefacedly departs. Having decided to leave the rented farm, Mrs. Derville meets Zepherine and tells her to avoid the fashionable gambler Jargon. Although Zepherine has lost money to Jargon and signed a £4,000 note, Mrs. Derville vows to help her. Later, while Jargon dozes in a summer house, Mrs. Derville manages to extract the note. At the party, Mrs. Derville tells Sir Caustic her story of elevated birth, large fortune, and the death of her parents when she was young. An uncle squandered her money and put her into a convent, but she eloped and married a poor Englishman who abandoned her after two years. Sir Caustic immediately identifies the husband as his son, and he tells Mrs. Derville "you have found a parent." With the £4,000 note gone, Jargon leaves. When Ap-Griffin arrives, asking for the jewels or the cash, Period gives him a receipt and hands the jewels to Bewley the rightful owner, who can now ask Zepherine to marry him. Mrs. Derville accepts Belford in his rightful character of Lord Orton.

Genest has little commendation for the play: "the dialogue is not bad, but most of the incidents improbable" (7: 439). Smith may have been at fault for trying to include too much, such as the large number of visual symbols—the cask of jewels, the miniature portrait of Mrs. Derville, and Zepherine's £4,000 note. Appearance and reality are central to the action. The too-frequent disguises, however, work against the play: Lord Orton takes the role of the poor Belford, while both Zepherine and Period impersonate Lord Orton. Mrs. Derville's assumed name shades her real past. Even though Mrs. Derville has come down in the world, she retains her cleverness and wit. That she has retired to a Welsh farm and expects to make it pay seems a dubious way to gain a subsistence. Mrs. Derville demonstrates the play's strengths through her kind actions and generous spirit, especially her helping Zepherine out of her difficulties.

MANUSCRIPT: Larpent 1253.

TEXT: Readex Microprint.

Which is the Man?, Hannah Cowley. First produced at CG on 9 February 1782, this five-act comedy was published the following year by C. Dilly. The play had twenty-three performances its first season and became a repertoire piece. The comedy continued to be popular, and it was reprinted in Inchbald's *Modern Theatre* (1809).

Before the play opens, Belville and Julia (the ward of Fitzherbert) have been privately married in Paris, but Belville has been called away on a diplomatic mission. While he is gone, Fitzherbert wants Julia to return to London, and she does so without being able to notify Belville. When the play opens, Lord Sparkle (a confirmed rake) seeks information from Mrs. Johnson about her lodgers, a Cornish brother and sister (Pendragon and Sophie), from his borough; he also finds Belville back in London. Then Beauchamp, in uniform, calls on Belville and tells him he's fallen in love. Meanwhile, Clarinda talks to her maid about the widow Lady Bell Bloomer who has supplanted her as the toast of the town; still, Clarinda plans to go to her rout that evening. At Lady Bell's, Julia meets Fitzherbert, who wants her to marry Belville, without naming him. He then calls on Belville and suggests marriage to his ward, without naming her. But Belville says he has already married in Paris and names Julia. Fitzherbert plans to punish Julia for not telling him by proposing she marry Pendragon. Lord Sparkle, who Beauchamp believes is responsible for his commission, asks him to find out Lady Bell's attitude toward his lordship. Belville learns that Lord Sparkle is trying to gain Fitzherbert's ward as a mistress, and goes to warn Fitzherbert. In order to avoid Fitzherbert, Julia follows the plan of her maid Kitty (actually arranged by Lord Sparkle) for Julia to take lodgings at his lordship's, though she doesn't realize the house is his. When Lord Sparkle comes in Julia realizes Kitty has betrayed her, but upon Beauchamp's arrival she asks for his protection which he willingly gives, taking her temporarily to his lodgings. When Clarinda calls upon him, Julia is unwilling to see her and hides in the next room. Belville then arrives, Julia is discovered, and Belville leaves in a jealous fit. Before the rout, Julia explains to Lady Bell why she was at Beauchamp's and that she's married to Belville. Fitzherbert comes to Julia, says he knows her situation, and will reconcile her with Belville. Lord Sparkle's indiscretions are exposed at the party, and Lady Bell gives herself to Beauchamp, praising British military patriots.

Julia's refusal to tell Belville the name of her guardian is unnatural and mars a play that is otherwise successful (Genest 6: 224–25). Despite this problem, Link points out the effective interplay between the two plots. In the various levels of society, manners of the age are an important component of the play. Although Lord Sparkle acts out the "fashionable dissipation" of the upper classes, he is also scheming and selfish in marked contrast to the soldierly Beauchamp, who is generous and honorable. The clever, young widow Lady Bell is set against the more jaded Clarinda, and Pendragon and Sophie represent country society who ape London elegance in less-than-successful ways. Cowley made some deletions and alterations in the play for her *Works*, published posthumously in 1813.

MANUSCRIPT: Larpent 584.

TEXTS: Readex Microprint. TEC Reels 3512: 4 (third edition, 1783); 4375: 23 (fourth edition, 1784); 4397: 9 (fifth edition, 1785); 3512: 3 (Dublin, 1783).

FACSIMILE EDITION: E-CED, with introduction by F. Link (NY: Garland, 1982).

The Whim, Lady Eglantine Wallace. Prohibited performance by royal licenser, this three-act comedy was published by W. Epps at Margate, 1795. L. W. Conolly (102–05) examined the manuscript and believes that the censorship of the play resulted from unfavorable remarks on the aristocracy and from radical political opinions. Genest (10: 201–03) thinks the censorship resulted from an unflattering allusion to Lady Jersey, mistress of the Prince of Wales. Lady Wallace defends her position in the "Address to the Public," which preceded the printed version, where she maintains the social utility of the drama. Not incidentally, the benefits from the play were to have gone to "the Hospital and the Poor of the Isle of Thanet." Moreover, she attacks a system that allows a freedom to the press but that censors the drama.

In this comedy, Lord Crochet, an antiquarian, has a "whim," wanting to bring back the virtues of Greece and Rome by declaring a Saturnalia for a day. The servants Fag and Nell are made master and mistress of the family, while Lord Crochet becomes the cook and his daughter Julia the maid to Nell. The servants on this day have license to comment (negatively) on the aristocracy, which takes a number of political turns. Fag, however, takes the reversal one step further and gives Julia to Captain Belgrave, who is in love with her, and Lord Crochet is forced, grudgingly, to consent.

The subversive elements in the play appear quite mild to today's reader, and the witty dialogue could very possibly have made the play successful. Fag, for example, charges the aristocracy with being "arrogant—false—in debt to tradesmen. . . . [They] give money only to girls and gaming [and] defame friends, without truth or humanity." And even Lord Crochet agrees: "What are their modern balls, masquerades, and assemblies, but nurseries of gamesters, loose women, and wretched husbands!" The servants want to reduce the tax burden and redistribute the wealth so that "every one should be able to pay for bread." Suppression of this satiric drama appears to be merely a way to limit discussion about social issues and about the failures of the ruling classes.

MANUSCRIPT: Larpent 1093.

TEXT: Readex Microprint.

Whim for Whim, Maria Edgeworth. This unpublished comedy was, according to Edgeworth's biographer Marilyn Butler, begun in November 1798 by Edgeworth and her father. The family privately presented the play in the Christmas season and a second time early in 1799. She submitted a manuscript of the play to R. B. Sheridan, but his rejection of the manuscript caused her to doubt her ability in dramatic form.

Butler says that *Whim for Whim* deals with several stratagems and subsequently the unmasking of Count Babelhausen. "Other members of the cast include an elderly baronet who hates everything old, a rich and whimsical widow, a disreputable French governess, and a rational heroine." The principal satiric targets include philosophers of the supposedly self-indulgent German school and their English dupes. "The play ends with the hero resolving that henceforth 'instead of pure reason, I will follow common sense'" (165).

MANUSCRIPT: Bodleian MS. Eng. misc. d. 648.

Who's the Dupe?, Hannah Cowley. This afterpiece, a two-act farce, was first performed at DL on 10 April 1779 and played fifteen times its first season. An extraordinarily popular piece, it was acted every season until the end of the century: Hogan in *LS* records 126 performances in twenty-two seasons. The source of Cowley's play is based on the subplot of Susanna Centlivre's *The Stolen Heiress* (performed at LIF on 31 December 1702). The play was published 30 April 1779 by J. Dodsley and seven other publishers. It was also included in Elizabeth Inchbald's *Collection of Farces* (1809).

The rich and self-made tradesman, Abraham Doiley, father of Elizabeth, attempts to arrange her marriage to Gradus, an Oxford scholar, compensating for his own lack of an academic education. However, she is in love with Granger. Elizabeth, wishing to have her own way, plots with her cousin Charlotte: Gradus will be taught fashionable manners and modern dress, while Granger will act "bookish." When Gradus reappears as a gallant, Doiley is ready to accept the knowledgeable-sounding Granger. To settle the marriage in his own mind, he will have the two engage in a contest to determine who speaks the best Greek: after Gradus provides a Greek epigram, Granger speaks latinate English nonsense. Gradus then points out that Granger spoke English, and Doiley says "'Twas no more like English, than I am like Whittington's cat." Granger wins Elizabeth, and Gradus settles for Charlotte, provided he return to his old-fashioned ways.

Much depends on the swift actions and plot manipulation of the farceurs cast in this clever piece. The character types are not new: the nouveau-riche tradesman and the stolid scholar have long been figures of fun. Nevertheless, some serious ideas are raised about women's education by Elizabeth in contrast to Gradus's pedantry. To show that women know enough to handle their own arrangements, Elizabeth and Charlotte engineer the men into new roles, and the women achieve their own ends.

MANUSCRIPT: Larpent 475.

TEXTS: Readex Microprint. TEC Reels 4334: 13 (Dublin, 1779); 4364: 11 (third edition, 1780); 3744: 4 (fourth edition, 1780); 4375: 24 (seventh edition, 1790).

FACSIMILE EDITION: E-CED, the 1779 printing, with introduction by F. Link (NY: Garland, 1982). The 1809 version in *A Collection of Farces and Other Afterpieces*, selected by Mrs. Inchbald (NY: Benjamin Blom, 1970).

The Widow and the Riding Horse; or, The Paradox, translated by Anne Plumptre. Thomas J. Dibdin, Jr., adapted Plumptre's translation of this one-act farce—written by Kotzebue—for the stage. Plumptre mentions the adaptation in the advertisement, saying that her "Translation is the original from which Mr. Dibdin, Junior, formed his pleasant Interlude of the *Horse and the Widow*, as performed at Covent Garden Theatre" (sig. [A2v]), where the first production occurred on 4 May 1799. R. Phillips published Plumptre's translation later in 1799.

Classified as "a dramatic trifle" on the title page, this farce turns on the last testament and will of William Fullarton, who specified that his son, Thomas Fullarton, should inherit £80,000—if he swears never to marry a widow or keep a riding (i.e., racing) horse. In the event either of these conditions is violated, the money would go by default to Fullarton's cousin. Because of his kind heart, Fullarton has married Angelica, a French widow, in Flanders. Although he asks her to remain silent about her previous marriage, she has made indiscreet remarks, and a suspicious cousin, who stands to inherit if Thomas fails in his vows, has sent a lawyer to investigate. From a nearby inn, Ronsard, a French emigrant and servant to Count Valcour, calls on Fullarton to get £3 to pay his master's losses at piquet to a lawyer. Ronsard says he must give Fullarton something in return and offers him his master's old nag. After inviting the Count to dinner, Fullarton finally acquiesces and takes the nag, only to have the lawyer arrive and charge him with having violated the terms of the will. Here the Count intervenes and says the nag is actually a mule. Having got round this technicality, Fullarton calls for Angelica to clear him of marrying a widow. When she enters the room and sees the Count, she shrieks since the Count is her husband who she thought had died in the war. Neither the Count nor Fullarton now lays claim to Angelica, who may be hanged for bigamy, but they ask the lawyer if a third marriage would receive the same treatment. When the lawyer says that it would not, both men offer Angelica to the lawyer, who accepts her for a financial allowance from Fullarton. She gladly leaves her former husbands as the Count offers to throw the nag into the bargain.

Although Plumptre calls the play as a "pleasant interlude," its implications are decidedly misogynistic: Angelica is disposed of by her two husbands as a chattel to a third husband, the lawyer Warbifax—and for the price of £10,000. While Plumptre cannot be blamed for the content, Kotzebue's implications reinforce tired stereotypes of women as "vixens."

MANUSCRIPT: Larpent 1255.

TEXT: Readex Microprint under Plumptre.

The Widow of Malabar, Mariana Starke. Based on Antoine Lemierre's *La Veuve du Malabar* (1770), Starke's three-act tragedy may have been produced privately at Mrs. Crespigny's theatre, though one contemporary source suggests not (*Gazetteer*, 24 January 1791, quoted in *LS* 5: 1251). The first public performance took place at CG on 5 May 1790 for the benefit of Elizabeth Brunton of the Norwich theatre, who took the role of Indamora. *The Widow of Malabar* was acted a number of times over several seasons in London and printed by William Lane in 1791. Starke, whose name does not appear on the title page, signed the dedication to Mrs. Crespigny.

Set in Malabar, India, the play begins just as a young Indian widow is to be immolated on her deceased husband's funeral pyre. The Rajah wishes to postpone the religious ceremony until a truce can be achieved with warring British leaders. The widow, Indamora, is told by Fatima, her attendant and a Persian, that the cruel tradition adds "to the various ills entail'd on woman." The long-suffering, stoical

Indamora acknowledges that she was not happily married; even though she loved a British "chief," she was forbidden to marry a Christian. When a young Brahmin arrives to conduct Indamora to the funeral pyre, he tells his story to the widow, and they turn out to be brother and sister. Meanwhile, Raymond, the British officer who was in love with Indamora, has granted a one-day truce "to these barbarians." He learns, however, that the ritual is proceeding, and he goes to stop it. Just as Indamora is about to be burned, the young Brahmin returns with the news that a British priest is pleading for Indamora's life. This gives the young Brahmin time to hide Raymond from assassination. The situation, however, seems doomed, and the funeral procession recommences. The young Brahmin arrives and pleads for his sister's life, but the chief Brahmin won't hear of it. Raymond then enters with his troops, driving off the Indians and seizing the chief Brahmin. In a move that emphasizes the superiority of Christianity, Raymond spares the life of the chief Brahmin. The young Brahmin then asks to be instructed in Raymond's religion. To appease his gods, the chief Brahmin stabs himself.

Starke shortened Lemierre's drama from five to three acts, by omitting "long declamatory scenes," which she was convinced would not have met the approval of an English audience. Still, despite her claim, she retained the basic plot, and only in a very "small measure" (her own words) did she make the work her own. Besides having the chief Brahmin stab himself to death upon being defeated (his French counterpart is merely dismissed), Starke gives the hero a British identity that in no way affects his role. The play becomes a hymn to Britain's civilized accomplishments, instead of a panegyric to France's greatness and an ode to King Louis. For what she presents as her "first Essay," Starke asked the Public's indulgence. Obviously, she had not yet mastered the art of dialogue, as evidenced by repartee such as "ah a sister!" or "A lover's—Hah," or "our Enemy alive!—Confusion!" Despite the problematic dialogue, *The Widow of Malabar* enjoyed a certain measure of success.

Both the British and Christianity triumph in this clash of cultures. The barbarians (the minority culture) lose out to the English, though both sides are dominated by powerful men—Raymond and the old Brahmin. The young Brahmin assists Indamora, and Raymond brings in the troops to win a Christian victory. More harmful to the drama than the patent Christian superiority are the number of coincidences which render unbelievable situations preposterous: for example, the young Brahmin just happens to be Indamora's brother.

MANUSCRIPT: Larpent 869.

TEXT: Readex Microprint.

The Widow Ranter; or, The History of Bacon in Virginia, Aphra Behn. This tragicomedy was posthumously produced at DL on 20 November 1689 and printed the following year for James Knapton with a prologue and epilogue by John Dryden. Behn's use of historical sources are documented by Charles L. Batten, Jr., in *RECTR* 13 (1974): 12–19, enlarging on an earlier essay by Anne Witmer and John Freehafer in *Library Chronicle* 34 (Winter 1968): 7–23. Owing to miscasting and injudicious cutting of the text, Behn's play did not succeed on stage and was not revived.

The events of the drama take place in the colony of Virginia, where there are three factions—the Indians, the settlers, and General Bacon and his army. The General had been asked by the settlers to protect them from the Indians, but then the town council disapproves of his methods. The play opens with Hazard arriving from England; he renews his acquaintance with Friendly, who suggests Hazard act as a cousin to old Surelove (presently in England) in order to meet Madam Surelove. In the same house lodges Friendly's inamorata, Chrisante. The town council, who are concerned about Bacon, includes the deputy governor, Wellman, and a boozy lot of justices, who are cowardly layabouts and who can be out-drunk by the Widow Ranter. Meanwhile, Bacon and his lieutenants (Fearless and Daring) are meeting with the Indians whose Queen, Semernia, laments that she married the Indian King before she met Bacon. After Bacon receives a letter from the council, an attempt is made to ambush him, but he survives and confronts the council. When they try to seize him, he and his followers beat them back and leave. The council offers a reward for the capture of Bacon, who then threatens to burn the town and to take all the women hostages. Upon a soldier's reporting that the Indians have started a war, Bacon turns to this fight. Bacon kills the King, but laments over his worthy antagonist. The Widow dresses as a man and comes to help Bacon's forces, but also to gain access to Daring, whom she loves. Two of the layabout justices, Whimsey and Whiff, are arrested for cowardly treason. Semernia, meanwhile, has dressed as an Indian brave, but she and others are attacked by Bacon, who fatally wounds her. Fearless wishes to rally Bacon to another attack, but his love of the slain Semernia causes him only to lament. When Daring tells them that their army is likely to be defeated, Bacon takes poison. As Bacon is dying, Daring returns with news of their victory. Bacon dies, and there is a reconciliation between the warring sides. Madam Surelove learns her husband has died, but it appears that she will marry Hazard. The Widow and Daring are united, as are Chrisante and Friendly, Dunce and Flirt. Whimsey and Whiff are sacked from the council.

The tragic action of Bacon and Semernia is set off by the satire on the cowardly members of the town council and by the various contrasting love affairs (Hume 221, 397–98). Several events set up ironic contrasts: the Widow dresses as a soldier to gain Daring, whereas Semernia, dressed as a brave, is killed by her lover Bacon, who then takes poison only to learn that his troops have won. The Ranters, a small sect, believed that earthly perfection was achieved and sin was overcome by perfect freedom, and perhaps the Widow accomplishes this. While Woodcock lauds the play, Link objects to the lack of unity: "Mrs. Behn is after everything at once: history, tragedy, heroic romance, intrigue, farce, and satire" (82). Indeed, the audience cannot easily discern the main plot: is it Bacon's war, his romance with the virtuous Semernia, the different social levels on which the various love affairs are conducted, or the Widow's winning of Daring? However, like a three-ring circus, there is something for everyone. And in this posthumous play, perhaps Behn was trying to convey a fullness of life which includes much—love and war, sadness and humor, cowardice and heroism.

TEXTS: Wing B1774. EEB Reel 1056: 13. Readex Microprint.

MODERN EDITION: *Works*, ed. Montague Summers (1915; NY: Phaeton, 1967) 4: 215–310. Behn, *Five Plays*, introduction by Maureen Duffy (London: Methuen, 1990), reprints Summers's edition: 205–295. Behn, *Oroonoko, The Rover and Other Works*, introduction by Janet Todd (London: Penguin, 1992): 249–325. Edited from the 1690 text, with introduction by Arron R. Walden (NY: Garland, 1993).

Widow's Tears, Jane M. Scott. The one-act burlesque was first performed at the Sans Pareil Theatre on 23 October 1817 and ran for thirteen nights. Although no text of the play survives, *The British Stage* praised the play and notes that it was "founded on Bickerstaffe's *Ephesian Matron*" (*Adelphi* 24).

The Widow's Vow, Elizabeth Inchbald. The source of this two-act farce is Joseph Patrat's *L'Heureuse Erreur* (1783). Inchbald's version was first produced at the Haymarket on 20 June 1786 and published the same year by G. G. J. and J. Robinson. A Dublin printing in 1786 was titled *The Neuter*, though the London printing retained *The Widow's Vow*.

After an unfortunate marriage contracted when she was young, the Countess had vowed to shun male companionship and never to marry again. When Isabella's brother the Marquis falls in love with the recluse, Isabella concocts a scheme to get them together. She sends her maid to "inform" the Countess that she plans to ridicule the Countess and her vow by coming herself disguised as the Marquis, and making her fall in love and marry a woman, all the while thinking it is a man. When the real Marquis, unaware of his sister's ruse, arrives, he is taken for his disguised sister. The Countess, wanting to have the last laugh, plays along beautifully and, feeling safe from any real entanglement, allows herself familiarities that shock the well-brought up Marquis. She goes so far as to agree to marry him, a decision she does not regret, even when Isabella's arrival puts an end to the game, for she has fallen for the charming Marquis, despite herself. Her uncle, Antonio, concludes the play by announcing that she must replace her just broken vow of solitude by "the vow to love, honour and obey" her new husband.

Inchbald exploited very well the comical potential of the mistaken sexual identity of the Marquis, which carried over to other characters as well. The audience, informed of the real situation, could laugh at the characters who thought they knew what was going on, when in fact they were themselves hoaxed. This complicity, the swiftness of dialogue, and the excellent acting ensured the farce a great success.

In the Advertisement, Inchbald states her indebtedness to Patrat's *L'Heureuse Erreur* "for the Plot of her Piece, and for the Plot alone" (sig. a4). She kept the main plot, i.e. the sister's stratagem, but discarded the subplot involving the Countess's brother, choosing to replace the latter by an old lecherous uncle, the comical Antonio. Contrary to what Kinne says, her plot is simpler than Patrat's, and her comedy of situation more apparent than in the original. However, Kinne's remarks concerning the cleverly depicted character of the uncle and the importance of the servants as further sources of farcical incident are quite correct. *The Widow's Vow* met with a favorable reception in England, as it did in America (Waldo notes nine performances from 1785 to 1796).

MANUSCRIPT: Larpent 736.

TEXT: Readex Microprint.

FACSIMILE EDITION: E-CED, with introduction by Paula R. Backscheider (NY: Garland, 1980).

A Wife in the Right, Elizabeth Griffith. Sent to the licenser as *Patience the Best Remedy; or, A Wife in the Right*, the play was scheduled to be performed 5 March 1772. Owing to Edward (Ned) Shuter's "indisposition" (i.e., drunkenness), this five-act comedy had to be postponed. Finally produced at CG on 9 March 1772, the play was withdrawn after one performance because of provocations by the audience. An edition of the play, published the same year by subscription, included the names of James Boswell, Edmund Burke, the Duke of Devonshire, the Duchess of Bedford, David Garrick, Sir Joshua Reynolds, and Elizabeth Montague.

Before Lord Seaton's marriage to Lady Seaton, she had been a great friend of Charlotte Melville. After the marriage, Seaton maintains a passion for Charlotte, but her affections are set on Colonel Ramsey. To avoid causing trouble between the Seatons, Charlotte takes lodgings with an old school friend, the widow Mrs. Frankly, who desires an intrigue with Seaton as well as having designs on Governor Anderson (Lady Seaton's uncle who is recently back from India). When he visits Mrs. Frankly, Seaton discovers Charlotte and on his knees implores her to return to their house. In the midst of his protestations, Lady Seaton walks in, having heard where Charlotte was lodging. Although upset, Lady Seaton handles the situation decorously, winning Seaton's love in the process. After a misunderstanding with Colonel Ramsey, Seaton warns the Governor about Mrs. Frankly's deficiency in money and virtue. Lord and Lady Seaton help Colonel Ramsey resolve his differences with Charlotte. When the Governor arrives, he is angry about what he perceives as Seaton's misinformation about Mrs. Frankly. Seaton shows him a letter from Mrs. Frankly, in which she calls the Governor the man she most detests. The Governor decides to remain single and to return to India.

Less sentimental than Griffith's other comedies, *A Wife in the Right* still has its share of reformation, middle-class sententiousness, and a benevolent view of human nature. Bevis points to a tighter construction in the first act before "it declines into a standard reform comedy" (1980: 53). The potential duel between Lord Seaton and Colonel Ramsey recalls Steele's *The Conscious Lovers*. Governor Anderson, who would like to buy a seat in parliament, has a love of Indian food and clothing, constituting an eccentric enough obsession to create a type of humours character.

MANUSCRIPT: Larpent 332. Readex Microprint of the manuscript.

TEXTS: Readex Microprint. TEC Reel 552: 40.

A Wife to Be Lett, Eliza Haywood. First produced at DL on 12 August 1723 with Haywood in the role of Mrs. Graspall (the wife of the title), this five-act comedy played three nights; it was not revived. Dan. Browne Jr. and Sam. Chapman published the play the following year.

The comedy has three plot lines. The first involves forced marriages: Fairman plans to marry his daughter Celemena to the Widow Stately's nephew—one Sneaksby—and his niece Marilla to Toywell, a rich fop. The second treats Amadea, who has been deserted by Sir Harry Beaumont, and hopes to regain him by disguising herself as a male servant to the Graspalls. The third exposes Graspall, a miser, who "lets" his wife to Sir Harry Beaumont. Being forced to marry against their wishes, Marilla and Celemena enlist their lovers, Courtly and Gaylove, to thwart Fairman's choices. Gaylove tells Toywell that Trusty, who holds Marilla's fortune, is financially ruined. Thinking Marilla hasn't a penny, Toywell rejects her. Celemena drops Sneaksby when he comes in drunk. Meanwhile, Amadea, in male dress, warns Mrs. Graspall of Sir Harry Beaumont's passion and recommends she see him less. When Graspall arrives at home, he tells his wife that for £2,000 he has given Sir Harry free access to her. Amadea, who has overheard this conversation, reveals to Mrs. Graspall that she is a woman, and Sir Harry's former fiancée: she asks Mrs. Graspall to appear to go along with her husband's arrangement to test Sir Harry, who regrets his previous love life. Mrs. Graspall, then, brings out Amadea and reunites her with Sir Harry. Still, Mrs. Graspall wishes to get revenge on her husband and asks Sir Harry and Amadea to help her by inviting everyone to dinner; Graspall grumbles over the expense but agrees. People begin to arrive. Courtly has won Marilla, and Fairman admits he was wrong about Sneaksby. Celemena accepts Gaylove with Fairman's approval. Before dinner, a scuffle occurs offstage: Sir Harry appears to have caught Amadea in male attire with Mrs. Graspall, who then turns on her husband and reports his forcing her to be for hire. Moreover, she has given the £2,000 to Amadea, who is now the wife of Sir Harry. Graspall regrets his covetousness and promises to reform. A subplot involves two servants—Jenny Dogood, a housekeeper to the rich Widow Stately, and Shamble, servant to Courtly. Because the Widow wishes to marry a man with a title, Shamble passes himself off as a knight and proposes to her; when the Widow Stately shows little interest, he acts demented until she accepts. After the marriage, the Widow is told that Shamble used to be a footman, but Gaylove suggests that the Widow buy Shamble a title.

Several hints for Haywood's play come from Congreve's *The Way of the World* (1700). Like Millamant and Mirabell, Celemena and Gaylove exchange verses. Like Sir Wilfull Witwoud, Sneaksby speaks a country language, and he gets drunk. Shamble woos the Widow Stately disguised as a knight, which is similar to Waitwell acting Sir Rowland and wooing Lady Wishfort. In this comedy, Haywood demonstrates Mrs. Graspall's integrity in several ways: first, she has Mrs. Graspall withstand the suits of Toywell and Sir Harry; next, Mrs. Graspall befriends Amadea; and, finally, Mrs. Graspall shames her husband by exposing his greediness.

TEXT: Readex Microprint of 1735 edition.

FACSIMILE EDITION: E-CED, with an introduction by V. Rudolph (NY: Garland, 1983), prints the 1724 edition.

A Wife to be Lett; or, The Miser Cured, Ann Minton. Eliza Haywood's comedy of 1723 was condensed into two acts by Minton. A. Seale printed and sold the text of the comedy in 1802. There is no record in Genest or Nicoll of this version being acted.

Graspall, the miser of the subtitle, offers and sells the services of his wife for £2000 to Sir Harry Beaumont, who has a passion for Mrs. Graspall. Before Harry can close the bargain with the virtuous Mrs. Graspall, his former inamorata, Amadea, derails the assignation by forgiving Harry his indiscretions. Harry is so stunned by Amadea's generosity that he proposes marriage to her. Mrs. Graspall asks their help to get revenge on her husband, and they assist in exposing Graspall's follies to the whole community and in getting him to repent his avaricious act. In the second plot, Marilla has been promised by her father's will to Toywell, a wealthy fop, and Celemena's father plans to have her marry Sneaksby, whose aunt pledges her estate to her nephew. Two gallants, Courtly and Gaylove, intrude on these plans and expose the moneygrubbing of Toywell and the foolishness of Sneaksby in order to win their admirers.

The text is almost word for word from Haywood. Minton's additions may be found in the opening, which she has trimmed. Minton has also cut out the subplot involving the Widow Stately, aunt to Sneaksby, and her wooing by Shamble, Courtly's valet, disguised as a knight. Many of Minton's condensed scenes delete all that is not essential to her borrowed plot. As in Haywood, the setting in Salisbury makes little use of the locality, but both plots expose the folly and vice of unworthy men. In her reduction, Minton places an emphasis on the women being released from incompatible men, who are easily duped. The "letting," prostituting, of Mrs. Graspall by her avaricious husband is corrected in this version by having "the miser cured," whereas Haywood adds no subtitle to suggest that stupidity and depravity have been corrected.

TEXT: Readex Microprint.

The Wife Well Managed; or, Cuckoldom Prevented, Susanna Centlivre. Although the author did not see a production of this farce in five scenes during her lifetime (it was refused a license), there was a performance at HAY on 2 March 1724 as an afterpiece. The cast list in the 1715 text, printed by S. Keimer, suggests the performers intended by Centlivre. J. Roberts reissued the farce with *The Gotham Election* in 1715. The play performed at Tottenham Court on 17 August 1732 appears to be a version of Centlivre's play. John Randall (i.e., Henry Carey) altered the play for a ballad opera, *The Disappointment*, without crediting Centlivre as the source. This ballad opera probably played in 1732, when S. Slow published it; the title page indicates it was acted at HAY (Burling 149). Another performance of Carey's ballad opera took place at York Buildings on 8 July 1734 (*LS* 3: 405).

Enamored of Father Bernardo, Lady Pisalto writes to invite him to an assignation. Don Pisalto intercepts the letter and writes back, saying that Bernardo will come to her just at twilight. Pisalto then informs his wife that he will be gone for several hours to see some lawyers in the evening. Pisalto borrows a habit from the priest and invites him to dinner. When Pisalto enters Lady Pisalto's room in a habit of Bernardo's order, there is talk of love until he whips out a rope and beats her. When Lady Pisalto's maid, Inis, enters the room, the beating stops. Pisalto leaves, doffs the habit, and returns as himself. Inis advises Pisalto that her mistress fell down the stairs, and Lady Pisalto refuses to dine with her husband and Bernardo. At dinner, Pisalto asks Bernardo to cure Lady Pisalto of "unclean Spirits," and the priest supplies himself with holy water. With Pisalto listening, Bernardo speaks amorously and kisses her, but when she sees the priest, Lady Pisalto flies up and begins to beat Bernardo; she is also joined by Inis. He throws holy water at them to purge them of evil spirits. Pisalto lets Bernardo out, and Lady Pisalto promises never to see the priest again.

Set in Lisbon, the play appears at first an invective against Catholic hypocrisy, because the would-be seducer is a priest, "an appropriate metaphor for the Catholic James Edward," as Pearson points out (224). The Whiggish political overtones, however, do not mask the emphasis of male domination through the physical force that Pisalto exercises. While Lady Pisalto does wish to cuckold her husband, Pearson believes "the brutal husband is not a good recommendation either for marriage or for the house of Hanover" (224). The play's misogyny damages Centlivre's political point and mars the feminist success she had with her previous play, *The Wonder*.

TEXTS: Readex Microprint. TEC Reels 481: 18 (Keimer); 2776: 4 (J. Roberts, as *A Cure for Cuckoldom; or, The Wife Well Manag'd*).

FACSIMILE EDITION: E-CED, with introduction by R. C. Frushell (NY: Garland, 1982) reprints the Keimer text.

The Wife with Two Husbands, translated by Elizabeth Gunning, later Plunkett. This tragicomedy was translated from R. C. Pixérécourt's *La Femme à deux maris*. Although this version was never acted, James Cobb made a three-act musical drama from Pixérécourt's play (acted DL, 1 November 1803). Whether or not he used Gunning's translation, published in 1803 by H. D. Symonds, is unclear. McMillan finds numerous differences between the two.

Despite its title, this work is not a comedy. Elisa Werner, the fifteen-year-old daughter of a German officer, falls in love with Isodore Fritz, a deserter and a rogue who kidnaps her and finally marries her. After six years of marital abuse, she leaves him and begs forgiveness from her stern and principled father who rejects her. Being sent a false death certificate, she believes herself free to marry the Count of Fersen, who loves her and whom she loves. She lives happily on her second husband's estate in the company of her son from her first marriage, Julius, who believes he is her protégé. Her father, whom she has hired as a farmer and who is now blind, lives near her, surrounded by her loving care, unaware that his wonderful mistress is no other than his daughter. One day Fritz reappears in her life, revealing to Julius that Elisa is his wife. Fritz's attempt to blackmail her fails. The Count knows everything about Elisa's past, and siding with her, tries to get rid of the scoundrel, not by handing him over to the military authorities, which would mean death by fire since he deserted, and, thus, dishonor for his wife and her son, but by shipping him to a far away place. As for Fritz, he plans on having the Count killed by his accomplice, but a brave servant of the Count thwarts his efforts and manages to have the villain assassinated instead. Papers found on the dead man reveal that the fake death certificate had been written by him: Elisa is vindicated and her father finally forgives her. The play ends with the Count stating: "A justly offended father, who affectionately grants his forgiveness, is a faint representation of the merciful goodness of the DIVINITY," underlining the power that patriarchal figures have over Elisa.

In her Preface, Gunning admits that the play, which had enjoyed a tremendous success in Paris, was declined for the piece was not, according to the manager Mr. Harris, "calculated for the English stage." She went ahead with the publication of her rendering which appears to be a literal translation, as she stated. In this faithful rendering of Pixérécourt's play, mistranslations are few, and might be attributed to carelessness, rather than a lack of knowledge of French, although failure to realize that "tromper" and its pronominal form "se tromper" have different meanings could indicate otherwise. What is more puzzling is the addition of a few words here and there, or of scenic indications not in the original. For example, the Count's last words read in French as simply: "An offended father, who forgives, is the most perfect representation of the divinity!" Gunning may have found them too succinct or too flat for a melodramatic work such as *The Wife with Two Husbands*, but alterations of this kind are rare.

TEXT: Readex Microprint.

William Thompson; or, Which is He?, Caroline Boaden. This farce was first produced at the Haymarket Theatre on 11 September 1829 and acted twenty-two times. It was published in Cumberland's British Theatre series without a date.

Julia is being forced by her father, Dr. Soothem, to marry William Thompson, a man she has never seen and the son of her father's old friend. The action is generated when two men named William Thompson show up at Dr. Soothem's house. Remarkably, the first William Thompson turns out to be a man who knows nothing about the engagement; he has, however, met Julia at a masquerade where they were both attracted to each other. Soon after the first William Thompson arrives, Julia receives a letter from her cousin, Miss Dormer, saying that "Mr. Thompson was engaged to her, but has been persuaded by his father to leave her, and pay his address to me, which she trusts I will not receive." Insisting that she will not be "a sharer in his injustice" (14), Julia vows to discourage William Thompson. When the second William Thompson arrives, a bailiff follows him, looking for a man by the same name who has taken property from Mr. Snip. In order to avoid arrest, the second William Thompson pays for the property in spite of his declared innocence. After discovering that another William Thompson has arrived, the first man tries to discourage his rival by telling him that Dr. Soothem has died. When Soothem himself appears, the second William Thompson does not know who he is, and they engage in a bewildering conversation: the former assuming that he is discussing his daughter's wedding plans and the latter assuming that a funeral is being arranged. As a result of the verbal confusion, Dr. Soothem identifies the second William Thompson as the disoriented patient he has been expecting, and he has his keepers seize his intended son-in-law. When Miss Dormer arrives,, she and Julia discover the identities of the two men, but they keep them a secret, hoping that Dr. Soothem will accept the first William Thompson as a son-in-law. Learning that the second William Thompson is not his patient, Dr. Soothem assumes that the man is an imposter, and the first William Thompson asks for the right to punish the man assuming his identity. Insisting that they duel, the first William Thompson terrifies the second into confessing that he has deserted Miss Dormer. The second William Thompson also "resigns all pretensions" (30) to Julia and promises to become engaged to Miss Dormer. In the final scene, Dr. Soothem agrees that Julia may marry the first William Thompson. After seeing him properly humbled, Miss Dormer accepts the second William Thompson.

Most of the comic situations result from confusion over the two William Thompsons and the two Julias (Miss Dormer's first name is also Julia). The popularity of the play may result from Boaden's deft handling of a complex plot, which functions to undermine the control that Dr. Soothem assumes he has over his daughter's marriage. Julia, Miss Dormer, and the first William Thompson take actions that help ensure that they can marry the mate of their own choosing.

TEXT: Readex Microprint of J. Cumberland's British Theatre series, vol. 23, n.d.

WILLIAMS, Anna (1706–1783). Perhaps best known as the blind woman who lived with Dr. Johnson, Williams deserves to be known for her interest in scientific experiments and for her written work. She is credited with one drama *The Uninhabited Island*, a version of P. Metastasio, *L'isola disabitata*, which is printed in her *Miscellanies in Prose and Verse* (London: T. Davies, 1766). The play is also attributed to John Hoole, who published a translation of Metastasio, 2 vols., 1767. Boswell does not mention the play in the *Life*. [*BD*, DBAWW, DNB, FCLE, Lonsdale]

WILMOT, Barbarina Ogle. See **DACRE**, Brand, Lady.

WILSON, Ann (fl. 1783). The author of a poetic drama, titled *Jephthah's Daughter*, printed in 1783 by W. Flexney. According to Lonsdale, this is not the Anne Wilson who published the poem *Teisa* (Newcastle, 1778). *BD* says the dramatic poem is a "strange heterogeneous piece, neither prose nor verse." [*BD*, Lonsdale]

WINCHILSEA, Countess of. See **FINCH**, Ann Kingsmill.

The Wise Man of the East, Elizabeth Inchbald. This five-act drama, adapted from *Das Schreibepult; oder, Das Gefahren der Jugend* by Kotzebue, was first produced at CG on 30 November 1799 and published the same year by G. G. and J. Robinson. It was acted fourteen times its first season. Inchbald included the play in her *Modern Theatre* (1811).

Claransforth, whose father has recently died in a fire, meets Ava Thoanoa, an Indian friend of his father's, who appears to have psychic powers. Mr. Metland, who has lost £12,000 in the fire, has two children—Ensign Metland (in the army) and Ellen (employed by Lady Mary Diamond). The two children visit their mother and give her half of their wages, unknown to their proud father. Rachel Starch wants her daughter Ruth to marry Claransforth, even though he is not of their Quaker faith. Ruth receives a letter from Ensign Metland, who wants to ask for her hand. When Claransforth goes to Lady Mary's, he protests his love for Ellen, but she points out their age difference (he's 34 and she's 17). Lady Mary then explains to Ellen that she is bait for Lady Mary's crooked pharo tables. Ellen decides to tell this to Claransforth. Meanwhile, the elder Metland receives a letter telling him that his creditors are planning to foreclose. When lawyer Lawley arrives, they find, in the desk given him as a legacy by Claransforth, Sr., his £12,000 in a secret drawer. Lady Mary reports that Ellen is missing. At Ava Thoanoa's house, Claransforth asks the sage's help in finding Ellen. The elder Metland goes to Claransforth's to return the £12,000 from the desk, but the son tells him it was Metland's all along. Also in the desk is a letter from Claransforth, Sr., who recommends Ellen to be his son's wife. Ava Thoanoa arrives with information that Ellen is safe. Claransforth goes with the sage to his lodgings. The "ghost" of Claransforth, Sr., (he has, in fact, escaped the fire and has acted the part of Ava Thoanoa) unites Claransforth with Ellen, and Ensign Metland with Ruth, with her consent and the approval of her parents.

The testing of the morals of Claransforth, Jr., is central to the action of the play, which involves three sets of parents and children. Claransforth's father in the disguise of an Indian acts the principal tester. Economics and class also play their roles: creditors always distress the poor, and the loss of money is a severe trial to the Metlands; although poor, they are moral, upright, and proud. The rich, on the other hand, are immoral, licentious gamblers. The adult Quakers are stock figures of fun in their rigidity. Timothy Starch says, for instance, "I seldom cry—and as seldom laugh. I keep my passions cool and steady, as I keep my countenance." Their daughter, Ruth, seems not to take after her parents. Inchbald's alterations from Kotzebue include the addition of the Quaker family, setting the play in London, and introducing the English class system and the intended seduction of Ellen.

MANUSCRIPT: Larpent 1271. Readex Microprint of manuscript.

TEXT: Readex Microprint of the 1799 edition.

FACSIMILE EDITION: E-CED, with introduction by Paula R. Backscheider (NY: Garland, 1980).

WISEMAN, Jane, later Holt (fl. 1701–1717). The little we know about this author of one blank-verse tragedy, *Antiochus the Great; or, The Fatal Relapse* (performed at LIF in November 1701, the quarto edition dated 1702), comes from Giles Jacob's *Poetical Registrar* (1719). She was a servant in the family of Mr. William Wright, Recorder of Oxford, and she had access to his library, "where, having a pretty deal of leisure Time, which she spent in Reading Novels and Plays, she began a Play, and finished it after she came to London." After Jane Wiseman's play was produced, "She married a young Vintner, whose Name was Holt; and with the Profits arising from her Play, they set up a Tavern in Westminster." From Abel Boyer's *Letters of Wit, Politicks and Morality* (1701), we know that she was a friend of Susanna Carroll, later Centlivre, and associated with a literary group, including other playwrights—notably George Farquhar and William Burnaby. In 1717, Wiseman published *A Fairy Tale . . . With Other Poems*, but she apparently wrote no other dramas. [*BD*, Cotton, DBAWW, FCLE, Hume, Kendall, Lonsdale, Pearson]

Witchcraft, Joanna Baillie. This five-act tragedy was published in the third volume of her *Dramas*, published by Longman, et al. in 1836. Like her earlier *Plays on the Passions*, *Witchcraft* is largely unified by Baillie's preoccupation with a single passion: jealousy.

Lady Dungarren's daughter Jessie is ill and the spirits of Grizeld Bane and Mary Macmurren are believed to visit her bedside. In order to dispel the effect that these "witches" have on the girl, Rutherford, the local minister, will pray at her bedside. On his way to see her, Rutherford comes upon Violet Murrey, the daughter of Lady Dungarren's closest girlfriend, meeting with her father, a man who is believed to be a murderer and dead. The plot is further complicated because Annabella, who is in love with Lady Dungarren's son, uses the community's fear of witchcraft to punish Violet, who has gained Dungarren's attention. Annabella tricks Bawldy, the herdboy of Dungarren, into stealing one of Violet's dresses to use as evidence against her. Dungarren himself begins to distrust Violet's loyalty when he sees her with another man (in fact, her father); nevertheless, he assists her when she is accused of witchcraft. Since she has promised her father to tell no one that he is still alive, Violet is unable to defend herself against any of these charges. Dungarren tries to help Violet escape the prison through a secret passage, but they are apprehended. Just before she is to be burned at the stake, Murrey suddenly appears to save his daughter. Soon after this, Bawldy explains how Annabella plotted against Violet, and Annabella is strangled by Grizeld. Violet pleads for her father, insisting that he is innocent. As Murrey is being led away, Fatheringham returns, proving the father's innocence and revealing that Grizeld has deluded herself into believing she is a witch.

As indicated, the end of the play is riddled with coincidences and implausibilities. In addition to the men who arrive at the last minute to save Violet and her father, the officers who arrive with Fatheringham also bring a decree from the King outlawing the punishment of witches. (Fatheringham, we learn, has been delayed because his ship was captured by pirates.) Both leading women in the play function as stereotypes: Violet is long-suffering and good, willing to burn at the stake before she breaks her promise to her father; and Annabella is capable of any kind of cruelty to revenge the woman favored by Dungarren. Unlike criticisms made of paternal figures in other plays by Baillie, there is no indication that Murrey was unwise when he forced his daughter to promise she would reveal to no one that he was still alive.

TEXT: Readex Microprint of *Dramas* (1836) 3: 1–164.

The Witlings, Fanny Burney. After the success of *Evelina*, Burney was encouraged by Mrs. Thrale and other friends to write a play and began work on this, her first comedy. When her father and his friend Mr. Crisp read the play in manuscript in 1779, they advised her to drop her plans for seeing it produced.

The comedy has five acts with one scene each. In the theatre conventions of the day, the heroine suddenly loses her fortune and the man she loves. The body of the play gives the heroine an opportunity to regain her man. In the course of events, Burney satirizes false learning, ignorance, and pretentiousness. Learned ladies come in for a large share of Burney's satiric attack: Lady Smatter (the Mrs. Malaprop of the piece) has formed a "club," the members of which have little understanding and no judgment. Intellectual affectation and vacuity are everywhere to be found in these superficially learned characters. Finally, Lady Smatter is forced to give her blessing to the parted lovers on the threat of being the subject of public lampoons and bawdy ballads.

Margaret Doody devotes an entire chapter to the play and to the circumstances of its censorship by her father and Mr. Crisp. She describes in detail Burney's very original contributions in the opening scene at a milliner's shop, the forgetfulness of most of the characters, and the creation of comic effects through frustration, incompleteness, and anticlimax (66–98).

MANUSCRIPT: New York Public Library, Berg Collection.

MODERN EDITIONS: Ed. Clayton J. Delery (East Lansing, MI: Colleagues, 1993); *The Meridian Anthology of Restoration and Eighteenth-Century Plays by Women*, ed. Katharine M. Rogers (NY: Penguin-Meridian, 1994): 290–406.

Wits Cabal, Margaret Lucas Cavendish, Duchess of Newcastle. A drama in two parts, printed in her *Playes*, published in 1662 by John Martyn, James Allestry, and Tho. Dicas. The play was not staged.

Divided into two parts, the action continues from the first to the second part. A core of unmarried, young women constitute the wits cabal (the term, as used in this play, refers to a private circle practicing and promoting wit). Each young woman has a slightly different focus on wit, suggested by their names—Ambition, Bon Esprit, Superbe, Faction, Pleasure, and Portrait. Grave Temperance and Mother Matron, two older women, sometimes enter the young women's discussions, providing sage advice. Pleasure's five waiting maids (Wanton, Idle, Ease, Excess, and Surfet), as well as Superbe's maid Flattery, enlarge the group when invited to contribute. At the women's invitation, several single men enter into their deliberations, talk with the women singly, or speak to each other in pairs. Again their names suggest their points of view: Heroick, Tranquillitous Peace, Inquisitive, Satyrical, Vain-glorious, Censure, Sensuality, Busie, and Frisk. While the use of verbal repartee is central to the play, marriage develops as a major subject for discussion. At one time or another, most of the women express what they expect in a mate. Ambition, for instance, wants a man who has achievements, while she herself desires fame. It is perhaps no surprise that she decides on Heroick. Bon Esprit wages verbal war with Satyrical, defeats him in the battle of wits, and finds his ability with language makes him the man she wants to marry. Of the older women, Grave Temperance refuses to marry, whereas Matron pursues Frisk despite the difference in their ages. The wits cabal discusses many elevated topics, such as the soul, true love, beauty vs. wit, grace, and poetry. In the end most women select their appropriate mate, or decide not to marry (Ease).

Much of the play has to do with language and how it is used. The ability to use language wittily seems more important than beauty, which most of the women feel is transient. In this play, more than her others, Cavendish employs classical mythology and lore with several characters referring to ancient tales. Most important, however, the wits cabal provides an educational setting where the women may air their different views and learn from each other. Pearson points out that more than half of the scenes involve only the women and their concerns (269).

TEXTS: Wing N868. EEB Reel 502: 11. Readex Microprint.

Wives as They Were, and Maids as They Are, Elizabeth Inchbald. First produced at CG on 4 March 1797, this five-act comedy enjoyed a run of twenty-four performances its first season. Originally titled *The Primitive Wife and Modern Maid*, it was published by G. G. and J. Robinson under its altered title in 1797. CG revived this popular comedy the following year.

Many years before the play opens, Sir William Dorrillon has gone to India to make his fortune, leaving his daughter Maria in England to be raised by Mr. Norberry and his sister. In the opening scene, Dorrillon has returned to London, and he has convinced Norberry to introduce him to his daughter under the assumed name of Mr. Mandred. He finds Maria a frivolous slave of fashion and one who cares little for her elders and their opinions. Moreover, Maria and her friend Lady Mary Raffle have gotten in debt by excessive gambling. Even though Maria tries to be friends with Mandred, his rigid, old-fashioned ways and obsolete attitudes make it difficult. Two suitors, Mr. Bronzely and Sir George Evelyn, compete for Maria's hand, but she acts the coquette and appears to care little for either. Her gambling debts, however, cause real concerns. When her creditors press for payment, Maria asks for Mandred's protection, only to have him turn her over to the bailiffs. Mandred finally bails out Maria without conditions, though he hopes she will avoid her "former follies and extravagances" (82); she also learns Mandred is actually her father, who accepts Evelyn as a son-in-law.

In a second plot, Norberry invites Lord and Lady Priory to stay with him since they have just come from the country, where they are in bed by ten and arise in the morning at five. Married eleven years, Lord Priory expects his young wife to be obedient, though he's aware "modern wives do as they like" (5). At a concert in Norberry's house, Bronzely, thinking he has found Maria in an unlit gallery, kisses instead Lady Priory. Though she cannot identify her assailant, she has cut a piece out of his coat.

Bronzely changes coats with Mandred, who is found with the offending coat and accused of affronting Lady Priory. Early the next morning, Bronzely goes to her to apologize for Mandred's conduct. When she meets Bronzely later that day with Lord Priory's permission, Lady Priory is deceived by Bronzely and driven to his house outside London, where she shames him into returning her to Lord Priory.

Despite the inclusion of several interesting characters, the play seems contrived. While the question of believability might not arise in the theatre, a reading of the play exposes the formulations invented for the purpose of contrasting an obedient wife with superficial maids. Lady Priory knows herself and deftly fends off Bronzely; however, Lord Priory distrusts appearances and doesn't appear to deserve her. Both plots use testing to validate the true feelings of various characters. This theme is most obvious in Dorrillon's acting as Mandred so he may discover Maria's character, but it also appears in Bronzely's attempt to elope with Lady Priory. By rejecting him, she passes the test admirably, whereas Lord Priory, who shows no confidence in his wife of eleven years, fails utterly.

MANUSCRIPT: Larpent 1155.

TEXT: Readex Microprint.

FACSIMILE EDITION: E-CED, with introduction by Paula R. Backscheider (NY: Garland, 1980).

The Woman Hater, Fanny Burney. This satiric comedy, written in 1800 or 1801, was neither printed nor produced. The genesis of the play has been traced by both Adelstein and Doody to Burney's earlier suppressed comedy *The Witlings*.

The title character, Sir Roderick, turns misogynist after he has been jilted many years before by a Miss Wilmot, who becomes Lady Smatter. When Sir Roderick's sister Elenora married Wilmot, the brother of Lady Smatter, Sir Roderick disowns her. Elenora later separates from Wilmot, and he goes to the West Indies. In a related situation, Sir Roderick, now a wealthy, old bachelor, wants his heir Jack Waverley to give up women and remain single. Although his uncle spends his time railing at women, Jack cannot stay away from them. When Wilmot and his daughter Joyce Wilmot arrive back in England, he discovers his wife was not unfaithful as he thought. After the Wilmots meet by chance, he learns that Sophia Wilmot is actually their daughter, and the dutiful child he has raised, Joyce Wilmot, was in fact born to their nurse and a journeyman shoemaker. When we see Joyce with Wilmot, she is quiet and well behaved, but once he is gone she is impudent and talkative. Discovering her real parentage, she is delighted to do as she pleases. Waverley, meanwhile, realizes how foolish his interest in Lady Smatter (and a jointure) is, and he returns to his first love Sophia Wilmot. The play concludes with several reversals and revelations, and long separated characters are reunited: the Wilmots reconcile, and even Sir Roderick and Lady Smatter get together.

Burney's directs her satire on the characters: Sir Roderick the stereotypical misogynist and Lady Smatter the female pedant. While Burney has been said to satirize the ignorance of Joyce Wilmot, Joyce is, according to Doody, "the most appealing character in the play, [because she] is hearty and life affirming. . . . The unmasking of Joyce as the false daughter is her way to freedom. . . .*The Woman Hater* exhibits a rebellious desire to cast off the trammels of the father-daughter relationship . . . for the good of both father and daughter" (305, 307–08). In addition, Doody believes this play, like Burney's other late comedies, examines injustice, separation, and reactions that are inadequate or inappropriate. It should be noted that the confused identity of many of the characters and the misunderstanding of women result largely from the men's stereotyping of them.

MANUSCRIPT: New York Public Library, Berg Collection.

The Woman Turn'd Bully, attributed to Aphra Behn. Produced at DG in March 1675, this five-act comedy may have been written by Behn, according to Summers (although he does not print the play). Cotton mentions the possible attribution, and Woodcock thinks Behn may have "collaborated" in the play. Link and Hargraves reject the ascription to Behn, and Pearson finds it "doubtful" that

Behn is the author. Hume and J. H. Smith mention only that the play's authorship is anonymous, whereas Goreau and Gewirtz ignore the play altogether. The play, licensed by Roger L'Estrange on 5 July 1675, was published by T. Dring, who also published Behn's *The Amorous Prince* (1671) and *The Dutch Lover* (1673).

Betty Goodfield flees to London from Derbyshire to avoid a forced marriage to Sir Alexander Simple, a country neighbor. Passing herself off as "Sir Thomas Whimsey" by dressing in men's clothes, Betty impersonates a town gallant, and "discourses out of Plays" (Dryden's *An Evening's Love* and Etherege's *The Comical Revenge*, according to J. H. Smith). Meanwhile, her brother Ned Goodfield comes to London from Cambridge to visit his friend Jack Truman at the Temple. Truman wants to introduce Goodfield to Lucia, lawyer Docket's niece and ward. Goodfield in turn wants Truman to meet his sister, Betty. As Truman and Goodfield talk with Lucia, Betty, unknown to them and playing the gallant, challenges both Goodfield and Truman to a duel. The next morning, when she faces Goodfield, Betty identifies Ned and he recognizes her. Ned introduces Betty to Truman, and while she loves him at first sight, Betty plans to test Truman's devotion. Matters become more complicated when Mrs. Goodfield comes to town to have papers for Betty's marriage drawn up by lawyer Docket. In a series of clever, if not always believable, maneuvers, the young people circumvent their elders and marry: Truman passes Betty's trials, and Lucia accepts Ned. Also, Truman recovers his family's lands from Docket, who is duped into marrying Mrs. Loveal, Mrs. Goodfield's woman.

Hume praises the "vivid characters, lively intrigue, and repartee [that] make the piece enjoyable" (303). Pearson observes the significance of cross-dressing in this and a number of other plays by Behn. Dressed as a male, Betty Goodfield is free of the usual restraints placed on women. Even after she is recognized as a woman, she sets up various trials for Truman and proves him a suitable match. Her unconventional actions may emanate from having an unorthodox mother. Mrs. Goodfield likes her Derbyshire ale: when she comes to London, she outdrinks lawyer Docket. In her carousing, she also smokes a pipe. If the comedy is by Behn, Mrs. Goodfield may be a prototype for the Widow Ranter, who appears in Behn's play by that name. The Widow Ranter is similarly idiosyncratic in her actions and conduct.

TEXTS: Wing W3322. EEB Reel 971: 12. Readex Microprint.

The Wonder: A Woman Keeps a Secret, Susanna Centlivre. This five-act comedy has some sources in Ravenscroft's *The Wrangling Lovers* (1677), but it is largely original with Centlivre. First produced at DL on 27 April 1714, the comedy was published the same year by E. Curll with a dedication to the Duke of Cambridge, Prince George Augustus (later George I). Robert Wilks and Anne Oldfield played Don Felix and Violante in the original production, and they are praised by Centlivre in her preface. In its opening season the play ran for six nights, but in the Garrick era its popularity blossomed as Garrick himself acted Don Felix, Maria Macklin was cast as Violante, and Kitty Clive as Flora. Both Clive and Garrick chose the play for their final performances.

Set in Lisbon (also the scene of *Marplot*), the play treats opposing ideas of freedom and confinement, jealously and trust, as well as varying concepts of honor. Before the events of the play, Felix has fought a duel and is a fugitive. Frederick, a Lisbon merchant, opens the play by calling on Lopez (Felix's father) for news about his son. Although he has no tidings, Lopez plans for his daughter, Isabella, to marry an old wealthy suitor. Frederick urges Lopez not to force Isabella into a mismatched union. After learning Felix plans to be at Frederick's house that night, Frederick meets Colonel Britton, an old friend who is returning to England, and he offers to let the Colonel, and his Scottish servant Gibby, lodge with him. When she hears from her father that her husband-to-be has arrived, Isabella pleads with him not to force her to marry, but he locks her in her room. She leaps out of the window into the arms of the Colonel, who carries her to the nearest house, belonging to Don Pedro, whose daughter Violante is awaiting her lover Felix. (Violante's father insists that she enter a convent, so he may claim her fortune.) When she and her maid, Flora, find the Colonel with Isabella in his arms, Violante recognizes Isabella, Felix's sister, and Isabella explains how she is being forced to marry against her will. Isabella then begs Violante to conceal her for two or three days—the secret of the subtitle. When she hears Felix will visit Violante, Isabella asks to hide from him because "he'll think his Honour blemish'd by my Disobedience" (19). After Isabella enters a closet, Felix greets Violante, but following a brief reunion Colonel Britton knocks at the window. Felix starts through the closet to find out who it is, but Violante stops him, saying her father is there asleep. Violante then opens the window and tells the Colonel to come the next day. While Felix is upset about having secrets kept from him, Violante tells him he should allow a woman to keep a secret by rule of honor. He leaves angrily when she won't divulge the secret.

Discovering his daughter has fled, Lopez arranges to have the Alguazil (a police unit) search Frederick's house, where Colonel Britton has just received a letter from Isabella asking him to meet her on the Terriero de Passa at five in the morning. Calling his servant Lissardo (just then trifling with Flora), Felix tells him that he plans to leave Lisbon forever. On hearing his father's arrival, Felix steps into the next room. As Lopez enters insisting the Alguazil search for Isabella, Felix steps out and stops them. The Alguazil want the reward for the capture of Felix, but Lopez offers a bond and gives them money to drink his health. Violante arrives in time to see a woman (Flora) flee from the house, and she declares a truce with Felix: if he will ask no more about the man at the window, she'll forgive the woman's presence.

At the Terriero de Passa, Colonel Britton meets the veiled Isabella who won't unmask but is ready to marry him: "Show yourself a Man of Honour, and you shall find me a Woman of Honour" (42). After she has gone, Britton sends Gibby to follow her, but he gets confused, finds Violante, follows her home, and learns her name. Inside, Isabella asks Violante to speak to Colonel Britton, and Violante, with some misgivings, agrees, and the Colonel asks to meet Isabella at the Terriero that evening at six. When Flora reports that Felix is coming, Violante tells the Colonel to step into her bed chamber. After his arrival, Felix appears to be reconciled with Violante when Flora warns them that her father is on his way. Just as Felix starts to go into her bed chamber, Violante stops him, but not before he has seen a man. Flora claps a riding hood on Felix, telling him not to say a word. When Violante's father enters, Flora introduces the disguised Felix as her mother, making excuses for her "mother's" sight and hearing before she takes Felix out. Pedro reminds Violante that she is to go to the convent next week and says he plans to go to the country for several days. After he leaves, Flora takes the Colonel out, unseen by Violante, who is frightened by Felix's swift return to search the bed chamber. As Felix goes in, Flora comes back and tells Violante that the Colonel has gone. When Felix finds he has been a jealous fool, he asks if Violante will marry him, but she puts it off until tomorrow. Having heard all, Isabella prepares to meet the Colonel at the Terriero.

Felix returns to Frederick's where he hears the Colonel tell of his escapade, and Frederick prevents violence between the two. At Violante's, Flora announces Felix has arrived and Isabella jumps into the closet. In a jealous rage, Felix reports the Colonel's story only to have Pedro return because his chariot broke down. Felix runs to the closet, but Isabella locks it from within. Felix insists on a discovery, and as he tries the closet door, Pedro enters. Violante tells her father a woman asked for her protection when pursued by this man, so she locked the woman in her closet. While Felix acts drunk, Pedro demands the closet be opened and Isabella in a veil crosses the stage, going to her assignation with the Colonel. In an aside Violante tells Felix to meet her at the Terriero where all mistakes will be rectified, and they leave separately. Lopez blunders in, searching for his daughter, but a servant reports all three (Isabella, Violante, and Felix) have gone to the Terriero. As both fathers go in pursuit of their children, Gibby comes to the house and an argument ensues. Before a fight breaks out, the newlyweds arrive. After both fathers learn their children are married, they leave angrily. Frederick enters and wishes the couples joy. Following a dance, Felix closes the comedy with praise of Violante.

The intricate plot shows *The Wonder* to be "an actor's play," as Frushell declares (xlix). Centlivre's clever handling of details in this intrigue comedy allows the actors to make the most of the disguises, mistakes, and confusion in visual stage business. The importance of timing in performance demands exacting choreography in getting the players in and out of doors on cue. The use of doors and windows as a means of ingress and egress sets up a metaphorical underpinning for the play. Locked doors keep unwanted people out, but the same locked doors keep others (usually women) inside, as a means of confinement, and also as a way to keep something or someone from being discovered. Keeping a secret may be a way to control information and maintain its safety. In comparison, open doors suggest freedom and liberty. Pearson points out the many locked rooms and gates, "Locks and Bars," a "Padlock," "Fetter" of duty, as well as confinement in a closet, chest, or nunnery (227). These contrast with Liberty, especially in one of Felix's concluding remarks that "every Man's Happiness consists in chusing for himself" (79). In the play, Pearson notes, "true love is a potent force for liberty, corrupt love is another form of imprisonment" (227). That Violante jeopardizes her relationship with Felix to assist Isabella dominates the action, and her steadfastness of purpose to her friend continues throughout the play. Interweaving the two plots together, Centlivre has herself created a wonder of contrasting themes and interlocking ideas that make the comedy one of the finest of the eighteenth century.

TEXTS: Readex Microprint of Bell's 1797 edition. TEC Reel 589: 20.

MODERN EDITION: *The Female Wits*, ed. Fidelis Morgan (London: Virago, 1981): 329–387.

FACSIMILE EDITION: E-CED, with introduction by R. C. Frushell (NY: Garland, 1982).

The World as It Goes; or, A Party at Montpelier, Hannah Cowley. This five-act comedy was produced only once under this title at CG on 24 February 1781. It was altered to *Second Thoughts Are Best* and mounted at CG on 24 March 1781, but it has never been printed.

MANUSCRIPT: Larpent 548.

-X-

Xarifa, Lady Dacre, earlier Barbarina Ogle Wilmot. This five-act tragedy was published in volume two of her collection *Dramas, Translations, and Occasional Poems* (John Murray, 1821). The play was not performed.

Set in Granada and the Spanish camps under the city walls. Albin Homad arrives with news for Xarifa that her father Moraizel, the leader of the Aben-Zurrah troops, has been captured by Don Juan, a Spanish general. Xarifa then goes to the King of Granada, Abdallah, asking for permission to meet with Don Juan. After meeting with Xarifa and Homad, Don Juan frees Moraizel who agrees he will not lead Granada's troops against the Moors. When they return to Granada, Abdallah expresses an interest in Xarifa, whom he forces to live in his palace until Homad (her betrothed) can distinguish himself by deeds of arms. Leading the Aben-Zurrah knights as they drive back the Spanish, Homad is overwhelmed by Don Juan, who disarms Homad but allows him to go free so that he can rescue Xarifa. Hearing that Homad is now Abdallah's prisoner, Xarifa agrees to marry the King if he will let Homad live. Angry that an Aben-Zurrah woman has become Queen, Alhamut and Ali make it appear as if Xarifa is plotting with Homad. Convinced that she has been disloyal, Abdallah announces that Xarifa will be executed unless her honor is successfully defended by a knight. Accepting the gauntlet, the disguised Don Juan and Homad succeed, forcing Alhamut to retract his accusation against the Queen and declare her innocent. After the King agrees to reclaim her as his wife, Xarifa stabs herself, asking that Don Juan prevent Homad from committing suicide. Xarifa dies, after declaring that she has freed herself from the King and will be reunited with Homad in Heaven.

While Don Juan's kind treatment of Homad might be difficult to understand, Lady Dacre foreshadows the fact that the young man is actually Don Juan's son. (Don Juan looks at Homad, a stranger, and instantly suspects his lineage. Only much later do father and son discover that they are wearing identical necklaces, establishing who Homad's mother was.) Even less easy to believe, perhaps, is Don Juan's ability to come to Granada and publicly defend the Queen's virtue. (Although Don Juan is supposedly disguised, Xarifa recognizes who he is.) Xarifa herself is a consistently strong protagonist, who initiates much of the action: she goes into enemy camp to rescue her father, she decides to marry the King to save Homad's life, and she commits suicide rather than remain married to Abdallah. It is hinted that Xarifa has converted to Christianity, abandoning her Muslim beliefs, but this play—unlike Lady Dacre's *Pedrarias*—is not primarily concerned with the superiority of Christianity over other more "primitive" religions.

TEXT: Readex Microprint. 2: 115–218.

-Y-

YEARSLEY, Ann Cromartie (1752–1806). With almost no formal education, Ann was married to John Yearsley; they had six children, and Ann sold milk from door to door. With the family in near poverty, Ann was assisted by Hannah More in her poetry and in gaining subscribers for Ann's *Poems on Several Occasions*, 1784 (Lonsdale gives June 1785 as the publication date). Now known as the "Bristol Milkmaid," Ann continued to write poetry, but she rejected More's acting as a trustee over her earnings, and the two became bitter enemies. Ann later turned her hand to drama: her first effort, *Earl Goodwin*, a historical tragedy, was produced at Bristol and Bath in 1789 and published in 1791. *BD* reports that two other plays, *The Ode Rejected*, a comedy, and *The Petticoat Government*, a farce, were advertised but never printed (2: 182). In 1793, Ann had opened a circulating library at Bristol Hot Wells, and later she published an historical novel, *The Royal Captive*, 1795. Her last collection of verse, *The Rural Lyre*, appeared in 1796. Her own failing health and deaths in the family caused her in 1803 to retire to Melksham, Wiltshire, where she died in 1806. [*BD*, BNA, DBAWW, DNB, EBWW, FCLE, Lonsdale, OCEL]

YORKE, Elizabeth Lindsay, Countess of Hardwick (1763–1858). Author of a dramatic entertainment, Yorke prepared the piece to be acted by adults for children. *The Court of Oberon; or, The Three Wishes* was privately produced at Wimpole Hall, near Cambridge, "about the year 1800." From 1801 to 1806, Count Hardwicke was Lord Lieutenant of Ireland, where she must have accompanied him. It was only in May 1831 that the play was printed (at the Shakespeare Press by W. Nicol) for "the aid of the distressed Irish, . . . whom the writer will ever remember with affectionate regard." T. H. Lacy provided an acting edition in 1854. [Inglis, Nicoll]

The Yorkshire Ghost, the Margravine of Anspach, formerly Baroness Elizabeth Berkeley Craven. This comedy, which was produced privately at Brandenburgh House on 21 July 1794, was apparently not printed. No manuscript of this play has been found.

The Young Couple, Jane Pope. This two-act comedy, adapted from Frances Sheridan's *The Discovery*, was produced at DL on Pope's benefit night, 21 April 1767. It was not repeated, nor was it printed. No manuscript of this play exists in the Larpent Collection. The title of this afterpiece was probably Pope's reference to the quarrelling young married pair,

Sir Harry and Lady Flutter, taken from a subplot in Frances Sheridan's full-length comedy.

The Young King; or, The Mistake, Aphra Behn. This tragicomedy, based on La Calprenède's *Cleopâtra* and Calderón's *La vida es sueño*, was probably produced at DG in September or October 1679 (Hume suggests March, based on references in the epilogue). The play was not printed until 1683, for D. Brown, T. Benskin, and H. Rhodes. The drama may be Behn's first excursion in attempting to write for the stage: she says she prepared an early draft in Surinam. Later, she could have altered the poetry to suit a drama in the heroic mode—written in couplets—for a production early in the 1670s. Clearly, revisions were made for the acting version almost ten years later, but vestiges of previous forms still exist. Link calls the play "an anachronism," belonging to duel-plot tragicomedies, more popular in the previous decade.

The pastoral opening of the play belies the turbulent action that will follow: Colonel Vallentio finds Urania, a Sythian woman, in a grove near the Dacian camp. Even though the two countries are at war, Vallentio agrees to arrange an interview with Princess Cleomena so Urania may request the freeing of her lover Amintas. Cleomena has come to the woods to find Clemanthis, whom she loves, though she does not know that he is in fact Thersander, the Sythian Prince in disguise. Cleomena agrees to Urania's suit. The scene shifts to "a Castle or Prison on the Sea," where Orsames, ignorant that he is Cleomena's brother and the Prince, learns philosophy from Geron, his elderly tutor. Because an oracle has said that he would be a bloody tyrant, Orsames has been confined all his life. His first meeting with someone other than his tutor occurs when Urania comes to find Amintas, who shields her from Orsames's violence. Amintas praises Urania's generosity and they leave. Meanwhile, Thersander admits to his page that he loves Cleomena, for "she scorns the little Customs of her Sex" (132), and when she comes to visit him, Thersander confesses his love. Even though he must keep his birth and name secret, Thersander declares he will set the crown of Sythia on her head. Honorius, Cleomena's uncle, appreciates the abilities of Clemanthis (Thersander) and offers him his fortune and his daughter, Olympia, in marriage. Thersander reels from the generosity, but he also perceives that it will mar his relationship with Cleomena. He's right; Cleomena is furious and threatens to stab him, but she cannot bring herself to murder the man she loves and banishes him. While war brews, Orsames is brought to Court where he's smitten with every woman he sees, even his mother, but he is so taken with Olympia that he puts the crown on her head. After he drinks some wine he falls asleep, and back in his cell Geron convinces Orsames it was all a dream. In the war, the Sythians with the help of Thersander defeat the Dacians. Still in love, Thersander returns to Cleomena disguised as Clemanthis. The Dacians draw names to see who will fight Thersander and the lot falls to Clemanthis. Since he cannot engage in single combat with himself, Thersander changes clothes with Amintas, and the two rig the fight. On his way to the battle, however, Amintas in Clemanthis's clothes is attacked by ruffians—hired by Artabazes—who sees Clemanthis as a rival. When Cleomena discovers the wounded knight, she dresses in Clemanthis's clothes and fights Thersander. Victorious against the "unknown" knight, Thersander, his father suggests, might marry Cleomena. Still thinking Thersander has killed Clemanthis, Cleomena goes to him disguised as a shepherd and stabs him. Severely wounded, Thersander urges his father to have the generosity to release her; he frees her—if she'll visit the wounded Prince. When she does, Cleomena discovers Clemanthis and Thersander are one and the same. The Dacian army, meanwhile, has set Orsames on the throne, and he arrives at Thersander's tent for the denouement. Amintas, with his wounds healed, has been married to Urania. Thersander will marry Cleomena, and Honorius gives Olympia to Orsames, who will rule the Dacians. The warring nations are now united: "The God of Love o'ercomes the God of War" (191).

The main plot, derived from La Calprenède's prose romance *Cleopâtra*, combines earlier pastoral elements with a later use of comic intrigue, whereas Behn's subplot originated in Calderón's *La Vida es Sueño* without the philosophical overtones of the Spanish dramatist. Notwithstanding that the two story lines come together in the final act, they appear as separate plots and have little reference to one another, though Loftis does find "a coherent relationship" (*The Spanish Plays of Neoclassical England* [New Haven: Yale UP, 1973] 137).

Hume classifies the play as a "romantic intrigue comedy," involving love, war, politics, and disguise (322). And disguise does play a key role: Cotton points out that both Thersander and Cleomena take the character of Clemanthis, promoting androgyny (168). Pearson labels Cleomena "an unconventional woman" and notes that the cross-dressing breaks down sexual stereotypes. The mental and physical agility of Cleomena moderates somewhat a fiery impetuosity. She insists on achieving her ends even if it means fighting with a man in single combat. Cleomena, dressed as an Amazon, is given command of the Dacian forces, while her uncle is only charged with "the Conduct of this hopeful Army" (139). It is curious that no punishment is given to Artabazes for setting ruffians on Amintas when he's dressed as Clemanthis. This, however, may promote the theme of generosity that frequently arises in the play, stressing the importance of forgiveness and unity.

TEXTS: Wing B1776; EEB Reel 121: 6 (1683). Wing B1777; EEB Reel 1518: 10 (1698). Readex Microprint of 1683 copy.

MODERN EDITION: *Works*, ed. Montague Summers (1915; NY: Phaeton, 1967) 2: 99–193.

Young Men and Old Women, Elizabeth Inchbald. Adapted from *Le Méchant* by J. B. L. Gresset (1747), this two-act farce was first produced at the Haymarket on 30 June 1792. It was performed six times as an afterpiece in its first season, but dropped after that. Originally titled *Lovers no Conjurors*, the farce was not printed during Inchbald's life.

Knaveston, in love with Fanny Prejudice, learns that his friend Sylvan is to marry her as part of an inheritance. To discourage Sylvan, he tells him that Fanny has many lovers and cannot be trusted; he then suggests that Sylvan act as a boorish fop in order to be rejected, but without losing the inheritance. Sylvan succeeds but, having fallen in love with Fanny, he tries to convince her that he is not a foolish coxcomb. Knaveston declares his passion but must hide as an old female fortuneteller, as does Sylvan (hence the title). In the end, Sir Samuel Prejudice, who always wanted to leave his property to a man who would love it as much as he does, gives his daughter's hand to Sylvan who had openly desired the legacy more than Fanny.

This farce relies on conventional elements such as violence (beating a dog), role playing (Sylvan acts a coxcomb), disguise and transvestism (the two young men as fortune tellers), and bodily noises (coughing whenever a certain character lies). It hardly explores, as Backscheider states in her introduction, "the dangers of deceit and impressions based on appearances" (xvi), but it does expose, wittingly or not, the low status of women at that time. Fanny makes it plain that she considers herself part of the marriage bargain as she tells her father: " I do not doubt that Mr. Sylvan will pay proper Respect to everything in your Possession and to me among the rest" (7). Her father echoes her even more crudely in the closing lines of the play as he admonishes Sylvan: "But remember you alter nothing—except my daughter—and you may alter her as soon as you please. For in Woman there is no Perfection, till they are made Wives and Mothers" (25).

Inchbald retained very little of Gresset's five-act comedy in verse. Her villain does not match Cléonte, who reminds one of Molière's sinister Tartuffe in his overtaking the household and in his ruthless schemes. Ariste, the virtuous and wise friend, is deleted in the adaptation. Florise, Géronte's (Sir Samuel's) sister, and Chloé (Fanny's mother) have been combined into the eccentric Mrs. Ambilogy (Sir Prejudice's sister). Infatuated with the young villain, she displays ridiculous actions because she still believes she can charm young men. Although she is forced into more lying by Sir Samuel's untractable mania for truth, Mrs. Ambilogy does not reach her full comical potential. Kinne calls Inchbald's work a "sad travesty of the Frenchman's excellent, though complex, comedy of character and manners" (226). The *European Magazine* describes the farce as "meager" and not worth comparing with Inchbald's earlier plays (22 [1792]: 64–65). The general disapproval must have contributed to Inchbald's decision not to print the farce.

MANUSCRIPT: Larpent 952. Readex Microprint of manuscript.

Manuscript transcribed in E-CED, with introduction by Paula R. Backscheider (NY: Garland, 1980).

The Younger Brother; or, The Amorous Jilt, Aphra Behn. This five-act comedy was posthumously produced at DL in February 1696 for three nights, with some additions and deletions (of dated Whig-Tory disputes in the second scene) by Charles Gildon. These deletions suggest that a draft of the play may date from as early as 1681–1683, though in *Oroonoko* (1688) Behn does mention a Colonel Martin who is celebrated in her "new comedy." J. Harris printed the play in 1696, the year of its production.

The younger brother of the title, George Marteen (alias Lejere), loves Mirtilla, the amorous jilt of the subtitle. While George is in France, his sister Olivia, dressed as a man, acts as a page to observe Mirtilla's activity. When George returns, however, Olivia must report that for financial reasons Mirtilla has married Sir Morgan Blunder, George's cousin. Olivia also says that Mirtilla has made advances toward her in her disguise as a male page. George decides to continue under the guise of Lejere so his older brother, Merlin, will not recognize him. Prince Frederick, George's friend, arrives to tell him he's infatuated with a woman named Mirtilla, and George resigns his former mistress to the Prince. Meanwhile, Merlin has turned rake and spends his time drinking with Morgan. When his father, Sir Rowland, learns this, he threatens to disown Merlin. Sir Rowland has determined his younger son George should marry the old but wealthy Lady Youthly, while he proposes to marry her granddaughter, Teresia. George is appalled at this proposal, but he's quite taken with Teresia. Sir Rowland orders Olivia to marry one Welborn, whom she has never seen. Olivia and Teresia vow to avoid these forced marriages. At a ball, George sees the Prince slip off with Mirtilla, and, as Lejere, George meets Welborn, who has fallen in love with a woman he encountered at the Mall. Olivia is, of course, the woman, as we learn when she spots him at the ball. Despondent over his loss of Mirtilla, George muses in the garden when Olivia tells him the house is on fire. George finds a ladder and saves the Prince and Mirtilla, who go to the Prince's rooms in Welborn's house. Here, George asks Olivia to pretend to be Mirtilla's lover so the Prince will realize the dissembling nature of Mirtilla's amorousness. But all does not go according to plan as Mirtilla hides Olivia beneath her train, allowing Olivia to slip out. Welborn invites Olivia, still in disguise, to stay: the joke turns on Olivia's taunting note to Welborn next morning proclaiming her real identity after they innocently sleep together. The same morning, George goes to Lady Youthly's house; because the old lady can't hear well, George feels free to woo Teresia, who admits a passion for him. To avoid being forced into unwanted marriages, they both agree to wed before their parents can stop them. George wants one more chance to show the Prince Mirtilla's treachery, and they observe Olivia becoming the object of Mirtilla's passion. The Prince leaps out ready to stab Olivia until she is discovered to be a woman, and George's sister. Mirtilla says she knew her page's sex all along. Welborn enters to find that Olivia, whom he's being forced to marry, is the woman he wants to marry. When Teresia arrives, George goes off with her to speak their vows. The newlyweds arrive at Lady Youthly's and ask Sir Rowland's indulgence, and he blesses George and Teresia, Welborn and Olivia. The Prince resigns Mirtilla to Morgan, who encourages visitation, and Lady Youthly takes consolation in her chaplin, Mr. Twang.

Behn reverts to the comedy of intrigue in her last play, but Link believes the play "suffers from too many plots and too little focus" (83). Interestingly enough, Behn returns to the theme of forced marriage, which began with her first play; *The Younger Brother* demonstrates a continuing and serious indictment of this practice. George, like Olivia and Teresia, must acquiesce to a marriage mandated by Sir Rowland. None of the three plans to accept this patriarchal demand without a spirited attempt to circumvent it. Olivia and Teresia see the urgency for haste, and they immediately put their plans into action. Their success shows wit and verve in achieving their ends. Another character who exploits her opportunities, though in a different way, is the unscrupulous Mirtilla, who manipulates every situation to her own advantage. Although Link describes Mirtilla as "heartless and amoral," he also points out how she "uses and exposes the hypocrisy of her society" (84). Mirtilla cynically declares to George that "all things in nature cheat, or else are cheated" (Summers text 370). Woodcock suggests that the play, through the character of Mirtilla, produces "a quality of violent moral disgust" (221). Although not one of her best plays, Behn's final comedy continues to treat significant social problems.

MANUSCRIPT: Bodleian Library, MS Rawlinson, poet. 195. O'Donnell notes that this manuscript "appears to be an eighteenth-century transcription from the printed copy" (162).

TEXTS: Wing B1778. EEB 203: 9. Readex Microprint.

MODERN EDITION: *Works*, ed. Montague Summers (1915; NY: Phaeton, 1967) 4: 311–399.

Youth's Glory, and Death's Banquet, Margaret Lucas Cavendish, Duchess of Newcastle. A drama in two parts printed in her *Playes*, published by John Martyn, James Allestry, and Tho. Dicas in 1662. The play was not produced.

The drama continues from the first to the second part, alternating within each part between the two plot lines. In the main plot, Lady Sansparelle has been encouraged by her father, Sir Thomas Love, to study the arts and sciences, and he acts as her tutor. While Lady Love objects to so much learning, Sansparelle herself enjoys the intellectual rigor and wishes to present her views in public lectures. Her father arranges occasions where Sansparelle may demonstrate her learning and oratorical abilities. Although the philosophers are dubious, Sansparelle overcomes their skepticism and speaks to even wider audiences until she becomes ill. Sir Thomas calls for physicians, but they report his daughter is dying. On her death bed, Sansparelle tries to comfort her father before she dies. Sir Thomas becomes distracted at his daughter's death and grows ill himself. When asked who is to preach his daughter's funeral sermon, Sir Thomas takes the task upon himself, delivers the sermon, and dies upon its conclusion. He is buried with his daughter. In a second plot, Lady Incontinent has left her husband for Lord de d'Amour only to find that his lordship is obliged to marry Lady Innocence. Incontinent remains as de d'Amour's mistress, but she is asked to raise Innocence and finish her education. In fact, Incontinent wants to corrupt the virtuous Innocence to rid herself of a rival. Meanwhile, de d'Amour falls for Innocence, causing Incontinent to make false allegations against the young woman. De d'Amour questions Innocence, who becomes melancholy at not being trusted, but she believes her guiltless nature will protect her. In desperation to denounce her rival, Incontinent arranges to have Innocence charged with theft of an expensive necklace, and she employs two maids to swear Innocent took the gold chain. A judge believes Innocence culpable, and she arranges her own funeral, repeating that she is guiltless of the crime before stabbing herself. De d'Amour finds the dying Innocence, who forgives her false witnesses. He grows so tormented that he blames himself for the false accusation. Questioning the maids, he discovers that Incontinent arranged the wicked act out of jealousy and malice. News is brought to de d'Amour that Incontinent has hanged herself and left a letter admitting her guilt. De d'Amour has Incontinent's body thrown in a field where it may be devoured by beasts.

The two plot lines in the play do not impinge on each other: characters in the Lady Sansparelle plot have no connections with the characters in the Lady Innocent plot. But thematically the plays juxtapose different concepts of two virtuous young women coming of age. Each plot could be read independently, but the movement from one plot to the other forces the reader to see the relationship between the two. Both Lady Sansparelle and Lady Innocence display virtue in their actions and speech, and neither will be corrupted by a male hierarchy. Sansparelle has no wish to marry, but Innocence has been pledged to de d'Amour by her father. Sir Thomas assists his daughter in every way he can, but Innocence has no supporters to assist her in the monstrous lies being told about her and is subject to the false accusations that follow, having only her own innocence to support her, but she believes that is enough. Sansparelle's several orations are mirrored in the events of Innocence's life and demise; even the funerals parallel each other. The alternating dramatic events in each plot give the play a unity that critics have neglected.

TEXTS: Wing N868. EEB Reel 502: 11. Readex Microprint.

-Z-

Zelmane; or, The Corinthian Queen, attributed to Mary Pix. This five-act tragedy was produced at LIF on 13 November 1704 and acted four more times that month. It was printed the following year by William Turner and sold by John Nutt. A contemporary attribution to Pix is in the *Diverting Post* of 28 October 1704 (*LS* 2: 80). The Epistle Dedicatory claims the play is based on an unfinished manuscript by "Mr. [William] M[ontfor]t." Elizabeth Barry performed the title role, and Anne Bracegirdle acted Antimora.

When Amphialus returns to Corinth victorious over the Arcadians, the chief minister Geronta reads the will of the deceased King Philemon, who has bequeathed his daughter Zelmane and the crown to Amphialus, provided it suits her. It does, but no one is aware that Amphialus has secretly wed the captive Arcadian Princess, Antimora, who is in a prison guarded by Pirotto. Zelmane will in time allow her half brother, Arbaces, to visit the Princess. Amphialus explains to his brother, Arcanes, that he loves Antimora, whereas Arcanes says he loves Zelmane. At the prison, Pirotto admits Amphialus, but listens to the conversation between the general and the captive: Amphialus wants their marriage kept secret, whereas Antimora thinks it should be published. Since he has army duties to perform, Amphialus leaves, while Pirotto gloats that he will have revenge on the general who replaced Pirotto's father. When Arbaces comes to woo Antimora, Pirotto says he has a scheme and stabs himself in the arm. While Pirotto goes to Zelmane, Arbaces is rebuffed by Antimora, and he starts to rape her when Arcanes enters and stabs Arbaces. Meanwhile, Pirotto has told Zelmane that Amphialus inflicted the wound; Geronta defends the general, but Pirotto details Amphialus's love of Antimora. In high dudgeon, Zelmane goes to the prison, where Pirotto stops the fight, but Arbaces is thought dead and carried off. Zelmane wants to put Antimora to death, but the captive Princess puts up a spirited defense. While Pirotto blames Arcanes, Geronta asks for evidence. Emotionally overwrought, Arcanes tells Zelmane of his love for her and returns a ring she gave him in childhood. Back in the palace, Amphialus has discovered that Zelmane has sentenced Antimora and Arcanes to death. The only way to save them is for Amphialus to wed Zelmane, and with many misgivings he marries her. Both Arcanes and Antimora say they would rather have died. Amphialus then tells the Queen of his previous marriage to Antimora: she pronounces Amphialus a traitor, banishes him from the kingdom, and will have the senate dissolve their marriage. In act five, the Corinthians are besieged by the Arcadians, and the Queen must call Amphialus back to defend them. Pirotto and Arbaces, who lived, are leading the Arcadian forces. But the Corinthian troops rally to Amphialus, and they defeat the Arcadians (Arbaces dies in battle and Pirotto has been fatally wounded). The Queen joins Amphialus and Antimora; she also will permit

Arcanes to woo her after her "wounded Heart" heals. Zelmane makes a final speech on the importance of virtue for rulers: Corinth can "Date her Glories from a Female Reign" (70).

Despite the involved plot, *Zelmane* has a number of strengths, not the least of which is the way the two women play off of each other. Zelmane proves to be an effective ruler unless her emotions overtake her, whereas the captive princess Antimora shows strong leadership qualities in her ability to argue forcefully. The play is placed in contexts of the theatrical milieu by two critics. Hume compares *Zelmane* to Joseph Trapp's popular *Alba-Mule* (performed January 1704) and finds *Zelmane* a better play, for it is "less turgid, and benefits from a better villain (Pirotto)" (475). Burling points out the strong affinities with John Banks's *The Unhappy Favourite* (1681), because each play revolves around a queen's conflict between political responsibility and love: "Both queens are forced for political reasons to dismiss their principal generals with whom they are in love. And both generals, while faithful servants to their queens are married to other women." While Banks's play ends tragically, Burling finds "the 'happy' ending of *Zelmane* . . . satisfying, if less theatrically interesting . . ." (*Curtain Calls* 319).

TEXT: Not in Readex Microprint. Not included in E. L. Steeves's facsimile edition of Pix's plays, E-CED (NY: Garland, 1982). The text is available at the Lilly Library, Indiana U, Bloomington, where we read the play.

APPENDICES

Abbreviations for Genres

B = Burlesque
BO = Ballad Opera
C = Comedy
CO = Comic Opera & burlettas
D = Drama, Serious
DD = Dramatic Dialogue
DN = Dramatic Form in a Novel
DSc = Dramatic Scenes
DwM = Drama with Music
E = Entertainment
F = Farce
HD = Historical Drama
HT = Historical Tragedy
Int = Interlude
Juv = Drama for Juveniles
Mas = Masque
MD = Melodrama
ME = Musical Entertainment
Med = Medley
O = Opera
P = Pantomime
Pre = Prelude
Pst = Pastoral
SdD = Sacred Drama
Sp = Spectacle
T = Tragedy
TC = Tragicomedy

Checklist of Women Playwrights in England, Ireland, and Scotland: 1660–1823

After each playwright's name, we give the birth and death dates (if known). For each play, we supply the genre of play, the title, production information, and publication dates (the place of publication is London, unless otherwise noted). Questionable authorship is indicated by the abbreviation "attrib" for "attributed to."

-A-

ABINGTON, Frances Barton (1737–1815)
C. attrib *Matrimony; or, The Sleep Walker* (produced CG, 27 Apr 1798). Not ptd. Abington's name does not appear on Larpent 1209.

T. *Almeda; or, The Neapolitan* (not acted). 1801.

ANSPACH, Lady Elizabeth Berkeley Craven, Margravine of (1750–1828)
C. *The Sleep Walker* (not acted). 1778. [microprint]
C. *The Miniature Picture* (produced Newbury Town Hall, 6 Apr 1780; DL, 24 May 1780). 1781. [microprint] Larpent 525.

CO. *The Silver Tankard; or, The Point at Portsmouth* (produced HAY, 18 July 1781). Songs, 1781. Larpent 564. [ms. microprint]

C. *The Statue Feast* (produced privately, Benham House, 1782). Lost.

Pst. *The Arcadian Pastoral* (produced privately, Burlington House, 1782). Lost.

C. *Le Philosophe Moderne* [in French] (not acted). 1790.

C. *The Yorkshire Ghost* (produced privately, Brandenburgh House, 1794). Lost.

T. attrib *The Robbers* (produced privately, Brandenburgh House, 1798). 1799.

O. *The Princess of Georgia* (produced privately, Brandenburgh House, 28 Feb 1798; CG, 19 Apr 1799). Songs, 1799. Larpent 1251. [ms. microprint]

Pst. *Love Rewarded* [in English and Italian] (not acted). 1799?

P. *Puss in Boots* (produced privately, Brandenburgh House, 1799). Lost.

D. *Nourjahad* (produced privately, Brandenburgh House, 1803). Lost.

F. *Nicodemus in Despair* (produced HAY, 31 Aug 1803). Lost. "Acted at Brandenburg House in 1803 as *Poor Tony*."

C. *Love in a Convent* (produced privately, Brandenburgh House, July 1805). Lost.

"ARIADNE" (fl. 1695–96)

C. *She Ventures and He Wins* (produced LIF, Sept 1695). 1696. [microprint] Wing S3054. EEB Reel 511: 43.

T. attrib *The Unnatural Mother* (produced LIF, fall? 1697). 1698. Wing U87. EEB Reel 1076: 21.

AUBERT, Penelope or Isabella (fl. 1715–20)

CO. misattrib *Harlequin Hydespes; or, The Greshamite* (produced LIF, 27 May 1719). [microprint] On the basis of the *Daily Courant* (24, 26, and 27 May 1719), Burling has identified the author as Mr. Aubert.

AUBIN, Penelope (1679–1731)

C. *The Merry Masqueraders; or, The Humourous Cuckold* (produced HAY, 9 Dec 1730). 1732. Printed as *The Humours of the Masqueraders*, 1733. Pirated as *The Masquerade; or, The Humourous Cuckold*, 1734 (Burling).

-B-

BAILLIE, Joanna (1762–1851)

A Series of Plays: [on] the Stronger Passions, 1798. [microprint]

T. *De Monfort* (produced DL, 29 Apr 1800 in an adaptation by J. P. Kemble). Larpent 1287.

T. *Count Basil*

C. *The Tryal*

A Series of Plays: [on] the Stronger Passions, 2nd series, 1802. [microprint of 2nd ed., 1802]

C. *The Election* (altered 1802 version and produced at Lyceum, 7 June 1817). Larpent 1971.

T. *Ethwald, in Two Parts*

C. *The Second Marriage*

Miscellaneous Plays, 1804. [microprint of 2nd ed., 1805]
T. *Constantine Paleologous; or, The Last of the Caesars* (produced Liverpool, Oct 1808). Larpent 1557.
T. *Rayner*
C. *The Country Inn*
T. *A Family Legend: A Tragedy* (produced Edinburgh, 29 Jan 1810). Edinburgh, 1810. Produced DL 29 Apr 1815. [microprint of 2nd ed., 1810; and of New York ed., 1810]
A Series of Plays: [on] the Stronger Passions, 3rd series, 1812. [microprint of 1821 ed.]
T. *Orra*
T. *The Dream*
C. *The Siege*
DwM. *The Beacon* (produced Edinburgh, 9 Feb 1815). Larpent 1846.
T. *Martyr*, 1826. [microprint]
D. *The Bride*, 1828. [microprint]
Dramas, in 3 vols., 1836. [microprint]
T. *Romiero*
C. *The Alienated Manor*
T. *Henriquez* (produced DL, 19 Mar 1836). CAM: BL Add. Ms. 42935 (13) ff. 274–314b.
T. *The Martyr*
T. *The Separation* (produced CG, 24 Feb 1836). CAM: BL Add. Ms. 42934 (18) ff. 770–816.
T. *The Stripling*
DwM. *The Phantom*
C. *Enthusiasm*
T. *Witchcraft*
T. *The Homicide*
D. *The Bride*
C. *The Match*

BALFOUR, Mary Devens (1755?–1820?)
D. *Kathleen O'Neil* (produced Belfast, 9 Feb 1814). 1814.

BARRELL, Maria Weylar (fl. 1770–90)
D. *The Captive* (not acted). 1790.

BARRYMORE, Mrs. W[illiam?] (fl. 1823)
E. *Evening Revels* (produced DL, 10 Nov 1823). Lost.

BEHN, Aphra (1640?–1689)
TC. *The Forced Marriage; or, The Jealous Bridegroom* (produced LIF, 20 Sept 1670). 1671. [microprint] Wing B1734. EEB Reel 446: 1.
C. *The Amorous Prince; or, The Curious Husband* (produced LIF, 24 Feb 1671). 1671. [microprint] Wing (1) B1717; Wing (2) B1718. EEB Reel 483: 3.
C. *The Dutch Lover* (produced DG, 6 Feb 1673). 1673. [microprint] Wing B1726. EEB Reel 445: 32.
C. attrib *The Woman Turned Bully* (produced DG, 24 Mar 1675). 1675. Wing W3322. EEB Reel 971: 12.
T. *Abdelazer; or, The Moor's Revenge* (produced DG, 3 July 1676). 1677. [microprint] Wing B1715. EEB Reel 167: 5.

C. *The Town Fopp; or, Sir Timothy Tawdry* (produced DG, Sept 1676). 1677. [microprint] Wing B1769. EEB Reel 446: 5.

C. attrib *The Debauchee; or, The Credulous Cuckold* (produced DG, Feb 1677). 1677. [microprint] Wing B4869. EEB Reel 484: 15.

C. *The Rover; or, The Banished Cavaliers* (produced DG, 24 Mar 1677). 1677. [microprint] Wing B1763. EEB Reel 446: 3.

C. attrib *The Counterfeit Bridegroom; or, The Defeated Widow* (produced DG, Sept 1677). 1677. [microprint] Wing M1983. EEB Reel 642: 123.

C. *Sir Patient Fancy* (produced DG, 17 Jan 1678). 1678. [microprint] Wing B1766. EEB Reel 203: 7.

C. *The Feign'd Curtizans; or, A Night's Intrigue* (produced DG, Mar 1679). 1679. [microprint] Wing (1) B1732; Wing (2) B1733. EEB Reel 203: 6.

TC. *The Young King; or, The Mistake* (produced DG, Sept 1679). 1683. [microprint] Wing B1776. EEB Reel 121: 6.

C. attrib *The Revenge; or, A Match in Newgate* (produced DG, June 1680). 1680. Wing B2084. EEB Reel 14: 4.

C. *The Second Part of The Rover* (produced DG, Jan 1681). 1681. [microprint] Wing B1765. EEB Reel 446: 4.

C. *The False Count; or, A New Way to Play an Old Game* (produced DG, Nov 1681). 1682. [microprint] Wing B1730. EEB Reel 203: 5.

C. *The Roundheads; or, The Good Old Cause* (produced DG, Dec 1681). 1682. [microprint] Wing B1761. EEB Reel 54: 6.

C. *Like Father, Like Son; or, The Mistaken Brothers* (produced DG, Mar 1682). Only prologue and epilogue ptd., Wing B1759. EEB Reel 1396: 13. Text lost.

C. *The City Heiress; or, Sir Timothy Treat-All* (produced DG, Apr 1682). 1682. [microprint] Wing B1719. EEB Reel 270: 7.

Pst. *The Wavering Nymph; or, Mad Amyntas* (produced 1683/84?). Two songs from the play ptd. in Behn's *Poems Upon Several Occasions*, 1684. Wing B1757. EEB Reel 525: 2. Text lost.

C. *The Luckey Chance; or, An Alderman's Bargain* (produced DL, Apr 1686). 1687. [microprint] Wing B1744. EEB Reel 1195: 10.

F. *The Emperor of the Moon* (produced DG, Mar 1687). 1687. [microprint] Wing B1727. EEB Reel 203: 4.

TC. *The Widow Ranter; or, The History of Bacon in Virginia* (produced DL, 20 Nov 1689). 1690. [microprint] Wing B1774. EEB Reel 1056: 13.

C. *The Younger Brother; or, The Amorous Jilt* (produced DL, Feb 1696). 1696. [microprint] Wing B1778. EEB 203: 9. MS: Bodleian Library MS Rawlinson, poet. 195.

BERRY, Mary (1763–1852)

C. *The Fashionable Friends* (produced DL, 22 Apr 1802). 1802. [1500–1800: microprint; 1800–1900 microprint of 3rd ed., 1802] Larpent 1344.

BOADEN, Caroline (fl. 1821–39)

C. *Quite Correct* (produced HAY, 29 July 1825). Not ptd. CAM: BL Add. Ms. 42874 (15) ff. 651–690b.

T. *Fatality* (produced HAY, 1 Sept 1829). 1829. CAM: BL Add. Ms. 42896 (10) ff. 651–690b.

F. *William Thompson; or, Which is He?* (produced at HAY, 11 Sept 1829). 1829. CAM: BL Add. Ms. 42897 (1) ff. 1–80.

F. *First of April* (produced at HAY, 31 Aug 1830). 1830. CAM: BL Add. Ms. 42903 (8) ff. 367–478.

D. *A Duel in Richelieu's Time* (produced at HAY, 9 July 1832). Not ptd. CAM: BL Add. Ms. 42917 (5) ff. 158–211b.
C. *Don Pedro the Cruel and Manuel the Cobbler* (produced Surrey Theatre, 1838). 1839.

BOOTH, Ursula Agnes (1740–1803)
F. *The Little French Lawyer* (produced CG, 27 Apr 1778). 1778. [microprint]

BOOTHBY, Frances (fl. 1669–70)
TC. *Marcelia; or, The Treacherous Friend* (produced summer?, 1669, Bridges DL). 1670. [microprint] Wing B3742. EEB Reel 172: 3.

BOWES, Mary Eleanor Lyon, Countess of Strathmore (1749–1800)
T. *The Siege of Jerusalem* (not acted). 1774.

BOYD, Elizabeth (fl. 1726–45)
BO. *Don Sancho; or, The Student's Whim* with *Minerva's Triumph; A Masque* (not acted). 1739. [microprint]

BRAND, Lady Dacre, Barbarina Ogle Wilmot. See **DACRE**.

BRAND, Hannah (d. 1821)
Poems and Plays, Norwich, 1798. [microprint]
HT. *Huniades; or, The Siege of Belgrade* (produced Norwich, 7 Apr 1791; King's, 18 Jan 1792). Larpent 896. [ms. microprint] Altered to *Agmunda* (produced King's, 2 Feb 1792). Larpent 932.
C. *Adelinda* (not acted).
C. *The Conflict; or, Love, Honor and Pride* (not acted).

BROOKE, Charlotte (1740–1793)
T. *Belisarius* (not acted). In *The Oracle*, 17 Oct 1795?

BROOKE, Frances Moore (1724–1789)
T. *Virginia* (not acted). 1756.
T. *The Siege of Sinope* (produced CG, 31 Jan 1781). 1781. [microprint] Larpent 545.
CO. *Rosina* (produced CG, 31 Dec 1782). 1783. [microprint] Larpent 612. [ms. microprint]
CO. *Marian* (produced CG, 22 May 1788). Airs ptd., 1788. 1800. [microprint of 1800 ed.] Larpent 805. [ms. microprint]

BRUNTON, Anna Ross. See **ROSS**, Anna.

BURGESS, Mrs. (fl. 1779–80)
C. *The Oaks; Or, The Beauties of Canterbury* (produced Canterbury, 1779?). Canterbury, 1780.

BURKE, Miss. (fl. 1793)
CO. *The Ward of the Castle* (produced CG, 24 Oct 1793). Songs, 1793. Larpent 992. [ms. microprint]

BURNEY, Fanny, later D'Arblay (1752–1840)
C. *The Witlings* (written 1779, not acted). 1993.
C. misattrib *The East Indian* (produced HAY, 16 July 1782). Not ptd. Larpent 596. [ms. microprint]

T. *Hubert de Vere* (written 1789–91, not acted). [in ms.]
T. *The Siege of Pevensey* (written 1789–91, not acted). [in ms.]
T. *Elberta* (fragment written 1789–91, not acted). [in ms.]
T. *Edwy and Elvina* (produced DL, 21 Mar 1795). Larpent 1058. [in 2 mss.]
C. *Love and Fashion* (written 1799, accepted by CG for production, but not acted). [in ms.]
C. *A Busy Day; or, An Arrival from India* (written 1800, accepted by CG for production, but not acted). 1983.
C. *The Woman Hater* (written 1800–01, but not acted). [in ms.]

BURNEY, Frances; niece of Fanny Burney (1776–1828)
T. *Tragic Dramas* (none acted). 1818.
T. *Aristodemus*
T. *Fitzormund; or, Cherished Resentment*
T. *Malek Adhel, The Champion of the Crescent*

BURRELL, Lady Sophia Raymond, later Clay (1750?–1802)
D. *Comala* (produced Hanover Square Rooms, 1792?). 1793. [microprint]
T. *Theodora; or, The Spanish Daughter* (not acted). 1800. [microprint]
T. *Maximian* (not acted). 1800. [microprint]

BURTON, Philippina, later Hill (fl. 1768–87)
C. *Fashion Display'd* (produced HAY, 27 Apr 1770). Not ptd. Larpent 308.

-C-

CARROLL, Susanna Freeman. See **CENTLIVRE**, Susanna Carroll.

CARSTAIRES, Christian (fl. 1786)
F. *The Hubble Shue* (acted?). 1786?

T. *The Carthusian Friar; or, The Age of Chivalry*. Written by a female refugee. 1793. [microprint]

CAVENDISH, Margaret Lucas, Duchess of Newcastle (1623–1673)
Playes (none acted). 1662. [microprint] Wing N868. EEB Reel 502: 11.
D. *Love's Adventures, 2 parts*
C. *The Several Wits*
D. *Youth's Glory and Death's Banquet, 2 parts*
D. *The Lady Contemplation, 2 parts*
D. *Wits Cabal, 2 parts*
T. *The Unnatural Tragedy*
C. *The Public Wooing*
C/TC. *The Matrimonial Trouble, 2 parts*
D. *Nature's Three Daughters: Beauty, Love, and Wit, 2 parts*
D. *The Religious*
C. *The Comical Hash*
D. *Bell in Campo, 2 parts*
C. *The Apocriphal Ladies*

D. *The Female Academy*

C. attrib *The Humourous Lovers* (produced LIF, 28 Mar 1667). 1677. [microprint] Wing N883. EEB Reel 393: 18.

Playes, never before printed (none acted). 1668. [microprint] Wing N867. EEB Reel 674: 2.

D. *The Bridals*

C. *The Convent of Pleasure*

F. *A Piece of a Play*, intended to be added to the prose version of *The Blazing World*

D. *The Presence*

C. *The Sociable Companions; or, The Female Wits*

CELISIA, Dorothea Mallet (1738–90)

T. *Almida* (produced DL, 12 Jan 1771). 1771. [microprint] Larpent 314.

CENTLIVRE, Susanna Carroll (1669?–1723)

TC. *The Perjured Husband; or, The Adventures of Venice* (produced DL, Oct 1700). 1700. [microprint] Wing C1671. EEB Reel 449: 15.

C. *The Beau's Duel; or, A Soldier for the Ladies* (produced LIF, June 1702). 1702. [microprint]

C. *The Stolen Heiress; or, The Salamanca Doctor Outplotted* (produced as *The Heiress*, LIF, 31 Dec 1702). 1703. [microprint]

C. *Love's Contrivance; or, Le Medecin Malgre Lui* (produced DL, 4 June 1703). 1703. [microprint]

C. *The Gamester* (produced LIF, Feb 1705). 1705. [microprint]

C. *The Basset-Table* (produced DL, 20 Nov 1705). 1706. [microprint]

C. *Love at a Venture* (produced New Theatre, Bath, 1706). 1706. [microprint]

C. *The Platonick Lady* (produced Queen's, 25 Nov 1706). 1707.[microprint]

C. *The Busie Body* (produced DL, 12 May 1709). 1709. [microprint]

C. *The Man's Bewitched; or, The Devil to Do about Her* (produced Queen's, 12 Dec 1709). 1710. [microprint]

F. *A Bickerstaff's Burying; or, Work for the Upholders* (produced DL, 27 Mar 1710). 1710. [microprint]

C. *Mar-plot; or, The Second Part of the Busie Body* (produced DL, 30 Dec 1710. 1711. [microprint]

C. *The Perplex'd Lovers* (produced DL, 19 Jan 1712). 1712. [microprint]

C. *The Wonder! A Woman Keeps a Secret* (produced DL, 27 Apr 1714). 1714. [microprint of Bell's 1797 ed.]

F. *The Gotham Election* (not acted). 1715. [microprint]

F. *The Wife Well Managed; or, Cuckoldom Prevented* (produced HAY, 2 Mar 1724). 1715. [microprint]

T. *The Cruel Gift; or, The Royal Resentment* (produced DL, 17 Dec 1716). 1717. [microprint]

C. *A Bold Stroke for a Wife* (produced LIF, 3 Feb 1718). 1718. [microprint of 1727 Dublin ed.]

C. *The Artifice* (produced DL, 2 Oct 1722). 1723. [microprint]

CHAMBERS, Marianne (fl. 1799–1812)

C. *The School for Friends* (produced DL, 10 Dec 1805). 1805. [microprint]

C. *Ourselves* (produced LYC, 2 Mar 1811). 1811. [microprint] Larpent 1663.

CHARKE, Charlotte Cibber (1713–1760)

F. *The Carnival; or, Harlequin Blunderer* (produced LIF, 17 Sept 1735). Lost.

F. *The Art of Management; or, Tragedy Expelled* (produced YB, 24 Sept 1735). 1735. [microprint]

Med. *Tit for Tat; or, The Comedy and Tragedy of War* [a puppet show?] (produced James St, 17 Mar 1743). Lost.

CIBBER, Susanna Maria Arne (1714–1766)
E. *The Oracle* (produced CG, 17 Mar 1752). 1752. Larpent 94. [microprint of 1763 ed.]

CLARKE, Lady Olivia (fl. 1819)
C. *The Irishwoman* (produced Crow-St, Dublin, 1819). Dublin & London, 1819.

CLIVE, Catherine "Kitty" Raftor (1711–1785)
B. *The Rehearsal; or, Bays in Petticoats* (produced DL, 15 Mar 1750). 1753. [microprint] Larpent 86.
F. attrib *The London 'Prentice* (produced DL, 23 Mar 1754). Lost.
F. *Every Woman in Her Humour* (produced DL, 20 Mar 1760). Larpent 174. [ms. microprint]
C. attrib *The Island of Slaves* (produced DL, 26 Mar 1761). Larpent 190.
F. *Sketch of a Fine Lady's Return from a Rout* (produced DL, 21 Mar 1763). Larpent 220. [ms. microprint]
F. *The Faithful Irish Woman* (produced DL, 18 Mar 1765). Larpent 247. [ms. microprint]

COCKBURN, Catharine Trotter. See **TROTTER**, Catharine.

COLLIER, Jane (1709?–1754?)
DD. coauthor with Sarah Fielding, *The Cry* (not acted). 1754.

F. *The Conjurer* (not acted). By a Lady. 1823.

T. *The Conquest of Corsica by the French* (not acted). By a Lady. 1771.

COOPER, Elizabeth (fl. 1735–40)
C. *The Rival Widows; or, The Fair Libertine* (produced CG, 22 Feb 1735). 1735. [microprint]
C. *The Nobleman; or, The Family Quarrel* (produced HAY, 17 May 1736). Lost.

C. *The Coquet's Surrender; or, The Humourous Punster* (produced HAY, 15 May 1732). 1732.

CORNELYS, Margaret (1723–1797)
C. *The Deceptions* (produced Crow-St., Dublin, 14 Mar 1781). Lost.

BO. *The Country Coquet; or, Miss in Her Breeches* (not acted). 1755.

C. *The Court Lady; or, The Coquet's Surrender* (not acted). By a Lady. 1733. A reissue of *The Coquet's Surrender*, 1732.

COWLEY, Hannah Parkhouse (1743–1809)
C. *The Runaway* (produced DL, 15 Feb 1776). 1776. [microprint] Larpent 402.
F. *Who's the Dupe?* (produced DL, 10 Apr 1779). 1779. [microprint] Larpent 475.
T. *Albina, Countess Raimond* (produced HAY, 31 July 1779). 1779. [microprint] Larpent 486 [ms. microprint]
C. *The Belle's Stratagem* (produced CG, 22 Feb 1780). 1782. [microprint of 1781 Dublin ed.] Larpent 513.
Int. *The School of Eloquence* (produced DL, 4 Apr 1780). Not ptd. Larpent 515.

F. *The World as It Goes; or, A Party at Montpelier* (produced CG, 24 Feb 1781). Larpent 548. Altered to *Second Thoughts Are Best* (produced CG, 24 Mar 1781). Not ptd.
C. *Which is the Man?* (produced CG, 9 Feb 1782). 1783. [microprint] Larpent 584.
C. *A Bold Stroke for a Husband* (produced CG, 25 Feb 1783). 1784. [microprint] Larpent 617.
C. *More Ways Than One* (produced CG, 6 Dec 1783). 1784. [microprint of 1784 Dublin ed.] Larpent 640.
C. *A School for Greybeards; or, The Mourning Bride* (produced DL, 25 Nov 1786). 1786. [microprint] Larpent 748.
HT. *The Fate of Sparta; or, The Rival Kings* (produced DL, 31 Jan 1788). 1788. [microprint] Larpent 791 & 792.
CO. *A Day in Turkey; or, The Russian Slaves* (produced CG, 3 Dec 1791). 1792. [microprint of 1793 ed.] Larpent 921.
C. *The Town Before You* (produced CG, 6 Dec 1794). 1795. [microprint] Larpent 1045, as *The Town as it is*.

CRAVEN, Elizabeth Berkeley, Baroness, afterward Margravine of Anspach. See **ANSPACH**.

CULLUM, Mrs. (fl. 1775)
D. *Charlotte; or, One Thousand Seven Hundred and Seventy Three* (not acted). 1775. [microprint]

CUTHBERTSON, Miss Catherine? (fl. 1793)
C. *Anna* (produced DL, 25 Feb 1793). Not ptd. Larpent 969. [ms. microprint]

-D-

DACRE, Brand, Lady; Barbarina Ogle Wilmot (1768–1854)
T. *Ina* (produced DL, 22 Apr 1815. 1815. Larpent 1803.
Dramas. Translations and Occasional Poems, 2 vols. 1821. Published as Lady Dacre.
T. *Ina*
T. *Gonzalvo of Cordova* (not acted)
T. *Pedrarias* (not acted)
T. *Xarifa* (not acted)
Juv. *Frogs and Bulls* (privately performed, 1834). 1838.

D'AGUILAR, Rose, later Lawrence (fl. 1799–1836)
T. *Gortz of Berlingen* (not acted). 1799. [microprint]

D'ARBLAY, Frances Burney. See **BURNEY**, Fanny.

DAVYS, Mary (1674–1731)
C. *The Northern Heiress; or, The Humours of York* (produced LIF, 27 Apr 1716). 1716. [microprint]
C. *The Self-Rival* (not acted). *Works*, 1725. [microprint]

De HUMBOLDT, Charlotte (fl. 1821–38)
T. *Corinth* (not acted). 1821; rev. ed. 1838. [microprint]

De la ROCHE-GUILHEN, Anne (1644–1707)
Mas. *Rare on tout* (produced at the Hall Theatre, Whitehall, 29 May 1677). 1677.

DEVERELL, Mary (b. 1737)
HT. *Mary Queen of Scots* (not acted). 1792. [microprint]

DN. *The Disguise* (not acted). By a Woman. 1771.

DUBOIS, Lady Dorothea Annesley (1728–1774)
ME. *The Magnet* (produced Marybone Gardens, 27 June 1771). 1771. [microprint]
ME. *The Divorce* (produced Marybone Gardens, 27 Aug 1771). 1771. [microprint]
ME. *The Haunted Grove* (produced Crow-St., Dublin, 1773). Lost.

T. *The Duke of Rochford* (not acted). By a Lady of Quality. Edinburgh, 1799?

-E-

EDGEWORTH, Maria (1768–1849)
C. *The Double Disguise* (written 1786, not publicly acted). [in ms.]
C. *Whim for Whim* (written 1798–99, not publicly acted). [in ms.]
In *The Parent's Assistant* (not acted). 1801.
C. *Old Poz*
Juv. *The Knapsack*
Juv. *Eton Montem*
C. *Comic Dramas* (not acted). 1817.
C. *The Rose, the Thistle, and the Shamrock*
C. *Love and Law*
C. *The Two Guardians*
Juv. *Little Plays for Children* (not acted). 1827.
C. *The Grinding Organ*
C. *Dumb Andy*
C. *The Dame School Holiday*

EDMEAD, Elizabeth Hull (fl. 1786–1832)
D. *The Events of a Day* (produced Norwich, 1795). Not ptd. Larpent 1100.

EDWARDS, Anna Maria (fl. 1783–87)
ME. *The Enchantress; or, The Happy Island* (produced Crow-St., Dublin, 1783). 1787. [microprint]

EDWARDS, Miss Christian (fl. 1776–87)
D. *Otho and Rutha* (not acted). Edinburgh & Dublin, 1780. Rev. 1787.

EGLETON, Jane Gifford (d. 1734)
BO. *The Maggot* (produced LIF, 18 Apr 1732). Lost.

C. *The Englishman in Bourdeaux [sic]* (not acted). By an English Lady Residing in Paris. 1764.

"EPHELIA" (1640s?–1681/82)
C. *Pair of Coxcombs Royal* (acted at a dancing school, 1679). Only prologue, epilogue, and two songs exist in her *Female Poems on Several Occasions*, 1679: 16–21. Wing P2030; EEB Reel 645: 13. Wing P2031 (1682). Text lost.

-F-

D. *The Fate of Corsica; or, The Female Politician* (not acted). By a Lady of Quality. 1732.

FAUCIT *or* **FAWCETT**, Anne Gaudry (1780?–1849); or **FAUCIT**, Harriet Elizabeth Diddear (1789–1857)
HD. *Alfred the Great* (produced Norwich, 16 May 1811). Not ptd. Larpent 1665.

FIELDING, Sarah (1710–1768)
DD. misattrib "Much Ado" and "Fashion" from her *Dialogues* in *Familiar Letters*, vol. 2. 1747.
DD. coauthor with Jane Collier, *The Cry* (not acted). 1754.

FINCH, Anne Kingsmill, Countess of Winchilsea (1661–1720)
TC. *The Triumphs of Love and Innocence* (not acted). 1903.
T. *Aristomenes; or, The Royal Shepherd* (not acted). 1713. [microprint]

FORSYTH, Elizabeth (fl. 1784–89)
T. *The Siege of Quebec; or, The Death of General Wolfe* (possibly acted in 1784?). Strabane, Ireland, 1789. [microprint]

FRANCIS, Ann Gittins (1738–1800)
SdD. *The Song of Solomon* (not acted). 1781.

FRASER, Susan (fl. 1809–16)
T. *Comala*. In *Camilla de Florian and other Poems*, 1809.

-G-

GARDNER, Sarah Cheney (fl. 1763–98)
C. *The Advertisement; or, A Bold Stroke for a Husband* (produced HAY, 9 Aug 1777). Not ptd. Larpent 435.
F. misattrib *The Female Dramatist* (produced HAY, 16 Aug 1782). Larpent 598.
Pre. *Mrs. Doggerel in Her Altitudes; or, The Effects of a West Indian Ramble* (produced HAY, 22 Apr 1795). Not ptd. Larpent 1101.
C. *The Loyal Subject* (not acted). [in ms.]
F. *Charity* (not acted). [in ms.]

GEISWEILER, Maria (fl. 1799–1800)
D. *The Noble Lie: A Drama* (not acted). 1799. [microprint]
D. *Poverty and Nobleness of Mind* (not acted). 1799. [microprint]

D. *Joanna of Montfaucon* (not acted). 1799. Larpent 1276 is a prologue to *Joanna* by Richard Cumberland (produced CG, 16 Jan 1800), based on Geisweiler's translation.

D. *Crime from Ambition* (not acted). 1799. [microprint of 1800 ed.]

GOLDSMITH, Mary (fl. 1800–04)

C. *She Lives; or, The Generous Brother* (4-act version produced, HAY, 7 Mar 1803; 5-act version produced at Margate, Feb 1803). 4-act version, Larpent 1284. [ms. microprint] 5-act version, Larpent 1399. Not ptd.

CO. *Angelina* (produced Margate, 1804). Larpent 1431. Not ptd.

GREEN, Mrs. (fl. 1756)

F. *Everybody to Their Own Liking* (produced Bath, 1756). Lost.

GRIFFITH, Elizabeth (1727–1793)

T. *Amana: A Dramatic Poem* (not acted). 1764. [microprint]

C. *The Platonic Wife* (produced DL, 24 Jan 1765). 1765. [microprint] Larpent 244.

C. *The Double Mistake* (produced CG, 9 Jan 1766). 1766. [microprint of 1766 Dublin ed.] Larpent 251.

C. attrib *Dorval; or, The Test of Love* (not acted). 1767. [microprint]

C. *The School for Rakes* (produced DL, 4 Feb 1769). 1769. [microprint]

C. attrib *The Father* (not acted). 1770.

C. *A Wife in the Right* (produced CG, 9 Mar 1772). 1772. [microprint] Larpent 332. [ms. microprint]

C. *The Barber of Seville; or, The Useless Precaution* (not acted). 1776. [microprint]

C. *The Times* (produced DL, 2 Dec 1779). 1780. [microprint] Larpent 499 [ms. microprint]

GRIFFITHS, Miss (fl. 1793)

C. attrib *Cross Partners* (produced HAY, 23 Aug 1792). 1792. Larpent 955.

GUNNING, Elizabeth, later Plunkett (1769–1823)

TC. *The Wife with Two Husbands* (not acted). 1803.

-H-

H——, Eleanor (fl. 1803)

D. *Matilda* (not acted). In *The Lady's Magazine*, 1803?

Int. *Half An Hour After Supper* (produced HAY, 25 May 1789). By a Lady. 1789.

HARDWICKE, Countess of. See **YORKE**, Elizabeth.

HARLOW, Elizabeth (fl. 1789)

C. *The English Tavern in Berlin* (not acted). Dublin and London, 1789. [microprint of Dublin, 1789]

HARRISON, Elizabeth (fl. 1724–56)

T. *The Death of Socrates*. In *Miscellanies on Moral and Religious Subjects, In Prose and Verse*, 1756.

HARVEY, Margaret (fl. 1814–22)
MD. *Raymond de Percy; or, The Tenant of the Tomb* (produced Sutherland, 1822). 1822.

HAYWOOD, Elizabeth "Eliza" Fowler (1693?–1756)
T. *The Fair Captive* (produced LIF, 4 Mar 1721). 1721. [microprint]
C. *A Wife to Be Lett* (produced DL, 12 Aug 1723). 1724. [microprint of 1735 ed.]
T. *Frederick, Duke of Brunswick-Lunenburgh* (produced LIF, 4 Mar 1729). 1729. [microprint of 1733 ed.]
BO. coauthor with William Hatchett *The Opera of Operas; or Tom Thumb the Great* (produced HAY, 31 May 1733) [microprint]
T. attrib *Arden of Faversham* (produced HAY, 21 Jan 1736). Not ptd.

HELME, Elizabeth (d. 1810)
Juv. *Cortez; or, The Conquest of Mexico* (not acted). 1800; rev. 1811.
Juv. *Pizarro; or, The Conquest of Peru* (not acted). 1800.

HEMANS, Felicia Dorothea Browne (1793–1835)
T. *The Vespers of Palermo* (produced CG, 12 Dec 1823). 1823. Larpent 2375.
T. *The Siege of Valencia* (not acted). 1823.
T. *DeChatillon; or, The Crusades* (not acted). 1839.
T. *Sebastian of Portugal* (fragment, not acted). 1839.

HILL, Isabel (1800–1842)
T. *The Poet's Child* (not acted). 1820. [microfilm]
C. *The First of May; or, A Royal Love Match* (produced CG, 10 Oct 1829). 1829. CAM: BL Add. Ms. 42897 (3) ff. 229–256.
D. *West Country Wooing* (produced HAY, June/Sept 1834). Not ptd. CAM: BL Add. Ms. 42927 (12) ff. 358–365b.
D. *My Own Twin Brother* (9 Sept 1834). Not ptd. CAM: BL Add. Ms. 42927 (15) ff. 430–452.
T. *Brian the Probationer; or, The Red Hand* (not acted). 1842.

HOFLAND, Barbara Wreaks, later Hoole (1770–1844)
Juv. *Little Dramas for Young People by Mrs. Hoole* (not acted). 1810.

HOLCROFT, Frances "Fanny" (1778/83–1844)
Translator of plays, published in her father's *Theatrical Recorder*, 1805–06.
T. *Philip the Second* (from Alfieri)
C. *From Bad to Worse* (from Calderon)
T. *Emilia Galotti* (from Schiller)
C. *Fortune Mends* (from Calderon)
C. *Minna von Barnhelm* (from Lessing)
C. *The Baron* (from Celenio)
T. *Rosamond* (from Weisse)
MD. *The Goldsmith* (produced at HAY, 23 Aug 1827). Not ptd. CAM: BL Add. Ms. 42885 (7) ff. 150–182b.

HOLFORD, Margaret Wrench (1761–1834)
C. *Neither's the Man* (produced Chester, Nov 1798). Chester & London, 1799. [microprint] Larpent 1231. [ms. microprint]
C. *The Way to Win Her* (not acted). Printed in *The New British Theatre*, 1814.

HOLT, Jane Wiseman, See **WISEMAN**, Jane.

HOOK, Harriet Horncastle (d. 1805)
CO. *The Double Disguise* (produced DL, 8 Mar 1784). 1784. [microprint] Larpent 646.

HOPER, [HOOPER?, Rachael? Harford] (fl. 1742–1760)
T. *The Battle of Poictiers; or The English Prince* (produced GF, 5 Mar 1747). Not ptd.
F. *The Cyclopedia* (produced HAY, 31 Mar 1748). Not ptd.
B. *Queen Tragedy Restored* (produced HAY, 9 Nov 1749). 1749. [microprint]

HORNBY, Mary (fl. 1819–20)
T. *The Battle of Waterloo* (not acted). Stratford-upon-Avon, 1819.
C. *The Broken Vow* (not acted). Stratford-upon-Avon, 1820.

HOUSTON, Lady (d. 1780)
C. *The Coquettes; or, The Gallant in the Closet* (produced Edinburgh, 1760). Not ptd.

HUGHES, Anne (fl. 1784–97)
Moral Dramas Intended for Private Representation (none acted). 1790. [microprint]
T. *Aspacia*
T. *Constantia*
T. *Cordelia*

HUMBOLDT, Charlotte de. See **De HUMBOLDT**.

-I-

I., P. (fl. 1786–88)
Juv. *Dramatic Pieces* (not acted). 1788.
The Good Mother-in-law
The Good Daughter-in-law
The Maternal Sister
The Reformation
The Contract
The Triumph of Reason

INCHBALD, Elizabeth Simpson (1753–1821)
F. *A Mogul Tale; or, The Descent of the Balloon* (produced HAY, 6 July 1784). Dublin, 1788. [microprint of Dublin ed., 1796] Larpent 661.
C. *I'll Tell You What* (produced HAY, 4 Aug 1785). 1786. [microprint] Larpent 700.
F. *Appearance Is Against Them* (produced CG, 22 Oct 1785). 1785. [microprint] Larpent 708.
F. *The Widow's Vow* (produced HAY, 20 June 1786). 1786. [microprint] Larpent 736.
D. *Such Things Are* (produced CG, 10 Feb 1787). 1788. [microprint] Larpent 761.
C. *The Midnight Hour* (produced CG, 22 May 1787). 1787. Larpent 775.
C. *All on a Summer's Day* (produced CG, 15 Dec 1787). Not ptd. Larpent 789. [transcription in E-CED by Paula Backscheider]
F. *Animal Magnetism* (produced CG, 29 Apr 1788). Dublin, 1789. [microprint 1792 Dublin ed.] Larpent 802.

D. *The Child of Nature* (produced CG, 28 Nov 1788). 1788. [microprint]
C. *The Married Man* (produced HAY, 15 July 1789). 1789. [microprint] Larpent 838.
F. *The Hue and Cry* (produced DL, 11 May 1791). Larpent 900. Larpent 1184. [ms. microprint] [transcription in E-CED by Paula Backscheider]
C. *Next Door Neighbours* (produced HAY, 9 July 1791). 1791. [microprint] Larpent 912.
F. *Young Men and Old Women* [*Lovers, No Conjurors*] (produced HAY, 30 June 1792). Not ptd. Larpent 952. [ms. microprint] [transcription in E-CED by Paula Backscheider]
C. *Every One Has His Fault* (produced CG, 29 Jan 1793). 1793. Larpent 967. [microprint]
C. *The Wedding Day* (produced DL, 1 Nov 1794). 1794. [microprint] Larpent 1044.
C. *Wives as They Were, and Maids as They Are* (produced CG, 4 Mar 1797). 1797. [microprint] Larpent 1155.
D. *Lovers' Vows* (produced CG, 11 Oct 1798). 1798. [microprint] Larpent 1226.
D. *The Wise Man of the East* (produced CG, 30 Nov 1799). 1799. [microprint] Larpent 1271. [ms. microprint]
D. attrib *The Egyptian Boy* (written 1802, not acted). Not ptd. Larpent 1348.
C. *To Marry, or Not to Marry* (produced CG, 16 Feb 1805). 1805. [microprint] Larpent 1438.
T. *The Massacre* (written 1792, not acted). 1833.
D. *A Case of Conscience* (written 1800, not acted). 1833.

ISDELL, Sarah (fl. 1805–25)
C. *The Poor Gentlewoman* (produced Crow-St., Dublin, 4 Mar 1811). Not ptd.
CO. *The Cavern* (produced Hawkins-St., Dublin, 1825). Not ptd.

-J-

JORDAN, Dorothy [Dorothy Bland] (1761–1816)
F. attrib *The Spoiled Child* (produced DL, 22 Mar 1790). Dublin, 1799. Larpent 862.

-K-

KEMBLE, Elizabeth Satchell (1762?–1841)
Pst. *Philander and Rose; or, The Bridal Day* (produced Manchester, 25 Apr 1785). Songs, Manchester, 1785. Larpent 689.

KEMBLE, Marie Therese DeCamp (1775–1836)
C. *First Faults* (produced DL, 3 May 1799). Not ptd. Larpent 1254.
Int. *Personation; or, Fairly Taken In* (produced DL, 29 Apr 1805). 1805?. Larpent 1447.
Int. *The Day After the Wedding; or, The Wife's First Lesson* (produced CG, 18 May 1808). 1808. Larpent 1549.
C. attrib *Match-making; or, 'Tis a Wise Child that Knows its own Father* (produced CG, 24 May 1808). Not ptd.
C. *Smiles and Tears; or, The Widow's Stratagem* (produced CG, 12 Dec 1815). 1815. Larpent 1889.

KENNEDY, Grace (1782–1824)
DN. *The Decision; or, Religion Must Be All, or Is Nothing* (not acted). Edinburgh, 1821.

DN. *Profession Not Principle; or, The Name of Christian is not Christianity* (not acted). Edinburgh, 1821.

KILLIGREW, Anne (1660–1685)
Pst. Pastoral Dialogues," in *Poems*, 1686. Wing K442. EEB Reel 189: 7.

-L-

LATTER, Mary (1722?–1777)
T. *The Siege of Jerusalem By Titus Vespasian* (produced Reading, 1768). In her *Miscellaneous Works*, 1763. [microprint]

LAWRENCE, Rose D'Aguilar. See **D'AGUILAR**.

LAWRENCE, Sarah [pseud A.B.C.] (fl. 1806–1846)
C. *Lausus and Lydia with Madam Bonso's Three Strings to Her Bow; or, Three Bows to Her String!!!* (not acted). 1806.

LEADBEATER, Mary Shackleton (1758–1826)
DN. *Cottage Dialogues Among the Irish Peasantry* (not acted). 1811.

LEAPOR, Mary (1722–1746)
T. *The Unhappy Father* (written c. 1745, not acted). In vol. 2 of her *Poems Upon Several Occasions*, 1751. [microprint]

LEE, Harriet (1757–1851)
C. *The New Peerage; or, Our Eyes May Deceive Us* (produced DL, 10 Nov 1787). 1787. [microprint] Larpent 787.
MD. *The Mysterious Marriage; or, The Heirship of Roselva* (not acted). 1798. [microprint]
MD. *The Three Strangers* (produced CG, 10 Dec 1825). 1826. CAM: BL Add. Ms. 42874 (1) ff. 3–109.

LEE, Sophia (1750–1824)
C. *The Chapter of Accidents* (produced HAY, 5 Aug 1780). 1780. [microprint] Larpent 526.
T. *Almeyda; Queen of Granada* (produced DL, 20 Apr 1796). 1796. [microprint] Larpent 1113. [ms. microprint]
C. *The Assignation* (produced DL, 28 Jan 1807). Not ptd. Larpent 1508.

LEFANU, Alicia Sheridan (1754–1817)
C. *The Sons of Erin; or, Modern Sentiments* (produced LYC, 11 Apr 1812). 1812. Larpent 1714.

LENNOX, Charlotte Ramsey (1729?–1804)
C. misattrib *Angelica; or, Quixote in Petticoats* (not acted). 1758. [microprint]
Pst. *Philander* (not acted). 1758. [microprint]
T. *The Greek Theatre of Father Brumoy*, 1759; includes trans.
Oedipus (from Sophocles)
Electra (from Euripides)
Philoctetes (from Sophocles)

C. *The Sister* (produced CG, 18 Feb 1769). 1769. [microprint] Larpent 291.
C. *Old City Manners* (produced DL, 9 Nov 1775). 1775. [microprint] Larpent 396.

F. *A Lesson for Lovers* (not acted). By a Lady. 1823.

LEWIS, Mary G. (fl. 1823–25?)
HD. *Cardiff Castle* (not acted). Published with *Zelinda* [a long poem]. 1823.

-M-

MACAULEY, Elizabeth Wright (1786?–1837)
MD. *Marmion* (probably produced Dublin, 1810 and Cork, 1811). Cork, 1811. [microprint]

McCARTHY, Charlotte (fl. 1745–67)
DD. *The Author and Bookseller* (not acted). 1765.

M'TAGGART, Ann Hamilton (1753?–1834)
Plays published anonymously in John Galt's *New British Theatre* (none acted). 1814.
T. *Theodora*
C. *A Search after Perfection*
D. *Villario*
T. *Hortensia*
T. *Constantia* (not acted). 1824.
D. *Valville; or, The Prejudices of Past Times* (not acted). 1824.

MANLEY, Delariviere (1672?–1724)
C. *The Lost Lover; or, The Jealous Husband* (produced DL, Mar 1696). 1696. [microprint] Wing M435. EEB Reel 36: 6.
T. *The Royal Mischief* (produced LIF, Apr/May 1696). 1696. [microprint] Wing M436. EEB Reel 36: 7.
T. *Almyna; or, The Arabian Vow* (produced Queen's, 16 Dec 1706). 1707. [microprint]
T. *Lucius, the First Christian King of Britain* (produced DL, 11 May 1717). 1717. [microprint]
C.? *The Double Mistress; or, 'Tis Well "Tis No More* (announced 1720, not acted). Lost.
D. *The Duke of Somerset* (not acted). Lost.
BO. misattrib *The Court Legacy* (not acted). 1733. [microprint]

C. *Manoeuvering* (not acted). Published anonymously in John Galt's *New British Theatre*, 1814.

MARISHALL, Jean. See **MARSHALL**, Jean.

MARSHALL, Jean (fl. 1766–89)
C. *Sir Harry Gaylove; or, Comedy in Embryo* (not acted). Edinburgh, 1772.

MARTIN, Mrs. (fl. 1823)
D. *Reparation; or, The Savoyards* (not acted). 1823.

METCALFE, Catharine (d. 1790)
T. *Julia de Roubigné* (produced Bath, 23 Dec 1790). Not ptd. Larpent 885.

The Little Country Visitor
The Distrest Family
The Village Wedding
The Mockingsbird's Nest
Juv. *The Two Cousins* (not acted). 1794.

PIX, Mary Griffith (1666–1709)
T. *Ibrahim, the Thirteenth Emperour of the Turks* (produced DL, May/June 1696). 1696. [microprint] Wing P2329. EEB Reel 506: 5.
F. *The Spanish Wives* (produced DG, Aug 1696). 1696. [microprint] Wing P2332. EEB Reel 396: 7.
C. *The Innocent Mistress* (produced LIF, June 1697). 1697. [microprint] Wing P2330. EEB Reel 506: 6.
C. *The Deceiver Deceived* (produced LIF, Nov 1697). 1698. [microprint] Wing P2327. EEB Reel 506: 3.
T. *Queen Catharine; or, The Ruines of Love* (produced LIF, June 1698). 1698. [microprint] Wing P2331. EEB Reel 1099: 3.
T. *The False Friend; or, The Fate of Disobedience* (produced LIF, May 1699). 1699. [microprint] Wing P2328. EEB Reel 506: 4.
C. attrib *The Beau Defeated; or, The Lucky Younger Brother* (produced LIF, Mar 1700). 1700. [microprint] Wing P2326. EEB Reel 1192: 3.
T. *The Double Distress* (produced LIF, Mar 1701). 1701. [microprint]
T. *The Czar of Muscovy* (produced LIF, Mar 1701). 1701.
C. *The Different Widows; or, Intrigue All-a-Mode* (produced LIF, Nov 1703). 1703. [microprint]
T. attrib *Zelmane; or, The Corinthian Queen* (produced LIF, 13 Nov 1704). 1705.
T. *The Conquest of Spain* (produced Queen's, May 1705). 1705. [microprint]
C. *The Adventures in Madrid* (produced Queen's, June 1706). 1706. [microprint]

PLOWDEN, Dorothea (d. 1827)
CO. *Virginia* (produced DL, 30 Oct 1800). 1800. [microprint] Larpent 1303.

PLUMPTRE, Anne (1760–1818)
D. *The Count of Burgundy* (not acted). 1798. [microprint]
D. *The Natural Son* (not acted). 1798. [microprint]
D. *The Force of Calumny* (not acted). 1799. [microprint]
D. *La-Peyrouse* (not acted). 1799. [microprint]
T. *The Spaniards in Peru; or, The Death of Rolla* (not acted). 1799. [microprint] 2nd ed., 1799, published as *Pizarro: The Spaniards in Peru; or The Death of Rolla* (same text).
D. *The Virgin of the Sun* (not acted). 1799. [microprint]
F. *The Widow and the Riding Horse; or, The Paradox* (not acted). 1799. [microprint]

PLUMPTRE, Bell (1761–1838)
D. *The Foresters; a Picture of Rural Manners* (not acted). 1799. [microprint]
D. attrib *The Guardian Angel* (not acted). 1802.

PLUNKETT, Elizabeth. See **GUNNING**, Elizabeth.

POLWHELE, Elizabeth (1650–1691)
T. *The Faithful Virgins* (produced LIF, c. 1670). MS: Bodleian Rawl. Poet. 195, ff. 49–78.

Mas.? *Elysium* (acted, 1669/70?). Lost.
C. *The Frolicks; or, The Lawyer Cheated* (written 1671, not acted) 1977. MS: Cornell U Lib. MS BD Rare P P77.

POPE, Jane (1743?–1818)
C. *The Young Couple* (produced DL, 21 Apr 1767). Not ptd.

PORTER, Anna Marie (1780–1832)
ME. *The Fair Fugitives* (produced CG, 16 May 1803). Songs. 1803. Larpent 1385.
T. attrib *Switzerland* (produced DL, 15 Feb 1819). Lost. Prologue: Larpent 2075.

PORTER, Jane (1776–1850)
T. *Egmont; or, the Eve of St. Alyne* (written 1817, not acted). Lost.
T. attrib *Switzerland* (produced DL, 15 Feb 1819). Lost. Prologue: Larpent 2075.
T. *Owen Prince of Powys; or, Welch Feuds* (produced 28 Jan 1822). Lost.

PYE, Jael-Henrietta Mendez (1737?–1782)
F. *The Capricious Lady* (produced DL, 10 May 1771). Not ptd. Larpent 323 [ms. microprint]

-R-

RAINSFORD, Mrs. (fl. 1794)
F. *The Speechless Wife* (produced CG, 22 May 1794). Songs, 1794. Larpent 1025.

RICHARDSON, Elizabeth (d. 1779)
C. *The Double Deception; or, Lovers Perplex'd* (produced DL, 28 Apr 1779). Not ptd. Larpent 478.

RICHARDSON, Sarah Watts (d. 1823/24)
T. *Ethelred* (not acted). [1809/1810].
T. *Gertrude* (not acted). [1810].

ROBE, Jane (fl. 1723)
T. *The Fatal Legacy* (produced LIF, 23 Apr 1723). 1723. [microprint]

ROBERTS, Miss R. (1730?–1788)
HT. *Malcolm* (not acted). 1779. [microprint]

ROBERTSON, Mrs. T. (fl. 1796)
ME. *The Enchanted Island; or, The Freeborn Englishman* (produced Wisbeach, 1796?). Not ptd.

ROBERTSON, Mrs. (fl. 1800)
MD. *Ellinda; or, The Abbey of St. Aubert* (produced Newark, 1800). Not ptd.

ROBINSON, Mary Darby, "Perdita" (1758–1800)
CO. *The Lucky Escape* (produced DL, 30 Apr 1778). Songs, 1778. [microprint of songs] Larpent 447.

CO.? attrib *Kate of Aberdeen* (not acted?). 1787.
F. *Nobody* (produced DL, 29 Nov 1794). Not ptd. Larpent 1046.
T. *The Sicilian Lover* (not acted). 1796. [microprint]

ROCHE-GUILHEN, Anne de la. See **De la ROCHE-GUILHEN**.

ROSS, Miss Anna, later Brunton (1773–?)
CO. *The Cottagers* (produced Crow-St., Dublin, 19 May 1789). 1788. [microprint]

RYVES, Elizabeth (1750–1797)
BO. *The Prude* (not acted). In *Poems on Several Occasions*, 1777.
Mas. *The Triumph of Hymen* (not acted). In *Poems on Several Occasions*, 1777.
C. *The Debt of Honour* (written 1777, not acted). Not ptd.
DD. *Dialogue in the Elysian Fields between Caesar and Cato* (not acted). 1784.

-S-

SANDERS, Charlotte Elizabeth (fl. 1787–1803)
Juv. *The Little Family* (not acted). 1797.
The Little Gamester
The Bird's Nest
The Foundling of Savoy
Juv. *Holidays at Home* (not acted). 1803.
The Governess
The Giddy Girl; or, Reformation
The Grandmother
The Errors of Education

SCOTT, Jane M. (fl. 1811–26)
E. *The Rout* (produced SP, 17 Nov 1806). Not ptd.
E. *Tempest Terrific* (produced SP, 17 Nov 1806). Not ptd.
Sp. *The Vision in the Holy Land; or, Godfrey of Bouillon's Dream* (produced SP, 17 Nov 1806). Not ptd.
Sp. *Battle in the Shadow* (produced SP, 12 Jan 1807). Not ptd.
ME. *Rural Visitors; or, Singularity* (produced SP, 12 Jan 1807). Not ptd.
E. *Spectrology of Ghosts* (produced SP, 12 Jan 1807). Not ptd.
ME. *Successful Cruize; or, Nobody Coming to Woo* (produced SP, 14 Nov 1807). Not ptd.
E. *Ulthona the Sorceress* (produced SP, 14 Nov 1807). Not ptd.
CO. *The Magistrate* (produced SP, 15 Feb 1808). Not ptd.
MD. *The Red Robber; or, The Statue in the Wood* (produced SP, 3 Dec 1808). Not ptd.
ME. *The Bashaw; or, Midnight Adventures of Three Spaniards* (produced 23 Jan 1809). Not ptd.
P. *Mother White Cap; or, Hey Up the Chimes* (produced SP, 27 Feb 1809). Not ptd.
P. *The Necromancer; or, The Golden Key* (produced SP, 11 Dec 1809). Not ptd.
MD. *Mary, the Maid of the Inn; or, The Bough of Yew* (produced SP, 27 Dec 1809). Not ptd. Larpent 1603.
CO. *The Two Misers of Smyrna; or, Mufti's Tomb* (produced SP, 8 Mar 1810). Not ptd.

MD. *Disappointments; or, Love in Castile* (produced SP, 3 Dec 1810). Not ptd. Larpent 1645.
P. *The Magic Pipe; or, Dancing Mad* (produced SP, 3 Dec 1810). Not ptd.
CO. *The Lowland Romp* (produced SP, 27 Dec 1810). Not ptd. Larpent 1648.
F. *The Animated Effigy* (produced SP, 12 Feb 1811). Not ptd. Larpent 1660.
P. *The Poison Tree; or, Harlequin in Java* (produced SP, 18 Nov 1811). Not ptd.
CO. *The Vizier's Son, The Merchant's Daughter, and The Ugly Woman of Bagdad* (produced SP, 16 Dec 1811). Not ptd. Larpent 1697.
CO. *Il Giorno Felice; or, The Happy Day* (produced SP, 24 Feb 1812). Not ptd. Larpent 1705.
Sp. *Asgard, the Daemon Hunter; or, Le Diable a la Chasse* (produced SP, 17 Nov 1812). Not ptd. Larpent 1741.
F. *Love, Honor, and Obey* (produced SP, 7 Dec 1812). Not ptd. Larpent 1746.
P. *Davy Jones's Locker; or, Black-Eyed Susan* (produced SP, 23 Dec 1812). Not ptd.
F. *The Forest Knight; or, The King Bewildered* (produced SP, 4 Feb 1813). Not ptd. Larpent 1757.
F. *Love in the City* (produced SP, 8 Mar 1813). Not ptd.
Sp. *Raykisnah the Outcast; or, The Hollow Tree* (produced SP, 22 Nov 1813). Not ptd. Larpent 1784.
P. *The Magicians; or, The Enchanted Bird* (produced SP, 23 Dec 1813). Not ptd.
F. *Whackham and Windham; or, The Wrangling Lawyers* (produced SP, 24 Jan 1814). Not ptd. Larpent 1790.
MD. *The Inscription; or, Indian Hunters* (produced SP, 28 Feb 1814). Not ptd. Larpent 1804.
F. *Eccentricities; or, Mistakes at Madrid* (produced SP, 26 Dec 1814). Not ptd. Larpent 1836.
F. *The Gipsy Girl* (produced SP, 9 Jan 1815). Not ptd.
P. *Harlequin Rasselas; or, The Happy Valley* (produced SP, 9 Feb 1815). Not ptd.
CO. *The Summer House* (produced SP, 16 Feb 1815). Not ptd. Larpent 1847.
F. *The Conjurer; or, Blaze in Amaze* (produced SP, 30 Oct 1815). Not ptd. Larpent 1882.
MD. *The Old Oak Chest; or, The Smuggler's Son and the Robber's Daughter* (produced SP, 5 Feb 1816). Duncombe, n. d. Larpent 1908.
MD. *The Stratagems; or, The Lost Treasure* (produced SP, 4 Mar 1816). Not ptd. Larpent 1913.
F. *The Dinner of Madelon* (produced SP, 16 Dec 1816). Not ptd. Larpent 1941.
MD. *Camilla the Amazon; or, The Mountain Robber* (produced SP, 6 Feb 1817). Not ptd. Larpent 1954.
MD. *The Lord of the Castle* (produced SP, 13 Oct 1817). Not ptd. Larpent 1989.
B. *Widow's Tears* (produced SP, 23 Oct 1817). Not ptd.
F. *The Row of Ballynavogue; or, The Lily of Lismore* (produced SP, 27 Nov 1817). Not ptd. Larpent 1994.
Pre. *The Fortunate Youth; or, Newmarket Hoax* (produced SP, 5 Jan 1818). Not ptd. Larpent 2005.
F. *The Three Crumps; or, Crooked Brothers of Damascus* (produced SP, 5 Feb 1818). Not ptd. Larpent 2005.
F. *The Two Spanish Valets; or, Lie Upon Lie* (produced SP, 2 Nov 1818). Not ptd. Larpent 2051.
DwM. *Fairy Legends; or, The Moon-light Night* (produced SP, 7 Dec 1818). Not ptd. Larpent 2057.
P. *The Fire Goblin and the Three Charcoal Burners* (produced SP, 26 Dec 1818). Not ptd.
F. *The Half-Pay Officer; or, Love and Honor* (produced SP, 18 Jan 1819). Not ptd. Larpent 2067.

SERRES, Olivia Wilmot (1772–1834)
O. *The Castle of Avola* (not acted). In *Flights of Fancy*, 1805.

SHERIDAN, Elizabeth "Betsy," later Lefanu (1758–1837)
F. *The Ambiguous Lover* (produced Crow-St., Dublin 1781). Lost.

SHERIDAN, Frances Chamberlaine (1724–1766)
C. *The Discovery* (produced DL, 3 Feb 1763). 1763. [microprint] Larpent 219.
C. *The Dupe* (produced DL, 10 Dec 1763). 1764. [microprint] Larpent 228.
C. *A Trip to Bath* (3 acts extant, not acted). 1984. MS: BL Add. Ms. 25975.

SHORT, Mrs. C. (fl. 1792)
Juv. *Dramas for the Use of Young Ladies* (not acted). 1792.
Domestic Woe
The Fortunate Disappointment

SMITH, Charlotte Turner (1749–1806)
Juv. *Rural Walks* (not acted). 1795.
Juv. *Rambles Further* (not acted). 1796.
C. *What is She?* (produced CG, 27 Apr 1799). 1799. [microprint] Larpent 1253.

C. *The South Briton* (produced Smock-Alley, Dublin, 24 Jan 1774; CG 12 Apr 1774). Dublin, 1774; London, 1774.

STARKE, Mariana (1762?–1838)
C. *The Sword of Peace; or, A Voyage of Love* (produced HAY, 9 Aug 1788). 1789. [microprint]
T. *The British Orphan* (produced at Mrs. Crespigny's private theatre, Camberwell, 1790). Not ptd.
T. *The Widow of Malabar* (may have been privately produced at Mrs. Crespigny's theatre, Camberwell, 1790; publicly produced CG, 5 May 1790). 1791. [microprint] Larpent 869.
T. *The Tournament* (not acted). 1800. [microprint]

STRATFORD, Agnes (fl. 1794–95)
T. *The Labyrinth; or, The Fatal Embarrassment* (not acted). Dublin, 1795.

STRATHMORE, Countess of. See **BOWES**, Mary Eleanor.

-T-

T. *Theodorick, King of Denmark* (not acted). By a Young Gentlewoman. Dublin, 1752.

THOMAS, Elizabeth Francis Amherst (1716–1779)
Pst. *Dramatick Pastoral* (produced Gloucester, 1762). 1762.

TOLLET, Elizabeth (1694–1754)
DwM. *Susanna; or, Innocence Preserved* (not acted). In *Poems on Several Occasions*, 1755. [microprint]

TRIMMER, Sarah Kirby (1741–1810/11)
Juv. *The Little Hermit; or, The Rural Adventure* (not acted). In *The Juvenile Magazine*, 1788.

TROTTER, Catharine, later Cockburn (1679–1749)
T. *Agnes de Castro* (produced DL, Dec 1695). 1696. [microprint] Wing C4801. EEB Reel 87: 12.

T. *The Fatal Friendship* (produced LIF, May/June 1698). 1698. [microprint] Wing C4802. EEB Reel 486: 26.
C. *Love at a Loss; or, Most Votes Carry It* (produced DL, 23 Nov 1700). 1701. [microprint] Later revised as *The Honourable Deceivers; or, All Right at the Last*. Lost.
T. *The Unhappy Penitent* (produced DL, 4 Feb 1701). 1701. [microprint]
T. *The Revolution of Sweden* (produced Queen's, 11 Feb 1706). 1706. [microprint]

TURNER, Margaret (fl. 1790)
Pst. *The Gentle Shepherd* (not acted). 1790. [microprint]

-U-

T. *The Unnatural Mother* (produced LIF, Sept/Oct 1697). By a Young Lady [Ariadne?]. 1698. EEB Reel 1076: 21.[microprint]

-V-

CO. *The Village Maid* (not acted). By a Young Lady. 1792.

-W-

WALLACE, Eglantine Maxwell, Lady (d. 1803)
C. *Diamond Cut Diamond* (not acted). 1787. [microprint]
C. *The Ton; or, Follies of Fashion* (produced CG, 8 Apr 1788). 1788. [microprint] Larpent 801.
C. *The Whim*, (prohibited by royal licenser). Margate, 1795. [microprint] Larpent 1093.
T. *Cortes* (not acted). Lost.

WEDDELL, Mrs. (fl. 1737–1742)
F. *The City Farce* (not acted). 1737. [microprint]
B. attrib *The Voyage up the Thames* (not acted). 1738.
T. *Incle and Yarico* (not acted). 1742. [microprint]

WEST, Jane Iliffe (1758–1852)
T. *Edmund Surnamed Ironside* (not acted). In *Miscellaneous Poems*, 1791. [microprint]
T. *Adela* (not acted). In *Poems and Plays*, vol. 2, 1799. [microprint]
C. *How Will it End?* (not acted). In *Poems and Plays* vol. 2, 1799. [microprint]
T. *The Minstrel; or, The Heir of Arundel* (not acted). In *Poems and Plays*, vol. 4, 1805.

WHARTON, Lady Anne Lee (1659?–1685)
T. *Love's Martyr; or, Witt Above Crownes* (written c. 1685, not acted). MS: BL Add. Ms. 28693.

WILLIAMS, Anna (1706–1783)
D. attrib *The Uninhabited Island* (not acted). In *Miscellanies in Prose and Verse*, 1766. [microprint]

WILMOT, Barbarina Ogle, later Brand, Lady Dacre. See **DACRE**.

WILSON, Ann (fl. 1783)
SdD. *Jephthah's Daughter* (not acted). 1783. [microprint]

WINCHILSEA, Countess of. See **FINCH**, Ann Kingsmill.

WISEMAN, Jane, later Holt (fl. 1701–17)
T. *Antiochus the Great; or, The Fatal Relapse* (produced LIF, Nov 1701). 1702. [microprint]

-Y-

YEARSLEY, Ann Cromartie (1752–1806)
HT. *Earl Goodwin* (produced Bath, Oct? 1789). 1791. [microprint] Larpent 846. [ms. microprint]
C. *The Ode Rejected* (announced, not acted). Lost.
F. *The Petticoat Government* (announced, not acted). Lost.

YORKE, Elizabeth Lindsay, Countess of Hardwicke (1763–1858)
E. *The Court of Oberon; or, The Three Wishes* (privately produced at Wimpole Hall, Cambridgeshire, c. 1800). 1831.

Chronological List of Plays by British Women Dramatists 1660–1823

We have tried to furnish 1) the exact production date if known ("n.d." shows we have been unable to determine the exact month or day); 2) the author's name, or a possible attribution marked "attrib"; 3) a short title, with subtitle added only for clarity; 4) the genre of play, and if a play is translated the author of the original is given; 5) the venue, or indication of a closet drama (not intended for the stage) or an unacted play (not produced and published in lieu of performance). Our list goes to 1854 and includes dramatists (such as Baillie and Mitford) who began writing plays before 1824 and continued writing beyond our terminal date of 1823. Female playwrights who began writing after 1823 are not included. The use of a question mark indicates an uncertain date or venue; "ms" indicates that the play remained in manuscript in its own day, though it may have been printed later (as Milhous and Hume have transcribed Polwhele's *The Frolicks*, for publication and Wallace has transcribed Burney's *The Busy Day*).

This classification scheme generally follows Cotton's plan in her *Women Playwrights in England, c. 1363–1750* (Lewisburg, PA: Bucknell UP, 1980).

date—author—title—genre—auspices

1662 Margaret Cavendish, Duchess of Newcastle—*Playes*—closet
Loves Adventures, *The Several Wits*, *Youth's Glory, and Death's Banquet*, *The Lady Contemplation*, *Wit's Cabal*, *Unnatural Tragedy*, *The Publick Wooing*, *Matrimonial Trouble*, *Nature's Three Daughters, Beauty, Love, and Wit*, *The Religious*, *The Comical Hash*, *Bell in Campo*, *A Comedy of the Apocriphal [sic] Ladies*, and *The Female Academy*

1663 10 Feb—Katherine Philips—*Pompey*—(T trans, P. Corneille)—Smock-Alley, Dublin

1667 28 Mar—attrib Margaret Cavendish, Duchess of Newcastle—*The Humourous Lovers*—(C)—LIF

1668 4 Feb—Katherine Philips—*Horace*—(T trans, P. Corneille)—Court
Margaret Cavendish, Duchess of Newcastle—*Plays, Never before Printed*—closet
The Sociable Companions, or The Female Wits, *The Presence*, *Scenes* (an appendix to *The Presence*), *The Bridals*, *The Convent of Pleasure*, and *A Piece of a Play* (intended for *The Blazing World*)

1669 n.d.—Frances Boothby—*Marcelia*—(TC)—Bridges St.

1670 20 Sept—Aphra Behn—*The Forced Marriage*—(TC)—LIF
n.d.—Elizabeth Polwhele—*The Faithful Virgins*—(T)—LIF?

1671 24 Feb—Aphra Behn—*The Amorous Prince*—(C)—LIF
ms—Elizabeth Polwhele—*The Frolicks*—(C)—unacted

1673 6 Feb—Aphra Behn—*The Dutch Lover*—(C)—DG

1675 June—attrib Aphra Behn—*The Woman Turned Bully*—(C)—DG

1676 3 July—Aphra Behn—*Abdelazer*—(T)—DG
Sept—Aphra Behn—*The Town Fopp*—(C)—DG

1677 Feb—attrib Aphra Behn—*The Debauchee*—(C)—DG
24 Mar—Aphra Behn—*The Rover*—(C)—DG
29 May—Anne Roche-Guilhen—*Rare on tout*—(Mas)—Court
Sept—attrib Aphra Behn—*The Counterfeit Bridegroom*—(C)—DG

1678 17 Jan—Aphra Behn—*Sir Patient Fancy*—(C)—DG

1679 Jan—Aphra Behn—*The Feign'd Curtizans*—(C)—DG
Sept/Oct—Aphra Behn—*The Young King*—(TC)—DG
n.d.—"Ephelia"—*Pair of Coxcombs Royal*—(C)—A Dancing School

1680 June—attrib Aphra Behn—*The Revenge*—(C)—DG

1681 Jan—Aphra Behn—*The Rover, part two*—(C)—DG
Nov—Aphra Behn—*The False Count*—(C)—DG
Dec—Aphra Behn—*The Roundheads*—(C)—DG

1682 Mar—Aphra Behn—*Like Father, Like Son*—(C)—DG
Apr/May—Aphra Behn—*The City Heiress*—(C)—DG

1684? attrib Aphra Behn—*The Wavering Nymph; or, Mad Amyntas*—(Pst.)—DG?

1685? ms—Anne Wharton—*Love's Martyr*—(T)—unacted

1686 16 Apr—Aphra Behn—*The Luckey Chance*—(C)—DL
Anne Killigrew—"Pastoral Dialogues"—(Pst.)—closet

1687 Mar—Aphra Behn—*The Emperor of the Moon*—(F)—DG

1688? Anne Finch, Countess of Winchilsea—*The Triumphs of Love and Innocence*—(TC)—closet

1689 20 Nov—Aphra Behn—*The Widow Ranter*—(TC)—DL

1690? Anne Finch, Countess of Winchilsea—*Aristomenes*—(T)—closet

1695 Sept—"Ariadne"—*She Ventures and He Wins*—(C)—LIF
Dec—Catharine Trotter—*Agnes de Castro*—(T)—DL

1696 Feb—Aphra Behn—*The Younger Brother*—(C)—DL
Mar—Delariviere Manley—*The Lost Lover*—(C)—DL

Apr/May—Delariviere Manley—*The Royal Mischief*—(T)—LIF
May/June—Mary Pix—*Ibrahim*—(T)—DL
Aug—Mary Pix—*The Spanish Wives*—(C)—DG

1697 June—Mary Pix—*The Innocent Mistress*—(C)—LIF
Sept/Oct—"A Young Lady"—*The Unnatural Mother*—(T)—LIF
Nov—Mary Pix—*The Deceiver Deceived*—(C)—LIF

1698 May/June—Catharine Trotter—*The Fatal Friendship*—(T)—LIF
June—Mary Pix—*Queen Catharine*—(T)—LIF

1699 May—Mary Pix—*The False Friend*—(T)—LIF

1700 Mar—attrib Mary Pix—*The Beau Defeated*—(C)—LIF
Oct—Susanna Centlivre—*The Perjured Husband*—(TC)—DL
23 Nov—Catharine Trotter—*Love at a Loss*—(C)—DL

1701 4 Feb—Catharine Trotter—*The Unhappy Penitent*—(T)—DL
Mar—Mary Pix—*The Double Distress*—(T)—LIF
Mar—Mary Pix—*The Czar of Muscovy*—(T)—LIF
Nov—Jane Wiseman—*Antiochus the Great*—(T)—LIF

1702 June—Susanna Centlivre—*The Beau's Duel*—(C)—LIF
31 Dec—Susanna Centlivre—*The Stolen Heiress*—(C)—LIF

1703 4 June—Susanna Centlivre—*Love's Contrivance*—(C)—DL
Nov—Mary Pix—*The Different Widows*—(C)—LIF

1704 13 Nov—attrib Mary Pix—*Zelmane*—(T)—LIF

1705 Jan—Susanna Centlivre—*The Gamester*—(C)—LIF
May—Mary Pix—*The Conquest of Spain*—(T)—Queen's
20 Nov—Susanna Centlivre—*The Basset-Table*—(C)—DL

1706 3 Jan—"A Young Lady" [M. N.]—*The Faithful General*—(T)—Queen's
11 Feb—Catharine Trotter—*The Revolution of Sweden*—(T)—Queen's
June—Mary Pix—*Adventures in Madrid*—(C)—Queen's
25 Nov—Susanna Centlivre—*The Platonick Lady*—(C)—Queen's
16 Dec—Delariviere Manley—*Almyna*—(T)—Queen's
n.d.—Susanna Centlivre—*Love at a Venture*—(C)—Bath

1709 12 May—Susanna Centlivre—*The Busie Body*—(C)—DL
12 Dec—Susanna Centlivre—*The Man's Bewitched*—(C)—Queen's

1710 27 Mar—Susanna Centlivre—*A Bickerstaff's Burying*—(F)—DL
30 Dec—Susanna Centlivre—*Mar-plot*—(C)—DL

1712 19 Jan—Susanna Centlivre—*The Perplexed Lovers*—(C)—DL

1714 27 Apr—Susanna Centlivre—*The Wonder! A Woman Keeps a Secret*—(C)—DL

1715 Susanna Centlivre—*The Gotham Election*—(F)—unacted
Susanna Centlivre—*The Wife Well Managed*—(F)—unacted (until 1724)

1716 27 Apr—Mary Davys—*The Northern Heiress*—(C)—LIF
17 Dec—Susanna Centlivre—*The Cruel Gift*—(T)—DL

1717 11 May—Delariviere Manley—*Lucius*—(T)—DL

1718 3 Feb—Susanna Centlivre—*A Bold Stroke for a Wife*—(C)—LIF

1719 27 May—misattrib Isabella Aubert—*Harlequin Hydespes*—(CO)—LIF

1721 4 Mar—Eliza Haywood—*The Fair Captive*—(T)—LIF

1722 2 Oct—Susanna Centlivre—*The Artifice*—(C)—DL

1723 23 Apr—Jane Robe—*The Fatal Legacy*—(T)—LIF
12 Aug—Eliza Haywood—*A Wife to Be Lett*—(C)—DL

1724 2 Mar—Susanna Centlivre—*The Wife Well Managed*—(F)—HAY

1725 Mary Davys—*The Self-Rival*—(C)—unacted

1729 4 Mar—Eliza Haywood—*Frederick, Duke of Brunswick-Lunenburgh*—(T)—LIF

1730 9 Dec—Penelope Aubin—*The Merry Masqueraders*—(C)—HAY

1732 18 Apr—Jane Egleton—*The Maggot*—(BO)—LIF
15 May—anon—*The Coquet's Surrender*—(C)—HAY
A Lady of Quality—*The Fate of Corsica*—(D)—closet

1733 31 May—Eliza Haywood—*The Opera of Operas*—(BO)—HAY
misattrib Delariviere Manley—*The Court Legacy*—(BO)—closet

1734 ms—Lady Mary Wortley Montagu—*Simplicity*—(C)—unacted

1735 22 Feb—Elizabeth Cooper—*The Rival Widows*—(C)—CG
17 Sept—Charlotte Charke—*The Carnival*—(F)—HAY
24 Sept—Charlotte Charke—*The Art of Management*—(F)—YB

1736 21 Jan—attrib Eliza Haywood—*Arden of Faversham*—(T)—HAY
17 May—Elizabeth Cooper—*The Nobleman*—(C)—HAY

1737 attrib Mrs. Weddell—*The City Farce*—(F)—unacted

1738 attrib Mrs. Weddell—*A Voyage up the Thames*—(B)—unacted

1739 Elizabeth Boyd—*Don Sancho; or, The Student's Whim*—(BO)—includes *Minerva's Triumph*—(Mas)—unacted

1742 attrib Mrs. Weddell—*Incle and Yarico*—(T)—unacted

1743 16 Mar—Charlotte Charke—*Tit for Tat*—(Med)—James St.

1747 5 Mar—Rachael? Hoper—*The Battle of Poictiers*—(T)—GF
misattrib Sarah Fielding—*Familiar Letters*—(two D)—closet
"Much Ado" and "Fashion"

1748 31 Mar—Rachael? Hoper—*The Cyclopedia*—(F)—HAY
n.d.—Laetitia Pilkington—*The Turkish Court; or London 'Prentice*—(B)—Capel-St., Dublin

1749 9 Nov—Rachael? Hoper—*Queen Tragedy Restored*—(B)—HAY
Laetitia Pilkington—The Roman Father—(T)—unacted

1750 15 Mar—Kitty Clive—*The Rehearsal; or, Bays in Petticoats*—(B)—DL

1751 Mary Leapor—*The Unhappy Father*—(T)—unacted

1752 Susannah Cibber—*The Oracle*—(E trans., St. Foix)—CG
A Young Gentlewoman—*Theodoric, King of Denmark*—(T)—closet

1754 23 Mar—attrib Kitty Clive—*The London 'Prentice*—(F)—DL
Sarah Fielding and Jane Collier—*The Cry*—(DD)—closet

1755 Elizabeth Tollet—*Susanna*—(DwM)—closet

1756 n.d.—Jane? Green—*Everybody to Their Own Liking*—(F)—Bath?
Elizabeth Harrison—*The Death of Socrates*—(T)—closet
Frances Brooke—*Virginia*—(T)—unacted

1758 Charlotte Lennox—*Philander*—(Pst)—closet
misattrib Charlotte Lennox—*Angelica; or, Quixote in Petticoats*—(C)—unacted

1759 10 Feb—Lady Elenora Houston—*The Coquettes*—(C)—Canongate, Edinburgh
Charlotte Lennox—*The Greek Theatre of Father Brumoy*—closet

1760 20 Mar—Kitty Clive—*Every Woman in Her Humour*—(F)—DL

1761 26 Mar—attrib Kitty Clive—*The Island of Slaves*—(C)—DL

1762 June?—Elizabeth Thomas—*Dramatick Pastoral*—(Pst)—Gloucester

1763 3 Feb—Frances Sheridan—*The Discovery*—(C)—DL
21 Mar—Kitty Clive—*Sketch of a Fine Lady's Return from a Rout*—(F)—DL
10 Dec—Frances Sheridan—*The Dupe*—(C)—DL

1764 Elizabeth Griffith—*Amana*—(T)—closet

1765 24 Jan—Elizabeth Griffith—*The Platonic Wife*—(C)—DL
18 Mar—Kitty Clive—*The Faithful Irish Woman*—(F)—DL
Hannah More—*The Search after Happiness*—(Pst)—closet
Charlotte MacCarthy—*The Author and the Bookseller* (DD)—unacted

1766 9 Jan—Elizabeth Griffith—*The Double Mistake*—(C)—CG
ms—Frances Sheridan—*A Trip to Bath*—(three acts of a C)—unacted
attrib Anna Williams—*The Uninhabited Island*—(D)—closet

1767 21 Apr—Jane Pope—*The Young Couple*—(C)—DL
attrib Elizabeth Griffith—*Dorval; or, The Test of Love*—(C trans, Diderot)—unacted

1768 n.d.—Mary Latter—*The Siege of Jerusalem By Titus Vespasian*—(T)—Reading

1769 4 Feb—Elizabeth Griffith—*The School for Rakes*—(C)—DL
18 Feb—Charlotte Lennox—*The Sister*—(C)—CG

1770 27 Apr—Philippina Burton—*Fashion Display'd*—(C)—HAY
attrib Elizabeth Griffith—*The Father*—(C trans, Diderot)—unacted

1771 12 Jan—Dorothea Celisia—*Almida*—(T)—DL
10 May—Jael Henrietta Pye—*The Capricious Lady*—(F)—DL
27 June—Lady Dorothea Dubois—*The Magnet*—(ME)—MG
n.d.—Lady Dorothea Dubois—*The Divorce*—(ME)—MG
A Lady—*The Conquest of Corsica by the French*—(T)—closet
Anne Penny—*The Birthday*—(E)—closet
A Lady—*The Disguise*—(DN)—closet

1772 9 Mar—Elizabeth Griffith—*A Wife in the Right*—(C)—CG
Jean Marshall—*Sir Harry Gaylove*—(C)—unacted

1773 n.d.—Lady Dorothea Dubois—*The Haunted Grove*—(ME)—Crow-St., Dublin

1774 12 Apr—A Lady—*The South Briton*—(C)—CG
18 Apr—Hannah More—*The Inflexible Captive*—(T)—Bath
Mary Eleanor Bowes, Countess of Strathmore—*The Siege of Jerusalem*—(T)—closet

1775 9 Nov—Charlotte Lennox—*Old City Manners*—(C)—DL
Mrs. Cullum—*Charlotte*—(D)—unacted

1776 15 Mar—Hannah Cowley—*The Runaway*—(C)—DL
Elizabeth Griffith—*The Barber of Seville*—(C trans, Beaumarchias)—unacted

1777 9 Aug—Sarah Cheney Gardner—*The Advertisement*—(C)—HAY
10 Dec—Hannah More—*Percy*—(T)—CG
Elizabeth Ryves—*The Prude*—(BO)—unacted
Elizabeth Ryves—*The Triumph of Hymen*—(Mas)—unacted
Elizabeth Ryves—*The Debt of Honour*—(C)—unacted

1778 Mar—Lady Elizabeth Craven—*The Sleep Walker*—(C)—Newbury

27 Apr—Ursula Booth—*The Little French Lawyer*—(F)—CG
30 Apr—Mary Darby Robinson—*The Lucky Escape*—(CO)—DL

1779 10 Apr—Hannah Cowley—*Who's the Dupe?*—(F)—DL
28 Apr—Elizabeth Richardson—*The Double Deception*—(C)—DL
6 May—Hannah More—*The Fatal Falsehood*—(T)—CG
31 July—Hannah Cowley—*Albina*—(T)—HAY
2 Dec—Elizabeth Griffith—*The Times*—(C)—DL
Miss R. Roberts—*Malcolm*—(HT)—unacted
ms—Fanny Burney—*The Witlings*—(C)—unacted

1780 22 Feb—Hannah Cowley—*The Belle's Stratagem*—(C)—CG
4 Apr—Hannah Cowley—*The School of Eloquence*—(Int)—DL
24 May—Lady Elizabeth Craven—*The Miniature Picture*—(C)—DL
5 Aug—Sophia Lee—*The Chapter of Accidents*—(C)—HAY
n.d.—Mrs. Burgess—*The Oaks*—(C)—Canterbury
Christian? Edwards—*Otho and Rutha*—(D)—closet

1781 31 Jan—Frances Brooke—*The Siege of Sinope*—(T)—CG
24 Feb—Hannah Cowley—*The World as It Goes*—(F)—CG
14 Mar—Margaret Cornelys—*The Deceptions*—(C)—Crow-St., Dublin
24 Mar—Hannah Cowley—*Second Thoughts are Best*—(F)—CG
5 Mar—Betsy Sheridan—*The Ambiguous Lover*—(F)—Crow-St., Dublin
18 July—Lady Elizabeth Craven—*The Silver Tankard*—(CO)—HAY
Ann Gittins Francis—*The Song of Solomon*—(SdD)—closet
attrib Elizabeth Montagu—*The Family Picture*—(C trans, Diderot)—closet

1782 9 Feb—Hannah Cowley—*Which is the Man?*—(C)—CG
16 July—misattrib Fanny Burney—*The East Indian*—(C)—HAY
July—Lady Elizabeth Craven—*The Statue Feast*—(C)—Benham House
16 Aug—misattrib Sarah Cheney Gardner—*The Female Dramatist*—(F)—HAY
31 Dec—Frances Brooke—*Rosina*—(CO)—CG
n.d.—Lady Elizabeth Craven—*The Arcadian Pastoral*—(Pst)—Burlington House
Hannah More—*Sacred Dramas*—(SdD)—closet
Moses in the Bulrushes, *David and Goliath*, *Daniel*, and *Belshazzar*

1783 25 Feb—Hannah Cowley—*A Bold Stroke for a Husband*—(C)—CG
6 Dec—Hannah Cowley—*More Ways Than One*—(C)—CG
Anna Maria Edwards—*The Enchantress*—(ME)—Capel-St., Dublin
Ann Wilson—*Jephthah's Daughter*—(SdD)—closet

1784 8 Mar—Harriet Horncastle Hook—*The Double Disguise*—(CO)—DL
6 July—Elizabeth Inchbald—*A Mogul Tale*—(F)—HAY
ms—Elizabeth Ryves—*Dialogue in the Elysian Fields between Caesar and Cato*—(DD)—unacted

1785 25 Apr—Elizabeth Kemble—*Philander and Rose*—(Pst)—Manchester
4 Aug—Elizabeth Inchbald—*I'll Tell You What*—(C)—HAY
22 Oct—Elizabeth Inchbald—*Appearance Is Against Them*—(F)—CG
ms—Mary O'Brien—*The Temple of Virtue*—(CO)—unacted

1786 18 May—A Lady—*The Peruvian*—(CO)—CG
20 June—Elizabeth Inchbald—*The Widow's Vow*—(F)—HAY
25 Nov—Hannah Cowley—*A School for Graybeards*—(C)—DL
Dec—Maria Edgeworth—*The Double Disguise*—(C)—private performance
n.d.—Christian Carstaires—*The Hubble-Shoe*—(F)—Edinburgh
P. I.—*Dramatic Pieces*—(Juv)—closet
The Good Mother-in-Law, *The Good Daughter-in-Law*, *The Reformation*, *The Maternal Sister*, and *Triumph of Reason*

1787 10 Feb—Elizabeth Inchbald—*Such Things Are*—(D)—CG
22 May—Elizabeth Inchbald—*The Midnight Hour*—(C)—CG
10 Nov—Harriet Lee—*The New Peerage*—(C)—DL
15 Dec—Elizabeth Inchbald—*All on a Summer's Day*—(C)—CG
n.d.—attrib Mary Darby Robinson—*Kate of Aberdeen*—(CO?)—Edinburgh?
Lady Eglantine Wallace—*Diamond Cut Diamond*—(C)—unacted
?ms—Sarah Cheney Gardiner—*Charity*—(F)—unacted
?ms—Sarah Cheney Gardiner—*The Loyal Subject*—(C)—unacted

1788 31 Jan—Hannah Cowley—*The Fate of Sparta*—(HT)—DL
8 Apr—Lady Eglantine Wallace—*The Ton*—(C)—CG
29 Apr—Elizabeth Inchbald—*Animal Magnetism*—(F)—CG
22 May—Frances Brooke—*Marian*—(CO)—CG
9 Aug—Marianna Starke—*The Sword of Peace*—(C)—HAY
28 Nov—Elizabeth Inchbald—*The Child of Nature*—(D)—CG
Sarah Kirby Trimmer—*The Little Hermit*—(Juv)—closet

1789 19 May—Anna Ross—*The Cottagers*—(CO)—Crow-St., Dublin
25 May—A Lady—*Half an Hour after Supper*—(Int)—HAY
15 July—Elizabeth Inchbald—*The Married Man*—(C)—HAY
3 Nov—Ann Yearsley—*Earl Goodwin*—(HT)—Bristol
?ms—Fanny Burney—*Hubert de Vere*—(T)—unacted
?ms—Fanny Burney—*The Siege of Pevensey*—(T)—unacted
?ms—Fanny Burney—*Elberta* (a fragment of a T)—unacted
Elizabeth Harlow—*The English Tavern in Berlin*—(C)—unacted

1790 22 Mar—attrib Dorothy Jordan—*The Spoiled Child*—(F)—DL
7 Apr—Marianna Starke—*The British Orphan*—(T)—Mrs. Crespigny's Private Theatre
5 May—Marianna Starke—*The Widow of Malabar*—(T)—CG
23 Dec—Catharine Metcalfe—*Julia De Roubigne*—(T)—Bath
n.d.—Mary O'Brien—*The Fallen Patriot*—(C)—Dublin?
Maria Weylar Barrell—*The Captive*—(D)—closet
Lady Elizabeth Craven—*Le Philosophe Moderne*—(C)—closet
Anne Hughes—*Moral Dramas*—closet
Aspacia—(T), *Constantia*—(T), *Cordelia*—(T)
Margaret Turner—*The Gentle Shepherd*—(Pst)—closet

1791 4 Jan—Amelia Alderson Opie—*Adelaide*—(T)—Plumptre's, Norwich
11 May—Elizabeth Inchbald—*The Hue and Cry*—(F)—DL
9 July—Elizabeth Inchbald—*Next Door Neighbors*—(C)—HAY
3 Dec—Hannah Cowley—*A Day in Turkey*—(CO)—CG

Elizabeth Pinchard—*The Blind Child*—(Juv)—closet
Jane West—*Edmund Surnamed Ironside*—(T)—closet

1792 18 Jan—Hannah Brand—*Huniades*—(HT)—DL
2 Feb—Hannah Brand—*Agmunda*—(HT)—DL
18 Apr—Eliza Parsons—*The Intrigues of a Morning*—(F)—CG
30 June—Elizabeth Inchbald—*Young Men and Old Women*—(F)—HAY
23 Aug—attrib Miss Griffiths—*Cross Partners*—(C)—HAY
30 Aug—Elizabeth Forsyth—*The Siege of Quebec*—(D)—Cork?
n.d.—Lady Sophia Burrell—*Comala*—(D)—Hanover Square Rooms?
Mary Deverell—*Mary Queen of Scots*—(HT)—closet
ms—Elizabeth Inchbald—*The Massacre*—(T trans, Mercier)—unacted
A Young Lady—*The Village Maid*—(CO)—closet
C. Short—*Dramas for the Use of Young Ladies*—(Juv)—closet
Elizabeth Pinchard—*Dramatic Dialogues*—(Juv)—closet
The Misfortunes of Anger, *Sensibility*, *The Little Trifler*, *The Little Country Visitor*, *The Distrest Family*, *The Village Wedding*, and *The Mocking Bird's Nest*
Hannah More—*Village Politics*—(DD)—closet

1793 29 Jan—Elizabeth Inchbald—*Every One Has His Fault*—(C)—CG
24 Oct—Miss Burke—*The Ward of the Castle*—(CO)—CG
25 Feb—Catherine? Cuthbertson—*Anna*—(C)—DL
A Female Refugee—*The Carthusian Friar*—(T)—closet

1794 22 May—Mrs. Rainsford—*The Speechless Wife*—(F)—CG
21 July—Lady Elizabeth Craven, Margravine of Anspach—*The Yorkshire Ghost*—(C)—Brandenburgh House
1 Nov—Elizabeth Inchbald—*The Wedding Day*—(C)—DL
29 Nov—Mary Darby Robinson—*Nobody*—(F)—DL
6 Dec—Hannah Cowley—*The Town Before You*—(C)—CG
Elizabeth Pinchard—*The Two Cousins*—(Juv)—closet

1795 21 Mar—Fanny Burney—*Edwy and Elvina*—(T)—DL
22 Apr—Sarah Cheney Gardner—*Mrs. Doggerel in Her Altitudes*—(Pre)—HAY
Oct?—Charlotte Brooke—*Belisarius*—(T)—closet?
n.d.—Elizabeth Edmead—*The Events of a Day*—(D)—Norwich
attrib Agnes Stratford—*The Labyrinth*—(T)—closet
Lady Eglantine Wallace—*The Whim*—(C)—forbidden to be acted by the Lord Chamberlain
Charlotte Turner Smith—*Rural Walks*—(Juv)—closet

1796 20 Apr—Sophia Lee—*Almeyda*—(T)—DL
Mrs. T. Robertson—*The Enchanted Island*—(ME)—unacted?
Mary Darby Robinson—*The Sicilian Lover*—(T)—unacted
Charlotte Turner Smith—*Rambles Further*—(Juv)—closet

1797 4 Mar—Elizabeth Inchbald—*Wives as They Were, and Maids as They Are*—(C)—CG
Maria Edgeworth—*Old Poz*—(Juv)—closet
Charlotte Sanders—*The Little Family*—(Juv)—closet
The Little Gamester, *The Bird's Nest*, and *The Foundling of Savoy*

1798 27 Apr—attrib Frances Abington—*Matrimony*—(C)—CG
11 Oct—Elizabeth Inchbald—*Lovers' Vows*—(D trans, Kotzebue)—CG
Nov/Dec—Margaret Holford—*Neither's the Man*—(C)—Chester
n.d.—Lady Elizabeth Craven, Margravine of Anspach—*The Robbers*—(T trans, Schiller)—Brandenburgh House
Joanna Baillie—*A Series of Plays: [on] the Stronger Passions*
De Monfort—(T), *Count Basil*—(T), and *The Tryal*—(C)
Hannah Brand—*Poems and Plays*—closet
Huniades—(T), *Adelinda*—(C), and *The Conflict*—(C)
Harriet Lee—*The Mysterious Marriage*—(MD)—unacted
Anne Plumptre—*The Count of Burgundy*—(D trans, Kotzebue)—closet
Anne Plumptre—*The Natural Son*—(D trans, Kotzebue)—closet
n.d.—Maria Edgeworth—*Whim for Whim*—(C)—privately performed

1799 19 Apr—Lady Elizabeth Craven, Margravine of Anspach—*The Princess of Georgia*—(O)—CG
27 Apr—Charlotte Smith—*What is She?*—(C)—CG
3 May—Maria Therese DeCamp Kemble—*First Faults*—(C)—DL
June—Lady Elizabeth Craven, Margravine of Anspach—*Puss in Boots*—(P)—Brandenburgh House
30 Nov—Inchbald—*The Wise Man of the East*—(D)—CG
n.d.—Lady Elizabeth Craven, Margravine of Anspach—*Love Rewarded*—(Pst)—acted Brandenburgh House?
ms—Fanny Burney—*Love and Fashion*—(C)—unacted
Maria Geisweiler—*The Noble Lie*—(D trans, Kotzebue)—closet
Maria Geisweiler—*Poverty and Nobleness of Mind*—(D trans, Kotzebue)—closet
Maria Geisweiler—*Joanna of Montfaucon*—(D trans, Kotzebue)—closet
Maria Geisweiler—*Crime from Ambition*—(D trans, Iffland)—closet
Rose D'Aguilar Lawrence—*Gortz of Berlingen*—(T trans, Goethe)—closet
Anne Plumptre—*The Widow and the Riding Horse*—(F trans, Kotzebue)—closet
Anne Plumptre—*La Perouse*—(D trans, Kotzebue)—closet
Anne Plumptre—*The Virgin of the Sun*—(D trans, Kotzebue)—closet
Anne Plumptre—*The Spaniards in Peru*—(T trans, Kotzebue)—closet
Anne Plumptre—*The Force of Calumny*—(D trans, Kotzebue)—closet
Belle Plumptre—*The Foresters*—(D trans, Iffland)—closet
Elizabeth Helme—*Cortez*—(Juv trans, Campe)—closet
Jane West—*Poems and Plays*, vols. 1–3—closet
Adela—(T), *How Will it End?*—(C), *Edmund Surnamed Ironside*—(T)

1800 29 Apr—Joanna Baillie, *De Monfort*—(T)—DL
30 Oct—Dorothea Plowden—*Virginia*—(CO)—DL
n.d.—Mrs. Robertson—*Ellinda; or, The Abbey of St. Aubert* —(MD)—Newark
n.d.—Elizabeth Lindsay Yorke, Countess of Hardwick—*The Court of Oberon*—(D)—privately acted Wimpole Hall
ms—Fanny Burney—*A Busy Day*—(C)—unacted
ms—Fanny Burney—*The Woman Hater*—(C)—unacted
ms—Elizabeth Inchbald—*A Case of Conscience*—(D)—unacted
Lady Sophia Burrell—*Theodora; or, The Spanish Daughter*—(T)—closet
Lady Sophia Burrell—*Maximian*—(T trans, T. Corneille)—closet
Maria Edgeworth—*Eton Montum*—(Juv)—closet

Elizabeth Helme—*Pizarro*—(Juv trans, Campe)—closet
Marianna Starke—*The Tournament*—(T trans, von Toerring)—closet

1801 Hannah More—*Reflections of King Hezekiah in his Sickness*—(SdD)—closet
A Lady, *Almeda; or, The Neapolitan Revenge*—(DN)—closet
Maria Edgeworth—*The Knapsack*—(Juv)—closet

1802 22 Apr—Mary Berry—*The Fashionable Friends*—(C)—DL
Joanna Baillie—*A Series of Plays: [on] the Stronger Passions, 2nd*
The Election—(C), *Ethwald, Two Parts*—(T), and *The Second Marriage*—(C)
Anne Minton—*A Wife to Be Lett*—(C)—unacted
ms—Elizabeth Inchbald, *The Egyptian Boy*—(D)—unacted

1803 7 Mar—Mary Goldsmith—*She Lives*—(C)—HAY?
16 May—Anna Marie Porter—*The Fair Fugitives*—(ME)—CG
31 Aug—Lady Elizabeth Craven, Margravine of Anspach—*Nicodemus in Despair*—(F)—HAY
n.d.—Lady Elizabeth Craven, Margravine of Anspach—*Nourjad*—(D)—Brandenburgh House
Elizabeth Gunning—*The Wife with Two Husbands*—(TC)—unacted
Eleanor H——.—*Matilda*—(D)—closet
Charlotte Sanders—*Holidays at Home*—(Juv)—closet
The Governess, *The Giddy Girl*, *The Grandmother*, and *The Errors of Education*

1804 Sept—Mary Goldsmith—*Angelina*—(CO)—Margate
Joanna Baillie—*Miscellaneous Plays*
Constantine Paleologous—(T), *Rayner*—(T), and *The Country Inn*—(C)

1805 16 Feb—Elizabeth Inchbald—*To Marry, or Not to Marry*—(C)—CG
29 Apr—Maria Therese DeCamp Kemble—*Personation*—(Int)—DL
July—Lady Elizabeth Craven, Margravine of Anspach—*Love in a Convent*—(C)—privately produced at Brandenburgh House
10 Dec—Marianne Chambers—*The School for Friends*—(C)—DL
Olivia Wilmot Serres—*The Castle of Avola*—(O)—closet
Jane West—*Poems and Plays*, vol. 4
The Minstrel—(T)—closet
Fanny Holcroft—*From Bad to Worse*—(C trans, Calderon)—closet
Fanny Holcroft—*Emilia Galotti*—(T trans, Lessing)—closet
Fanny Holcroft—*Philip the Second*—(T trans, Alfieri)—closet

1806 17 Nov—Jane M. Scott—*The Rout*—(E)—SP
17 Nov—Jane M. Scott—*Tempest Terrific*—(E)—SP
17 Nov—Jane M. Scott—*Vision in the Holyland*—(Sp)—SP
Fanny Holcroft—*The Baron*—(C trans, Celernio)—closet
Fanny Holcroft—*Fortune Mends*—(C trans, Calderon)—closet
Fanny Holcroft—*Rosamond*—(T trans, Weisse)—closet
Fanny Holcroft—*Minna von Barnhelm*—(C trans, Lessing)—closet

1807 12 Jan—Jane M. Scott—*Battle in the Shadows*—(Sp)—SP
12 Jan—Jane M. Scott—*Rural Visitors*—(ME)—SP

12 Jan—Jane M. Scott—*Spectrology of Ghosts*—(E)—SP
28 Jan—Sophia Lee—*The Assignation*—(C)—DL
14 Nov—Jane M. Scott—*Ulthona the Sorceress*—(E)—SP
14 Nov—Jane M. Scott—*Successful Cruise*—(ME)—SP
n.d.—Sydney Owenson—*The First Attempt*—(CO)—Dublin

1808 15 Feb—Jane M. Scott—*The Magistrate*—(CO)—SP
18 May—Maria Therese DeCamp Kemble—*The Day After the Wedding*—(Int)—CG
24 May—attrib Maria Therese DeCamp Kemble—*Match-making*—(C)—CG
7 Nov—Joanna Baillie—*Constantine Paleologous*—(T)—Liverpool
3 Dec—Jane M. Scott—*The Red Robber*—(MD)—SP

1809 23 Jan—Jane M. Scott—*The Bashaw*—(ME)—SP
27 Feb—Jane M. Scott—*Mother White Cap*—(P)—SP
11 Dec—Jane M. Scott—*The Necromancer*—(P)—SP
27 Dec—Jane M. Scott—*Mary, the Maid of the Inn*—(MD)—SP
Susan Fraser—*Comala*—(T)—closet

1810 29 Jan—Joanna Baillie—*A Family Legend*—(T)—Edinburgh
8 Mar—Jane M. Scott—*The Two Misers of Smyrna*—(CO)—SP
3 Dec—Jane M. Scott—*The Magic Pipe*—(P)—SP
3 Dec—Jane M. Scott—*Disappointments*—(MD)—SP
27 Dec—Jane M. Scott—*The Lowland Romp*—(CO)—SP
Sarah Richardson—*Ethelred*—(T)—closet
Sarah Richardson—*Gertrude*—(T)—closet
Barbara Hoole Hofland, *Little Dramas for Young People by Mrs. Hoole*—(Juv)—closet

1811 12 Feb—Jane M. Scott—*The Animated Effigy*—(F)—SP
2 Mar—Marianne Chambers—*Ourselves*—(C)—DL
4 Mar—Sarah Isdell—*The Poor Gentlewoman*—(C)—Dublin
16 May—Harriet Faucit *or* Fawcett—*Alfred the Great*—(HD)—Norwich
18 Nov—Jane M. Scott—*The Poison Tree*—(P)—SP
16 Dec—Jane M. Scott—*The Vizier's Son, the Merchant's Daughter*—(CO)—SP
n.d.—Elizabeth Wright Macauley—*Marmion*—(MD)—Dublin and Cork
Mary Shackleton Leadbeater—*Cottage Dialogues Among the Irish Peasantry*—(DN)—closet

1812 24 Feb—Jane M. Scott—*Il Giorno Felice*—(CO)—SP
11 Apr—Alicia Sheridan Lefanu—*The Sons of Erin*—(C)—DL
17 Nov—Jane M. Scott—*Asgard the Demon Hunter*—(Sp)—SP
7 Dec—Jane M. Scott—*Love, Honor, and Obey*—(F)—SP
23 Dec—attrib Jane M. Scott—*Davy Jones's Locker*—(P)—SP
Joanna Baillie—*A Series of Plays: [on] the Stronger Passions, 3rd* —closet
Orra—(T), *The Dream*—(T), *The Siege*—(C), and *The Beacon*—(DwM)

1813 4 Feb—Jane M. Scott—*The Forest Knight*—(F)—SP
8 Mar—Jane M. Scott—*Love in the City*—(F)—SP
22 Nov—Jane M. Scott—*Raykisnah the Outcast*—(Sp)—SP
23 Dec—Jane M. Scott—*The Magicians*—(P)—SP

1814 24 Jan—Jane M. Scott—*Whackham and Windham, The Wrangling Lawyers*—(F)—Sp
9 Feb—Mary Balfour—*Kathleen O'Neil*—(D)—Belfast
28 Feb—Jane M. Scott—*The Inscription*—(MD)—SP
26 Dec—Jane M. Scott—*Eccentricities*—(F)—SP
Printed in *New British Drama*, 4 vols., ed. John Galt
Margaret Holford—*The Way to Win Her*—(C)—unacted
Anne M'Taggart—*Hortensia*—(T)—unacted
Anne M'Taggart—*A Search after Perfection*—(C)—unacted
Anne M'Taggart—*Theodora*—(T)—unacted
Anne M'Taggart—*Villario*—(D)—unacted
An anonymous woman—*Manoeuvering*—(C)—unacted

1815 9 Jan—Jane M. Scott—*The Gipsy Girl*—(F)—SP
9 Feb—Jane M. Scott—*Harlequin Rasselas*—(P)—SP
16 Feb—Jane M. Scott—*The Summer House*—(CO)—SP
22 Apr—Barbarina Wilmot, Lady Dacre—*Ina*—(T)—DL
30 Oct—Jane M. Scott—*The Conjurer; or, Blaze in Amaze*—(F)—SP
12 Dec—Maria Therese DeCamp Kemble—*Smiles and Tears*—(C)—CG
Charlotte Nooth—*Clara*—(T)—closet

1816 5 Feb—Jane M. Scott—*The Old Oak Chest*—(MD)—SP
4 Mar—Jane M. Scott—*The Stratagems*—(MD)—SP
16 Dec—Jane M. Scott—*The Dinner at Madelon*—(F)—SP

1817 6 Feb—Jane M. Scott—*Camilla the Amazon*—(MD)—SP
7 June—Joanna Baillie—*The Election*—(C)—Lyceum
13 Oct—Jane M. Scott—*The Lord of the Castle*—(MD)—SP
23 Oct—Jane M. Scott—*Widow's Tears*—(B)—SP
27 Nov—Jane M. Scott—*The Row of Ballynavogue*—(F)—SP
Maria Edgeworth—*Comic Dramas in Three Acts*—closet
Love and Law—(C), *The Two Guardians*—(C), and *The Rose, the Thistle, and the Shamrock*—(C)
Jane Porter—*Egmont*—(T)—unacted

1818 5 Jan—Jane M. Scott—*Fortunate Youth*—(Pre)—SP
5 Feb—Jane M. Scott—*The Three Crumps*—(F)—SP
2 Nov—Jane M. Scott—*Two Spanish Valets*—(F)—SP
7 Dec—Jane M. Scott—*Fairy Legends*—(DwM)—SP
26 Dec—Jane M. Scott—*The Fire Goblin*—(P)—SP
Frances Burney, niece of Fanny Burney—*Tragic Dramas*
Malek Abdul—(T trans, Mme Cottin), *Aristodemus*—(T trans, Vincenzo Monti), and *Fitzormond*—(T)

1819 18 Jan—Jane M. Scott—*The Half-Pay Officer*—(F)—SP
15 Feb—Jane Porter—*Switzerland*—(T)—DL
n.d.—Lady Olivia Clarke—*The Irishwoman*—(C)—Crow-St., Dublin
Mary Hornby—*The Battle of Waterloo*—(T)—closet

1820 Isabel Hill—*The Poet's Child*—(T)—closet
Mary Hornby—*The Broken Vow*—(C)—closet

1821 Barbarina Wilmot, Lady Dacre—*Dramas, Translations, and Occasional Poems*
Ida (T), *Gonzalvo of Cordova* (T), *Pedarias* (T), and *Xarifa* (T)
Charlotte de Humboldt—*Corinth*—(T)—closet

1822 28 Jan—Jane Porter—*Owen Prince of Powys*—(T)—DL
Apr—Margaret Harvey—*Raymond de Percy*—(T)—Sutherland

1823 15 Mar—Mary Russell Mitford—*Julian*—(T)—CG
10 Nov—Mrs. Barrymore—*Evening Revels*—(E)—DL
12 Dec—Felicia Dorothea Browne Hemans—*The Vespers of Palermo*—(T)—CG
Felicia Dorothea Browne Hemans—*The Siege of Valencia*—(T)—closet
A Lady—*Lesson for Lovers* and *The Conjuror*—(F)—unacted
Mary G. Lewis—*Cardiff Castle*—(HD)—closet
Mrs. Martin—*Reparation*—(D)—closet

1824 Anne M'Taggart—*Constantia*—(T)—unacted
Anne M'Taggart—*Valville*—(D)—unacted

1825 29 July—Caroline Boaden—*Quite Correct*—(C)—HAY
10 Dec—Harriet Lee—*The Three Strangers*—(MD)—CG
n.d.—Sarah Isdell—*The Cavern*—(CO)—Hawkins-St., Dublin

1826 4 Nov—Mary Russell Mitford—*Foscari*—(T)—CG
Joanna Baillie—*Martyr*—(T)—closet

1827 23 Aug—Fanny Holcroft—*The Goldsmith*—(MD)—HAY
Mary Russell Mitford—*Dramatic Scenes*—(DSc)—closet
Cunigunda's Vow, *The Fawn*, *The Wedding Ring*, *Emily*, *The Painter's Daughter*, *Fair Rosamond*, *Alice*, *Henry Talbot*, *The Siege*, *The Bridal Eve*, *The Captive*, and *The Masque of the Seasons*
Maria Edgeworth—*Little Plays for Children*—(Juv)—closet
The Grinding Organ, *Dumb Andy*, and *The Dame School Holiday*

1828 9 Oct—Mary Russell Mitford—*Rienzi*—(T)—DL
Joanna Baillie—*The Bride*—(D)—closet

1829 1 Sept—Caroline Boaden—*Fatality*—(T)—HAY
11 Sept—Caroline Boaden—*William Thompson*—(F)—HAY
Oct—Isabel Hill—*The First of May*—(C)—CG

1830 31 Aug—Caroline Boaden—*First of April*—(F)—HAY

1832 9 Jul—Caroline Boaden—*A Duel in Richelieu's Time*—(D)—HAY

1833 Sydney Owenson, Lady Morgan—*Dramatic Scenes from Real Life*—(DSc)—closet
Manor Sackville, *The Easter Recess*, and *Temper*

1834 9 Sept—Isabel Hill—*My Own Twin Brother*—(D)—EOH
2 Jul—Mary Russell Mitford—*Charles I*—(T)—Victoria

n.d.—Isabel Hill—*West Country Wooing*—(DSc)—HAY
Barbarina Wilmot, Lady Dacre—*Frogs and Bulls*—(Juv)—privately produced at Hoo

1835 20 Apr—Mary Russell Mitford—*Sadak and Kalasrade*—(O)—Lyceum

1836 Joanna Baillie—*Dramas*—mostly closet
Romiero, The Alienated Manor, Henriquez, The Martyr, The Separation, The Stripling, The Phantom, Enthusiasm, Witchcraft, The Homicide, The Bride, The Match
24 Feb—*The Separation*—(T)—CG
19 Mar—*Henriquez*—(T)—DL

1838 Aug—Caroline Boaden—*Don Pedro the Cruel and Manuel the Cobbler* (C)—Surrey Theatre

1839 Felicia Dorothea Browne Hemans—*Dramatic Works*—closet
De Chatillon—(T)
Sebastian of Portugal—(fragment of a T)

1841 12 Apr—Mary Russell Mitford—*Inez de Castro*—(T)—City of London Theatre

1842 Isabel Hill—*Brian the Probationer*—(T)—closet

1851 Joanna Baillie—*Dramatical and Poetical Works*
[all plays previously published]

1854 Mary Russell Mitford—*Dramatic Works*—closet
Otto of Wittelsbach (T) and *Gaston de Blondville* (T)